Frommer's

D0446081

Montana
& Wyoming

Here's what the critics say about Frommer's:

"Amazingly easy to use. Very portable, very complete."
—*Booklist*

♦

"The only mainstream guide to list specific prices. The Walter Cronkite of guidebooks—with all that implies."
—*Travel & Leisure*

♦

"Complete, concise, and filled with useful information."
—*New York Daily News*

♦

"Hotel information is close to encyclopedic."
—*Des Moines Sunday Register*

♦

"Detailed, accurate and easy-to-read information for all price ranges."
—*Glamour Magazine*

Other Great Guides for Your Trip:

Frommer's Yellowstone and Grand Teton National Parks

Frommer's National Parks of the American West

Frommer's USA

Frommer's Utah

Frommer's Colorado

Frommer's Rocky Mountain National Park

Frommer's®

3rd Edition

Montana & Wyoming

by Geoff O'Gara & Dan Whipple

IDG Books Worldwide, Inc.
An International Data Group Company
Foster City, CA • Chicago, IL • Indianapolis, IN • New York, NY

ABOUT THE AUTHORS

Dan Whipple is a writer in Broomfield, Colorado. He has lived, traveled, and worked in the Rocky Mountain West for more than 25 years.

Geoff O'Gara writes travel guides, fiction, and nonfiction on natural resource issues from his home in Lander, Wyoming, where he also works for Wyoming Public Television. His next book is *What You See in Clear Water* (Knopf).

IDG BOOKS WORLDWIDE, INC.

An International Data Group Company
919 E. Hillsdale Blvd.
Suite 400
Foster City, CA 94404

Find us online at **www.frommers.com**

ISBN 0-02-863697-X
ISSN 1088-2650

Editor: Vanessa Rosen
Production Editor: Stephanie Lucas
Photo Editor: Richard Fox
Staff Cartographers: John Decamillis and Roberta Stockwell
Design by Michele Laseau
Page creation by Natalie Evans, Carl Pierce, and Angel Perez

SPECIAL SALES

For general information on IDG Books Worldwide's books in the U.S., please call our Consumer Customer Service department at 1-800-762-2974. For reseller information, including discounts, bulk sales, customized editions, and premium sales, please call our Reseller Customer Service department at 1-800-434-3422.

Manufactured in the United States of America

5 4 3 2 1

Contents

List of Maps

AN INVITATION TO THE READER

In researching this book, we discovered many wonderful places—hotels, restaurants, shops, and more. We're sure you'll find others. Please tell us about them, so we can share the information with your fellow travelers in upcoming editions. If you were disappointed with a recommendation, we'd love to know that, too. Please write to:

Frommer's Montana & Wyoming, 3rd Edition
IDG Travel
1633 Broadway
New York, NY 10019

AN ADDITIONAL NOTE

Please be advised that travel information is subject to change at any time—and this is especially true of prices. We therefore suggest that you write or call ahead for confirmation when making your travel plans. The authors, editors, and publisher cannot be held responsible for the experiences of readers while traveling. Your safety is important to us, however, so we encourage you to stay alert and be aware of your surroundings. Keep a close eye on cameras, purses, and wallets, all favorite targets of thieves and pickpockets.

WHAT THE SYMBOLS MEAN

✪ Frommer's Favorites

Our favorite places and experiences—outstanding for quality, value, or both.

The following abbreviations are used for credit cards:

AE	American Express	EURO	EuroCard
CB	Carte Blanche	JCB	Japan Credit Bank
DC	Diners Club	MC	MasterCard
DISC	Discover	V	Visa
ER	EnRoute		

FIND FROMMER'S ONLINE

www.frommers.com offers up-to-the-minute listings on almost 200 cities around the globe—including the latest bargains and candid, personal articles updated daily by Arthur Frommer himself. No other Web site offers such comprehensive and timely coverage of the world of travel.

The Best of Montana & Wyoming

by Geoff O'Gara & Dan Whipple

The area around Montana and Wyoming is sometimes called the "last, best place," but we've been living in the Northern Rockies long enough to hold a less romantic view: This is the *best* place indeed for wilderness, for history still writ on the landscape, and for capable, helpful neighbors; but it's the *last* place to go for French *haute cuisine*, a Puccini opera, or a bells-and-whistles amusement park. You can still get a whiff out here of the dust of the Old West (which is really not that old), but you should be cautioned that some of those red-nosed cowboys in Livingston are just pretenders, CEOs from back East who've bought themselves an open horizon.

Dan Whipple and I have put together here a thorough but sometimes idiosyncratic list of places to go, places to stay, things to do. Hopefully his strengths will cover my deficits and vice versa—he can tell you about golf, and I know where to paddle. We've covered the well-known (and deserving) sites and events, but we've also thrown in a few eccentric delights, too.

1 The Best Vacation Experiences

- **Glacier National Park** (MT): The best vacation spot in Montana is also the most obvious one. By the standard of other crowded national parks, this spectacular country is virtually undiscovered. Step a short ways off the road and you can easily find wild places that seem untouched by the crowds. You'll encounter fabulous scenery, as well as a parade of wildlife. See chapter 4.
- **The Lewis & Clark Trail** (MT): If you want to get a feel for the terrain of plains and foothills and mountains, and take in some American history at the same time, follow the trail of explorers Meriwether Lewis and William Clark through Montana. Two centuries after Jefferson sent these explorers west, you can follow their Voyage of Discovery through every kind of landscape the Rockies have to offer. You can get a guide to the trail from Travel Montana, 1424 9th Ave., P.O. Box 200533, Helena, MT 59620-0533 (☎ **800/847-4868;** visitmt.com). See chapter 7.
- **Yellowstone National Park** (WY): It's the crown jewel of American parks, and it remains the prime attraction in the Rocky Mountains. This unique park offers visitors an extraordinary combination of wilderness, wildlife, and geothermal wonders. See chapter 10.

Montana

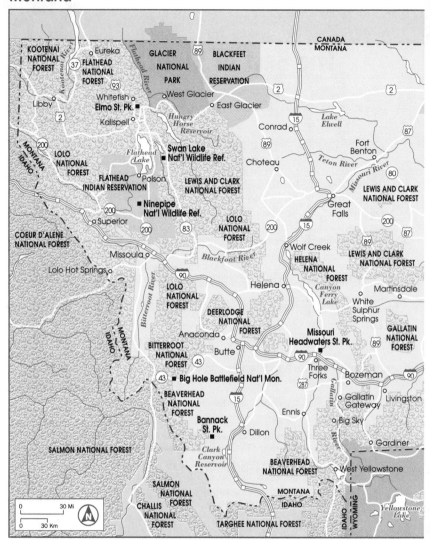

- **The Grand Tetons** (WY): The Grand Tetons are an excellent short course in Rocky Mountain parks for travelers with less time: magnificent peaks rising from the Snake River plain, alpine lakes, wildflowers, and wildlife, in a relatively small park that can be seen in a few days. You can climb to the top of the Grand under the tutelage of experienced guides, or take a gentler climb up trails around Jenny Lake, or float the Snake River. See chapter 11.

2 The Best Outdoor Adventures

- **Exploring the Bob Marshall Wilderness** (MT): The 1.5-million-acre Bob Marshall Wilderness Complex in northwest Montana is one of America's most spectacular wild places. Lace on your hiking boots, tie on your bandanna, and take to the high country in Montana's northwest corner. See chapter 5.

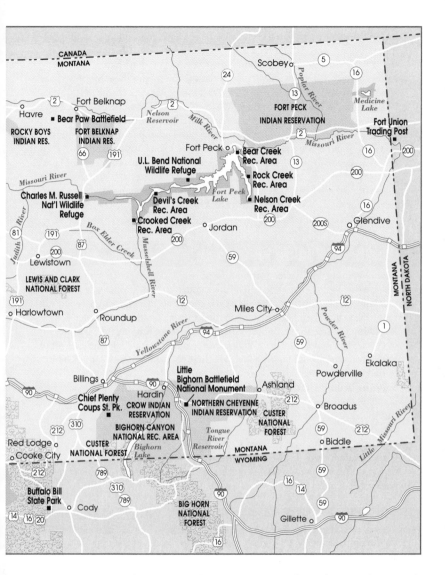

- **Enjoying the Yellowstone Backcountry** (WY): Outfitters from ranches around Yellowstone National Park will take you into the deep wilderness that surrounds the busy attractions at the park's center, and there you'll get a flavor of the wild as rich as the Rockies can offer. If you have the experience, you can go on your own—paddling Yellowstone Lake, backpacking into Bechtel Falls, telemark skiing the powder on Togwotee Pass. Outfitters aren't cheap, but they provide pack animals, knowledge of the best backcountry fishing, safety in bear country, and gourmet campfire meals. See chapter 10 for details.

- **Climbing Over the Tetons** (WY): Some folks who see the Tetons' jagged profile aren't content merely to gaze: They need to bag a peak. If you enjoy yourself more on top than on the bottom, there are two climbing schools (**Exum Mountain Guides,** ☎ **307/733-2297;** and **Jackson Hole Mountain Guides,** ☎ **800/239-7642**) that will train you and guide you to the top of the Grand, or one of the other peaks in the chain. The view is sensational and the accomplishment thrilling, and though there are moments where you'll feel exposed, you're roped to expert guides who minimize the risk. But you don't have to summit to enjoy this park—a gentle climb up trails at the mountains' base by Jenny Lake will take you to waterfalls, scenic views, and tranquility. See chapter 11.

- **Battling the Wind River Canyon Whitewater** (WY): Located on the Wind River Indian Reservation, this white-water adventure is closed to private rafters and all but one outfitter—so, unlike the Snake and other popular rivers, your trip down the Wind is yours alone. The steep-walled canyon has dramatic views, deep drops, and good fishing. At the end of the day, you're only a few miles from Thermopolis, where you can soothe yourself in the hot springs at several pools and spas. For your river trip, choose from half-days, whole days, and lunch in a riverbank tepee, with **Wind River Canyon Whitewater** (☎ **307/864-9343**). See Thermopolis in chapter 12.

3 The Best Wildlife Viewing

- **Bear Watching in Glacier National Park** (MT): The experience of watching wildlife run wild at Glacier National Park is tough to beat. It's almost a guarantee that you'll see mountains, but with a little energy and a lot of courage, you can see grizzlies and black bears basking in their natural habitat. See chapter 4.
- **Searching for Life in the Bob Marshall Wilderness Complex** (MT): Just south of Glacier in the Bob Marshall Wilderness Complex, roam a full complement of Rocky Mountain wildlife—although you have to wander into the backcountry to find it. See chapter 5.
- **Spotting Wildlife in the Lamar Valley** (WY): You can see wildlife in many parts of Yellowstone, including the meadows across from the Old Faithful complex. But the richest trove of wildlife is in the park's northeast corner, a less-traveled corridor that leads to the northeast entrance and Cooke City. This is where several packs of wolves were reintroduced in 1990, bison and elk graze, and grizzly bears are often seen. To the astonishment of biologists, the wolves continue to appear in full view of travelers along the road. If you're patient, you may spot a grizzly. See chapter 10.

4 The Best Organized Activities

- **Exploring Glacier** (MT): You can spot wildlife and spend the night in a rustic chalet in Glacier National Park with **Glacier Wilderness Guides** (☎ **800/ 521-7238**)—one of the longest-running guide services in this part of the country. They'll even carry your gear for you. See chapter 4.
- **Getting Outdoors Near Bozeman** (MT): **Northern Rockies Natural History Safari** (☎ **406/586-1155**) will help you explore the backcountry that sits just north of Yellowstone via guided hikes, snowshoeing expeditions, and river-running tours. See chapter 8.
- **Fly-Fishing on the Snake River** (WY): **Crescent H. Ranch Rivermeadows** (☎ **307/733-3674**) works with Orvis (the equipment manufacturer) to provide fishing lessons as well as guided trips. See chapter 11.
- **Bagging Grand Teton** (WY): To learn how to climb Grand Teton or even just learn how to rope up and scramble, sign up with **Jackson Hole Mountain Guides** (☎ **800/239-7642**). See chapter 11.

- **Riding & Camping Along Butch Cassidy's Outlaw Trail** (WY): **Equitor** (☎ **800/545-0019;** www.ridingtours.com) arranges organized trips along this trail in Wyoming's largely unchanged Hole-in-the-Wall country. See chapter 13.

5 The Best Scenic Drives

- **Going-to-the-Sun Road** (Glacier National Park, MT): The 50-mile Going-to-the-Sun Road bisects the park from West Glacier to St. Mary (from southwest to northeast), offering spectacular views of glaciated valleys, mountain wildflowers, curious mountain goats, and towering peaks. Because of heavy snowfall, the road doesn't open until early June, when you can drive up and watch workers dynamite through the last wall of snow. See chapter 4.
- **Beartooth National Scenic Byway** (MT and WY): Take your time on this cloud-kissing drive: Stop at the pullouts and gaze into the deep canyons, toe the snowfields that hang on well into the summer, lean over for a close look at the minute flowers that bloom more than 10,000 feet above sea level. There are small planes that can't fly this high, but you can drive the switchbacks over Beartooth Pass between Red Lodge and Cooke City, and down into Wyoming and Yellowstone National Park. See chapter 8.
- **The Road from Billings Through Little Bighorn Battlefield to Devils Tower** (MT and WY): This trip will take a few days, but provides a snapshot of some interesting Western history. From Billings, you'll head east to the rolling, grassy hills where Custer and his troops met their fate, then south to Sheridan, Wyoming, for a step back in time to an authentic Western town. Heading east, you'll travel through a mix of forest and grassland scenery to Devils Tower, which is now receiving its due as a national monument. Then it's back to Billings through the isolated southeast corner of Montana. See chapters 9 and 13.

6 The Best Winter Vacations

- **Skiing on a Big Mountain** (MT): No lines, lots of powder, lots of skiing in the trees, plenty of runs for every level of skier. The Big Mountain is one of the best resorts in the northwestern United States, still relatively undiscovered. More than half the mountain is geared to the intermediate skier, but there is plenty of terrain for experts and beginners at the **Big Mountain Ski and Summer Resort** in Whitefish, MT (☎ **800/858-5439**). See chapter 5.
- **Cross-Country Skiing** (MT): In Big Sky, Montana, the cross-country skiing at the **Lone Mountain Range** (☎ **800/514-4644**) can't be beat. There's more than 36 miles of trails for every level of skier and lots of room to get off into the backcountry powder. See chapter 8.
- **Wintering at Old Faithful** (WY): The chilly season in Yellowstone is increasingly popular, and it's bound to grow now that the Old Faithful Snow Lodge has been transformed into a handsome, comfortable facility. You can take a snowcoach into the park or ride your own snowmobile, then put on your cross-country skis for a quiet ski to the Lone Star Geyser or some other attraction. Equipment rentals are available. Call the park concessionaire, **AmFac,** at ☎ **307/344-7311.** See chapter 10.
- **Snowmobiling Through the High Country** (MT and WY): There is now a linkage of groomed snowmobile trails running from the southern end of Wyoming's Wind River Mountains up through Yellowstone National Park to

Wyoming

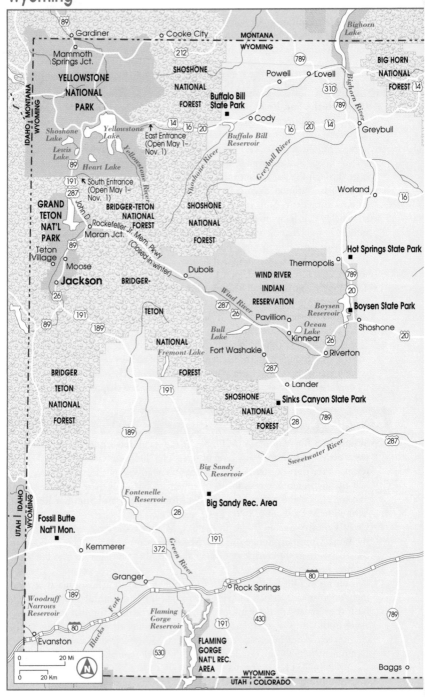

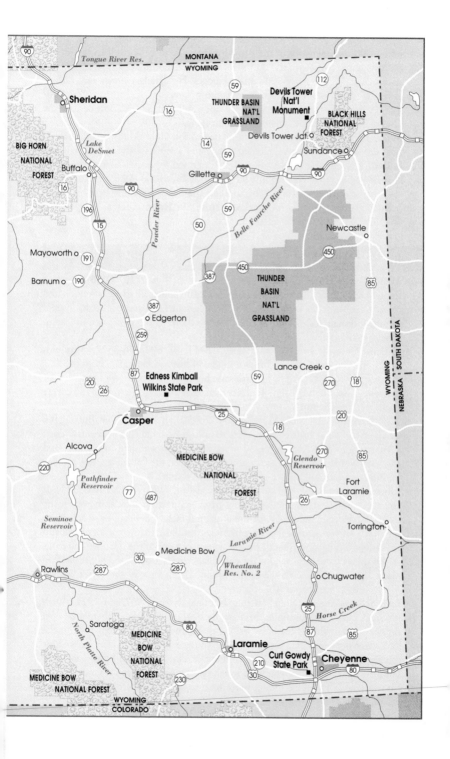

join a 500-mile network of trails in Montana. It's an eerie thrill to race across pillowy, moonlit snow in the thin night air on the Continental Divide. You can spend your night in strategically spaced lodges. For details, contact Travel Montana (☎ 800/548-3390) or the Wyoming Division of Tourism (☎ 800/225-5996). For more information on snowmobiling in Yellowstone and the Grand Teton area, flip to chapters 10 and 11.

- **Skiing on a Bigger Mountain** (WY): The Jackson Hole Ski Resort offers a vertical drop that will take your breath away, and a variety of ways to get to the bottom, from double black diamonds to intermediate slopes. Skiers who like a challenge will come here, and mix the visit with some ballooning, tours of the elk refuge, and other adventures. Upgrades like the new quad lift at Apres Vous are occurring every year. Try the **Jackson Hole Ski Resort** (Teton Village, WY; ☎ 307/733-2292). See chapter 11.

7 The Best Hotels & Resorts

- **Many Glacier Hotel** (Glacier National Park, MT; ☎ 602/207-6000): The best thing about Many Glacier, apart from its elegant mien, its friendly service, and its cozy rooms, is the setting, hard by Swiftcurrent Lake and in the shadows of Mount Grinnell and Mount Wilbur. Many Glacier is the best place to stay in Glacier National Park. See chapter 4.
- **Gallatin Gateway Inn** (Gallatin Gateway, MT; ☎ 800/676-3522): Very old-world, the Gallatin Gateway Inn is a model of historical elegance from the days of luxury railroad travel. The Spanish-style building has vast interior spaces, large enough to be a railroad station all its own. The food in the restaurant is very good, too. See chapter 8.
- **The Pollard** (Red Lodge, MT; ☎ 800/765-5273): You can join Buffalo Bill Cody on the guest register at the Pollard, a historic hotel that proves you don't need to sprawl all over the place to set the highest standard of comfort and elegance. Nestled snugly on picturesque Main Street, the Pollard features a wood-burning fireplace and a three-story gallery. See chapter 8.
- **The Old Faithful Inn** (Yellowstone National Park, WY; ☎ 307/344-7311): If you ever wonder whether there is really art in architecture, look at the way rustic simplicity and monumental structure of the inn make a perfect fit just across the way from one of nature's most astonishing creations. A lattice of logs climbs to an 85-foot ceiling, and you can either find peace at one of the small writing desks in the upper balconies, or join the convivial crowds around the big stone fireplace. If you want one of the corner rooms with a view of the geyser, reserve 2 years ahead. See chapter 10.
- **Lake Yellowstone Hotel** (Yellowstone National Park; ☎ 307/344-7311): With its Greek pillars and sunroom, this hotel defies the notion that only rough-hewn timber and bunkhouse furniture belong in Yellowstone. It harkens back to the days when big bands played on summer evenings and Victorian gents dressed for dinner. The tall windows and high ceiling of the sunroom fill the space with soothing light, and when you want to take in the night air, you are a brief stroll from the lake. The huge dining room feels relaxed and uncrowded. See chapter 10.
- **Rusty Parrot Lodge** (Jackson, WY; ☎ 307/733-2000): The Rusty Parrot manages to create the quiet, luxurious atmosphere of a country inn despite a location in the heart of Jackson. So you can enjoy the amenities of the lively downtown

and still escape for a relaxing evening by a river rock fireplace, or for a tailor made omelet at the expansive breakfast. The Body Sage, a spa to take away pains and blemishes, is a bonus. See chapter 11.

8 The Best Guest Ranches

The ranch vacation is one of the treats this area offers that really can't be duplicated elsewhere. You can live a *City Slickers* fantasy and ride out with the 'hands, or you can fish the stream and spend quiet hours on the porch. Meals are generally served family style in a central lodge. The following ranches were chosen for maintaining some of the dusty flavor of a real ranch while providing first-rate service, good accommodations, and amenities.

- **Triple Creek Ranch** (Darby, MT; ☎ 406/821-4600): This place is wonderful if you can afford it. Pretty much the perfect guest ranch, where guests are pampered like European royalty, the prices reflect it. It has all the traditional dude ranch activities, or you can just swim in the pool or work out in the fitness room. See chapter 5.
- **Lone Mountain Ranch** (Big Sky, MT; ☎ 800/514-4644): Lone Mountain Ranch is a winter and summer resort that has views into the Spanish Peaks Wilderness Area. In winter there are 65 kilometers (about 36 miles) of cross-country trails over terrain that will challenge every level of skier. In summer, you can ride, hike, fish, or simply relax and eat in the popular restaurant. There are bird walks with naturalists, and forays into Yellowstone. See chapter 8.
- **Lost Creek Ranch** (Moose, WY; ☎ 307/733-3435): Positioned next door to a national park with a beautiful view of the Tetons on one side and the Gros Ventres on the other, Lost Creek layers on the comforts and activities. You can ride, hike, swim, fish, float, play tennis, shoot skeet, play billiards, and eat gourmet food. Regulars return every year, and there are only 10 cabins, but if you can get a reservation, it's worth it. See chapter 11.
- **Eaton Ranch** (Sheridan, WY; ☎ 800/210-1049): This is one of the oldest dude ranches in the country, but it remains a working cattle ranch as well, running bovines and dudes on 7,000 acres of private land and Bighorn National Forest. It's a bigger operation than some of the smaller dude outfits. If you really want to work in the saddle, sign up for the spring drive when they bring the horses back to the ranch. See chapter 13.

9 The Best Bed & Breakfasts

- **Copper King Mansion** (Butte, MT; ☎ 406/782-7580): This is the lavishly restored home of original Butte Copper King William Clark, built in 1888 for $260,000. There are 30 rooms on three floors. It's decorated in a lush "modern Elizabethan" style. The ornamentation, from the frescoed ceilings to the pipe organ in the third-floor ballroom, reflects Clark's love of opulence. See chapter 6.
- **The Sanders** (Helena, MT; ☎ 406/442-3309): Built in 1875, this historically important B&B has been beautifully restored by Bobbi Uecker (no relation to former ballplayer Bob) and Rock Ringling (a fourth-generation descendant of the famous circus family). The Italianate brick-and-shingle mansion is located in Helena's historic district, and you'll settle on original 1875 furniture under the eyes of portraits hung by the original owner, U.S. Sen. Wilbur Fiske Sanders. See chapter 6.

- **Howlers Inn Bed-and-Breakfast** (Bozeman, MT; ☎ **406/586-0304**): Not only are the accommodations here first-class, but you get to run with the wolves . . . or at least watch. Located on 42 acres in Bridger Canyon, the Howlers Inn is also home to eight resident wolves, who live in a large penned area adjacent to the main house. The rooms here are large and well appointed, complete with views of the Absaroka and Bridger mountains. See chapter 8.
- **Spahn's Big Horn Mountain Bed & Breakfast** (Big Horn, WY; ☎ **307/ 674-8150**): There's lots to enjoy here: the 100-mile view from a secluded mountaintop; a rustic hideaway tucked amid the Bighorn Mountains that features a massive three-story living area and rooms decorated with country quilts and lodgepole furniture; and the chance to take a wildlife safari and search for a glimpse of moose, elk, or ever-present deer that inhabit the area. See chapter 13.

10 The Best Low-Cost Lodging

- **Swiftcurrent Motor Inn** (Glacier National Park, MT; ☎ **602/207-6000**): Though the accommodations are spartan, in Glacier National Park this is the cheapest, nicest place. The Swiftcurrent Motor Inn is located about a mile upstream from Many Glacier Hotel, but it attracts an entirely different crowd. The people who stay here are younger, less well-to-do, and active. The Inn is in a spectacular setting at the base of two mountains. See chapter 4.
- **Hibernation House** (Whitefish, MT; ☎ **800/858-5439**): Hibernation House at the Big Mountain in Whitefish offers virtually ski-in-ski-out convenience for the price of a motel down the hill. All of the rooms are exactly alike, pretty small with a double bed and a set of bunk beds. See chapter 5.
- **Golden Eagle Lodge** (Big Sky, MT; ☎ **800/548-4488**): It's always tough to find affordable places in a ski resort. If you want to ski Big Sky and keep the price down a little for the family, then the Golden Eagle Lodge is the best bet. It provides basic ski area rooms, nothing fancy, with enough beds for a family in the suites—queen beds for the grown-ups and bunks for the kids. You can also get lift ticket-plus-room deals through the Lodge. See chapter 8.
- **Roosevelt Lodge Cabins** (Yellowstone National Park; ☎ **307/344-7311**): These thin-walled, thin-mattress cabins hark back to early in the last century, when the inexpensive assembly-line Fords made travel a more democratic adventure. The most bare-bones of these cabins are called "Rough Riders," and the shower and toilet are a short hike away. But you're here in the beautiful northeast corner of the park. See chapter 10.
- **Colter Bay Village** (Grand Teton National Park; ☎ **800/628-9988**): If you don't mind bunk beds and woodstoves, then jump at this bargain and spend your nights by Jackson Lake in a big canvas tent mounted on a cement slab. You can make this into a fun family outing, telling scary stories late into the night while you listen to the snap of twigs outside as shadowy critters make their way through the woods. See chapter 11.
- **Hostelx** (Teton Village, WY; ☎ **307/733-3415**): If you've come to Jackson to ski, not to nestle in a spacious luxury suite, and you haven't got a deep pocket, here's an alternative that puts you right at the foot of the ski hill at a bargain-basement rate. It's not a dormitory, either—you get a private room for up to four people, and there's a fireplace lounge for hanging out. See chapter 11.

11 The Best Dining Experiences

- **Snowgoose Grille** (in St. Mary's Lodge, St. Mary, MT; ☎ **406/732-4431**): This is one of two excellent restaurants around Glacier National Park. Call the cuisine adventurous Montana food. While you can get beef or bison steak, you can also get wild boar, buffalo oysters, and buffalo tongue. The restaurant is located at the eastern entrance to Glacier in St. Mary's Lodge. See chapter 4.
- **Marianne's at the Wilma** (Missoula, MT; ☎ **406/728-8549**): Chef Marianne Hoyt is a veteran of the Missoula restaurant scene, and with each incarnation, her restaurants get better and better. If nothing else, the decor—call it art deco honky-tonk—in this restaurant makes it worth the trip. See chapter 5.
- **Rocco's** (Kalispell, MT; ☎ **406/756-5834**): The Italian food at Rocco's alone makes a trip to Kalispell worthwhile. Portions are vast, and tomato-based sauces aren't the only ones on the menu. The legend surrounding the place is an involved one about an American prisoner of war in World War II who was shot down over Italy. See chapter 5.
- **Buck's T-4 Restaurant** (Big Sky, MT; ☎ **406/995-4111**): This is the place to test your palate for game tolerance. Buck's has an extensive menu of game meats, and they are always brilliantly done. See chapter 8.
- **The Chico Inn at Chico Hot Springs** (Pray, MT; ☎ **800/468-9232**): The vegetables served here are grown at the resort's own greenhouse. Although the game is raised here, it's served expertly, along with beef, lamb, and other Rocky Mountain staples. Portions are generous and beautifully presented. Check out the *Easy Rider* motorcycle in the bar while you're here. See chapter 8.
- **The Blue Lion** (Jackson, WY; ☎ **307/733-3912**): This is an old stalwart, still serving some of the best food in the region, with delicious game dishes like grilled elk loin in peppercorn sauce, and fresh seafood flown in daily. It's a cozy two-story clapboard building across from the town park, with dining on the deck in the summer. It's also expensive. See chapter 11.
- **Jenny Lake Lodge Dining Room** (Grand Teton National Park; ☎ **307/543-2831**): The six courses (from prime rib of buffalo to smoked sturgeon ravioli) of food served for dinner here are good enough to distract you from the scenery outside. You may be roughing it in the park, but you'll need to dress properly at this establishment. See chapter 11.
- **Nani's Genuine Pasta House** (Jackson, WY; ☎ **307/733-3888**): Tucked away in the back of a low-rent motel, this is the best Italian cooking in Wyoming (and Italian is the one cuisine that excels here, besides steak and beans). There is a menu of *classico* dishes, then a second menu changed monthly highlighting the dishes of a different region of Italy. See chapter 11.
- **Ciao Bistro** (Sheridan, WY; ☎ **307/672-2838**): Prawns in cognac cream. That sort of thing. You can run up quite a bill from the à la carte menu, but it's hard to stop when the food is this good. A small place with an unassuming exterior and a good wine list. See chapter 13.

12 The Best Fishing

The hundreds of alpine lakes in the high country often serve up voracious trout during the brief summer seasons when ice melts and insects hatch. The fishing is especially good at Montana's **Mission Mountains** and the Wind River Mountains within the boundaries of the **Wind River Indian Reservation** in Wyoming (be sure and get a reservation license). See chapters 5 and 12.

But more often fly-fishing aficionados come to try their guile on flowing water. Here are some of the best stream fisheries in the region:

- **The Madison** (Yellowstone, MT): Brown trout are not native to this area, but no one's asking them to leave—on this popular river running from Yellowstone National Park into Montana, they're the big attraction. The Madison eventually joins up with its "holy trinity" counterparts, the Jefferson and Gallatin, at the Missouri headwaters near Three Forks, but a lot of anglers fish it around West Yellowstone, where you can find good guides. The Madison can be fished year-round, but watch out for restrictions during early spring runoff. See chapter 8.

- **The Snake** (WY): It seems somehow fitting that the menacing-sounding Snake River is home to a feisty strain of cutthroat trout, making it one of the most satisfying Western rivers to fish. With picture-perfect scenery and the resort town of Jackson within casting distance, this Wyoming river gets a lot of casts, but it's still an angler's paradise. Different stretches from Jackson Lake into Idaho are good at different times of the year, so seek the advice of local guides. See chapter 11.

- **Sunlight Basin** (WY): The Clark's Fork of the Yellowstone, Wyoming's only designated Wild and Scenic River, rewards anglers with spectacular scenery and an abundance of rainbows and cutthroats. It's a steep canyon, hard to get in and out of. Sunlight Creek will provide pan-size brook trout that can be enjoyed on long summer evenings alongside its crystal-clear waters. See chapter 12.

- **The Miracle Mile** (WY): Out in fairly open plains country south of Casper, this stretch of the North Platte River produces lunker brown and rainbow trout, and some walleye, too, since it's between two reservoirs, Seminoe and Pathfinder. Fishermen float this stretch, which is actually several miles long, and they also like the upstream area of the North Platte around the town of Saratoga. See chapter 14.

13 The Best Golf Courses

- **Old Works** (Anaconda, MT): Jack Nicklaus has created a beautiful course that is as much fun to play as it is beautiful to look at. The course wonderfully integrates the rocky bluffs, the historical nature of the old copper-processing sites, and prairie grasses and sage. The black sand in the vast bunkers is not only pleasing to the eye, it's fun to hit out of (it's not fun to hit into, of course). See chapter 6.

- **Teton Pines** (Jackson, WY): You won't find a more beautiful view from any golf course in the country—except maybe the neighboring Jackson Hole club—with the granite Grand Teton looming over every shot. This Arnold Palmer design is not that long unless you're foolish enough to play from the gold tees, but water comes into play on nearly every hole. Take lots of golf balls. See chapter 11.

14 The Best Museums & Historical Sites

- **C.M. Russell Museum Complex** (Great Falls, MT; ☎ **406/727-8787**): This is a spectacular collection of the West's best-known and best-loved artist, as well as other fine artists. The museum has many of Russell's original paintings and bronzes, and includes a tour of his studio and home. See chapter 7.

- **Yellowstone Art Museum** (Billings, MT; ☎ **406/256-6804**): The Yellowstone Art Museum is nationally renowned for showcasing Montana's best artists, from Charley Russell to Deborah Butterfield and Russell Chatham. See chapter 9.
- **Buffalo Bill Historical Center** (Cody, WY; ☎ **307/587-4771**): An art museum, a firearm gallery, the memorabilia of the West's great showman, and exhibits about the Plains Indians comprise the finest museum in the Rocky Mountains. See chapter 12.
- **Fort Laramie** (Eastern Wyoming; ☎ **307/837-2221**): Life at a military outpost during the days of the Oregon Trail and Indian Wars is faithfully re-created here. Interpreters in costume wander among the 22 buildings, including the barracks, the guardhouse, and a bakery. See chapter 13.

15 The Best Rodeos

- **Jaycee Bucking Horse Sale** (Miles City, MT; ☎ **406/232-2890**): For real rodeo aficionados, this is the place to find the future stars of the rodeo circuit: horses, not people. This is where horses aspiring to a career in the main arena must earn their spurs. Horse racing, barbecues, and a street dance also highlight the weekend event, held annually in May. See chapter 9.
- **Cheyenne Frontier Days** (Cheyenne, WY; ☎ **800/227-6336**): Tough bulls, pancake breakfasts, top country music acts, and a party on every corner have sustained Cheyenne's annual rodeo fest as the "Daddy of 'em All" for more than a century. See chapter 14.

16 The Best Places to Experience Native American Culture

- **Crow Fair** (MT; ☎ **406/638-2601**): One of the country's largest gatherings of Native Americans, Crow Fair takes place the third weekend in August. The fairground is covered with a mélange of tepees and campsites. Traditional dances and the haunting songs of tribes from around the country make this one of the great Native American gatherings in the country, and certainly one of the largest. See chapter 9.
- **Arapaho Sun Dance** (Wind River Indian Reservation, WY; ☎ **307/332-3060**): Various Plains Indian tribes now embrace the Sun Dance, but this gathering every summer is one of the most festive that's open to non-Indians. Visitors cannot bring cameras, and must be quiet and respectful during the 4-day ceremony. See chapter 12.

17 The Best Learning Vacations

- **Glacier Institute** (Glacier National Park, MT; ☎ **406/755-1211**): You can go hard or take it easy in Glacier Institute's field classes in and around the park. Offerings are comprehensive—geology and spirit; photography and forests. Classes run from 1 day to 1 month—though most are only a day or two. See chapter 4.
- **Pine Butte Guest Ranch Summer Trips and Workshops** (Choteau, MT; ☎ **406/466-2158**): Operated by the conservation group Nature Conservancy since 1978, Pine Butte has some of the best naturalist guides in the two states and offers weeklong workshops each spring and fall, with special attention to the bears in the area and their habitat. Located on 18,000 acres along the eastern

Rocky Mountain front, Pine Butte also offers the usual dude ranch activities—riding, hiking, and swimming. See chapter 7.

- **Yellowstone Association Institute** (Lamar Valley, Yellowstone National Park; ☎ **307/344-2294;** www.YellowstoneAssociation.org): This association, which is located at the old Buffalo Ranch in Yellowstone's Lamar Valley, offers more than 100 winter and summer courses, covering everything from wildlife tracking in the snow to wilderness medicine to the history of fur trappers on the plateau. The courses, some of which are offered for college credit, run from 2 to 5 days, with forays into the field, and lectures and demonstrations at the Institute's cramped quarters. Participants are generally friendly and supportive, sharing meals and stories in the common kitchen. Prices are reasonable, and some classes are specifically oriented to families and youngsters. See chapter 10.

- **The National Outdoor Leadership School** (Lander, WY; ☎ **307/332-6973**) takes youngsters and adults on journeys into wilderness areas around the world to learn how to take care of themselves and their companions on expeditions. The emphasis is on skills and leadership techniques, but there is also a great deal of naturalist lore passed along. NOLS has branches all over the world, but its largest operations are in Wyoming. See chapter 12.

18 The Best Performing Arts & Cultural Festivals

- **Flathead Festival** (Whitefish, MT; ☎ **406/862-7708**): Though coordinated out of Whitefish, this is an area-wide Flathead Lake music festival that runs through the month of July in venues around the region. It includes classical, blues, rock, folk, and other music styles. You can request the schedule of upcoming performances by early spring. In recent years, the festival has brought world-class operas to the area in addition to their annual summer concert series, one of the state's premier cultural attractions. See chapter 5.

- **International Wildlife Film Festival** (Missoula, MT; ☎ **406/728-9380**): Begun in 1977, this film festival has become a required festival for international filmmakers who specialize in wildlife. It goes for a week in early April, and includes panel discussions and workshops, as well as screenings of the world's best wildlife films. See chapter 5.

- **Montana Cowboy Poetry Gathering** (Lewistown, MT; ☎ **406/538-5436**): Held each year in mid-August, this is a rhyming good time for the bow legged and horse-drawn set. In addition to a healthy dose of range rhyme, there are arts-and-crafts shows, and booths full of leather. The event is held at the Yogo Inn and is coordinated by the chamber of commerce. See chapter 7.

- **Grand Teton Music Festival** (Jackson, WY; ☎ **307/733-1128**): Under the energetic direction of Eiji Oue, the festival gathers musicians from orchestras around the country for a summer program of classical music, mixed with the occasional Duke Ellington tribute. Top international soloists appear, and there is a fine chamber-music program, too. See chapter 11.

Planning a Trip to Montana & Wyoming

2

by Geoff O'Gara

Few things can ruin a much-anticipated vacation more than poor planning: arriving at a national park in mid-January, only to discover that it's closed until early May, for example. Similarly, you don't want to turn up with a suitcase full of shorts and T-shirts during months when snowstorms occur. This chapter is designed to assist you in sorting out the details that could make the difference between a trip you'll never forget and one you'd rather not remember.

1 The Regions in Brief

MONTANA

GLACIER COUNTRY & THE NORTHWEST CORNER   This includes Glacier National Park, the Flathead Valley and northwest corner of the state, and Missoula, one of Montana's three largest cities. Each year the park draws millions of visitors who come to see the combination of soaring peaks, varied wildlife, and innumerable lakes and streams that comprise this natural haven. The **Going-to-the-Sun Road,** a 50-mile scenic highway that cuts through the heart of the park from southwest to northeast, makes the park highly accessible to visitors. Elsewhere in the region, the increasingly popular Big Mountain draws downhill skiers, and Flathead Lake is a magnet because of its excellent water sports and quality golf courses. One of the fastest-growing areas in the state, the **Flathead Valley** shelters an interesting mix of residents: Farmers and loggers share ski lifts and trout streams with transplanted urbanites and big-bucks entrepreneurs, all looking for their slice of paradise. On the southern edge of the region is **Missoula,** a vigorous college town with fine restaurants, interesting shops, and bits and pieces of Montana history.

SOUTHWESTERN MONTANA   The people of this area in the central part of the state are extremely diversified. **Helena,** a town centered around arts and politics (though not necessarily in that order), has a beautiful historic district filled with classic architecture, and access to tremendous fishing on the Missouri River. **Butte,** on the other hand, is working hard to overcome the decay caused by the exploitation, then abandonment, of its mines. A town that once prospered, it is searching for a new identity—perhaps as a silicone capital or movie set. Other areas in this part of the state are full of lore, though not of the political kind. Vigilantes and corrupt sheriffs dominate the stories of the "ghost towns" of Virginia City and Nevada City, both of which are kept alive today by tourists seeking a realistic glimpse into the area's past.

MISSOURI RIVER COUNTRY   The most distinctive trait of this region, which stretches interminably from the mountains to the eastern border, is its prairies, which roll along in repetitive mundanity for hundreds of miles. One of the least populated areas in the state, its major population center is **Great Falls,** which is set to inaugurate a new Lewis and Clark Interpretive Center; likewise, the X-33 space program will be relocated to the town's Malmstrom Air Force Base. U.S. Highway 2, or the **Hi-Line**—that long stretch of pavement that runs across the northern part of the state—is made up of a series of farms and ranches that perpetuate the homesteader life. New farming equipment and techniques and satellite dishes by the house are just modern polish on an old tune. Residents cling to U.S. Highway 2 for every means of survival since most of the roads that connect to it are dirt and gravel and hardly worthy of travel in the winter months.

SOUTHCENTRAL MONTANA (YELLOWSTONE COUNTRY)   Though this region is almost a twin of the northwest part of the state in many ways—a nearby national park, renowned ski resorts, a university, heavy tourism—it has a personality of its own. The city of **Bozeman** has its own set of tourist attractions and an environment with more of a cowboy bearing, since ranching still thrives throughout the region. Anglers come from all over the world to fish these blue-ribbon trout streams, but the main attraction in this part of the state is **Yellowstone National Park.** Still, even the valleys that lead to it—the Madison, Gallatin, and Paradise—are spectacular destinations themselves.

EASTERN MONTANA   The geography in this part of Montana is no different from its neighboring region to the north, but there are more people and things to do here. **Billings** is the supply center for eastern Montana and northern Wyoming. It's easily the largest city in Montana and has grown in the last half of the 20th century without the helpful hand of tourism that the western side of the state has seen. The Bighorn Canyon and the Yellowtail Dam draw their share of visitors, especially hunters and fishermen, but this region's main attraction is **Little Bighorn Battlefield,** where Gen. George Armstrong Custer led the Seventh Cavalry to defeat at the hands of the Sioux and the Northern Cheyenne.

WYOMING

YELLOWSTONE PLATEAU   Yellowstone sits atop a volcanic caldera that periodically blows its top—about every 600,000 years—but in the interim provides a largely intact ecosystem of roughly 2 million acres. Protected by the national park and surrounding forests from much development, Yellowstone provides habitat no longer found elsewhere in the Lower 48, home to herds of bison, elk, grizzly bears, trumpeter swans, Yellowstone cutthroat trout, and more subtle beauties like wildflowers and hummingbirds. The geothermal area is greater than any other in the world, with mud pots, geysers, and hot springs of all color, size, and performance, indicative of a complex plumbing system that pulls water down into the earth's crust and regurgitates it at high temperatures. More than three million visitors come here annually, not just to pay homage to Old Faithful, but also to fish, hike, camp, and boat.

THE TETONS & JACKSON HOLE   The Tetons are a young range, abrupt and sharp-edged as they knife up from the Snake River valley. And while the peaks get top

The Regions of Montana & Wyoming

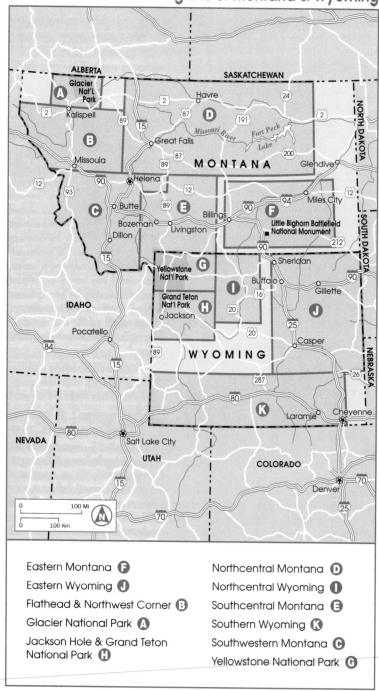

Eastern Montana **F**

Eastern Wyoming **J**

Flathead & Northwest Corner **B**

Glacier National Park **A**

Jackson Hole & Grand Teton
National Park **H**

Northcentral Montana **D**

Northcentral Wyoming **I**

Southcentral Montana **E**

Southern Wyoming **K**

Southwestern Montana **C**

Yellowstone National Park **G**

billing, it's the valley of Jackson Hole that provides the more varied environments and experiences. **Grand Teton National Park** is regarded by most visitors as scenically superior to its northern neighbor, with shimmering lakes, thickly carpeted forests, and towering peaks that are blanketed with snow throughout most of the year. It's a most accessible park—you can catch its breathtaking beauty on a quick drive-by—but there are lakes and waterfalls and even better views and adventures that you'll get to if you leave your car and take to the trails and waterways. The Tetons are especially popular with mountain climbers, who scale its peaks year-round. Elsewhere in the valley you can float the lively Snake River, visit the National Elk Refuge in the winter, or play cowboy at one of the dude and guest ranches that dot the valley. Skiers and snowboarders have a blast at the resorts here, as well as Grand Targhee on the other side of Teton Pass. And the snug town of **Jackson,** with its antler-arched town square and its busy shops, offers everything from classy art galleries to noisy two-step cowboy bars.

NORTHCENTRAL WYOMING   This is the sort of basin settlers were looking for when they came this way in the 19th century—mountain ranges on all sides and cradling wide, ranchable bottomlands, and some mineral wealth to pay for ranch kids' college educations. More and more, though, the oil and gas development, sheep herding and cattle driving, and beet and wheat growing are giving away to recreation and tourism. The beautiful mountains here—the Wind Rivers, the Owl Creeks, the Absarokas, the east side of the Bighorns—get less attention than, say, the Tetons, and that only makes them more attractive. Historically, the area learned its lessons in tourism from the West's greatest showman, Buffalo Bill Cody, who helped build the fun-loving town that still bears his name. The rodeo and great museum of **Cody** are joined by other attractions, including the Bighorn Canyon National Recreation Area, the hot springs of **Thermopolis,** and the **Wind River Indian Reservation,** home to the Shoshone and the Arapaho peoples.

EASTERN WYOMING   The plains don't begin when you pass east over the Continental Divide; there's another mountain range to cross, and another—first the Bighorns, then the Black Hills—before you're really out there on the howling flats. The **Bighorns** are a treasure of steep canyons, snow-crowned peaks, good fishing, and good hiking, and at their feet sit two of Wyoming's nicest communities, **Sheridan** and **Buffalo.** Some of the prize ranches in this country have become some of the best dude ranches in the country. Farther east, across the plains beyond the energy boomtown of **Gillette,** stands the 1,280-foot landmark of **Devils Tower,** and along Wyoming's eastern border rise the Black Hills. The region's other claim to fame lies in its history. This is the land of Butch Cassidy and his Hole-in-the-Wall Gang (also known as the Wild Bunch), of cattle rustlers, cowboys, and outlaws.

SOUTHERN WYOMING   To the millions of drivers who cross Wyoming on I-80, this is the empty quarter, mostly barren, windswept sagebrush plains. It is that, but it also has its own mountainous corner—the craggy **Medicine Bow**—a lot of history, and mineral wealth of many varieties, from natural gas to trona. More discerning travelers will not see a wasteland: They'll follow the routes of Oregon Trail pioneers (you can still find the wagon-wheel ruts and graves), get off the freeway to visit historic sites like Fort Laramie, and throw out a fishing line on the North Platte near Saratoga or in Flaming Gorge Reservoir south of Green River. In this country you'll find both old and new—from the re-created 1880s gold rush town of **South Pass City** to the capital city of **Cheyenne,** where the city throws the biggest rodeo party in the West during July's Frontier Days.

2 Visitor Information

MONTANA

Travel Montana, P.O. Box 200533, 1424 9th Ave., Helena, MT 59620-0533 (☎ **800/VISIT-MT** or 406/444-2654; visitmt.com) provides information about Big Sky country and specific locales in Montana.

They put out two well-designed **Vacation Guides**—one for summer, one for winter—including information about museums, national monuments and battle-fields, scenic driving tours, and events. A special section describes how road travelers can retrace the Lewis and Clark and Nez Perce trails. The companion *Travel Planner* provides more detailed information, including contacts with agencies that can provide information, travel services such as airlines and rental car agencies, and listings by town of places to stay and eat, with charts specifying price ranges and such amenities as hot tubs and disabled access. Travel Montana will also provide you with separate guides to some of Montana's more popular sports: snowmobiling, fishing, and skiing, as well as site-specific guides for each of the six travel regions divined by the state's travel experts: Glacier Country in the northwest, Gold West Country in the south-west, Russell Country in northcentral Montana, Yellowstone Country in southcentral Montana, Missouri River Country in the northeast, and Custer Country in the southeast.

For additional information about attractions, facilities, and services in specific Montana destinations—national parks, cities, or towns—contact the **Montana Chamber of Commerce,** Box 1730, Helena, MT 59624 (☎ **406/442-2405**), for the address and phone number of the nearest chamber office.

WYOMING

The **Wyoming Business Council Tourism Division,** I-25 at College Drive, Cheyenne, WY 82002 (☎ **800/225-5996** or 307/777-7777; www.wyomingtourism.org), distributes the *Wyoming Vacation Guide*, another fine-looking guide with information about sights and towns in the state's five travel areas: Devils Town/Buffalo Bill Country in the north and east; Oregon Trail/Rendezvous Country in central Wyoming; Medicine Bow/Flaming Gorge along the southern border; Jackson Hole/Jim Bridger country in the west; and Grand Teton and Yellowstone; as well as special features on everything from geology to adventure travel. The nitty-gritty of agency contacts, accommodations, and eateries is in the *Wyoming Vacation Directory*, which goes beyond motels to list guest ranches and B&Bs. Call ☎ **800/225-5996** to request a free copy.

INFORMATION ON PUBLIC LANDS

So much of the fun to be had in the Northern Rockies takes place out of doors, so here are some key resources. **Glacier National Park** can be contacted at Superinten-dent, Glacier National Park, West Glacier, MT 59936 (☎ **406/888-7800;** www.nps.gov/glac). **Yellowstone National Park** can be reached at Visitors Services, Yellowstone National Park, Box 168, Yellowstone National Park, WY 82190 (☎ **307/344-7381;** www.nps.gov/yell). For information on **Grand Teton National Park,** write to P.O. Drawer 170, Moose, WY 83012, call ☎ **307/739-3600,** or log onto www.nps.gov/grte.

The **U.S. Forest Service** has information about national forests and wilderness areas in Montana, as well as **Bridger-Teton National Forest** in Wyoming, at the

Weather Conditions

For up-to-date information on current weather, contact the **National Weather Service** at ☎ **406/449-5204** (Montana) or **307/772-2468** (Wyoming). Statewide **road conditions** are available by calling ☎ **800/226-7623** (Montana), or **888/WYO-ROAD** or 307/635-9966 (Wyoming).

Northern Region Office, Federal Building, 200 E. Broadway, Box 7669, Missoula, MT 59807 (☎ **406/329-3511;** www.fs.fed.us/r1). The rest of Wyoming's forests, as well as the Thunder Basin National Grassland, are covered by the Rocky Mountain Region Office, P.O. Box 25127, Lakewood, CO 80225 (☎ **303/275-5350;** www.fs.fed.us/r2).

The federal **Bureau of Land Management** also manages millions of acres of recreational lands and can be reached at its Wyoming state office, 5353 Yellowstone Rd., Cheyenne, WY 82003 (☎ **307/775-6256**), or its Montana state office, 222 N. 32nd St., Billings, MT 59101 (☎ **406/255-2888**).

For information on Montana state parks, fishing, and hunting, get in touch with **Montana Fish, Wildlife and Parks,** 1420 E. 6th Ave., Helena, MT 59620 (☎ **406/444-2535;** fwp.state.mt.us). This organization also offers a 900-number information line (☎ **900/225-5397**) on a wide variety of recreational topics, for $1.50 per minute. In Wyoming, contact **Wyoming State Parks and Historic Sites,** 122 W. 25th St., Herschler Bldg., 1-E, Cheyenne, WY 82002 (☎ **307/777-6323;** commerce.state.wy.us/sphs/index1.htm). For hunting and fishing, contact **Wyoming Game and Fish,** 5400 Bishop, Cheyenne, WY 82003 (☎ **307/777-4600;** gf.state.wy.us).

3 Money

Traveler's checks are accepted throughout both states and can be purchased at any bank for a small fee. Don't expect to be able to cash a personal check. Most restaurants and shops will allow you to use your credit cards, although some of the smaller, mom-and-pop establishments still refuse to go to the trouble. Some of the more exclusive dude ranches do not accept credit cards, either. In Montana, Canadian currency is accepted at the current conversion rate, although some businesses from time to time offer services or goods at par.

ATMS

ATMs are linked to a national network that most likely includes your bank at home. **Cirrus** (☎ **800/424-7787;** www.mastercard.com/atm/) and **PLUS** (☎ **800/843-7587;** www.visa.com/atms) are the two most popular networks; check the back of your ATM card to see which network your bank belongs to. Use the 800 numbers to locate ATMs in Montana and Wyoming. Be sure to check the daily withdrawal limit before you depart. Most banks in resort towns in the Montana/Wyoming area have ATM machines.

TRAVELER'S CHECKS

These days, traveler's checks seem less necessary because most cities have 24-hour ATMs that allow travelers to withdraw small amounts of cash as needed—and thus avoid the risk of carrying a fortune around an unfamiliar environment. Many banks, however, impose a fee every time a card is used at an ATM in a different city or bank.

What Things Cost in Montana & Wyoming	U.S.$
Expensive double in Missoula	$99
Mid-range double in Jackson	$145
Cabin (double) at Lake Yellowstone	$77
Guest ranch vacation in Sheridan area, family of four, 1 week	$4,200
Breakfast buffet at Old Faithful Inn	$7
Dinner for two w/ wine at the Blue Lion, Jackson (expensive)	$85
Good seats at Cheyenne Frontier Days Rodeo, 1 night	$18
Cafe latte at Coal Creek Coffee Co., Laramie	$2.25
Guided 1-day fly-fishing trip on the blue-ribbon North Platte (Wyoming)	$325
Adult lift ticket at Big Mountain in Whitefish, Montana	$40
Adult 2-day ticket to Buffalo Bill Historical Center, Cody	$10
Research on wolf/coyote behavior at Yellowstone Ecosystems Studies (per week)	$1,295
View from Beartooth Pass, south of Red Lodge, MT	$0

If you're withdrawing money every day, you might be better off with traveler's checks—provided that you don't mind showing identification every time you want to cash a check.

You can get traveler's checks at almost any bank. **American Express** offers denominations of $10, $20, $50, $100, $500, and $1,000. You'll pay a service charge ranging from 1% to 4%. You can also get American Express traveler's checks over the phone by calling ☎ **800/221-7282;** by using this number, AmEx gold and platinum cardholders are exempt from the 1% fee. AAA members can obtain checks without a fee at most AAA offices.

Visa offers traveler's checks at Citibank locations nationwide, as well as several other banks. The service charge ranges between 1.5% and 2%; checks come in denominations of $20, $50, $100, $500, and $1,000. **MasterCard** also offers traveler's checks. Call ☎ **800/223-9920** for a location near you.

CREDIT CARDS

Credit cards are invaluable when traveling. They are a safe way to carry money and provide a convenient record of all your expenses. You can also withdraw cash advances from your credit cards at any bank (though you'll start paying hefty interest on the advance the moment you receive the cash, and you won't receive frequent-flyer miles on an airline credit card). At most banks, you don't even need to go to a teller; you can get a cash advance at the ATM if you know your PIN number. If you've forgotten your PIN number or didn't even know you had one, call the phone number on the back of your credit card and ask the bank to send it to you. It usually takes 5 to 7 business days, though some banks will provide the number over the phone if you tell them your mother's maiden name or pass some other security clearance.

THEFT   Almost every credit-card company has an emergency 800-number that you can call if your wallet or purse is stolen. They may be able to wire you a cash advance off your credit card immediately, and in many places, they can deliver an emergency credit card in a day or two. The issuing bank's 800-number is usually on the back of the credit card—though of course that doesn't help you much if the card was stolen. The toll-free information directory will provide the number if you dial ☎ **800/ 555-1212.** Citicorp Visa's U.S. emergency number is ☎ **800/336-8472.** American Express cardholders and traveler's check holders should call ☎ **800/221-7282** for all money emergencies. MasterCard holders should call ☎ **800/307-7309.**

If you opt to carry traveler's checks, be sure to keep a record of their serial numbers, separately from the checks of course, so you're ensured a refund in just such an emergency.

4 When to Go

The northern Rockies are spectacular three seasons of the year, but they aren't the three seasons you might guess. Summer, autumn, and winter are the times to visit. The days are sunny, the nights are clear, humidity is low. A popular song once romanticized "Springtime in the Rockies," but that season—or what most people think of as spring-time—lasts about 2 days in early June. The rest of the spring season is likely to be chilly with spitting snow or rain, as most of the annual moisture in these states falls during March and April. Spring is when the weather is the most treacherous.

Summer is the best season to visit Montana for hiking, fishing, camping, and wildlife watching. It will be warm during the day and cool at night. Average highs in July run from 76° in **Bozeman** to 89° in **Miles City,** and lows at night from 40° to 60°. In **Wyoming,** the average high temperatures in July range from 85° to 95°—at this elevation, it almost never gets above 100°, and it's dry. The plains tend to get hotter than the mountains.

Montana's Average Monthly Temperatures (High/Low)

	Jan	Feb	Mar	Apr	May	Jun	Jul	Aug	Sep	Oct	Nov	Dec
Billings	36/12	44/17	52/24	63/33	72/42	81/50	89/55	88/53	76/43	66/34	49/23	38/14
Bozeman	33/13	38/18	44/23	55/31	64/39	74/46	82/52	81/51	70/42	59/33	43/23	34/15
Missoula	30/15	37/21	47/25	58/31	66/38	74/46	83/50	82/49	71/40	57/31	41/24	30/16
W. Yellowstone	24/0	30/4	37/10	46/20	58/29	69/37	79/41	76/39	65/31	52/23	34/12	23/1

Wyoming's Average Monthly Temperatures (High/Low)

	Jan	Feb	Mar	Apr	May	Jun	Jul	Aug	Sep	Oct	Nov	Dec
Casper	33/12	37/16	45/22	56/30	67/38	79/47	88/54	86/52	74/42	61/32	44/22	34/14
Cheyenne	38/15	41/18	45/22	55/30	65/40	74/48	82/55	80/53	71/44	60/34	47/24	39/17
Cody	34/12	40/17	47/23	56/31	66/40	76/49	84/55	82/53	71/43	61/35	45/24	36/15
Devils Tower	34/4	39/10	48/18	60/28	70/38	80/47	88/53	87/50	76/39	64/28	46/17	35/7
Jackson	26/4	32/7	41/16	51/24	62/30	72/37	82/41	80/39	70/31	58/23	39/16	27/5
Sheridan	33/9	38/15	46/22	57/30	66/39	77/47	86/53	85/52	73/41	62/32	45/20	35/10
Yellowstone	28/8	33/12	39/16	48/26	59/34	70/42	80/47	78/46	67/37	54/29	38/19	29/10

Fall brings spectacularly clear days, cool clear nights, and calm winds up until late October, when things get iffy again. If you've forgotten what the stars look like on a clear autumn night, fall in the Rockies will remind you. Weather is changeable, how-ever, and snow is possible—likely, even—in the high country, so don't try an extended backpacking trip unless you are experienced and well prepared. Actually, this is a requirement year-round; we've been caught in mountain snowstorms in July and August.

Winter is a glorious season here, though not for everyone. It can be very cold. Lows in Havre or Butte, West Yellowstone or Jackson average single digits in January. And it can be very windy in some parts of these states, especially on the plains. But the air is crystalline, the snow is powdery, and the skiing is fantastic. If you drive around Montana and Wyoming in the winter *always* carry sleeping bags, extra food, flashlights, and other safety gear. Your cell phone will not work in large areas of Montana and Wyoming. You need to be prepared to survive if your car breaks down, if you are blown off the road or if a blizzard or snow squall makes further progress impossible. Every resident has a horror story about being caught unprepared in the weather. Only the north entrance at Yellowstone National Park is open to automobiles in the winter. Lodging is available in the park at Mammoth and Old Faithful only. Ski resort towns like Jackson and Kalispell stay lively all winter, but summer tourist towns like Cody are rather quiet.

Northern Rockies Calendar of Events

January

- **Montana Pro Rodeo Circuit Finals.** Montana's best cowboys compete in the final round of this regional competition in Great Falls. Call ☎ **406/727-8115** for information. Second or third weekend in January.
- **Stage Stop Sled Dog Race.** Some of the top mushers in the world come to compete in this race around the Wind River Mountains, run in stages like the bicycling Tour de France, with festive overnight stops in towns along the way. Call ☎ **307/734-1163.** Late January to early February.

February

- **Wyoming Winter Fair.** They hold this one indoors in Lander, except for the chariot races. There are booths galore, music, entertainment, a livestock competition, and a big dance. Call ☎ **307/332-4011** for information. First week in February.
- **Winternational Sports Festival.** A multisport competition with tennis, racquetball, speedskating, soccer, swimming, and skiing events held in Anaconda and Butte, Montana. Call ☎ **800/735-6814** for information. Begins first weekend in February, continuing each weekend into April.
- **Race to the Sky.** This weeklong event is the longest continuous dogsled race in the Lower 48. It starts in Helena and ends in Missoula. Call ☎ **406/442-4008** for information. Second Saturday in February.
- **Cowboy Ski Challenge.** Novelty ski races and rodeo events take center stage during this Jackson, Wyoming, event that includes cowboy poetry readings, Dutch-oven cook-offs, and a barn dance. Call ☎ **307/733-3316** for information. Mid-February.

March

- **Big Mountain Doug Betters Winter Classic.** Celebrity ski benefit held near Whitefish, Montana, with proceeds going toward medical care for children. Call ☎ **406/862-3501** for information. Second Friday and Saturday of March.
- **Ski Joring.** A competition rooted in the Scandinavian tradition of pulling a skier behind a horse, in Red Lodge, Montana. Call ☎ **406/446-1718** for information. Early March.
- **St. Patrick's Day.** Montana's biggest 1-day celebration, held in Butte, includes a parade, various musical events, and lots of Irish mirth. Call ☎ **406/723-5042** for information.
- ✪ **C.M. Russell Auction of Original Art.** The finest Western art auction in the country, with exhibitors and attendees from around the world. Great Falls, Montana. Call ☎ **406/727-8787** for information. Mid-March.

- **World Snowmobile Expo.** Snowmobile dealerships from around the world display their new sleds in West Yellowstone, Montana, with test rides and demonstrations. Call ☎ **406/646-7701** for information. Second or third weekend in March.

April

- **International Wildlife Film Festival.** A unique, juried film competition in Missoula, Montana, with more than 100 entries from leading wildlife filmmakers. Call ☎ **406/728-9380** for information. Early April.
- ✪ **Pole, Pedal, Paddle Race.** This original race marks the end of the ski season in Teton Village, Wyoming, with a relay that combines skiing (downhill and cross-country), biking, and boating. Call ☎ **307/733-6433** for information. Early April.
- **Cowboy Songs and Range Ballads.** With scholarly underpinning, the Buffalo Bill Historical Center in Cody, Wyoming, stages a gathering of real cowboy song and storytelling. Call ☎ **307/587-4771** for the schedule. Mid-April.

May

- ✪ **Miles City Bucking Horse Sale.** A "3-day cowboy Mardi Gras," this stock sale in Miles City, Montana, features street dances, parades, barbecues, and, of course, lots of bucking broncos. Call ☎ **406/232-2890** for information. Third weekend in May.
- **Annual Whitewater Festival.** Downriver and slalom kayaking races on the Flathead's "Wild Mile," near Bigfork, Montana. Call ☎ **406/837-5888** for information. Third weekend in May.
- **Elk Antler Auction.** Nearly 10,000 pounds of bull-elk antlers are auctioned off in Jackson's town square. Call ☎ **307/733-3444** for information. Late May.

June

- **Happy Jack Mountain Music Festival.** Bluegrass and fiddles prevail over this festival of mountain music in Cheyenne, Wyoming. Call ☎ **307/777-7519** for information. Early June.
- **Woodchoppers Jamboree & Rodeo.** Historic mountain town hosts contests including log-rolling, along with rodeo. Encampment, Wyoming. Call ☎ **800/592-4309** for details. Mid-June.
- ✪ **Plains Indian Powwow.** Indian dancers from around the region compete in various dance categories, accompanied by traditional drum groups, on the Robbie Powwow Garden next to the Buffalo Bill Historical Center in Cody, Wyoming. Call ☎ **307/587-4771**. Mid-June.
- **Strawberry Festival.** A 1-day celebration of the strawberry in downtown Billings, Montana, with food vendors, arts and crafts, and live music. Call ☎ **406/259-5454** for information. Mid-June.
- ✪ **Chugwater Chili Cook-Off.** Thousands of hot-food pilgrims come to the Diamond Guest Ranch west of Chugwater, Wyoming, to taste the spicy contenders in this contest. Call ☎ **307/322-2322** for information. Mid-June.
- **Lewis & Clark Festival.** Commemoration of Lewis and Clark's journey in and around Great Falls, Montana, with historic reenactments, buffalo roasts, and float trips. Call ☎ **406/761-4434** for information. Late June.
- **Little Big Horn Days.** A 4-day festival of ethnic food and performances in Hardin, Montana, featuring Custer's Last Stand Reenactment. Call ☎ **406/665-1672** for information. Last weekend in June.
- **Shoshone Treaty Days/Eastern Shoshone Powwow and Indian Days.** A celebration of Native American tradition and culture that's followed by one of

Wyoming's largest powwows and all-Indian rodeos, in Fort Washakie, Wyoming. Call ☎ **307/332-9106** for information. Late June.

July

- **Cody Stampede.** There's rodeo nights all summer in Cody, but this long weekend is the big one, and the rodeo ring excitement carries over to street dances, fireworks, and food. Call ☎ **800/207-0744.** July 1 to 4.

- ✪ **Grand Teton Music Festival.** Fine musicians drawn from around the world join this orchestra for a summer in the mountains. A varied classical repertoire includes numerous chamber concerts and some premieres in Teton Village, Wyoming. Call ☎ **307/733-1128** for information. Mid-July through August.

- **Frontier Festival.** The Buffalo Bill Historical Center in Cody, Wyoming, hosts exhibits of frontier skills—rawhide braiding and blacksmithing, among others—along with competitions and entertainment. Call ☎ **307/587-4014** for information. Mid-July.

- **Legend of Rawhide Reenactment.** An overeager gold miner comes to an untimely end in this production of the popular, if apocryphal, Western legend in Lusk, Wyoming. Call ☎ **307/334-2950** for information. Second weekend in July.

- **Fiesta Days.** Street fair, big sales, and dance, topped by an Outhouse Obstacle Race, in Rawlins, Wyoming. For information contact ☎ **307/324-4111.** Second weekend in July.

- ✪ **North American Indian Days.** The Blackfeet Reservation hosts a weekend of native dancing, singing, and drumming, with crafts booths and games, in Browning, Montana. Call ☎ **406/338-7276** for information. Second week of July.

- ✪ **International Climbers Festival.** Speakers, music, demonstrations, and climbing at the famed Wild Iris and other rock faces in Fremont County attract rock climbers from around the world to this gathering in Lander, Wyoming. Call ☎ **307/332-6697.** Second weekend in July.

- **Yellowstone Jazz Festival.** This music camp gathers young musicians for tutelage by some big names from the jazz world, followed by a series of performances in Powell and Cody, Wyoming. Call ☎ **307/587-3898** for information. Mid-July.

- ✪ **Flathead Festival.** A 2-week concert series in Flathead Valley, Montana, featuring a variety of music from headline musicians in valley-wide settings. Call ☎ **406/257-0787** for information. Mid- to late July.

- **Bannack Days.** Frontier crafts, music, and drama re-create the Old West in the ghost town of Bannack, Montana. Call ☎ **406/834-3413** for information. Third weekend in July.

- **Montana State Fiddlers Contest.** A 2-day event in Polson, Montana, featuring competitions as well as impromptu and organized jam sessions among the state's best. Call ☎ **406/883-5969** for information. Third weekend in July.

- ✪ **Frontier Days.** One of the country's most popular rodeos, the "Daddy of 'em All" entertains standing-room-only crowds during a full week of rodeo events in Cheyenne, Wyoming. Call ☎ **800/227-6336** for information. Last full week of July.

August

- ✪ **Sweet Pea Festival.** A full-fledged arts festival in Bozeman, Montana, with fine art, headliner musicians, and various entertainment for all ages. Call ☎ **406/586-5421** for information. First full weekend in August.

- **Outlaw Trail Ride.** Participants saddle up and spend a week riding through the Hole-in-the-Wall Country where Butch and Sundance once hid, around the southern end of the Bighorn Mountains and in the sandstone country near Kaycee. Call ☎ 800/362-RIDE for information. Second week in August.
- **Grand Targhee Bluegrass Festival.** A 3-day celebration of music, arts, food, and entertainment in Jackson, Wyoming. Call ☎ 800/827-4433 for information. Mid-August.
- **Wind River Rendezvous.** A buffalo barbecue highlights this black powder, buckskinner event in Dubois, Wyoming. Call ☎ 307/455-2556 for information. Mid-August.
- ✪ **Crow Fair.** By far one of the biggest and best Native American gatherings in the Northwest, with dancing, food, and crafts in Crow Agency, Montana. Call ☎ 406/638-2601 for information. Mid-August.
- **River Festival and Wyoming Microbrewery Competition.** Held on the banks of the North Platte River in Wyoming, this float and festivity features brews from around the state. For details call ☎ 307/326-8855. Third weekend in August.
- **Montana Cowboy Poetry Gathering.** A 3-day event featuring readings and entertainment from the real McCoys in Lewistown, Montana. Call ☎ 406/538-5436 for information. Late August.
- **Big Sky Indian Powwow.** A celebration of various Native American tribes and their cultures, with traditional dancing, blanket trading, and authentic Native American food. In Helena, Montana. Call ☎ 406/442-4120 for information. Last weekend in August.

September

- **Fort Bridger Rendezvous.** At the re-created outpost of legendary scout Jim Bridger in Wyoming, mountain men gather to show their skills and hawk their wares. Call ☎ 307/789-2757 for information. Labor Day weekend.
- **Lander Jazz Festival.** Traditional jazz bands from around the country play in concerts, at street dances, and in the bars of Lander, Wyoming. For more information call ☎ 800/433-0662. Labor Day Weekend.
- **Nordicfest.** A Scandinavian celebration in Libby, Montana, featuring a parade, a juried craft show, headliner entertainment, and an international Fjord horse show. Call ☎ 406/293-6838 for information. First weekend following Labor Day.
- **Western Design Conference.** Western-style furniture and clothing fashions on the runway, in Cody, Wyoming. Call ☎ 888/685-0574 for more information. Third week in September.
- ✪ **Buffalo Bill Historical Center Art Show and Patrons Ball.** Big art sale to support the museum, and a black-tie dinner and ball, one of the Rockies' premier (and only) formal social events. Cody, Wyoming. For information call ☎ 307/578-2777 or 307/578-4032. Late September.
- **Oktoberfest.** A celebration of fall, German-style, with live music, good food, and better beer in Livingston, Montana. Call ☎ 406/222-0850 for information. Late September.

October

- **Flathead International Balloon Festival.** Pancake breakfasts, barbecues, and skydiving center around hot air balloon competitions in Flathead Valley, Montana. Call ☎ 406/756-9091 for information. Early October.
- ✪ **Microbrewery Festival.** Buy a mug and sample beers from various Pacific Northwest microbreweries. On the Big Mountain, near Whitefish, Montana. Call ☎ 406/862-1900 for information. Mid-October.

December
- **Dogsled Races.** A week's worth of dogsled racing in Anaconda, Montana, from 15 to 50 miles daily, including poker runs, passenger races, and a stampede race. Call ☎ **406/563-2675** for information. First week in December.
- **Christmas Strolls and Parades.** Statewide, Montana and Wyoming. Check with local chambers of commerce for specific dates and locations.

5 The Active Vacation Planner

There aren't too many people coming to the Rockies for amusement parks or opera festivals—the attraction here is the outdoors, and the fastest-growing sector of tourism is adventure travel, where you cut some of those civilized ties and get the adrenaline pumping. Every section of this book has suggestions for what you can do outside in the enviable setting of the Northern Rockies, but listed here, if you need them, are some general ideas to get you started.

Let's get the cautions out of the way first: For many visitors, this is a big jump in **altitude**—give yourself a few days to acclimate before you embark on strenuous exercise, and remember that the air is a little thinner. The **weather** in the northern Rockies is capricious—it can snow in July, or give you a serious burn (remember how thin the protective atmosphere is) in February. Be cautious around **wildlife,** particularly with children: Bison are not big sheepdogs, and bears are not stuffed animals; they are wild animals that can turn on you suddenly if you get too close. Finally, remember that you may be in one of the few regions still largely untrampled by man, so try not to **litter** in the plains or mountain wilderness.

ACTIVITIES A TO Z

BACKCOUNTRY SKIING   There is nothing as thrilling as skiing deep, untracked powder in completely wild terrain. The hard part can be getting there, strapping on skis and climbing through deep, soft snow. To enjoy this sport you need a good set of telemark skis, good information about where to go, and expert knowledge of snow conditions and avalanche risks. Among the best places to pursue this sport is **Togwotee Pass** in Bridger-Teton National Forest in Wyoming. Otherwise, check at local ski shops and ask at the headquarters of national forests and state parks. The **Jackson Hole Ski Resort** in 1999 decided to allow skiers to ski "out of bounds" beyond the areas groomed and patrolled—as long as they sign waivers. Check with other ski resorts about forest areas around the lifts that might be accessible for backcountry adventures.

BIKING   Mountain biking is a fast-growing sport: Some folks take it easy, pedaling their way to wild country on smooth, easy-grade paths; others are looking for a fast ride down on bumpy, steep trails that can send you head over heels. Bring your own bike or rent from one of the many local bike shops around the region; they will usually assist you in planning a local day trip equal to your fitness level and ability. Bicycling on roads is also popular, but there are limitations: While automobile traffic on many roads is light, there isn't much room, because most of the roads have only one lane of traffic in each direction and skimpy shoulders—**Yellowstone roads** are among the worst. Nor are drivers in this region terribly respectful of bicyclists. So be watchful, research your routes so you can keep to the wider roads, and always wear that helmet.

BOATING & SAILING   Serious sailors are not likely to put down roots at this altitude; even weekend sailors would be wise to look elsewhere for their kind of fun. But if you insist on trying, you'll find a few sails spread on the bigger lakes of these mountains. You can take a pretty big boat on pretty big **Flathead Lake,** or **Jackson Lake,**

Are You a Dude or a Guest?

A century ago, it was common courtesy in the West for ranches to feed and lodge travelers who stopped by on their treks across the great empty spaces. Gradually it became acceptable to accept a few dollars from guests, and by the 1920s a ranch visit was a full-fledged vacation, and "dude" had entered the Wyoming vocabulary.

When you make your ranch reservations out West, it's wise to know the difference between a "dude" and a "guest." A dude ranch only accepts visitors for at least a week, and they give you the whole package: riding, fishing, trips to the rodeo, family-style meals. Dude ranchers look down their noses at "guest" ranches, which will take overnight guests and charge extra for activities like riding.

---

or even **Yellowstone Lake,** if you're careful about the weather. Smaller boats like Hobie Cats in some ways better suit the sudden, swirling winds typical of these mountains.

Powerboating is another matter; if you've got a motor, pack a lunch and head for any of the many lakes that dot Montana and Wyoming's landscape. **Canyon Ferry** is a popular Montana waterskiing spot, and you'll see Wyoming powerboats cruising **Boysen Reservoir** or the many impoundments on the **North Platte.** Just make sure to check around locally regarding access if you're uncertain about it. All types of boats are available locally for rent, so never fear if you don't have your own.

CROSS-COUNTRY SKIING   If you don't plan to pound down the backcountry powder on telemark skis, but you like a little quiet cardiovascular workout during the winter, cross-country skiing can be practiced on any flat, open meadow or plain where there's snow on the ground. Scores of guest ranches now groom trails for both track and "skate" skiing, and almost every ski resort in the region has a trail system, though you may have to buy a ticket. If you don't want to pay to ski, **Forest Service logging roads** are typically used for cross-country trails. Many golf courses are also regularly groomed for track skiing; some are even lighted for night skiing. **Best place to cross-country ski in Montana:** West Yellowstone, training ground of U.S. Nordic and Biathlon ski teams; **in Wyoming:** Jackson Hole area and Grand Teton National Park.

DOWNHILL SKIING   There are 13 downhill ski areas in Montana and 11 in Wyoming, scattered amid the towering mountain ranges found predominantly in the western parts of both states. Breathtaking summit vistas are standard fare and slopes are less crowded than the major areas in neighboring states. Usually operating from late November to mid-April, and with comparatively shorter lift lines and less expensive lift tickets than most other ski areas in the country, Montana and Wyoming ski resorts are great values for the ski enthusiast. Don't fret if you're not skiing black-diamond runs; all ski resorts have acres of beginner and intermediate trails, and seasoned instructors provide lessons at extremely affordable prices. More and more often, you'll find telemark skiers honing their skills on packed resort slopes. **Best ski scene in Montana:** Big Sky Resort near Bozeman is the biggest in Montana, with runs for all abilities, and Whitefish's Big Mountain prides itself on a family atmosphere; **in Wyoming:** the Jackson Hole area wins hands down, with Jackson Hole Ski Resort, Snow King, and Grand Targhee ski hills all in close proximity.

DUDE RANCHES   The dude ranch is the fabled Western experience come to life: daily rides by horseback, cowboy coffee beneath an expansive blue sky, campfire sing-alongs with rope tricks, and homemade food served family-style in rustic lodges. But you won't end the day in a smelly bunkhouse—accommodations are usually in a comfortable cabin or lodge. You need not have any riding experience before your visit; ranch "hands" are trained to assist even the greenest of greenhorns. **Best places in Montana:** the Paradise and Gallatin valleys in the southwest; **in Wyoming:** the Sheridan area and the Wapiti Valley west of Cody.

FISHING   Trout grown in the wild have a different flavor and character than those hatchery-raised fish you find in more crowded states—that's why serious trout anglers comes to the Rockies. Montana and Wyoming have long been known for world-class fly-fishing, their streams and creeks teeming with native trout—rainbow, brook, brown, mackinaw, golden, and cutthroat—as well as kokanee salmon, yellow perch, largemouth bass, and northern pike. Warmwater species include sauger, channel cat-fish, and smallmouth bass. **Best places to fish in Montana:** on any one of the world-class, blue-ribbon streams in the southwest part of the state; **in Wyoming:** the North Platte River near Saratoga and the Miracle Mile, or the high lakes of the Wind River Indian Reservation.

GOLF   Golfers not familiar with Montana or Wyoming will be pleasantly surprised at the number of exceptional courses found in both states, particularly in Bigfork and Anaconda, Montana (where a Nicklaus-designed course opened in 1997). Summer's long days make this a perfect place to play a round (or two), especially when you take into consideration that average daily temperatures and humidity are much lower here than at destinations in Florida. This isn't much of a secret anymore, so set your tee times well in advance. **Best Montana courses:** the Old Works, Anaconda; Eagle Bend, Whitefish; **in Wyoming:** the Jackson Hole Golf and Tennis Club; Teton Pines, Jackson.

HIKING   Hiking gives you the extra added bonus of moderate to strenuous cardio-vascular exercise while you're touring the areas. The most important factor to consider when embarking on a hike is the ratio of distance traveled to elevation gained, so be certain to study topographical maps to find this information before setting out. The elevation you will gain over the course of the hike, much more so than the actual dis-tance you will travel, is the better indication of how difficult the hike will be. Be sure to wear comfortable hiking shoes that have been broken in or you may spend the rest of your trip limping around with blistered feet. If you plan on hiking in prime grizzly country, be sure to carry bear mace and check with rangers for what to do in case you actually see one (also see the factoid in chapter 4, "Bear Warning"). **Best places to take a hike in Montana:** Glacier National Park. **In Wyoming**: the Wind River Mountains or the Bighorn Mountains.

MOUNTAINEERING: ROCK & ICE CLIMBING   The northern Rockies pro-vide a spectacular setting for climbers in search of a peak experience. There are superb opportunities for climbers to experience the year-round beauty of Montana and Wyoming's mountains, whether you seek a daylong rock climb during the height of summer in Montana's Beartooths or a technical climb up one of the faces of the

Montana Fishing Permits

Fishing permits are required in all Montana state waters for all nonresidents over the age of 15. A license for the period March 1 through the following February is $45. A consecutive 2-day license is $10. Licenses are available from the Montana Depart-ment of Fish, Wildlife and Parks, 1420 E. 6th St, Helena, MT 59620 (☎ **406/444-2535**); at any local FWP office; or from most sporting goods stores, outfitters, or tackle shops.

Tetons. Ice climbing is becoming a hot ticket in the dead of winter, when many of the world's finest climbers congregate in Cody, Wyoming, for unforgettable winter mountaineering. Not for the faint of heart, the sport is highly technical and requires extreme fitness and stamina. **Best place to climb in Montana:** Granite Peak, the state's highest; **in Wyoming:** Grand Teton National Park or Wild Iris south of Lander.

SNOWBOARDING   Forget all those stereotypes you've heard about snowboarders: This sport is a simple combination of speed, air, and style. If you've never done it, realize that you may have a very sore butt during your first few days of trying to learn how to ride (although seasoned shredders swear that the learning curve is much shorter than that for skiing). If you're not new to the sport, you'll find Montana and Wyoming ski areas to be snowboard-friendly. If you're *really* into riding, ask around at local ski shops for winter backcountry options or summer snowboarding—**Glacier Park's Logan Pass** is a popular Fourth of July hike 'n' ride destination. **Best place in Montana and Wyoming:** The Big Mountain.

SNOWMOBILING   With more than 3,000 miles of trails in Montana and 1,300 in Wyoming, snowmobilers have a vast winter playground to explore. Though sled rental shops are plentiful, machines are in high demand, so you're wise to make a reservation well in advance of your arrival. Though snowmobiling doesn't require an extreme level of physical fitness, you have to be able to adequately handle the snowmobile and be well-versed in safety measures since avalanches are common in the areas some of these trails traverse. Snowmobiles are prohibited in Glacier National Park, but they are still allowed to operate on groomed trails in Yellowstone. **Best bet for sledding in Montana:** West Yellowstone and the Seeley Lake Valley; **in Wyoming:** Yellowstone National Park.

WATER SPORTS: CANOEING, KAYAKING, RAFTING & SAILING   Paddlers have got a wealth of choices here, whether they want to kayak Class IV white water or canoe beneath osprey on an alpine lake. Montana is particularly rich in rivers worth floating: the Flathead, the Blackfoot, the Madison, the Clarks Fork near Missoula, the Dearborn, the Yellowstone, and more, even the big old Missouri. In Wyoming there is less variety, but some fine stretches of river on the Snake, the Platte, the Hoback, or Wyoming's own Clarks Fork through Sunlight Basin. If you choose white-water rafting, the most popular summer water sport in these parts, you leave the driving to someone else, though you may be asked to paddle. It's a thrilling way to spend a morning, day, or entire week, as long as you don't mind getting soaked, and it's open to anyone regardless of skill or age. The smaller rivers have no dams to regulate flows, which means kayakers seeking fast, scary runs should come during runoff in June, while canoeists wanting to relax and bird-watch can easily handle the upper Snake or Flathead late in the summer. **Best places to paddle in Montana:** For thrills, try the Yellowstone River at Gardiner; **in Wyoming:** the Snake River.

CHOOSING AN OUTFITTER

If you're just getting started as an outdoor adventurer, you might wisely hire an outfitter to train and guide you in the ways of the wild. Even if you know your way around a snow cave or the Exum Route up Grand Teton, you might prefer to pay someone else to handle the logistics of food, shelter, and planning, so you can just enjoy yourself. Give that some thought, then check your bank account, because outfitters can be expensive.

When considering an outfitter, ask yourself what you expect to get out of the trip. Think about things like group size, activity level, and guide expertise. Do you mind sleeping in a tent every night? Do you want to travel with a small group or be part of

Finding a Licensed Outfitter

The Montana Board of Outfitters will provide you with a booklet listing all licensed outfitters and guides in the state for a nominal fee. Request one by writing to the Montana Board of Outfitters and Professional Guides, Arcade Building, 111 N. Jackson, Helena, MT 59620, or call them at ☎ **406/444-3738.** A similar Wyoming directory is available by writing to the **Wyoming Outfitters and Guide Association,** P.O. Box 2284, Cody, WY 82414, or by calling ☎ **307/527-7453.**

a larger one? With strangers, or friends? Is your fitness level appropriate to the type of trip you want to take? Do you want to try a new approach— like packing llamas— or go into an area you've never explored before? Evaluate your own limitations honestly—your health, your outdoor experience, your travel comfort zone.

Make sure that the company is up-to-date with state licenses and Forest Service permits, if applicable. An outfitter without a license is breaking the law, but so are you, if you hire one. Find out how well the company knows the area where you're going, and ask for references from people they've taken on similar trips. Inquire who will actually accompany you—often it's not the boss—and about the guide's background and experience. Get a firm price, including extras like airport transfers, meals, or equipment rentals.

Here are some travel outfitters that help arrange trips of all varieties—including trips where you might try several different angles, like combining rafting with visits to historic sites—in our region. They are essentially brokers who work with reputable outfitters, either offering a completely planned package or helping clients create tailor-made itineraries:

Your Ride Tours (☎ **307/577-1226**) in Wyoming tailors sightseeing tours across the state year-round. Participants can travel via bus, mountain bike, or even horse-drawn wagon. Your Ride also offers customized educational tours—such as the ecology of Yellowstone or the history of the Oregon Trail. Reservations are required 2 to 6 months in advance, depending on the mode of transportation desired.

Also try **American Wilderness Experience,** P.O. Box 1486, Boulder, CO 80306 (☎ **800/444-0099;** www.awetrips.com); and **Off the Beaten Path** (☎ **800/445-2995**), 27 E. Main St., Bozeman, MT 59715.

6 Tips on Insurance, Health & Safety

INSURANCE

The cost of your trip will usually include liability coverage for any accidents that may occur as a result of your outfitter's negligence. Ask, and check your personal health insurance policy for details regarding medical emergencies. Your homeowner's insurance should cover stolen luggage. The airlines are responsible for $1,250 on domestic flights if they lose your luggage; if you plan to carry anything more valuable than that, keep it in your carry-on bag. Some credit/charge-card companies may insure you against travel accidents if you buy plane, train, or bus tickets with their cards. Before purchasing additional insurance, read your policies and agreements carefully. Call your insurers or credit/charge-card companies if you have any questions. American Express and certain gold and platinum Visa and Master-Cards offer automatic flight insurance against death or dismemberment in case of an airplane crash.

If you do require additional insurance, try one of the companies listed below. But don't pay for more than you need. For example, if you need only trip cancellation insurance, don't purchase coverage for lost or stolen property. Trip cancellation insurance costs approximately 6% to 8% of the total value of your vacation.

Access America, 6600 W. Broad St., Richmond, VA 23230
(☎ **800/284-8300**)
Travel Guard International, 1145 Clark St., Stevens Point, WI 54481
(☎ **800/826-1300**)
Travel Insured International, Inc., P.O. Box 280568, East Hartford, CT 06128 (☎ **800/243-3174**)
Travelex Insurance Services, P.O. Box 9408, Garden City, NY 11530-9408
(☎ **800/228-9792**)

SAFETY

It goes without saying that life jackets, helmets, pads, and other protective gear are essential when pursuing an outdoor adventure. If you aren't bringing your own, make sure that the shop you are renting from will also provide you with safety equipment.

Winter backcountry explorers should always be equipped with a shovel, a sectional probe, and an avalanche transceiver, since avalanches are common. If you're exploring during the summer, carry a can of pepper spray (bear mace), an effective deterrent to bears, available at local sporting goods stores.

If your wilderness activity takes you to a body of water, have extra clothes available in case you get wet, preferably wool and fleece fabrics, which wick away moisture. Many Western streams, rivers, and lakes are glacier-fed, and run high during spring months; they can be difficult to negotiate and are extremely cold.

When driving during the winter months, even on highways, four-wheel drive or at least front-wheel drive is wise, because of how quickly conditions can worsen. At all times of the year, it's a sensible precaution to carry a sleeping bag and flashlight.

HYPOTHERMIA   Hypothermia is an abnormally low body temperature resulting from exposure to cold and aggravated by exhaustion, wetness, and wind. It is a leading cause of death among outdoor recreationists. It occurs when your body gets so cold that it can no longer warm itself. It is not limited to cold weather; you can get hypothermia on a summer day that suddenly turns stormy. Always dress in layers and be prepared for bad weather, especially if you will be away from your car or lodging for an extended amount of time. When a partner gets hypothermia, you should join him or her in a sleeping bag and use your body warmth to assist.

7   Tips for Travelers with Special Needs

FOR TRAVELERS WITH DISABILITIES

While efforts are being made in national parks and state facilities to accommodate people with disabilities, the less-developed areas of Wyoming and Montana often pose accessibility problems. The **Montana Independent Living Project** (☎ **800/735-6457**) operates an information and referral service for travelers with disabilities, providing information relating to such topics as accessibility, recreation, and transportation.

The Wyoming Business Council Division of Tourism, in conjunction with the Department of Vocational Rehabilitation, offers an incredible free guide to disabled persons touring the state. *Access Wyoming* provides readers with important restaurant and hotel listings complete with visual alarm clock information, TDD numbers, and wheelchair-accessible facilities throughout the state. For a copy of the guide, contact the Wyoming Division of Tourism, I-25 at College Drive, Cheyenne, WY 82002 (☎ **800/225-5996** or 307/777-7777).

Also note that the **National Park Service** issues free "Golden Access Passports," which entitle disabled visitors and a guest to free admission into national parks, forests, and wildlife refuges. Get them at park entrances. **Amtrak** (☎ **800/ USA-RAIL**) and **Greyhound** (☎ **800/231-2222**) both provide assistance and discounts for travelers with disabilities.

Eagle Mount is committed to creating unparalleled recreational opportunities for people of all ages with disabilities. Adaptive ski techniques and personalized instruction are utilized in Eagle Ski programs at the following Montana ski areas: **Bridger Bowl and the Bohart Ranch** (☎ 406/586-1781), **Red Lodge Mountain** (☎ 406/245-5422), and **Showdown** (☎ 406/454-1449).

Travelers with disabilities can join **The Society for the Advancement of Travel for the Handicapped (SATH),** 347 Fifth Ave., Suite 610, New York, NY 10016 (☎ **212/447-7284;** fax 212/725-8253; www.sath.org) for $45 annually, $30 for seniors and students, to gain access to their vast network of connections in the travel industry. They provide information sheets on travel destinations, and referrals to tour operators that specialize in traveling with disabilities. Their quarterly magazine, *Open World for Disability and Mature Travel,* is full of good information and resources. A year's subscription is $13 ($21 outside the U.S.).

Travelers with disabilities may also want to consider joining a tour that caters specifically to them. One of the best operators is **Flying Wheels Travel,** 143 W. Bridge (P.O. Box 382), Owatonna, MN 55060 (☎ 800/535-6790). They offer various escorted tours and cruises, with an emphasis on sports, as well as private tours in minivans with lifts. Other reputable specialized tour operators include **Access Adventures** (☎ 716/889-9096), which offers sports-related vacations; **Accessible Journeys** (☎ 800/TINGLES or 610/521-0339), for slow walkers and wheelchair travelers; **The Guided Tour, Inc.** (☎ 215/782-1370); **Wilderness Inquiry** (☎ 800/728-0719 or 612/379-3858); and **Directions Unlimited** (☎ 800/533-5343).

Many of the major car-rental companies now offer hand-controlled cars for disabled drivers. **Avis** can provide such a vehicle at any of its locations in the U.S. with 48-hour advance notice; **Hertz** requires between 24 and 72 hours of advance reservation at most of its locations. **Wheelchair Getaways** (☎ **800/873-4973;** www.blvd. com/wg.htm) rents specialized vans with wheelchair lifts and other features for the disabled in more than 100 cities across the United States.

FOR GAY & LESBIAN TRAVELERS

The murder of gay Laramie student Matthew Shepard in 1998 sent shock waves far beyond Wyoming's borders, and discouraged many gay and lesbian travelers from coming to the northern Rockies. Gay-oriented travel agencies confirm this, and none presently offer specifically gay and/or lesbian group tours to Montana or Wyoming. Nevertheless, there are gay communities in the region's larger cities—Billings, Bozeman, Helena, Missoula, Casper, Laramie, Jackson, and Cheyenne—and while these two states could generally be considered conservative regarding alternative lifestyles, communities are generally tolerant of locals who have come out.

If you are trying to identify resorts comfortable with openly gay or lesbian guests, your best bet is to search the Internet. Though many gay and lesbian travel sites have no listings for Montana or Wyoming, a few do, like **Gaywired.com Travel** at www.gaywired.com/travel.htm or "Outwest Adventures" offered by **Friends Travel** at home.earthlink.net/~friendstravl/index-new.htm.

The **International Gay & Lesbian Travel Association (IGLTA)** (☎ 800/448-8550 or 954/776-2626; fax 954/776-3303; www.iglta.org) links travelers with the appropriate gay-friendly service organization or tour specialist. With around 1,200 members, it offers quarterly newsletters, marketing mailings, and a membership directory that's updated quarterly. Membership often includes gay or lesbian businesses but is open to individuals for $150 yearly, plus a $100 administration fee for new members. Members are kept informed of gay and gay-friendly hoteliers, tour operators, and airline and cruise-line representatives. Contact the IGLTA for a list of its member agencies, who will be tied into IGLTA's information resources.

FOR SENIORS

U.S. citizens over the age of 62 can purchase the **Golden Age Passport,** which allows unlimited access to any U.S. national park for a one-time fee of $10.

The **American Association of Retired Persons (AARP),** 601 E St. NW, Washington, DC 20049 (☎ 202/434-2277; www.aarp.org), and the National Council of Senior Citizens, 925 15th St. NW, Washington, DC 20005 (☎ 202/347-8800), both offer members various travel benefits. Similarly, many hotels and attractions in both states offer a discount to senior citizens. Be sure to ask for this discount before you make your reservation or purchase a ticket; and have proof of your age (driver's license or passport).

Travelers 55 or older may want to join other seniors on a lively trip with **Elderhostel,** 75 Federal St., Boston, MA 02110-1941, (☎ 877/426-8056; www.elderhostel.org), which runs numerous programs throughout Montana and Wyoming during the summer and winter. Generally, the courses offer informative presentations on culture, history, and crafts in settings as varied as universities and alpine lake cabins. Programs generally run less than a week, and participants in this region may find themselves meeting Native Americans, listening to a historian talk about the fur-trapping area, or learning to make beef jerky.

FOR FAMILIES

Be sure to ask about family discounts for accommodations before making your reservations. If you plan to stay a week at a ski resort or dude ranch, you may find a better value by renting a condominium or lodge than multiple rooms. Ski areas often offer packages that include accommodations and lift tickets; check with the ski resort's reservation service for current prices. Before booking any type of room, event, or activity, be sure to inquire if there are discounts for children or age restrictions. Know exactly what you're buying before you leave home: "Does the per-person cost include meals and activities?" for example. You can also consult **Families Welcome!,** 92 N. Main, Ashland, OR 97520 (☎ 800/326-0724 or 541/482-6121), which is a travel company that specialize in worry-free vacations for families.

A tip: Find out exactly what a motel means when it advertises a "continental breakfast." If it's coffee and donuts, that probably won't be enough for the kids. However, for many motels the definition of a "continental breakfast" means cereal, juice, toast, pastries, and beverages, which can save a family of four around $25 for morning meals.

FOR STUDENTS

Students looking for a good lodging value should check out hostels. Though Montana and Wyoming have an unusually short list of statewide hostels, it changes from year to year—as this edition goes to press, the only nationally affiliated hostel in these two states is in East Glacier Park. But it's a beaut—a two-story log building with deep porches where you can stay for $12 per night. To join, make reservations, or keep abreast of any additional hostels, contact **Hostelling International-American Youth Hostels,** 733 15th St. NW, Suite 840, Washington, DC 20005 (☎ 202/783-6171; www.hiayh.org. A 12-month membership is free for anyone under 18, costs $25 for adults (ages 18 to 54), $15 for seniors (over 54), or $250 for a life membership. Included in the cost of membership is a publication titled *Hostelling North America,* a thorough directory of member hostels, but these days you can go to the Web site and bring up a current map and listing of hostels.

With three national parks within their borders, Montana and Wyoming are popular destinations for students, regardless of the season. Many choose to work in a national park during the summer or a ski resort in the winter. If you're interested in obtaining a summer park job, contact **Glacier** (☎ 406/888-5441), **Yellowstone** (☎ 307/344-7381), or **Grand Teton** (☎ 307/739-3399) national parks directly for more information and applications.

8 Getting There

BY PLANE

Travelers flying into Montana can choose to land in one of the state's six major airports: Billings, Bozeman, Great Falls, Helena, Kalispell, or Missoula. Air service to these airports is provided by the following airlines, although only Billings can boast of service from all three: **Delta** (☎ 800/221-1212), **Northwest** (☎ 800/225-2525), and **United** (☎ 800/241-6522). Delta's commuter affiliate is **Skywest** (☎ 800/453-9417), and Northwest's is **Horizon** (☎ 800/547-9308). The busiest of the smaller connection airlines is **Big Sky** (☎ 800/237-7788).

In Wyoming, Jackson, Casper, Cheyenne, Cody, Gillette, Laramie, Riverton, Rock Springs, and Sheridan all have airports with commercial intrastate airline service. Presently, the two major airlines serving the state are **Delta** (☎ 800/221-1212) and **United** (☎ 800/241-6522), with seasonal service to Jackson by **American Airlines** (☎ 800/433-7300). Commuter carriers in Wyoming have confused travelers in recent years by frequently changing affiliations and schedules, but currently they include **Skywest** (the Delta Connection) (☎ 800/453-9417) and **Great Lakes Aviation** (United Express) (☎ 800/241-6522).

FLYING FOR LESS: TIPS FOR GETTING THE BEST AIRFARES

Here are some easy ways to save on airfare:

1. Consolidators, also known as bucket shops, are a good place to find low fares. Consolidators buy seats in bulk from the airlines and then sell them back to the public at prices below even the airlines' discounted rates. Their small boxed ads usually run in the Sunday newspaper's travel section at the bottom of the page. Before you pay, however, ask for a confirmation number from the consolidator and then call the airline itself to confirm your seat. Be prepared to book your ticket with a different consolidator—there are many to choose from—if the airline can't confirm your reservation. Also be aware that bucket shop tickets are usually nonrefundable or rigged with stiff cancellation penalties, often as high as 50% to 75% of the ticket price.

     Council Travel (☎ 800/226-8624; www.counciltravel.com) and **STA Travel** (☎ 800/781-4040; www.sta.travel.com) cater especially to young travelers, but their bargain-basement prices are available to people of all ages. **Travel Bargains** (☎ 800/AIR-FARE; www.1800airfare.com) was formerly owned by TWA but now offers the deepest discounts on many other airlines, with a 4-day advance purchase. Other reliable consolidators include **1/800-FLY-CHEAP** (www. 1800flycheap.com); **TFI Tours International** (☎ 800/745-8000 or 212/ 736-1140), which serves as a clearinghouse for unused seats; or "rebators" such as **Travel Avenue** (☎ 800/333-3335 or 312/876-1116) and the **Smart Traveller** (☎ 800/448-3338 in the U.S., or 305/448-3338), which rebate part of their commissions to you.

2. Search the Internet for cheap fares—though it's still best to compare your findings with the research of a dedicated travel agent, if you're lucky enough to have one, especially when you're booking more than just a flight. A few of the better-respected virtual travel agents are Travelocity (www.travelocity.com) and Microsoft Expedia (www.expedia.com). Each has its own little quirks—Travelocity and Expedia, for example, require you to register with them—but they all provide variations of the same service. Just enter the dates you want to fly and the cities you want to visit, and the computer roots out the lowest fares. Expedia's site will e-mail you the best airfare deal once a week if you so choose. Travelocity uses the SABRE computer reservations system that most travel agents use, and has a "Last Minute Deals" database that advertises really cheap fares for those who can get away at a moment's notice.

3. Great last-minute deals are also available through a free e-mail service, provided directly by the airlines, called E-savers. Each week, the airline sends you a list of discounted flights, usually leaving the upcoming Friday or Saturday, and returning the following Monday or Tuesday. You can sign up for all the major airlines at once by logging on to Smarter Living (www.smarterliving.com), or go to each individual airline's Web site.

4. Join a travel club such as **Moment's Notice** (☎ 718/234-6295) or **Sears Discount Travel Club** (☎ 800/433-9383, or 800/255-1487 to join), which supply unsold tickets at discounted prices. You pay an annual membership fee to get the club's hotline number. Of course, you're limited to what's available, so you have to be flexible.

BY CAR

In Montana, **I-90** runs east-west from St. Regis to Wyola, near the Wyoming border southeast of Billings. **I-94** goes east from Billings to Glendive and the North Dakota border. **U.S. Highway 2,** called the "Hi-Line," is another east-west alternative, stretching across the northern reaches of Montana from Bainville to Troy. The major interstate traversing the state from north to south is **I-15,** from Sweetgrass to Monida.

Wyoming is crossed through the southern part of the state by **I-80,** a huge trucker route from Egbert in the east to Evanston in the west. **I-90** begins in the northcentral part of the state near Ranchester and comes out in the northeast near Beulah. Just outside Buffalo is I-90's junction with **I-25,** a north-south route that runs through Cheyenne. The western part of the state north of Rock Springs is dominated by U.S. highways and secondary state-maintained roads.

BY TRAIN

Amtrak's *Empire Builder* (☎ **800/872-7245**) provides rail service along the northern tier of Montana, traveling west from Chicago and east from Seattle. The train stops in the following towns along the Hi-Line (U.S. Highway 2, east-west): Wolf Point, Glasgow, Malta, Havre, Shelby, Cut Bank, Browning, East Glacier, Essex, West Glacier, Whitefish, and Libby. Now and then the train returns to its Wyoming route when there is track or weather trouble in Colorado—an indication that train travel in

Montana Driving Distances

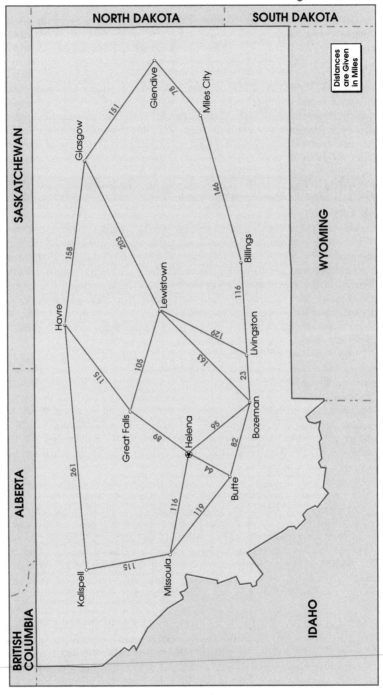

Distances are Given in Miles

NORTH DAKOTA   SOUTH DAKOTA

SASKATCHEWAN

WYOMING

ALBERTA

BRITISH COLUMBIA

IDAHO

Glendive
Miles City
Glasgow
151
78
146
Billings
158
203
116
Lewistown
Havre
Livingston
129
105
163
23
Great Falls
Helena
Bozeman
89
95
82
115
64
Butte
116
119
Kalispell
261
Missoula
115

37

this part of the country is an inconsistent mode of transportation, certainly not anything to set your watch by. Still, a trip on the *Empire Builder* can be an unhurried meditation on the American landscape from the Rockies to the West Coast.

BY BUS

Greyhound (☎ 800/231-2222) can provide you with information on specific routes to Montana's and Wyoming's most popular destinations from other cities around the country. Be sure to inquire about discounts on advanced ticket purchases and reduced fares for foreign travelers. **Rimrock Stages** (☎ 800/255-7655) operates bus lines through Montana. Some Wyoming feeder routes are covered by **Powder River Bus Lines** (☎ 307/635-1327).

9 Getting Around

BY CAR

With a weak public transportation infrastructure and long distances between towns, an automobile is essential in these parts, particularly if you plan to get off the beaten path (the exception would be a ski vacation where you stay at the resort). Most paved roads are well-maintained—in fact, road repair crews are a much bigger hazard than potholes. Be forewarned that many of the less-accessible places require driving down dirt or gravel roads, far from the nearest tow truck. There is also a high incidence of cracked windshields—one reason you might consider renting a car (and checking that little $1 insurance box) instead of driving your own if you plan to explore these out-of-the-way places.

If you plan to get off the highway, rent accordingly: You'll need front-wheel drive at least, and if you're going onto the bentonite roads of the desert or foothills, you'd better get four-wheel drive. In the winter, even the interstate can turn glassy and treacherous.

Car rentals are available in every sizable city in the state and at airports. Widely represented agencies include **Alamo** (☎ 800/327-9633), **Avis** (☎ 800/831-2847), **Budget** (☎ 800/527-0700), **Hertz** (☎ 800/654-3131), and **Thrifty** (☎ 800/699-1025). We give detailed lists of car-rental agencies in particular areas throughout the book.

Montana now has speed limits—75 m.p.h. on the interstates, and 70 m.p.h. and slower on secondary roads, depending on the road condition and contour.

The interstate speed limits in Wyoming are 75 m.p.h., while the speed limits for two-lane roads throughout the state are as posted (usually 55 or 65 m.p.h.). The limits are enforced fairly strictly, particularly in construction areas, where fines are doubled.

For information on current driving conditions in **Glacier National Park,** call ☎ 406/888-5441; in **Yellowstone National Park,** call ☎ 307/344-7381. It's important to check, when you're planning a trip, because the parks are working through a backlog of road repair, and one entrance or another may be subject to long delays.

ROAD CLOSINGS IN GLACIER **Going-to-the-Sun Road** in Glacier National Park is closed in winter, usually from mid-October to early June; its opening depends on current weather and road conditions. Call the park at ☎ 406/888-5441 to find when tentative openings and closings are scheduled. However, during the winter, you can drive Going-to-the-Sun Road for 10 miles from West Glacier along Lake McDonald to the road closure. **U.S. highways 2 and 89**—with access to East Glacier and St. Mary, respectively—are plowed regularly.

Wyoming Driving Distances

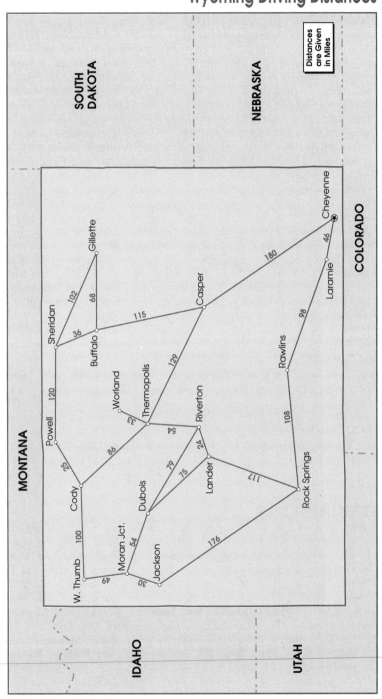

Distances are Given in Miles

ROAD CLOSINGS IN YELLOWSTONE   In the winter, the only access into Yellowstone National Park by car is the northern entrance at **Gardiner, Montana,** which is kept open to get supplies to Cooke City, just outside the park's northeast gate. The west entrance, just outside the town of West Yellowstone, Montana, is open to wheeled vehicles from April to November and during the winter to snowmobiles. The south entrance is from Grand Teton National Park and is open to wheeled vehicles from May to November and to snowmobile traffic from December to March. The east entrance is 52 miles west of Cody and is open to wheeled traffic from May to September and to snowmobiles from December to March. The northeast entrance, at **Cooke City, Montana,** is open throughout the year to wheeled vehicles, but in the late fall, when the Beartooth Pass is closed, the only route to Cooke City is through the Gardiner entrance.

Take extra precautions when driving in winter, since some highways may be restricted to four-wheel-drive vehicles or those equipped with tire chains or snow tires (these highways will be clearly marked). If the transportation department or highway patrol determines that a road is hazardous, roads may be closed by a barrier. If you encounter a roadblock during winter, choose an alternate route: Passing a road barrier is a misdemeanor offense and punishable by fine and/or imprisonment. Make sure your trunk is equipped with the following safety items: a shovel and a small bag of sand or cat litter in case you get stuck in snow or ice; a first-aid kit; jumper cables; wool blankets or sleeping bag; and an ice scraper/snow brush. Always carry drinking water, summer or winter.

Above all, drive slower, don't make any sudden turns or stops, and watch for wildlife: Some animals gravitate to the warmth of asphalt during cold weather.

HITCHHIKING   Unless you're literally on the road—between the painted lines on either side—or happen to be sticking your thumb out in a location where signs are posted to the contrary, hitchhiking is perfectly legal in Montana. For your personal safety, make sure that you are well off the shoulder of the road and watch for those signs: Where designated illegal, hitchhiking is a misdemeanor offense and can carry fines of up to $500.

In Wyoming, hitchhiking is illegal and can set you back $750 and/or land you in the slammer for up to 6 months. According to the Highway Patrol office in Cheyenne, fines and jail time are unlikely, but they do mean business when they ask you to get off the roadside.

BY ESCORTED TOUR

If you're short on time, an escorted tour may provide you with the most thorough trip, even though you'll be traveling in a large group and observing a rigid time schedule. One particular advantage is that tour companies are staffed with knowledgeable operators who will be able to enhance your understanding of the area. The following companies provide escorted tours of specific areas in Montana and Wyoming including Glacier, Yellowstone, and Grand Teton national parks: **Aventours** (☎ 406/587-5226), **Common Man Tours** (☎ 406/446-2329), **Montana's First Connection** (☎ 406/652-8839), **High Country Discovery** (☎ 406/267-3377), **Northwest Passage** (☎ 406/256-9793), **Rocky Mountain Tours** (☎ 406/862-4648), **Tauck Tours** (☎ 800/468-2825), and **Tours by Maitland** (☎ 406/755-8687).

Fast Facts: Montana & Wyoming

AAA   If you're a member of the American Automobile Association and you have a breakdown on the road, call ☎ **AAA-HELP** for 24-hour emergency roadside service (but you should expect things to take a while here).

American Express   American Express travel-service representatives are located across the state. To automatically connect with the nearest agent, call ☎ **800/221-7282.**

Area Code   The statewide area code for Montana is **406.** The Wyoming area code is **307.** Intrastate long-distance calls also require these prefixes.

Banks/ATM Networks   Banks in Montana and Wyoming are generally open Monday through Thursday from 9am to 4pm with extended hours to 6pm on Friday. Some are open on Saturday from 9am to noon. They are closed on Sunday. Automated teller machines are generally available for cash transactions at any time of the day; most are compatible with Cirrus, Cash Card, and PLUS system networks.

Business Hours   Most businesses in the states operate at least 5 days each week and many are also open on weekends. Generally speaking, retail shops open around 10am and close at 6pm. During the two peak tourist seasons in summer and winter, many businesses extend their hours. In smaller towns, don't be surprised to find a hastily penned note on the door if the snow or sunshine conditions are perfect: Many business owners have been known to take their share of "powder days" with no advance notice.

Car Rentals   See "Getting Around," earlier in this chapter.

Climate   See "When to Go," earlier in this chapter.

Driving Rules   See "Getting Around," earlier in this chapter.

Emergencies   Throughout most of Montana and Wyoming, call ☎ **911** for any emergency requiring the police, firefighters, or emergency medical technicians. Where 911 is not available, dial **0** and the operator will connect you to the appropriate emergency service provider.

Gambling   The legal gambling age in Montana is 18, and it's a habit that's easily indulged—you'll find videogambling machines in restaurants, taverns, and filling stations. The two most popular are poker and keno (a game of chance similar to bingo). Although some bars have real poker tables, old-fashioned keno message boards are disappearing and are most likely to be found in bars or restaurants on the eastern side of the state. In Wyoming, gambling is illegal (though the issue seems always up for debate).

Information   See "Visitor Information," earlier in this chapter.

Liquor Laws   The legal age for the purchase or consumption of alcohol is 21 in both states. All liquor stores in Montana are state-controlled with minimum hours of 10am to 6pm, although individual stores may be open longer. Most are closed on Sunday. Liquor may also be bought at bars with package licenses during their operating hours. Beer and wine are available at convenience stores and supermarkets from 8:30am to 2am.

Lodging   The following companies provide reservation services for statewide lodging options in Montana and Wyoming: **Room Search Network** ☎ 800/869-7666), **America's Lodging Network** (☎ 800/341-8000), **Adventure Connections of Montana** (☎ 800/441-2286), **Adventures in Montana** (☎ 800/473-4343), and **American West Adventures** (☎ 800/952-9996). For a central reservations service representing more than 60 facilities in the Flathead Valley, call ☎ **406/862-5500. AHH-West** can book you a room at one of the West's premier historic hotels. Call ☎ **303/546-9040** for more information on this lodging option in the Rocky Mountains. **Bed & Breakfast Western Adventure** (☎ **406/585-0557**) is a reservation service devoted to bed-and-breakfast inns, homes, and ranches in Montana, Wyoming, and Idaho—each listing has been interviewed and inspected—and is one of the region's most trusted consultants.

Newspapers/Magazines   There are three major newspapers in Montana and at least one of them will be available wherever you may find yourself in the state: The *Missoulian,* the *Great Falls Tribune,* and the *Billings Gazette.* You'll also find *USA Today* on street corners throughout the state. A regional edition of the *Wall Street Journal* is available in most bigger towns and cities but any copy of *The New York Times* you may stumble upon is almost guaranteed to be 1 week late. In Wyoming, the *Casper Star-Tribune* is the only statewide paper, while the *Wyoming Tribune-Eagle* is Cheyenne's daily, the next-biggest paper. The *Billings Gazette* circulates in Wyoming's northeast corner, and provides Wyoming news.

Pets   Pets are sometimes allowed at hotels in these two states—much more often than in the rest of the country. Dogs are not allowed in many parks and recreational areas, though, and if that's the case, please don't break the rules—it's usually a matter of safety, since many of these areas are in bear country.

Police   Dial ☎ **911** or **0** (for the operator) to reach the police.

Safety   While driving through Montana and Wyoming, it is a good idea to carry plenty of water, both for drinking and for your car. Cities are often separated by great distances, although you'll find that people who live in the more remote areas of the state are usually very helpful to stranded motorists. If traveling in the winter, make sure there are plenty of warm blankets in the trunk.

Taxes   There is currently no sales tax in Montana, and no personal income tax in Wyoming. You might want to consider living on the border, doing your shopping in Montana but keeping your domicile in Wyoming. The odd tax structures of both states—highly dependent on mineral and oil and gas taxes—are debated in the legislatures every year. Wyoming's sales tax amounts to 5% statewide, and the state also allows communities to impose a "bed" tax aimed at tourists. In Montana there is a resort tax imposed on gift and souvenir-type items in certain resort communities around the state.

Time Zone   Montana and Wyoming are located in the mountain time zone and both states observe daylight saving time from spring to fall.

Weather   See "When to Go," earlier in this chapter.

For Foreign Visitors 3

The pervasiveness of American culture around the world may make you feel that you know the USA pretty well, but leaving your own country still requires an additional degree of planning. This chapter will help prepare you for the more common problems that visitors may encounter.

1 Preparing for Your Trip

ENTRY REQUIREMENTS

For up-to-the minute information, check at any U.S. embassy or consulate for current information and requirements. You can also plug into the **U.S. State Department's** Internet site at **http://state.gov**.

VISAS The U.S. State Department has a **Visa Waiver Pilot Program** allowing citizens of certain countries to enter the United States without a visa for stays of up to 90 days. At press time these included Andorra, Argentina, Australia, Austria, Belgium, Brunei, Denmark, Finland, France, Germany, Iceland, Ireland, Italy, Japan, Liechtenstein, Luxembourg, Monaco, the Netherlands, New Zealand, Norway, San Marino, Slovenia, Spain, Sweden, Switzerland, and the United Kingdom. Citizens of these countries need only a valid passport and a round-trip air or cruise ticket in their possession upon arrival. If they first enter the United States, they may also visit Mexico, Canada, Bermuda, and/or the Caribbean islands and return to the United States without a visa. Further information is available from any U.S. embassy or consulate. Canadian citizens may enter the United States without visas; they need only proof of residence.

Citizens of all other countries must have (1) a valid passport that expires at least 6 months later than the scheduled end of their visit to the United States, and (2) a tourist visa, which may be obtained without charge from any U.S. consulate.

OBTAINING A VISA To obtain a visa, the traveler must submit a completed application form (either in person or by mail) with a 1½-inch-square photo, and must demonstrate binding ties to a residence abroad. Usually you can obtain a visa at once or within 24 hours, but it may take longer during the summer rush from June through August. If you cannot go in person, contact the nearest U.S. embassy or consulate for directions on applying by mail. Your travel agent or airline office may also be able to provide you with visa applications and instructions. The U.S. consulate or embassy that issues your visa will determine whether you will be issued a multiple- or single-entry visa and any restrictions regarding the length of your stay.

British subjects can obtain up-to-date passport and visa information by calling the **U.S. Embassy Visa Information Line** (☎ **0891/200-290**) or the **London Passport Office** (☎ **0990/210-410** for recorded information).

IMMIGRATION QUESTIONS   Telephone operators will answer your inquiries regarding U.S. immigration policies or laws at the **Immigration and Naturalization Service's Customer Information Center** (☎ **800/375-5283**). Representatives are available from 9am to 3pm, Monday through Friday. The INS also runs a 24-hour automated information service, for commonly asked questions, at ☎ **800/755-0777.**

MEDICAL REQUIREMENTS   Unless you're arriving from an area known to be suffering from an epidemic (particularly cholera or yellow fever), inoculations or vaccinations are not required for entry into the United States. If you have a disease that requires treatment with narcotics or syringe-administered medications, carry a valid signed prescription from your physician to allay any suspicions that you may be smuggling narcotics (a serious offense that carries severe penalties in the U.S.).

DRIVER'S LICENSES   Foreign driver's licenses are mostly recognized in the U.S., although you may want to get an international driver's license if your home license is not written in English.

FOR RESIDENTS OF THE UNITED KINGDOM   To pick up an application for a regular 10-year passport (the Visitor's Passport has been abolished), visit your nearest passport office, major post office, or travel agency. You can also contact the London Passport Office at ☎ **020/7271-3000** or search its Web site at www.open. gov.uk/ukpass/ukpass.htm. Passports are £21 for adults and £11 for children under 16.

CUSTOMS
WHAT YOU CAN BRING IN

Every visitor over 21 years of age may bring in, free of duty, the following: (1) 1 liter of wine or hard liquor; (2) 200 cigarettes, 100 cigars (but not from Cuba), or 3 pounds of smoking tobacco; and (3) $100 worth of gifts. These exemptions are offered to travelers who spend at least 72 hours in the United States and who have not claimed them within the preceding 6 months. It is altogether forbidden to bring into the country foodstuffs (particularly fruit, cooked meats, and canned goods) and plants (vegetables, seeds, tropical plants, and the like). Foreign tourists may bring in or take out up to $10,000 in U.S. or foreign currency with no formalities; larger sums must be declared to U.S. Customs on entering or leaving, which includes filing form CM 4790. For more specific information regarding U.S. Customs, call your nearest U.S. embassy or consulate, or the **U.S. Customs** office at ☎ **202/927-1770** or www.customs. ustreas.gov.

WHAT YOU CAN BRING HOME

U.K. citizens returning from a non-EC country have a customs allowance of: 200 cigarettes; 50 cigars; 250g of smoking tobacco; 2 liters of still table wine; 1 liter of spirits or strong liqueurs (over 22% volume); 2 liters of fortified wine, sparkling wine or other liqueurs; 60cc (ml) perfume; 250cc (ml) of toilet water; and £145 worth of all other goods, including gifts and souvenirs. People under 17 cannot have the tobacco or alcohol allowance. For more information, contact HM Customs & Excise,

Passenger Enquiry Point, 2nd Floor Wayfarer House, Great South West Road, Feltham, Middlesex, TW14 8NP (☎ **020/8910-3744,** or 44/181-910-3744 from outside the U.K.), or consult their Web site at www.open.gov.uk.

For a clear summary of **Canadian** rules, write for the booklet *I Declare,* issued by **Revenue Canada,** 2265 St. Laurent Blvd., Ottawa K1G 4KE (☎ **613/993-0534**). Canada allows its citizens a $500 exemption, and you're allowed to bring back, duty-free, 200 cigarettes, 2.2 pounds of tobacco, 40 imperial ounces of liquor, and 50 cigars. In addition, you're allowed to mail gifts to Canada from abroad at the rate of C$60 a day, provided they're unsolicited and don't contain alcohol or tobacco (write on the package "Unsolicited gift, under $60 value"). All valuables should be declared on the Y-38 form before departure from Canada, including serial numbers of valuables you already own, such as expensive foreign cameras. *Note:* The $500 exemption can only be used once a year and only after an absence of 7 days.

INSURANCE

Although it's not required of travelers, health insurance is highly recommended. Unlike many European countries, the United States does not usually offer free or low-cost medical care to its citizens or visitors. Doctors and hospitals are expensive, and in most cases will require advance payment or proof of coverage before they render their services. Policies can cover everything from the loss or theft of your baggage and trip cancellation to the guarantee of bail in case you're arrested. Good policies will also cover the costs of an accident, repatriation, or death. See "Tips on Insurance, Health & Safety" in chapter 2 for more information. Packages such as **Europ Assistance** in Europe are sold by automobile clubs and travel agencies at attractive rates. **Worldwide Assistance Services, Inc.** (☎ **800/821-2828**) is the agent for Europ Assistance in the United States.

Though lack of health insurance may prevent you from being admitted to a hospital in nonemergencies, don't worry about being left on a street corner to die: The American way is to fix you now and bill the living daylights out of you later.

INSURANCE FOR BRITISH TRAVELERS   Most big travel agents offer their own insurance, and will probably try to sell you their package when you book a holiday. Think before you sign. **Britain's Consumers' Association** recommends that you insist on seeing the policy and reading the fine print before buying travel insurance. **The Association of British Insurers** (☎ **020/7600-3333**) gives advice by phone and publishes the free *Holiday Insurance,* a guide to policy provisions and prices. You might also shop around for better deals: Try **Columbus Travel Insurance Ltd.** (☎ **020/7375-0011**) or, for students, **Campus Travel** (☎ **020/7730-2101**).

INSURANCE FOR CANADIAN TRAVELERS   Canadians should check with their provincial health-plan offices or call **HealthCanada** (☎ **613/957-2991**) to find out the extent of their coverage and what documentation and receipts they must take home in case they are treated in the United States.

MONEY

CURRENCY   The U.S. monetary system is simple: The most common bills (all ugly, all green) are the $1 (colloquially, a "buck"), $5, $10, and $20 denominations. There are also $2 bills (seldom encountered), $50 bills, and $100 bills (the last two are usually not welcome as payment for small purchases). Note that redesigned $100 and $50 bills were introduced in 1996, and a redesigned $20 bill in 1998. Expect to see redesigned $10 and $5 notes in the year 2000. Despite rumors to the contrary, the old-style bills are still legal tender.

There are six denominations of coins: 1¢ (1 cent, or a penny); 5¢ (5 cents, or a nickel); 10¢ (10 cents, or a dime); 25¢ (25 cents, or a quarter); 50¢ (50 cents, or a half dollar); and, prized by collectors, the rare $1 piece (the older, large silver dollar and the newer, small Susan B. Anthony coin). A new gold $1 piece will be introduced by the year 2000.

Note: The "foreign-exchange bureaus" so common in Europe are rare even at airports in the United States, and nonexistent outside major cities. It's best not to change foreign money (or traveler's checks denominated in a currency other than U.S. dollars) at a small-town bank, or even a branch in a big city; in fact, leave any currency other than U.S. dollars at home—it may prove a greater nuisance to you than it's worth.

TRAVELER'S CHECKS Though traveler's checks are widely accepted, make sure that they're denominated in U.S. dollars, as foreign-currency checks are often difficult to exchange. The three traveler's checks most widely recognized are **Visa, American Express,** and **Thomas Cook.** Be sure to record the numbers of the checks, and keep that information separate in case they get lost or stolen. Most businesses are pretty good about taking traveler's checks, but you're better off cashing them in at a bank (in small amounts, of course) and paying in cash. *Remember:* you'll need identification, such as a driver's license or passport, to exchange a traveler's check.

CREDIT CARDS & ATMs Credit cards are the most widely used form of payment in the United States: **Visa** (BarclayCard in Britain), **MasterCard** (EuroCard in Europe, Access in Britain, Chargex in Canada), **American Express, Diners Club, Discover,** and **Carte Blanche.** You must have a credit or charge card to rent a car. There are, however, a handful of stores and restaurants (especially in Montana and Wyoming) that do not take credit cards, so be sure to ask in advance. Most businesses display a sticker near their entrance to let you know which cards they accept.

It is strongly recommended that you bring at least one major credit card. Hotels, car-rental companies, and airlines usually require a credit-card imprint as a deposit against expenses, and in an emergency a credit card can be priceless.

Automated teller machines (ATMs) allow you to draw U.S. currency against your bank and credit cards. Check with your bank before leaving home, and remember that you will need your personal identification number (PIN) to do so. Most ATMs accept Visa, MasterCard, and American Express, as well as ATM cards from other U.S. banks. Expect to be charged up to $3 per transaction, however, if you're not using your own bank's ATM. And remember that interest on a cash advance on a credit card starts the minute you withdraw the money.

One way around these fees is to ask for cash back at grocery stores that accept ATM cards and don't charge usage fees. Of course, you'll have to purchase something first.

SAFETY

Montana and Wyoming have much lower crime rates than urban areas of the U.S., and violence against strangers is very rare. Crimes like carjacking are virtually unknown. Crimes against property happen, though, and it is a good idea to lock your car, and use common sense in public—don't flaunt cash or credit cards, keep cell phones out of sight when not in use, don't stray into unsavory-looking neighborhoods.

Always stay alert. Avoid deserted areas, especially at night, and don't go into public parks at night unless there's a concert or similar occasion that will attract a crowd.

Remember also that hotels are open to the public, and in a large hotel, security may not be able to screen everyone entering. Always lock your room door—don't assume that once inside your hotel you are automatically safe and no longer need to be aware of your surroundings.

DRIVING SAFETY   Always try to park in well-lit and well-traveled areas if possible. If you leave your rental car unlocked and empty of your valuables, you're probably safer than locking your car with valuables in plain view. Never leave any packages or valuables in sight. If someone attempts to rob you or steal your car, don't try to resist—report the incident to the police department immediately by calling ☎ **911.**

2 Getting to the U.S.

Flying into Montana and Wyoming from outside the U.S. is not much harder than flying there from within the U.S.—which is not to say it is easy. There are no direct flights from any foreign countries to either Montana or Wyoming. Travelers have to go through one of the hub cities. However, several major U.S. airlines with international connections serve the states.

If you travel on **Northwest** (☎ **800/447-4747** for international reservations, 0990-561000 in London, or 03/3533-6000 in Tokyo; www.nwa.com), you'll probably fly through Seattle. On **United** (☎ **800/538-2929** for international reservations, or 0120/11-44-66 in Japan; www.ual.com) you'll probably go through Denver. And on **Delta** (☎ **800/241-4141** from the U.S., Puerto Rico, and Virgin Islands; **800/221-1212** from Canada; or **800/327-2850** from Japan; www.delta-air.com), the trip will take you through Salt Lake City. **American** (☎ **020/8572-5555** from England) may take you through Salt Lake City as well. One of the charms of Montana and Wyoming is that they are remote, but this remoteness means that it may take you 8 hours of travel to reach them, even after you arrive in the U.S.

The major airports in Montana are Billings, Bozeman, Great Falls, Helena, Kalispell, and Missoula. Billings is served by **Northwest, Delta,** and **United.** The others are served by Northwest and Delta.

In Wyoming, the major airports are in Casper and Jackson. **American** and **Delta** serve Jackson from Salt Lake City; **United** has service from Denver. Casper is primarily served by **United Express** from Denver and **Skywest** (☎ **800/453-9417**) from Salt Lake City.

AIRLINE DISCOUNTS   The idea of traveling abroad on a budget is something of an oxymoron, but travelers can reduce the price of a plane ticket by several hundred dollars if they take the time to shop around. For example, overseas visitors can take advantage of the APEX (Advance Purchase Excursion) reductions offered by all major U.S. and European carriers. For more money-saving airline advice, see "Getting There," in chapter 2. For the best rates, compare fares and be flexible with the dates and times of travel.

IMMIGRATION & CUSTOMS CLEARANCE   Visitors arriving by air, no matter what the port of entry, should cultivate patience and resignation before setting foot on U.S. soil. Getting through immigration control may take as long as 2 hours on some days, especially on summer weekends, so be sure to have this guidebook or something else to read. Add the time it takes to clear Customs, and you'll see that you should make a 2- to 3-hour allowance for delays when you plan your connections between international and domestic flights.

In contrast, for the traveler arriving by car or rail from Canada, the border-crossing formalities have been streamlined to the vanishing point. People traveling by air from Canada, Bermuda, and some places in the Caribbean can sometimes clear Customs and Immigration at the point of departure, which is much quicker.

There are three 24-hour service ports of entry into Montana from Canada (and vice versa): **Roosville,** the farthest west, en route from Cranbrook, B.C. (☎ **406/ 889-3865); Sweetgrass,** in the center near Glacier National Park, en route from Calgary (☎ **406/335-2434);** and **Raymond,** the farthest east en route from Regina (☎ **406/895-2664).** There are also 12 seasonal ports, which vary their hours and seasons of operation. For information on whether or not a specific seasonal port is open, contact one of the 24-hour ports.

3 Getting Around the U.S.

BY PLANE   Some large airlines (for example, Northwest and Delta) offer travelers on their transatlantic or transpacific flights special discount tickets under the name **Visit USA,** allowing mostly one-way travel from one U.S. destination to another at very low prices. These discount tickets are not on sale in the United States and must be purchased abroad in conjunction with your international ticket. This system is the best, easiest, and fastest way to see the United States at low cost. You should obtain information well in advance from your travel agent or the office of the airline concerned, since the conditions attached to these discount tickets can be changed without advance notice.

BY TRAIN   International visitors can also buy a **USA Railpass,** good for 15 or 30 days of unlimited travel on Amtrak (☎ **800/USA-RAIL).** The pass is available through many foreign travel agents. Prices in 1999 for a 15-day pass are $285 off-peak, $425 peak; a 30-day pass costs $375 off-peak, $535 peak. (With a foreign passport, you can also buy passes at some Amtrak offices in the United States, including locations in San Francisco, Los Angeles, Chicago, New York, Miami, Boston, and Washington, D.C.) Reservations are generally required and should be made for each part of your trip as early as possible.

Amtrak (☎ **800/872-7245)** stops along Montana's northern tier at Browning, Cut Bank, Essex, Glacier National Park, Glasgow, Havre, Libby, Malta, Shelby, West Glacier, Whitefish, and Wolf Point. Amtrak doesn't run through Wyoming.

BY BUS   Although bus travel is often the most economical form of public transit for short hops between U.S. cities, it can also be slow and uncomfortable—certainly not an option for everyone (particularly when Amtrak, which is far more luxurious, offers similar rates). **Greyhound/Trailways** (☎ **800/231-2222),** the sole nationwide bus line, offers an **International Ameripass** that must be purchased before coming to the United States, or purchased at the Greyhound International Office at the Port Authority Bus Terminal in New York City. The pass can be obtained from foreign travel agents and costs less than the domestic version. 1999 passes cost as follows: 7 days ($179), 15 days ($269), 30 days ($369), or 60 days ($539). Foreigners can get more info on the pass at www.greyhound.com, or by calling ☎ **212/971-0492** from 14:00 to 21:00 GMT or 402/330-8552 at all other times. In addition, special rates are available for senior citizens and students.

BY CAR   The most cost-effective, convenient, and comfortable way to travel around Montana and Wyoming is by car. The interstate highway system connects cities and towns all over the country; in addition to these high-speed, limited-access roadways, there's an extensive network of federal, state, and local highways and roads. Some of the national car-rental companies include **Alamo** (☎ 800/327-9633), **Avis** (☎ 800/331-1212), **Budget** (☎ 800/527-0700), **Dollar** (☎ 800/800-4000), **Hertz** (☎ 800/654-3131), **National** (☎ 800/227-7368), and **Thrifty** (☎ 800/367-2277).

If you plan on renting a car in the United States, you probably won't need the services of an additional automobile organization. If you're planning to buy or borrow a car, automobile-association membership is recommended. **AAA, the American Automobile Association** (☎ **800/222-4357**), is the country's largest auto club and supplies its members with maps, insurance, and, most important, emergency road service. The cost of joining runs from $63 for singles to $87 for two members, but if you're a member of a foreign auto club with reciprocal arrangements, you can enjoy free AAA service in America.

Fast Facts: For the Foreign Traveler

Automobile Organizations   Auto clubs will supply maps, suggested routes, guidebooks, accident and bail-bond insurance, and emergency road service. The **American Automobile Association (AAA)** is the major auto club in the United States. If you belong to an auto club in your home country, inquire about AAA reciprocity before you leave. You may be able to join AAA even if you're not a member of a reciprocal club; to inquire, call AAA (☎ **800/222-4357**). AAA is actually an organization of regional auto clubs, so look under "AAA Automobile Club" in the White Pages of the telephone directory. AAA has a nationwide emergency road-service telephone number (☎ **800/AAA-HELP**).

Business Hours   Offices are usually open weekdays from 9am to 5pm. Banks are open weekdays from 9am to 3pm or later and sometimes Saturday mornings. Stores, especially those in shopping complexes, tend to stay open late: until about 9pm on weekdays and 6pm on weekends.

Currency & Currency Exchange   See "Entry Requirements" and "Money" under "Preparing for Your Trip," above.

Drinking Laws   The legal age for purchase and consumption of alcoholic beverages is 21; proof of age is required and often requested at bars, nightclubs, and restaurants, so it's always a good idea to bring ID when you go out. Beer and wine can often be purchased in supermarkets in Montana, but not in Wyoming. Hard liquor in Montana is available in state liquor stores, open from 8am to 5pm Monday through Saturday. In Wyoming, liquor, beer, and wine can be purchased 7 days a week at independent liquor stores.

Do not carry open containers of alcohol in your car or any public area that isn't zoned for alcohol consumption. The police can, and probably will, fine you on the spot. And nothing will ruin your trip faster than getting a citation for DUI ("driving under the influence"), so don't even think about driving while intoxicated.

Electricity   Like Canada, the United States uses 110 to 120 volts AC (60 cycles), compared to 220 to 240 volts AC (50 cycles) in most of Europe, Australia, and New Zealand. If your small appliances use 220 to 240 volts, you'll need a 110-volt transformer and a plug adapter with two flat parallel pins to operate them here. Downward converters that change 220 to 240 volts to 110 to 120 volts are difficult to find in the United States, so bring one with you.

Embassies & Consulates   There are no foreign consulates in Wyoming or Montana. All embassies are located in the nation's capital, Washington, D.C.

Some consulates are located in major U.S. cities, and most nations have a mission to the United Nations in New York City. If your country isn't listed below, call for directory information in Washington, D.C. (☎ **202/555-1212**) for the number of your national embassy.

The embassy of **Canada** is at 501 Pennsylvania Ave. NW, Washington, DC 20001 (☎ **202/682-1740;** www.cdnemb-washdc.org). Other Canadian consulates are in Buffalo, New York; Detroit; Los Angeles; New York; and Seattle.

The embassy of the **United Kingdom** is at 3100 Massachusetts Ave. NW, Washington, DC 20008 (☎ **202/462-1340**). Other British consulates are in Atlanta, Boston, Chicago, Cleveland, Houston, Los Angeles, New York, San Francisco, and Seattle.

Emergencies   Call ☎ **911** to report a fire, call the police, or get an ambulance anywhere in the United States. This is a toll-free call (no coins are required at public telephones).

If you encounter travelers' problems, check the local telephone directory to find an office of the **Traveler's Aid Society,** a nationwide, nonprofit, social-service organization geared to helping travelers in difficult straits. Their services might include reuniting families separated while traveling, providing food and/or shelter to people stranded without cash, or even emotional counseling. If you're in trouble, seek them out.

Gasoline (Petrol)   Petrol is known as gasoline (or simply "gas") in the United States, and petrol stations are known as both gas stations and service stations. Gasoline costs about half as much here as it does in Europe (about $1.40 per gallon at press time), and taxes are already included in the printed price. One U.S. gallon equals 3.8 liters or 0.85 Imperial gallons.

Holidays   Banks, government offices, post offices, and many stores, restaurants, and museums are closed on the following legal national holidays: January 1 (New Year's Day), the third Monday in January (Martin Luther King, Jr. Day), the third Monday in February (Presidents' Day, Washington's Birthday), the last Monday in May (Memorial Day), July 4 (Independence Day), the first Monday in September (Labor Day), the second Monday in October (Columbus Day), November 11 (Veterans' Day/Armistice Day), the fourth Thursday in November (Thanksgiving Day), and December 25 (Christmas). Also, the Tuesday following the first Monday in November is Election Day and is a federal government holiday in presidential-election years (held every 4 years, and next in 2000).

Legal Aid   The foreign tourist will probably never become involved with the American legal system. If you are "pulled over" for a minor infraction (for example, of the highway code, such as speeding), never attempt to pay the fine directly to a police officer; this could be construed as attempted bribery, a much more serious crime. Pay fines by mail, or directly into the hands of the clerk of the court. If accused of a more serious offense, say and do nothing before consulting a lawyer. Here the burden is on the state to prove a person's guilt beyond a reasonable doubt, and everyone has the right to remain silent, whether he or she is suspected of a crime or actually arrested. Once arrested, a person can make one telephone call to a party of his or her choice. Call your embassy or consulate.

Mail   If you aren't sure what your address will be in the United States, mail can be sent to you, in your name, c/o General Delivery at the main post office of the city or region where you expect to be (call ☎ **800/275-8777** for information on the nearest post office). The addressee must pick mail up in person and must produce proof of identity (driver's license, passport, etc.). Most post offices will hold your mail for up to 1 month, and are open Monday to Friday from 8am to 6pm, and Saturday from 9am to 3pm.

Generally found at intersections, mailboxes are blue with a red-and-white stripe and carry the inscription U.S. MAIL. If your mail is addressed to a U.S. destination, don't forget to add the five-digit postal code (or ZIP code), after the two-letter abbreviation of the state to which the mail is addressed.

At press time domestic postage rates were 20¢ for a postcard and 33¢ for a letter. For international mail, a first-class letter of up to one-half ounce costs 60¢ (46¢ to Canada and 40¢ to Mexico); a first-class postcard costs 50¢ (40¢ to Canada and 35¢ to Mexico); and a preprinted postal air letter costs 50¢.

Taxes   In the United States there is no value-added tax (VAT) or other indirect tax at the national level. Every state, county, and city has the right to levy its own local tax on all purchases, including hotel and restaurant checks, airline tickets, and so on. In Montana, there's no sales tax; hotel tax is 4% of the room rate. In Wyoming, sales tax is 2%, but depending on the county it can be as high as 6%. There's a lodging tax that varies from county to county, but it can be as high as 9% of the regular room rate.

Telephone, Telegraph, Telex & Fax   The telephone system in the United States is run by private corporations, so rates, especially for long-distance service and operator-assisted calls, can vary widely. Generally, hotel surcharges on long-distance and local calls are astronomical, so you're usually better off using a **public pay telephone,** which you'll find clearly marked in most public buildings and private establishments as well as on the street. Convenience grocery stores and gas stations always have them. Many convenience groceries and packaging services sell **prepaid calling cards** in denominations up to $50; these can be the least expensive way to call home. Many public phones at airports now accept American Express, MasterCard, and Visa credit cards. **Local calls** made from public pay phones in most locales cost either 25¢ or 35¢. Pay phones do not accept pennies, and few will take anything larger than a quarter.

Most long-distance and international calls can be dialed directly from any phone. **For calls within the United States and to Canada,** dial 1 followed by the area code and the seven-digit number. **For other international calls,** dial 011 followed by the country code, city code, and the telephone number of the person you are calling.

Calls to area codes **800, 888,** and **877** are toll-free. However, calls to numbers in area codes **700** and **900** (chat lines, bulletin boards, "dating" services, and so on) can be very expensive—usually a charge of 95¢ to $3 or more per minute, and they sometimes have minimum charges that can run as high as $15 or more.

For **reversed-charge or collect calls,** and for person-to-person calls, dial 0 (zero, not the letter O) followed by the area code and number you want; an operator will then come on the line, and you should specify that you are calling collect, or person-to-person, or both. If your operator-assisted call is international, ask for the overseas operator.

For **local directory assistance** ("information"), dial ☎ **411;** for long-distance information, dial 1, then the appropriate area code and 555-1212.

Telegraph and telex services are provided primarily by Western Union. You can bring your telegram into the nearest Western Union office (there are hundreds across the country) or dictate it over the phone (☎ **800/325-6000**). You can also telegraph money, or have it telegraphed to you, very quickly over the Western Union system, but this service can cost as much as 15% to 20% of the amount sent.

Most hotels have **fax machines** available for guest use (be sure to ask about the charge to use it), and many hotel rooms are even wired for guests' fax machines. A less expensive way to send and receive faxes may be at stores such as Mail Boxes Etc., a national chain of packing service shops (look in the Yellow Pages directory under "Packing Services").

There are two kinds of telephone directories in the United States. The so-called **White Pages** list private households and business subscribers in alphabetical order. The inside front cover lists emergency numbers for police, fire, ambulance, the Coast Guard, poison-control center, crime-victims hotline, and so on. The first few pages will tell you how to make long-distance and international calls, complete with country codes and area codes. Government numbers are usually printed on blue paper within the White Pages. Printed on yellow paper, the so-called **Yellow Pages** list all local services, businesses, industries, and houses of worship according to activity with an index at the front or back. (Drugstores/pharmacies and restaurants are also listed by geographic location.) The Yellow Pages also include city plans or detailed area maps, postal ZIP codes, and public transportation routes.

Time   The continental United States is divided into **four time zones:** eastern standard time (EST), central standard time (CST), mountain standard time (MST), and Pacific standard time (PST). Alaska and Hawaii have their own zones. For example, noon in New York City (EST) is 11am in Chicago (CST), 10am in Billings and Jackson (MST), 9am in Los Angeles (PST), 8am in Anchorage (AST), and 7am in Honolulu (HST).

Montana and Wyoming are in the Mountain Time Zone.

Daylight saving time is in effect from 1am on the first Sunday in April through 1am the last Sunday in October, except in Arizona, Hawaii, part of Indiana, and Puerto Rico. Daylight saving time moves the clock 1 hour ahead of standard time.

Tipping   Tipping is so ingrained in the American way of life that the annual income tax of tip-earning service personnel is based on how much they should have received in light of their employers' gross revenues. Accordingly, they may have to pay tax on a tip you didn't actually give them.

Here are some rules of thumb:

In hotels, tip **bellhops** at least $1 per bag ($2 to $3 if you have a lot of luggage) and tip the **chamber staff** $1 to $2 per day (more if you've left a disaster area for him or her to clean up, or if you're traveling with kids and/or pets). Tip the **doorman** or **concierge** only if he or she has provided you with some specific service (for example, calling a cab for you or obtaining difficult-to-get theater tickets). Tip the **valet-parking attendant** $1 every time you get your car.

In restaurants, bars, and nightclubs, tip **service staff** 15% to 20% of the check, tip **bartenders** 10% to 15%, tip **checkroom attendants** $1 per garment, and tip **valet-parking attendants** $1 per vehicle. Tip the **doorman** only if he has provided you with some specific service (such as calling a cab for you). Tipping is not expected in cafeterias and fast-food restaurants.

Tip **cab drivers** 15% of the fare.

As for other service personnel, tip **skycaps** at airports at least $1 per bag ($2 to $3 if you have a lot of luggage) and tip **hairdressers** and **barbers** 15% to 20%.

Tipping ushers at movies and theaters, and gas-station attendants, is not expected.

Toilets   You won't find public toilets or "rest rooms" on the streets in most U.S. cities, but they can be found in hotel lobbies, bars, restaurants, museums, department stores, railway and bus stations, or service stations. Note, however, that restaurants and bars in resorts or heavily visited areas may reserve their rest rooms for the use of their patrons. Buy a cup of coffee or a soft drink, which will qualify you as a patron. Large hotels and fast-food restaurants are probably the best bet for good, clean facilities.

4 Glacier National Park

by Dan Whipple

Glacier National Park—named to describe the 48 slow-moving glaciers that carved awe-inspiring valleys throughout this expanse of nearly one million acres—exists because of the efforts of George Bird Grinnell, a 19th-century magazine publisher and co-founder of the Audubon Society. Following a pattern established with Yellowstone and Grand Teton, Grinnell lobbied for a national park to be set aside in the St. Mary region of Montana, and in May 1910 his efforts were rewarded. Just over 20 years later, it became, with its northern neighbor Waterton Lakes National Park in Canada, Glacier-Waterton International Peace Park—a gesture of goodwill and friendship between the governments of the two countries.

The park is conspicuously different from those parks to the south. With spewing geysers and wildlife, Yellowstone attracts travelers that crowd and almost clutter its narrow roads. Grand Teton entrances visitors with its revered, cathedral-like spires that grasp the sky overhead. Glacier beckons with equally stunning though somewhat smaller peaks (many covered year-round with glaciers), verdant mountain trails that cry out for hikers, and the sheer diversity of its plant and animal life.

Majestic and wild, this vast preserve continues to overwhelm visitors as much as any other national park in the Lower 48. Every spring, Glacier is a postcard come to life: Wildflowers carpet its meadows; bears emerge from months of hibernation; and moose, elk, and deer again play out the drama of birth, life, and death in the wilderness. The unofficial mascot in these parts is the grizzly, a refugee from the High Plains who now inhabits the Montana mountains.

Man has left his imprint on the park, of course—the patter of feet has taken an environmental toll. But park management continues to successfully maintain the delicate balance between tourism and preservation. Nature is at work as well: The glaciers are receding (the result of global warming, some say), and avalanches have periodically ravaged Going-to-the-Sun Road, the curving, scenic 50-mile road that bisects the park. For the time being, the park is intact and very much alive, a treasure in a vault that is open to visitors.

If your time is limited, simply motor across Going-to-the-Sun Road, viewing the dramatic mountain scenery. Longer-term visitors will find diversions for both families and hard-core adventurers; while some hiking trails are suitable for tykes, many more will challenge those determined to conquer and scale the park's tallest peaks. Glacier's

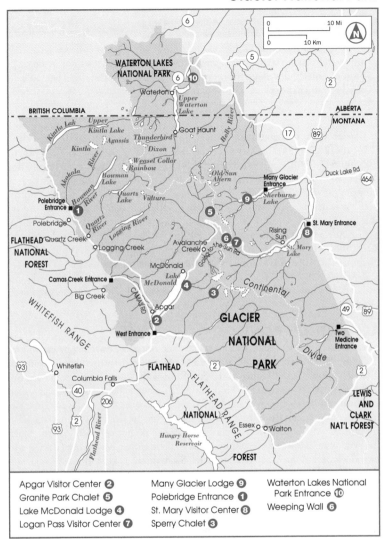

Apgar Visitor Center ❷
Granite Park Chalet ❺
Lake McDonald Lodge ❹
Logan Pass Visitor Center ❼
Many Glacier Lodge ❾
Polebridge Entrance ❶
St. Mary Visitor Center ❽
Sperry Chalet ❸
Waterton Lakes National
Park Entrance ❿
Weeping Wall ❻

lakes, streams, ponds, and waterfalls are equally engaging. Travelers board cruise boats to explore the history of the area; recreational types fish, row, and kayak.

To truly experience Glacier requires slightly more effort, interest, and spunk than you'd expend at, say, drive-through Yellowstone. Sure, you can glimpse her sights from behind the windshield—but abandon the pavement for even the easiest and shortest of the hundreds of hiking trails, and you'll find a window into her soul.

1 Just the Facts

GETTING THERE

The closest cities to the park with airline service are **Kalispell,** 29 miles southwest of the park; and **Great Falls,** 143 miles southeast of the park.

If you only have a day at Glacier, the best use of your time is to drive across Going-to-the-Sun Road, viewing the dramatic mountain scenery. Get out at Logan Pass Visitor Center and walk up the boardwalk Hidden Lake Nature Trail behind it. This may be your chance to see a mountain goat.

Glacier Park International Airport, north of Kalispell at 4170 U.S. Hwy. 2 (☎ 406/257-5994), is serviced by **Delta** (☎ 800/221-1212), **Horizon** (☎ 800/547-9308), and **Northwest** (☎ 800/225-2525). **Great Falls International Airport** (☎ 406/727-3404) has daily service on Delta, Horizon, Northwest, and **Frontier** (☎ 800/432-1359).

If you're driving, you can reach the park from U.S. 2 and 89. Rental cars are available in Kalispell, Great Falls, Whitefish, East Glacier, and West Glacier. **Avis** (☎ 800/831-2847), **Budget** (☎ 800/527-0700), and **National** (☎ 800/227-7368) all have counters at Kalispell's airport. **Hertz** (☎ 800/654-3131) and **National** (☎ 406/453-4386) have counters at Great Falls International Airport.

Amtrak's *Empire Builder* (☎ 800/872-7245), a Chicago-Seattle round-trip route, makes daily stops at West Glacier and Essex year-round. The train also stops at East Glacier, but only from May through October.

ACCESS/ENTRY POINTS

There are six entrances to Glacier National Park, but those traveling by car will most likely use **West Glacier** on the west and **St. Mary** on the east. These entrances are located at either end of Going-to-the-Sun Road with West Glacier on the southwest side and St. Mary on the east. From the park's western boundary, you can enter at **Polebridge** to access Bowman and Kintla lakes, or take the mostly gravel **Camas Road** to Going-to-the-Sun. Essex, East Glacier, Two Medicine, Cut Bank, and Many Glacier are primarily designed to access specific places and do not take you into the heart of the park by car. However, the most popular of these entrances is **Many Glacier,** which provides access to the Many Glacier Hotel, Swiftcurrent Lake, and many backcountry trails. **East Glacier** takes you into Glacier Park Lodge and hiking trails at the southeastern corner of the park. The **Two Medicine** entrance is only about 4 miles north of East Glacier on MT 49, with auto access to Lower Two Medicine Lake and Two Medicine Lake, as well as hiking trails to Pumpelly Pillar and over Pitamakan Pass. Essex is strictly a backcountry access point to Scalplock Mountain and backcountry campgrounds along Old Creek and Park Creek. **Cut Bank** is a dirt road, closed in winter, with only backcountry access to Triple Divide Pass and the northern route to Pitamakan Pass.

Caution: Entrance is severely restricted during winter months when Going-to-the-Sun Road is closed. See section 2, "Driving the Park," later in this chapter for more information.

VISITOR CENTERS

To receive information about the park before your trip, write the Superintendent, **Glacier National Park,** West Glacier, MT 59936 (☎ 406/888-7800; www.nps.gov/glac). The **Glacier Natural History Association** has many publications sold throughout the park; for a catalog, write the association at P.O. Box 428, West Glacier, MT 59936.

For up-to-date information on park activities once you arrive, check in at visitor centers located at **Apgar, Logan Pass,** and **St. Mary.** St. Mary is open from mid-May through mid-October; Logan Pass, from mid-June through mid-October; and Apgar, from May through October (and weekends during the winter). Park information may also be obtained from the **Many Glacier Ranger Station** or park headquarters in **West Glacier.** General park information is available about Glacier at ☎ **406/ 888-7800,** or on the Web at **www.nps.gov/glac**; or about Waterton at ☎ **403/ 859-5133,** or **parkscanada.pch.gc.ca/waterton.** The **Alberta Information Center** is located in a conspicuously postmodern building in West Glacier, providing information about Waterton-Glacier and other attractions in Alberta. There are also numerous exhibits about Canadian life and culture, including a full-size replica skeleton of Tyrannosaurus rex, and a fully uniformed, red-coated Royal Canadian Mounted Policeman, who is, alas, a mannequin.

FEES & BACKCOUNTRY PERMITS

Rangers are on duty at most entry points to collect fees, issue backcountry permits, and answer questions.

FEES   A season pass costs $20 and allows unlimited entry to Glacier National Park for 1 year. A vehicle pass good for 7 days costs $10. A pass for walk-ins, bicycles, and motorcycles, also good for 7 days, is available for $5. A separate entrance fee is charged for visitors to Waterton Lakes National Park. For $50, you can buy a **Golden Eagle Passport,** which allows unlimited entry into any national park in the United States for the calendar year. U.S. citizens over the age of 62 can purchase the **Golden Age Passport,** which allows unlimited access to any U.S. national park for a one-time fee of $10. And for travelers with disabilities, there's the **Golden Access Passport,** which offers the same unlimited access, and is available free of charge.

BACKCOUNTRY PERMITS   These permits must be obtained in person from the visitor centers at the Apgar Backcountry Permitting Station, St. Mary Visitor Center, or the ranger stations at Many Glacier, Polebridge, or Two Medicine. Visitors who enter Glacier's backcountry from the Canadian side (at Goat Haunt or Belly River in Waterton) can get a permit at the Waterton Visitor Reception Centre, but only with a credit card. **During summer months,** permits may be obtained no earlier than 24 hours before your trip. There is a $4 per-person per-night charge for backcountry camping. Trips are limited to 6 nights, with no more than 3 nights allowed at each campground. Campsites are limited. A single site has a maximum occupancy of four persons—so, groups of five have to reserve two campsites, which can be tricky during the crowded summer months. Stoves are required in most areas (no open fires) and pets are not permitted on the trails.

To assure a spot and avoid the hassle, order an Advance Reservation Backcountry Trip planner from Backcountry Reservations, GNP, West Glacier, MT 59936; sending them your dates with a check for $20 will reserve your spot in the wilderness.

Due to lower demand in winter, camping permits are available up to 7 days in advance. A few rules do take effect beginning each November 20, so double-check at visitor centers for details.

REGULATIONS

The following regulations apply to visitors.

BIKES   Bikes are restricted to established roads, bike routes, or parking areas, and are not allowed on trails. Restrictions apply to the most hazardous portions of Going-to-the-Sun Road during peak travel times from around mid-June to Labor Day; call

Traveling Through the Park Without a Car

Going-to-the-Sun Shuttle Bus Service (☎ **406/888-5431**) runs mid-size historic motorcoaches from virtually every major hotel and campground to other points in the park. Costs for the shuttle service range from $2 for a short distance to $44 for a one-way long-distance excursion. Reservations are recommended. If you plan to mostly drive anyway, you'll do yourself a favor by letting the shuttles do the work for you. If you're hiking, hiking shuttles are also available to pick you up and take you back to your car for about $8.

ahead to find out when the road will be closed to bikers. During low-visibility periods caused by fog or darkness, a white front light and a back red reflector are required. A few campsites for bicyclists are held until 9pm at Apgar, Sprague Creek, Avalanche, Rising Sun, and St. Mary campgrounds, for $3 per person.

From June 15 through Labor Day, bikes are prohibited between Apgar Campground and Sprague Creek Campground between 11am and 4pm. It takes about 3 hours and 45 minutes to ride from Sprague Creek to Logan Pass.

BOATING   While boating is permitted on some of Glacier's lakes, motor size is restricted to 10 hp. Gas-powered boats are prohibited on Two Medicine Lake, but electric motorboats are allowed. A detailed list of other regulations is available at park headquarters and staffed ranger stations. Park rangers may inspect or board any boat to determine regulation compliance.

CAMPING   Camping is permitted only at designated locations and is strictly prohibited on the roadside.

FISHING   A fishing license is not required within the park's boundaries. But there are guidelines, so check with rangers at visitor centers for regulations. Also, keep in mind that since the eastern boundary of the park abuts the Blackfeet Indian Reservation, you may find yourself fishing in tribal waters. To avoid a problem, purchase a $5 use permit from businesses in the gateway towns. The phone for the **Blackfeet Nation** is ☎ **406/338-7406.** The permit covers fishing, hiking, and biking. Some waters run through state-administered land, so you'll need a state license. Check in at a local fishing shop to make certain you are legal.

PETS   All pets must be on a leash no longer than 6 feet, and under physical restraint or caged while in the park. Pets are not allowed indoors at any of the park's gift shops, restaurants, or visitor centers, or on any trails.

VEHICLES   Travel on wheeled vehicles, including bicycles, is prohibited on park trails. Park regulations prohibit vehicles over 21 feet long and 8 feet wide on the 24-mile stretch of Going-to-the-Sun Road between Avalanche Campground and Sun Point on St. Mary Lake.

WHEN TO GO

Glacier is magnificent at any time of the year. But it's not always easily accessible. Most visitors come **in summer** and it seems as if they all drive along the Going-to-the-Sun Road. The 52-mile two-lane road is open from late May or early June until the third Monday in October, depending upon the weather. During summer months, sunrise is around 5am, and sunset is at nearly 10pm, so there's plenty of time for exploring. The shoulder seasons of **spring and fall** see budding wildflowers and seasonal colors, but these sights can only be viewed from the park's outer boundaries and a limited stretch of the scenic highway.

In winter, Glacier is shut off from the motorized world. Even snowmobiles, which are allowed in Yellowstone, are prohibited. All unplowed roads become trails for snowshoers and cross-country skiers, who rave about the vast powdered wonderland. Guided trips into the backcountry are a great way to experience the park in winter, or you can strap on a pair of snowshoes and explore it on your own. A popular skiing expedition is to go as far up the Going-to-the-Sun Road as your energy permits. Wintertime temperatures average between 15° and 30° F, but extreme lows can reach 30° below. Average winter snowfall is more than 138 inches, and it snows about half the time from November through February.

Avoiding the Crowds

If you want to avoid the crowds, travel in the off-season before mid-June, when the park begins to fill, and after Labor Day, when families traveling with youngsters have returned home. (August is the busiest month in *all* of the parks.) If that's not possible, consider the following: Since most people congregate in close proximity to the major hotels, find a trailhead that is equidistant from two major points and head for the woods.

The Going-to-the-Sun Road is nearly always jammed in the summer daylight hours. If you can, make the trip before 8:30 in the morning. In July and August, the parking lot at Logan Pass Visitor Center fills to capacity. Try to visit early in the day or late in the afternoon.

RANGER PROGRAMS

When you enter the park, you'll be given the park's publication *Nature with a Naturalist,* which lists the naturalist-led programs offered at Glacier and Waterton. There is a wide variety of hikes, boat trips, campfire programs, and family programs among other activities offered. A number of them are specifically designed to be accessible for those in wheelchairs. Children are welcome on interpretive activities, but should be accompanied by an adult. In another program, members of the Salish, Kootenai, and Blackfeet tribes give 45-minute campfire presentations at locations around the park. The park has a *Junior Ranger Newspaper* available at the visitor centers that lists seven activities to introduce youngsters between 6 and 12 years of age to the habitats in Glacier. Most programs are free, although those including boat trips may have a small fee associated. For schedules, check the park newspapers or call ☎ **406/ 888-7800.**

TIPS FOR TRAVELERS WITH PHYSICAL DISABILITIES

Information on facilities and services for those with disabilities is available at any of the visitor centers in the park, although most of the park's developed areas are fully accessible by wheelchair. The park's *Accessibility in Glacier National Park* publication describes current programs and services for visitors with disabilities. *Note:* Groups may request special programs by contacting the Chief of Interpretation at park headquarters 2 weeks before arrival.

FOR THE VISUALLY IMPAIRED   Small-scale relief maps, park brochure recordings, and tactile nature items are available at the Apgar, Logan Pass, and St. Mary visitor centers. All other park facilities—rest rooms, restaurants, campgrounds, gift shops—are accessible with some assistance.

FOR THE MOBILITY IMPAIRED   The Trail of the Cedars is the park's sole wheelchair-accessible trail, although a bike path at Apgar also provides magnificent views of the park's scenery. Wheelchairs are available for loan at the Apgar Visitor Center and almost all of the park's facilities are fully accessible.

FOR THE HEARING IMPAIRED   Interpreters provide written synopses of most slide and campfire programs prior to the event. If you plan on hiking, note that five of the park's self-guided nature trails have printed brochures available at the trailhead. General park information is available by TDD at ☎ **406/888-5790.** An interpreter may be available to sign at the *Nature with a Naturalist* programs. Call ☎ **406/ 888-7939** a week in advance to make arrangements.

ORGANIZED TOURS & ACTIVITIES

Narrated boat tours from Lake McDonald, St. Mary, Two Medicine, and Many Glacier are offered daily from mid-June to mid-September by Glacier Park Boat Co. These "scenicruises" combine the comfort of an hour-long lake cruise with a short hike or picnic. Spectacular views of Lake McDonald sunsets, the Grinnell Glacier, and the panoramic rugged cliffs ringing St. Mary Lake are just a few of the possible photo opportunities you may have while enjoying a cruise. The boats typically depart every other hour, usually five times each day, although schedules are subject to change in late season or if the weather is inclement. For a complete listing of departure times and dates, contact **Glacier Park Boat Co.** at P.O. Box 5262, Kalispell, MT 59903 (☎ **406/257-2426**). Listed below are seasonal phone numbers for cruises at the following locations: **Lake McDonald** (☎ **406/888-5727**), **Many Glacier** (☎ **406/732-4480**), **Two Medicine** (☎ **406/226-4467**), and **St. Mary** (☎ **406/732-4430**).

Coach tours are given aboard a scarlet 1936 "Jammer" coach—so named because of the standard transmissions that grind on the steep climbs—along Going-to-the-Sun Road and north to Waterton. These coaches, with their roll-back tops, are an excellent (even preferred) method of transportation along this scenic route. Their drivers provide the commentary, and you don't have to get vertigo peering over the roadside. They also offer hiker express and Amtrak pickup. The tours are conducted by **Glacier Park, Inc.** After May 15, you can call ☎ **406/888-5431.** Prior to May 15, coach schedules can be requested directly from them at Dial Tower, Phoenix, AZ 85077-0928 (☎ **602/207-6000**). Interpretive van tours of the Going-to-the-Sun Road conducted by Blackfeet guides originate from East Glacier, Browning, and St. Mary. Contact **Sun Tours** (☎ **800/786-9220** or 406/226-9220). One of the visitors on Sun Tour told me he thought this was the best guided tour he'd ever taken, because the guides lived in the area and really knew what they were talking about.

SPECIAL ACTIVITIES

Scenic helicopter tours of Glacier are offered by **Glacier Heli Tours** (☎ **800/ 879-9310**) and **Kruger Helicopters** (☎ **800/220-6565**). Prices range from $60 to $90 for 1- to 2-hour tours, depending on your destination. All are located within 2 miles of West Glacier off U.S. Highway 2. Fees for a 1-hour tour are about $150 per person.

✪ **Glacier Institute** (☎ **406/755-1211;** www.gigisys.net/glacinst; e-mail: glacinst@digisys.nat) conducts field classes and seminars each summer to look at the geologic, wildlife, and spiritual contributions of the park. Classes run from 1 day to 1 month—most are only a day or two, and cost less than $75—and cover subjects from photography to forests. The fees include instruction, transportation, park fees, and college credit (if any). You can gather fall mushrooms, work on your journal-keeping skills, improve your writing, or search out the elusive harlequin duck.

2 Driving the Park

Because of the massive piles of rock that surround a visitor, it is impossible to drive Glacier without drawing comparisons to Grand Teton. At Teton, unless you hit the

Vehicle Regulations

Park regulations prohibit vehicles more than 21 feet long and 8 feet wide on the 24-mile stretch of Going-to-the-Sun Road between Avalanche Campground and Sun Point on St. Mary Lake. If you are traveling in a vehicle exceeding the 21-foot limit, park it at one of the parking areas located at Avalanche Campground and Sun Point and take the **Going-to-the-Sun Shuttle Bus Service** (see above).

hiking trails, the mountains keep their distance. But, in Glacier, as you drive, the mountain peaks will envelop you.

GOING-TO-THE-SUN ROAD

If you plan only a day or two in Glacier, the most important thing to do is to drive **Going-to-the-Sun Road,** the 50-mile road that bisects the park between West Glacier and St. Mary. Points of interest are clearly marked along this road by interpretive signs, and correspond to the park brochure *Points of Interest Along the Going-to-the-Sun Road,* which is available at visitor centers. Bring plenty of film.

The road gains more than 1,400 feet in 32 miles, and is very narrow in places. Visitors with a fear of heights may consider taking a coach. And because of the road's narrowness, oversized vehicles and trailers must use U.S. Highway 2.

As you begin the drive from the West Glacier entrance, you'll pass the largest of the 653 lakes in Glacier—**Lake McDonald.** Numerous turnouts along the way present opportunities to photograph the panoramic views of the lake with its mountainous backdrop. You can see **Sacred Dancing Cascade** and **Johns Lake** after an easy, half-mile hike from the roadside through a red cedar/hemlock forest. The trailhead for this hike is 2 miles north of the Lake McDonald Lodge along Going-to-the-Sun Road.

The **Trail of the Cedars** is a short, handicapped-accessible boardwalk trail thickly carpeted in vibrant, verdant hues. This is also the beginning of the Avalanche Lake Trail, a 2.1-mile hike to the foot of Avalanche Lake, one of the most popular day-hikes in the park. The Trailhead is about 5.5 miles north of Lake McDonald Lodge, just past the Avalanche Creek Campground.

Almost exactly halfway along Going-to-the-Sun is the overlook for Heaven's Peak, the massive snow-covered mountain to the south that you've just driven around. This is also the jumping-off point for **The Loop Trail,** which can take you into Granite Park Chalet. Just 2 miles farther is the **Bird Woman Falls Overlook.** Bird Woman Falls drops in a wondrous bounty of water from a hanging valley above the road. Next along the road is the oft-photographed **Weeping Wall,** which is a wall of rock, with water pouring forth.

At the 32-mile mark from West Glacier is **Logan Pass,** one of the park's busiest areas and the starting point for the hike to **Hidden Lake,** one of the park's most popular. There's a visitor center here atop the Continental Divide, which has a small display about the wildlife, flora, and geology of the area, and a larger area selling books and such.

As you head downhill, you'll reach the turnout for **Jackson Glacier,** the most easily recognizable glacier in the entire park; followed by **Sunrift Gorge** and **Sun Point,** which are accessible via two short trails rife with wildlife.

WINTER ROAD CONDITIONS   Going-to-the-Sun Road is open seasonally, usually from early June to mid-October, although it may be open earlier or later, depending on weather conditions. Call the park at ☎ **406/888-7800** to find out

> ## Picnicking Tips
>
> The best picnicking spot on the Going-to-the-Sun Road is at the **Sun Point Lake** parking spot, which is also the trailhead for the 0.7-mile round-trip to Baring Falls, a trail that follows the shoreline of the lake. It's located about 9 miles east of the Logan Pass Visitor Center, or 9 miles west of the St. Mary Visitor Center. From the picnic area, the views across the lake to the mountains are unrivaled in the park. For a truly spectacular experience, get there at sunrise.

when tentative openings and closings are scheduled. During the winter, you may drive Going-to-the-Sun Road for 10 miles from West Glacier along Lake McDonald to the road closure; this is a popular destination for cross-country skiers.

OTHER DRIVES

THROUGH THE LOWER HALF OF THE PARK Circumnavigating the lower half of the park is easily accomplished in 1 long day. You'll experience Glacier's splendor and get a bird's-eye view of Big Sky country in the process. After a leisurely breakfast in West Glacier, you'll be in East Glacier in plenty of time for lunch at the Glacier Park Lodge (see "Where to Stay," below) and at St. Mary or Many Glacier for dinner. To complete this counterclockwise loop from West Glacier, hop onto U.S. Highway 2 and head along the park's southern boundary to Essex and East Glacier, then north to St. Mary.

The road between West Glacier and East Glacier—it's approximately 52 miles—is a well-paved, two-lane affair that winds circuitously around the western and southern edges of the park and follows the Middle Fork of the Flathead River. As you descend to the valley floor, you'll travel through beautiful, privately owned Montana ranch- and farmland. Shortly after entering the valley, look to the north and admire the park's massive peaks. The **Goat Lick** parking lot, on U.S. Highway 2 just east of Essex, gets you off the beaten path and provides a view down into a canyon carved by the Flathead River; if you have time, take the short hike down to the stream.

Beyond East Glacier, as you head east on MT 49 and north towards Two Medicine, you'll notice that the earth appears to fall off. The contrast is inescapable—mountains tower in the west, but to the east the Hi-Line begins, sporting a horizon that extends so far and so flat as to seemingly lend credence and legitimacy to the Flat Earth Society. But round a bend on the Two Medicine Road and suddenly find yourself faced with three mountains (Appistocki Peak, Mount Henry, and Bison Mountain) bare of vegetation but as red as their Southwestern counterparts. The difference here is that the crevasses are filled with snow, even in mid-August. Ten miles later, continuing the route northward on U.S. Highway 89, you'll come across a 180° to 220° panorama of mountain peaks, valleys, ridges, and forested mountains that truly characterize Glacier's personality. Conclude the bottom half of your long loop by wending downward from these high elevations to the village of St. Mary.

TO POLEBRIDGE There are two ways to see the park's western boundary, and to access the Polebridge area in the north; one is slow and uncomfortable, the other slightly faster and *less* uncomfortable. The **North Fork Road** (Highway 486) from Columbia Falls takes about an hour to negotiate. It's a sometimes paved, mostly gravel and pothole stretch that follows the North Fork of the Flathead River. Not much is there besides water and scenery, but the area around Polebridge is a popular place to take in Montana's natural beauty without modern-day distractions like telephones and TVs.

Camas Road, just inside the park's West Glacier entrance, also runs to Polebridge. However, it's totally unpaved, takes an hour longer, and is much harder on driver, passenger, and equipment. Unless you are a glutton for punishment, I suggest you take the faster route and spend that extra hour relaxing on a riverbank.

3 Outdoor Pursuits

BOATING   You can take advantage of some of those 653 lakes with a boat rental at various spots. At Apgar and Lake McDonald, you will find kayaks, canoes, rowboats, and motorboats. Only human-powered or electric motorboats are available at Two Medicine. At Many Glacier you can rent kayaks, canoes, and rowboats. For details, call **Glacier Park, Inc. (GPI)** at ☎ **406/257-2426.**

FISHING   Glacier's streams and lakes are habitat for whitefish, kokanee salmon, arctic grayling, and five kinds of trout. Try the North Fork of the Flathead to fish for cutthroat and bull trout and any of the three larger lakes in the park (Bowman Lake, St. Mary Lake, and Lake McDonald) for rainbow, brook trout, and whitefish. The North Fork and Middle Fork of the Flathead require a fishing license from the state of Montana.

HIKING   Glacier is a wilderness park. Most of it is inaccessible by car, and the best way to see it is on foot. Glacier's 1,600 square miles have 151 trails, totaling 753 miles. You can hike 106 miles along the Continental Divide alone.

Trail maps are available at outdoor stores in Whitefish and Kalispell as well as at the major ranger stations at each entry point. Before striking off into the wilderness, however, check with the nearest ranger station to determine the accessibility of your destination, trail conditions, and recent bear sightings. This may save you a lot of headache (even in the summer months) if you plan a high-country hike and 10 miles into the trip a ranger turns you back. Also note that the trail maps don't show elevation changes or many terrain features beyond lakes and the tallest peaks. If you plan to do any extensive hiking, it is best to purchase a U.S. Geological Survey topographic map.

The Park Service asks you to stay on trails to keep from eroding the fragile components of the park. Also, snowbanks shouldn't be traversed, especially the steeper ones. You should have proper footwear and rain gear, enough food, and, most important, enough water, before approaching any trailhead. A can of pepper spray can also come in handy when you're in grizzly habitat. If you're planning to hike in Canada, be sure to purchase the bear spray in Canada, not in the U.S., as Customs will not allow you to take most U.S.-made pepper sprays across the border. See "Exploring the Backcountry," below, for notable hiking trails and further information.

HORSEBACK RIDING   Horseback riding at East Glacier is provided by **Two Medicine River Outfitters** (☎ **406/226-9220**), located a stone's throw from the front door of the lodge; the company offers hourly and half-day rides into the nearby wilderness. **Mule Shoe Outfitters** (☎ **406/888-5121**) offers similar rides from corrals at Apgar, Lake McDonald, and the Many Glacier Corral. Mule Shoe has 1- and 2-hour rides through the varied terrain of Glacier.

MOUNTAIN CLIMBING   The peaks of Glacier Park rarely exceed 10,000 feet in elevation, but don't let the surveyors' measurements fool you. Glacier has some incredibly difficult climbs, and you must inquire at the ranger station regarding climbing conditions and closures. Climbers die here every summer. In general, the peaks are unsuitable, except for experienced climbers or those traveling with experienced guides. An excellent reference for climbers is *A Climber's Guide to Glacier National Park* by Gordon Edwards (Falcon Press).

RAFTING & FLOAT TRIPS   Though the waters that are actually in the park don't lend themselves to white-water rafting, the boundary forks of the Flathead River are some of the best in the northwest corner of the state. For just taking it easy and floating on your back in the summer sun, the North Fork of the Flathead River stretching from Polebridge to Columbia Falls and into Flathead Lake is ideal. Portaging in Polebridge can be difficult if there's not a good sport waiting for you downstream, however. The same may be said for the Middle Fork of the Flathead, which forms the southern border of the park.

For white-water voyagers, the North Fork of the Flathead River (Class II, III) and the Middle Fork (Class III) are the best bets. Inquire at any ranger station for details and conditions, since flow rates change dramatically as snow melts or storms move through the area.

The Middle Fork is a little more severe and isn't the sort of river you enjoy with an umbrella drink in your hand. The names of certain stretches of the Middle Fork are terror-inspiring in themselves (the Narrows, Jaws, Bonecrusher) and to assuage that terror, several outfitters offer expert and sanctioned guides to make sure you're not floating downstream facedown in the river of life.

The **Montana Raft Company** (☎ **800/521-7238** or 406/387-5555; fax 406/387-5656; www.glacierguides.com; e-mail: giguides@cyberport.net) is an arm of Glacier Wilderness Guides that offers rafting trips in Glacier and the surrounding area. Prices range from half-day adult for $38 (child $29), to a 3-day trip at about $430 per person. Prices cover all necessary equipment and food. Trips are scheduled throughout the season. The full-day trip puts in at Cacadilla about 15 miles up the Flathead River. You'll paddle down the relatively calm upper portion, stop for lunch, then be ready for the Class II and Class III white water below Moccasin Creek.

Great Northern Whitewater Raft & Resort (☎ **800/735-7897** or 406/387-5340; www.gnwhitewater.com; e-mail: white2o@digisys.net) offers white-water rafting, kayaking, and drift boat fishing. Full-day raft trips are $71 for adults, $46 for children (12 and under); full-day fishing trips are $295. Horseback riding and rafting combos are also available by arrangement. You can choose between trips where you paddle, or where a guide paddles for you. Other options include scenic and white-water trips, and an 8-mile barbecue dinner trip that leaves at 3pm. Adults with a little previous water experience can take a guided funyak trip—a buoyant inflatable kayak that handles the water better than a kayak.

SNOWSHOEING & CROSS-COUNTRY SKIING   Glacier has many cross-country trails, the most popular of which is the **Upper Lake McDonald Trail** to the Avalanche picnic area. This 8-mile trail offers a relatively flat route up Going-to-the-Sun Road with views of McDonald Creek and the mountains looming above the McDonald Valley. For the advanced skier, the same area presents a more intense 10.5-mile trip that heads northwest in a roundabout fashion to the Apgar Lookout. The most popular trail on the east side is the **Autumn Creek Trail** near Marias Pass. However, avalanche paths cross this area, so inquire about current weather conditions. Yet another popular spot is in Essex along the southern boundary of the park at the Izaak Walton Inn.

4 Exploring the Backcountry

Glacier offers every kind of backcountry experience, from 1-mile day hikes to 2-week treks. Consider your fitness level, backcountry experience, and interests, then get some advice from one of the visitor center rangers. They can provide you with area maps showing little detail. A topographical map is highly recommended if you're going for

---

Bear Warning

To remind you yet again: Glacier is grizzly country. Make noise when you walk, don't cook near where you sleep, and don't sleep in the same clothes you cooked in.

---

more than a short walk. An excellent backcountry guide for Glacier is *Trail Guide to Glacier National Park,* by Eric Molvar (Falcon Press).

Backcountry campgrounds have maps at the entrance to show you the location of each campground, the pit toilet, food preparation areas, and, perhaps most important, food storage areas. If you fish while camping, it's recommended you exercise catch-and-release so as to avoid attracting wildlife in search of food. If you eat the catch, be certain to puncture the air bladder and throw the entrails into deep water at least 200 feet from the nearest campsite or trail.

If you plan an extended hike, let someone know your route and when you expect to get back. Take a flashlight, in case you take longer than you think. Carry a map, rain gear, and extra clothing. It's possible to hike many trails in walking shoes or sneakers, but every time I do it, I wish that I'd stopped to put on my hiking boots.

Drink lots of water. And if you carry it in, carry it out. Don't leave anything behind.

AN OUTFITTER Glacier Wilderness Guides (☎ **800/521-7238** or 406/387-5555; fax 406/387-5656; www.glacierguides.com) is the exclusive hiking guide service in the park. They will put together any kind of trip for you, or offer weekly departures for 3-, 4-, and 6-day trips. Prices vary depending on the trip, but you can figure on spending $100 to $120 per person per day. They also rent equipment and provide "Sherpa service" where the guide will carry your gear. The season runs from May to September.

NOTABLE HIKING TRAILS

FROM TWO MEDICINE CAMPGROUND These trails consist of moderate-length hikes with moderate elevation gains on trails that are accessed most easily by boat, and longer hikes (5 to 8 miles) with elevation gains of nearly one-half mile. Hardly a hike, the easiest is to **Running Eagle Falls** along a one-third-mile trail that winds through a heavily forested area to a large, noisy waterfall. The trailhead is about 1 mile away on the road to the Two Medicine campground. Similarly, the **Appistoki Falls Trail** is a short jaunt to a waterfall.

The most popular hiking path is the **Twin Falls Trail,** which originates at the campground. Hikers may walk the entire 3.8-mile distance to Twin Falls on a clearly identified trail, or boat across Two Medicine Lake to the foot of the trailhead and hike the last mile. More aggressive outdoor types will continue on the **Pitamakan Pass Trail,** a 7-mile-long trail that intersects the **Nyak Creek** and **Cut Bank trails.**

Upon reaching Old Man Lake, you can return on the same route or complete a loop by continuing on the **Dawson Pass Trail** back through Twin Falls to the campground.

Also from Two Medicine, if you want a serious backcountry hike, try the **Dawson-Pitamakan Loop.** This difficult, 19-mile hike traverses Rising Wolf Mountain, at 9,513 feet the area's most prominent feature. There are backcountry campsites at Old Man Lake and at No Name Lake. The trail offers panoramas of the park's interior and of many alpine lakes. You'll encounter lots of steep ups and downs.

KINTLA LAKE TO UPPER KINTLA LAKE This 24-mile round-trip hike skirts the north shore of Kintla Lake above Polebridge for about 7 miles before climbing a couple of hundred feet. This stretch of the Boulder Pass hike is a breeze. However, once you hit Kintla Creek you may want to reconsider going any farther. With 12 miles under your belt at this point, climbing 3,000 feet may not seem like a great idea. The trail, once it breaks into the clear, offers views of several peaks, including Kinnerly Peak to the south of Upper Kintla Lake. The **trailhead** is located 14 miles north of Polebridge after a drive along a gravel road. The trail begins at the western tip of Kintla Lake.

BOWMAN LAKE   This trail (14 miles to Brown Pass) is similar to the Kintla Lake hike in difficulty, and, like the Kintla Trail, passes the lake on the north. After a hike through the foliage, the trail climbs out of reach of anyone in bad shape, then ascends 2,000 feet in less than 3 miles to join the Kintla Trail at Brown Pass. A left turn takes you back to Kintla Lake (23 miles), a right takes you to Goat Haunt at the foot of Waterton Lake (9 miles). To reach the **Bowman Lake trailhead,** go 0.3 miles north of Polebridge, then turn east (right) up the Bowman Creek road. The road ends after 6 miles at the southeast end of Bowman Lake, from which the trails radiate.

QUARTZ LAKE   Cross the bridge over Bowman Creek. The entire loop is 12 miles and runs a course up and over a ridge and down to the south end of Lower Quartz Lake. From there it's a level 3-mile hike to the west end of Quartz Lake, then it's 6 miles back over the ridge farther north (and higher up) before dropping back to Bowman Lake. An interesting aspect of this trail is evidence of the Red Bench Fire of 1988, which took a chunk out of the North Fork area.

LAKE MCDONALD-TROUT CREEK LOOP   This is a good workout if you're moping around Lake McDonald Lodge sipping coffee and skipping rocks off the lake. This hike is straight up and straight down. The trail to the foot of Trout Lake and back is roughly 8 miles and begins from the north end of Lake McDonald.

THE HIGHLINE TRAIL   This relatively easy hike, which gains only 200 feet in elevation over 7.6 miles, begins at the Logan Pass Visitor Center and skirts the Garden Wall at elevations of more than 6,000 feet to Granite Park Chalet. Keep an eye on your watch to be certain you'll have enough time for the return hike to Logan Pass. You can continue on from the chalet to "the Loop," the aptly named section of Going-to-the-Sun Road where the trail actually terminates (an additional 4.2 miles), although you'll need to plan for a shuttle back to your car.

THE HIDDEN LAKE NATURE TRAIL   This is a short, easy walk on a boardwalk path to an overlook of Hidden Lake. I've hiked this trail with my mother and my in-laws and they all made it to the top and back with a minimum of puffing and complaining. I've gone up here four or five times, and every time there has been a mountain goat hanging around at the top. No kidding. This trail starts at the Logan Pass Visitor Center and goes east and uphill from there. The hike is about a mile one-way.

PIEGAN PASS-TO-MANY GLACIER   If you're looking for a longer, tougher hike from Logan Pass, try this hike. You pick up the trail at Sunrift Gorge about 6 miles on the east side of Logan Pass Visitor Center. It's a 12.5-mile walk up over Piegan Pass, past Grinnell Glacier and Grinnell Lake to Josephine and Swiftcurrent lakes before reaching Many Glacier Lodge. There are long stretches of up (and of down) walking.

ST. MARY FALLS   This is another pretty easy walk, about 0.8 mile, that takes you to a rushing falls of the St. Mary River. It is a well-padded, gently sloping hiking path, suitable for seniors in tennis shoes or sandal-clad children bouncing along to keep their bear bells jingling. The falls themselves are easily worth the trip, a raging white torrent gushing through a narrow cleft in the rock and dropping perhaps 60 feet to the racing green river below. The roar of the cascade is prodigious and satisfying.

CHALETS

Two of the park's most popular destinations, Granite Park and Sperry chalets—National Historic Landmarks built by the Great Northern Railway between 1912 and 1914—are subjects of an extensive restoration project. The **Granite Park Chalet** is a hiker's shelter only. Guests must bring their own food, water, cooking and eating utensils, flashlights, and sleeping bags. Rooms and beds are provided, as are a kitchen with a cooking stove and dining room. No public water is available, so bring your own. The chalet has 12 rooms (all single bunk beds), and sleeps two to six per room. Cost is $60 per night per person, plus $10 per person if you want bed linens. For reservations at Granite Park Chalet, call **Glacier Wilderness Guides** (☎ **800/521-7238** or 406/387-5555; www.glacierguides.com). **To get here,** you'll have to walk about 3 miles from The Loop trailhead off the Going-to-the-Sun Road, or about 6 miles on the trail to Swiftcurrent Pass at the end of Many Glacier Road from the east side.

The **Sperry Chalet** is more of a full-service facility; it opened in 1999 for the first time since 1992. It's an impressive stone edifice in the center of the wilderness. For reservations contact **Belton Chalets** at ☎ **888/345-2649** or www.ptinet.net/sperrychalet. **To get here,** walk about 4 miles from the road, up Snyder Creek, then toward Gunsight Mountain. The trailhead is opposite the entrance to Lake McDonald Lodge on the lower portion of Going-to-the-Sun Road.

5 Camping

INSIDE THE PARK

Stop at any ranger station for information on closures and availability, or consult the chart below for information on amenities and fees.

Glacier offers the RV and tent camper seven campgrounds that are accessible on paved road: **Apgar,** near the West Glacier entrance; **Avalanche Creek,** just up from the head of Lake McDonald; **Fish Creek,** on the west side of Lake McDonald; **Many Glacier,** in the northeast part of the park; **Rising Sun,** on the north side of St. Mary Lake; **St. Mary,** on the east side of the park; and **Two Medicine,** on the southeast part of the park near East Glacier. **Sprague Creek,** near the West Glacier entrance, offers a paved road but does not allow towed vehicles. Though utility connections are not provided at these sites, fireplaces, picnic tables, washrooms, and cold running water are located at each campground. The nightly fee is $10 to $12 and campsites are obtained on a first-come, first-served basis only. Reservations are not accepted.

A few sites for bicyclists are held until 9pm at Apgar, Sprague Creek, Avalanche, Rising Sun, and St. Mary campgrounds, for $3 per person.

NOTES ON THE CAMPGROUNDS

Despite its proximity to the center of the hotel and motel activity, the **Many Glacier Campground** is a well-treed, almost secluded campground that provides as much privacy in a public area as we've seen anywhere. The campground has adequate space for recreational vehicles and truck/camper combinations, but space for trucks pulling trailers is limited. It is a veritable mecca for tent campers. The **Avalanche Campground** is situated in the bottom of the valley near Lake McDonald in a heavily treed area immediately adjacent to the river. The **Two Medicine Campground** lies in the shadow of the mountains near three lakes and a stream. It is a well-treed area that has beautiful sites, plenty of shade, and opportunities to wet a fishing line or dangle your feet in cool mountain water. Two Medicine is a little out of the way of the typical Glacier traveler, and may offer a little more solitude. The **Cut Bank Campground** road is not paved. But it's only 5 miles from the pavement to the ranger station and campground. The road and campground are best suited to recreational vehicles 21 feet or shorter.

Amenities for Each Campground in Glacier National Park

Campground	# of Sites	Fee	Max RV Length	Flush Toilets	Disposal Stations	Boat Access
Apgar	196	$12	25 sites; up to 40'	Yes	Yes	Yes
Avalanche	87	$12	50 sites; up to 26'	Yes	Yes	No
Bowman Lake*	48	$10	RVs not recommended	No	No	Yes
Cut Bank*	19	$10	RVs not recommended	No	No	No
Fish Creek	180	$15	3 sites; up to 35'	Yes	Yes	No
Kintla Lake*	13	$10	RVs not recommended	No	No	Yes
Logging Creek*	8	$10	RVs not recommended	No	No	No
Many Glacier	110	$12	13 sites; up to 35'	Yes	Yes	Yes
Quartz Creek*	7	$10	RVs not recommended	No	No	No
Rising Sun	83	$12	3 sites; up to 30'	Yes	Yes	Yes
Sprague Creek	25	$12	no towed units	Yes	No	No
St. Mary	148	$15	25 sites; up to 35'	Yes	Yes	No
Two Medicine	99	$12	13 sites; up to 32'	Yes	Yes	Yes

Campgrounds are accessible only by narrow dirt roads. RVs are not recommended.

CAMPGROUNDS IN GATEWAY COMMUNITIES

During the busy season, it's recommended that you reserve these campsites at least 1 month in advance.

IN EAST GLACIER

Y Lazy R. Box 146, East Glacier, MT 59434. ☎ **406/226-5573.** 10 tent sites, 30 RV sites. $10 tent; $15 full hookup.

Situated just off U.S. Highway 2, this campground is conveniently located within walking distance of East Glacier and is the closest to town with laundry facilities. Plan to arrive early if you want to snag one of the few sites with trees. This place is a great value and an ideal place to plant the RV before heading off to explore the region.

IN ST. MARY

Johnson's of St. Mary. St. Mary, MT 59417. ☎ **406/732-4207.** Fax 406/732-5517. 50 tent sites, 65 RV sites. $14 tent; $18 RV with electricity and water only, $20 full hookup. MC, V.

From April through September (depending on the weather) this is where you want to camp if you can get a spot. The campground is located near the southern end of Lower St. Mary Lake and provides an inexpensive overnight stop with access to the east side of the park and the tourist facilities at the St. Mary Lodge. There are also showers ($2) and a Laundromat.

IN WEST GLACIER

Glacier Campground. P.O. Box 447, 12070 U.S. Hwy. 2, West Glacier, MT 59936. ☎ **406/387-5689.** 80 tent sites, 80 RV sites, 5 cabins. $15 tent; $18 full hookup; $30–$40 cabin.

This campground—1 mile west of West Glacier on U.S. Highway 2—is the closest campground outside the park. Set amid a forested area overgrown with evergreens, it's

Bear Watching

If you haven't had the good (or bad) luck to run into a bear during your back-country adventures, you can still get a guaranteed sighting under your belt at the **Great Bear Adventure**, 10555 U.S. Hwy. 2 E., in Coram, near West Glacier. This 10-acre compound is the home of four healthy, free-roaming black bears, including one 750-pounder. The path you drive through the compound—actually, it's a private residence with a backyard full of bears—is approximately a mile long. Because of the unscheduled and unpatterned manner of feeding, they are constantly foraging for food just as they do in the wilderness. Open 10am to 7pm. Adults $4, children $2. Cash only.

a quiet, comfortable place to retreat under the shade of the trees, especially on hot summer days. Most sites have water and electric hookups; the balance is perfect for tent camping. Five rather primitive cabins are also available, but furnishings are modest: sleeping beds with mattresses and electricity, but no plumbing or kitchen facilities. Recreational facilities include volleyball, horseshoes, and a basketball court; also on the premises are a Laundromat and teensy general store that has little to offer except a fresh quart of milk or a T-shirt.

Lakeside Resort. 540 Belton Stage Rd., West Glacier, MT 59936. ☎ **406/387-5601.** 21 tent sites, 14 RV sites, 9 cabins. $16–$20 site; $70–$98 cabin.

Located 3 miles west of West Glacier and approximately 1 mile from U.S. Highway 2 is this cabin and campground arrangement, an alternative to potentially crowded park campgrounds. Situated on a 235-acre lake surrounded by private homes and summer cottages, the resort is far from the madding crowd (though still close to the park itself). Seven of the nine cabins are on the lakefront, all of them equipped with bathrooms and showers. The only distraction may be the sound of powerboats.

North American RV Park & Campground. P.O. Box 130449, Coram, MT 59913 (on U.S. Hwy. 2 about 5.5 miles west of West Glacier). ☎ **406/387-5800.** 18 tent sites, 91 RV sites (45 full hookups, 46 electric only). $13–$23.

This is a large, convenient, and conspicuous campground, close to Glacier National Park and Hungry Horse Reservoir. The RV park is associated with the **Wildlife Museum** next door. Here you'll find preserved most of the animals indigenous to this area. The museum is closed in winter. Admission is $3 for adults and $2 for children; hours are 9am to 9pm daily, May 1 to October 31.

West Glacier KOA. Box 215, West Glacier, MT 59936. ☎ **800/562-3313** or 406/ 387-5341. Fax 406/387-5209. E-mail: wgkoa@netrix.net. $21 tent; $28 full hookup. Drive 2.5 miles west on U.S. Hwy. 2, then 1 mile south on a paved road.

This is a neat, modern facility with a store, ice cream parlor, and playground. The campsites are wooded, and a few small cabins are available. The campground also sponsors occasional wildlife slide shows and lectures.

BACKCOUNTRY CAMPING

If it's the backcountry you're bent on seeing, Glacier has 63 backcountry campgrounds. Fortunately, many are at lower elevation, so inexperienced backpackers have an opportunity to take advantage of them. For an accurate depiction of your itinerary's difficulty, and advice on what may be needed, check with rangers in the area you contemplate visiting. One of the main sources of danger is bears. Backcountry permits are available at ranger stations, and requests for sites can be made 24 hours in advance. There is no fee for a permit.

6 Where to Stay

INSIDE THE PARK

With only one exception, Glacier Park, Inc. (GPI) operates the hostelries in Glacier National Park. Lake McDonald Lodge, Glacier Park Lodge, and Many Glacier Hotel are first-tier properties that have been popular destinations since early in the century. Swiftcurrent Motor Inn is typical of the casual motel-style properties at the other end of the spectrum, providing decent but undistinguished accommodations for less money. Although the lodges have a considerable stately charm, they don't have spas or air-conditioning. They also don't have televisions in the rooms.

Reserve well in advance. August dates may fill before the spring thaw. For more information on the following properties or to make a reservation, contact **Glacier Park, Inc.,** Viad Tower, Phoenix, AZ 85077-0928 (☎ **602/207-6000** for reservations; www.glacierparkinc.com). GPI does not accept pets at any of its facilities.

Apgar Village Lodge. Apgar Village, Box 410, West Glacier, MT 59936. ☎ **406/888-5484.** Fax 406/888-5273. www.westglacier.com. E-mail: lodging@westglacier.com. 50 units. TV. $59–$89 motel room; $73–$210 cabin. DISC, MC, V. Closed mid-Oct to Apr.

The Apgar Village Lodge is located on the south end of Lake McDonald and is one of two lodgings in Apgar Village. There's a wide variety of lodging available here, but the best places—reserve early—are along Lake McDonald Creek and on the banks of the lake. You might be able to catch a glimpse of the beavers working on a dam in the creek. There are nine river cabins, and several motel rooms overlooking the creek. The cabins are much nicer than they look on the outside. Five large cabins have been completely remodeled, with two bedrooms; most of them have kitchens with stoves and refrigerators. Some of the small ones tend to be a little dark, and the towels aren't big enough. Fans of the film *Beethoven II* might recognize the scenery—the movie was shot here.

✪ **Glacier Park Lodge.** Glacier National Park, MT 59936. ☎ **406/226-9311.** www.glacierparkinc.com. 154 units. TEL. $131–$192 lodge; $233 suite. DISC, MC, V.

Located just inside the southeast entrance at East Glacier, this is GPI'S flagship inn. This imposing timbered lodge stands as a stately tribute to the Great Northern Railroad and its early attempts to lure tourists to Glacier. The hotel is stylish and impressive, but not luxurious. The rooms are fairly small—a common complaint in these old railroad hotels, built when travelers' expectations were different—with spartan furnishings. You didn't come to Glacier to sit in your room, though, and most of the activity occurs in the lobby and grounds outside. The carefully manicured lawn and blooming wildflowers frame the grounds in colors spectacular enough to rival the mountain backdrop. The interior features massive Douglas fir pillars, some 40 inches in diameter and 40 feet tall. A wooden deck outside the lounge provides an excellent spot for cocktails, reading, or a late-afternoon snooze. A glass-enclosed breezeway connects the main building to the annex; the oak chaise lounges provide an ideal spot to watch the sun rise.

Dining/Diversions: There is always a crowd at the dining rooms of the park hotels, and the dining room of the Glacier Park Hotel is no exception. If you want to eat here, make your reservation as soon as you arrive. The room is nice, though a bit institutional in feel. The food, however, is ordinary and overpriced. The menu consists mostly of beef and seafood, though it varies somewhat from year to year. The service is friendly and enthusiastic but can be uneven, since the park facilities rely almost entirely on college students from around the country for staff.

Presentations and entertainment include Blackfeet explaining the history and culture of their tribe, naturalists' programs or an employee-performed rock 'n' roll revue.

Amenities: The hotel has a pool and a nine-hole golf course, and can arrange horseback rides for you during your stay. There is also a small chip-and-putt golf course that occupies most of the front lawn and is very popular in the evenings. The Native American Trading Post offers traditional souvenirs, as well as artwork and clothing from tribal artisans.

Lake McDonald Lodge. Glacier National Park, MT 59936. ☎ **602/207-6000.** www.glacierparkinc.com. 62 units in lodge and motel, 38 cottage rooms (some without private bathroom). TEL. $81–$130 double. DISC, MC, V.

The Lake McDonald Lodge looks and feels like a lodge in the old style. It's small compared to the other GPI park lodges, only two stories and without the towering open lobby featured at Many Glacier and Glacier Park Lodge. The ambience is altogether more cozy. Situated on the shore of the park's largest lake, it provides a fine base for exploring the western part of the park. A center for boating activity, scenic cruises depart daily, or you can rent your own boat by the day ($75 motor; $40 row) or hour ($15 motor; $8 row). Rooms in the Stewart Annex and well-preserved cabins are comfortable but less desirable. Be sure to inquire as to whether yours has a private bathroom. Common lounging areas are furnished with heavy couches, sofas, and chairs that surround a stone fireplace. The lodge houses a dining room, gift shop, and lounge; a coffee shop, post office, and sundries store are also on the grounds.

⚙ **Many Glacier Hotel.** Glacier National Park, MT 59936. ☎ **602/207-6000.** www.glacierparkinc.com. 211 units. TEL. $103–$175 lodge room; $190 suite. DISC, MC, V.

Many Glacier is a vast, sprawling four-story structure on Swiftcurrent Lake. It's the most popular lodging in the park, and with good reason. The setting is beautiful, and there's a wide variety of activities to embark on from here—boating, hiking, and bird-watching, to name but a few. And the wildlife wanders around as if it owns the place (which I guess it does, in a way). The rooms are a little larger than the ones usually associated with a Northern Pacific hotel. But this was never a "railroad hotel." Completed in 1915, it was one of a network of chalets —others were Sperry and Granite— that visitors rode to on horseback. The chalets were set 1 day's ride apart.

Comfortably furnished rooms with decks overlooking the lake are available, some carpeted and some with hardwood floors. The views are spectacular as Mount Grinnell and Mount Wilbur wake you for breakfast. Wandering bears are more than a rumor around Many Glacier. In a stay here in 1990, taking a walk around Swiftcurrent and Lake Josephine, I saw a very large black bear strolling in a gentlemanly fashion along the shore of Josephine. We were alarmed at first—he was getting closer to us—but were finally disappointed when some other visitors unknowingly scared him off into the wooded country. You'll almost certainly see bears in August when the huckleberries ripen.

A dining room, coffee shop, gift shop, and lounge are all located in the hotel; nightly cabaret performances begin mid-summer.

Rising Sun Motor Inn. Glacier National Park, MT 59936. ☎ **602/207-6000.** www.glacierparkinc.com. 63 units. $81–$87 double. DISC, MC, V.

Located 6.5 miles from St. Mary, just off Going-to-the-Sun Road, the Rising Sun is just another motel, lacking charisma. The complex is made up of a restaurant, a motor inn, cottages, a camp store, a gift shop, and a service station. The rooms are just

The Other Gateway Communities

If the convenience of staying on Glacier's back porch is important to you, the places listed on the following pages are your best bets. However, in surrounding communities not necessarily classified as gateway towns, you'll find a greater variety of accommodations. See "Where to Stay" in the Whitefish, Kalispell, and Columbia Falls sections of chapter 5 for listings of places that might be more in line with your needs if the park is merely a 1- or 2-day part of your vacation.

rooms, comfortable enough. The main advantage is that St. Mary Lake is across the street. There's a lot of asphalt and plain brown buildings here, along with 28 motel rooms, 9 of which are located in the same building as the camp store, and 35 rooms in duplex cottages.

Swiftcurrent Motor Inn. Glacier National Park, MT 59936. ☎ **602/207-6000.** www.glacierparkinc.com. 88 units (most cabins without private bathroom). TEL. $40–$87 double. DISC, MC, V.

The Swiftcurrent Motor Inn is located about a mile upstream from Many Glacier Hotel, but it attracts an entirely different crowd. The people who stay here are younger, less well-to-do, active. The accommodations are—how to put this delicately?—rustic. Quaint. Spartan. The Swiftcurrent was built in 1936 as a motor hotel, the first in the park specifically directed at tourists arriving by car rather than train. There are three circles of cabins and two motel-style units, all set back in the trees. Only two of the cabin units have private bathrooms; the rest are two or three rooms with beds. The motel rooms all have private bathrooms and in fact are comparable in quality to many of the fancy lodge rooms—but they lack other lodge amenities. They are very cheap, however, compared with other places within the park. The Inn is in a spectacular setting at the base of two mountains. From here you can see the Ptarmigan wall, a huge rock band across the horizon, in places only 7 feet thick, where two glaciers rubbed against each other in a romance over geologic time. The inn sits in a wildlife migratory path. So there really will be bear and elk and moose in the parking lot. The Italian Garden Ristorante serves a mean garlic and artichoke-heart pizza.

Village Inn. Glacier National Park, MT 59936. ☎ **602/207-6000.** www.glacierparkinc.com. 36 units (12 with kitchenette). $90–$142 double. DISC, MC, V.

Not to be confused with Apgar Village Lodge (see above), the Village Inn is the smallest of the properties operated by GPI in Glacier. Located in Apgar Village, the inn is convenient to the general store, cafes, and boat docks. Like its counterparts throughout the park, the Village Inn is comfortably outfitted with modest furnishings, making it a cozy and convenient place to set up camp. Though there's no dining room on the property, the restaurants of Lake McDonald and Apgar are all close by. Apgar Village bustles with activity during the summer and is a great choice for families.

IN GATEWAY COMMUNITIES
IN EAST GLACIER

Backpacker's Inn. P.O. Box 94, East Glacier, MT 59434. ☎ **406/226-9392.** E-mail: serranos@digisys.net. 3 cabins (sleeping 20 people). $10 per person. DISC, MC, V. Closed mid-Oct to Apr.

This dorm-style hostel consists of three cabins—one for men, one for women, and one coed—each sleeping up to six people (the coed cabin sleeps eight). At $10 per person, the price is right, but don't expect the rooms to include much more than a bed. The rooms are booked out of Serrano's Restaurant (see "Where to Dine," below).

Brownies Grocery and AYH Hostel. P.O. Box 229, East Glacier, MT 59434. ☎ **406/ 226-4426** or 406/226-4456. www.grizzlyadventures.com. 10 units, 2 family rooms (all with shared bathroom). AYH members $12–$17, $30 family room; nonmembers $15–$23, $35 family room. DISC, MC, V. Closed Oct to early May, depending on the weather.

Reservations are recommended at this popular combination grocery store/hostel, which offers comfortable rooms at extremely affordable prices. Dorm and family rooms are located on the second floor of a rustic, older log building with several common rooms for guests to share, including a porch, kitchen, bathrooms, and laundry.

East Glacier Motel and Cabins. 1107 MT 49, East Glacier, MT 59434. ☎ **406/226-5593.** E-mail: 102164.356@compuserve.com. 11 cabins, 6 motel rooms. $45–$65 double. DISC, MC, V. Pets accepted.

This is a small place across the street from The Restaurant Thimbleberry. The motel rooms are very nice, recently remodeled, average size, done in pastel colors. The cabins are small, with low ceilings, a small refrigerator, and two-burner stove. The prices are very low for the area, however, and the rooms were sparkling clean.

Jacobson's Cottages. P.O. Box 216, East Glacier, MT 59434. ☎ **406/226-4422.** 12 units. $59–$63. DISC, MC, V. Closed Nov–Apr.

Located down the street from Glacier Park Lodge, these quaint cottages are small but comfortable. And while they aren't equipped with either TVs or kitchens (with one exception), entertainment and good food are short walks away with the Restaurant Thimbleberry a half block down the street and Two Medicine a 4-mile drive.

Mountain Pine Motel. MT 49, East Glacier, MT 59434. ☎ **406/226-4403.** 25 units. TV. Summer, $55–$60 double; May 1–June 15 and Sept 15–Oct 1, $44–$54 double. AE, DC, DISC, MC, V. Small pets accepted.

This property is a one-story, 1950s-type motel that provides clean, well-furnished rooms equipped with cable TV—a very rare phenomenon in Glacier area motels. It is in a shaded, timbered area on MT 49. Most standard rooms have two queen-size beds, reading chairs and table, chest, and bathrooms with tub-shower combinations. They're clustered around a small green and timbered courtyard. There is also a large three-bedroom log house available with a view of the mountains. Someone will meet you at the Amtrak station, if you arrive by train.

IN ESSEX

Glacier River Retreat. HC36 Box 11A (mile marker 173.4 on U.S. Hwy. 2), Essex, MT 59916. ☎ **406/888-9001.** www.cyberport.net/glacierriverretreat. 4 units. $120 (2-night minimum) double. MC, V.

Open only since 1998, these are two modern duplex cabins, each unit sleeping up to four. They are good-size units, with kitchens and two bedrooms each. The arched ceilings add to the feeling of openness. The cabins are located in a deeply wooded setting. It is a short walk to fishing in the Flathead River. A sauna and recreation room are available. Luxury-seekers, take note: The rooms don't have phones, air-conditioning, or televisions.

✪ **Izaak Walton Inn.** P.O. Box 653, Essex, MT 59916. ☎ **406/888-5700.** Fax 406/ 888-5200. www.izaakwaltoninn.com. E-mail: izaakw@digisys.net. 30 units, 3 suites, 4 caboose cottages. $98 double; $150 suite; $475 caboose (3-night minimum). MC, V.

Built in 1939, this inn originally housed railway workers who kept the tracks free of winter snow. It now has three floors of rooms, a restaurant on the first floor, and a downstairs tavern. The rooms are not large, but they are beautifully kept and furnished. Each has a private bathroom, and some of the bathrooms are encircled at the top by smoked glass bearing the mountain goat insignia of the Northern Pacific. There are no phones or televisions in the rooms. Some have, in addition to the double beds, futon couches that can be folded out for another bed. The halls are decorated in railroad memorabilia. Unlike a lot of Glacier places, the inn is booming in winter. Skiers are attracted to its 30 miles of groomed trails. A new pavilion will house a covered ice rink in winter. There is also a Finnish sauna.

○ **Paola Creek Bed & Breakfast.** HC 36 Box 4C (at mile 172.8 on U.S. Hwy. 2), Essex, MT 59916. ☎ **888/311-5061** or 406/888-5061. Fax 406/888-5063. www.wtp.net/ go/paola. E-mail: paola@in-tch.com. 4 units. $120 double. MC, V. Personal checks accepted.

This B&B (pronounced pay-ola) sits back in the woods with a beautiful view of Mount St. Nicholas in the distance. The rooms are small but beautifully decorated, very comfortable and each with a private bathroom. The centerpiece of the place is the great room, a large open living room dominated by a three-story river rock chimney of the large fireplace. There is also a large deck out back where you can sit in awe of the Glacier Park peaks. Kelly Hostetler, who owns the place with her husband Les, provides a full breakfast and evening wine and hors d'oeuvres as part of the price. She'll also cook a gourmet dinner for guests for an additional $25 per plate. Paola Creek attracts a vigorous outdoor crowd who are up and out in the morning for hiking, kayaking, or fishing on the Flathead River. While it is about 15 miles from here to the West Glacier park entrance, I highly recommend a stay here.

IN POLEBRIDGE

North Fork Hostel and Square Peg Ranch. P.O. Box 1, Polebridge, MT 59928. ☎ **406/888-5241.** www.nfhostel.com. E-mail: nfhostel@nfhostel.com. 15 bunks, 2 cabins, 2 log homes. $13 bunk; $25 cabin; $50 log home. AE.

Next to the North Fork of the Flathead River, the North Fork Hostel is basic. The guys' dorm is upstairs and the girls' dorm is downstairs. Serious bikers, hikers, and river rats stay here. The office-lobby-living room is comfortably jumbled with 10 years of *National Geographic*, two dogs (one of them a blind spaniel, the other a grouchy German Shepherd), and a couple of stray guitars, kept in tune. On one sign at the entrance, owner John Frederick says, "I can't be here all the time. Make yourself comfortable. Pick a bunk." There are some cabins and trailers in the back, just large enough to accommodate the beds that fill them. This is truly a hostel from the 1960s.

Polebridge Mercantile and Cabins. P.O. Box 42, Polebridge, MT 59928. ☎ **406/ 888-5105.** 4 cabins, 1 tepee. $20 tepee; $30–$55 cabin. Children stay free. MC, V.

No running water, let alone bedding —it's bring your own sleeping bag at the Merc. Each cabin has propane cooking stoves and lights, and the views out over the west side of Glacier National Park make the $35 price tag a steal, especially if you brought the kids. This may sound like an adventure in hell, but Polebridge is a happening spot in the summer when all the river rats and seasonal residents converge for good times and tall tales about the rapids they've run and their mountaineering adventures. The Mercantile sells canned goods, hot sandwiches, and T-shirts, to remind you, no doubt, of the great times you had in the cabins. There is a bakery with great baked goods.

IN ST. MARY

St. Mary Lodge. U.S. Hwy. 89 and Going-to-the-Sun Rd., St. Mary, MT 59417. ☎ 406/732-4431. Fax 406/732-9265. www.glcpark.com. 57 units, 19 cabins and cottages. A/C TEL. $89–$145 room or cabin; $285 cottage. AE, DISC, MC, V. Closed Oct 2 to Mother's Day.

Owner Roscoe Black has built himself quite an empire here on the east edge of Glacier National Park. The accommodations are very nice, the restaurant is excellent, the gift shop is huge, and they sell 7 tons of chocolate a year. Even the highway going by is newly repaved. The cheaper units are small but bright with golden logs. The furniture is lodgepole. The six cottages on the hill—which will hold four adults and rent for $285 per night in season—are the best luxury accommodations anywhere in or near the park. They have a living room, full kitchen, two bedrooms, spacious decks, a good-size bathroom with a tub, and gas barbecue grills. There are only six of them, and they rent out so fast that Black says he wishes he'd built twice as many. The cottages sit high on a hill, and the view from the decks out over St. Mary Lake are spectacular. Most of the rest of the lodge units are also air conditioned, the only ones in the Glacier to have it. (Although, frankly, I was too cold with the air-conditioning on. It is called "glacier" for a reason, after all.)

Dining: When Roscoe Black met owner Mike Arp of the Paradise Valley's Chico Hot Springs, Arp said to him, "So, I finally get to meet the owner of the second-best restaurant in Montana." I wouldn't give the "Montana's best" title to St. Mary Lodge's **Snowgoose Grille** (or to Chico either, for that matter), but it is certainly in the top ten. The restaurant specializes in elegant preparation of Montana-style food like wild boar, elk medallions, buffalo, and their signature fresh St. Mary Lake whitefish. They are aided in these efforts by having their own bakery, butcher shop, and smokehouse. Dinners are pricey. There's also a cafe and pizza place.

Amenities: The lodge makes its own buffalo sausage, hot dogs, and jerky, for sale on the premises. There are a coffee/chocolate shop, a gas station, a Laundromat, and a vast and unpredictable gift shop. This is where you'll find the best outdoors store anywhere in the vicinity of the park, **Trail & Creek Outfitters** (☎ 406/732-4431, ext. 332).

IN WEST GLACIER

Belton Chalets and Lodge. U.S. Hwy. 2, West Glacier, MT. ☎ **406/888-5000.** Fax 406/888-5005. www.beltonchalet.com. E-mail: belton@digisys.com. 32 units. $95–$175. AE, MC, V.

This old chalet and lodge immediately across from the railroad station has recently been completely refinished to the elegance of a turn-of-the-century railroad hotel. The rooms are small, simple, and old-fashioned. There are no phones or televisions in them. The bathrooms are also small. But the feel of the place is comfortable, and the staff is very friendly. Many of the rooms have individual balconies looking out over the rounded timber hills in the near distance, the foothills to Glacier National Park. There is a restaurant and bar with the hotel, in a separate building down the hill (see "Where to Dine").

Great Northern Chalets. 12127 U.S. Hwy. 2, West Glacier, MT 59936. ☎ **800/735-7897** or 406/387-5340. www.gnwhitewater.com. E-mail: white2o@digisys.net. 6 chalets. $110–$250. DISC, MC, V.

Located near West Glacier, Great Northern Chalets offers log chalets of a decidedly Nordic *stabbur* look. The gingerbread balconies face landscaped flower gardens and a pond, with mountain views in the distance. A 16-foot indoor hot-tub spa is on the property, as are a volleyball court that doubles as a sandbox for children, and a pond that is used for fly-fishing instruction. Two types of chalets are offered, the largest being a beautifully furnished two-story, two-bedroom unit with three queen-size beds, a full bathroom upstairs, and half bathroom downstairs. Smaller chalets have one large upstairs bedroom with two queen beds, a spiral staircase, and a downstairs level with a full-size sleeper sofa and a kitchen with service for six. This is also headquarters for white-water rafting, kayaking, and fishing expeditions.

Mountain Timbers. P.O. Box 94, West Glacier, MT 59936. ☎ **800/841-3835** or 406/387-5830. Fax 406/387-5835. E-mail: mtnmbrs@digisys.net. 7 units (3 with shared bathroom), 1 chalet (3 bedrooms, 2 bathrooms). $75–$85 double with shared bathroom, $95–$125 double with private bathroom; $250 chalet (3-night minimum). AE, MC, V.

Tucked away on the other side of the Flathead River near the south side of the park is this cozy B&B. Situated on 260 acres, the beautiful 5,000-square-foot lodge offers easy access to the park and more than 10 miles of gorgeous hiking and biking trails of its own. It's an excellent spot for avoiding park crowds. After days spent outdoors, evenings may be spent soaking in the hot tub or lounging in the library. During winter months the lodge is transformed into an excellent base for cross-county skiers, with more than 10 miles of well-groomed trails that are even good enough for the locals.

Vista Motel. P.O. Box 98, West Glacier, MT 59936. ☎ **406/888-5311.** 26 units. TV. $60–$190 double. AE, DISC, MC, V. Closed Nov–Feb.

Perched atop a hill at the west entrance to Glacier National Park, the Vista boasts tremendous views of the mountains. It's strictly a strip motel, old but pretty well preserved. The owner is a serious Denver Broncos fan, if that influences your choice one way or the other. Accommodations are not luxurious, but rooms are clean and comfortable, and there's an outdoor heated pool. It's a lot cheaper than the competition.

West Glacier Motel. 200 Going-to-the-Sun Rd., West Glacier, MT 59936. ☎ **406/888-5662.** 32 units. TV. $59–$68 double. DISC, MC, V.

Formerly the River Bend Motel, this property has two locations. Half of the units are in West Glacier on the Going-to-the-Sun Road, about 1 mile from the park entrance, and a second set of units is 1 mile away on a forested piece of ground that presents panoramic views of the park. This 1950s-style motel, in addition to its location and property, boasts television sets despite the fact that there is virtually no reception. However, the prices can't go wrong during peak season, and rates drop dramatically the week before Labor Day. Cabins are better suited to family use, since they come with two or three queen-size beds, kitchens completely equipped for cooking, and a dishwasher.

7 Where to Dine

INSIDE THE PARK

You'll find above-average food served at above-average prices in the dining rooms at the major properties. **Glacier Park Lodge** has the Goatlick Steak & Rib House and the Teepee Room; **Lake McDonald Lodge** has the Cedar Dining Room and Lounge; **Many Glacier Hotel** has the Ptarmigan Dining Room. The dining rooms open with the park and close sometime in September, depending on the facility. At each dining room, breakfast is served from 6:30 to 9:30am; lunch from 11:30am to 2pm; and dinner from 5:30 to 9:30pm. Coffee and snack shops open either at 7 or 8am and close at 9pm.

The alternatives include second-tier restaurants in close proximity to the hotels, most of which are comparable to chain restaurants. The coffee shop at the **Rising Sun Motor Inn** serves hearty American fare; the Italian Garden at the **Swiftcurrent Motor Inn** serves meals from 6am to 10pm. Breakfast prices range from $4 to $7; lunch and dinner feature combinations of salads, sandwiches, pasta dishes, and lasagna, or "create your own" pizza. At **Apgar,** you'll find the **Cedar Tree Deli,** which specializes in sandwiches, ice cream, and cold drinks; and Eddie's Cafe, a family dining arrangement. There are two restaurants at **Lake McDonald.** The informal one is Russell's Trail's End, where you'll find breakfast costing from $3 to $7. Lunch and dinner menus are the same: mostly sandwiches, soups, and salads between $6 and $11. The nicer restaurant in the lodge offers beef tenderloin, roast duckling, seared mountain trout, roast turkey, Alaskan salmon, pasta, chicken, and steaks from $13 to $20. Breakfast buffet is $8.50 and lunch runs from $6 to $10.

IN GATEWAY COMMUNITIES
IN EAST GLACIER

Glacier Village Restaurant. 304–308 U.S. Hwy. 2, East Glacier. ☎ **406/226-4464.** Breakfast $3–$5; lunch $4–$7; dinner $8–$17. MC, V. Daily 6am–10pm. Closed Oct–Apr. AMERICAN.

This family-owned, seasonal restaurant is one of the few full-service joints in the area that serves three meals, starting with breakfast at 6am. It's actually two in one: a cafeteria on one side and a full-service restaurant on the other. Portions are healthy and prices are moderate, but don't expect anything too exotic. The cafeteria half dishes up great home-style food with standards like yummy waffles and pancakes made from homemade batter, as well as a hearty chicken pot pie. The restaurant side is equally impressive, with a menu that includes medallions of pork with raspberry sauce and a succulent smoked chicken breast spinach salad.

Restaurant Thimbleberry. 112 Park Dr., East Glacier. ☎ **406/226-5523.** Breakfast $2.50–$6; lunch $4–$6.50; dinner $9–$15. DISC, MC, V. Daily 7am–9:30pm. Closed Oct–Apr. AMERICAN.

The food is good here at all the meals but it's most famous for gigantic breakfasts. I ordered one blueberry pancake and couldn't finish it. The decor is charming, a rugged pine motif, and the staff is very friendly. For dinner try the cornmeal-dusted St. Mary's Lake whitefish. There's also a number of vegetarian and low-fat entrees.

✪ **Serrano's.** 29 Dawson Ave., East Glacier. ☎ **406/226-9392.** Reservations recommended. Main courses $8–$14. DISC, MC, V. Daily 5–10pm. Closed Oct–Apr. MEXICAN.

In East Glacier, if you're only going to eat one dinner, eat it at Serrano's. The farther north you go, the warier you should be of Mexican restaurants. But Serrano's only claims a kind of Mexican-California-Southwest influence, and the food succeeds very well. The seafood enchilada, with shrimp and scallops, was excellent. The night I arrived, a windstorm a few days earlier had blown down a tree in the backyard; children, waiting for their parents to finish eating, had for a generation swung in the tree upon an auto tire. The wind had also blown down a gate to the street, which owner Renee Serrano was trying to put back up. I offered to help, we got it done, and she offered to buy me one of their world-famous margaritas. Frankly, all margaritas taste pretty much alike to me. I had a beer from their large selection of microbrews. The place is busy with both locals and tourists.

IN POLEBRIDGE

Northern Lights Saloon. Polebridge (next to the Polebridge Mercantile). ☎ **406/888-5669.** Main courses $7–$11. MC, V. Memorial Day to Labor Day, daily 11am–2pm and 4–9pm; off-season hours vary, usually on weekends, so call ahead. AMERICAN.

Polebridge is where the serious Glacier outdoorspeople hang out. And the Northern Lights Saloon is where they go to have a beer and a burger. In the dictionary, under the phrase "middle of nowhere," they have a picture of Polebridge. This small restaurant, located squarely in the middle of Polebridge, gets enough crowds in summer that you actually may have to wait for a table. The fact that there are only four or five tables exacerbates the problem. The customers are usually folks who have spent the last few days in the backcountry, on the river, or in one of the primitive lodging choices that Polebridge offers. The saloon is a classic Western hangout. The food consists of burgers, turkey burgers, and falafel burgers.

IN WEST GLACIER

The nightlife in West Glacier consists primarily of long walks, or having a beer at the bar portion of the **West Glacier Restaurant and Bar,** a hangout for locals that they call "Frieda's." It's very friendly, and you may find yourself drafted as a partner for a game of pool.

The Belton Tap Room and Grille. U.S. Hwy. 2, West Glacier (across from the west entrance to the park and from the Glacier Amtrak Station). ☎ **406/888-5000.** Breakfast $2.50–$8; dinner $9–$25. AE, MC, V. AMERICAN.

This restaurant, located in restored buildings that were once the Great Northern Railroad Chalet, serves up respectable food geared toward American tastes—steaks, chicken, ribs, trout, and salmon. And although this place is deep within the heart of the meat-and-potatoes Rockies, steamed vegetables come with the meal. The large stone fireplace dominates the tap room, which serves several kinds of brewed-in-Montana beers.

Glacier Highlander Restaurant. U.S. Hwy. 2, West Glacier (across from the west entrance to the park and from the Glacier Amtrak Station). ☎ **406/888-5427.** Breakfast $3–$5; lunch $5–$7; dinner $7–$14. DISC, MC, V. Daily 7am–9pm. Closed Nov 2–Mar 31. AMERICAN.

This is the spot to satisfy the sweet tooth; a baker is on hand, so the pies are well worth the stop, and the cinnamon rolls are breakfast giants. The Highland Burger is, by any standard, a great hunk o' beef, and the fresh trout is a dinner specialty.

Heaven's Peak Restaurant. 12130 U.S. Hwy. 2, West Glacier. ☎ **406/387-4754.** Reservations not accepted. Lunch $7–$10; dinner $12–$20. DISC, MC, V. Daily 11am–3pm and 5–10pm. AMERICAN.

West Glacier's newest eating facility is in a massive log building right off the highway. A large deck overlooks a beautiful sculpted rock garden and manicured grounds and provides comfortable seating but, alas, also provides road noise. The chef is proud of the fact there is no deep fryer on the property, nor is anything other than fresh ingredients used in meal preparation. Specialties include a buffalo roulade, a thin, pounded steak rolled and stuffed with chorizo; and duck prepared with Flathead cherries. The luncheon menu includes several salads, as well as various sandwich dishes. The Huckleberry crème brûlée and the dense chocolate tri-layer avalanche are irresistible for dessert. They are open roughly from the summer solstice to the fall equinox.

ESSENTIAL SERVICES

EAST GLACIER   The **Glacier Park Trading Company** (☎ 406/226-4433), which is situated on U.S. Highway 2, just outside the park, has some fresh and canned goods. There is a deli shop in back, with fresh sandwiches. Other services at East Glacier include a service station, a post office, several gift shops, a small market with a narrow choice of fresh meats and produce as well as beer and wine, and fishing and camping accessories.

WEST GLACIER   A service station, post office, and gift shop are located in this compound, as is the **West Glacier Bar,** a small darts-and-pool tavern that serves adult beverages and doubles as a retail liquor store. The **West Glacier Restaurant** serves food starting with breakfast at 7am and ending with dinner at 10pm. The bar, however, is a jumping little place of an evening as the guides and facility employees filter in after work to flirt. The bar and restaurant are located just outside the West Glacier entrance to the park.

ST. MARY   The **St. Mary Supermart** (☎ **406/732-4431**) has fresh produce, canned goods, and beverages including beer and wine. Expect to pay tourist-town prices. There's a magazine rack and post office.

8 A Side Trip to Browning & the Blackfeet Indian Reservation

127 miles NW of Great Falls; 68 miles E of West Glacier; 160 miles W of Havre

According to Native American legend, the Blackfeet were named because their moccasins were blackened with soot from fires or paint. *Siksika,* the "Blackfooted People," became their tribal name, and they eventually grew into four bands: the Blackfeet in Montana and the Kaina, Pikani, and Siksika of Alberta, Canada. Today the Blackfeet maintain a humble existence near the beautiful lands that were once their own, with about half of the tribal enrollment of 14,000 living on the reservation near the east side of Glacier National Park. **Browning,** the tribal headquarters, is a gateway town to Glacier, but many visitors pass through quickly in anticipation of the end of the prairies and the beginning of the mountains.

ESSENTIALS

GETTING THERE   To reach Browning, follow U.S. Highway 89 south from St. Mary 32 miles, or take U.S. Highway 2, 12 miles east of East Glacier. Browning is about 69 miles east of West Glacier on Highway 2.

SPECIAL EVENTS   Browning holds **North American Indian Days** in mid-July. This 4-day celebration draws visitors from across the region to view Native Indian dance competitions, games, and sporting events at the Blackfeet Tribal Campgrounds, which are adjacent to the **Museum of the Plains Indian.**

WHAT TO SEE & DO

The **Museum of the Plains Indian** is a fairly modest effort, but it has one of the best collections of Indian dress in the West. It also features some very good art by local Blackfeet artists. Between June 1 and September 30, there is a $4 fee for adults, $1 for children ages 6 to 12. The rest of the year, it's free.

A **Blackfeet Historic Site Tour** is offered daily through Blackfeet Tours and Encampment. Half- and full-day tours depart from the **Museum of the Plains Indian,** and pickups can be arranged from any of the park's hotels, lodges, or campgrounds in either the St. Mary or East Glacier area. For information on these and other programs—including arts and crafts workshops, Blackfeet Elders Storytelling Campfires, or mini-powwows—contact **Blackfeet Tours and Encampment,** Box 271, Babb, MT 59401 (☎ **800/215-2395**).

A large and eclectic art collection is on display at the intersection of U.S. highways 2 and 89, in the **Bob Scriber Hall of Bronze** (☎ **406/338-5425**). The building does not look like an art gallery—it looks more like a warehouse on its last legs. The 20-foot-tall, 15-foot-long bucking horse and cowboy, and the equally impressive

Brahma bull and bullrider that are in front of the building are both products of an artist who has been called "the foremost sculptor in America" by H. McCracken, curator of the Whitney Gallery of Western Art. Scriber did 1,200 bronzes over a 47-year career. He died in January 1999 at the age of 84. The museum consists of two segments, a wildlife exhibit—Scriber started out as a taxidermist—and the bronze section. There are hundreds of bronzes here, arranged by subject: rodeo, animals, Indians, and so on. There's a $5 admission fee. You can spend more if you want to, though. The bronzes are for sale, for prices ranging from $250 to $150,000.

9 A Side Trip to Waterton Lakes National Park

190 miles NW of Great Falls; 342 miles S of Edmonton, Alberta

Waterton Lakes National Park and Glacier are one park separated by an international boundary. The terrain is much the same. But Canada is a foreign country, and you'll be pleasantly reminded of that in a visit to Waterton, where you can still get British high tea and a biscuit, if you're so inclined.

The parks have been designated the Waterton/Glacier International Peace Parks to commemorate the "long history of peace and friendship" between the U.S. and Canada. Waterton Lakes was made a national park first, in 1895, with Glacier being designated 15 years later. The joint international designation came in 1932, and in 1995, the peace park became a World Heritage site.

Waterton is where the Canadian mountains meet the vast rolling prairies that stretch away east to Saskatchewan. The park provides excellent habitat for elk, moose, grizzly and black bears, mountain sheep, and much other wildlife.

ESSENTIALS

American and Canadian money is freely accepted in both Glacier and Waterton. Stores provide change in the local currency after adjusting for the current exchange-rate differential (about 30% in 1999).

GETTING THERE From the eastern entrance of Glacier National Park at St. Mary, drive north through Babb, until you reach the intersection of MT 17—it's very well marked. Head northwest to the Canadian border, where MT 17 becomes Canada Highway 6 (remember, you need proof of citizenship—and a driver's license doesn't always work). Head down into the valley until you reach the park entrance on your left.

VISITOR INFORMATION The park's only **Visitor Reception Centre** is just inside the park, on the same road you used coming in (☎ **403/859-5133**).

EXPLORING THE PARK

Unlike most "park villages," Waterton Village actually *is* a village. It looks like it would be a nice place to live. As you cruise the perimeter of the lake headed for Waterton Village, you'll pass three large lakes, the habitat of bald eagles that are often perched atop the snags of dead trees. The park bears a passing resemblance to Grand Teton in that its attractions spread across a narrow valley floor. But the valley is narrower and three-fourths of it surrounded by peaks, so the overall effect is cozier and equally dramatic.

By most standards, it's also windier here—though locals say that they don't acknowledge the wind unless there are whitecaps in the rest room toilets at the Prince of Wales Hotel (see "Where to Stay," below). The Prince of Wales actually does sway noticeably in a high wind, although signs assure us that it is not a concern.

Hiking, biking, and boating on the lake are the most popular pastimes. Many of the 191 miles of trails are accessible from town. They range in difficulty from short strolls to steep treks for overnight backcountry enthusiasts. Hiking permits may be obtained at the visitor reception center up to 24 hours in advance of your trip, or they may be reserved by calling ☎ **403/859-5133.**

BIKING   All of Waterton's roads are open for bicycling, though they are narrow and potentially hazardous since they are shared with automobiles. Waterton allows biking on some trails. Check at the visitor center to find out which ones.

HIKING   The first thing a lot of people do at Waterton Park is hike the **Bear's Hump Trail.** It is the park's most popular path—but not necessarily the easiest. The trail starts at the visitor center. Only about three-quarters of a mile long, it gains 700 feet in elevation from bottom to top. That is steep, squared. You'll be rewarded with a panoramic view of the park. The hike is called Bear's Hump because of the shape of the mountain, not because you're likely to run into bears—though, of course, you never know.

Right at the edge of Waterton Park, at **Cameron Falls,** Cambrian rocks are exposed from the period 600 million years ago when life exploded on earth. This is the oldest exposed formation in the Rocky Mountains.

For 20 years, the 10.8-mile **Crypt Lake Hike** has been rated as one of Canada's best hikes. The trailhead is reached by taking a 2-mile boat ride across Upper Waterton Lake. After that, the trail leads past Hellroaring Falls, Twin Falls, and Burnt Rock Falls before reaching Crypt Falls and a passage through a 60-foot rock tunnel. The elevation gain is 2,300 feet. It can be done in 3 hours (plus time on the boat) if you're in good shape.

A second extended tour is from the marina and heads south across the international boundary to **Goat Haunt,** Montana, an especially popular trip because of the sightings of bald eagles, bears, bighorn sheep, deer, and moose, as well as numerous unusual geologic formations. For details regarding the boat shuttle, call ☎ **403/859-2362.**

The **International Peace Park Hike** is a free guided trip held on Saturdays from the end of June through the end of August. Participants meet at the Bertha Trailhead at 10am and spend the day on an 8.5-mile trail that follows Upper Waterton Lake. At the end of the trail, hikers return via boat to the main dock. Adult fare is C$10 (US$7); children's fare C$5 (US$3.60).

The day I hiked in **Red Rock Canyon,** there were three mountain sheep in the parking lot at the end of the canyon road, begging food from motorcyclists. Why they preferred motorcyclists, I can't say. Some evolutionary adaptation, no doubt. There is a wonderful nature trail here, a short, easy trek through time—0.7 miles, 65 million years—when the shallow sea that once lay here exposed and then oxidized mudstone rock to the color of a Merlot. The rocks are banded with white slashes through the formations, portions that didn't oxidize because they were not exposed to the air from the receding and returning sea. The Red Rock Canyon Road is also an area of fairly frequent bear sightings.

WHERE TO STAY

For complete lodging information contact **central reservations** for the Waterton area (☎ **800/215-2395**). While the **Prince of Wales Hotel** (see below) is clearly the flagship on this lake, alternate arrangements can be made at **Kilmore Lodge** (☎ **403/859-2334**). This cozy country inn on Emerald Bay, at the north end of the lake, has an antique decor. Bedrooms have down comforters and a dining room and lounge are on the premises. Waterton's newest property is the **Lodge at Waterton Lake** (☎ **888/985-6343** or 403/859-2150). In the heart of Waterton Village, the lodge offers lake and mountain views; some rooms have fireplaces, whirlpool tubs, and kitchenettes. Other facilities include a health center, spa, and indoor pool.

The Prince of Wales Hotel. Waterton Lakes National Park, AB T0K 2M0. ☎ **403/859-2231,** or 602/207-6000 off-season. 87 units. TEL. C$212–C$275 (US$142–US$184) double; C$499 (US$300) suite. MC, V. Closed Oct–Apr.

As you drive into Waterton Park Village, the Prince of Wales Hotel dominates a hilltop in the near distance like some gingerbread Swiss UFO. The only things taller than this until you get to Calgary are the mountains. Built in 1927 as the only Canadian link in the railroad's chain of park hotels, this seven-story monstrosity oozes old-world charm and New World ambition—from its stained-glass windows on the entry doors to the concierge in the kilt to the china and crystal and Princess Diana plates on sale in the gift shop. The rooms are still railroad hotel rooms, small, but with European-style baths with wraparound curtains. They have dark paneled wainscoting and heavily upholstered chairs. The lobby has vast picture windows that look out over upper Waterton Lake and the mountains beyond. The Prince of Wales—named for the popular prince, later Edward VII of England, who abdicated to marry American commoner Wallis Simpson—serves a traditional British high tea from 2:30 to 4pm daily.

CAMPING

There are 13 designated wilderness campgrounds with dry toilets and surface water, some of which have shelters.

At the west end of the village is **Townsite Campground,** a Canada Park Service–operated facility with 235 sites that's an especially popular jumping-off spot for campers headed into the park's backcountry. Prices range from C$15 to C$21 (US$11 to US$15); half of the sites have electricity and sewage disposal; also available on the premises are kitchen shelters, washrooms, and shower facilities. The campground is right on the lake, with beautiful views of the mountains beyond.

WHERE TO DINE

All of the village's restaurants are within a 2-block area on Waterton Avenue (which the locals call Main Street). So despite the fact that many buildings aren't numbered, you'll have no problem finding places to eat or shop.

Waterton Park Family Cafe (no phone) has indoor dining on plastic chairs and tables, and meals are modestly priced; breakfast prices average C$5 to C$8 (US$3 to US$6), and dinner runs C$11 to C$15 (US$8 to US$10). Just up the street, **Zum's** (☎ **403/859-2388**) is a busy, inviting place with a family-oriented menu but lower prices. More luxurious surroundings, and slightly higher prices, are found at **Kootenai Brown Dining Room** (☎ **403/859-2211**), at the Bayshore Inn, considered the luxury spot on the lake. The order of the day is steaks, chicken, rack of lamb, and the occasional seafood entree; prices range from C$15 to C$22 (US$10 to US$16). The food is ordinary, but come here for the peaceful porch overlooking the lake. **New Frank's Restaurant** (☎ **403/859-2240**) serves conventional Western fare that includes beef, chicken, and spaghetti, with prices ranging from C$12 to C$28 (US$8 to US$21), as well as a Chinese menu that includes an all-you-can-eat evening buffet.

Missoula, the Flathead & the Northwest Corner

5

by Dan Whipple

The northwest corner of Montana is the mythological Montana, the one you probably wanted to visit when you set out for the Big Sky. This is the country of sheer, snow-capped mountains, and bottomless crystal lakes. It's a land of barely explored wilderness, of steel-toed lumberjacks, a land peopled with the ghosts of trappers, mountain men, and Blackfeet.

It's also a booming recreational area. The central point of the region is Flathead Lake, which boasts the somewhat cumbersome distinction of being the "Largest Natural Freshwater Lake West of the Mississippi." The lake was gouged during the last glaciation about 12,000 years ago. It is very deep in places—386 feet out toward the middle—with 128 miles of shoreline, much of it taken up by vacation homes. Anglers will appreciate the fact that trophy trout, salmon, perch, and whitefish all take up residence here. And vacationers seeking a quiet getaway will be pleased by the fact that despite the busy summer season on the lake, it doesn't *feel* crowded here, and there are plenty of places to get off by yourself.

Besides Flathead Lake, there's hiking, biking, fishing, boating, golf, parasailing, and nearly any other outdoor activity known to man in the area from Whitefish to Missoula. In winter, there are fine alpine ski areas, excellent cross-country skiing, snowshoeing, snowboarding, and inner tubing accessible north to south.

Also here is the nation's largest wilderness complex, **the Bob Marshall-Great Bear-Scapegoat Wilderness,** which includes some of the most rugged, beautiful, untrammeled country in the lower 48 states. The magnificent Chinese Wall, a vast monolith on the spine of the Continental Divide, is a symbol of wilderness in Montana, as is the grizzly bear, who rules here even when humans venture in for a visit.

1 Scenic Drives

Two major roads run through the northwest corner: U.S. Highway 93, north to south; and U.S. Highway 2, which runs east to west. MT 200, one of the state's most scenic drives, bisects the lower section of the region.

U.S. Highway 93 heads north from the Bitterroot Valley south of Missoula to the Canadian border. Much of the road slices beneath jagged peaks poking at the skyline. It's especially pretty early in the morning or early evening, when the light softens the rugged landscape. North of Missoula in the Flathead Valley near St. Ignatius and the spectacular Mission Mountains, the valley opens. At **Polson,** you've reached the southern portion of Flathead Lake, which stretches 28 miles to the north. In some places it is 8 miles wide. North of the lake are Kalispell, Whitefish, and Columbia Falls, gateway towns to nearby Glacier National Park. The last oasis in Montana is the border village of Eureka, just minutes south of the Canadian border.

Plan on spending an afternoon making your way around Flathead Lake, which is ringed by snowcapped mountains and bright blue skies. On the east side, you can pick ripe cherries and explore the art galleries and Western boutiques of Bigfork; and on the west side, you should taste a creamy huckleberry shake, poke through the antique stores, and visit an award-winning winery.

2 Missoula

200 miles E of Spokane, Washington; 213 miles NE of Lewiston, Idaho; 339 miles W of Billings; 115 miles NW of Helena; 115 miles S of Kalispell

Missoula's current marketing slogan is "We Like It Here," and it's pretty obvious that they do. The reason is clear—Missoula is in a beautiful valley along the Clark Fork River, with a relatively mild climate that is more influenced by the Pacific Northwest than the high Rockies.

Since it's home to the University of Montana, the crowds in Missoula's vibrant downtown are young, long-haired, and Birkenstocked rather than grizzled and cowboy-booted. A lot of the West's best writers —Deirdre McNamer, Bill Kittredge, Jim Crumley, Annick Smith, James Lee Burke, Jon Jackson, David Quamman and many others—live in or near the city.

The great outdoors—be it fly-fishing on the Bitterroot, downhill skiing, hiking in the Selway-Bitterroot, or cross-country skiing on Lolo Pass—is probably what most attracts these types to the area. The outdoors figures heavily in Missoula-area politics as well. There is a strong pro-environment sentiment among the populace.

ESSENTIALS

GETTING THERE **Delta** (☎ 800/221-1212), **Horizon** (☎ 800/547-9308), **Skywest** (☎ 800/453-9417), and **Northwest** (☎ 800/225-2525) all have flights into the Missoula International Airport at Johnson Bell Field, northwest of downtown on U.S. Highway 93.

I-90 leads into Missoula from the west (Washington State and Idaho) and the east (Billings and Bozeman). From Salt Lake City, I-15 leads up through Idaho and intersects with I-90 at Butte. For information on **road conditions** in Missoula, call ☎ 406/728-8553. For statewide conditions, call ☎ 800/332-6171. Avalanche information can be obtained by calling either the **Lolo National Forest Weekend Report** (☎ 406/549-4488) or the **U.S.D.A. Forest Service** (☎ 800/281-1030).

The bus terminal, 1660 W. Broadway (☎ 406/549-2339), is served by **Greyhound** (☎ 800/231-2222), which offers east-west service and usually has considerably more passengers than the other, smaller companies. **Rimrock Stages** (☎ 800/255-7655) serves intrastate Montana travelers.

VISITOR INFORMATION **The Missoula Chamber of Commerce,** 825 E. Front (☎ 406/543-6623; www.missoulachamber.com) has brochures, city maps, and area maps for outdoor activities, shopping, dining, and tours for most of northwestern Montana.

GETTING AROUND Several rental car agencies, including **Avis** (☎ 800/831-2847), **Budget** (☎ 406/543-7001), **Hertz** (☎ 800/654-3131), and **National**

Northwest Montana

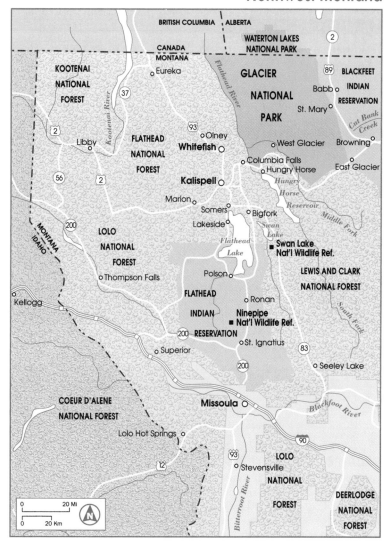

(☎ **800/227-7368**), maintain counters at the airport; or try **Rent-a-Wreck,** 2401 W. Broadway (☎ **406/721-3838**). **Payless** has an airport shuttle service to its office at 200 S. Pattee at the Holiday Inn (☎ **800/PAYLESS** or 406/728-5475); or there's **U-Save,** 3605 Reserve (☎ **406/721-2191**).

Missoula's city bus line is **Mountain Line Transit,** 1221 Shakespeare (☎ **406/ 721-3333**). It doesn't run late at night or on Sundays.

Taxi service is available through **Yellow Cab, Inc.** (☎ **406/543-6644**).

ORIENTATION   Missoula's layout is relatively straightforward—remember that downtown is bisected by the Clark Fork River, and become acquainted with the locations of the three bridges, which provide access to the university and points south. Trails alongside the river are suitable for strolling, though you'll share them with runners and bikers.

Baseball Under the Stars

Missoula has recently been awarded the franchise of the **Missoula Osprey** (an affiliate of the Montreal Expos), a minor league baseball team in the Pioneer League. As of this writing, Osprey home games were being played at the American Legion Lindborg-Cregg Field. Take Reserve Street to Spurgin Road, turn west 1 mile to Tower Road, then turn left. However, the city plans to build the team a new home, and a debate about the location of the new park was raging. For ticket information call ☎ 406/543-3300 or visit www.missoulaosprey.com.

SPECIAL EVENTS   ✪ **The International Wildlife Film Festival,** which began in 1977, is the longest-running such film festival in the world. Founded by internationally known bear biologist Dr. Charles Jonkel, the festival recognizes scientific accuracy, artistic appeal, and technical excellence through a juried competition. Highlights of the 1-week festival, held annually in early April, include three daily screenings, workshops and panel discussions, a wildlife photo contest, and various wildlife art displays. Contact the festival at Fort Missoula (☎ **406/728-9380**) for details.

Out to Lunch at Caras Park (☎ **406/543-4238**) is a popular summer series featuring live entertainment and numerous food vendors from 11:30am to 1:30pm every Wednesday from June through August. Missoula's carousel is also located at this riverfront park (see below).

GETTING OUTSIDE

One of the first things you notice if you look up in Missoula is a giant M on Mount Sentinel. The trail to the M is a popular hike, a steep zigzag that rewards the determined hiker with panoramic views of the valley. Mount Sentinel is also a favorite spot for hang gliders. You can obtain information and maps of recreation areas before leaving town at the **Bureau of Land Management,** 3255 Fort Missoula Rd. (☎ **406/329-3914**).

ORGANIZED ADVENTURES

Venture West Vacations (☎ **406/825-6200;** P.O. Box 7543, Missoula, MT 59807) arranges a variety of Montana and Idaho area adventures, primarily horsepacking, fishing, hunting, rafting, backpacking, cabin rentals, and dude-ranch visits. **Garnet Historical Tours,** 36085 Washoe Rd., Bonner, MT 59823 (☎ **406/244-5523**), presents an opportunity to go horseback riding and absorb some Montana history in the process. The tours, which begin 30 miles east of Missoula, wind through places like Elk Creek, Charlie Ellis, Reynolds City, Warren Park, and the Mountainview Mill, and eventually reach Garnet, Montana's last gold camp. **Garnet Ghost Town,** located high in the cold mountains, is one of the best-preserved old mining camps in the West. This collection of old wooden buildings offers the look and feel of a mining camp from a hundred years ago. The roads up to Garnet are dirt and treacherous. The road from the south is particularly rough. The road leading in from the north through the **Lubrecht Experimental Forest** has a number of spectacular views of the valley below.

BIKING

The best place to cycle is at the **Rattlesnake National Recreation Area.** To get there, drive northeast on Van Buren to Rattlesnake Drive. Be sure to consult one of the free

Missoula

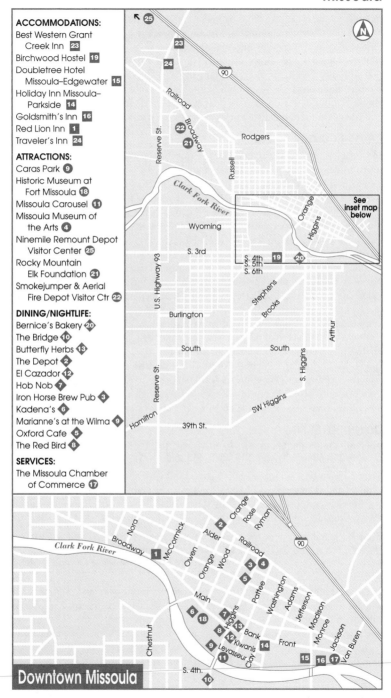

ACCOMMODATIONS:
Best Western Grant
 Creek Inn 23
Birchwood Hostel 19
Doubletree Hotel
 Missoula–Edgewater 15
Holiday Inn Missoula–
 Parkside 14
Goldsmith's Inn 16
Red Lion Inn 1
Traveler's Inn 24

ATTRACTIONS:
Caras Park 9
Historic Museum at
 Fort Missoula 18
Missoula Carousel 11
Missoula Museum of
 the Arts 4
Ninemile Remount Depot
 Visitor Center 25
Rocky Mountain
 Elk Foundation 21
Smokejumper & Aerial
 Fire Depot Visitor Ctr 22

DINING/NIGHTLIFE:
Bernice's Bakery 20
The Bridge 10
Butterfly Herbs 13
The Depot 2
El Cazador 12
Hob Nob 7
Iron Horse Brew Pub 3
Kadena's 6
Marianne's at the Wilma 9
Oxford Cafe 5
The Red Bird 8

SERVICES:
The Missoula Chamber
 of Commerce 17

Downtown Missoula

trail maps available at bike shops before setting out. Bikes are prohibited in the wilderness portion of the recreation area. **Montana Snowbowl** ski area also has trails for the serious mountain biker. For information, contact ☎ **406/549-9777.** To rent bikes, contact **Open Road Bicycles and Nordic Equipment,** 517 S. Orange St. (☎ **406/549-2453**); or **Bicycle Hangar,** 1801 Brooks (☎ **406/728-9537**). In summer, **Snowbowl** (see "Downhill Skiing" below) offers mountain biking. You and your bike can ride the lift to the top, or you can pedal on trails at the base. Five bike trails range from intermediate to expert in difficulty, and from 1 to 8 miles in length.

CROSS-COUNTRY SKIING

Missoula has hundreds of square miles of cross-country ski terrain within 30 miles of town. In nearby Garnet, the absence of gold turned a once-prosperous mining town into a ghost town that's now become a magnet for cross-country skiers at the **Garnet Resource Area.** With more than 50 miles of trails and a remote location, this area offers a backcountry experience. And while out there, many like to stay in Garnet's **old-fashioned miner's cabins;** for details, see "Where to Stay," below. Getting there can be an arduous task in winter. Take I-90 east to MT 200, turn east for 5 miles to Garnet Range Road, then go south along the Forest Service Road.

There are 150 miles of marked cross-country ski trails scattered through the Lolo National Forest ☎ **406/329-3814.** Popular areas include **Pattee Canyon, Seeley Lake,** and **Lolo Pass.** The **Pattee Canyon Complex,** 5.5 miles south of town, offers several trails that range in difficulty from a short 1.6-kilometer trail to a longer 5.4-kilometer trail, but don't count on them being groomed. At Lolo Pass, there's an information center at the top of the pass with maps and permits sales. To get here, take U.S. Highway 12 west from Lolo for about 30 miles.

The **Lubrecht Experimental Forest** is operated by the University of Montana's Forestry Department (☎ **406/243-0211**) and has six ski trails. To reach Lubrecht from Missoula, take I-90 east to MT 200 to Greenough and make a right just past the post office. Less than a half-mile down is the Lubrecht camp.

DOWNHILL SKIING

Marshall Mountain Ski Area. Take I-90 east to MT 200, and proceed for 7 miles. ☎ **406/258-6000.** Lift tickets $17 adults, $15 students, $10 children. Open daily Nov–Apr.

Marshall is an unassuming ski hill as these things go, not too steep. It's popular with families, and is an excellent place for youngsters to learn to ski. Because of its lower, warmer elevation, its season is a little shorter than Snowbowl's. The night skiing for $9 is a bargain.

Montana Snowbowl. From I-90, exit at Reserve St.; head north on Grant Creek Rd., and turn left on Snowbowl Rd. ☎ **406/549-9777.** www.montanasnowbowl.com. Lift tickets $28 adults, $13 children; senior citizen, student, and half-day rates available. Open Wed–Mon late Nov to early Apr.

There are 2,600 feet of vertical drop at Snowbowl, much of it in steep runs suitable only for experts. There's not a lot of terrain for beginners here, but the hardcore skier will have a ball. Eighty percent of the runs are for intermediate, expert, and advanced skiers, with another 700 acres for the extreme skier. Snowbowl has 30 rooms for rent during the winter, most without private baths. The bar and restaurant has recently been doubled in size, and rentals and instruction are available.

FISHING

The **Clark Fork River,** which runs through town, has had its share of environmental problems and concerns over the years. A cleanup effort that began in the 1970s has gone a long way towards cleaning it up, but it's never going to be an angler's first choice. Fishing downtown is your worst alternative. The **Bitterroot River** and **Rock Creek** are better bets for trout. Though Rock Creek has been known as a blue-ribbon trout stream, the Bitterroot has multiple public access areas near the highway. Rock Creek has a full-service campground at **Elkstrom's Stage Station,** a mile off I-90 on Rock Creek Road (☎ **406/825-3183**), but the RV campground, showers, toilets, store, and swimming pool do nothing to contribute to its primitiveness. The Missoula office for the **Montana Department of Fish, Wildlife, and Parks,** 3201 Spurgin (☎ **406/542-5500**), will direct you to some fine fishing spots, including Siria, a more remote site 30 miles up Rock Creek Road.

Whether guiding you along Missoula's Clark Fork River or helping you pick out the perfect fly, Grizzly Hackle, 215 W. Front St. (☎ **800/297-8996** or 406/721-8996; www.grizzlyhackle.com) can help you with your fly-fishing vacation. Seasoned guides lead you to fishing holes along the Lower Clark Fork, the Bitterroot, and the Blackfoot rivers, as well as Rock Creek, in search of native rainbow, Westslope cutthroat, and German browns. The company also runs the Lodge on Butler Creek, not far from Missoula, for $125 per night for two. Grizzly Hackle advocates catch-and-release and barbless fishing and donates 5% of all fly sales to Trout Unlimited and the Clark Fork Coalition to help keep rivers healthy.

GOLF

Farther north, there are a number of great golf courses, but in Missoula the golf is only average. The nine-hole **Highlands Golf Club,** located on 102 Ben Hogan Dr. (☎ **406/728-7360**), is a short, hilly, public course with wickedly gyrating greens. The clubhouse is located in the historic Greenough Mansion and restaurant. Another nine-hole course is located on the **University of Montana** campus (☎ **406/728-8629**). The **Larchmont Golf Course,** 3200 Old Fort Rd. (☎ **406/721-4416**), the only public course within city limits with 18 holes, is a long, fairly tough track that the big hitters will like.

HIKING

An easy hike follows the **Kim Williams Trail,** along either side of the Clark Fork River through downtown. The trail was named for a deceased, much-beloved newspaper columnist. Just outside of town is the **Rattlesnake National Recreational Area and Wilderness.** To get there, drive northeast on Van Buren to Rattlesnake Drive. The Rattlesnake covers 59,000 acres, 33,000 of which are congressionally designated wilderness. Camping is prohibited within 3 miles of the road because of the heavy use the area receives. Drive northeast on Van Buren to Rattlesnake Drive. For a copy of *Trails Missoula,* a free brochure listing your options, contact the Missoula Chamber of Commerce (☎ **406/543-6623**).

There are two state parks in the Missoula area: Beavertail Hill and Council Grove. **Beavertail Hill** is located on the Clark Fork and is open May through September, with excellent river access and shady cottonwood trees lining the river banks. There is a day-use charge of $4; campers pay $9 per night. **Council Grove** is where the Hellgate Treaty establishing the Flathead Indian Reservation was signed. Open for day use only, the park has interpretive displays and picnic facilities. Take the Reserve Street exit from I-90 and drive 2 miles south, then 10 miles west on Mullan Road.

The Lolo Trail is an interesting hike. This trail was created by the constant use of the Nez Perce, Salish and other tribes who lived in the area and moved back and forth across Lolo Pass.

You can explore a 0.4-mile section of the original trail at **Howard Creek,** 18 miles west of the intersection of U.S. Highway 93 and U.S. Highway 12 in Lolo. Or you can hike a 5-mile section of the trail from **Lee Creek Campground to the Idaho border.** The campground is 26.5 miles west of the highway intersection in Lolo.

SNOWMOBILING

The areas around Missoula have more than 500 miles of groomed trails in a number of popular snowmobiling areas. In Lolo Pass, for instance, there are 150 miles of groomed trails connecting the Lolo and Clearwater national forests. There are four other nearby designated areas—Superior, Skalkaho Pass, Seeley Lake and Lincoln—each with approximately as many miles of groomed trails. For a guide to area snowmobiling, contact the Missoula Convention and Visitors Bureau, ☎ **800/526-3465.**

WHITE-WATER RAFTING & KAYAKING

Lewis & Clark Trail Adventures, 912 E. Broadway (☎ **800/366-6246** or 406/728-7609; www.trailadventures.com; e-mail: raft@montana.com), offers no-nonsense white-water rafting on the Salmon River during excursions through the heart of the Frank Church No Return Wilderness. The main trip is on a 120-mile stretch of Idaho white water, where you can expect to see mountain goats, bighorn sheep, elk, deer, eagles, and otters. Other excursions take in the Lochsa River, the Alberton Gorge of the Clark Fork River, and the Missouri River (through areas in which Lewis and Clark made their famous trek). Trips run May through September. Hiking, biking, and historic tours on the Lolo Trail are also available. Five- to seven-day trips on the Salmon River run from $380 to $945 per person, depending on dates and length. One-day trips on the Lochsa or through Alberton Gorge range from $49 to $125 per person. Guided hikes on the Lolo Trail are between $65 and $110 per person.

The woman-owned **Pangaea Expeditions,** 1610 Sherwood (☎ **888/721-7719** or 406/721-7719; www.bigsky.net/pangaea), offer trips through Alberton Gorge, 35 miles west of Missoula, on the Blackfoot River and through Hellgate Canyon. The homemade lunch served on the trips is fabulous. Half-day trips are $30 per person; full-day floats cost $55.

The Clark Fork and the Blackfoot Rivers are the settings for white-water adventure with **10,000 Waves** (☎ **800/537-8315** or 406/549-6670; www.10000-waves.com; e-mail: waves@bigsky.net). The company specializes in self-paddling rafts. Half-day and full-day floats feature thrilling white-water rapids along high mountain rivers and through steep, narrow canyons. Half-day trips are $30 per person; full-day floats cost $55 (includes lunch). The self-bailing rafts enable the paddler to focus on the sport, not survival. If you want an even bigger thrill, consider renting an inflatable kayak. Rates are $30 for 2 hours, $45 for a half day, and $70 for a full day. 10,000 Waves also offers a rafting and kayaking trip and guided tour of Garnet Ghost town for $85.

SEEING THE SIGHTS

You can organize your own tour and check out the architectural highlights of the "Garden City" by picking up a copy of the Chamber of Commerce brochure *Historical Walking/Driving Tour.* For further information contact the Missoula Historic Preservation Office, ☎ **406/523-4650.**

The **Farmers Market** at Market Plaza (☎ **406/777-2636** or 406/549-0315) is the place to be during summer for organic vegetables, fresh flowers, and a diverse collection of "Made in Montana" crafts and art objects. It's open Tuesday and Saturday mornings from 9am.

Historical Museum at Fort Missoula. Fort Missoula Rd. ☎ **406/728-3476.** www. ftmslamusem.com. $2 adults, $1 seniors and students, free for children under 6. Memorial Day–Labor Day, Mon–Sat 10am–5pm, Sun noon–5pm; Labor Day–Memorial Day, Tues–Sun noon–5pm.

Fort Missoula, one of Montana's first military posts, was established in 1877, when Chief Joseph of the Nez Perce led his tribe toward Canada. Now the home of the National Guard and Reserve units, Fort Missoula has as its main attraction this museum, which houses rotating art exhibits in its indoor galleries. A guided tour takes you through a Western town as it existed around the turn of the 20th century, along with several old buildings subsequently moved to the site—an 1880 carriage house, a homestead cabin, an 1863 church, and other buildings. The museum has added a new outdoor summer theater. Tickets cost $12 adult, $10 senior/student, $6 child, and are available by calling ☎ **800/655-3871** or by inquiring in person.

Aerial Fire Depot and Smokejumper Center. Adjacent to Missoula International Airport, U.S. Hwy. 93. ☎ **406/329-4900.** Free admission. Memorial Day–Labor Day, daily 8:30am–5pm. Tours available on the hour beginning at 10am; no tours noon–2pm; last tour begins 4pm.

This is the nation's largest training base for smokejumpers, firefighters who parachute into remote areas of national forests to combat wildfires. This facility offers a fascinating look at the life of a Western firefighter, beginning with the days when pack animals were an important part of backcountry fire fighting, through the 1939 advent of the smokejumper, up to today's heroes. The Aerial Fire Depot Visitor Center features murals, educational videos, a reconstructed lookout tower, and exhibits of firefighters that illustrate the lives and history of these rescue workers. The center also talks about the important role of fire in forest ecology.

Historic Ninemile Remount Depot Visitor Center. 22 miles west of Missoula on I-90, 4 miles north of Exit 82. ☎ **406/626-5201.** Free admission. Memorial Day–Labor Day, daily 8:30am–5pm.

This visitor center, along with the Smokejumper Center, will educate you in the early-day methods of rugged fire fighting in the Northern Rockies, when pack animals were a vital part of a firefighter's "equipment." Listed on the National Register of Historic Places, the depot appears today much as it did when it was constructed by the Civilian Conservation Corps in the 1930s. Unlike those at the Smokejumper Center, all tours are self-guided.

Art Museum of Missoula. 335 N. Pattee. ☎ **406/728-0447.** $2. Wed–Sat noon–6pm, Tues noon–8pm.

Changing exhibits at this downtown museum feature regional, national, and international art with a special emphasis on art of the Western states. Associated programs include films, concerts, lectures, tours, and children's events.

Rocky Mountain Elk Foundation. 2291 W. Broadway. ☎ **800/225-5355** or 406/523-4545. Free admission. Mon–Fri 8am–6pm, Sat–Sun 9am–6pm.

Though a relatively young conservation organization, the Rocky Mountain Elk Foundation has made a large contribution to conserving elk and elk habitat. There is a display here of trophy elk heads—some with world record racks—and a diorama of the other animals that share elk habitat: bears, coyotes, mountain sheep, rabbits, and lynxes. There are also an art gallery, small theater, and gift shop.

ESPECIALLY FOR KIDS

A remarkable community effort, **the Missoula Carousel** was a project begun with nothing more than unrealistic optimism and turned into the first carousel built in decades in the United States. During planning, funding, and assembly stages of the project, Missoula relied on the kindness of others to make it happen. The handcarved and hand-painted horses are the result of thousands of hours of labor from volunteer workers, most of whom were novices trained in the art of carving and painting. A treat for kids, adults will also marvel at this merry-go-round by the river at downtown's **Caras Park,** which is located at the spot where Higgins Avenue crosses the Clark Fork River.

SHOPPING

Global Village World Crafts, 519 S. Higgins (☎ **406/543-3955**) is a project of the Jeannette Rankin Peace Resource Center, selling jewelry, clothing, and musical items from communities around the world. **Butterfly Herbs,** 232 N. Higgins Ave. (☎ **406/728-8780**), features an eclectic collection of items, including fresh herbs, jewelry, coffee mugs, teapots, and handmade paper and candles. If you begin to feel the bohemian spirit and suddenly want your own pair of Birkenstocks, just go next door to **Hide & Sole,** 236 N. Higgins (☎ **406/549-0666**), for re-shodding.

   Pipestone Mountaineering, 101 S. Higgins (☎ **406/721-1670**), has an excellent range of outdoor gear for serious climbers, river runners, and campers.

   Missoula is home to an impressive literary community, and the city's bookstores are among the state's best, including **Fact and Fiction,** 216 W. Main (☎ **406/721-2881**). New Age literature is available at **Earth Spirit Books,** 135 E. Main (☎ **406/721-2288**). The largest newsstand in Missoula is the **Garden City News,** 329 N. Higgins (☎ **406/543-3470**), which specializes in daily newspapers from both coasts, as well as from the Rocky Mountain area. Vintage, rare, and first edition books are available from **Bird's Nest Books** (☎ **406/721-1125**) at 219 N. Higgins. **Great Northern Book Co.,** at 109 W. Main (☎ **406/721-3311**), specializes in kids' books.

   If you're looking for clothes, the **Bon Marche,** 110 N. Higgins (☎ **406/542-6000**), is an old standard and Missoula's only downtown department store. **Rainbow's End,** at 113 W. Main (☎ **406-829-1800**), is the last refuge of hippie clothing for women.

   If you haven't found that perfect Montana gift yet, try the **Moose Creek Mercantile,** 314 N. Higgins (☎ **406/543-6503**), a vast collection, much of it on wildlife themes. **Native Earth Trading Co.** (☎ **406/543-4331**), 111 W. Main, has both contemporary and traditional Indian art.

   Monte Dolack is one of the best-known artists in Montana. His often humorous posters and prints are available at 139 W. Front St. in the **Monte Dolack Gallery** (☎ **406/549-3248**). The gallery features works of other prominent Montana artists, including Mary Beth Percival. Other galleries include **Art Attic,** 123 South Ave. W. (☎ **406/728-5500**), and the **Museum of Fine Arts** in the PAR/TV Building on the campus of the University of Montana (☎ **406/243-2019**).

WHERE TO STAY

Information on rental of **old-fashioned miner's cabins** at the ghost town of Garnet is available by contacting the **Garnet Preservation Association,** Box 20029, Missoula, MT 59801-0029 (☎ **406/329-1031**); get information on camping at Missoula's **Bureau of Land Management,** 3255 Fort Missoula Rd., Missoula, MT 59804 (☎ **406/329-3914**).

HOTELS & MOTELS

Best Western Grant Creek Inn. 5280 Grant Creek Rd., Missoula, MT 59802. ☎ **888/543-0700.** Fax 406/543-0777. 126 units. A/C TV TEL. $70–$120 double. AE, MC, V.

Situated close to a freeway off-ramp, this Best Western is a relatively new property in Missoula. The quality of the rooms and services is what you'd normally associate with a higher-priced chain. There's an indoor swimming pool, steam room, sauna, and fitness center. Deluxe suites have a fireplace, two television sets, a dining area, a desk, a closet, and a view. Conventional rooms have two queens or one king bed. A "continental breakfast" is included in the room rate. There is no restaurant or bar on the premises, though many are nearby.

Birchwood Hostel. 600 S. Orange, Missoula, MT 59801. ☎ **406/728-9799.** 22 beds in 4 dorm units and 1 private room. $9–$25. No credit cards.

A traditional European-style hostel, the Birchwood is closed during the day from 9am to 5pm. It's located just 4 blocks south of the Clark Fork River and 12 blocks west of the university. With 22 bunks, it's one of the largest hostels in Montana. The hostel is especially popular with bicycle tours and offers inside bike storage and bike rental. You can bring your own linens or rent some for $1. Open year-round, the Birchwood is a good value if you don't mind the spartan lifestyle. Hostel guests are expected to clean up after themselves and do a 10-minute chore before leaving in the morning. If the car is available, the staff will send someone to pick you up from the airport for a gas donation.

Doubletree Hotel Missoula-Edgewater. 100 Madison St., Missoula, MT 59802. ☎ **800/547-8010** or 406/728-3100. 171 units. A/C TV TEL. $99 double. AE, DISC, MC, V.

This is the premier hotel facility in Missoula. Located along the Clark Fork, the riverview rooms offer just that, a large room with a beautiful view of the river and the University of Montana. This is the businessperson's destination, with meeting rooms available. The lobby area is nicely finished, with a gift shop that sells Western American souvenirs, clothing, and trinkets. Rooms on the second level have balconies, some overlooking the swimming pool. An outdoor swimming pool with a jetted tub and an exercise room with Nautilus equipment round out the amenities. The Edgewater dining room, serving lunch and dinner, is just off the lobby. The wooden deck outside the lounge is a fine spot for a cocktail over the Clark Fork River.

The Fort at Lolo Hot Springs. 38500 W. U.S. Hwy. 12, Lolo, MT 59847. ☎ **406/273-2201.** www.fortlolohotsprings.com. 34 units. $52–$72 double. MC, V.

This hot springs resort, 25 miles west of Lolo, only 7 miles from Idaho, is an especially popular winter destination—the cross-country skiing on Lolo Pass is excellent; snowmobilers also flock here. The Fort is upgrading its facilities, adding a large new building that will house a Lewis & Clark interpretive exposition, two hot tubs, a dinner theater, and a convention center. Since the fabled hot springs are a separate operation, there's a fee to soak in them.

There are 18 rooms in the lodge, and 16 in a motel-style unit. It's called the Fort because the design is a little like television's old Fort Apache. The motel rooms are large and less expensive than those in the lodge, but they are spare in the decor department. The **Eatery** and the **Saloon** provide pretty ordinary food and drink for guests, who can also enjoy fishing, horseback riding, and hiking in nearby Lolo National Forest. There are also an outdoor hot springs swimming pool and an indoor hot springs soaking pool.

Goldsmith's Bed & Breakfast. 809 E. Front St., Missoula, MT 59802. ☎ **406/721-6732.** Fax 406/543-0045. www.goldsmithsinn.com. 7 units. TEL. $95–$119 double. Rates include full breakfast. AE, MC, V.

This B&B is in a beautiful 1911 brick home right on the Clark Fork River, just across the river from the University of Montana. Four of the seven rooms are suites with televisions and sitting rooms. All rooms have private baths. Some also have fireplaces or reading nooks. Request the Clark Fork Suite to get a Japanese bath that you can soak in while you look out at the river. The Goldsmith name is famous in Missoula for making fabulous ice cream, and you can get some right next door at Goldsmith's Waterfront Pasta House. The home is the former residence of Clyde Duniway, the second president of the University of Montana.

Red Lion Inn. 700 W. Broadway, Missoula, MT 59802. ☎ **800/733-5466** or 406/728-3300. Fax 406/728-4441. 76 units. A/C TV TEL. $69–$89 double. AE, DC, DISC, MC, V. Pets accepted, $5 per night.

The comfortable motel-style Red Lion, which sits close to downtown, is a good bet for families. The outdoor heated pool is open year-round and parents can take a dip in the hot tub. And even though the hotel is close to the road, I found it not noisy at all. There is a Chinese restaurant, **Mah Wing's,** next door, but since you're so close to Missoula's downtown restaurants, you may want to eat elsewhere. The rooms are large and comfortable. The staff was also very friendly and helpful.

Traveler's Inn. 4850 N. Reserve, Missoula, MT 59802. ☎ **800/862-3363** or 406/728-8330. 28 units. A/C TV TEL. $50 double. AE, DISC, MC, V. Pets accepted.

This one-story, white stucco building located off the interstate at Exit 101 isn't the most exciting place to stay, but it is less expensive than the downtown motels. Basic rooms are furnished with queen-size beds, and nonsmoking rooms are available. The closest place to grab a bite is Rowdy's, a family diner located on the property. If the place is booked, just keep searching along Reserve Street or Motel Row, as it's known, and you're bound to find something.

A GUEST RANCH

✪ **West Fork Meadows Ranch.** 52 Coal Creek Rd., Darby, MT 59829. ☎ **800/800-1437** or 406/349-2468. 7 cabins. $990–$1,290 per person per week. Minimum stay may be required. AE, DC, MC, V.

A charming blend of Old West and European traditions makes this guest ranch unique. You won't lack for things to do at West Fork Meadows, and chances are you'll meet other interesting people from all corners of the globe. Operated by Guido and Hanny Oberdorfer, themselves transplanted Europeans, West Fork Meadows caters to an international market. The main lodge is the picture of rustic Western charm, but its Black Horse Inn is pure international elegance, serving five-course dinners in an intimate setting. The Selway Saloon is open daily until midnight, convenient to the lodge's cozy living room and outside deck. Cabins are carpeted, either one-bedroom/one-bath or three-bedroom/two-bath combinations, and are equipped with wood-burning stoves or fireplaces as well as wonderful covered porches. Summer brings with it horseback rides, fly-fishing, hiking, and canoeing; winter ranch activities include snowmobiling, sleigh rides, cross-country skiing, and horse rides.

WHERE TO DINE
EXPENSIVE

The Depot. 201 W. Railroad Ave. ☎ **406/728-7007.** Reservations recommended. Main courses $16–$23. AE, DC, DISC, MC, V. Sun–Thurs 5:30–10:30pm, Fri–Sat 5:30–11pm. STEAKS/SEAFOOD.

The Depot is the choice of the Montana literati for its upscale atmosphere and good food. Not only have I eaten here with writers Bill Kittredge and Annick Smith, but I've also seen writers Deirdre McNamer and Bryan DiSalvatore patronize this joint. The decor is along the contemporary cowboy and western theme. You might try the scallop casserole: scallops and mushrooms in white wine, Swiss cheese, and cream sauce. The beef menu features prime rib, New York strip, and filets; specialties include the garlic-roasted filet and fresh range veal chop served with fresh mushrooms and heavy cream. There is a huge wine list, including even some hard-to-find 1989 Bordeaux, which was one of the finest recent vintages. They go for $95 to $145 a bottle, though.

✪ **Marianne's at the Wilma.** 131 S. Higgins Ave. ☎ **406/728-8549.** Reservations recommended. Main courses $6–$26. Tues–Thurs 11am–3pm and 5:30–9pm, Fri 11am–3pm and 5:30–11pm, Sat 5:30–11pm, Sun brunch 9am–3pm. CONTINENTAL.

Everything about this restaurant is first class, starting with the transformation of the Wilma—an old-fashioned movie palace—into an art-deco dining extravaganza. The arched ceiling is painted blue and the walls and columns in the room are yellow. There is also a new attractive patio. The food, while expensive by Montana standards, is also first-rate. Executive chef Marianne Forrest is a veteran of the Missoula dining scene. She originated the Hob Nob restaurant (see below). The menu includes thresher shark (which was not a native Montana fish last time we checked) and a fajita-style cherry smoked flank steak.

The Red Bird. 120 W. Front St. ☎ **406/549-2906.** Reservations recommended. Lunch $6–$12; dinner $15–$22. AE, DISC, MC, V. Tues–Fri 11am–2:30pm and Tues–Sat 5–9:30pm. ECLECTIC.

The casual Red Bird is tucked in the alley on the ground floor of the art deco Florence Building. Chef Christine Staggs has brought fine creative cuisine to Missoula's restaurant explosion. The menu changes seasonally. All the entrees are fresh and superbly prepared. One of Staggs's personal favorites is halibut in saffron, lobster, zucchini, and red pepper cream sauce. It's served on a bed of geometrically fried potatoes, for a remarkable presentation. It's best to come here with a reservation.

MODERATE

El Cazador Restaurant. 101 S. Higgins. ☎ **406/728-3657.** Lunch $5–$7; dinner $7–$12. No credit cards. Daily 11am–8pm. MEXICAN.

This is the fifth addition to a family-owned chain of Mexican restaurants located in Washington, Oregon, and Idaho. Among the moderately priced entrees are typically Americanized tacos, enchiladas, burritos, and such. The dinner menu is slightly more interesting, since it includes seafood specialties with shrimp, crab, and prawns in various concoctions. For a downtown, sit-down restaurant that serves something besides hamburgers and fries, this is not a bad option, though the environment is as plain as an uncooked tortilla.

Hob Nob. In the Union Club, 217 E. Main. ☎ **406/542-3188.** Reservations required for parties of 6 or more. Lunch $5–$9; dinner $12–$14. No credit cards. Mon–Fri 11am–9pm, Sat 5pm–midnight. AMERICAN/VEGETARIAN.

The sign outside the Hob Nob says, "Union Hall" in stark black-and-white. It can be a little hard to find. Inside, though, the restaurant is a funky, eclectic place with bad art on the walls and great live jazz one night a week—usually Thursday. This is an excellent place for either vegetarians or carnivores. Try the artichoke braised chicken.

INEXPENSIVE

✪ **Bernice's Bakery.** 190 S. 3rd St. W. ☎ **406/728-1358.** Most items $2–$5. No credit cards. Mon–Sun 6am–midnight. BAKED GOODS.

Bernice's is one of Missoula's most popular spots. This small, out-of-the-way place, known for its delicious baked goods, is a great place for breakfast. In addition to an outstanding crunchy homemade granola, Bernice's sells buttery croissants filled with flavored cream cheeses, an excellent complement to the freshly brewed gourmet coffee that's also a staple. Organic juices, teas, and decaf have all been recently added to the menu.

The Bridge. 515 S. Higgins. ☎ **406/542-0002.** Main courses $13–$19. No credit cards. Sun–Thurs 5–10pm, Fri–Sat 5–11pm. CONTINENTAL.

The Bridge is a very popular restaurant on the second floor above the Crystal Theater. There's always a wait on weekends. Order several appetizers rather than a dinner—they'll all be delicious and it's the best way to sample the restaurant's variety. The best entrees are the vegetarian lasagna, eggplant Parmesan, and shrimp and sun-dried tomato linguine; there are also a number of thin-crusted pizzas on the menu. It's within walking distance of the major hotels, so you can take a nice stroll across the river to get there.

Kadena's. 231 W. Front St. ☎ **406/549-3304.** Reservations not accepted. Lunch $4–$6; dinner $6–$8. MC, V. Mon–Thurs 11am–7:30pm, Fri 11am–8pm, Sat 11am–6pm. GOURMET DELI.

Located near the downtown riverfront and carousel, Kadena's is a fresh dining alternative with an extensive selection of unusual salads, pastas, entrees, and sandwiches, including Cajun chicken with linguine or eggplant olivada. The atmosphere is deli style, and meals are served at plastic tables and plastic chairs; still, there's a wonderful view of the riverfront and the Carousel. Best bets here are the Chicken Kadena (sliced chicken breast with fresh vegetables sautéed in a sherry-sesame sauce), Front Street Fried Noodles (roast pork tenderloin with fresh vegetables and linguine sautéed in teriyaki sauce), and Angel Hair Primavera.

The Oxford Cafe. 337 N. Higgins. ☎ **406/549-0117.** Breakfast $3–$6; lunch $3–$5; dinner $5–$8. Daily 24 hours. AMERICAN.

You probably don't really want to eat at the Ox, as its known, but you have to go in and look around. This dismal cafe is a Missoula institution. There was once a cook here who opened the eggs for the omelets by tossing them up to the ceiling, where they cracked on the pressed tin overhead then dropped into his hands, ready to be spread in the sizzling grease. When a customer orders the brains and eggs—admittedly not often—the waitress shouts to the cook, "He needs 'em!" There might be a guy sitting at the bar playing some country tunes on his guitar in exchange for beer. The noon poker game starts at 2pm. No sleeping in the poker room. No checks. No exceptions. The Oxford card room is the gathering place for the toughest, tightest poker players in western Montana. Other restaurants—all better than the Oxford—come and go, but the Ox endures, a testament to greasy food, live keno calling, and bottled American beer.

MISSOULA AFTER DARK
WATERING HOLES FOR ANY TASTE

There are plenty of watering holes in Missoula, whether your buzz of choice is alcohol- or caffeine-induced. **Sean Kelly's,** 130 W. Pine (☎ **406/542-1471**), serves Irish, pub-style food—bangers and mash, pot roast, Irish stew. The weekend jazz is wonderful. There are also pool tables in the back. **Butterfly Herbs** at 232 N. Higgins Ave. (☎ **406/728-8780**) has a distinct 1960s feel. It's the perfect place to order up an ordinary cup of java, or an exotic beverage from an extensive specialty espresso menu. **The Iron Horse Brew Pub** at 100 W. Railroad Ave. (☎ **406/728-8866**) is home to Bayern, a microbrew made next door. If you're feeling particularly cocky, ask for a beer in the boot—then see if you can drink it all.

THE PERFORMING ARTS

The **Montana Repertory Theater,** located at the University of Montana campus
(☎ 406/243-4581), is the state's only Equity company, performing new and classical
works. The **Missoula Children's Theater** is the largest touring children's theater in the
United States, performing original musical productions and featuring hundreds of talented children from communities across the States, Canada, and the Pacific Rim. The
theater season starts early in July and continues through the end of April. The **Missoula Community Theater** provides a year-round calendar of family entertainment.
Both the Children's Theater and the Community Theater are located at 200 N. Adams
(☎ 406/728-1911).

The **Missoula Symphony Orchestra and Chorale,** 131 S. Higgins in the Wilma
Building (☎ 406/721-3194), is composed of university students, Missoula residents,
and other regional musicians, often performing with featured guests in the historic
Wilma Theater. The **String Orchestra of the Rockies,** P.O. Box 8265 (☎ **406/
243-5371**), a statewide professional string ensemble, is based in Missoula and performs regularly there. The **University of Montana Music Department,** Music Recital
Hall at the University of Montana (☎ **406/243-6880**), often brings in outstanding
musicians performing in the university's remarkable recital hall. Regularly scheduled
recitals include solo and ensemble performances by faculty and students.

3 A Detour into the Bitterroot Valley

Extends 89 miles S of Missoula to the Idaho border

The Bitterroot Valley has become a second home and retirement home paradise for
folks who have fallen in love with the Missoula-area mountains, but not with the
Missoula-area traffic. Though not as well known as other areas of the state, the fly-fishing in the Bitterroot River is excellent, making it a preferred destination for anglers.

The Bitterroot has the reputation as Montana's banana belt, because the microclimate in the valley offers a long growing season. A lot of Missoula-area golf fanatics
head to Hamilton in February because the golf course there greens up for play so
much earlier than the ones even a few miles farther north.

GETTING AROUND & VISITOR INFORMATION   For maps, brochures, and
sage advice about the area and its happenings, stop at the **Bitterroot Valley Chamber
of Commerce,** which has offices at 105 Main St., Hamilton, MT 59840
(☎ 406/363-2400).

DRIVING TOURS

A driving tour through the area will take you on a long, narrow loop beginning in
Missoula, heading south to the Idaho border, and returning. You'll travel south on
U.S. Highway 93 to Florence, then cross the Bitterroot River and travel south on MT
203/263 through a 32-mile area filled with interesting landmarks, reconnecting with
U.S. Highway 93 at Hamilton. On your return trip, come back straight up U.S.
Highway 93 through Hamilton and Victor, Darby, and Sula. As an alternative, continue south beyond Sula to MT 43, the road that leads to Wisdom. Doing so will take
you winding through the valley and canyons of the Bitterroot Mountains, and you'll
finally emerge at the Big Hole Battlefield.

If you are feeling very brave, and you don't mind getting your car beaten up on a
rough dirt road, take the Skalkaho Pass Road to the east of Hamilton. Pick up Route
38 just south of Hamilton—up Skalkaho Creek. The pavement runs out after a few
miles, and you'll drive over a rocky, pitted narrow road up through the Sapphire
Mountains. Go slowly; the exposure to the south is as extreme as that of the Going-

to-the-Sun Road in Glacier, but without the guardrails. But the views of forested hills are unsurpassed. It takes about 2 hours to cover the 54 miles to the **Anaconda Pintler Scenic Route,** MT 1, which you pick up around Georgetown Lake.

GETTING OUTSIDE

The Bitterroot Valley runs south along the Bitterroot River between the Bitterroot Range to the west and the Sapphire Mountains to the east. The Bitterroot Range is the site of the Selway Bitterroot Wilderness, which at 1.3 million acres is one of the nation's largest wilderness areas. Numerous trailheads are located off major highways between Lolo and Darby. You can get information about hiking in the wilderness from the Darby Historic Center/Darby Ranger Station (☎ **406/821-3913**), open Monday to Saturday 9am to 5pm and Sunday from 1 to 5pm.

The Lake Como Recreation Area is a popular day use and camping area with swimming, hiking, and boating. To get there, go 4 miles north from Darby on U.S. Highway 93. Turn west on Lake Como Road and go about 2.5 miles to the area. There are 20 camping units in two different campgrounds and a cabin on the lake available for rental at $50 per night. Reservations for the cabin can be made at the Darby Ranger Station.

If it's fly-fishing you're seeking, it's important to know that **Riverbend fly-fishing** (☎ **406/363-4197;** e-mail: rvrbend@montananet.com) is one of the longest-running acts in the Montana guiding business, and has been under the same management for more than 14 years. Owner Chuck Stranahan is a nationally known flytier, with a number of his patterns chosen for the Jack Dennis fly tying book, the Bible of the business. Riverbend customizes trips for its customers, with an emphasis on the Bitterroot River, though trips also go to other rivers in western Montana. The company specializes in instruction. Guided trips cost $285 per day for one or two people.

SEEING THE SIGHTS

The west side of the valley has fishing access as well as places to spend money, eat, and stay. The historic section of the valley is on the east side of the river, and is accessible at Florence, Stevensville, Victor, Pinesdale, and Hamilton.

Following are a lot of attractions you'll come across if you start driving at the north end of MT 203/269 and head south.

Eight miles south of Florence on MT 203, you'll hit the **Lee Metcalf National Wildlife Refuge** (☎ **406/777-5552;** www.fws.gov), which is free and is open dawn to dusk. This newly created wetland habitat was formed by dikes and dams that impound the water of several streams. It has helped to improve migratory waterfowl habitats and has created a nesting success, but a number of other species benefit as well, including osprey and deer. A short loop trail, open from mid-July to mid-September, leads around several ponds and blinds in the refuge's southwest corner. The picnic area is open year-round, and has 2 miles of walking trails. Hunting for waterfowl is permitted on designated ponds in the fall duck hunting season. Bow hunting for deer is permitted in season as well. Near the entrance is the well-preserved exterior of the 1885 **Whaley Homestead,** an excellent example of vernacular frontier architecture. You can drive around the refuge on the dirt road and come out in Stevensville, the next stop on the tour.

Stevensville is the oldest town in Montana, the result of the early missionary work of the indefatigable Jesuit Fr. Pierre DeSmet, who founded **St. Mary's Mission** in 1841. The mission is a small log and white board paneled structure with a bell tower and an important place in the development of Montana—it was the first permanent structure in Montana. John Owen bought the mission from the Jesuits in 1850, and established a trading post, Fort Owen. Though the issue of who first found gold in Montana will doubtless never be established, in Owen's diary in 1852 he wrote a cryptic statement: "Hunting gold. Found some."

From here, continue south on MT 203 to Hamilton and the Marcus Daly Mansion. Montana copper king Marcus Daly never did anything on a small scale, and his house is no exception. The **Marcus Daly Mansion** (☎ **406/363-6004**) is a spectacular Georgian Revival mansion with classical porticoes. It occupies 24,000 square feet on three floors with 24 bedrooms, 14 bathrooms, and 7 fireplaces. The mansion was finished in 1910, after Daly's death, and his widow Margaret lived there in the summers until her own death in 1941. It's open daily from April 15 to October 15. Admission costs $6 for adults, $5 for seniors, $4 for students; there are tours on the hour from 11am to 4pm.

On the opposite side of the river, the village of Hamilton, several blocks long and 4 blocks wide, is worth a leisurely stroll since most of the businesses here are small, locally owned, and often interesting. The largest outdoor/sporting goods store is **Mountain Outfitters,** 205 W. Main (☎ **406/363-1560**). Nearby is **Robbins,** 209 W. Main (☎ **406/363-1733**), a nice shop that sells home furnishings, crystal china, and gourmet kitchen accessories. The **Friendly Giant Espresso Company,** 252 W. Main St., sells all manner of espresso drinks and adjoins the **Chapter One** bookstore, featuring new and used books and periodicals. At last count there were 27 antique dealers listed in the Bitterroot antique dealers brochure; for your copy, contact the Bitterroot Valley Chamber of Commerce (see "Getting Around & Visitor Information," above). Perhaps the most remarkable store in Hamilton is the **Main Street Rug Co.** (☎ **406/363-0339**), 126 Main St., which has a vast collection of Oriental rugs for sale, assembled by owner Miriam Kalamian.

WHERE TO STAY

Hamilton Super 8, 1325 N. 1st, Hamilton, MT 59840 (☎ **800/800-8000** or 406/363-2940), is a clean, typically budget-minded motel with a location central to the Bitterroot Valley. The same holds true for the **Best Western Hamilton Inn,** 409 S. 1st St., Hamilton, MT 59840 (☎ **800/426-4586** or 406/363-2142), though the advantage here is the presentation of an excellent breakfast buffet, and the fact that some rooms are equipped with microwaves and refrigerators.

Blackbird's Fly Shop and Lodge. 1754 U.S. Hwy. 93, Victor, MT 59875. ☎ **406/ 642-6375.** www.blackbirds.com. E-mail: blackbrd@bitterroot.net. 5 units. $125–$185 per person per night for room and meals; $350 per person per night for room, meals, and guided fishing.

This is a combination fly shop and lodge offering a full guiding service. In addition to supplying the necessary gear for fly-fishing, the outfit also organizes trips for guests. Fishing the Bitterroot River is the specialty here, but trips also go up to the blue ribbon Rock Creek early in the season. The rooms in the lodge are large and have four-poster beds and down comforters. A 1,000-square-foot deck overlooks the river.

Triple Creek Ranch. 5551 West Fork Stage Rd., Darby, MT 59829. ☎ **406/821-4600.** Fax 406/821-4666. www.triplecreekranch.com. E-mail: tcr@bitterroot.net. 19 cabins. A/C TV TEL. $510–$995 per couple per night. Rate includes meals, drinks, and activities. AE, DISC, MC, V.

This is one of the most elegant—and expensive—guest ranches in the West, with pool, tennis courts, putting green, horseback riding, hiking, and many other activities. This is an adults-only resort that encourages guests to relax and do things according to their own schedules. The luxury cabins have a sitting area, king bed, wet bar, and double steam shower. Tennis rackets, fly-fishing gear, and horses are available to guests. The ranch, which is owned by the CEO of Intel, is only one of two Montana properties to meet the Relais & Châteaux standards. The *Wall Street Journal* called a stay here "roughing it Robin Leach style."

Dining: The **Triple Creek Dining Room** serves gourmet cuisine. It's open to the public in the evenings, but during the summer season—June, July, and August—it's filled with resort guests, and it's very difficult to get a reservation.

Amenities: Rates include all meals, drinks, a wet bar in the cabin, pool, hot tub, fly-casting lessons, putting green, and tennis. Massage is available. There are a concierge, room service, laundry, newspaper delivery, secretarial services, and free videos, as well as conference and business center facilities.

Trout Springs Bed-and-Breakfast. 721 Desta St., Hamilton, MT 59840. ☎ **888/ 67-TROUT** or 406/375-0911. Fax 406/375-0988. www.troutsprings.com. E-mail: Tsprings@bitterroot.net. 6 units. TV. $80–$115 double. DISC, MC, V.

This is a large, beautiful bed-and-breakfast that has been lovingly handcrafted by owners Maynard and Brenda Gueldenhaar. Maynard does iron work and his craft is on display here in the fixtures and in an elegantly designed freestanding circular staircase. Trout Springs has its own trout pond, and fish caught in it can be cooked up for you for breakfast. The rooms are spacious; all have private baths and king-size beds. Outside, you're next to the river for nature walks, fishing, or viewing the several moose that hang around nearby waiting to have their pictures taken.

WHERE TO DINE

Don't expect much in the way of fine dining in the Bitterroot Valley. If all your outdoor activities have you craving a juicy steak, try **Victor Steakhouse,** U.S. Highway 93, Victor (☎ 406/642-3300). The **Spice of Life Cafe,** 163 S. Second St., in Hamilton (☎ 406/363-4433) has offerings ranging from Thai chicken to Japanese sesame noodles. **Wild Oats Cafe and Coffeehouse** at 217 Main St. in Hamilton (☎ 406/363-4567) is a good breakfast and lunch place in a spare cafe-style setting.

A SIDE TRIP: SKIING & HOT SPRINGS IN LOST TRAIL PASS

Lost Trail Pass is a remote and undiscovered corner of Montana about 80 miles south of Missoula on the Idaho border. This area is heavily timbered, but not very heavily populated. It's also off the beaten path, since even the portions of Idaho that Route 93 accesses here are sparsely peopled. Most travelers go up I-15. Yet this corner of the state is very pretty, though the peaks have more of a pine and pastoral aspect, rather than the forbidding rock crags that dominate the skyline farther north.

With Lost Trail Powder Mountain, Lost Trail Hot Springs, and Camp Creek Inn, this pass area is an unforgettable winter vacation destination for those who loathe big crowds and the attendant ski scene.

Lost Trail Powder Mountain ski area plans to expand into a long, steeper area adjacent to the existing hill, with two new lifts. Currently, however, this small ski area is mostly intermediate, with lots of light powder. Beginner runs cover 20% and the black diamonds are 20%. If you like to ski the bumps but aren't a fanatic about it, the moguls develop on the intermediate runs in the afternoon, just in time to wear you out completely. The lift ticket prices are an excellent value at $16 for adults and $8 for children 12 and younger; kids 5 and younger ski free. For more information on Lost Trail Powder Mountain, write P.O. Box 311, Conner, MT 59827. Ski reports are available during the season at ☎ 406/821-3211. The ski area is 90 miles south of Missoula at the Montana-Idaho border, one-eighth of a mile from U.S. Highway 93.

Just down the hill to the north from the ski area is the unpretentious lodge and hot springs, **Lost Trail Hot Springs Resort,** 8221 U.S. Hwy. 93 S., Sula, MT 59871 (☎ **800/825-3574** or 406/821-3574). The lodge offers summer raft trips, horseback riding, and fishing. It isn't fancy by lodge standards, but the food in the restaurant, which overlooks the hot springs pool, is good, though it is heavily American—burgers and pizzas. Nightly rates are $53 to $89 for lodge rooms, and $63 to $89 for cabins.

Nightly group rates start at $375 for the Clark Lodge, which sleeps 12; and $400 for the Sacajawea, which sleeps 23 in four furnished main rooms with lofts, and 20 in a downstairs bunk area.

The **Camp Creek Inn B&B,** 7674 U.S. Hwy. 93 S., Sula, MT 59871 (☎ **406/821-3508**) is a homestyle gathering place without a lot of bells and whistles, but with nice and simple rooms. There are three rooms in the main house—with graceful hardwood floors—and two cabins. The owners of Camp Creek Inn also own the Lost Trail Powder Mountain ski area, so the Inn is especially set up for skiers who want to overnight during the winter. Winter packages include lift tickets, lodging, and breakfast. Summer visitors can bring their horses and board them during the stay. Rooms are $45 for a single, $55 for a double. There are many miles of Forest Service trails in the area for hiking and riding.

4 The Flathead Indian Reservation & St. Ignatius

42 miles N of Missoula; 75 miles S of Kalispell

The Confederated Salish and Kootenai tribes make their home on the Flathead Indian Reservation, with tribal headquarters for the 1.2-million-acre reservation in Pablo. The tribes, however, own only slightly more than 50% of the land within reservation boundaries.

The change in culture for the tribes came quickly when fur traders, homesteaders, and the missionaries of the Catholic Church headed west. Founded in the early 1850s by Jesuit priests, the town of **St. Ignatius** is nestled in the heart of the Mission Valley. One of the valley's larger small towns, St. Ignatius has a modest Flathead Indian Museum and trading post on the highway.

Wildlife conservation and land management have played big parts in the lives of the tribal members. The **Mission Mountain Wilderness** was the first wilderness area officially designated as such by a tribe in the United States. Hiking in the wilderness area requires the purchase of a $6 tribal permit from the Flathead Reservation Confederated Salish-Kootenai Tribes, Box 278, Pablo, MT 59855 (☎ **406/675-2700**). The Mission Mountain Wilderness is located in the Missions Mountain Range, east of U.S. Highway 93. Numerous gravel roads lead up to the trailheads.

The St. Ignatius Mission was established in 1854, as an offshoot of the missionary work of the famous Jesuit Fr. Pierre DeSmet. A Fr. Hoecken began the mission in a small log cabin, which is still on the premises and serves as the visitor center. In 1891, the mission added this magnificent brick church in its ministry to the Indians. The ceiling is decorated with 58 murals, depicting scenes from the old and new testaments, by Brother Joseph Carignano, an Italian Jesuit without formal art training, and a kind of Mission Valley Michelangelo.

The National Bison Range (☎ **406/644-2211**), just west of St. Ignatius on reservation land, is just 7 miles southwest of Charlo on Highway 212. The 18,500 acres here contain between 350 and 500 bison, the remnants of a national bison herd that once totaled 60 million. The visitor center has a small display about the history and ecology of bison in America. The 13-mile Red Sleep Road goes through four different habitat types—grasslands, riparian, montane forest, and wetlands. You'll also see deer, bighorn sheep, antelope, and maybe an occasional coyote or black bear. There's a trail here for people with physical disabilities. Gates are open 9am to 7pm daily; the visitor center is open from 8am to 7pm weekdays, 9am to 7pm weekends. Cost is $4 per car.

If you're more interested in feather than fur, check out the **Ninepipe National Wildlife Refuge,** which is next to U.S. Highway 93, 5 miles south of Ronan. Established in 1921, the refuge has 2,000 acres of water, marsh, and grassland for the double crested cormorant and the bald eagle, among other migrating birds. There is a picnic area at Ninepipe Dam on the west side of the refuge. Fishing is permitted in some areas at Pablo Reservoir, but a tribal permit is required. For information on tribal fishing regulations, call ☎ **406/675-2700.**

GETTING THERE   St. Ignatius is located 32 miles north of Missoula on U.S. 93.

WHERE TO STAY   The **Mandorla Ranch Retreat Bed & Breakfast** (☎ **406/745-4500**) can provide a comfortable place to hang your hat while you explore this beautiful valley. The **Ninepipes Lodge** (☎ **406/644-2588**) across from the refuge is also a respectable motel.

SIDE TRIP TO HOT SPRINGS

Hot Springs is a town of hand-painted signs and potholed streets, tucked into a cul-de-sac of low Montana mountains. It offers a time capsule trip back to the era of primitive hot tubbing, before California took over the business. Lots of visitors swear by the local waters' therapeutic qualities, especially as a palliative for arthritis. Situated southwest of Polson, just off Highway 28, the tiny community is about an hour-and-a-half from Flathead Lake.

The **Symes Hotel,** 209 N. Wall (☎ **888/305-3106** or 406/741-2361), is a vaguely pinkish, Alamo-like structure that aspires to be art deco. You can rent rooms or tubs in stalls that can be filled with the famous waters. Some rooms have their own tubs, and there are two tubs and a large hot tub outside.

Rooms run from $29 to $80 a night, in a bewildering combination of options. All of them are furnished like a 1940s war movie.

Wild Horse Hot Springs (☎ **406/741-3480**), 5 miles northeast of town, offers another primitive soak in blue concrete tubs. This place is located several miles down a dirt road. The private rooms are each outfitted with a "plunge," toilet, shower, steam room, and furniture that your grandmother would have found old-fashioned. But some people swear by the place. One arthritic client has come down from Canada every year for 3 weeks since the mid-1960s. There are only two rooms to sleep in here.

The free **Camas Bath** is located at the end of Spring Street, a small concrete pool with the same valuable waters. For more information, the **Hot Springs Chamber of Commerce** can be reached at ☎ **406/741-5642.**

5 The Flathead Lake Area: Somers, Polson & Bigfork

Bigfork: 92 miles N of Missoula; 15 miles SE of Kalispell

This is one of the most beautiful areas in Montana. Glacier's towering peaks rise from the valley floor on the east and the mountains of the Flathead National Forest define the edge of the valley to the west. This is forest country and cow country and alfalfa country—with a velvet-green valley floor, green and granite mountains, and, on a sunny day, a dramatic deep-blue ceiling.

This part of Montana offers something for everyone, whether your interests lie indoors or out. There are water sports on the lake, and hikes lead to sparkling mountain streams with views. But if you want to shop or see a play, you can easily spend your day inside the shops, galleries, and theater of Bigfork.

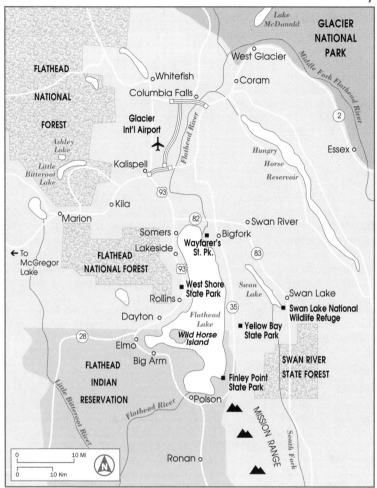

With much of this area lying within the tribal lands of the Salish-Kootenai, there is also a long-standing native heritage.

ESSENTIALS

GETTING THERE   The nearest airports are **Glacier International,** north of the lake between Kalispell and Columbia Falls (see chapter 4 for airlines), and the **Johnson Bell Airport** in Missoula (see section 2 of this chapter for airlines). Bigfork is just over a 30-minute drive from Glacier International; Polson is roughly midway between the two. For rental cars, **Avis** (☎ **800/331-1212**), **Budget** (☎ **800/527-0700**), **Hertz** (☎ **800/654-3131**), and **National** (☎ **800/227-7368**) maintain counters at each airport.

VISITOR INFORMATION   Your best bet for information on the south end of the lake is the **Port Polson Chamber of Commerce,** P.O. Box 677, Polson, MT 59860 (☎ **406/883-5969**). For goings-on north, contact the **Bigfork Chamber,** 645 Electric Ave. (☎ **406/837-5888**). **Travel Montana** (☎ **800/541-1447**) and **Glacier Country** (☎ **800/338-5072**) can supplement this information.

GETTING OUTSIDE

The Flathead is one of those places where you see the serious golfer and the serious backpacker in the same spot, sometimes in the same body. The golfing is excellent on several courses, and the backpacking, hiking, and fishing are even better. Fishing, boating, and "yachting" are popular sports for those who can afford to practice them. If your plans take you to one of the lakes or trails on the Salish-Kootenai Reservation, don't forget to buy a tribal permit. For fishing gear, fishing licenses, and tribal permits, go to **Tom's Tackle** at the south end of the lake in Polson, at 108 E. 1st St. (☎ **406/883-6209**).

BOATING

Boat rentals are also available at the **Bigfork Marina and Boat Center** (☎ 406/837-5556), **Kwa Taq Nuk Resort** (☎ 800/882-6363), **Flathead Boat Rentals** (☎ 406/857-3334), and **Marina Cay Resort** (☎ 406/837-5861).

A sailboat excursion is available from **Averill's Flathead Lake Lodge** (☎ **406/837-5569**) on two classic racing sloops designed by L. Francis Herreshoff. Fewer than a dozen of these 50-foot "Q-Boats" remain in the world. Two have been restored there. There are four 2-hour cruises daily. Fixed-keel sailboats can be launched at the state parks around Flathead Lake. Big Arm, Yellow Bay, and Somers have fishing accesses. Because winds may blow hard during the afternoon, only ballasted boats are recommended on the main portion of the lake.

Montana Fish, Wildlife & Parks has designated a **Flathead Lake Marine Trail,** showing point-to-point campsites and landing points that a human-powered craft like a canoe or kayak can reach in 1 day. You can obtain a brochure on the trail from the MFW&P (☎ **406/444-2535**) or from the Flathead Area Chamber of Commerce in Kalispell (☎ **800/543-3105**).

CRUISES

Excursion cruises are a good way for visitors to check out Flathead Lake. The 65-foot *Far West* (☎ **406/857-3203**) is one of the area's oldest, with daily dinner cruises and Sunday brunches. One of the finest charter boats on the lake, *Lucky Too,* is based at Marina Cay (☎ **406/257-5214**). **Pointer Scenic Cruises** (☎ **406/837-5617**) offers charter rides on high-speed powerboats that cruise to ancient petroglyphs viewable only by boat; this company also offers explorations of Wild Horse Island. Located just south of Bigfork on Highway 35, the **Bayview Resort and Marina** at Woods Bay on the east side of the lake (☎ **406/837-4843**) provides private sunset cruises. The **Port of Polson** *Princess* (☎ **406/883-2448**) takes a 3-hour tour, leaving the Kwa Taq Nuk resort marina in the early afternoon and making a loop around Wild Horse Island (no stops) before heading back. If it's a Montana sunset you're after, take the 2-hour sunset cruise, departing in the late afternoon, and look west. This evening cruise costs $12 for adults, $5 for children.

FISHING

Fishing the southern half of the lake requires a Salish-Kootenai tribal permit, which you can purchase at stores in Polson or at the tribal headquarters in Pablo. The brochure *Fishing the Flathead* is available from the **Flathead Convention and Visitor Association** (☎ **800/543-3105**). It provides information on 14 different fishing opportunities, as well as an outline of the licensing and catch and release regulations. This brochure includes information on Whitefish Lake, Flathead Lake, Swan Lake, and several other lesser known lakes where you will be able to catch some fish but avoid the crowds. To increase your odds of snagging something besides a log, contact **Glacier Fishing Charters** (☎ 406/892-2377). Also, **Big Fork Outdoor**

Expeditions (☎ 406/837-2031) will outfit a fishing trip—or a mountain biking, climbing, or hiking expedition—with qualified guides who know the area. On the Swan River, you can take a fishing float with **Outlaw River Runners** (☎ 406/837-3529).

GOLF

Flathead Lake has two golf courses—one terrific, the other just pretty good—overlooking its shores. In Polson, the 18-hole **Polson Country Club** public course is the pretty good one, situated just off the lake on U.S. Highway 93 (☎ 406/883-8230). A round of 18 is $24. The course is fairly short, under 6,800 yards from the tips and only 6,079 from the white tees. But it's very pretty and beautifully maintained.

The terrific course is **Eagle Bend Golf Club** (☎ 406/837-7300), a challenging Jack Nicklaus-designed track with views of Flathead Lake and the surrounding mountains, located in Bigfork just off the highway on Holt Drive. The 18-hole course is only 6,200 yards from the white tees, but it's harder than Chinese arithmetic. There are 27 excellent holes of golf here. It's $50 for 18 holes, $27 for 9. This has been called one of the country's top 50 courses by *Golf Digest.* Be sure to call ahead for a tee time. Contact the **Flathead Valley Golf Association** (☎ 800/392-9795) for a free visitor's guide and information regarding all of the area courses. Contact the **Flathead Convention and Visitor Bureau** (☎ 800/543-3105) for a copy of another excellent brochure called *Golf Montana's Flathead Valley.*

HIKING

I know we've said it before, but all these areas are bear country. Make noise, be careful. Don't surprise them and they won't surprise you.

Besides strolling by the lake at one of the marinas or state parks, the best bet for trekking is in the **Jewel Basin,** a designated hiking area north of Bigfork. More than 30 miles of hiking trails make it a great place for day-hiking as well as overnights. Before dropping into the actual basin, you'll get a great look at the Flathead Valley and Flathead Lake. For free maps of some of the more popular trails, inquire locally at one of the **Forest Service** offices in Kalispell (☎ 406/755-5401) or Bigfork (☎ 406/837-5081). To reach the head of the hiking area, take MT 83 from either Bigfork or Somers, turn north onto Echo Lake Road, and follow the signs.

A short hike, not far from Bigfork and about 45 minutes from the trailhead, will take you to **Estes Lake.** Take Highway 209 out of Bigfork. Turn south at the Ferndale fire station. When the road forks, take the right fork, County Road 498. It's about a 7-mile drive from there to the parking area.

A slightly more ambitious, but still short, hike goes up to **Cold Lakes** in the **Mission Mountain** Wilderness. Take MT 83 south to County Road 903. Turn right (west), then follow the road to the trailhead. The hike is about an hour one-way.

RAFTING

The **Flathead Raft Company** (☎ 800/654-4359) runs half of its outfit from Polson at Riverside Park on U.S. Highway 93, and half from Bigfork. Tours go down the South Fork of the Flathead River, and include a swing through the Buffalo Rapids and Kerr Dam.

SKIING

Opened in December 1998, the **Blacktail Mountain Ski Area** (☎ 406/844-0999; www.blacktailmountain.com) is a big step toward making the Flathead Lake region a full-blown year-round resort area. There's an average annual snowfall of 250 inches, which ought to be enough. The area is starting out relatively small with 200 developed acres, two double chairs, a triple lift, and a beginner lift. The hill is excellent for beginner and intermediate skiers, with 1,400 vertical feet of drop. Seventy percent of the runs are rated intermediate and only 15% are black diamonds. There are two restaurants, a lounge ski rental, and a ski school. Lift tickets cost: adults, $24 full, $17 half-day; 7 to 18 years old, $15 full, $12 half-day; ages 70 and older and 7 and younger, free. Lifts open at 9:30am and close at 4:40pm, Wednesday to Sunday and holidays. The area is located 14 miles west of Lakeside on Blacktail Mountain Road.

EXPLORING THE AREA

Miracle of America Museum. 58176 U.S. Hwy. 93, Polson, MT 59860. ☎ **406/883-6804.** $2.50 adults, $1 for children 3–12. Summer, daily 8am–8pm.

This is an extensive collection of stuff dedicated to explaining how America came to be the way it is. Like most of these efforts, it is heavily weighted toward the military and conquest sides of the story. There are plenty of guns, uniforms, and battle memorabilia. But unlike a lot of the roadside museums, there is at least some effort to explain what you're looking at. There's also a collection of antique Harley-Davidsons, some dating back to 1915, and some which look like the one that Steven McQueen jumped the fence with in *The Great Escape.*

The Mission Mountain Winery. U.S. Hwy. 93, Dayton. ☎ **406/849-5524.** Apr–Oct, tastings daily until 5pm.

Montana's only winery is located here on Flathead Lake, producing award-winning Merlot along with Chardonnay and pale ruby champagne. Tours of the small facility are free and take about 15 minutes. The winery produces 6,000 cases of wine a year. Although 80% of the wines produced here are white, the winery considers even the reds to be the finer vintages. The pinot noir grapes are grown in orchards around Flathead Lake.

Bigfork Summer Playhouse. 526 Electric Ave., Bigfork. ☎ **406/837-4886,** or 406/837-4876 for show times and reservations. www.montanaweb.com/playhouse. Tickets $20 adults, $12 children.

Bigfork has earned a fine regional reputation for its summer stock theatrical productions. The summer musical repertory is performed by rising college-age stars. Nightly performances of Broadway shows are scheduled from the end of May until the end of August. Past hits have included *Big River, The Adventures of Huckleberry Finn, Oklahoma, West Side Story, Guys and Dolls,* and *Li'l Abner.*

SHOPPING

Bigfork is the town to find Montana chic. The main street, Electric Avenue, is littered with a variety of galleries, gift shops, boutiques, and bookstores. And it's only 4 blocks long. For visitors who can't stand to go more than 5 minutes without buying something, **Twin Birch Square,** at 459 Electric Ave., is a two-level, pine log shopping mall. **Kakuli** (☎ **406/837-1367**) sells hand-blown glass artworks made from recycled glass in Swaziland, and handbags from Kenya. **Rock 'n' River** (☎ **406/837-7275**) has Montana monogrammed shirts, quilts, and gifts. At **Electric Avenue Books** (☎ **406/837-6072**), 524 Electric Ave., browsers are treated to piano jazz performances by 85-year-old Nina Russell on Sunday afternoons. If you're lucky, you may also see a big-name artist accompanying her. The **Eric Thorsen Studio,** 547 Electric Ave., handles artwork from the well-known sculptor. He is best known for the sculptures he has created for Trout Unlimited, the Wild Turkey Federation, and Ducks Unlimited (at last count more than 12,000

A Visit to Wild Horse Island

Wild Horse Island, one of the largest islands in the inland United States, is run as a wildlife preserve by the Montana Division of Fish Wildlife and Parks (☎ **406/752-5501**). It contains one of the last remnants of Montana's endangered palouse prairie plant and provides a habitat for bighorn sheep, mule deer, coyote, and a few wild horses. The island was originally created more than 17,000 years ago as a result of heavy glacial activity that formed the entire area. Sensitivity to this unusual environmental preserve by the human visitors is essential—please leave no traces of your visit. The park is open for day use only, and can only be reached by boat. Take your own or rent one from the **Big Arm Resort and Marina** (☎ **406/849-5622**). Several boat tours go to Wild Horse Island as well. You can take one from Bigfork with **Pointer Scenic Cruises** (☎ **406/837-5617**). Note: There are no visitor services here.

fund-raising pieces in total). His two-level gallery is a display case for bronze and wood creations; on the second level is the artist's studio, where visitors are encouraged to observe the artist at work.

Doors away is the gallery of **Ken Bjorge** (☎ **406/837-3839**), 603 Electric Ave., who also creates life-size studies of wildlife in bronze. Don't be surprised to find yourself standing next to a 6-foot tall crane or eagle while he works his craft in your presence. Next door to Bjorge's studio is **Two River Gear** (☎ **406/837-3474**), which deals in fly-fishing gear and info, and Patagonia wear. This shop is also owned by Bjorge, who is an avid fly fisherman himself. **Artfusion,** 471 Electric Ave. (☎ **406/837-3526**), is an eclectic gallery that represents more than 60 contemporary Montana artists and craftspeople. Around the corner at **Bay Books & Prints,** 350 Grand Ave. (☎ **406/837-4646**), there are rare books and first editions. The owners carry an extensive collection of books about the explorers Lewis and Clark, some very rare and in good condition.

If you're looking for an authentic yet unusual gift item with a Western theme, visit the **Great Montana Mercantile and Trading Post,** 469 Electric Ave.; or **Swan River Trading Company,** 459 Electric Ave. At **Brookies Cookies,** 191 Mill St., you'll find blue-ribbon cookies and desserts; you can start the day here with a jolt since Brookies opens at 6:30am.

Shopping in **Polson** at the other end of Flathead Lake is less of an upscale experience. The 3-block Main Street shopping district has few galleries. There is a good antique store, though, the **Antique Emporium,** actually two shops at 323–325 Main St. (☎ **406/883-3045**). Out on U.S. Highway 93, there is a three-store strip mall, the anchor store for which is **Three Dog Down,** 61547 U.S. Hwy. 93 (☎ **800/DOG-DOWN**). This funky down outlet sells comforters, coats, pillows, duvets, and other cold-weather gear. Owner Robert A. Ricketts is a former opera singer who moved from Cincinnati to Polson to start a low-key dream business. Prices for high quality down goods are lower here than in more fashionable metropolitan stores. Next door in the same strip, **Clayton's of Montana,** 61541 U.S. Hwy. 93, sells fine jewelry and gifts, including a wide variety of Native American gold and silver jewelry, artwork, and hand-carved elk and wood sculptures.

WHERE TO STAY

There are five campgrounds in Flathead Lake State Park, each located at a different point around the lake: Big Arm (☎ **406/849-5255**) and West Shore (☎ **406/**

844-3901) on the west side of the lake; and Finley Point (☎ **406/887-2715**), Yellow Bay (☎ **406/837-4196**), and Wayfarers (☎ **406/752-5501**) on the east shore. The phone numbers are operational only in summer. You can also call ☎ **406/755-5501** for information on any of these state park campgrounds, open from May through September.

Accommodations on and near the lake include guest ranches, water-oriented resorts with the gamut of recreational opportunities, and clean, though modest, rooms that are a place to rest after a day on the road. Less expensive options to the ranch vacation or area resorts include **The Bayshore Resort Motel** (☎ **406/844-3131**); each unit has a kitchenette and some come with a boat slip.

❂ **Averill's Flathead Lake Lodge.** P.O. Box 248, Bigfork, MT 59911. ☎ **406/837-4391.** Fax 406/837-6977. www.averills.com. E-mail: fll@digisys.net. 2 lodges, 20 cabins. $1,980 per person per week (based on 1-week minimum stay). Rate includes all meals and ranch activities. AE, MC, V.

For an all-around vacation experience, this is the best on the lake. A beautiful log lodge surrounded by thousands of acres of forest is your home base for all activities, which include horseback riding, boating, and fishing. The Western experience is done up right at this place, complete with sing-alongs, campfires, and barn dances. The location and the atmosphere of this place (the Averills perfectly combine a ranching lifestyle with the summer vacation experience) make this one of the top picks in the state. Twenty two- and three-bedroom cabins are scattered around the property and feature simple yet tasteful Western-style furnishings. Meals are served family-style in the main lodge.

Hotel Bigfork. 425 Grand Ave., Bigfork, MT 59911. ☎ **406/837-7377.** 6 units. TV. $65–$85 double. DISC, MC, V.

The six rooms of this hotel are located over a popular restaurant and nightspot. Understandably, the noise from downstairs can be a problem. But to compensate, two of the rooms have large sliding glass doors opening on to a deck and to a view of Flathead Lake beyond. When you aren't trying to sleep, try the restaurant for lunch or dinner—the menu includes steaks, baby back ribs, and whitefish, and the atmosphere is pleasant, and there's a nice view of the lake. Rock 'n' roll from the sound system drowns out the bar patrons' talk about their golf game.

Kwa Taq Nuk Resort at Flathead Bay. 303 U.S. Hwy. 93, Polson, MT 59860. ☎ **800/528-1234** or 406/883-3636. Fax 406/883-5392. www.kwataqnuk.com. E-mail: bwktn@ptinet.net. 112 units. A/C TV TEL. $64–$124 double. AE, DC, DISC, MC, V.

This Best Western affiliate is a top-draw resort managed and owned by the Salish and Kootenai Indian tribes. It's the nicest property on the Polson end of the lake and offers a restaurant, marina, and art gallery. It's also the best decorated, with interesting and artful Native American works on the walls. Lakeside rooms have commanding views, enhanced by decks furnished with chairs and cocktail tables. All the rooms are large and amply furnished.

The main lobby level is home to both a lounge and a restaurant, which provide stunning lakeside views. You can also eat or drink in the sunshine out on the deck. The retail operation is a combination gift shop-art gallery, so you'll find typical tourist souvenirs as well as authentic Western art produced by regional artists. The lower level has a large, comfortable sitting area with a large-screen cable television, swimming pool, and casino. It's the most expensive property on this end of the lake, but with the amenities it's worth the extra money.

Marina Cay Resort and Conference Center. 180 Vista Lane, Bigfork, MT 59911. ☎ **800/433-6516** or 406/837-5861. Fax 406/837-1118. www.marinacay.com. E-mail:

mcr@marinacay.com. 125 units. A/C TV TEL. $65–$99 room; $199–$265 condo; $145–$275 suite. AE, DC, DISC, MC, V.

Marina Cay is an elegant resort right on the water and right in the town of Bigfork. The rooms are very large, and most open to a view on the water. The place attracts a few of the Montana glitterati. The night I stayed, L.A. Lakers center Shaquille O'Neal was playing Frisbee on the front lawn. Rooms here are good sized, and there is a wide variety to choose from. But the walls are thin and noise carries easily from room to room.

Dining/Diversions: Quincy's at Marina Cay is a good restaurant, just a shade below Bridge Street and Showthyme in its food quality. But it's still very good, and in fact a lot of folks rate it higher. It looks out on the marina and the food is excellent. A second restaurant, **Champs,** serves food year-round in a sports bar, casino-style atmosphere. The outdoor **Tiki** lounge serves drinks by the pool under flaring gas lamps.

Amenities: Pool and hot tubs, boat rentals, parasailing (☎ **406/837-2161**), and fishing charters sponsored by **A-Able Fishing Charters.**

The Osprey Inn. 5557 U.S. Hwy. 93 S., Somers, MT 59932. ☎ **800/258-2042** or 406/857-2042. Fax 406/857-2019. www.ospreybnb.com. E-mail: ospreyinn@cyberport.net. 5 units. $90–$110. All rates include full breakfast. MC, V. Open only in summer.

Sharon and Wayne Finney have created a comfortable bed-and-breakfast right on the western edge of the lake. Rooms are large, comfortably furnished, and homey. The Finneys urge you to make yourself at home, and their B&B gives you very much a feeling that you're visiting family. Most of the rooms have private baths, though their most popular venue is a cabin next to the main house that does not. However, the bathroom is only a few steps away in the main house. Included in the list of amenities is a hot tub, a canoe for the guests' use, a nice fireplace, and a player piano. There's a campfire by the lake each night.

Port Polson Inn. 502 U.S. Hwy. 93 E., Polson, MT 59860. ☎ **800/654-0682** or 406/883-5385. Fax 406/883-3998. www.imalodging.com/lodges/w154.html. 44 units. A/C TV TEL. $79–$175. AE, MC, V.

Although it's right by the highway, this is a very nice motel with an excellent view of the lake. The rooms are large and very clean, and there are two apartments and three suites. The outdoor hot tub has a view of the lake, and there's an exercise room, as well as an indoor hot tub. Some rooms have kitchens and views overlooking the lake to Wild Horse Island.

Swan River Inn. 360 Grand Ave., Bigfork, MT 59911. ☎ **406/837-2220.** Fax 406/837-4618. 3 units. $90–$165. Rates include breakfast. MC, V.

Swan River Inn has a decidedly European feel. There are only three rooms at the inn, all overlooking Flathead Lake. The large log cabin suite is decorated to resemble, well, a log cabin. The Victorian suite is also large, with turn-of-the-century elegance. The art deco suite hearkens back to the 1920s. All have beautifully restored bathrooms.

The **Swan River Cafe and Dinner House** serves steak, pork loin, rack of lamb, and a number of chicken and pasta dishes. In contrast to the Swiss architecture of the building's exterior, the Grotto is a recent makeover that converted an average lounge into a beautiful Spanish facility complete with heavy wood furniture, stucco walls, and wrought-iron fixtures.

WHERE TO DINE

Bigfork has cornered the market on fine dining on the lake. Flathead residents from Whitefish and Kalispell routinely make their way to Bigfork to eat and take in a play at the Bigfork Summer Playhouse.

✪ **Bridge Street Gallery Restaurant.** 408 Bridge St., Bigfork. ☎ **406/837-5825.** Reservations recommended. Lunch $4–$9; dinner $10–$20. AE, MC, V. Summer, Tues–Sun 11am–2pm and 5:30–10pm; winter, Tues–Sat 5:30–10pm. CONTINENTAL/INTERNATIONAL.

It is a close race for Bigfork's best restaurant between Bridge Street and Showthyme (see below). The menu is varied and adventurous, including elk chops, East London shepherd's pie, and tamarind tea smoked duck. The halibut is baked in a coconut and macadamia nut crust. The buttermilk mashed potatoes are wonderful. A new solarium was added in 1999. The restaurant started out as a gallery with a little food on the side, and it's now a fine restaurant with a little art on the side. There are changing art exhibits throughout the season.

The Montana Grill. 5480 U.S. Hwy. 93 S., Somers. ☎ **406/857-3889.** Main courses $8–$32. AE, DISC, MC, V. Mon–Thurs 11:30am–3:30pm and 5–9:30pm, Fri–Sat 11:30am–3:30pm and 5–10pm, Sunday 9am–2:30pm (brunch) and 5–9:30pm. CONTINENTAL.

This is a relatively new restaurant, done in a beautiful Montana pine log building but with a decidedly continental mood to the menu. The huckleberry roast duck is a local favorite, and the ribs are a good standby. The downstairs pub also serves an inexpensive dinner menu of burgers and the like. L.A. Lakers coach Phil Jackson had dinner here the week before I arrived. The table side flambé for two is a real showstopper. You can choose from bananas Foster, cherries jubilee, or wild huckleberries over vanilla ice cream.

✪ **Showthyme.** 548 Electric Ave., Bigfork. ☎ **406/837-0707.** Reservations recommended. Main courses $12–$17. AE, DISC, MC, V. Daily from 5pm. AMERICAN.

When you ask locals what the best restaurant in town is, they'll tell you Showthyme—the restaurant that's located next to the summer playhouse. The atmosphere is a little bit New York, a little bit Montana. With chefs named Blu Funk and Rose Funk, you know the food has to be colorful. The grilled tuna, which is only offered as a special, is excellent. Or try the roasted duck or the Jamaican jerked pork loin.

Tiebuckers Pub and Eatery. 75 Somers Rd., Somers. ☎ **406/857-3335.** Reservations required for parties of 8 or more. Main courses $12–$18. AE, DISC, MC, V. Summer, Tues–Sat 5–10pm; winter, Tues–Sat 5–10pm. AMERICAN.

Somers is a very small community on Flathead Lake that has the look of a northern California hill town that hasn't been discovered yet. Tiebuckers is a pretty good restaurant that offers decent, affordable food. The atmosphere is nothing special. The dining room is spare but comfortable. The playing cards stuck to the ceiling are a nice touch—put there by a magician who often performs on weekends. The restaurant serves buffalo, ostrich, squab, and alligator, if your tastes run to the exotic meats. If you're not excited about those, the chicken or ribs in grandpa's sauce are excellent alternatives.

The Village Eatery. River St. at Osborne, Bigfork. ☎ **406/837-5251.** Lunch $6–$11; dinner $10–$15. DISC, MC, V. Daily 11am–2am. BURGERS/PIZZA.

The red neon sign outside says EAT HERE. You could do worse.

This loud, hip, young, ski area kind of place without the ski area is a good choice for inexpensive pizzas and burgers. If you prefer a quieter atmosphere, avoid the bar and head to the dining area to enjoy such creations as the Jimmy Buffet pizza with chicken, mozzarella, and lime tomato cilantro salsa. There's a pool table and Ping-Pong table to keep the kids occupied.

THE PERFORMING ARTS

In addition to the troupe of the Bigfork Summer Playhouse (see "Exploring the Area," above), Flathead Lake visitors can take in a play by the **Polson Players,** an equally talented group of thespians who take to the stage at the Mission Valley Performing Arts Center. Call the **Port Polson Chamber of Commerce (☎ 406/883-5969**) for current information on plays, ticket prices, event dates, and times.

6 The Swan Valley

Extends 91 miles S of Bigfork; Southern End: 33 miles E of Missoula; 90 miles W of Helena

The 50-mile stretch of MT 83 from Columbia Falls to Swan, Condon, and Seeley lakes is far removed from Flathead Lake's tourist attractions. Though less traveled, the road boasts vistas even more lovely than those seen from U.S. Highway 93, its cousin to the west. Opportunities for watching wildlife are quite good, since Seeley Lake, Summit Lake, and Alva Lake, all excellent recreational areas, lie close to the highway.

Swan Valley seems more authentically "Montana" than other, busier areas. Perhaps because the area isn't developed for tourists. Though some think the timber industry clear-cuts are an eyesore, the remainder of this thinly populated area is crowned with snowcapped mountains and accessible lakes. Swan Valley seems remote compared to the nearby larger towns—an hour from Missoula, 2 hours from Helena—and I would guess that it'll remain undiscovered for some time. In winter, snowmobiling, cross-country skiing, and even sled-dog mushing are the sports of choice in this out-of-the-way wonderland. Be sure to watch out for deer year-round along MT 83, especially at dawn and dusk—and remember, they usually travel in small groups.

Seeley Lake is one of the places where you can hear the "long-drawn, unearthly howl, probably more like that of a wolf than any other bird" of the loon. So said Henry David Thoreau. The loon is a symbol of north-country wilderness, and an appropriate one for this quiet and beautiful area.

ESSENTIALS

GETTING THERE   Other than being air-dropped like a parcel of supplies, the only way to get into the Swan Valley is by MT 83. Airports in **Kalispell (☎ 406/257-5994**) and **Missoula (☎ 406/543-8631**) are almost equidistant from the Swan. The town of Seeley Lake is 48 miles from Missoula. Take MT 200 east from Missoula 33 miles to MT 83 north. It's 42 miles from Kalispell to Swan Lake in the northern portion of the valley. Take U.S. 93 south to MT 82 east, then MT 83 south. Statewide road reports are available by calling **☎ 800/332-6171;** for weather reports, call **☎ 406/449-5204.**

VISITOR INFORMATION   The Swan isn't exactly a self-promoter. Though several businesses rely on tourists, the valley-wide tendency is to remain small. The **Swan Lake Chamber of Commerce,** Stoney Creek Road, Swan Lake, MT 59911 (**☎ 406/886-2279**), can send you information on local happenings. For general information about Glacier Country, which includes the Swan Valley, call **☎ 800/338-5072** or 406/756-7128.

GETTING OUTSIDE

Densely forested and marked by a sparkling chain of lakes, the Seeley-Swan Valley offers a variety of activities for the outdoor enthusiast, with a vast network of Forest Service trails making year-round recreational opportunities for hiking, mountain biking, and fishing. The **Seeley Lake Ranger District,** Seeley Lake (**☎ 406/**

677-2233; www.fs.fed.us/welcome.html), will provide you with a detailed map of these trails upon request. The district office is 3 miles north of Seeley lake near mile marker 18 of Highway 83. Winter sports in the Swan Valley center around cross-country skiing and snowmobiling, along the same Forest Service trails and logging roads that are popular with bicyclists and hikers in summer. One of the most popular summer activities is the **Clearwater River Canoe Trail,** a 3.5-mile leisurely run down the river to the north end of Seeley Lake. The put-in is at the end of Forest Service Road 17597 and ends at the canoe landing at the ranger station.

If you want to hike by yourself, the Forest Service publishes *Seeley Lake Area Recreation Opportunities,* which outlines a number of hikes in the national forest and wilderness areas. For a fairly short and interesting family hike, try the **Morrell Falls Trail,** a 2.5-mile hike from the trailhead to a series of cascades, the largest of which drops 90 feet. From Clearwater Junction travel north on Highway 83 for 15 miles. Turn east on Cottonwood Lakes Road 477, and go 1.1 miles. Turn north on West Morrell Road 4353, then go 6 miles. Turn east on Pyramid Pass Road 4364 and go a quarter mile. Turn north on Morrell Falls Road 4364 and go a mile to the trailhead.

OUTFITTERS & GUIDES   Swan Valley is home to several experienced guides who know parts of this vast territory like the toughened backs of their leathery hands. Guided pack trips on horseback usually run from $165 to $200 per person per day with a normal trip into the Bob Marshall Wilderness usually lasting a week. **Buck Creek Guide Service** (☎ **406/754-2471**) offers trips that focus on natural history and local culture. **JM Bar Outfitters** (☎ **406/825-3230**) of Clinton, a tiny town south of the wilderness area, offer trips into the Bob Marshall Wilderness that may include hunting and fishing, photography, and sightseeing ventures. Good pack trips into the Bob Marshall take at least 5 days, with 10-day trips being a little longer than normal, but certainly worthwhile. Expect to pay around $1,000 per person for a trip, with longer trips costing closer to $1,500. In Clearwater, the **Monture Face Outfitters** (☎ **406/244-5763**) offers summer backpacking trips, hunting, and fishing in the Bob Marshall Wilderness. **Montana Equestrian Tours,** P.O. Box 1280, Swan Valley, MT 59826 (☎ **406/754-2900**), offers several-day horseback tours of the valley for experienced riders. Tours begin in the Seeley Lake area and go out to three or four different lodging facilities. Rides are 17 to 25 miles per day at a relatively lively pace. Weather doesn't slow the riders down, so if it's raining, you'll be out there in it. Along the way you can expect to see elk, deer, and occasionally a bear. Trips begin on Sunday and conclude on Friday.

WHERE TO STAY

✪ **The Emily A. Bed-and-Breakfast.** MT 83 (Mile Marker 20), Seeley Lake, MT 59868. ☎ **406/677-3474.** Fax 406/677-2474. www.thcemilya.com. E-mail: slk3340@montana. com. 6 units (3 with private bathroom). $115 double; $150 suite. Rates include full breakfast. MC, V. Pets accepted.

The Emily A. is a thoroughly modern, two-story bed-and-breakfast beautifully situated on the Clearwater River, in the middle of a stunning mountain meadow. It's located about 5 miles north of the town of Seeley Lake at the 20-mile marker. The lodge is decorated in a distinctly Western theme, emphasized by blonde pine logs. There is a large, open great room dominated by a river rock fireplace, with an upper tier lounge for sitting, reading, or watching television. The new sunroom boasts views of Swan Valley and the Mission Mountains in addition to a wide variety of wildlife that wanders right outside the B&B's door. The facility offers canoes for its guests to explore the waters that beckon just off the rear deck. The suite, with two bedrooms, a kitchen, and a private deck, is ideal for families.

The Lodges on Seeley Lake, 2156 Boy Scout Rd., Seeley Lake, MT 59868. ☎ **800/ 900-9016.** Fax 406/677-3806. www.lodgesatseeleylake.com. 11 units. TV. $65–$200 double. MC, V.

One of only two lodges right on Seeley Lake, this 1920 lodge and cabins operation is being gradually renovated. The cabins are spacious and beautifully decorated, complete with upholstered chairs and queen beds. All the rooms have televisions and private baths. Fortunately, the modern conveniences have been added without sacrificing the rustic feeling of the lodge. The best thing here though, remains the peaceful views of the lake from the beachfront, and of the wilderness beyond. The lodges have boats for guests to take out for fishing or recreation.

Swan Valley Super 8. Between mile markers 46 and 47 on MT 83 (P.O. Box 1278), Condon, MT 59826. ☎ **800/800-8000** or 406/754-2688. Fax 406/754-2651. 22 units. TV TEL. $56–$59 double. AE, DC, DISC, MC, V.

This is the only chain hotel in the Seeley-Swan Valley. The rooms are just motel rooms, though the setting is spectacular. And the building is pretty, a two-level log structure that doesn't look like many other Super 8s. A continental breakfast is available in the lobby.

GUEST RANCHES & RESORTS

Double Arrow Resort. P.O. Box 747, Seeley Lake, MT 59868. ☎ **800/468-0777** or 406/677-2777. Fax 406/667-2922. www.doublearrowresort.com. E-mail: slk2087@ montana.com. 25 units. $70–$550. Call for off-season rates. DISC, MC, V.

Double Arrow is 2 miles south of Seeley Lake on MT 83 and near the Bob Marshall Wilderness Area. The resort has just about any activity that a Montana-bound vacationer could want—golf, tennis, fishing, riding, hiking, mountain biking. There are also guided fly-fishing and float trips available on the Blackfoot River. In the winter, there's cross-country skiing, snowmobiling, and sleigh riding. You can get accommodations suited to nearly any taste, from relatively inexpensive rooms in the main lodge, to cabins, to a full-sized four-bedroom lodge all to yourself. The cabins are large and comfortably furnished, with sitting areas featuring upholstered chairs and sofas.

Off-site rides to trailheads in the wilderness area offer opportunities for guests to explore Clearwater Valley, Horseshoe Hills, and the Morrell Falls National Recreation Trail. Two all-weather tennis courts and an enclosed pool with a hot tub keep them busy afterwards. There are currently nine holes of golf in place, and back nine is being added, to be ready for play in 2001. The public is welcome at **The Seasons Restaurant,** which offers fine dining—mostly well-prepared beef and seafood—and a Sunday brunch.

Holland Lake Lodge. S.R. Box 2083, Condon, MT 59826. ☎ **800/648-8859** or 406/ 754-2282. 15 units, including 6 cabins. $78 double; $85–$140 cabin. AE, DISC, MC, V. Head south of Condon and 4 miles east of MT 83; look for signs.

Holland Lake Lodge is a 75-year-old dude range and lodge that the new owner is rapidly upgrading from grungy rustic to genteel rustic. All of the renovated cabins have new bathrooms, carpets, and drapes. They are bright and clean and have a view of Holland Lake, but they don't have televisions. The lodge rooms share two bathrooms. All the beds have down quilts, and all the baths have thick Egyptian cotton towels. Horseback riding trips and boat rentals to use on the lake off the back deck are available, though they cost extra. The hikes from here into the Bob Marshall Wilderness are many and varied, and the views from the front lawn of The Bob and the Mission Mountain Wilderness to the west are unparalleled. This is not an upscale Montana dude ranch, but it is an excellent effort to preserve a historic Montana lodge and provide an authentic Montana experience. The lodge also has a very good restaurant, run by a chef trained in France. The Holland Lake pot roast is an excellent house specialty.

There is an extensive wine list—especially when you consider you're at the end of the road. Dinners, which require reservations, run from $12 to $20.

✪ **Lake Upsata Guest Ranch.** P.O. Box 6, Ovando, MT 59854. ☎ **800/594-7687.** 8 cabins. $220 per adult per night, $190 per child per night. 3-day minimum stay. Rates include all meals and activities. No credit cards.

This family-oriented guest ranch is located along the southern border of the Bob Marshall Wilderness Area within shouting distance of Missoula and Seeley Lake. Horseback riding is still the number-one activity at the ranch, although fly-fishing instruction (on the nearby Blackfoot River) is part of the arrangement for guests. Hiking is another key ingredient of this experience, and the managers have organized several hikes that allow visitors to see wildlife and learn about the area's flora. Crafts, horseback instruction, hiking, and boating are part of a popular 5-day program for kids. Other activities here include tours to Garnet, a nearby ghost town, and tube riding and kayaking on the Blackfoot River. Meals are served family-style in the main lodge. The traditional Saturday night steak/chicken/hamburger barbecue will continue to be a staple, but daily menus change and include baked ham, Yankee pot roast, trout, and roast turkey.

Tamaracks Resort. P.O. Box 812, Seeley Lake, MT 59868. ☎ **800/477-7216** or 406/677-2433. Fax 406/677-3503. www.tamarackresort.com. E-mail: heagy@aol.com. 14 cabins. $78–$185 cabin. DISC, MC, V.

Tamaracks started out as a homestead in 1916 and became a resort in 1930. It is right on Seeley Lake with 1,700 feet of lakefront. The resort has a 1940s feel to it, with lots of room between the cabins, screened-in porches, and an attached campground. The cabins are clean and comfortable in the old style, though not large. They offer boat and canoe rental, a basketball court, horseshoe pits, and volleyball in the summer, and cross-country ski, skate, and snowmobile rentals in winter. A new cabin and a hot tub will be in place by 2000.

White Tail Ranch. 82 Whitetail Ranch Rd., Ovando, MT 59854. ☎ **888/987-2624.** Fax 406/793-5043. www.whitetailranch.com. E-mail: whitetail@montana.com. 10 cabins. $100–$175 per person per night (3-night minimum). No credit cards. Well-behaved pets accepted.

Close to both Missoula and Helena, this guest ranch is nonetheless another of those "in the middle of nowhere" properties in the Blackfoot Valley, 9 miles from MT 200. But upon arriving, your first and biggest challenge will be to determine which of the many available activities suit your tastes. There's fly-fishing on Salmon-Trout Creek (which runs through the middle of the property), horseback riding, mountain biking, and hiking. There are also children's programs. The area is a photographer's paradise as well. During winter months it's an excellent spot for cross-country skiing and snowmobiling. Accommodations are in 10 guest cabins on the creek, with views of both the mountains and the woods. Meals are served family-style in the main lodge. All the cabins are newly redecorated and now have private baths.

WHERE TO DINE

In Seeley Lake, the best spot for breakfast or lunch may be the **Filling Station Restaurant and Bar** (☎ 406/677-2080), and the best cup of hot chocolate is undoubtedly at the **Stage Station** (☎ 406/677-2227). Both restaurants are in the heart of town.

Lindey's Restaurant. MT 83. ☎ **406/677-9229.** Main courses $14–$19. No credit cards. May 1–Sept 30, daily 5–10pm; Oct 1–Apr 15, Tues–Sun 5–9pm. Closed April 16–April 30. STEAKS.

Apart from the dining room at the Double Arrow Resort (see "Where to Stay," above), this is easily the best restaurant in the area. A carbon copy of a sister restaurant in Minnesota that has achieved national acclaim, Lindey's makes ordering easy: There are only three dinner choices—chopped sirloin, prime sirloin, and special sirloin—all of which are accompanied by the restaurant's famous greaseless hash browns as well as a tossed green salad. Seating is in a comfortable glass-enclosed space with views overlooking the lake and the seaplane landing area. To acknowledge tiny appetites, there's a special "dinner sharing" arrangement that allows two people to order one steak and two plates for an additional $5.25. The restaurant takes checks from just about anywhere.

7 The Bob Marshall Wilderness Complex

45 miles S of Big Fork; 78 miles NE of Missoula; 80 miles W of Great Falls

The Bob Marshall Wilderness Complex is the largest wilderness area in the lower 48 states, covering 1.5 million acres, or about 2,400 square miles. We hate to keep picking on Rhode Island for these comparisons, but the Bob, as it is usually called, is more than twice the size of that state.

The complex includes the Bob Marshall Wilderness proper, and the Great Bear and the Scapegoat wilderness areas. It abuts Glacier National Park, creating a huge area of relatively untouched country extending nearly half the width of Montana from the Canadian border. Marshall himself was one of the earliest advocates of wilderness for its own sake in the U.S., and the nearly one million acres of wild lands that bear his name were among the areas designated by the federal Wilderness Act of 1964. The Great Bear and Scapegoat were set aside in the 1970s.

Just south of Glacier National Park, the complex occupies nearly the entire territory that lies between the boundaries of U.S. Highway 2 to the north, MT 83 to the west, MT 200 to the south, and Highways 287 and 89 to the east. Access points along these roads occur infrequently and are poorly marked, so keep your eyes peeled.

The wilderness area has become very popular with hikers and horsepackers over the years, leading to a curious pattern of trail deterioration. Federal budget austerity allows the U.S. Forest Service little funding for trail maintenance, and while heavy traffic on the most popular trails has led to their corrosion, many of the secondary trails have virtually disappeared. Quite a few trails that are marked on topographical maps of the area are faint or nonexistent on the ground. You should know fundamental trail-finding and direction skills—how to read a topo map—in case a trail dies out or is covered by snow banks.

GETTING THERE   Day hiking is best done near **Holland Lake.** Take MT 83 south 61 miles from Bigfork, or north 20 miles from Seeley Lake, to reach the **Holland Lake Lodge** and the trails. Trail 42 from the north side of Holland Lake connects with Trail 110 to reach the Necklace Lakes just inside the Wilderness boundaries. To reach the Holland Lake Falls and Upper Holland Lake before crossing the Wilderness boundary at Gordon Pass, take Trail 415 a short way until it joins Trail 35. This trail, taken to its end, stretches from the western boundary into the center of the park near the South Fork of the Flathead River (not a day-hike).

EXPLORING THE AREA

For information, maps, and advice about traveling in the Bob Marshall Wilderness complex, contact one of the six ranger stations monitoring the wilderness. In the **Lewis and Clark National Forest:** Rocky Mountain Ranger District, 1102 Main Ave. NW, Box 340, Choteau, MT 59242 (☎ **406/466-5341**). In the **Flathead National Forest:** the Spotted Bear and Hungry Horse Ranger Districts, 8975 U.S. Hwy. 2 E., Hungry Horse, MT 59919 (☎ **406/758-5376**), or the Swan Lake Ranger District, P.O. Box 370, Bigfork, MT 59911 (☎ **406/837-5081**). In the **Lolo National Forest:** Seeley Lake Ranger District, HC 31 Box 3200, Seeley Lake, MT 59868 (☎ **406/ 677-2233**). In the **Helena National Forest:** Lincoln Ranger District, Box 219, Lincoln, MT 59639 (☎ **406/362-4265**). An excellent guide book to the area is *The Trail Guide to the Bob Marshall Country,* by Erik Molvar (Falcon Press).

The most popular destination in the Bob is the **Chinese Wall,** a striking rock formation that stands more than 1,000 feet tall and stretches for 11 miles through the wilderness on the western boundary of the **Sun River Game Preserve**. One of the more well-traveled trails and easy accesses to the Chinese Wall is along the South Fork of the Sun River on the Holland Lake-Benchmark Trail (see below). From the east, reach the Chinese Wall by taking Trail 202 at Benchmark for 5 miles to Trail 203, then continue on this trail for roughly 11 miles before taking the Indian Creek Trail, Trail 211, to the south end of the Chinese Wall at White River Pass, elevation 7,590 feet. The Chinese Wall is unmistakable and is one of the most recognizable geologic formations in Montana. The USGS topographical maps for the trip are Slategoat Mountain, Prairie Reef, and Amphitheatre Mountain.

The high meadows at the base of the wall are very fragile, and overnight camping is prohibited all along the base. So plan your trip to allow time to reach a camping area away from the base.

Towering peaks run great lengths through the Bob and stand as some of the tallest, and certainly the most dramatic, sites in the northwest part of the state outside Glacier National Park. **Holland Peak,** just north of Holland Lake on the wilderness area's western boundary, is a spectacular 9,356-foot giant that can be seen from afar but cannot be accessed directly. A short day-hike is available from the Holland Lake Lodge (see "Where to Stay," in the Swan Valley section, above) into the wilderness to **Holland Falls.** From the trailhead to the falls is only about 1.5 miles (Holland Lake topo), an easy hike with only 240 feet of elevation gain. This trail is designated for hikers only, and horses, bikes, and other pack animals are prohibited.

Once inside the wilderness area, **Big Salmon Lake** (Pagoda Lake, Big Salmon Lake East, and Big Salmon Lake West topos) is a wonderful destination for the photographer, as it captures the length and the beauty of Holland Peak's east face. To reach Big Salmon Lake, take Trail 42 from the Holland Lake Lodge on the west side of the Bob to Trail 110. It's a very long day-hike, and a reasonable 2-day hike through the Swan Range to Big Salmon Lake.

Located one-third of the way in on the **Holland Lake-Benchmark Trail** (a 60-mile trail that takes roughly a week to traverse the midsection of the Bob), Salmon Lake is simple purity without sight or sound of civilization. This trail also runs just south of the Chinese Wall.

North, in the Great Bear, is the impressive **Great Northern Mountain.** This 8,705-foot peak towers over the northeast part of the Great Bear Wilderness and can be viewed from many different points along the roadsides near the wilderness areas. You'll need a couple of vehicles if you don't have someone who can pick you up where you exit the Bob at the end of your journey. Park at Holland Lake if you plan on making it your terminus, or at Benchmark, west of Augusta, if you plan on ending there.

If you begin on the east side, the trail follows the South Fork of the Sun River on Trails 202 and 203 before moving west along Indian Creek on Trail 211. This takes you, as mentioned above, to the south end of the Chinese Wall at White River Pass. From there, you'll take Trail 138 along the South Fork of the White River until you reach the White River and Trail 112. This trail takes you to the South Fork of the Flathead River at White River Park. Across the river is Murphy Flats and Trail 263 along the river to Trail 110. This long trail takes you along Big Salmon Lake and the Swan Range, and then to Holland Lake outside the Bob's western boundary.

To reach the summit of Great Northern, you'll have to do some off-trail hiking—8 miles, if you make a round-trip. From Martin City, just northeast of Columbia Falls on U.S. Highway 2, take the East Side Reservoir Road (38) for just more than 15 miles to Highline Loop Road (1048). Take this road for just more than a half-mile across the bridge to the "trailhead." Start along the left side of the creek until the landscape opens up. Trudge up to the ridge, then along it, to Great Northern's summit.

The majestic **Scapegoat Mountain** is the dominating jewel of the Scapegoat Wilderness Area. Surrounded by cliffs, this 9,204-foot summit is easily the most prominent feature in the southern part of the wilderness complex.

Wildlife abounds in the Bob, with grizzly bears being the most feared and the most difficult to spot. Moose and deer are common. Elk gather each fall for mating at the base of the Chinese Wall in the Sun River Game Preserve on the wilderness's east side. There are lots of birds, including the ptarmigan, a brown bird resembling the quail, which changes the color of its plumage each winter to snow white.

HELPFUL TIPS   Some things to remember when camping: Before you set out, contact and consult a ranger at one of the district ranger stations mentioned below about distances, the wisdom of your itinerary, and restrictions. You can also pick up a topographical map. Carry plenty of water and water containers. Remember when loading up your pack that this is the weight you'll likely endure for a week or so. Restrictions are few. No vehicles are allowed in the area: It's as simple as that. This includes bicycles. To get around in the Bob you either walk or ride on an animal's back. It might also help to remember, too, that hunting is allowed, making backpacking in the Bob a little less inviting in the fall. Wear bright colors and make lots of noise.

8 Kalispell

115 miles N of Missoula; 249 miles E of Spokane, Washington

Despite being in the center of Montana's primary vacation and tourism region, Kalispell doesn't offer much in the way of tourist amenities. It is a business and industrial hub, but not much of a destination for recreational visitors. It is nonetheless in a beautiful setting, and centrally located for visits to Flathead Lake, skiing in Whitefish, or hiking and touring in Glacier National Park. If you come to Kalispell after visiting Glacier or the Bob Marshall Wilderness, it will seem positively urban. It has all the modern inconveniences, including a large mall and long waits at traffic lights.

ESSENTIALS

GETTING THERE   **Glacier Park International Airport** is located north of town at 4170 U.S. Hwy. 2 (☎ 406/257-5994). **Delta** (☎ 800/221-1212 or 406/257-1030), **Horizon** (☎ 800/547-9308 or 406/752-2209), and **Skywest** (☎ 800/453-9417) have daily flights.

U.S. Highway 2 will get you here from the east or west. From Missoula, U.S. Highway 93 leads north into town on a scenic 120-mile route that takes you past

Flathead Lake. The drive usually takes a solid 2.5 hours, no matter what the season. RVs amble along the gradually curving road during summer (to the frustration of most other drivers!), and icy conditions warrant added caution and reduced speeds during the winter. **Statewide weather updates** are available by calling ☎ **800/332-6171** and 406/755-4949 for **road information** in the Kalispell area.

Amtrak stops at the Whitefish depot, just 15 miles north of Kalispell. The bus terminal is located at 1301 U.S. Hwy. 93 S. (☎ **406/755-4011**).

VISITOR INFORMATION   The **Flathead Convention and Visitor Association** is located at 15 Depot Park, Kalispell, MT 59901 (☎ **800/543-3105** or 406/756-9091), and offers not only practical information concerning Kalispell, but provides information on year-round valley lodging, activities, and attractions, including Glacier National Park, Big Mountain Ski Resort, and Flathead Lake.

GETTING AROUND   For rental cars, **Avis** (☎ 800/831-2847), **Budget** (☎ 800/527-0700), **Hertz** (☎ 800/654-3131), and **National** (☎ 800/227-7368) maintain counters at the airport. **Rent-a-Wreck** at 1194 U.S. Hwy. 2 (☎ 800/654-4642 or 406/755-4555) and **U-Save** at 1010 U.S. Hwy. 2 (☎ 800/262-1958 or 406/257-1900) both offer discount car rentals.

For taxi service, call Kalispell Taxi and Airport Shuttle at ☎ 406/752-4022.

GETTING OUTSIDE

Kalispell isn't exactly a destination for the person looking for outdoor recreation, but it's near the epicenter of Glacier Park and Flathead Lake, and therefore busies up during both the summer and ski season.

BIKING   Since biking on U.S. Highway 2 or U.S. Highway 93 is not a great idea, cyclists usually head to the back roads. **Whitefish Stage Road** runs parallel to U.S. Highway 93 (from 93, go east on Reserve to reach it) and offers some great views of the mountains in a bucolic environment. For area information, **Bikology** at 155 N. Main (☎ **406/755-6758**) offers all kinds of bicycle accessories and rentals.

FISHING   There is good fishing on the main Flathead River between Columbia Falls and Kalispell for trout and whitefish. There is good shore access at Pressentine, which is 5 miles north of Kalispell on Highway 2 (follow the fishing access signs). Or you can float from Pressentine down river to Old Steel Bridge.

GOLF   Golfers should head to **Northern Pines Golf Club** (☎ **800/255-5641** or 406/751-1950 for tee times), which is 2 miles north of Kalispell on Highway 93. It has already been called the second best course in Montana and the seventh best new course in the entire country by *Golf Digest*. Designed by two-time U.S Open champion Andy North and architect Roger Packard, it offers a front nine of links-style play with British Open rough. The back nine is a different style, heavily treed along the Stillwater River. The course is fairly long at 7,000 yards. Cost is $39 for 18 holes, $21 for nine. **Buffalo Hill** (☎ **406/756-4548**), just off Highway 2 north of town at 1176 N. Main St., is an older course that's very hilly, with lots of trees and lots of memorable holes that can have serious golfers brushing up on their cursing. Cost is $33 for 18 holes, $14 for nine.

HIKING   **Lone Pine State Park** (☎ **406/755-2706**) is an attractive state park with a few hiking trails. Go west on U.S. Highway 2. At the intersection with Meridian, you'll see signs for the park sending you left (south). Take this road for about 5 miles (in the curve to your right, the road becomes Foys Lake Road) to the park. Once you're there, take in the views of the valley below or hike on the trails.

SEEING THE SIGHTS

Woodland Park, on the east edge of town at Woodland Park Drive, is a little spot that offers visitors a place to sit down in the sun and relax if they want to kill a day outside without killing themselves. There's a lagoon with ducks and a swimming pool. Walking tracks skirt the park.

Conrad Mansion. 330 Woodland Ave. ☎ **406/755-2166.** $7 adults, $1 children. May–Oct, daily 9am–8pm. Closed Nov–Apr. Turn east from Main on 3rd St. Go east until you reach Woodland.

This 23-room Victorian mansion takes up most of a city block. Built in 1895 by Missouri River freighter Charles E. Conrad, the mansion has been beautifully refurbished with period furniture. Tour guides are dressed in Victorian costume and cheerfully explain the history of Conrad and his palatial home. The beautifully kept grounds also make for a peaceful, short walk.

Hockaday Museum of Art. 302 2nd Ave. E. ☎ **406/755-5268.** www.hockadaymuseum. org. $2 adults, $1 seniors and students. Tues and Thurs–Sat 10am–6pm, Wed 10am–8pm.

The Hockaday is six galleries of art located in a former Carnegie library. The museum focuses on the works of Montana artists, both contemporary and historic, including Russell Chatham, Ace Powell, and Robert Scriver. There are tours, a gift shop, and an "Arts in the Park" program each July. The Hockaday has a very fine regional reputation for the quality of its programs.

SHOPPING

Whether you're a mall shopper or a downtown thrifter, you'll find places to divert your attention in Kalispell. The **Kalispell Center Mall** at 20 N. Main St. has more than 40 stores and restaurants. Just up the street, downtown Kalispell has a few stores of its own. **Norm's News** has the latest newspapers from around the globe as well as a comprehensive magazine rack and espresso bar. **Books West** (☎ 406/752-6900) is the downtown book shop on 1st and Main. The **Western Outdoor Store** (☎ 406/756-5818), 48 Main St., has a vast collection of Western gear for sale, and an antique store in the basement. There are 4,000 pairs of cowboy boots, sterling silver Western belt buckles, and, for the wanna-be dude, cowboy hats in all sizes and shapes. The **Rocky Mountain Outfitter** (☎ 406/752-2446), 135 Main St., has all the gear you'll need for hiking nearby trails and scaling the peaks. You can also rent kayaks and canoes if you want to head out on the water on your own.

   Artworks Cooperative Gallery at 124 Main St. (☎ **406/752-3341**) has pieces by many local artists on mostly Western themes—you can even buy an artistic broom here. **Columbine Glassworks** (☎ **406/752-7174**) at 140 Main St. has stained glass and artworks in many other media.

WHERE TO STAY

Best Western Cavanaugh's Outlaw Hotel. 1701 U.S. Hwy. 93 S., Kalispell, MT 59901. ☎ **800/237-7445** or 406/755-6100. Fax 406/756-8994. www.Bestwestern.com/cananaughsoutlawhotel. E-mail: rdominick@cavanaughs.com. 250 units. A/C TV TEL. $99 double; $134–$350 suite. AE, DC, MC, V.

This is the largest property in Kalispell. It's located on the main highway just south of downtown. Standard rooms are accented by light-colored pine furniture and watercolors and floral patterns on bed and window coverings. All rooms come with coffeemakers, radio, and terry-cloth bathrobes. Business services include modem connections, fax, copiers, printers, and an air express drop-off box just outside the lobby. The dining room is more formal than in most mid-range hotels. To get away from the formal side of things, head to the on-site handball courts, tennis court, or swimming pools (one of which is enclosed). Other services include a men's and women's styling salon and massage service, as well as a Western art gallery and gift shop.

Cavanaugh's at Kalispell Center. 20 N. Main (attached to the Kalispell Center Mall), Kalispell, MT 59901. ☎ **800/325-4000** or 406/752-6660. Fax 406/652-6628. www.cavanaughs.com/hotels/kalispell/index.html. E-mail: rdominick@cavanaughs.com. 146 units. A/C TV TEL. $125 double; $128–$200 suite. AE, DC, DISC, MC, V.

Cavanaugh's is located inside the Kalispell Center Mall, as is the Fireside Lounge, a wide-open sitting area decorated in a Southwestern theme. Rooms are spacious, and some overlook the patio/garden area outside. More expensive suites include kitchenettes and whirlpool baths. The Atrium is the hotel's restaurant. The food is respectable, though conventional. But the skylights and atrium-style windows offer a nice dining experience on sunny summer days.

Diamond Lil Inn. 1680 U.S. Hwy. 93 S., Kalispell, MT 59901. ☎ **800/843-7301** or 406/752-3467. Fax 406/752-3489. E-mail: diamondlilinn@in-tch.com. A/C TV TEL. $52–$75 double. AE, MC, V.

This boisterous hotel is across the street from the Outlaw Inn, and offers rooms for considerably less. The rooms are fairly large, but they face the parking lot or the swimming pool and hot tubs. As might be expected from the name, there is a casino associated with the hotel, the Rose, which also has a lounge and restaurant. The restaurant is inexpensive and offers a fairly nice atmosphere, in a riverboat gambler sort of way.

Four Seasons Motor Inn. 350 N. Main, Kalispell, MT 59901. ☎ **800/545-6399** or 406/755-6123. Fax 406/755-1604. www.fourseasonsmotorinn.com. 101 units. A/C TV TEL. Summer, $58–$82 double; winter, $39–$64 double. AE, DC, DISC, MC, V.

This is a very nicely kept older, independent motel. The rooms are bright, clean, and good sized with full shower/baths. They are done in light earth tones, with nice artwork on the walls of lake and Glacier Park scenes. The rooms are in three different buildings that flank the parking area. None of them has a view to speak of, but this motel offers a nice, inexpensive alternative to the chains. There's also a Jacuzzi and meeting rooms.

Hampton Inn. 1140 U.S. Hwy. 2 W., Kalispell, MT 59901. ☎ **406/755-7900.** Fax 406/755-5056. www.northwestinns.com. E-mail: hamptonk@digisys.net. 120 units. A/C TV TEL. $78–$213 double. AE, DISC, MC, V.

Kalispell's Hampton Inn is a very nice three-story brick structure surrounded by lovely landscaping. The fairly large rooms have king-size beds or two queens. The lobby has a comfortable sitting area in front of a large dome fireplace, enhanced by colorful log furniture with leather cushions. Amenities include a glass-enclosed swimming pool; and an exercise room with stair climbers, bicycles, and treadmill. A business center provides a personal computer, fax modem lines, calculators, copier machines, and printer for guests. Hampton Inn has a 100% guarantee for accommodations, friendly and efficient service, and clean, comfortable surroundings—if you're not satisfied for any reason, you get your money back. This Kalispell hotel won the Pinnacle of Excellence Award in 1998, from among 450 Promus hotels in its category for service and quality. In my experience, the Hampton Inns are the best of the motel chains for guest service and consistent high quality of rooms. They are a little pricier, too.

✪   The Kalispell Grand Hotel. 100 Main St., Kalispell, MT 59901-4452. ☎ **800/858-7422** or 406/755-8100. Fax 406/752-8012. www.vtown.com/grand. E-mail: grand@vtown.com. 40 units. A/C TV TEL. $68–$115 double. AE, DISC, MC, V.

The Kalispell Grand is an old hotel done in the Old West tradition. Located right downtown, the hotel has been beautifully refurbished. The rooms are small, with small bathrooms, but adequate. But the historic ambience makes up for this minor failing. The lobby is the centerpiece of the hotel, with cherry wood walls and historical memorabilia. And the wolf-whistling parrot in the lobby can make a person feel downright attractive.

WHERE TO DINE
MODERATE

✪ **Alley Connection.** 22 1st St. ☎ **406/752-7077.** Reservations recommended. Lunch $2–$5; dinner $6–$13. AE, DISC, MC, V. Tues–Thurs 11am–2:30pm and 5–9pm, Fri–Sat 11am–2:30pm and 5–9:30pm. CHINESE.

The best place in the valley for Chinese cuisine, the Alley Connection took several years to reach its current state of grace. What started out as a small, one-room operation has become two tastefully but simply decorated dining rooms, which serve up excellent fare. Meals of chow mein, sweet-and-sour pork, and Szechwan chicken may be ordered separately or in the more popular family-style. Lunch is a great deal for less than $6 and service is always quick and dependable.

Cafe Max. 121 Main St. ☎ **406/755-7687.** Reservations strongly recommended. Main courses $19–$24. AE, MC, V. Mon–Sat 5:30–9:30pm. CONTINENTAL.

If First Avenue West gives Kalispell a San Francisco-style restaurant, then the new Cafe Max is the New York influence. The place is small, elegant, busy, and always booked. The food is excellent, elegantly prepared and presented. I had the rack of lamb, which was perfectly done and included garden fresh vegetables. The tables aren't tucked in as close as in a New York restaurant of the same size, but it's tighter than you would expect in a Montana restaurant. The restaurant expects to get a liquor license in the near future.

First Avenue West. 139 1st Ave. W. ☎ **406/755-4441.** Lunch $5–$8; dinner $9–$20. AE, DISC, MC, V. Mon–Sat 11am–10pm, Sun 5–9pm. ECLECTIC.

It may be common elsewhere, but Romano's Restaurant at First Avenue West is one of the few places in Montana where you can get alligator for dinner. The choices include alligator Florentine and alligator Alfredo. But alligator is just the tail end of the distribution of an extensive and varied menu. There's also crab, calamari, pork, steak, veal, and duck. The atmosphere is very San Francisco, with lots of light from large windows and exposed duct work in the ceilings. And the alligator is only about $16.

✪ **Rocco's.** 3796 U.S. Hwy. 2 E. ☎ **406/756-5834.** Most items $10–$18. AE, DISC, MC, V. Tues–Sun 5–10pm. ITALIAN/STEAKS/SEAFOOD.

You get to Rocco's after a seemingly interminable drive east of Kalispell on Route 2 toward the airport. It's worth the trip, though. Rocco's has something of a reputation among locals of not being as good as it once was, but I found the food to be terrific. The chicken and shrimp pasta special in a homemade stone-ground Dijon mustard sauce was excellent. I also recommend the *fettucine pescatora* —with fish, clams, scallops, mussels, and shrimp in a garlic cream sauce. The portions are vast. Models of airplanes are suspended from the ceiling, and the large windows offer some nice mountain views.

INEXPENSIVE

The **Avalanche Creek Coffeehouse** (☎ 406/257-0785) at 38 1st Ave. E. offers coffee, espresso, and bakery items if you need a break from wandering.

The Bulldog. 208 1st Ave. E. ☎ **406/752-7522.** Lunch $4–$6; dinner $8–$12. AE, DISC, MC, V. Mon–Fri 11am–2am; Sat 4pm–2am. STEAKS/SEAFOOD.

Decorated as an English pub, the Bulldog is a steak place with a sense of humor. The menu is fairly varied if conventional, but the barbecue duck breasts in huckleberry barbecue sauce stand out. If you're feeling adventurous, try the full elephant roasted on a spit for $29,000. The waitress assured me that it could be ready in 15 minutes because the elephants are parboiled ahead of time.

Moose's. 173 N. Main St. ☎ **406/755-2337.** www.montanaweb.com/mooses. Reservations not accepted. Most items $4–$14. No credit cards. Daily 11am–2am. PIZZA/SANDWICHES.

Very dark inside, Moose's is filled with softball players, soccer players, their kids and fans, and guys named Lefty planning their next golf outing. The food consists of pizza and sandwiches, very inexpensive, and pretty good for the price. The beer is served in frosted mugs, an important feature after a long evening on the softball field. Whatever you do, don't blow the moose horn.

Ozzy's. 92 N. Main St. ☎ **406/752-8111.** Main courses $6–$12. Sun–Thurs 5–9:30pm, Fri–Sat 5–10pm. MC, V. BURGERS.

Ozzy's is a sports-themed bar and casino that is locally famous for its burgers. You can also get ribs and chicken, and a cold brew. The place is a long thin restaurant, not terribly inviting, but they do make a good burger.

The Trattoria On Main/Norm's News. 34 Main St. ☎ **406/755-5500.** Reservations not accepted. Most items $3–$6. No credit cards. Summer, Mon–Sat 7am–10pm, Sun 8am–4pm; winter, Mon–Sat 7am–6pm, Sun 8am–4pm. SOUPS/SANDWICHES.

Norm's is a modernized, old-fashioned soda fountain, with racks of magazines and daily newspapers from all around the world.

The menu includes soups, salads, pizzas, and a few light sandwiches, as well as a soda fountain spread serving up the likes of a banana split or a turtle sundae (two layers of ice cream, hot fudge, caramel, and salted pecans). Norm's is especially great in the mornings when you just want to have a cup of coffee and read the paper from Australia. The food is very inexpensive.

9 Whitefish

12 miles N of Kalispell

Whitefish has grown a lot as a resort community, attracting people from all over the country, and making it Montana's fastest growing area. Long-time residents have feared it will become another Jackson Hole, but that hasn't happened yet. In fact, as national park gateway communities go, Whitefish is fairly sedate.

Whitefish is almost two different towns—the town itself and the Big Mountain. The busy season in town is the summer, and room rates in town are correspondingly higher during the summer. This may seem odd for a ski town, but Glacier National Park attracts about two million visitors a year, while the ski area only brings in only about 300,000.

Up on the mountain, however, the peak season is winter, especially the Christmas vacation. So if you don't mind the winding 5-mile drive up (or down) the Big Mountain road, you can find slightly less expensive accommodations in the appropriate season.

ESSENTIALS

GETTING THERE   Whitefish is easier to get to than virtually any other Montana vacation town. It's a quick drive up U.S. Highway 93 from Kalispell. Statewide weather updates are available by calling ☎ **406/449-5204;** for Whitefish, call ☎ **406/755-4829.** Call ☎ **800/332-6171** for statewide road reports and ☎ **406/755-4949** for road information in the Whitefish area.

Glacier International Airport is 10 minutes away between Columbia Falls and Kalispell. **Delta** (☎ **800/221-1212**), **Northwest** (☎ **800/225-2525**), **Big Sky** (☎ **800/237-7788**), and **Horizon** (☎ **800/547-9308**) have daily flights.

The **Amtrak** (☎ **800/USA-RAIL**) station is shared with **Burlington Northern** at the edge of downtown in the renovated and charmingly attractive depot. Trains arrive daily from the west at 7:15am and from the east at 9:20pm. The bus terminal is located at Stump's Pumps, a convenience store on the corner of Baker and Second across from the library and city hall. There is one **Rimrock Stages** (☎ **406/862-6700**) daily arrival from Missoula at 6:30pm; the bus to Missoula leaves at 10am.

VISITOR INFORMATION   The **Whitefish Chamber of Commerce** is located at Mountain Mall on Highway 93 on the south edge of town. Here you'll find just about everything you need in the way of brochures, area maps, and travel information (☎ **406/862-3501**).

GETTING AROUND   **Budget** (☎ **800/248-7604**) and **National** (☎ **800/227-7368**) maintain counters at Glacier International Airport. Other companies renting cars in Whitefish include **Dollar** (☎ **800/457-5335** or 406/862-1210), **Ford** (☎ **800/344-2377** or 406/862-3825), **Hertz** (☎ **800/654-3131** or 406/862-1210), and **Payless** (☎ **800/729-5377** or 406/755-4022). **Whitefish Taxi** can be reached at ☎ **800/377-1521** or 406/862-0587.

SPECIAL EVENTS   Whitefish is home to the ✪ **Flathead Festival** (☎ **406/862-7708**), an outstanding arts organization that coordinates musical events valley-wide.

You can request their schedule of upcoming performances by early spring. In recent years, the festival has brought world-class operas to the area in addition to their annual summer concert series, one of the state's premier cultural attractions.

GETTING OUTSIDE

To explore the outdoor adventures available in the area, contact **Rising Sun Outdoor Adventures,** 215 Sonstelie Lane, Kalispell, MT 59901 (☎ **406/862-5934**). The company organizes sailing adventures on Flathead Lake, custom horseback and float trips on nearby rivers, and mountain-biking and hiking tours. White-water rafting is on the Middle Fork of the Flathead River near the Great Bear Wilderness, over rapids named Jaws, Bonecrusher, and Repeater. Mountain biking is typically on closed logging roads near the Glacier Park entrance. The daily rate for rafting is $120, mountain bikes are rented for $20 a day, and an all-day sail on the lake is $300. For all kinds of outdoor equipment or apparel, check out **Silvertip** at 33 Baker St. (☎ **406/862-2600**); **Sportsman & Ski Haus** at the Mountain Mall (☎ **406/862-3111**); or **Ski Mountain Sports,** 200 Wisconsin St. (☎ **406/862-7541**).

BIKING

Whitefish is a wonderland for mountain bikers. The same old logging roads that make the hiking only average make the biking excellent. Big Mountain has added 20 miles of single-track bike trails. The trails are free, but the area offers a ride to the top on the chairlift for you and your bike for $17.75. The Big Mountain offers five graded mountain biking trails, the longest of which, graded as intermediate, is 8 miles. There's also a short half-mile trail for beginners and two expert trails of about a mile each. The **Big Mountain Bike Academy** (☎ 406/862-1995) offers a 2½-hour guided mountain tour ($75), and private mountain biking lessons ($15/hr). Trails lead across the mountain to entrances at Glacier National Park, Whitefish Lake, and Hellroarin Basin. Bicycle rentals are available as well. Another Whitefish operation shares the expertise for mountain bikers seeking adventure on seemingly undiscovered paths. **Glacier Cyclery,** 336 E. Second (☎ 406/862-6446), provides excellent service and maintenance as well as rentals, area maps, and up-to-date information for the serious mountain biker. This outfit has been ranked among the 100 best cycle shops in a pool of 6,800 independent dealers. For a less challenging ride, you can make the 20-mile round-trip on paved roads to the head of Whitefish Lake.

BOATING

The boating is excellent on Whitefish Lake. You can rent waterskiing boats, fishing boats, paddleboats, and personal watercraft from the **Whitefish Lake Lodge Marina** (☎ 406/862-9283) between mid-May and mid-September. Fees vary from $12 for a canoe (1-hour minimum) to $70 per hour for a water-ski boat (2-hour minimum). There are twilight boat cruises on Sunday and Thursday evenings.

CAMPING

Whitefish Lake State Park is tucked on the outskirts of town in a nicely wooded area near Whitefish Lake. Call the **Department of Fish, Wildlife, and Parks** (☎ 406/752-5501) for additional information. For the RV crowd, or those just looking for a hearty chuckwagon supper during the summer months, there's the **Diamond K RV Park** on U.S. Highway 93 (☎ 406/862-4242), which also has a limited number of tent sites, along with an on-site laundry and store. The **Whitefish KOA Kampground** (☎ 406/862-4242) is about 2 miles south of town on U.S. Highway 93 and has 76 sites ($19–$25 each) and 10 small cabins ($38–$42).

CROSS-COUNTRY SKIING

The **Big Mountain** (see below) offers 12 kilometers of very challenging cross-country trails. The **Glacier Nordic Club** maintains 15 kilometers of trails on the Whitefish Lake Golf Course and another 1.6 kilometers across the street near the Grouse Mountain Lodge.

These provide an excellent outing on the hilly golf course. A small donation allows skiers to enjoy both sides of the street, and yearly passes are available. For information, contact the **Outback Ski Shack** at Grouse Mountain Lodge (☎ 406/862-3000), which also rents skis and other equipment and apparel, and offers lessons. They are located in a tiny building behind the hotel and just off the track. The Flathead Convention and Visitor Association (see "Essentials," in section 8, above) provides a free outline of trails in or near Whitefish, as well as a list of equipment sales and rental operations.

DOGSLEDDING

Dog-Sled Adventures (☎ 406/881-BARK) lets you explore the mountains around Whitefish "at the speed of dog." The guided 12-mile rides in two-person sleds run through Stillwater State Forest, 2 miles north of Olney. Each trip takes about 2 hours and the sleds are equipped with blankets and elk-hide furs to keep you warm. The dogs pulling the sleds, mostly mixed breeds, were all rescued by the owners from unwanted homes or animal shelters and trained as sled dogs. A sled ride costs $100, or $50 per person, and includes a cup of hot chocolate and homemade cookies at the end of your ride.

DOWNHILL SKIING

✪ **The Big Mountain Ski and Summer Resort.** P.O. Box 1400 (12 miles north of Whitefish on Big Mountain Rd.), Whitefish, MT 59937. ☎ **800/858-5439** or 406/862-1900. Fax 406/862-2955. www.bigmtn.com. E-mail: bigmtn@bigmtn.com. Lift tickets $40 adults, $30 senior citizens, $27 children; half-day rates available. AE, DISC, MC, V. Late Nov–Apr open daily. From Whitefish, head over the viaduct to Wisconsin for 3 miles until you see the flashing yellow light. Turn right on Big Mountain Rd. and proceed 9 miles to the Big Mountain Village.

Lots of powder, lots of skiing in the trees, plenty of runs for every level of skier. With an annual snowfall of 300 inches, night skiing for $12, nine lifts, a vertical drop of 2,300 feet, and virtually no lines, the Big Mountain is one of the best resorts in the northwestern United States. More than half the mountain is geared to the intermediate skier, but there is plenty of terrain for experts and beginners. The expert runs are pretty steep—not as steep as Jackson's Teton Village but steep enough. There are never any crowds at Big Mountain, even in the holiday seasons, so though the prices have gone up over the years, you can spend your time skiing rather than waiting in lift lines.

The most recent improvement in the skiing side of the mountain is the addition of a lift that services almost 550 acres of new terrain, most of it for advanced or expert skiers. The lift is 3,500 feet long, but takes only 7 minutes to negotiate a 1,200-vertical-foot rise. Ski school options include half-day group lessons for kids ($18) and private lessons starting at $50 per hour. There are 10 restaurants in the village or on the hill and full-service ski rental.

For après ski food and entertainment, the Big Mountain holds its own. Food and beverage at the mountain are provided by **Moguls Bar and Grille,** a casual, full-service restaurant and bar with a menu chock full of Italian and American food. **Summit House** is a cafeteria that dishes up burgers and the like during the daytime; Mexican buffet dinners are served on some evenings. The **Hellroaring Saloon and Eatery** serves both lunch and dinners in a typical après ski atmosphere.

In summer, you can take gondola rides to the top of the mountain ($9.50 adults, $7.25 children and seniors), or go horseback riding with **Horsepower Adventures** (☎ **406/862-2900**), or mountain bike on the trails (bike rentals are available).

FISHING

It's not the Madison Valley, but Whitefish does have some hot spots for anglers wanting to try their hand. **Tally Lake** is a deep hole located north of Whitefish off U.S. Highway 93. Five miles north of town, turn left onto the Tally Lake Road (signs will direct you). You can expect cutthroat, rainbow, kokanee, brook trout, and whitefish.

In town, across the viaduct toward the Big Mountain lies **Whitefish Lake.** If you can handle all the recreationists hovering about like flies, the lake offers some pretty good lake trout. Northern pike can be found here, and rainbow and cutthroat can be nabbed on dry flies in the evening. The **Lakestream Flyshop,** 15 Central (☎ **406/862-1298**), is the best resource in town for information about fly-fishing the Flathead River and local streams. It's also a great spot for a fly-fisherman to construct a wish list, since the store sells all types of fly-fishing equipment, clothing, books, flies, dustcatchers, and memorabilia. The staff here provides full-service fly-fishing, tying, and rod-building services, in addition to good advice.

GOLF

The **Whitefish Lake Golf Club,** U.S. Highway 93 N. (☎ **406/862-4000**), is the only 36-hole golf facility in the state. Built in the 1920s, the golf club's trees have grown up over the last 75 years or so.

A Brewery in Whitefish

The glass-enclosed brewing "tower" at the **Great Northern Brewing Company,** on Central and Railway (☎ **406/863-1000**), gave birth to the original Black Star beer; the company has since added five new products. For a seat in the tasting room or a self-guided tour, call ahead of your planned arrival. The tasting room is open in summer from Monday to Saturday noon to 6pm, in winter 3 to 7pm.

While not especially long, the course requires that you use all the clubs in your bag (and maybe some you forgot), offering wide variety of shots. Almost all the fairways are lined with trees. There are few fairway bunkers, but they have strategic placement around the greens. Both 18 hole set-ups measure a little more than 6,500 yards from the tips. There is also a driving range and putting green. I don't think this is as good as the newer Meadow Lake (see Columbia Falls, below) for the modern game, but it is a very fun track. Greens fees are $29 for 18, $17 for nine holes. Carts rent for $24.50. **Par 3 on 93,** Highway 93 S. (☎ **406/862-7273**), is a nine-hole executive course on Highway 93 south of town. The greens fees are $8.

HIKING

The hiking in the immediate Whitefish area is not great. For the most part trails either stay in the woods so that you don't see anything, or they go along old logging roads—which make for good mountain biking, but less interesting hiking. The most popular trail in town is the **Danny On Trail** to the summit of the Big Mountain. Named for a Forest Service ecologist who was killed in a ski accident on the Big Mountain in 1979, it begins in the Big Mountain Village and ascends the south face of the mountain on four different paths. There's a 3.8-mile trek from the top of the lift along the ridge to Flower Point and back. It takes about 2 hours. The most demanding walk is 5.6 miles from the base of the ski area to the top of the hill and then along the ridge. You can ride the lift back down. Snow can be a problem in late spring and even the early months of summer.

SNOWBOARDING

Snowboarders will find kindred spirits—as well as an extensive line of boards and apparel—at **Snowfrog,** in the Alpine Village Center at 903 Wisconsin (☎ **406/862-7547**). The staff here will fill you in on the local snowboarding scene on the Big Mountain and other spots in the Flathead Valley. Downtown, the **Stumptown Snowboards** (☎ **406/862-0955**) at 128 Central Ave. can also serve the hammerheads in your party.

SNOWMOBILING

Contact the **Flathead Snowmobilers Association** (☎ **406/752-2561**) for current conditions and reports, then head north on U.S. Highway 93 for about 30 miles to **Loon's Echo Resort** (☎ **406/882-4791**) for any and all snowmobile adventures you may want or need; it has access to hundreds of miles of trails from state forest lands.

SHOPPING

The main shopping area of Whitefish is on Central Avenue and stretches for 3 blocks. For a ski town, the shopping frenzy here is fairly subdued. The largest bookshop in town is **Bookworks,** 110 Central Ave. (☎ **406/862-4980**), which stocks the best in nature books, regional writing, and children's literature; it's also the source of current hardcover and paperback best-sellers. **Montana Art and Trading,** 216 Central Ave. (☎ **800/555-9049** or 406/862-9317), has some unusual and beautiful handmade paper art work on Native American themes. The **Artistic Touch,** 209 Central Ave. (☎ **406/862-4813**), sells self-described "Montana crafts of merit." The gallery is operated by a jeweler who exhibits an eclectic, diverse group of sculptures in all types of media—expect glazed wall sculptures, pottery mobiles suspended from the ceiling, wood and wire combinations, and even a full-size, handmade marimba. **The Tomahawk Trading Company,** 131 Central Ave. (☎ **406/862-9199**), has a large selection of Indian-made jewelry. The **Bear Mountain Mercantile,** 237 Central Ave. (☎ **406/862-8382**), is chock-full of gimcracks, knickknacks, and souvenirs, many with a bear theme.

WHERE TO STAY
IN & AROUND TOWN

✪ **Best Western Rocky Mountain Lodge.** 6510 U.S. Hwy. 93 S., Whitefish, MT 59937. ☎ **800/862-2569** or 406/862-2569. Fax 406/862-1154. www.rockymtnlodge.com. E-mail: info@rockymtnlodge.com. 79 units. A/C TV TEL. $69–$119 double; $99–$169 suite. Rates include breakfast. AE, CB, DC, DISC, EURO, JCB, MC, V.

Located on the Highway 93 commercial strip just south of downtown, this is a very fine Best Western. The larger rooms, done in tasteful pastels, have their own kitchens and fireplaces. There are king and queen beds, coffeemakers in every room, and balconies on some of them. Standard rooms are average size. There are a complimentary continental breakfast, Jacuzzi, exercise room, and ski bus service.

Duck Inn. 1305 Columbia Ave., Whitefish, MT 59937. ☎ **800/344-2377** or 406/862-3825. Fax 406/863-2533. www.duckinn.com. 10 units. Winter $79 double; winter, $59 double. No credit cards.

This is the best value in the Whitefish area. The building is right off the Highway 93 strip, overlooking the Whitefish River. The rooms are very large, every one with a private bath with a deep soak tub, and a fireplace. There is a lovely lobby area, and the hot tub is in a broad-windowed room overlooking the river. Even though it's right in town, the location gives the illusion of the serene, quiet countryside. The owners are also own the Ford car-rental agency, and guests at the inn get unlimited mileage with their rentals.

✪ **The Garden Wall Inn.** 504 Spokane Ave., Whitefish, MT 59937. ☎ **888/530-1700** or 406/862-3440. www.wtp.net/go/gardenwall. E-mail: garden@digisys.net. 4 units. $85–$125 double; $175 suite. Rates include full breakfast. MC, V.

The Garden Wall prides itself on providing the little luxurious extras. For instance, guests receive a tray of coffee in their rooms a half-hour before breakfast. The hotel is full of country charm—it was built in the '20s, and all of the furnishings are period antiques, including claw-footed tubs and art deco dressers, depending on your room. All the details are perfect, right down to the towels, which are large and fluffy enough to dry two adults. Breakfast is a gourmet event, and afternoons end with hors d'oeuvres and complimentary beverages. The owner, Rhonda Fitzgerald, a ski instructor herself, caters to cross-country and downhill skiers.

✪ **Good Medicine Lodge.** 537 Wisconsin Ave., Whitefish, MT 59937. ☎ **800/860-5488** or 406/862-5488. Fax 406/862-5489. www.wtp.net/go/goodrx. E-mail: goodrx@digisys.com. 9 units. A/C TEL. $85–$145 double. Rates include full breakfast. AE, DISC, MC, V.

The Good Medicine Lodge is an already excellent place that is continually improving itself. The two best rooms have been upgraded recently, adding gas-fired potbellied stoves and new furnishings. Several second-floor rooms have beautiful views of the mountains in Glacier National Park, and ground floor rooms have their own patios on the green backyard. Rooms are large, modern, and clean, decorated with various themes—golf, Western, Indian. The clientele tends to be the active type, but also includes older folks from warmer climes who come to Whitefish for a white Christmas—or other special occasions.

✪ **Grouse Mountain Lodge.** 1205 U.S. Hwy. 93 W., Whitefish, MT 59937. ☎ **800/ 321-8822** or 406/862-3000. Fax 406/862-0326. www.grmtlodge.com. 145 units. A/C TV TEL. $159–$209 double. AE, DISC, MC, V.

Grouse Mountain Lodge is Montana's premier vacation lodge property, and is especially popular as a meeting place for businesses. Golfers have to love the fact that it's immediately adjacent to the 18th hole of one of Whitefish Lake's two golf courses. The lodge combines luxury accommodations, fine service, and good food to provide a memorable experience. The standard hotel-like rooms are called the executive rooms. The executive deluxe rooms all overlook the golf course from the third floor, with vaulted ceilings and large living areas. The loft rooms—there are 12 of them, 10 with kitchens and 2 with sauna tubs—have a spiral staircase, which leads to an upper sleeping loft, which has a king-size bed and a curtained-off area with two more beds. The only knock here is that the bathrooms aren't on the same level as the sleeping area. All rooms are equipped with ironing boards, coffeemakers, bathrooms with fluffy oversized towels, and terry-cloth robes.

Dining: The lodge houses the popular **Logan's Bar and Grill.** The food is very good, if a little pricey. You can also eat on the deck overlooking the course.

Amenities: Indoor pool, golf, cross-country skiing, meeting rooms for business meetings. The **Montana Adventure Company** (☎ **877/223-0742**) has a desk in the lobby and can arrange tee times, raft trips, trial rides, or dog-sledding.

Hidden Moose Lodge, 1735 E. Lakeshore Dr. (on the road to Big Mountain), Whitefish, MT 59937. ☎ **888/733-6667** or 406/862-6516. www.wtp.net/go/hiddenmoose. E-mail: seemoose@digisys.net. 8 units. $69–$140 depending on season. AE, DISC, MC, V.

The centerpiece of this new property is the vaulted, high-ceilinged great room with the vast river rock chimney fireplace. But the large, comfortable rooms are perfectly done as well. Guests can have their gourmet breakfast on their own decks if they wish. Even the bathroom mirrors are appointed with handmade iron work. Their sign on the road is almost invisible, so it's important to know that the lodge is located about a mile-and-a-half from town on the road to Big Mountain. I drove by the place twice before I got the right spot. Hidden Moose has canoes and bikes available for guests at no charge.

Loon's Echo Resort. 1 Fish Lake Rd., Stryker, MT 59933. ☎ **800/956-6632** or 406/ 882-4791. www.loonsecho.com. 5 units, 5 cabins. $100–$130 double; $90–$215 cabin. Discounts for extended stays. DISC, MC, V.

North on U.S. Highway 93 is the small town of Stryker, about 30 minutes from Whitefish. Conceived more than a decade ago as a retreat for those seeking an escape from the Flathead Valley, Ed and Gayle Hynes's Loon's Echo Resort changed its tune in 1995 when a multimillion-dollar renovation transformed some rustic cabins into a full-service resort. The main lodge, finished in 1995, is a Tudor-framed building covered by a Spanish-tiled roof; inside, the main lodge has a very Western feel (though many of the appointments are English antiques). This place exudes comfort, especially leather sofas that make watching a big-screen television almost enjoyable. The pool, a short walk below the TV room, is so small it's almost decorative; adjacent is a bar area also furnished with leather couches. The restaurant is fantastic and certainly not what you'd expect to find out here in the backwoods.

✪ **North Forty Resort.** 3765 Hwy. 40 W., Whitefish, MT 59937. ☎ **800/775-1740** or 406/862-7740. Fax 406/862-7741. www.northforty.com. 30 units. TV TEL. Winter $89–$139 double; summer $105–$185 double. AE, DISC, MC, V.

Nestled in the pines along Highway 40 between Whitefish and Columbia Falls, the North Forty is a great place to stay if you don't like being in town but still want to be close. Even the small cabins are pretty big. The smaller duplex cabins all have large living areas, fireplaces, kitchens, front porches, and barbecue grills. The North Forty is located in a serene and quiet area off the main highway, but it has televisions and telephones in each room. There is a cross-country ski/hiking trail located at the north end of the property. And a hot tub in the center of the resort for when you're done skiing.

Quality Inn Pine Lodge. 920 Spokane Ave., Whitefish, MT 59937. ☎ **800/305-7463** or 406/862-7600. Fax 406/862-7616. www.thepinelodge.com. 75 units. A/C TV TEL. $50–$195 double. AE, CB, DC, DISC, MC, V.

The Pine Lodge takes its name from the massive pine pillars that hold up the entry way and the porches. But the timbers seem more an architectural afterthought than an integral part of the design. The bedrooms are standard-sized, with one or two queen-size beds. There's an exercise room, an outdoor hot tub and guest laundry, and a continental breakfast. This inn is a step above the usual chain hotel.

✪ **Whitefish Lake Lodge Resort.** 1399 Wisconsin Ave., Whitefish, MT 59937. ☎ **800/735-8869** or 406/862-2929. Fax 406/862-3550. www.wfil.com. E-mail: wfil@wfil.com. 30 units. $125–$455. AE, MC, V.

The two-story condos available here may be the nicest accommodations in two states. They include a very large tiled kitchen, a dining area, a deck overlooking Whitefish Lake and the marina, and a large loft bedroom, as well as a downstairs bedroom. The living room is tastefully appointed and large mirrors on the far wall make a large room look even larger. The hotel-style units are much smaller—almost cramped, but they also have excellent furnishings. Managers require high maintenance standards to remain in the rental pool. Each of the one- to three-bedroom units has a spacious living area decorated in earth tones and accented with regional art and a gas fireplace; some even have sofa beds. The fully equipped kitchens include double sinks, four-burner stoves and ovens, full-size refrigerators, dishwashers, generous counter space, and tableware for six. Master bedrooms, some with mirrored double closets, have king-size beds and combination baths. Bedrooms and second baths are located well away from the main living-dining areas. In summer, there is a full-service marina with boat rentals. There's even a large parking lot for storing boat trailers.

ON THE BIG MOUNTAIN

The Big Mountain is a full-service ski area, working to attract local skiers, Canadian and American vacationers, and families. It provides a wide variety of accommodations to fit every pocketbook. You can reach central reservations at ☎ **800/858-5439.** Ask about discounted lift and lodging packages. If you're looking for a house or condo instead of a hotel, inquire at **Anapurna Properties** (☎ **800/243-7547;** www.anapurnaproperties.com) and **Big Mountain Alpine Homes** (☎ **800/858-5439;** www.bigmtn.com). Most are available for rent on a nightly basis. You can get a low-end condo or house for as little as $510 a week, or as much as $1,500. A video rental library is available, as is a heated indoor pool.

Alpinglow. Big Mountain Village, Whitefish, MT 59937. ☎ **406/862-6966.** Fax 406/862-0076. www.alpingdlow.com. E-mail: info@alpingdlow.com. 54 units. A/C TV TEL. $104–$134 double. AE, DISC, MC, V.

Alpinglow is located virtually at the base of gondola in the Big Mountain Village. The rooms are standard fare, clean, done in pastels, with televisions and phones. The valley-side rooms offer spectacular views of Flathead Lake. On a clear day, you can see almost to Polson. The restaurant has broad picture windows, a deck looking out over the lift base, and respectable if unimaginative sandwiches. The Alpinglow was the first recreational condo built in Montana, and it's showing its age a little around the edges.

Edelweiss. 3898 Big Mountain Rd., Whitefish, MT 59937. ☎ **800/228-8260** or 406/862-5252. Fax 406/862-3009. www.stayatedelweiss.com. E-mail: info@stayatedelweiss.com. 50 units. TV TEL. Winter $94–$162 double. AE, MC, V.

The Edelweiss has some very nice large rooms, all with kitchens, full baths, and fireplaces. Many of the rooms have panoramic views of the valley below. Convenient to the lifts, the Edelweiss has a large hot tub and a Finnish dry-heat sauna, and there's a laundry on the premises. Residents also have access to the indoor swimming pool at Anapurna Properties (see above).

Hibernation House. 3812 Big Mountain Rd., Whitefish, MT 59937. ☎ **800/858-5439** or 406/862-1982. Fax 406/862-1956. E-mail: hibehaus@bigmtn.com. 42 units. TEL. $65–$95 double. Rates include breakfast. AE, DISC, MC, V.

This is the least expensive place on the hill, popular with high school and college groups, ski teams, and families on budgets. All of the rooms are exactly alike, pretty small with a double bed and a set of bunk beds. Each room has its own television—a relatively recent development—but people still like to congregate in the lobby, where there is a large-screen TV. You can ski right to the back door on a groomed trail, and it is only a short walk to a lift in the morning. The full breakfast is very popular.

✪ **Kandahar Lodge.** 3824 Big Mountain Rd., Whitefish, MT 59937. ☎ **800/862-6094** or 406/862-6098. Fax 406/862-6095. www.vtown.com/Kandahar. E-mail: Kandahar@vtown.com. 48 units. TV TEL. $125–$380 double. AE, DISC, MC, V.

Kandahar combines the genteel ambience of an old-fashioned lodge with the requirements of an up-tempo modern ski area. The rooms are large, elegantly appointed. Many come with kitchenettes. All the beds have down comforters. The large loft bedrooms have vaulted ceilings, giving an airy feel to the rooms. Kandahar, by the way, is an ancient Afghan city purportedly founded by Alexander the Great. Why this has anything to do with a ski area in Montana, someone there will cheerfully explain to you. I couldn't follow it, myself.

Dining: The Cafe Kandahar is the best restaurant on the Big Mountain which, ski-area food being what it is, is not that high a recommendation. And the prices are reasonable.

Amenities: Skiing, spa, Jacuzzi, steam room, and locking ski storage.

Kintla Lodge. Big Mountain Village, Whitefish, MT 59937. ☎ **800/858-5439** or 406/862-1960. Fax 406/862-2955. www.bigmtn.com/resort. E-mail: bigmtn@bigmtn.com. 14 units. $165–$500 double, depending on season. AE, DISC, MC, V.

Kintla is the newest of the places on the mountain, opening in 1998. It is very upscale lodging, the only place on the mountain with an elevator serving its four floors. That's something people appreciate more than you might think after a day of skiing. A three-bedroom, three-bath unit goes for $500 a night in peak season. All units have wood-clad French doors opening onto a patio, stone flooring in the entry and kitchens, individual ski storage, and other appointments. Kintla is so close to the lift that they actually had to move part of it to build the lodge. There is no restaurant on the premises, but the village's tonier shops are located on the ground level outside.

Ptarmigan Village. 3000 Big Mountain Rd., Whitefish, MT 59937. ☎ **800/552-3952** or 406/862-3594. Fax 406/862-6664. www.ptarmiganvillage.com. E-mail: ptarmigan@ digisys.net. 50 units. TV TEL. $70–$245 condo. MC, V.

This is a very extensive condo set-up that is spread over a lower portion of the Big Mountain. Units feature vaulted ceilings, fireplaces, and fully equipped kitchens. The unit I had included a CD player (pretty unusual in rented lodgings, even in the digital age) and a spiral staircase down to the bedrooms. The decks overlook a woody area where signs warn about increased black bear activity in the summer. There are indoor and outdoor pools and tennis courts and a nice pond where kids can spy out the turtles hiding in the reeds in summer.

WHERE TO DINE

A good deli sandwich is available at the **Rocky Mountain Food Traders Market and Deli,** located at 905 Wisconsin Ave. (☎ **406/862-5838**), east of the city center.

✪ **The Buffalo Cafe.** 516 3rd St. ☎ **406/862-2833**. www.digisys.net/buffalocafe/. Reservations not accepted. Breakfast and lunch $3–$6. AE, MC, V. Mon–Fri 6:30am–2pm, Sat 7am–2pm, Sun 9am–2pm. Closed Tues, July to Sept 15. MEXICAN/AMERICAN.

Buffalo Cafe has your basic cafe atmosphere. Breakfast is traditional—eggs, pancakes, French toast, and the like—at prices lower than you might expect in a tourist town. Though this is not a Mexican restaurant per se, the menu includes several different Mexican entrees, including Craig's Burrito (a local favorite), a "Big Ol' Taco," and a chorizo enchilada. Alternatively, there's always a chicken fillet or Reuben sandwich.

The Out of the Blue Bakery Cafe. 3rd and Spokane. ☎ **406/862-6232**. Breakfast $3–$6; dinner $8–$26. AE, DISC, MC, V. Breakfast and lunch Tues–Sun 7am–3pm; dinner Thurs–Sun 5–10pm. BREAKFAST/BAKED GOODS.

The breakfast pastries are baked fresh here. Prices are higher than in many other places, but food proportions are larger and on a sunny day there's the opportunity to sit outside on a deck. Egg dishes are called "scrambles" and incorporate traditional items as well as a veggie scramble and a tofu scramble. Specialties are huevos rancheros, tofu rancheros, and fried rice with tofu and fresh veggies. At dinner you can get a buffalo rib eye, wild boar, shrimp, chicken, or tofu disguised as chicken.

Truby's. 115 Central Ave. ☎ **406/862-4979**. Dinner $7–$9. AE, MC, V. Sun–Thurs 11am–10pm, Fri–Sat 11am–midnight. PIZZA/BURGERS.

I should probably first confess that I am not crazy about pizza. But I was intrigued by Truby's eclectic approach to the all-American dish. Here you can get wood-fired, Thai-style, Athenian, veggie, or design-your-own pizza. The crusts are thin and crispy. I had a pizza called the Peking duck. Now in my gastronomic opinion, real Peking duck is the highest plateau to which the culinary arts can aspire. Peking duck pizza falls several levels below that, but it was an interesting and different approach to pizza. Truby's has a happening atmosphere with blues on the PA, lots of customers. and a cheerful staff.

✪ **The Tupelo Grille.** 17 Central Ave. ☎ **406/862-6136**. Reservations recommended for large parties. Dinner $11–$19. AE, MC, V. Daily 5:30–9:30pm. CONTINENTAL/CAJUN.

Tupelo is the best restaurant in the downtown area, especially for those with a taste for New Orleans-style food. Cajun pasta (chicken, smoked sausage, and tomatoes seasoned with cilantro and chilies, sautéed and finished with cream) and a Cajun Creole combo (a platter of shrimp Creole crawfish etoufée and chicken and sausage jambalaya) are specialties.

Whitefish Grill. 235 Central Ave. ☎ **406/862-3354.** Breakfast $4–$7; dinner $14–$17. No credit cards. Mon–Sat 8:30am–9pm. HEALTHY FOOD.

The Whitefish Grill is a small restaurant tucked away at the end of a narrow hallway in the back of a retail building. The trademark here is that everything served is fresh. The proprietors have developed a "heart smart" menu with low-fat entrees. Prices are slightly higher than at similar establishments, but the quality of the food is worth it. Among the specialties are the "House Toaster," which includes mushrooms, tomatoes, and bacon topped with cheddar served on a slice of toast. Breakfast is served until 3pm.

The house specialty at dinner is the roast duck served with fresh huckleberry sauce.

✪ **Whitefish Lake Restaurant.** U.S. Hwy. 93 N. (at the Whitefish Golf Course). ☎ **406/862-5285.** Reservations recommended. Lunch $4–$7; dinner $16–$24. AE, MC, V. Summer, daily 11am–3pm and 5:30–10pm; winter, 5:30–10pm. CONTINENTAL.

There are Montanans who will enter the Whitefish Lake Restaurant as their horse in the "best restaurant in the state" sweepstakes. Located at the public golf course, it is generally conceded to be the best restaurant in Whitefish. It's housed in a building that was constructed in 1936 as a WPA project. The dining room has an almost church-like atmosphere, dark, quiet, with large log beams and wagon-wheel chandeliers hanging from the ceiling. There are stained glass mountain scenes on the walls. Tables are covered with traditional Scottish tablecloths, and a large stone fireplace provides warmth on those chilly fall and early spring evenings. The menu for the evening meal covers the culinary landscape, from vegetarian pasta to 14-ounce prime rib, lamb shank, and roast duckling; fresh seafood may include lobster, king crab, halibut, or Pacific salmon. The wine list includes an impressive collection of French and Cali-fornia whites and reds. As formal as a golf club ever gets, it's the only place in White-fish that approaches dressy.

The Whitefish Times Coffeehouse and Restaurant, 334 Central. ☎ **406/862-2444.** Breakfast and lunch $2–$5; dinner $4.50–$8. Mon–Sat 7am–10pm, Sun 10am–5pm. COFFEEHOUSE.

The Whitefish Times is a modest restaurant and a great coffeehouse. It's like having your morning coffee in a rich person's library. There are magazines and newspapers to read in the rattan-backed chairs pulled up to the oak tables, or on the sofas. There are three nightly specials for dinner, as well as quiche, soups, and sandwiches.

WHITEFISH AFTER DARK

There's not much going on in Whitefish after hours except the bar scene, concentrated in a 2-block area on Central Avenue. A pub crawl begins at the **Palace Bar and Spirits,** a rather seedy joint that promises live rock and roll on weekends and holidays and $2 hamburgers. Follow that with a time-out at **Kacey's,** which is equally seedy but has more character; its clientele tends to be older and more local, and the walls are cov-ered with wildlife pictures and patriotic slogans. A third stop could be at **Great Northern,** which compared to the other two joints, is upscale. This place is jumping on the weekends after 7pm. Your final stop: the **Bulldog Saloon.** Not just a bar, the Bulldog turns out a pretty good burger, too.

10 Columbia Falls

11 miles N of Kalispell; 9 miles E of Whitefish

Columbia Falls gets a bad rep not only for being the home of Plum Creek, a smoke-billowing institution seen for miles even at night, but also for its not-so-subtle lack of spirit. Unlike Great Falls, where the falls are out of town and (gasp!) dammed,

Columbia Falls goes you one better by not having any falls at all. The redeeming features and equalizers are the town's proximity to Glacier National Park, and lodging rates that are somewhat less expensive—it's a good fallback location if you have trouble finding a room in Whitefish. Residents here are real Montanans, something of an enigma in an area being inundated with out-of-staters setting up house.

ESSENTIALS

GETTING THERE   **Glacier International Airport** is 10 minutes away on U.S. Highway 2 between Columbia Falls and Kalispell. **Delta** (☎ **800/221-1212**), **Northwest** (☎ **800/225-2525**), and **Horizon** (☎ **800/547-9308**) have daily flights. The closest **Amtrak** station is in Whitefish, 10 miles to the northwest.

Statewide weather updates are available by calling ☎ **406/449-5204;** for Columbia Falls, call ☎ **406/755-4829.** Call ☎ **800/332-6171** for **statewide road reports** and **406/755-4949** for **road information** in the Columbia Falls area.

VISITOR INFORMATION   The **Columbia Falls Area Chamber of Commerce,** P.O. Box 312, Columbia Falls, MT 59912 (☎ **406/892-2072**), can provide you with pertinent area information. The chamber and the **U.S. Forest Service** jointly operate an information cabin in Maranette Park on Route 2 near the center of town. Columbia Falls is located in **Travel Montana's Glacier Country;** request information from them at Box 1396, Dept. 8403, Kalispell, MT 59903 (☎ **800/338-5072** or 406/756-7128).

GETTING AROUND   The only car-rental agency actually located in Columbia Falls is **Dollar** (☎ **406/892-0009**).

GETTING OUTSIDE

Two of the best-kept secrets in this part of the state are the **North and South Lion lakes.** To find them, follow the signs to the west side of the Hungry Horse Reservoir. Less than 5 miles after turning off of Highway 40, you will come to a cutoff to the North Lion Lake and, within a hundred yards, arrive at South Lion Lake.

Both are well protected, quiet, and for the most part undiscovered by tourists—excellent for picnicking, fishing, or swimming.

There is a road around **Hungry Horse Reservoir,** a 110-mile round-trip that you can start from the town of Hungry Horse. Hungry Horse is 9 miles south of West Glacier or 6 miles east of Columbia Falls on U.S. Route 2. There's a small visitor center at Hungry Horse Dam (☎ **406/387-5241**). This is an excellent drive for seeing wildlife. You're almost certain to see at least an elk, and maybe a moose or bear. It's also a great place for fishing.

GOLF

Columbia Falls is home to one of Montana's best golf courses, **Meadow Lake** (at the Meadow Lake Resort; see "Where to Stay," below). About 6,700 yards from the back tees, the course is very challenging, especially the greens, which are "speed sensitive" and have lots of nearly invisible breaks in them. The fairways are fairly wide but lined with intimidating large trees. To reserve a tee time, call ☎ **406/892-7601.**

HIKING

Columbia Mountain, Glacier National Park, and the Jewel Basin are nearby, but the **Great Northern** is the grandpappy of 'em all in these parts. If you want a leisurely stroll with moderate difficulty, stick to the Danny On Trail on the Big Mountain in Whitefish. If you want 8 hours of hardship, then the Great Northern is for you. To get there, take U.S. Highway 2 to Martin City, then turn onto the East Side Reservoir Road (38) for 15 miles. At that point, turn east to Highline Loop Road (1048), and from here you should be able to see the approach route. The hike goes up the 8,705-foot high Great Northern Mountain in the Great Bear Wilderness. While there's not an official trail, enough people have beaten a path to the summit that one is clear enough to make out. This isn't a leisurely walk, nor is it the most well-publicized hike in the area, but it is the most rewarding for those willing to make the effort. The views of Glacier and the Hungry Horse Reservoir are remarkable.

EXPLORING THE TOWN: KITSCH & CAMP

Remember when your dad used to drive the family to the beach? Whenever you drove past the "Tent of Miracles" or the "Cave of 10,000 Rattlesnakes" or the "Fabulous Mystery House," you'd beg Dad to stop. He always ignored you and drove on as if you hadn't spoken. Columbia Falls offers you the chance to find out what these attractions are all about.

Big Sky Waterslide & Miniature Greens, at the junction of U.S. Highways 2 and 206 (☎ **406/892-5025**), is the main attraction and a good place to cool off. It is the largest such park in the state of Montana. If you've always wanted to reenact the snow scenes from *The Shining* without the snow (and who hasn't?), then the **Amazing Fun Center,** at U.S. Highway 2 E., Coram (☎ **406/387-5902**), is your place. Like rats hunting for an odorless cheese, tourists often enter the Fun Center's maze and emerge hours later. **Grizzly Go Kart,** 7480 U.S. Hwy. 2 E., Columbia Falls (☎ **406/892-3132**), offers a track for those wanting to make a run for an imaginative Grand Prix. Baseball fans and golfers will feel right at home here with the addition of a batting cage and mini-golf course. The **House of Mystery,** 7800 U.S. Hwy. 2 E., Columbia Falls (☎ **406/892-1210**), offers a vortex (you'll just have to go in to find out) and other bewilderments. **Just for Fun,** 1910 U.S. Hwy. 2 E., Columbia Falls (☎ **406/892-7750**), is that place you passed coming into town from the west with the giant jackalope.

WHERE TO STAY

✪ **Meadow Lake Resort.** 100 St. Andrews Dr., Columbia Falls, MT 59912. ☎ **800/321-4653** or 406/892-7601. Fax 406/892-0330. www.meadowlake.com. E-mail: mdwlake@meadowlake.com. 24 units. A/C TV TEL. $79–$129 at inn; $89–$439 condo or home. AE, MC, V.

Meadow Lake offers a wide variety of excellent accommodations in a modern-resort style. Development focuses on the golf course, which is one of the best in the state. Rooms are stylish in the modern sense and many of the condo units have Jacuzzis. The resort has a recreation center with Nautilus weight machines and aerobic equipment. There are a large pool and hot tub. The inn features standard-sized hotel rooms with a king bed, double sleeper sofa, a large bathroom with double vanity sinks, and a veranda or patio. The condos come in suites (a single room with kitchen, bath and, usually, a Jacuzzi), or one- and two-bedroom versions.

They all have fireplaces, full kitchens, convenient washer and dryer access, private deck with barbecue, VCR, and stereo. Even if you haven't come for golf, this is still the best place to spend the night.

Dining/Diversions: Tracy's Restaurant is a cozy place to enjoy lunch or dinner after a round or two of golf during the summer or skiing in winter. If you plan to visit during the summer, ask if the resort is hosting a Flathead Festival concert; past headline acts appearing on the course have included America, the Nitty Gritty Dirt Band, and Emmylou Harris (although you still have to buy a ticket).

Amenities: Dry cleaning and laundry service, in-room massage, video rentals, conference rooms area available for an extra charge. There is a self-service Laundromat in the inn.

Park View Inn Bed & Breakfast. 904 4th Ave. W., Columbia Falls, MT 59912. ☎ **888/830-9410** or 406/892-7275. E-mail: halls@digisys.net. 4 units, 3 cabins. $69–$125 double.

This is a pleasant bed-and-breakfast in downtown Columbia Falls. It has four rooms in the house, and three cabins on the grounds. A full breakfast is offered to those staying in the house, but the cabins have their own kitchens. The nicest unit by far is the honeymoon suite, a three-room cabin with a Jacuzzi and leather sofas.

Western Inn/Glacier Mountain Shadow Resort. At the intersection of U.S. hwys. 2 and 206, Columbia Falls, MT 59912. ☎ **800/766-1137** and 406/892-7686. Fax 406/892-4575. 22 units. TV TEL. $75 double. AE, DISC, MC, V.

This recently renovated, low-cost hostelry offers clean, comfortable accommodations with prices to match their modesty. Single rooms come with one queen-size bed, and double rooms have two queen-size beds. Also available for rent are tepees. The accommodations are no better or worse than those found in a typical low-cost national chain. There are also 18 RV campsites here for about $20 each. The inn offers a continental breakfast.

WHERE TO DINE

The Back Room of the Nite Owl. U.S. Hwy. 2 E. ☎ **406/892-3131.** Most items $6–$13. No credit cards. Mon–Sat 4–10pm, Sun 2–9:30pm. AMERICAN.

This greasy spoon in the back room of the Nite Owl Cafe is off the main drag in Columbia Falls. You'll be pleasantly surprised by what The Back Room has to offer— roasted chicken, spare ribs, and country ribs (small chunks cooked in barbecue sauce) are all delicious and reasonably priced. Fry bread is the house specialty and comes with meals instead of standard bread items. The pizza and salad buffet each Sunday is a bargain for less than $6.

6 Helena & Southwestern Montana

by Dan Whipple

This region is where the state of Montana came of age, changing in a few short years from an outback of fur traders and individual explorers to a bustling, wide open mining camp. Butte was once the "Richest Hill on Earth," and rich gold strikes were made at Helena's Last Chance Gulch and Virginia City's Alder Gulch. Bannack, another gold mining boomtown, was the first territorial capital.

The area has calmed down somewhat since then. The Berkeley Pit is filling with water. The Anaconda copper smelter is shut down, and the Old Works is now a golf course. Helena is a business-like state capital, the seat of state politics.

But in the Big Hole, you can still see some ranching and farming done the old-fashioned way, stacking hay with beaver slides, and sleds drawn by draft horses to feed cattle in the winter. There are plenty of fishing and outdoor opportunities here and in the mountains that cover the area.

Not all has been lost in the area. This region has undergone quite a bit of historic preservation. The old prison at Deer Lodge can give you a perspective on frontier justice, and the preserved mining towns of Nevada City and Virginia City can give you a flavor of the boomtown, mining camp life.

1 Scenic Drives

Two high-speed highways—Interstates 90 and 15—run north to south through the region, but the best roads to take are the well-kept back roads, the state and county highways that follow unlikely and out-of-the-way paths. Traveling from Anaconda to Dillon could be done via the interstate in good time, just over an hour. But a better, less-frequented route through the Big Hole Valley runs east of the Continental Divide and the Anaconda-Pintler Wilderness Area. A good stopping point is Wisdom, which has the dubious distinction of being one of the coldest places in the Lower 48, and the turnoff for the Big Hole Battlefield. Driving farther south on MT 278 takes you to Jackson, then Bannack State Park, before ending at I-15 south of Dillon. From Dillon, drive north on MT 41 to Twin Bridges and the junction with MT 287. This road runs south through the Old West towns of Sheridan, Laurin, Alder, Nevada City, and Virginia City, before ending in Ennis at U.S. Highway 287.

Southwestern Montana

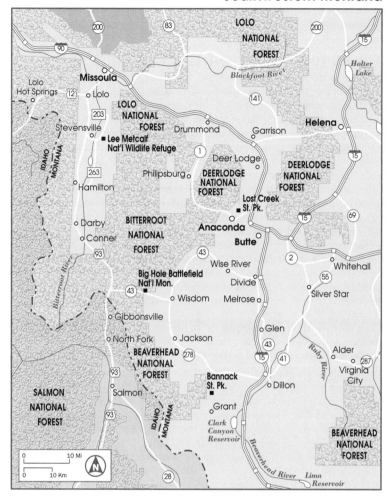

DRIVING TOUR #1: THE BIG HOLE VALLEY

This short loop tour takes you through the Big Hole Valley, nicknamed "Land of 10,000 Haystacks." Begin in Dillon, the largest of the towns in this area, and keep your eye out for white-tailed and mule deer in the morning and early evening. Travel north on I-15 to Divide, then take MT 43 southwest to Wisdom. This is a tiny town with little other than its residents and the scenery to recommend it, but the Big Hole National Battlefield (described in detail later in this chapter) is a short drive west on MT 43 and is well worth the trip.

After that, head back to Wisdom and take MT 278 towards Dillon. Along the way stop in Jackson for a soak in the hot springs, or tour Montana's territorial capital city, Bannack, just 28 miles farther, off MT 278. As you stroll the boardwalks you'll discover the ease with which you can lose yourself in the state's early history—a microcosm that reflects the entire Old West. This drive is great during the summer, when haystacks fill the fields and the Bannack Days celebration re-creates early events in

Montana's history. It's not so tame during winter months, though, when roads are icy and caution is required (so a tow truck won't be).

DRIVING TOUR #2: THE PINTLER SCENIC ROUTE

This tour is best enjoyed during summer, when area attractions open their doors to visitors and long summer days extend daylight hours.

This scenic route takes you from the mining city of Anaconda on a loop tour with ghost towns, historic buildings, and wildlife. Starting in Anaconda, where you can visit the copper smelting display at the Copper Village Museum or admire an old art deco theater, **The Washoe,** which was ranked fifth in the nation by David Naylor *(American Picture Palaces)* for its architectural value—you'll head on little-traveled roads into a mountainous area that rivals any in the state.

Northwest of Anaconda on MT 1 lies **Georgetown Lake,** a popular tourist destination in summer and winter, when anglers and skiers flock to the lake and nearby ski area, Discovery Basin. There are dogsled races here on a winter Sunday. Continue on MT 1 to Drummond, known as the "Bull Shipper's Capital of the World."

Heading southeast on I-90 will take you to **Deer Lodge,** home to the state prison, historic **Grant Kohrs Ranch,** and the **Towe Ford Museum,** which features a slightly depleted collection of nearly 110 antique Fords and Lincolns—restored, original models from the early 1900s to the present day. Highway 273 takes you back to Anaconda.

2 Helena

64 miles N of Butte; 115 miles SE of Missoula; 89 miles S of Great Falls

Modern Helena is a government town, a bustling community of politicians, lobbyists, and bureaucrats during the week. On the weekends, they all turn into outdoors fanatics, heading to the lakes or mountains or ski areas in winter.

In the olden days, Helena was a boomtown, built on gold mining. Last Chance Gulch was named when four miners said they had one last chance to hit it big in the West. The town boomed in the gold rush of 1865. During the height of this prosperity, only Manhattan could boast of more millionaires than the small Montana city. And along the way, the town recorded an alarming number of murders and robberies. In 1935, the town was devastated by earthquakes. Beginning October 3, more than 2,000 tremors rocked the city, causing millions of dollars in damage.

After Helena took capital rights from Virginia City in 1875, Marcus Daly, a Butte copper king with more than just a bystander's interest in the capital's location, decided to steal it away from Helena and move it to Anaconda, 25 miles from Butte. This touched off a political war that echoes throughout the state even today. As we all now know, Daly's efforts proved unsuccessful.

ESSENTIALS

GETTING THERE   Skywest (☎ 800/453-9417), **Delta** (☎ 800/221-1212), **Horizon** (☎ 800/547-9308 or 406/442-0930), and **Big Sky** (☎ 800/237-7788) provide commuter links to larger airports in Montana and other Western states from **Helena Regional Airport** (☎ 406/442-2821), northeast of the city on Skyway Drive off U.S. Highway 15.

The **bus depot** is located downtown at 3122 U.S. Hwy. 12 E. (☎ 406/442-5860), with service on **Rimrock Stages,** a Trailways affiliate (☎ 800/255-7655).

It's easy to drive to Helena. From the east or west, take I-90; turn off and head north toward Helena. From the north or south, I-15 leads right into town.

Helena

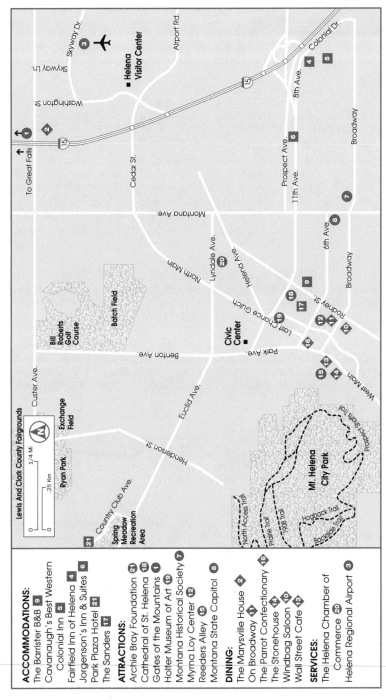

ACCOMMODATIONS:
The Barrister B&B 9
Cavanaugh's Best Western
Colonial Inn 5
Fairfield Inn of Helena 4
Jorgenson's Inn & Suites 6
Park Plaza Hotel 21
The Sanders 17

ATTRACTIONS:
Archie Bray Foundation 21
Cathedral of St. Helena 18
Gates of the Mountains 1
Holter Museum of Art 19
Montana Historical Society 7
Myrna Loy Center 12
Reeders Alley 15
Montana State Capitol 8

DINING:
The Marysville House
On Broadway 2
The Parrot Confectionary 16
The Stonehouse 14
Windbag Saloon 5
Wall Street Cafe 13

SERVICES:
The Helena Chamber of
Commerce 20
Helena Regional Airport 3

139

Helena, au natural

Thomas McBride (☎ **406/443-5286**), a river rafter, naturalist, storyteller, and wildlife photographer, provides river-floating trips designed to allow you to see, understand, and connect with nature. Subjects include environmental issues, wildlife, vegetation, geologic formations, and photography instructions. McBride is a well-known and popular photographer who combines his artistic eye with a deep environmental understanding. Raft trips are $100 minimum for a day.

VISITOR INFORMATION   A good starting point for local activities and area maps is the **Helena Area Chamber of Commerce** at 225 Cruse, Helena, MT 59601 (☎ **800/7-HELENA** or 406/442-4120; fax 406/447-1532; www.helenamt.com). There is an information office run by the chamber out near the airport at Cedar Street off I-15. Another source is the state tourism office, **Travel Montana,** the mother lode for brochures and information around the region and the state (Helena is located in Travel Montana's Gold West Country). Contact them at 1424 N. 9th Ave., Helena, MT 59620 (☎ **800/VISIT-MT** or 406/444-2654).

GETTING AROUND   Car-rental agencies include **Avis** (☎ 406/442-4440), **Enterprise** (☎ 406/449-3400), **Hertz** (☎ 406/449-4167), and **National** (☎ 406/442-8620).

GETTING OUTSIDE

A walking tour of the city will give you a capsule of the history of the Old West. A brochure, "The Heart of Helena," offers a comprehensive guide and tour map that will put you in the center of activities and bring meaning to your tour. To receive a copy, contact the **Helena Area Chamber of Commerce** (☎ **800/7-HELENA** or 406/442-4120).

FISHING

There are several stretches of prime fishing along the upper stretch of the Missouri River. The section from **Toston Dam** downstream to **Canyon Ferry Lake** offers brown and rainbow trout in the 2- to 10-pound class. Floating with large streamers, wet flies, and lures is the most popular and productive way to catch these fish as they make their way upriver to spawn. The fishing gets progressively better from late spring to fall. The section below **Hauser Dam** to **Beaver Creek** offers a chance for really big trout. Other popular fishing areas include **Park Lake** 15 miles southwest of Helena, **Lake Helena,** and the **Smith River** to the east of the Big Belt Mountains.

   Paul Roos Outfitters, 326 N. Jackson, Helena, MT 59624 (☎ **406/442-5489**), offers customized fly-fishing trips on the Smith River, considered in fishing circles one of the best not just in the state, but the world. Guides are helpful since river access is restricted to a limited number of permit holders by the Department of Fish and Wildlife.

HIKING

Mount Helena City Park covers 628 acres on Mount Helena, a 5,468-foot peak that looks over the city. Nine trails, seven of which are easily accessible, cover the park, the easiest of which, the **1906 Trail,** follows the base of the limestone cliffs past Devil's Kitchen to the 5,468-foot summit. To reach the beginning of the 1906 Trail, take Park Avenue to Clarke Street and turn west. Go south on Harrison to Adams Street, then west on Adams. The trailhead is at the picnic area at the end of Adams Street.

Hogback Trail is a rough and rocky hike that leads from the peak to the exposed Hogback Ridge.

There are more than 700 miles of trail in the Helena National Forest. The **Trout Creek Canyon Trail** offers a spectacular view of Hanging Valley. Helena is also the gateway to the **Gates of the Mountain Wilderness.** For a serious hike, you can go to **Mann Gulch,** the site of a Forest Fire in August 1949. Fifteen firefighters parachuted into Mann Gulch at about 6pm on August 5. By the next morning, 10 were dead and two died later from their injuries. The incident is the subject of Norman MacLean's book, *Young Men and Fire.* You can get more information about hiking into Mann Gulch from the Helena Ranger district (☎ **406/449-5490**). **Gates of the Mountain Boat Tours** (see below) offers considerably less strenuous boat tours of Mann Gulch along the Missouri River.

ROCKHOUNDING

Helena was founded on gold mining, and the area is still well known for its gemstones, particularly Montana sapphires. Sapphires, a variety of the mineral corundum, are harder than any natural stone except a diamond. The Helena area has seven commercial areas that allow visitors to dig for sapphires. The city also has the only commercial heat treating facility in the state. Heat treating removes the stone's original cloudy appearance and enhances the brilliance, which can approach that of a diamond. Garnets, moss agates, fossils, and hematite can also be uncovered by diligent treasure seekers. See the listing for the **Spokane Bar Sapphire Mine & Gold Fever Rock Shop,** below, under "Seeing the Sights." Or contact the Sapphire Gallery (☎ **800/525-0169**), Margaret Reed Custom Gems (☎ **406/475-3284**), Eagles' Nest Trading Post (☎ **406/475-3176**), or Eldorado Bar (☎ **406/442-7960**).

SKIING

Great Divide Ski Area. P.O. Box SKI, Marysville, MT 59640. ☎ **406/449-3746.** Lift tickets $20 adults, $10 seniors, $10 children, free for children 5 and under with adult; rate reductions at noon and 4pm. Take Exit 200 off I-15, then go west on MT 279 to Marysville Rd.

Great Divide is a local ski hill, not a destination resort. Its ticket prices are low, as are the speed of its lifts, compared to, say, the Big Mountain. It is also pretty tough, with 55% of its runs rated for advanced or expert skiers, 30% intermediate and 15% beginner. There are 50 designated runs and two open bowls.

There are two free ski instruction sessions for entry-level skiers, one at 10am and another at 1pm; KIDSKI is a daily program from 1 to 3pm for children ages 4 to 6, which includes a snack and equipment rental. Private lessons are also available through the ski school.

SNOWMOBILING

Three major trail systems are within a 30-minute drive of Helena. The Minnehaha-Rimini area grooms 120 miles of trails, and the Marysville and Magpie-Sunshine areas, with views into the Gates of the Mountains Wilderness, each groom 45 miles of trails. Guided tours can be arranged through the **Helena Snowdrifters.** For details on these tours, as well as specific trail information, contact the Snowdrifters at 1813 N. Oakes, Helena, MT 59601 (☎ **406/449-2685**).

WATER SPORTS

Canyon Ferry Lake Recreation Area, managed jointly by the federal Bureau of Land Management and the Bureau of Reclamation (☎ **406/475-3319** or 406/475-3310), is a 25-mile-long lake within 20 minutes of Helena. In the spring, summer, and fall, the lake is primarily a rainbow trout fishery, but it does have 24 recreation and camping areas, and boat ramps. The lake is especially popular with water-skiers and water-tubers, though you'll see sailboats racing as well. More than 1,000 eagles migrate through Canyon Ferry each year from mid-October to mid-December, and people come from all over the state and around the country to watch them feed on spawning kokanee salmon below the dam. The **Canyon Ferry Visitor Center,** 7661 Canyon Ferry Rd., ☎ **406/475-3128,** is open from 11am to 5pm from Memorial Day to Labor Day, and from 8am to 4pm on Saturday and Sunday from the end of October until early December. To get to the visitor center, take Canyon Ferry Road east from Helena about 9 miles.

Two Helena-area state parks center around man-made lakes: **Spring Meadow Lake** (day use only) and **Black Sandy** at the Hauser Reservoir. Spring Meadow is a 30-acre, spring-fed lake on Helena's western edge, noted for its clarity and depth. Open to non-motorized boats only, the lake is popular for swimming and fishing. To reach Spring Meadow Lake, take U.S. Highway 12 west, then head north on Joslyn to Country Club. One of the only public parks on the shores of Hauser Reservoir, Black Sandy is an extremely popular weekend boating, fishing, and waterskiing takeoff point. To get to the Hauser Reservoir, drive 7 miles north of Helena on I-15, then 4 miles east on Route 453, then follow signs 3 miles north on a county road.

SEEING THE SIGHTS

Last Chance Gulch was so named because a quartet of gold-seeking prospectors declared the spot to be their "last chance" to strike it rich. It came to be one of the richest gold-producing areas in the world and remains one of Helena's main streets. Located downtown, this historic area combines Helena's colorful past with a contemporary freshness. Architecturally significant buildings, many of which are listed on the National Register of Historic Places, house espresso shops and boutiques, while ultra-modern sculptures depict historical events. Interpretive markers are scattered along the pedestrian mall, with historical information relating to period construction. **Kumamoto Prefecture** in Japan is Montana's "sister state," and the prefecture maintains a cultural center at 34 N. Last Chance Gulch (☎ **406/449-7904**). Visitors are welcome, and it's free. Concrete tables with checkerboard tile inlays can be found at the south end of Last Chance Gulch, a great place for chess or checkers.

Archie Bray Foundation. 2915 Country Club Ave. ☎ **406/443-3502.** www. archiebray.org. MC, V. Gallery open Mon–Sat 10am–5pm, Sun 1–5pm, with ceramic art for sale. Visitors may take a self-guided walking tour of the grounds during daylight hours.

Archie Bray, a Helena resident and enthusiastic supporter of the arts, established this artistic colony for potters in 1951 at the brickyard and kilns of the Western Clay Manufacturing Company. Over the years it has become a premier testing ground for ceramic artists, working together to share ideas and techniques. Like discarded toys, various playful sculptures dot the lawns, some more inconspicuously than others. Of special note are several larger, freestanding monuments by Robert Harrison, most notably *A Potter's Shrine,* dedicated to Bray and incorporating some materials up to 100 years old; *Tile-X,* stacked drain tiles in the shape of a pyramid; and *Aruina,* a monument of brick and tile whose four arches frame the surrounding Helena landscape. Because of the intimate nature of each individual resident's art-making process, visitors are asked to respect their privacy. There is an annual summer resident artist exhibit and sale running from mid-June to mid-August each year. The foundation will be 50 years old in 2001, and is having a number of special events to celebrate between June 21 and 23.

Kleffner Ranch Tours. ☎ **406/227-6645.** www.kleffnerranch.com. $5 adults, $2.50 children. June 1–Sept 30, tours at 10am and 2pm Mon–Sat, 2pm Sun. Take U.S. Hwy. 12–287 through East Helena, then go south 1 mile on Hwy. 518. You'll see the barn, then turn in at the second cattle guard.

This is a really cool tour, with a really cool story behind it. The Kleffner Ranch is a working cattle ranch with an unusual history. The ranch was founded by William Child in 1888, a silver speculator who was ruined in the Panic of 1893. Child killed himself in the main ranch house that year, after the ranch was foreclosed by U.S. Sen.-elect Wilbur Fisk Sanders. Before his downfall, Child had built a stone octagonal ranch house, the oldest of its type west of the Mississippi, and a barn large enough to house a full-court basketball arena on the upper level. After Child's death, the ranch was vacant until 1916, when a family took it over. They became broke during the Depression, and it was vacant until Paul Kleffner bought it in 1943, who with his wife spent the next 50 years restoring the property. Kleffner now lives on the ranch by himself (his wife has Alzheimer's and lives in a nursing home), and as a hobby, he gives the tours of this interesting property himself.

Last Chance Tours. Tours leave from the Montana State Historical Society Building, 22 N. Roberts. ☎ **888/423-1023** or 406/442-1023. www.lctours.com. $5 adults, $4.50 seniors, $4 children. Mid-Apr to late Sept; tour times vary seasonally.

The train engine on wheels pulls you around Helena on a tour of its historic sites, like the Atlas Block, the Montana Club, the old governor's mansion, and other sites. This is a great way to get oriented in Helena and learn a few things about the town at the same time.

Montana State Capitol. Montana Ave. and 6th St. ☎ **406/444-4789.** Free admission; no charge for tours. Building open Mon–Fri 8am–6pm. Montana Historical Society gives daily tours on the hour Mon–Sat 10am–5pm, Sun 11am–4pm; call ahead to make group reservations.

Montana's beautiful state capitol building is undergoing extensive renovations that will keep it closed to visitors until sometime in early 2001, when Montana's biennial legislature next meets. Until then, visitors will have to be satisfied with a look at the Charles M. Russell mural of *Lewis and Clark Meeting Indians at Ross' Hole* in the House chamber, which is the only area open to the public. But don't feel too bad. Even the governor had to move his office. The renovation will attempt to bring some of the historic grandeur back that was lost in renovations made in the 1960s.

Situated on 14.1 acres, the building was designed by architects Charles Bell and John Kent in the late 1800s. It's decorated in the French Renaissance style with frescoes, stained glass, and murals. The dome, faced with copper, rises 165 feet. Inside are murals by noted Montana artists Charlie Russell, Edgar Paxson, and Ralph DeCamp. The grounds of the state capitol building in Helena are a designated state park, with the formal grounds and flower gardens visited by thousands of people each year (they will be open during the renovations).

The Montana Historical Society. 225 N. Roberts St. ☎ **800/243-9900** or 406/ 444-2694. www.his.mt.gov. Museum: Memorial Day–Labor Day, daily 8am–6pm; winter, Mon–Sat 8am–6pm. Library and archives: Mon–Fri 8am–5pm, some Sat.

The Montana Historical Society maintains a library and archives, as well as a museum, and publishes a quarterly magazine, *Montana, the Magazine of Western History.* The **Montana Homeland Gallery** displays the history of the occupation of Montana going back 11,500 years. On display are petroglyphs, dinosaur bones, and implements of the earliest Native Americans and first European settlers. Walls are adorned with calendars dating back to 1906, some of which have profit and loss calculations scribbled on them by their rancher-owners. An entire wall is covered with the *Fairy Alphabet,* an artistic creation of F. Y. Cory, a hard-working ranch wife near Canyon Ferry. Each letter of the alphabet is illustrated by hand-drawn renderings of fairies, babies, animals, and wildlife, and each has its own meaning.

The **Mackay Gallery** has a permanent display of original Charlie Russell masterpieces—more than 60 artworks, including oils, watercolors, sculptures, and Russell's famous illustrated letters—that showcase one of the West's most remarkable artists. The **Haynes Gallery** displays the work of Jay Haynes, a photographer who came west in 1876 with the Northern Pacific Railroad to photograph farms of the Red River Valley and Black Hills of the Dakota Territory. Haynes eventually produced more than 10,000 views of Yellowstone's features and structures, and created a tourist-coach business along the way.

Guided tours of the original **governor's mansion,** located at 304 N. Ewing, are also available through the society. This Queen Anne–style mansion with the distinctive checkerboard background was constructed in 1888 for entrepreneur William A. Chessman, who built it for his wife and two children. The state acquired the mansion in 1913 and governors resided here for half a century, during which time it lost much of its original historical flavor. However, restoration of the building began in 1969 with the support of the city. During summer, tours operate on the hour from noon to 5pm Tuesday to Sunday. After Labor Day, call for information on setting an appointment to view this magnificent home.

Cathedral of St. Helena. 530 N. Ewing. ☎ **406/442-5825.** Open to public, unless services are taking place; hours vary. Call to arrange a free tour.

The Cathedral of St. Helena was completed in 1924, modeled on a church in Cologne. Its beautiful twin 230-foot spires seem ready to soar heavenward on their own, filigreed and light. The Cathedral of St. Helena is decorated with magnificent Bavarian stained-glass windows, handcarved oak pews, hand-forged bronze light fixtures, and Carrara marble statues. At one time it was open to all and sundry who wandered by, but a sign now says, "Sadly, we are sometimes unable to leave the cathedral open when unattended." So if you want to see the inside, it is safest to call ahead. Masses are held here daily.

Holter Museum of Art. 12 E. Lawrence St. ☎ **406/442-6400.** www.holtermuseum.org. Admission by donation. June–Sept, Mon–Sat 10am–5pm, Sun noon–5pm; Oct–May, Tues–Fri 11:30am–5pm, Sat–Sun noon–5pm.

Considered one of the premier galleries in the state, the Holter displays artwork in 5,400 square feet and features 10 to 14 different shows each year, all of which display a diversity of media and styles. Specializing in contemporary Western art, the museum provides exhibition space for local as well as nationally prominent artists. The Holter is the home of the **Western Rendezvous of Art,** an annual summer exhibit spotlighting noted Western artists. The museum also runs an extensive summer arts education program for youngsters.

Gates of the Mountains Boat Tours. I-15 (Gates of the Mountains exit), 18 miles north of Helena (P.O. Box 478, Helena, MT 59624). ☎ **406/458-5241.** www.gatesofthemountains. org. $8.50 adults, $7.50 seniors, $5.50 children 4–17, free for children under 4. June–Sept; call for cruise schedule departures and returns.

Meriwether Lewis coined the name "Gates of the Mountains" while plying this portion of the Missouri with his party. At almost every bend in the waterway, the towering rock formations seemed to block their passage, only to magically open up as they drew closer. Visitors can have an experience similar to Lewis's through a boat tour of this scenic riverway on the *Pirogue,* the *Sacajawea II,* or the *Hilger Rose.* The 105-minute cruises take you through the mountain "gates" to a picnic area where wildlife photography opportunities abound. If you'd like, you can choose to return on a later boat and take a hike into the nearby Gates of the Mountains Wilderness Area or explore Native American pictographs on the limestone rocks. Mann Gulch, the setting of Norman Maclean's *Young Men and Fire,* and the site where 12 smokejumpers perished, is within hiking distance. Markers indicate where each of the men fell.

Spokane Bar Sapphire Mine & Gold Fever Rock Shop. 5360 Castles Dr., Helena, MT 59602. ☎ **406/227-8989** or 877/344-4367. www.crom.net/~gemking. Daily 9am–5pm; winter hours vary. From I-15, take York Rd. east to mile marker 8. Turn right on Hart Lane and left on Castles Rd.

If you've come to rockhound, this sapphire mine south of Hauser Lake is the place for you. With a plan for everyone—couples can dig all day for $52 plus concentrate (there's a five-bucket minimum)—this sapphire mine will get the entire family into the spirit of Montana's early pioneers. The mine, 150 feet below ancient river levels, is a good source of green-blue sapphires, the most common type found. The location yields sapphires, garnets, gold nuggets, and an occasional topaz. The record sapphire taken from here was 155 carats.

SHOPPING

Last Chance Gulch is a 4-block-long pedestrian mall. Though it is not exclusively a shopping area, the office buildings are liberally interspersed with boutiques, restaurants, pubs, and places for the kids to play. Informational kiosks are located in the center of this walking mall and at its north end. **Main News,** 9 N. Last Chance Gulch (☎ **406/442-6424**), is a tobacco shop with newspapers from various statewide and regional cities. It's located in the **Atlas Block,** one of a group of historically significant architectural structures in Last Chance Gulch. Helena's main areas were leveled several times in the last 125 years or so, once by earthquakes (in 1935) and several times by fire in the 19th century and again in 1928. The Atlas Block is carved with salamanders, in mythology impervious to fire. The **Upper Missouri Artists Gallery,** 25 S. Last Chance Gulch (☎ **406/457-8240**), is tucked in the back of a courtyard on the downtown walking mall. The gallery showcases Montanans' original art that includes hand-thrown pottery, pastels, wood-turned art, handcrafted jewelry, and a wide variety of oil and watercolor paintings. Just around the corner, at 19 S. Gulch Dr., is the **Ghost Art Gallery** (☎ **406/443-4536**), which features art on Western and nature themes. **Cobblestone Clothing,** 46 S. Last Chance Gulch, sells women's clothing with a modern Western theme (☎ **406/449-8684**).

Reeder's Alley is a quaint shopping area that has a distinctly European feel. Its brick streets are home to a tightly packed group of old mining shanties that have been converted into contemporary retail stores, though serious shoppers will find the pickings somewhat slim.

ESPECIALLY FOR KIDS

The Parrot Confectionery. 42 N. Last Chance Gulch. ☎ **406/442-1470.** Mon–Sat 9am–6pm.

Kids and adults alike will love this candy shop, established in 1922. The Parrot serves up its original cherry phosphates and caramel cashew sundaes from the soda fountain and beneath its charming collection of ceramic elephants. Family-owned, the Parrot has provided gourmet chocolate and candy to Helena for more than 75 years, and loyal customers attest that the place and its product haven't changed a bit. In addition to its Helena clientele, the Parrot supplies candy to chocoholics from nearly every state in the union. It's known for its signature parrot confection, chocolate-covered caramels, and many other candies. They also have a "secret recipe" chili for lunch.

WHERE TO STAY

The Barrister Bed-and-Breakfast. 416 N. Ewing, Helena, MT 59601. ☎ **800/823-1148** or 406/443-7330. Fax 406/442-7964. www.wtp.net/go/montana/sites/barrister.html. E-mail: barrister@rcisys.net. 5 units. A/C TV. $90–$125 double. Rates include full breakfast. AE, DC, DISC, MC, V. Pets accepted.

Located directly across the street from the cathedral, the Barrister is one of many elegant homes near the original governor's mansion. Built in 1874, it was renovated in 1992 and opened as a B&B in 1993. The rooms are large and nicely appointed, each with a private bathroom—though some are across the hall. The third floor is a two-bedroom apartment that rents for $125 per night but is usually leased on longer term, by the week or month. Many of the rooms have their own fireplaces, with stained glass windows and high ceilings. The common areas include a sun porch, den, TV room and library, and office.

Cavanaugh's Best Western Colonial Hotel. 2301 Colonial Dr. (just off I-15 at U.S. Hwy. 12), Helena, MT 59601. ☎ **800/422-1002** or 406/443-2100. Fax 406/449-8815. www.cavanaughs.com. 149 units. A/C TV TEL. From $89 double. AE, DC, DISC, MC, V.

This is a fairly upscale property, with a winding circular stairway to the second floor that you might expect Scarlett O'Hara to come sweeping down at any moment. It also has an ambitious new owner. But a lot about the place screams, "1955!" I don't think it's that old, but portions are showing signs of wear, like the carpets in the halls, for instance. But the rooms are huge for motel rooms, and the location right by the interstate is convenient for travelers. Some rooms also offer panoramic views of the valley and mountains beyond. The suites include king-size beds, refrigerators, microwaves, and the largest closets I've ever seen in a motel room. The hotel also features its own restaurant and lounge, as well as two swimming pools—one indoor and one outdoor.

Fairfield Inn of Helena. 2150 11th Ave., Helena, MT 59601. ☎ **800/228-2800** or 406/449-9944. Fax 406/449-9949. www.marriott.com/fairfieldinn. A/C TV TEL. $74–$80 double. AE, DC, DISC, MC, V.

This hotel run by Marriott is new, clean, and up to Marriott standards. The rooms are average size, and there is no restaurant or lounge on the premises, though a continental breakfast is available daily. There's also an indoor pool, whirlpool, and fitness center.

Jorgenson's Inn & Suites. 1714 11th Ave., Helena, MT 59601. ☎ **800/272-1770** or 406/442-1770. Fax 406/449-0155. 116 units. A/C TV TEL. $39–$98 double. AE, DC, DISC, MC, V.

Jorgenson's has been a Helena institution for more than 40 years, and the older residents, in particular, will send you to the restaurant next door for dinner (though I'm not going to). As you might expect in an older place, the rooms are a little smaller than those in some of the newer motels, but they all have data ports for the phones. Guests also have access to the fully equipped fitness center across the street. There's also a business center, a pool, and a free airport shuttle.

Park Plaza Hotel. 22 N. Last Chance Gulch, Helena, MT 59601. ☎ **800/332-2290** in Montana, or 406/443-2200. 71 units. A/C TV TEL. $75–$79 double. AE, DC, DISC, MC, V.

This seven-story hotel is on the pedestrian mall at Last Chance Gulch. It has undergone a number of changes in recent years, and in 1999 was seeing another renovation in the process of becoming a Holiday Inn. The rooms are nice, though, with over-stuffed chairs, desks, and double beds. JD's Lounge, a high-energy sports bar/dance hall that's the center of rock and roll activity in Helena, is just off the lobby.

⭐ **The Sanders.** 328 N. Ewing, Helena, MT 59601. ☎ **406/442-3309.** Fax 406/443-2361. www.sandersbb.com. E-mail: thefolks@sandersbb.com. 7 units. A/C TV TEL. $90–$112 double. Rates include full breakfast and afternoon refreshments. AE, DC, DISC, MC, V.

The Sanders is a lesson in Montana history all on its own. Built and owned by Wilbur Fisk Sanders in 1875, the B&B has been beautifully restored by Bobbi Uecker (no relation to former ballplayer Bob) and Rock Ringling (a fourth-generation descendant of the famous circus family). Sanders was Montana's first U.S. senator and made his reputation by vigorously prosecuting the infamous Plummer gang in Virginia City. The Uecker-Ringlings are only the third owners of the property, and they purchased it with nearly all of its furnishings, most brought in by Sanders himself. You will sleep on beds from 1875 and look at the same pictures that Sanders did. One was painted by his wife, an important Western suffragette in her day. Bobbi Uecker's enthusiasm shows in every detail, from the fine breakfasts where she's willing to accommodate every kind of dietary restriction, to the afternoon refreshments. My favorite accouterment was the elephant "bridle" marked with a big round disc reading "The Greatest Show on Earth."

CAMPING

Kim's Marina and RV Resort, 8015 Canyon Ferry Rd. (20 miles west of town), Helena, MT 59601 (☎ **406/475-3723**), has a complete resort facility that includes comfortable cabins situated on the lakefront. Canoes, deck boats, and paddleboats are for rent on a daily basis. You'll find 50 tent and 60 RV sites as well as tennis, volley-ball, horseshoes, and boat rentals. **The Lakeside Resort,** 11 miles east of Helena on York Road near Hauser Lake (☎ **406/443-3932**), is an RV park that is open year-round with 70 full hookups and an on-site bar, restaurant, beach, and picnic area. **The Canyon Ferry RV Park,** 750 Canyon Ferry Rd., Helena (☎ **406/475-3811**), has full hookups, a Laundromat, showers, and daily, weekly, or monthly rates. North of town 3 miles on Montana Avenue is the **Helena Campground and RV Park,** with green grass and shade, an all-you-can-eat breakfast, and an ice cream social in season. It's located at 5820 N. Montana Ave. (☎ **406/458-4714**).

For more primitive sites, the Bureau of Reclamation and Bureau of Land Management jointly run several campgrounds between Townsend in the south and Helena along U.S. 287 at Canyon Ferry Lake. From south to north, they are: **Indian Road Recreation Area** (1 mile north of Townsend on U.S. 287, milepost 75), **Silos** (7 miles north of Townsend on U.S. 2878, milepost 70), and **White Earth Campground** (13 miles north of Townsend on U.S. 287 to Winston). The Indian Road Recreation Area offers a fishing pond for children and visitors with disabilities.

WHERE TO DINE

Apart from the year-round eateries mentioned below, **The Hollows,** 26 N. Last Chance Gulch (☎ **406/443-2288**), serves breakfast and sandwiches daily during the summer. **Flickers Coffee House,** 101 N. Last Chance Gulch (☎ **406/443-5567**), is a nice place to sit in an overstuffed chair and have a cup of coffee.

The Marysville House. In Marysville, a 45-min. drive from Helena. Take U.S. 15 North to Exit 200, MT 279. Go north on MT 279 for 23 miles; turn left at the sign for Marysville for 7 miles to find this living ghost town. No phone. Meals from $10. No credit cards. Year-round Thurs–Sat; hours vary with the seasons. STEAKS/SEAFOOD.

Every Rocky Mountain state has a barely surviving ghost town that for some reason attracts the mountain cabin crowd and a steakhouse. Marysville, an 1870 gold mining town, once boasted a population of 4,000. And the Marysville House is the steakhouse at which they've all been eating. It is not as inaccessible as the directions suggest. The ski area is further up the road, and the dirt road is a good, smooth one. Located in what was once a train depot, the Marysville House serves steaks, lobster, and crab legs in a rustic setting that only enhances its romantic anonymity. The no-nonsense meals come with corn on the cob and beans. Guests have their choice of dining inside or out. And how's this for low-key Americana: Meals are served on paper plates, horseshoes can be found out back, and you can eat at a picnic table in the front yard.

Montana City Grill and Saloon. Montana City, 5 miles south of Helena on I-15. ☎ **406/449-8890.** Main courses $9–$20. AE, DC, DISC, MC, V. Sun–Thurs 11am–9pm, Fri–Sat 9am–10pm. STEAKS.

This is a nice, sunny place that specializes in beef, fish, chicken, pasta, and huckleberry ribs. The good but unimaginative food is served in a newly renovated dining room filled with woods and pastels. There's a pool table and the clearest big screen television I've ever seen in the saloon.

On Broadway. 106 Broadway. ☎ **406/443-1929.** Reservations not accepted. Main courses $10–$20. AE, DC, DISC, MC, V. Mon–Sat 5:30–10pm. ITALIAN.

Located in an upscale brick building near Last Chance Gulch, On Broadway is the place to go in Helena for good Italian food. It's dressed up like any other fern-laden bar/restaurant, but the food is anything but typical, with artful combinations of meats and vegetables, fresh herbs, and pasta highlighting a menu with Italian subtitles. A local favorite is the *Petti di Pollo alla Broadway*, a chicken breast topped with fresh mushrooms and cheese, then baked in a mornay sauce with mozzarella. The fish menu is the most imaginative, headed up by blackened tuna and oven-roasted salmon.

The Stonehouse. 120 Reeder's Alley. ☎ **406/449-2552.** Reservations recommended. Lunch $6; dinner $11–$17. AE, DC, DISC, MC, V. Sun–Thurs 11:30am–2pm and 5:30–9pm, Fri–Sat 5–10pm. STEAKS/SEAFOOD.

Within short walking distance of the shopping area on South Last Chance Gulch, the Stonehouse is a local favorite. In recent years it has received such awards as "Best Seafood," "Best Romantic Dinner," "Best Restaurant," and "Best Prime Rib." Your best bets are the evening specials, which include Nebraska corn-fed steaks and prime rib dinners, the latter of which are offered in 10- to 30-ounce servings and cost $13 to $25. Fresh seafood is flown in twice a week from Seattle, so the menu may include salmon, halibut, oysters, or shrimp scampi. The interior is divided into two rooms; the front is decorated in pinks and blues with seating at Early American-style tables with high-backed chairs. The back room is surrounded by a stone wall with an ersatz waterfall in front of a boring mountain mural.

The Wall Street Cafe. 62 S. Last Chance Gulch. ☎ **406/443-6215.** Breakfast and lunch $5–$7. Mon–Fri 7am–4pm, Sat 8am–3pm. COFFEE/SANDWICHES.

This small cafe is located at the end of the Last Chance Gulch pedestrian mall. It's a fine way to start the day, with pastry or some organically grown coffee. Lunches consist of sandwiches and salads. All the sandwiches at lunch are $5, and all the salads, $4, with daily soups and soup-salad-sandwich combos available. Artwork from local artists changes monthly.

Windbag Saloon. 19 S. Last Chance Gulch. ☎ **406/443-9669.** Reservations recommended. Lunch $3–$7; dinner $4–$15. AE, DISC, MC, V. Wed–Sun 5:30–9:30pm; off-season days and hours may vary. CONTEMPORARY AMERICAN.

Helena residents love this restaurant like you'd love an eccentric aunt: She's the most interesting relative you have and you always have a great time at her place. Who cares if she has a checkered past? So what if one of the cleanest and most respected bordellos in all of Montana once operated in the location where the restaurant now enjoys its own flourishing business? At least it's respectable, continuing in its tradition as a focal part of Helena's nightlife. Try one of a long list of microbrews in the meantime, or order something from the extensive, though mostly french-fried, collection of appetizers.

THE PERFORMING ARTS

Make it a point to visit the **Myrna Loy Center for the Performing Arts,** 15 N. Ewing St. (☎ **406/443-0287**). Formerly the Lewis and Clark County Jail, the Myrna Loy (named after one of Helena's most famous residents and a silver-screen legend) is a multidisciplinary cultural center of regional significance. Within its castlelike facade are a 40-seat cinema and a 200-seat performance hall, along with galleries that focus on regional art of all descriptions. The state-of-the-art facilities, where you can see the latest foreign films or attend one of the "Helena Presents" programs, are second to none in Montana.

3 Butte & Anaconda

Butte: 64 miles S of Helena; 120 miles SE of Missoula; 82 miles W of Bozeman; 150 miles NW of West Yellowstone

Butte may not be most people's idea of a vacation destination, but in many ways the town is the hidden soul of Montana. Butte's emergence in the 19th century as a hell-raising, wide-open mining town drew a lot of people to the state, including a variety of racial and ethnic groups that might not otherwise have contributed to the state's character. Butte has always been a strong union town in a state and region that disdain union activity. This union and socialist tradition from the rip-roaring days has made a lasting contribution to a strong progressive political tradition.

Butte used to be called "the richest hill on earth," for its production of copper, silver, and other precious metals. During the 1880s, Butte was the world's largest copper producer. In 1955, the world's richest hill became the beginning of one of the world's largest holes, the Berkeley Pit, which provided more cost-efficient open pit mining of copper. The pit expanded and swallowed up a lot of the town, like some voracious dragon. It is mostly closed now, filling with water, a giant clean-up problem now being dealt with by the federal Environmental Protection Agency.

But while Butte is proud of its rowdy past, it looks firmly to the future. It boasts Montana Tech, an arm of the University of Montana system. And full-time residents are flocking here for jobs in the city's emerging high tech industry.

If you can look past the signs of decline, Butte is full of rich history (very rich, in fact), colorful citizens, and a sort of blue-collar San Francisco-style charm. Physically, Butte is built along the sides of steep hills, which give it a cozy coastal-town feel.

Anaconda was the "company town," formed when copper king Marcus Daly extended his copper empire 24 miles west. The community was spared the name "Copperopolis."

ESSENTIALS

GETTING THERE   The **Bert Mooney Airport,** 111 Airport Rd. (☎ **406/ 494-3771**), is served by **Horizon** (☎ 800/547-9308), **Northwest** (☎ 800/ 225-25225), and **Skywest** (☎ 800/453-9417).

Travel Tip ──

When traveling to this part of the state, many folks decide to fly in to Salt Lake City, Utah. It's a 5.5-hour drive north through some spectacular country to get to this neck of the woods.

───

Butte is located right at the junction of Interstates 90 and 15. For **current road conditions in Butte and Anaconda,** call ☎ **800/266-7623;** call ☎ **406/449-5204** for **current weather information.**

The **Greyhound** station in Butte is located at 103 E. Front (☎ **406/723-3287**).

VISITOR INFORMATION   The **Visitors Center and Transportation Center,** 1000 George St., Butte, MT 59701-7901 (☎ **800/735-6814;** www.butteinfo.org) is located just off Exit 126 near the intersections of I-15 and I-90. The center is a user-friendly building just off the freeway, close to a wetlands area where you can take a breather from driving while watching wild ducks, geese, and muskrats go about their business.

The **Anaconda Chamber of Commerce,** 306 E. Park, Anaconda, MT 59711 (☎ **406/563-2400**), can give you information on Butte's sister city. Both Butte and Anaconda fall into **Travel Montana's Gold West Country,** 1155 Main, Deer Lodge, MT 59722 (☎ **406/846-1943**), where information requests yield brochures devoted to area attractions and driving tours.

GETTING AROUND   Car-rental agents in Butte include **Avis** (☎ 406/ 494-3131), **Budget** (☎ 406/494-7573), **Enterprise** (☎ 406/494-1900), **Hertz** (☎ 406/782-1054), and **Payless** (☎ 406/723-4366).

The **Butte-Silver Bow Transit System** city buses run from 7am to 5:45pm Monday to Friday; for information on fares and stops, call ☎ **406/723-8262. City Taxi** is located at 3 S. Main (☎ **406/723-6511**).

SPECIAL EVENTS   One of the largest immigrant groups to settle in Butte was the Irish. Some of Butte's wide-open wildness returns on St. Patrick's Day, when this mining museum of a town turns into a miniature Dublin each March 17 in one of the biggest American St. Patrick's Day celebrations outside of New York City. If you happen to be of Finnish extraction, or simply require a more obscure reason to party in Butte, you may want to arrive a few days earlier, when the city takes time off to honor St. Urho, patron saint who reputedly drove grasshoppers from Finland. Contact the **Visitor Center** (☎ 800/735-6814) for the dates and times of these activities.

GETTING OUTSIDE

Lost Creek State Park, a few miles outside of Anaconda, is a great place to camp or hike or simply look around. At the and of the road into the park, an asphalt path— about 125 yards long—will take you to Lost Creek Falls, which tumble over a 50-foot drop. There are also mountain goat and bighorn sheep in residence. Several hiking trails lead off from the road. Among the most interesting things here are not the living things, but the rocks. Exposed on the tops of some cliffs is the 1.3-billion-year-old Newman Formation, a Precambrian rock that's among the oldest exposed rocks in the lower 48 states. This is a primitive park, without services (and without charge). There are 25 campsites, suitable mostly for tents and car campers. Drive 1½ miles east of Anaconda on MT 1, then 2 miles north on Secondary 273, then 6 miles west.

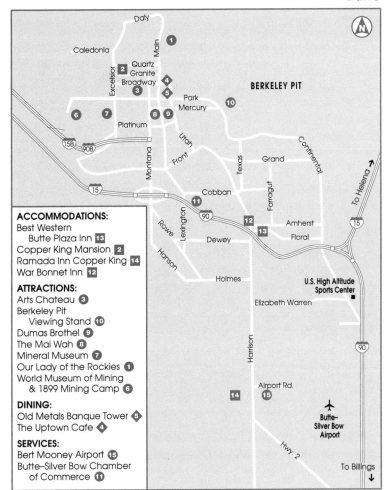

ACCOMMODATIONS:
Best Western
    Butte Plaza Inn 13
Copper King Mansion 2
Ramada Inn Copper King 14
War Bonnet Inn 12

ATTRACTIONS:
Arts Chateau 3
Berkeley Pit
    Viewing Stand 10
Dumas Brothel 9
The Mai Wah 8
Mineral Museum 7
Our Lady of the Rockies 1
World Museum of Mining
    & 1899 Mining Camp 6

DINING:
Old Metals Banque Tower 5
The Uptown Cafe 4

SERVICES:
Bert Mooney Airport 15
Butte–Silver Bow Chamber
    of Commerce 11

GOLF

The ✪ **Old Works,** 1205 Pizzini Way, Anaconda (☎ **406/563-5989**), is a golf course, but it is also a work of art. This is your tax dollars at work, and you can feel good about it. The course is built on a Superfund site that has been a blight on the landscape since 1884, when the upper works began to process 500 tons of copper ore daily under Marcus Daly's voracious eye. By 1887 the lower works were necessary because of the demand. The Old Works closed in 1902, when the new Washoe Smelter—the big tower you can see from anywhere in the valley—took over all the processing. The golf course was designed by Jack Nicklaus, a tough, fair, and challenging layout that even eight handicappers are willing to play from the white tees. The black sand traps, the old processing works, the vast forbidding black tailings piles, are all worked beautifully into the layout of the course. This is one of the finest courses, not just in Montana, but in America. $36 for 18 holes, $48 with cart, per person. To reach the course, take Commercial Street to N. Cedar Street, turn north, then east (right) on Pizzini Way.

Butte Touring Tips

The **Old No. 1 trolley tour** leaves from the Butte Visitor Center for a 1½-hour tour of the city's key attractions. Stops include the Berkeley Pit tunnel, where you'll have at least 10 minutes to explore the mine shaft, and the World Museum of Mining. Drivers are chosen for their knowledge of the town's history.

There's also an 18-hole course at nearby **Fairmont Hot Springs** (see "Where to Stay," later in this chapter). **Highland View Golf Course** (☎ 406/494-7900), at Stodden Park in Butte, has two separate nine-hole courses, one of which is a par 3.

ROCK CLIMBING

Spire Rock and the **Humbug Spires** are the two most popular routes for rock climbers. In Butte, **Pipestone Mountaineering,** at 829 S. Montana St. (☎ 406/782-4994), can give you leads on the local climbing scene.

ROCKHOUNDING

Within the Continental Divide east of Butte and its mountains to the south, diligent rockhounders can find smoky quartz, amethyst, epidote, and tourmalines. Ask the curator at the Mineral Museum (see "Seeing the Sights") for leads on local hot spots. The Butte Mineral and Gem Club has mining claims on Crystal Park 20 miles southwest of Wise River that are free and open to the public.

SKIING

In addition to **Discovery Basin,** you're within range of **Maverick Mountain** (see section 4, "Dillon & the Big Hole," later in this chapter).

Discovery Basin. 45 miles west of Butte on MT 1, off I-90 (P.O. Box 221, Anaconda, MT 59711). ☎ **406/563-2184.** Fax 406/563-7036. E-mail: peter@skidiscovery.com. Lift tickets $24 adults, $12 children 12 and younger and seniors; half-day $18 beginning at 12:30pm. Inquire about special group rates. AE, DC, DISC, MC, V.

This is another one of those Montana ski resorts that would fall somewhere in the middle if you made a list ranking them for nearly any category. The vertical drop isn't the longest, but it's not the shortest, either. If you are in the area, you'll find that the runs on the mountain are equal parts beginner, intermediate, and expert. Five kilometers of groomed trails will satisfy the Nordic skier or you can blaze your own trail through untracked snow.

While the scenery equals or exceeds that of other areas in the state, the real plus here is the resort's proximity to Fairmont Hot Springs, a 4-season facility where soaking and swimming are year-round favorites (see "Where to Stay," later in this chapter). Ski rentals and instruction are available (private lessons are $25 per hour) as well as cafeteria-style food.

There are no hotels at the ski area; the nearest accommodations are at Fairmont Hot Springs or in Butte and Anaconda.

SNOWMOBILING

The Anaconda Snowmobile Club (☎ 406/563-8182) can point you to the nearest trail or take you on a guided tour, most of which explore the vicinity of Georgetown Lake. The four major trail systems include Carp Ridge, which terminates at the Anaconda-Pintler Wilderness boundary; Echo Lake, at the midpoint of Georgetown Lake and Discovery Basin Ski area; Peterson Meadows, a popular spot for cookouts and picnics; and Red Lion Racetrack Lake, with ridgetop views of surrounding peaks.

SEEING THE SIGHTS

For information on the **Pintler Scenic Route,** a driving tour that begins in Butte, see section 1 of this chapter.

The Berkeley Pit is rumored to be visible—along with the Great Wall of China—from the moon. It is located just off Continental Drive in Butte. Starting in 1955, nearly 1.5 billion tons of material were removed from the pit before mining ceased in 1982—including more than 290 million tons of copper ore. A short walk through a dimly lit tunnel (fully accessible for those with disabilities) takes you to an observation deck where you can view the pit, which is currently filling with groundwater at a rate of about 7 million gallons per day. To keep birds from landing on the polluted water, they sometimes use flares, firecrackers or even guys in boats waving their arms. The water flows through several thousand miles of underground pit tunnels through the mineralized zones, and becomes heavily acidic. The viewing stand is at the east end of Mercury Street in the heart of downtown. The pit is open to the public during daylight hours from March through November.

The 585-foot **Anaconda Smelter Stack,** just off MT 1, on the outskirts of Anaconda, is one of the tallest standing brick structures in the world and is designated a Montana State Park, though there is no public access. Once considered the largest copper-smelting stack in the entire world, all 58 stories of the desolate shaft rise starkly to meet the Montana sky. It is broad enough around the top to drive a six-horse team and wagon. Or so they say.

Our Lady of the Rockies. 434 N. Main, Butte (gift shop and information center). ☎ **800/800-5239** or 406/782-1221. Free admission. Summer, Mon–Sat 9am–5pm, Sun 10am–5pm; winter, limited hours. Tours depart daily during summer from the Butte Plaza Mall, 3100 Harrison Ave., for $10 adults, $9 children 13–17, $5 children 5–12, and free for children under 5. For tour reservations call ☎ **406/494-2656.**

When you look up to the eastern heights above Butte, you'll see the large white statue of Our Lady of the Rockies in a notch at the top of a hill. The statue was built "in the likeness of Mary, Mother of Jesus." But the statue is advertised as non-denominational and dedicated to women everywhere, especially mothers. Private cars are not allowed up to the site, but bus tours leave the Butte Plaza Mall at 3100 Harrison Ave. If you don't have time for a tour, but are interested in learning more about Our Lady of the Rockies, visit the information center and gift shop for a look at a panoramic mural of the statue. There is also a video detailing the construction: Four hundred tons of concrete were used just for the statue's base.

✪ **Arts Chateau.** 321 W. Broadway, Butte. ☎ **406/723-7600.** www.artschateau.org. $6 family, $3 adults, $2.50 AAA members, $2 seniors, $1 children 16 and under. Summer: Tues–Sat 10am–5pm, Sun noon–5pm; winter: Tues–Sat 11am–4pm. Tours available.

Anaconda Touring Tips

You can take the **Vintage Bus Tour of Historic Anaconda** from the Chamber of Commerce visitor center, 306 E. Park (☎ **406/563-2400**), Monday through Saturday at 10am and 2pm. The cost is $4 adults, $1.50 children. The tour includes a stop and inside tour of the fabulous Washoe Theater, which usually is only open at 8pm. The chamber also has a historic walking tour brochure for $2, but you won't see the inside of the Washoe unless you get lucky (see below).

Built in 1898 for Charles Clark, son of copper king William A. Clark, the Butte-Silver Bow Arts Chateau is an impressively restored mansion and art gallery. Stained-glass windows, beveled glass, ornate wrought iron, and intricately detailed woodwork contribute to the mansion's turn-of-the-century elegance. The home's magnificent staircase leads to a second-story museum, filled with period furniture, and the gallery, which houses traveling displays by Montana artists in a much more modern setting. The two galleries have exhibits that change every 6 weeks. Other highlights include the 4th-floor ballroom, which replicates a grand hunting lodge, and the first-floor gift shop, with hundreds of "Made in Montana" items for sale.

World Museum of Mining & 1899 Mining Camp. Montana Tech Campus. ☎ **406/723-7211.** $4 adults, free for children under 12. Summer, daily 9am–9pm; spring and fall, limited hours. Go uphill to the campus of Montana Tech, past the statue of Marcus Daly, where a sign in the middle of the street will direct you to the museum.

This popular museum is set up as the 1899 Hellroarin' Gulch mining town. It's on the site of the Orphan Girl mine which, though not a blockbuster by Butte standards, managed to produce 7.6 million ounces of silver, along with lead and zinc. A good way to get an overview of the museum is to ride the Orphan Girl Express, a three-car train pulled by an underground trammer engine. The ride will explain the history of mining and of Butte. The mining town is set up with typical businesses and buildings of the mining era here, with explanations of each of their functions in the community. There's also a hard rock mining hall with tools of the trade and examples of types of framing timbers used underground.

Mineral Museum. Montana Tech Campus (take Park St. to the Montana Tech Campus and follow the signs to the museum). ☎ **406/496-4414.** Free admission. Summer, daily 9am–6pm; after Labor Day and before Memorial Day, Mon–Fri 9am–4pm; May, Sept, and Oct, Sat–Sun 1–5pm.

The mineral museum displays only a percentage of the mineral specimens that belong to Montana Tech's Mineral Museum, though that still makes for a pretty impressive mineral display. The explanation of the minerals consists entirely of their identification and place of origin. One display features a comprehensive display of fluorescent minerals, starkly illuminated by ultraviolet lights. One of the area's most exciting discoveries, a 27.5-ounce gold nugget found in the Highland Mountains south of Butte, is also on display.

Dumas Brothel. 45 E. Mercury St., Butte. ☎ **406/723-6128.** Tours $3.50. Daily 9am–5pm.

Opened in 1890 as a "parlor house," the Dumas was once at the heart of Butte's red-light district. It was the city's longest-running house of prostitution, closing in 1982. Under the guidance of Norma Jean Almodovar, a former Los Angeles policewoman, and later a call girl in Beverly Hills, the Dumas Brothel is being turned into a museum of prostitution. Almodovar says that when the long-closed rooms in the basement were opened, they revealed "intact time capsules"—cigarette packs, liquor bottles, playing cards, and a rare White Cross model no. 26 metal vibrator, made in the pre-WWI era. While Almodovar's project has received the unlikely support of the Butte Chamber of Commerce, it has not been universally applauded.

The Mai Wah. 17 W. Mercury St., Butte. ☎ **406/494-5595.** Minimal admission fee, free for children. Summer only, Tues–Sat 1–3pm.

Adjacent to China Alley, the Mai Wah and Wah Chong Tai buildings stand as tributes to Butte's early Asian population. With a first-floor mercantile and second-floor noodle parlor, the Mai Wah provided a segment of the city's ethnic community with jobs after the mines were exhausted. Today the buildings house exhibits and memorabilia honoring the rich Asian history of the area.

✪ **Washoe Theater.** 305 Main St., Anaconda. ☎ **406/563-6161.** Tickets $4 adults, $2 children 11 and under. Fri–Tues, open 8pm; Wed and Thurs, 7pm.

The Washoe shares the distinction with New York City's Radio City Music Hall of being the last two theaters done in the art deco style. I've been in both, and the Washoe is the more impressive. The brick exterior is unimpressive, and when you see it you'll wonder what all the fuss is about. But inside, this is a Movie Palace with a capital P (and a capital M, I guess). It's a work of art in cerulean, salmon, beige, and yellow, with a fabulous curtain. If you arrive at midday, the theater is usually closed. It is still a working movie theater, and doesn't open until eight. But if owner Jerry Lussy is there, he'll turn on the lights and let you look around. Or you can take the Chamber of Commerce tour (see above).

WHERE TO STAY

Best Western Butte Plaza Inn. 2900 Harrison Ave., Butte, MT 59701. ☎ **800/543-5814** or 406/494-3500. Fax 406/494-7611. www.bestwestern.com/butteplazainn. E-mail: butteplazainn@in-tch.com. 134 units. A/C TV TEL. $79–$89 double. AE, CB, DC, DISC, MC, V. Pets accepted, $50 deposit.

This property is the best motel in the area because of its facilities, services, restaurants, and location next to the freeway. Rooms are small but quiet and clean, all with either king- or queen-size beds, with a data port on all the phones. The European breakfast buffet, included in the room price, includes thinly sliced meats and cheeses, fruits, muffins, hot or cold cereals, and juices and coffee. Next door, **Perkins Family Restaurant** is open 24 hours a day and serves traditional family fare. **Hops** is a pub and casino decorated in the style of an English pub and accented with dark cherry wood. The recreation area includes an indoor pool, sauna, steam room, whirlpool, and fitness center.

✪ **Copper King Mansion.** 219 W. Granite St., Butte, MT 59701. ☎ **406/782-7580.** 5 units (2 with private bathrooms). $65–$95 double. AE, DISC, MC, V.

This huge home was built for William Clark in 1888 for $260,000. There are 30 rooms on three floors. It is a lush "modern Elizabethan" style which Clark is said to have favored. The home is privately owned, but tours are offered for $5. The intricate woodwork is remarkable and the owners have collected a large number of opulent furniture from the period to furnish it. There are even a few original pieces from the period of Clark's ownership. In the third-floor ballroom, there's an 825-pipe Estey organ as well as a private collection of clothing and memorabilia dating back to the late 1800s; a small chapel, complete with the stations of the cross, is discreetly located to the side.

In addition to being a lavishly restored period mansion, the house is a bed-and-breakfast. All the rooms but one are very large—the butler's room is seldom rented out—and beautifully furnished. There are parquet floors downstairs, and the octagon-shaped reception room, the billiard room, and the library all reflect Clark's love of luxury.

Antique lamps and chandeliers, ornate frescoed ceilings, and etched amber transoms complement the rooms' original furniture, including two matching African mahogany sleigh beds. If you stay at the B&B, you can sleep in the copper king's room, but you have to get up early. The tours start at 9 am and run until 5, when the mansion is closed to the public so that the night's guests can be admitted.

Fairmont Hot Springs Resort. 1500 Fairmont Rd., Fairmont, MT 59711. ☎ **800/ 332-3272** or 406/797-3241. www.fairmontmontana.com. E-mail: fairmontmt@aol.com. 158 units. A/C TV TEL. $109–$299 double. AE, CB, DC, DISC, MC, V.

Fairmont Hot Springs is an oasis between Bozeman and Missoula. It's a great place for families, with a huge water slide and pool, a golf course, horses, tennis, and cross-country skiing in the winter. Plus, of course, hot springs. The ski area Discovery Basin is only about 30 minutes away. The regular rooms are a little small, but they all have balconies, and the suites are as large as one could want. By resort standards, the cost is modest.

Ramada Inn Copper King. 4655 Harrison Ave. S., Butte, MT 59701. ☎ **800/332-8600** or 406/494-6666. 150 units. A/C TV TEL. $60–$70 double. Senior rates and family packages available. AE, CB, DC, DISC, MC, V.

This is a very nice motel property in the rapidly fading Ramada franchise. The exterior brick work provides a nice entrance, and the rooms are large and quiet, though a little sparsely furnished. There's a pool, hot tub, and guest laundry. The dome located in the back of the building is the city's only indoor tennis facility. The Savoy Dining Room prepares slow-cooked beef ribs in a subdued atmosphere.

War Bonnet Inn. 2100 Cornell, Butte, MT 59701. ☎ **800/423-1421** in Montana, 800/443-1806 elsewhere in the U.S., or 406/494-7800. Fax 406/494-2875. www.wbibutte. com. E-mail: warbonnet@wbibutte.com. 134 units. A/C TV TEL. $56–$89 double. AE, DC, DISC, MC, V. Pets accepted, $8 per night.

The War Bonnet is a good choice for families, with the largest rooms in town, and a very gracious staff. It has room service, which is fairly unusual in Montana motels. Its location next door to Father Sheehan City Park, with baseball diamonds, tennis courts, and a jogging track, is a plus, along with the dining room, the Apache. The hotel has an indoor pool, a sauna, and a hot tub.

WHERE TO DINE

Butte's ethnic tradition is most evident in its food, with pasties (pronounced "PASS-tees," or "PAH-stees" if you're British) ranking high on the list. If you've never tried one of these Cornish meat-filled pastries, you're in for a treat. Purveyed at nearly every eating establishment in the city, pasties are an essential part of the Butte experience.

Jim and Clara's. 311 E. Park, Ancaonda, MT 59711. ☎ **406/563-9963** or 406/563-2311. Reservations recommended Thurs–Sat. Main courses $9–$12. AE, MC, V. Mon–Sat 5pm until the last diner leaves. STEAKS/SEAFOOD.

This is a classic Montana steak place, with black Naugahyde booths and steaks that are too big to finish in one sitting. Thursday nights, you can get the large T-bone for $13. You also get the salad bar, spaghetti, and potato (that's not "spaghetti or potato"). One of the most popular dishes is the gourmet seafood plate for $30, which includes a small lobster tail, crab legs, and scallops. There's also an extensive menu for seniors and kids (without such large appetites) with items that run from $8 to $12. I thought the food was great, and all my friends thought so, too. (But how many naugas died to provide those booths?)

Old Metals Banque Tower. 8 W. Park (at Main). ☎ **406/723-6160.** Reservations recommended, especially on weekends. Lunch $4–$15; dinner $6–$15. DISC, MC, V. Call for days and hours; at press time, they were due to change. MEXICAN.

When restoration began on this deteriorated downtown building in 1989, original marble, African mahogany, solid copper window frames, and an intricate 22-inch vaulted plaster ceiling were discovered and a fine dining establishment was born. Built in 1898 to house the State Savings Bank by Marcus Daly and designed by famous turn-of-the-century architect Cass Gilbert, the Old Metals Banque Tower is today best known for the excellent food found inside its doors. An elegant, early-San Francisco atmosphere pervades the Old Metals Banque. It is a charming place to dine, though you'd never realize it's known locally for its Mexican food. Though you'll find a selection of meats on the menu, including steaks and seafood, the emphasis is on "clean" foods and low-fat items. The chef caters to special needs and will prepare food to order if the ingredients are on hand. Espresso and microbrews are also served.

✪ **The Uptown Cafe.** 47 E. Broadway. ☎ **406/723-4735.** www.montana.com/uptown. Reservations recommended. Lunch $3–$7; dinner $7–$25. AE, DISC, MC, V. Mon–Fri 11am–2pm and Mon–Sat from 5pm. CONTINENTAL.

The Uptown Cafe is a white-tablecloth restaurant in a no-tablecloth town. Despite the fact that the environment is casual and unpretentious, the restaurant continues to present five-course meals built around halibut (flown in fresh from Alaska) and Montana beef. The favorite starter is Clams Maison, succulent clams, crab, and artichokes prepared in white wine and butter. Other choices include soup—gazpacho if you're lucky—several types of salads, a pasta dish, and the main course. It makes you wonder if this is really Butte. During summer months, the cafe has an early-bird special: cheese ravioli, chicken dishes, or curried pork, served with a Caesar salad and French bread for $8.50—that's the best deal in Montana.

A SIDE TRIP TO DEER LODGE

Deer Lodge is home to Montana's state prison, which isn't ordinarily a recommendation for a tourist destination. And we won't recommend any places to stay, because you probably won't want to spend the night. But there are a collection of museums here that make Deer Lodge worth a morning's stop—especially if you're a car buff or a fan of ranching life.

As you enter Deer Lodge from the west on 275, you'll pass the **Grant-Kohrs Ranch National Historic Site,** another of the National Park Service's marvelous facilities. The ranch is set up to demonstrate the history and traditions of ranch life in the West. The ranch itself was founded in the late 1850s when Johnny Grant, a Canadian trader, moved here, eventually building up a herd of 2,000 cattle. He worked it only for a few years, then sold it to Conrad Kohrs. The ranch was scattered over Montana, Idaho, and Colorado, comprising more than 10 million acres, 32,000 of which are in this Deer Lodge section. It includes 89 structures, 23,000 artifacts, and a 1,500-acre cultural landscape maintained as a small-scale ranch. There are a series of farm buildings, including a bunk house and thoroughbred horse barns, and some Belgian draft horses on the property, and occasional living history presentations. The cost is $4 a car or $2 per person (☎ 406/846-3388). Open to the public daily except on Thanksgiving, Christmas, and New Year's Day.

Gold was discovered near Deer Lodge in 1862, an early precursor of the gold rush that reached full bloom in the discoveries at Bannack and Virginia City. One of the consequences of this gold rush is a little further downtown, the castle-like **Old Montana Prison,** at 1106 Main St., Deer Lodge, MT 59722 (☎ **406/846-3111**). The thievery and lawlessness that prevailed during the gold rush was initially dealt with by vigilantes, but the need for a prison was eventually solved by the construction of this prison, which took in its first prisoner in 1871. It was used until 1979, when another facility was built about 5 miles from here.

You can take a self-guided tour of the prison. Cell blocks, maximum security areas, crenelated guard towers, and the towering arches of the "Sally Port" gate are the attractions here, as well as a tribute to officers killed in the line of duty at the **Montana Law Enforcement Museum.** The Old Prison and the Law Enforcement Museum are only two of a collection of museums in Deer Lodge, which are all covered under one admission fee ($7.95). The prison complex also houses the **Old Prison Auto Museum,** the **Powell County Museum, The Frontier Montana Museum,** and **Yesterday's Playthings.** The museum complex is open to the public year-round. Summer hours: daily, Memorial Day to Labor Day, 8am to 9pm; winter hours, Sunday to Tuesday noon to 4pm, Wednesday to Saturday 10am to 4pm. Extended hours in April, 8:30am to 5:30pm.

The **Old Prison Auto Museum** currently houses more than 100 exquisitely restored automobiles—mostly Fords, but also a number of others. You can see a Model A Snowmobile, a World War II Ford Jeep, and a "Bootleggers Special" Lincoln, along with the infamous Edsel. There is also a collection of Mustangs, and an unusual Ford Fairlane with a retractable hard top.

The **Frontier Montana Museum** has a collection of the tools that were used to win the West. There is a nice exhibit on Colt "peacemakers" and their effect on the keeping of the peace. There are also saddles, spurs, and a saloon set-up.

The vast weapons collection at the **Powell County Museum,** 1193 Main St. (☎ **406/846-3294**) includes long guns and handguns from 1776 to 1956, as well as vintage jukeboxes and coin-operated slot machines. The museum is open Memorial Day to Labor Day, noon to 5pm, and is closed in winter.

Yesterday's Playthings, 1017 Main St. (☎ **406/846-1480**), is a doll and toy museum. The collection of Genevieve Hostetter is displayed here, with dolls of all descriptions: artistic, ethnic, advertising, and Native American. The collection also features dollhouses, toys, and trains, and can be viewed from Memorial Day to Labor Day, 9am to 5pm; closed in winter.

For additional information on these and other activities in Deer Lodge, contact the **Powell County Chamber of Commerce,** 1171 Main St., Deer Lodge, MT 59722 (☎ **406/846-2094**), or **Gold West Country,** 1155 Main St., Deer Lodge, MT 59722 (☎ **406/846-1943**).

4 Dillon & the Big Hole

Dillon: 65 miles S of Butte; 141 miles N of Idaho Falls, Idaho

In early Western parlance, a "hole" was a valley surrounded by steep mountains. And Big Hole is, well, a big "hole," in this old sense of a valley. It is a vast expanse of hay meadows, sagebrush flats, and ranch land ringed by towering mountains in the distance. These hay meadows have also given the Big Hole its nickname of the "valley of 10,000 haystacks," which may be a rare case of Rocky Mountain understatement.

But while there are lots of haystacks, there aren't many people. This region is the least densely populated in Western Montana. Beaverhead County, which is as large as Connecticut and Rhode Island combined, has only about 8,000 residents, and most of those live in Dillon, the county's largest town.

Dillon is an agricultural town, still dependent on local farmers and ranchers rather than tourism or industry. The population jumps from 5,000 to 15,000 to 20,000 people each year around Labor Day during the event known as **"Montana's Biggest Weekend."** Among the draws are a county fair, which is wrapped around a PRCA Rodeo that draws some of Montana and Wyoming's best cowboys, as well as live musical entertainment. If you plan on attending, book a room at least 3 months in advance.

The scenic loop that takes you around this valley is one of the state's more popular driving tours, and is described in section 1 of this chapter.

ESSENTIALS

GETTING THERE   **The Dillon Airport** is located at 2400 Airport Rd. with paved runways for light planes. See Butte and Anaconda "Essentials," earlier in this chapter, for information on the closest airport to the Big Hole Valley for commercial flights, car rentals, Amtrak service, and bus schedules. Dillon is located on I-15, about 67 miles south of Butte and 78 miles from Anaconda.

Since this area is a popular destination for snowmobilers, visitors are encouraged to call the **avalanche advisory** (☎ 406/587-6981) before setting out on a sledding trip. For **current road conditions** in the Big Hole Valley, call ☎ 800/332-6171 or 406/449-5204 for **current weather information.**

VISITOR INFORMATION   The **Dillon Visitor Information Center** (Beaverhead Chamber of Commerce) is located in the Old Union Pacific Railroad at 125 S. Montana St., Dillon, MT 59725 (☎ 406/683-5511). You can also contact **Gold West Country,** 1155 Main St., Deer Lodge, MT 59722 (☎ 406/846-1943), for information on the entire Big Hole Valley.

GETTING OUTSIDE

Beaverhead County has several natural hot springs, including **Jackson Hot Springs Lodge** (see "Where to Stay," later in this section), and **Elkhorn Hot Springs,** which is located about 10 miles off Route 278 on a gravel road. Go west of Dillon on 278 about 30 miles, then turn north toward Polaris at the sign. Follow the road through Polaris to Elkhorn Hot Springs, about 5 miles further. These waters provide a therapeutic complement to various winter activities, most notably snowmobiling, downhill skiing, and cross-country skiing.

OUTFITTERS & ORGANIZED TRIPS

Bad Beaver Bikes, Skis, and Tours at 25 E. Helena, Dillon (☎ 406/683-9292) is a full-service facility that coordinates forays into the Beaverhead National Forest with customized mountain-biking trips. All trips include meals and transportation to and from the ride site, and multi-day trips include lodging. Tour rates begin at $80 per person for a 1-day outing and range upwards from $150 per person/day for multi-day tours. A second full-service shop with the same facilities is now open at 312A W. Main St., Ennis, MT 59759 (☎ 406/682-5291). **Dillon's Backcountry Bike and Boards,** 35 E. Bannack (☎ 406/683-9696), rents and sells mountain bikes and cruising bikes.

Montana High Country Tours, 1036 E. Reeder, Dillon (☎ 406/683-4920; www.mhct.com; e-mail: montana@mhct.com), is operated by a sixth-generation Montanan. The company offers year-round guiding services, including fly-fishing, horseback riding, big-game hunting, and snowmobiling. Whether you're a sportsman looking to bag that elusive elk or a family longing for some quality time together, Russ Kipp has plenty of experience in arranging a unique outdoor adventure. His most popular trips center around southwest Montana's classic trout streams, picturesque limestone canyons, and stunning mountain ranges. Prices range from $625 for a 3-day/4-night snowmobiling package that includes sled (with fuel), lodging, meals, insurance, and equipment to $2,750 for a 5-day bighorn sheep-hunting trip including meals, lodging, and pack.

FISHING

The Big Hole, Beaverhead, and Poindexter Rivers are all within easy reach of Dillon, and Jefferson is only half an hour away by car. The fishing season begins early in the year when other streams may still be clearing, and extends into October. Big Hole fishermen can find several trout species, including the eastern brook, German brown, and golden. The **Clark Canyon Reservoir** provides good fishing for rainbow trout. Arctic grayling, ling, and whitefish also populate the waters of the Big Hole Valley. **The Beaverhead-Deerlodge National Forest,** 420 Barrett St., Dillon, MT 59725 (☎ **406/683-3900**) can provide you with a free "Lake and Fish Directory" covering all the waters in the forest. If you want to stay at a fishing lodge, check out **Craig Fellin's Big Hole River Outfitters** (see "Where to Stay," below).

For licenses, equipment, and advice on hot spots, check with the locals in Dillon at **Frontier Anglers,** 680 N. Montana (☎ **406/683-5276**). You can arrange a trip on any of the local rivers with **Tom Smith's Backcountry Angler,** 426 S. Atlantic St., Dillon, MT 59725 ☎ **406/683-3462.** Smith has been guiding in Montana since 1983, and in the winter he guides fishing trips in the Florida Keys. In Twin Bridges (just up MT 41), your best bet for fishing equipment and outfitting services is the **Four Rivers Fishing Co.,** 205 S. Main (☎ **800/BRN-TROUT**). Aficionados of the fishing world should stop at the **R.L. Winston Rod Co.,** also in Twin Bridges, at 500 S. Main (☎ **406/684-5674;** www.winstonrods.com), for a look at some of the finest fly rods in the world. Tours of the museum are given each weekday at 2pm, where you can learn what makes a great fly rod. Or if you're in the market, you can buy a rod for, say, $750.

HIKING

Hike along the **Continental Divide National Scenic Trail** in the **Anaconda-Pintler Wilderness** for interesting geologic discoveries, fabulous scenery, and views of wildlife: elk, moose, mule deer, antelope, and even black bears are all indigenous to the region. Covering parts of the Bitterroot and Beaverhead-Deerlodge National Forests, this 158,500-acre wilderness spans 40 miles on the Continental Divide over four counties. Highways with access to the area are U.S. 93 on the west, MT 38 and MT 1 from the north, and MT 43 from the east and south. The **Wise River Ranger District,** Box 100, Wise River, MT 59762 (☎ **406/832-3178**), can direct you to the area's most traveled trails. You can also obtain a *Recreation Directory for the Beaverhead-Deerlodge National Forest,* which describes many of the trails on the forest. The guide is available for free from **Beaverhead-Deerlodge National Forest,** 420 Barrett St., Dillon, MT 59725 (☎ **406/683-3900**).

HORSEBACK RIDING

Diamond Hitch Outfitters, 3405 Ten Mile Rd., Dillon, MT 59725 (☎ **800/ 368-5494**), offers 2-hour rides, half-day trips, and full-day trips in the Pioneer Mountains. As an alternative, evening horseback rides include a campfire cookout. More adventurous overnight and extended, backcountry rides are also available. Rates range from $25 per hour to $700 for a 5-day trip.

SKIING

In addition to **Maverick Mountain,** you're pretty close to **Lost Trail Powder Mountain.** See "A Detour into the Bitterroot Valley" in chapter 5 for complete details.

Maverick Mountain. Maverick Mountain Rd. (P.O. Box 475), Polaris, MT 59746. ☎ **406/834-3454.** Lift tickets $18 adults, $11 children 6–12, free for children 5 and under. Late Nov to early Apr, Thurs–Sun and holidays 9:30am–4:30pm. Take MT 287 west off U.S. Hwy. 15 to the Polaris Rd. for 13 miles.

Located in the Beaverhead National Forest, 35 miles west of Dillon, Maverick Mountain is a small area that attracts mostly local skiers. It has 18 runs with 2,000 vertical feet of skiing. It remains uncrowded because it has not generally become a destination ski resort—though there are some nice places to stay nearby. About half the runs are rated for the expert skier. There are some wide-open bowls, meadows, winding runs, and steep chutes. The lift tickets are very inexpensive. The area gets enough snow—200 inches yearly—to offer some nice powder days. Rentals and lessons are available for downhill skis and snowboards. There's a child care facility, but call ahead to reserve a spot. A nursery facility is also available by reservation. There are no lodging facilities at the ski area. Cafeteria-style meals are available at the base lodge or you can grab a hot toddy at the Thunder Bar.

SNOWMOBILING

The Wise River trail system features 150 miles of groomed trails in the Big Hole Valley area, including **Anderson Meadows**—which leads to backcountry lakes and a rental cabin—and **Lacy Creek,** with 10 miles of groomed and ungroomed trails to five high mountain lakes. **The Wise River Jackpine Savages,** Box 115, Wise River, MT 59762 (☎ **406/832-3258**), are the local sledding authorities; call them for trail specifics.

NATURE PRESERVES & WILDERNESS AREAS

One of the Bureau of Land Management's Backcountry Byways, the **Big Sheep Creek Canyon** offers the opportunity to observe the majestic bighorn sheep in their spectacular natural habitat. The 50-mile byway begins in Dell, Montana, on I-15, 24 miles north of the Montana-Idaho border, and passes beneath the high rock cliffs of Big Sheep Canyon to the head of Medicine Lodge Creek. From here, it's just a short drive down to the Medicine Lodge Valley to MT 324, just west of Clark Canyon Dam.

Clark Canyon Recreation Area, a man-made lake 20 miles south of Dillon on I-15, is a popular spot for waterskiing or trout fishing. Lewis and Clark's Camp Fortunate is located on the northwestern shore of the reservoir, where camping and boat launching facilities are also available.

Two Dillon area landmarks are designated state parks because of the historical significance attached to them as a result of the Lewis and Clark expedition. **Clark's Lookout** (☎ **406/834-3413**) provided the explorers with a vantage point from which to view their route and is reached by taking the MT 41 exit from U.S. Highway 90. Drive one-half mile east, then another half mile north on a county road. **Beaverhead Rock,** 14 miles south of Twin Bridges on MT 41 (☎ **406/994-4042**), was a tribal landmark recognized by expedition scout Sacajawea. Both parks are day use only.

SEEING THE SIGHTS

Based in Dillon or elsewhere in the valley, you can branch off to see **Big Hole National Battlefield;** see section 5 of this chapter for complete details.

The **Pioneer Mountain Scenic Byway** is a 4-mile drive that begins on MT 278 west of Dillon or along MT 43, south of the Wise River. Only the northern 28 miles of the road are currently paved, though there are plans to pave the rest eventually. Driving between the east and west Pioneer Mountain Ranges, you'll experience alpine meadows, jagged peaks, and ghost towns with numerous opportunities along the way to camp, fish, or watch wildlife. Near Coolidge (as you drive south) you'll see the old railroad bed of the Montana Southern Railway. This was the last narrow gauge railroad built in the U.S., to serve the Elkhorn mine.

There's not much of a shopping scene in Dillon or the Big Hole Valley, but the town's **Patagonia Outlet store,** 34 N. Idaho, ☎ **406/683-2580,** offers fleece pullovers and other popular outdoor gear. Right next door, at 36 N. Idaho, is

Red Rocks Lakes National Wildlife Refuge: A Haven for the Trumpeter Swan

Though well off the beaten path in the Centennial Valley, 28 miles east of Monida (about an hour south of Dillon), the **Red Rock Lakes National Wildlife Refuge** is often called the most beautiful wildlife refuge in the United States. The refuge was established in 1935 to protect the rare trumpeter swan, and it is here that the endangered species has been brought back from near extinction after a century of being hunted for their meat and feathers (quill pens were a hot item in the 1800s). It was feared that these beautiful creatures, which have wingspans of 7 to 8 feet, had been completely wiped out, until biologists discovered several dozen here in 1933. (They're also found along the Pacific Coast and in Alaska.)

This is the largest population in the lower 48 states—300 to 500 of the rare birds continue to nest and winter at the refuge. They mate for life and often return to the exact same nest each year to tend their eggs and cygnets. The best place to view the trumpeters is in the open areas near Upper Red Rock Lake, from late April through September.

In addition to the swan population, the 40,000-acre refuge is home to moose, deer, elk, antelope, fox, great blue herons, sandhill cranes, ducks, and geese; more than 50,000 ducks and geese may be seen during times of migration.

The multi-use refuge is a popular spot for hiking, mountain biking, and canoeing; check with the **U.S. Fish and Wildlife Service,** Mountain Prairie Region, P.O. Box 25486 DFC, Denver, CO 80225 (☎ **303/236-7920,** or locally 406/276-3536), for regulations concerning these activities within refuge boundaries. The refuge lies just beyond the town of Monida, off I-15 well south of Dillon; you'll take a gravel road the remainder of the way.

Sagebrush Sewing Works, ☎ **406/683-2329,** which offers outdoor gear for everyone except the fly-fisherman. **The Bookstore,** 26 N. Idaho, ☎ **406/683-6807,** makes it three in a row on the main drag. It has an excellent selection of contemporary, popular Western and Native American literature.

Beaverhead County Museum. 15 S. Montana, Dillon. ☎ **406/683-5027.** Free admission. Mon–Fri 1–5pm.

The Beaverhead County Museum is located in the center of town next to the depot building. It's housed in an 1890s settler's cabin moved to the spot. Inside there is a little bit of everything from the pioneer era—clothes, tools, cooking utensils, furnishings, typewriters. There's also a number of stuffed animals from the surrounding area. Like a lot of western county museums, though, this one seems more interested in preserving the names of the families who donated items than in telling a coherent historic story.

Western Montana College Gallery/Museum. 710 S. Atlantic, Dillon. ☎ **800/WMC-MONT** or 406/683-7126. Free admission. Mon–Thurs 10am–3pm.

The most exciting exhibit at this gallery and museum is the Seidensticker Wildlife Collection of big-game trophies. The collection features animals from the far-flung locales of Africa and Asia as well as North American game. Student art is also featured on a rotating basis.

WHERE TO STAY

In addition to the hotels listed below, two other cookie-cutter chain options in Dillon are the **Comfort Inn,** 450 N. Interchange (☎ **800/442-4667** or 406/683-6831), with rooms in the $40 to $60 range; and the **Super 8 Motel,** 550 N. Montana (☎ **800/800-8000** or 406/683-4288), which has double rooms for $58.

The Best Western Paradise Inn. 650 N. Montana, Dillon, MT 59725. ☎ **800/528-1234** or 406/683-4214. Fax 406/683-4216. 65 units. A/C TV TEL. $44–$70 double; $70–$80 suite. AE, DISC, MC, V.

The Paradise Inn is a comfortable two-story facility set back from one of Dillon's busier streets. The basic rooms are moderately appointed and cozy but the penthouse suites are well worth the indulgence, with huge bathtubs and large living areas. There is a heated swimming pool in a separate building to the front of the property along with a hot tub and exercise equipment.

Hotel Metlen. 5 S. Railroad Ave., Dillon, MT 59725. ☎ **406/683-2335.** 46 units. $18–$27 double. No credit cards.

When I asked the staff at the Metlen Hotel how many rooms could be rented in the place, they said they didn't know. Even the woman who does the cleaning didn't know how many rooms there are. It varies, I guess on the stage of renovation and the energy of the renovators. It is a little hard to tell whether the Metlen is being restored or simply falling down. But the rooms are very cheap, and some of them are quite nice. Room number 12, for instance, has a modern private bath (only two rooms do have private baths; most are shared with at least one other room), and new paint and wood-work. The erratic sleeping accommodations aside, this is a must-stop in Dillon for anyone interested in seeing what an old Montana watering hole looks like. Go to the back room and check out the large solid oak bar; it was once part of a joint in Ban-nack owned by the notorious outlaw Henry Plummer. Built in 1897 by Joe Metlen, the building was one of the premier hotels of its day, with an opening attended by local and regional dignitaries. The huge brick building, listed on the National Register of Historic Places, has three stories and includes two bars, a casino, and a card room, with live country-and-western music on the weekends.

Jackson Hot Springs Lodge. Jackson, MT 59736. ☎ **406/834-3151.** Fax 406/834-3157. www.jacksonhotsprings.com. E-mail: hotresort@jacksonhotsprings.com. 12 cabins. $65–$114 cabin. MC, V. Pets accepted with additional fee.

When I was at the Jackson Hot Springs Lodge, a new arrival came into the lobby/bar/pool room, stared up at the collection of animal heads on the wall, and exclaimed, "This is what you really expect a lodge to look like." Jackson Hot Springs combines some of the feeling of a mountain lodge with an informal cowboy-style atmosphere. The rooms are large with pine log beds, and the grounds are nicely land-scaped with gardens. On the other hand, you would not be too surprised to see a cowboy ride his horse up to the bar and order a drink (for the horse). The large hot springs pool—35 × 70 feet—is free to guests and available to others for a $5 fee ($3.50, 12 and under). Don't go on Wednesdays, though, because that's when it's emptied and cleaned, and it takes all day to fill up again. There is a small restaurant on the premises, with a menu that changes each night. Dinner goes for $11 to $22, depending on the meal of the day.

A FISHING LODGE

Craig Fellin's Big Hole River Outfitters. Box 156, Wise River Rd., Wise River, MT 59762. ☎ **406/832-3252.** Fax 406/832-3254. E-mail: wsr2352@montana.com. 4 units. $2,500 per person per week. Rates include all meals, drinks, fishing guide, boat, and tackle. No credit cards.

This is one of the finest fly-fishing lodges in the West. You can catch every species of trout—rainbow, brown, cutthroat, grayling, and brook. The Big Hole River is the only one in the lower 48 that still has native grayling in it, and the fine guides at Fellin's will help you find them. The food is excellent and the accommodations are comfortable, though not luxurious. You will likely have moose bedding down behind your cabin, and there are often moose and deer in front of the lodge in the evening. Fellin's is best for the experienced angler. Beginners probably won't catch many fish. Craig is also an avid golfer, and he's set up a putting green on the property. You can practice your putting, and combine fishing with a golf day at the Old Works course in Anaconda.

CAMPING

Beaverhead Marina, 1225 Hwy. 324, Dillon (☎ **406/683-2749**), is only 20 miles from town and offers an RV park with fishing in the Clark Canyon Reservoir. Visitors here will find 31 sites for RVs and two tent campsites and campground showers. Sites are available on a nightly, weekly, or seasonal basis. Facilities here include a small grocery store, fishing supplies, and RV dump station and boat access ramps.

Jefferson River Camp, off MT 41 South in Silver Star (☎ **406/684-5577**), offers full RV hookups, tent sites, and tepee rentals. The campground is located on a cattle ranch a short distance from the confluence of the Ruby, Beaverhead, and Big Hole Rivers, which unite to form the Jefferson. Campers have private access to one-half mile of the Jefferson; fly-fishing and fly-tying instruction are available with prior notice.

The **Maverick Mountain RV Park & Cabins,** P.O. Box 460–516, Polaris, MT 59746 (☎ **406/834-3452**), is situated along a National Scenic Byway near Polaris. Nightly, weekly, and monthly rates are available with full hookups.

WHERE TO DINE

It seems as if every town under the sun has a Sweetwater Cafe, although in Dillon it's called the **Sweetwater Coffee,** but the result is the same: freshly brewed coffee, some pastries, and six seats for visitors. This one's downtown at 23 N. Idaho (☎ **406/683-4141**). **Stageline Pizza** is at 24 S. Idaho (☎ **406/683-9004**). Order take-out and head down to the riverbank to enjoy a beautiful Montana sunset.

Big Hole Crossing Restaurant. Main St., Wisdom. ☎ **406/689-3800.** Reservations not accepted. Breakfast $2–$7; lunch $4.50–$8; dinner $8–$18. MC, V. May–Nov, 7am–9pm; Dec–Apr, Mon and Wed–Thurs 8am–7pm, Fri 8am–8pm, Sat–Sun 7am–7pm. AMERICAN.

This is a very nicely turned out restaurant, with a black tiled counter seating area. The food is good, and inexpensive. But it runs toward pretty typical beef, chicken, and seafood. It's popular with the Forest Service and BLM types for lunch, which I always consider a good sign, because those work up quite an appetite wrestling mountain lions, corralling grizzly bears, and arguing with ranchers about riparian habitat improvements. The Big Hole Crossing offers "Words from Wisdom" along with its daily specials on the chalkboard. There were seven kinds of homemade pie on the menu the day I was there. I had the bumbleberry, but I still don't know what it is. Bears probably eat it when they're done with the BLM guys.

Blacktail Station. 26 S. Montana, Dillon. ☎ **406/683-6611.** Lunch $6–$8; dinner $8–$45. DISC, MC, V. Mon–Thurs 11am–10pm, Fri 11am–11pm, Sat–Sun 4–10pm. STEAKS/SEAFOOD.

Located in a basement on Montana Street, Blacktail Station used to be the Mine Shaft, and some of the decorations from its past life still remain—like trophies. It's a more upscale, more yuppie-ish place than you'd expect in agricultural Dillon; Ansel Adams prints now adorn the walls as well as the hard rock mining detritus. The food is very good. The steak almost melts in your mouth. The twice baked potato is very popular, though it costs a little more. Try not to sit by the kitchen—you won't be able to avoid hearing a disembodied voice shouting out servers' names when the food is ready.

The Lion's Den. 725 N. Montana, Dillon. ☎ **406/683-2051.** Lunch $5–$7; dinner $9–$19. MC, V. Mon–Fri 11am–2pm and daily 5–10pm. AMERICAN.

The Lion's Den is classic Montana beef, right down to the cowboy-booted guys at the bar debating what to name the new horse. Opened in 1955, this is one of Dillon's oldest eating establishments, serving steak, seafood, and a little pizza if you really need it. The bar has a pool table and casino, and the jangly notes emanating from the video poker games to entice players are especially grating.

Los Carmelitas. 221 S. Montana, Dillon. ☎ **406/683-9368.** Lunch $4–$6; dinner $6–$10. DISC, MC, V. Daily 11am–8pm. MEXICAN.

Los Carmelitas, which is across the street from the visitor center, focuses on traditional Mexican-cum-American meals. Lunches are nachos, salads, enchiladas, burritos, and tacos; evening meals are more substantial versions of the same basic *platos*. The atmosphere is very basic, square tables, metal chairs. If you want a cold beer with your food, bring your own, as this restaurant doesn't have a liquor license.

Papa T's. 10 N. Montana, Dillon. ☎ **406/683-6432.** Reservations not accepted. Lunch $5–$9.50; dinner $5–$15. MC, V. Daily 11am–10pm. PIZZA.

Papa T's is a favorite place with local families. It's a vast room where mom and dad can get respectable food and the kids can run around without getting on anyone's nerves. There are video games lining one wall, and a little kiddies' carousel for the tykes. There's even a Ms. Pacman game. The food is basic American, burgers, chicken Philly steak, and pizza. The formula has worked for more than 17 years. The restaurant is named for owner Tom Lohman, whose kids all call him "Papa." If you're lucky, co-owner Evelyn Lohman will tell you all this in her soft, inquiring voice—and a lot of other things about Dillon, as well.

TWIN BRIDGES

Just up MT 41 a piece from Dillon, a faded billboard just outside of town proclaims Twin Bridges to be the platinum capital of the Western world, an odd designation for a town that seems to be much more famous regionally for great fishing. "Floating Flotillas & Fish Fantasies" is the name given to the tiny town's annual summer festival held in mid-July, with highlights that include the extremely popular floating parade on the Beaverhead, dances, and a barbecue. Locals are even given the chance to show their skills at fly-casting, fly-tying, and wader racing. For additional information about the Twin Bridges area and scheduled activities, contact the **Chamber of Commerce** at ☎ **406/684-5259.**

WHERE TO STAY

Healing Waters Fly-Fishing Lodge. 270 Tuke Lane, Twin Bridges, MT 59754. ☎ **406/684-5960.** www.flyfishing-inn-montana.com. 5 units. $425 per person per day. Rate includes meals and guide services. DISC, MC, V. Personal checks accepted.

Greg and Janet Lilly recently purchased this 6-acre plot, which came with a stone and hand-hewn log lodge. The Lilly name is synonymous with fishing in Montana, so it's no surprise that they've opened a hospitality center for anglers. The lodge and its dining, living, and fly-tying rooms—not to mention its five guest rooms—are a magnet for anglers working the waters of the three nearby streams under the tutelage of Greg and his guide staff. The package here includes rooms and meals (Janet prepares the daily fare), fly-fishing and guide service, and views from the front deck of the Ruby, Tobacco Root, and Greenhorn mountains. Henry Winkler ("The Fonz") is a fan of this spot.

WHERE TO DINE

The Old Hotel. 101 E. Fifth Ave. ☎ **406/684-5959.** Reservations required. Main courses $16–$21. MC, V. Personal checks accepted. May 18–Oct 18, Tues–Sat 11am–2pm and 5:30–9:30pm, Sun 7:30am–2pm; Oct to Dec open 3 days a week. Closed Dec to Apr. CONTINENTAL.

This remarkable restaurant is right on the highway in an out-of-the-way spot. Gourmet meals are served in a restored two-story brick building furnished with a hodgepodge of beautiful wooden antiques. Hostess Jane Waldie has engaged the services of a cordon bleu chef to prepare magnificent beef, chicken, and pasta dinners nightly during the summer months. An extensive wine cellar features French, Italian, and California labels. The second level has been converted to a two-room B&B; accommodations are nice, but not up to the standards of a higher-class B&B.

5 Big Hole National Battlefield

76 miles W of Dillon; 106 miles S of Missoula

The flight of the Nez Perce across Montana in 1877 is the most heroic and epic story of the Indian war period. About 800 non-treaty Nez Perce left the Wallowa area of Idaho in June of 1877. They eluded the pursuing forces of the United States until early October, attempting to join Sitting Bull in the relative safety and freedom of Canada. When they surrendered—from exhaustion and starvation, not from military defeat—on October 5, 1877, only 431 remained.

The **Big Hole National Battlefield** commemorates the flight of the Nez Perce over 1,200 miles of some of the roughest land in the lower 48 states, through Yellowstone National Park, across Montana's high plains, outwitting and outfighting the U.S. cavalry. There were several battles along the way, but the major one was fought here. Between 60 and 90 members of the band were killed. Only 12 of the dead were warriors—the rest were women, children, and the elderly. The military lost 29 dead and 40 wounded.

The Nez Perce had traditionally lived in eastern Washington, Idaho, and Oregon. They had always maintained good relations with the United States. They assisted Lewis and Clark in 1805, caring for the expedition's members when they arrived in their country sick, tired, and low on provisions. They gave them provisions, two dugout canoes, and guides. The Nez Perce were also the subjects of the first major Protestant mission effort among the Indians, when the stern and domineering Eliza Spaulding—an associate of the later martyred Marcus Whitman—urged them to give up their traditional ways in return for eternal salvation.

The Nez Perce's problems came to a head in 1860, when gold was discovered. Most were sent to reservations, but Joseph—known as "Young Joseph"—led a non-treaty band to live on his traditional homeland in the Wallowa Valley. Pressure from settlers eventually led to an order forcing Joseph's band onto a reservation.

In the summer of 1877, several Nez Perce braves ignored advice from the tribal elders and attacked and killed four white settlers in Oregon to exact revenge for the earlier murder of a father of one of the braves. This attack raised the ire of settlers, and the cavalry was called in to hunt down the Nez Perce. On June 1, 1877, Joseph's band crossed the swollen Snake River, fleeing to Canada.

Skirmishes erupted along the way in Idaho before the Nez Perce entered Montana, fleeing from U.S. Army troops under the leadership of Gen. Oliver O. Howard. When the Nez Perce reached the Big Hole Valley, they decided to make camp, thinking all the while that they had outrun the army troops, for a short time at least.

However, in addition to Howard's troops behind them, a second group of soldiers, under the command of Col. John Gibbon, was advancing up the Bitterroot Valley toward the unsuspecting tribe. On the morning of August 9, 1877, Gibbon's soldiers, along with a contingent of local volunteers, attacked the sleeping tribe in what is today known as the Battle of the Big Hole. Many lives were lost, including many Nez Perce women and children. Less than 48 hours after they'd set up camp, the remaining Nez Perce once again found themselves fleeing for their lives and their freedom. They headed toward Canada, although the U.S. Army troops caught up to them at Bear Paw, only 40 miles from the Canadian border. The capture of Joseph's tattered band was the last major military effort of the Indian War period.

The Battle of Big Hole is somewhat unusual among Indian fights in that a number of descriptions of the battle exist, many from the Indian point of view. Andre Garcia, a scout and adventurer, married a Nez Perce woman, In-who-lise, who was wounded in the battle. In his marvelous book *Tough Trip Through Paradise,* he says that he visited the battlefield 2 years later and human bones and skulls were still scattered everywhere.

Begun as a military reserve in 1883, the area became a national monument in 1910 and was designated a national battlefield in 1963. Today, the National Park Service maintains an interpretive center for visitors, where rangers help visitors understand the significance of the battle that occurred at Big Hole. Guided tours, a museum, exhibits, a bookstore, movies, and two self-guided walking trails are open and available to the public.

Trails begin at the lower parking lot and lead to several points of interest. **The Nez Perce Camp,** where soldiers surprised the sleeping tribe, is considered sacred ground. The **Siege Area** marks the place where soldiers were besieged for nearly 24 hours as the Nez Perce fought to save their families from certain death. A fairly steep walk will lead you to the **Howitzer Capture Site,** where soldiers suffered a heavy blow as Nez Perce warriors captured and dismantled the military weapon. This spot affords a spectacular view of the battlefield and surrounding area.

Big Hole Battlefield represents only a small fraction of the Nez Perce's tragic flight across the West. The 1,200-mile Nez Perce (Nee Me Poo) National Historic Trail follows the entire route of the Nez Perce War, from Wallowa Lake, in northwestern Oregon, to Bear Paw Battlefield in northcentral Montana (see chapter 7). Crossing four states, the trail features several Nez Perce war sites with interpretive markers telling the story of the tribe's fight for freedom. The trail is administered by the U.S.D.A. Forest Service, which can provide you with an excellent map of the four-state area.

GETTING THERE From Missoula, you can reach the Big Hole Battlefield by going south on U.S. Highway 93 through the Bitterroot, 80 miles to Lost Trail Pass. Then turn east 16 miles to the site. From Butte, go south on I-15 to MT 43 west for 51 miles to Wisdom, then continue west on MT 43 to the site for about 10 miles. From Dillon, take route 278 west to Wisdom, then go west on MT 43 for 10 miles.

VISITOR INFORMATION You can obtain a pamphlet with an auto tour of the flight of the Nez Perce through the Big Hole, Horse Prairie, and Lemhi valleys from the National Park Service, Big Hole National Battlefield, Box 237, Wisdom, MT 59761 (☎ **406/689-3155**); or from the Beaverhead-Deerlodge National Forest, 420 Barrett St., Dillon, MT 59725 (☎ **406/683-3900**).

The **Big Hole Battlefield Visitor Center,** P.O. Box 237, Wisdom, MT 59761 (☎ 406/689-3155), is open daily (except on Thanksgiving, Christmas, and New Year's Day) with summer hours from 8am to 6pm and winter hours from 8am to 4:30pm. Admission is $4 per car, $2 per bike. Picnic tables are located at the lower parking lot, though there are no camping or overnight facilities on the premises. Fishing and hunting are allowed within the battlefield's boundaries as provided by Montana law, but are restricted on private land adjoining the battle site. Montana laws apply in the adjacent national forest.

The nearest facilities—restaurants, gas stations, grocery stores, and lodgings—are located in Wisdom, 10 miles to the east.

6 The Old Mining Towns: Virginia City, Nevada City & Bannack

Virginia City: 72 miles SE of Butte; 67 miles S of Bozeman; 84 miles NW of West Yellowstone

Virginia City and Nevada City have both a boisterous and colorful history and present. They are old towns, but they aren't ghost towns. In fact, Virginia City is one of the oldest continuously occupied towns in the West.

In 1863, a group of miners led by Bill Fairweather took $180 in their first day of gold panning from a creek, which they later named Alder Gulch after the trees growing on the bank. A gold rush soon followed and a mining town grew. The nation was in the midst of the Civil War, and the Southern sympathizers in the crowd wanted to name the new city Varina after Jefferson Davis's wife. But G.G. Bissell, a northerner and a miners' judge, said, "I'll see you damned first." He wrote "Virginia" on the founding document instead, a sort of a compromise, but since Virginia housed the capital of the Confederacy, no one complained.

The dusty main drag of Bannack also pays silent tribute to the mining era. Bannack has its own colorful history. One writer said, "It is probable that there never was a mining town of the same size that contained more desperadoes and lawless characters than did Bannack during the winter of 1862 to '63."

Just as the cities have very interesting and significant pasts, so do they have a present that reflects Montana's pride in the part these two towns played in the state's culture.

The restoration of Virginia City began in 1946 when Charles and Sue Bovey began the painstaking task of preserving and restoring many of the structures you see in town today. Most of the buildings were erected during Virginia City's heyday as the state's second territorial capital.

In 1991, following the deaths of Sue and Charles, son Fred Bovey determined that he was unable to continue to operate the properties and attractions. He decided to sell the whole kit and caboodle, including millions of dollars of antiques (Sotheby's estimate: $60 million). The State of Montana and Montana Historical Society attempted to have the area designated a national park, but to no avail. Even the National Trust for Historic Preservation got into the act, declaring Virginia City an endangered historic site.

Finally, partly because of a public outcry and due to the efforts of Governor Marc Racicot, the 1997 Montana legislature took dramatic fiscal measures and agreed to fund the $6.5-million purchase (such a bargain), and added $3 million for operational purposes. Today, the cities operate under the supervision of the Montana Historical Society and its foundation.

GETTING THERE   Virginia City and Nevada City are 13 miles west of Ennis on MT Route 287. From Bozeman take MT 84 west to Norris, then go south on U.S. 287 to Ennis, then west on MT 287 to the sites. From Butte, take I-90 east to the Whitehall exit (MT 55), then go south 27 miles to Twin Bridges. From Twin Bridges, take MT 287 east 30 miles to the sites. They are only about a mile apart, with Nevada City being the further west.

Bannack is located about 15 miles west of Dillon on Route 278, then south on a gravel road at the sign for Bannack State Park.

VISITOR INFORMATION   There are remains of many other Montana ghost towns in this part of the state; it's just that information about them is often hard to find and the towns themselves even harder. Your best bet: Contact the **Virginia City Chamber of Commerce,** P.O. Box 218, Virginia City, MT 59755 (☎ **800/ 829-2969;** www.virginiacitychamber.com; e-mail: townofvc@3rivers.net), and **Gold West Country,** 1155 Main St., Deer Lodge, MT 59722 (☎ **406/846-1943**). These two agencies can provide you with free information about the historic ghost towns of Montana. While you're at it, request copies of two brochures that will enhance your visit to the area: *Walking Tour,* a historical, block-by-block guide to Virginia City; and *A Walking Tour of Nevada City, Montana.*

The attractions in Virginia City (and all of them in Nevada City) are run by Historic Virginia City, Inc., P.O. Box 314, Virginia City, MT 59755 (☎ **406/ 843-5331**), and they're only open during the peak summer season, from Memorial Day to Labor Day. Before driving in this area during winter, check on weather conditions and road reports statewide (☎ **800/332-6171**).

VIRGINIA CITY

As Virginia City boomed after Bill Fairweather's discovery, it became the site of a dramatic ordeal of Western lawlessness and revenge that has fueled a thousand cowboy movie plots. Much of Virginia City's history was driven by the vigilante movement and it launched the career of Wilbur Fisk Sanders, who eventually went to Washington as Montana's first U.S. senator. It also ended the careers of a number of what they called road agents.

By 1864, when the Montana Territory was created by President Abraham Lincoln, nearly 30,000 people were living along the gulch's 8 miles. Virginia City was named territorial capital in 1865—taking that title from Bannack, virtually a ghost town by then—and held the position until 1875. For many years after its founding, the only currency acceptable to Virginia City merchants was gold dust.

As the town boomed, the incidence of robberies and murders increased. These robberies could only have taken place with foreknowledge by the perpetrators, usually called "road agents." The miners' sheriff, Henry Plummer, who had "persuaded" the sheriffs in Bannack, Nevada City, and Virginia to turn over their duties to him, turned out to be the leader of the road agents. As sheriff, he knew the timing of the gold movements.

No legal relief was possible, because the nearest officials to administer an oath were 400 miles away. In 1863, when a popular miner, Dutchman Nicholas Thiebalt, was murdered for $200, the other miners were outraged. The killer, George Ives, was captured and tried by a miners' court, then hanged. The site of his hanging is preserved in Nevada City. The local residents formed "vigilance committees" to capture and bring the road agents to justice. They hanged at least 21 more of the road agents— including Plummer—and some order was restored to the area.

Virginia City is a the largest of the two towns. Nevada City is entirely a ghost town, a collection of original and transplanted buildings from the period. There is a beautifully restored train, the **Alder Gulch,** that makes seven round-trips daily between the two.

SEEING THE SIGHTS

Virginia City, though, has a number of operating commercial enterprises interspersed with the historical stuff. Along the main thoroughfare you'll find the village centerpieces: the **Fairweather Inn,** the **Wells Fargo Overland Company building,** and the **Virginia City Historical Museum.** One of the oldest structures, the **Montana Post Building,** once housed the state's first newspaper; the paper's original press is still used locally for menus, playbills, and placards.

You should start your visit to Virginia City at the **Visitor Center and Museum Store,** at the end of Main Street. The center has photos and a brief explanation of the history of the town, and a friendly staff of volunteers. The government shut down gold mining for good in 1942, and a few years later the Boveys began buying up the property.

The **Virginia City Players** completed its 50th season in 1999, operating out of the Smith and Boyd Livery Stable, built in 1900. The players are Montana's oldest professional acting company. For information on show times, prices, and days for the Virginia City Players, call ☎ **406/843-5377.**

A little farther up the hill is the **Hangman's Building.** On January 4, 1864, the building was still being constructed, and a stout beam was exposed in the unfinished structure. The vigilantes took advantage of this situation to hang four of the road agents. The **Virginia City–Madison County Historical Museum** (☎ **406/843-5500**), also on the main street, has some photos of the vigilantes on exhibit and a nice collection of period clothing. Museum visits are $2 per person and $5 per family.

Up above the town, looking down over the main street, is **Boot Hill,** the last resting place of a several road agents, who required hasty burial after they died with their boots on.

If you *really* want to see the Old West come to life, check out a **Brewery Follies** production. Famous statewide for their cabaret-style revues and entertaining period melodramas, both companies perform most nights during the summer. The Brewery Follies now have a loyal following of their own, with hand-set flyers proclaiming this "A Remarkable Revue in a Cabaret Atmosphere!" For information on show times and days for the Brewery Follies call ☎ **406/843-5218.**

WHERE TO STAY

The **Fairweather Inn** at 315 W. Wallace (☎ **800/648-7588** or 406/843-5377) is a small hotel located right in the middle of downtown Virginia City with a great upstairs porch, a fun place to sit and people-watch. Though most of the rooms are tastefully decorated in an Old West theme, a few of them are distinguished by odd combinations of bright paint and mismatched quilts. Only five of the hotel's 15 rooms have private baths; the rest are rooming house–style. Rooms rent for $40 to $50.

The **Virginia City Campground and RV Park,** P.O. Box 188, Virginia City, MT (☎ **406/843-5493;** e-mail: vccamp@3rivers.net), has 15 trailer and RV units, and 17 tent camping sites. The campground is located just east of downtown. Tent sites are $15 and the trailer sites are $18 to $20.

Bennett House Country Inn. 115 E. Idaho, Virginia City, MT 59755. ☎ **877/843-5220** or 406/843-5220. www.bennetthouseinn.com. E-mail: stay@bennetthouseinn.com. 7 units, 1 cabin. $65–$80. AE, MC, V.

There is not a great deal of housing choice in either Nevada City or Virginia City. Both of the best places to stay in Virginia City are bed-and-breakfasts, right across the street from one another. The Bennett House is an eclectically furnished B&B with friendly folks running the place. All the rooms have shared baths, though the proprietors hope to add private baths to two rooms by the 2000 season. The nicest room is the honeymoon suite, with a large bay window on the second floor.

Sanders-Vanderbeck Center. 118 E. Idaho St., Virginia City, MT 59755. ☎ **406/843-5474.** www.svcenter.org. E-mail: svc@3rivers.net. 4 units (none with private bathroom). $75–$85. MC, V.

The Sanders-Vanderbeck Center is dedicated to the arts and humanities, sponsoring symposia and performances ranging from performing arts to fly-fishing. In addition to enjoying the cultural events here, guests can rent rooms in the B&B. The rooms are comfortable but small. The house was the home of the ubiquitous Wilbur Fisk Sanders, and is reputed to be the oldest continuously inhabited house in Montana.

WHERE TO DINE

Banditos. Wallace Ave. ☎ **406/843-5492.** Main courses $9–$23. MC, V. Mon–Sat 5:30–9:30pm. Closed in winter. MEXICAN.

There's not a lot of great food in Virginia City, but Banditos has drawn good reviews. The vegetable chiles rellenos are terrific and the atmosphere is nice—the restaurant is housed in the 1899 brick Buford Block. A little farther down the street, the **Roadmaster Grille** sells food out of the backs of 1950s cars, made into booths. It's very American.

NEVADA CITY

The distance between Nevada City and Virginia City is only a mile or so, but back in the days before the vigilance committees formed, it was a dangerous mile. Miners dared not go between the two cities after dark. One miner known as Dutch Fred was waylaid by a robber. When the highwayman found that Fred had only $5 with him—and paper money, not gold dust, at that—the bandit cursed and told him, "If ever you come this way with only $5, I'll shoot you." The robber shot Dutch Fred anyhow, wounding him in the arm.

Nevada City is now safer, a collection of wooden buildings, including an open air museum depicting the gold mining and settlement period of the area's turbulent history. Nevada City also exists as the result of Charles Bovey's diligence and dedication to the preservation of history. Though Nevada City was once a thriving mining camp, most of the buildings in town today were originally located elsewhere. Entry fees to the Nevada City site are $5 for adults, $4 for seniors, and $3 for kids.

In the mid-1950s, Bovey began to re-create an authentic Western town with buildings he'd accumulated around the West. The buildings are authentic, though their setting may not be. It looks like a perfect cowboy movie set, though, and has in fact been used for a couple of oaters, including *Missouri Breaks, Little Big Man,* and *Return to Lonesome Dove.*

Nevada City was the site of the resurgence of law and order in these Montana mining camps. Two thousand people reportedly came to town to watch the trial of George Ives for the murder of Nicholas Thiebalt. Emotions were running high on both sides, and it was in the face of these feelings that Wilbur Fisk Sanders began his place in Montana history by courageously prosecuting Ives before the crowd. The spot where Ives was hung is marked in town.

SEEING THE SIGHTS

With your walking-tour booklet in hand, begin your excursion behind the **Nevada City Hotel,** where you can view the state's only double-decker outhouse, and stroll along the streets to see what a Western mining town might have looked like. Boardwalks pass barber shops, homes, a schoolhouse, and even an Asian section. Some of the buildings are closed, but many include period furnishings and wares.

When you hear a cacophony of horns and whistles, follow the noise to the **Nevada City Music Hall,** located next door to the hotel. There you can see the "famous and obnoxious horn machine from the Bale of Hay Saloon!" A sign on the machine begs visitors not to miss hearing the machine that has driven 28 changemakers, 72 bartenders, and near a million tourists to the brink of insanity! The music hall is a fascinating place to spend an hour listening to the many music machines and reading about their history. It's one of the largest collections of its kind on display in the United States today. The building was originally the Canyon Lodge Recreation Hall in Yellowstone.

Across the street is the railroad museum, where you can board the **Alder Gulch** for the short train ride to Virginia City. The museum has an observation car once used by Calvin Coolidge and the last "Catholic chapel car" in the world. The train runs every hour, and costs $5.

WHERE TO STAY & EAT

You can believe the **Star Bakery's** claim that it has the best biscuits and gravy in town—it's also the *only* restaurant in town. Best known for its breakfasts, the small restaurant begins serving home-style food at 7 in the morning and closes after lunch. It's small, but full of cozy country charm. The kids will love the old-fashioned soda fountain.

Just an Experience Bed-and-Breakfast. 1570 MT 287, Virginia City, MT 59755. ☎ **406/843-5402.** www.bbhost.com/anexperience. 5 units. $50–$75. DISC, MC, V.

If you want something more modern than the Nevada City Hotel and Cabins, this B&B is your only other choice in Nevada City proper (dare we say, "downtown Nevada City?"). Two of the rooms in the house share a bath, and one has a private bath. The rooms are large, with iron-post beds. The cabins are quite large, with enough room for six people, and include loft bedrooms for the kids and full kitchens. There are no televisions or telephones in any of the rooms or cabins. Pets are permitted outdoors only, not indoors. The original log house here was first built in 1864. It has been remodeled and incorporated into a modern cedar-sided home.

Nevada City Hotel and Cabins. Nevada City, MT. ☎ **800/648-7588** or 406/843-5377. 30 units. $55–$80. MC, V. Closed Oct to mid-May.

Entering this hotel is like taking a step back in time. It was originally a stage stop near Twin Bridges, and still has the cool musty smell of a mining camp hotel. The building was constructed in the 1860s. Most of the rooms are small and spare, but the upstairs Victorian suites are huge, furnished in rough but exquisite Victorian style, complete with polished burlwood furniture and private baths. If you rent a cabin, be certain to lock your door—many tourists have no idea that the cabin is actually rented and may try to come inside.

BANNACK

Montana's first territorial capital, Bannack was the site of the state's first big gold strike in 1862. With more than 60 of the town's original buildings preserved for visitors, the tumbledown town is a stark reminder of the heyday of the frontier: vigilantes stalking road agents stalking prospectors, in a favored place where the rivers yielded gold dust.

Born out of the discovery of placer gold in 1862, Bannack quickly grew to a town of 3,000 people, largely composed of those hoping to strike it rich. Blacksmiths, bakeries, stables, restaurants, hotels, dance halls, and grocery stores rapidly sprang up to complement an expanding mining industry.

Bannack became the first territorial capital and the site of the first territorial legislative session in 1864. But the placer veins in Grasshopper Creek were thin. Only a few years later, it was a ghost town, and the boosters of the capital movement had turned their attention to Virginia City and the richer mines at Alder Creek.

Henry Plummer killed his first local man in Bannack in Goodrich's saloon. The victim was Jack Cleveland, who had threatened another man about a debt, which the other man had already paid. Cleveland bragged that he wasn't afraid of him. Plummer, apparently a bystander, got to his feet, cursed Cleveland, roared, "I'm tired of this," and commenced to shooting. Cleveland got the worst of it, dying 3 hours later.

Plummer was an enigmatic outlaw. He was considered a "gentleman" by the standards of the era. He married a schoolteacher, though she left him after only 10 weeks of wedded bliss. Only a few weeks before he was hanged, he held an elaborate dinner for territorial officials, including the governor and some of the vigilantes, for which he had ordered a $60 turkey from Salt Lake City. His guests apparently saw nothing unusual about enjoying the hospitality of a man they had already decided to hang.

VISITOR INFORMATION   Designated a state park in 1954, Bannack is open year-round. Summer hours are 7am to 9pm; winter hours 8am to 5pm. There are a visitor center, camping and picnic grounds, a group use area, and hiking trails. Other lodging facilities are available in nearby Dillon (see section 4 of this chapter). Day-use fees are $4 per vehicle, $1 per person, and $8 for a campsite ($7 in the off-season).

Bannack is located 4 miles south of MT 278, 25 miles west of Dillon. To get there, turn west off I-15, 3 miles south of Dillon. Head west 20 miles on MT 278, then south 4 miles on a gravel road, suitable for all vehicles. For additional information, call ☎ **406/834-3413.**

A SPECIAL EVENT   Bannack Days, staged annually during the third weekend in July, is a 2-day event commemorating the history and heritage of Montana's early pioneers with activities centering around frontier crafts, music, pioneer food, and dramas. A black powder muzzle loader shoot, Sunday church services, and horse-and-buggy rides bring the "toughest town in the West" to life and is fun for the entire family.

7

The Hi-Line & Northcentral Missouri River Country

by Dan Whipple

An early writer on agricultural subjects once wrote, "Of all the things that live and grow upon this earth, grass is the most important." Northcentral Montana and the Hi-Line was once a wilderness of grass, tall enough to roll in the wind like the sea, home to a million antelope and 60 million buffalo. Another observer wrote that "you could graze all the cattle of the world upon this plain." This portion of Montana remains classic cattle and wheat country, the true home of the cowboy. In *High, Wide and Handsome,* Joseph Kinsey Howard wrote that in this country, by 1883, "the cowboy, with leather chaps, wide hat, gay hand-kerchief, clanking silver spurs and skin-fitting high-heeled boots . . . had become an institution."

Lewis and Clark reported vast herds of buffalo on the plains, at one time reporting laconically "a thousand." When the adventurers entered Montana in 1805 just past the confluence of the Yellowstone and Missouri Rivers, they saw their first grizzly bear, and Lewis made the first extensive description of the animal for science.

As you travel along here, you're closely following the trail of Lewis and Clark to the portage of the Great Falls. In the city of Great Falls, you should take time to visit the Lewis and Clark National Historic Trail Interpretive Center and experience vicariously one of the great American adventures. This portion of the state is also Charles M. Russell country, the landscape that Russell memorialized (and sometimes lamented) in his famous Western paintings and bronzes.

But the country isn't all history and vanished mythology. There's plenty of outdoor activity, especially fishing and boating on Fort Peck Lake, bird-watching on the C.M. Russell National Wildlife Refuge, rafting on the wild and scenic Missouri River, or skiing in some of the region's ski areas.

1 Scenic Drives

DRIVING TOUR #1: KINGS HILL SCENIC BYWAY

The Kings Hill Scenic Byway is a 71-mile drive through the Little Belt Mountains and the Lewis and Clark National Forest. You pick it up about 22 miles southeast of Great Falls, where U.S. Highway 87 and U.S. Highway 89 divide. Take U.S. Highway 89 south toward the small mountain towns of Monarch and Neihart. From the south, take U.S. Highway 89 north from just east of Livingston on I-90. For a

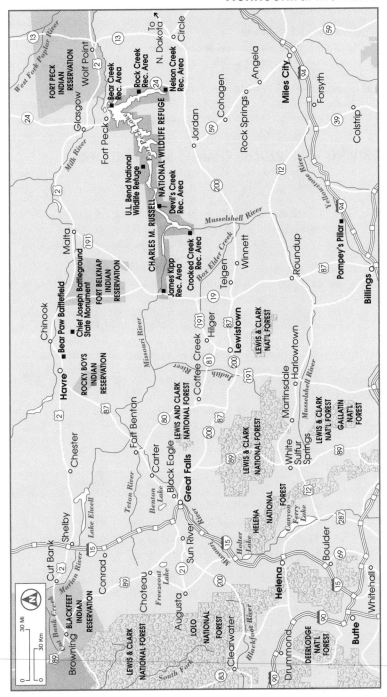

leisurely tour, you can watch the wildlife and the scenery, then visit the ghost towns at Castle Town and Hughesville, and the historic mining site at Glory Hole. For the more active trip, go to **Sluice Boxes State Park** just north of Monarch to hike along the abandoned rail line there, or fish in Belt Creek. In winter, there is cross-country skiing at the Silver Crest Trail System (just north of Showdown ski area, see below), and snowmobiling at Kings Hill. Snowmobile and ski rentals are available at Kings Hill. Memorial Falls has a nature trail that is accessible to visitors with disabilities. There are camping sites and national forest access points at numerous spots along the highway.

DRIVING TOUR #2: THE CHARLES M. RUSSELL TRAIL

The Judith Basin inspired the work of one of the West's seminal artists, Charles M. Russell. This drive on U.S. Highway 87/MT 200 between Great Falls and Lewistown provides an intimate look at the unsettled West through Russell's eyes. The drive is lovely in a pastoral way, but it helps to have a copy of the interpretive guide of the trail from **Russell Country, Inc.** (☎ **800/527-5348** or 406/761-5036; russell. visitmt. com/) if you want to get the full force of the Russell experience. The guide uses Russell's art to illuminate the history of the basin.

The highway was designated the Russell trail by the Montana legislature. The scruffy cowhands and toughened Indians that Russell painted have been mostly replaced by carefully tended fields of grain, but with the help of Russell's art and a little imagination, you can put yourself back in the saddle in 1880s Montana.

From Great Falls, you go through the towns of Raynesford, Geyser and Moccasin, taking in the history of the Blackfeet, the wolves of the basin in Stanford, and the role of the railroads in Hobson. Spring and fall are the best times to match Russell's color palette with that of the surrounding landscape. If you're traveling between May and September, be sure to stop at The Charles M. Bair Family Museum (☎ **406/ 572-3314;** www.bairmuseum.org) in Martinsdale (see below).

There are roadside turnouts along the highway for many of the 25 interpretive sites, including the settings for two of Russell's best-known paintings, *Buffalo in Winter* and *Paying the Fiddler.* Yogo Creek Road (266) and Memorial Way (487) are single-lane gravel roads included in the tour, but they are not recommended for RVs.

2 Great Falls

89 miles N of Helena; 219 miles NW of Billings

Great Falls is a big city on the plain. An important cog in the U.S. military strategy, it is the control point for a number of U.S. ICBMs (Intercontinental Ballistic Missile). Malmstrom Air Force Base is also the launching point for the new X-33, the space shuttle of the future.

But the country around Great Falls looks much as Charlie Russell found it and painted it at the end of the last century. Russell made his home Great Falls, and did much of his painting in his studio here.

Lewis and Clark came through with the Corps of Discovery, making an extremely strenuous 18-mile portage around the falls. It is a sign of Great Falls' progress that it is now known as the electric city, because the falls that Lewis and Clark marveled at have been tamed by a series of dams to provide electric power.

ESSENTIALS

GETTING THERE   Great Falls serves as the hub for northcentral Montana east of the Rockies. The Great Falls International Airport has daily service from **Delta**

Great Falls

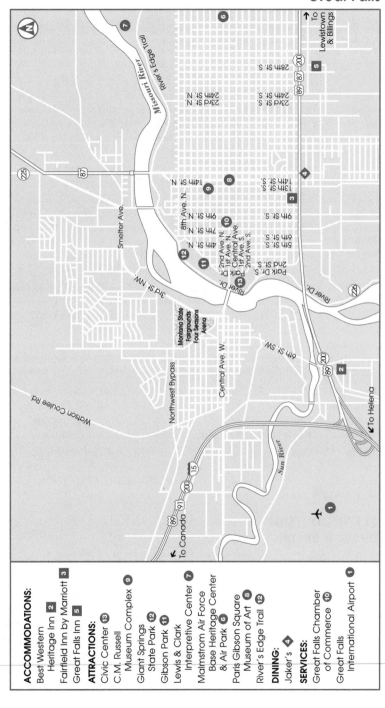

ACCOMMODATIONS:
Best Western
Heritage Inn **2**
Fairfield Inn by Marriott **3**
Great Falls Inn **5**

ATTRACTIONS:
Civic Center **13**
C.M. Russell
    Museum Complex **9**
Giant Springs
    State Park **12**
Gibson Park **11**
Lewis & Clark
    Interpretive Center **7**
Malmstrom Air Force
    Base Heritage Center
    & Air Park **6**
Paris Gibson Square
    Museum of Art **8**
River's Edge Trail **12**

DINING:
Jaker's **4**

SERVICES:
Great Falls Chamber
    of Commerce **10**
Great Falls
    International Airport **1**

(☎ 800/221-1212), **Northwest** (☎ 800/225-2525), **Horizon** (☎ 800/547-9308), and **Big Sky** (☎ 800/237-7788). Shelby, 88 miles northwest, provides the closest **Amtrak** service (☎ 800/872-7245). You can rent a car there with Ford Mercury (☎ 800/823-6737.

Great Falls is located on I-15, which runs north-south from Butte on I-90 to Helena, then through Great Falls, and then north to Canada. From Missoula, you can take MT 200 east, or you can take I-90 a little southeast, pick up U.S. Highway 12, and go east to Helena, then north to Great Falls. MT 200 is more scenic. From Billings, you can take MT 87 north to Lewistown and then west to Great Falls. Or you can go west on I-90 to Livingston, then take MT 89 and the Kings Hill Scenic Byway (see the driving tour earlier in this chapter) northwest to Great Falls. From Bozeman take U.S. Highway 287 at Three Forks, then I-15 to Great Falls.

VISITOR INFORMATION   Request tour information from Russell Country, Inc., at P.O. Box 3166, Great Falls, MT 59403 (☎ **800/527-5348** or 406/761-5036; travel.mt.gov/Russell/). The Great Falls Chamber of Commerce is at 710 1st Ave. N. There is also a visitor center at the Broadwater Overlook at 10th Avenue South and Second Street South, by the tall flagpole (☎ **800/735-8535**). For a Great Falls road report call ☎ **406/453-1605;** for statewide road reports call ☎ **800/226-7623.**

GETTING AROUND   The best way to get around Great Falls and environs is by car. Rental franchises in town include **Avis** (☎ 800/331-1212), **Enterprise** (☎ 800/736-2227), **National** (☎ 800/227-7368), **Rent-a-Wreck** (☎ 800/962-5344), and **Hertz** (☎ 800/654-3131).

You can also use public transit. Great Falls Transit System operates eight lines from early morning to early evening during the week. No service on Sundays or holidays. Call ☎ **406/727-0382** for information.

AN ORGANIZED TOUR   To see the town, take the 2-hour Historic Trolley tour, $10 for adults, $5 children 2 to 12, with one stop at the Rainbow Falls. You pick up the tour at the visitor information center at the Broadwater overlook. Call ☎ **406/771-1100** for information or go to seemontana.com/greatfalls/tours.

A SPECIAL EVENT   Great Falls hosts the Lewis and Clark Festival each year at the end of June. Events include history and natural history workshops, tours, food booths, and children's activities. For information call ☎ **406/727-8733.** For tickets call ☎ **406/454-0157.**

GETTING OUTSIDE
FISHING & BOATING
Great Falls is the unofficial dividing line for cold- and warm-water fish. You can fish for trout from Giant Springs. Or there are quite a few guides and tours available on the Missouri. For 2- to 7-day fishing and white-water trips on the Missouri, try **Montana River Outfitters,** 923 10th Ave. N., Great Falls (☎ **800/800-8218** or 406/761-1677; www.mt-river-outfitters.com). You can also paddle the Upper Missouri in 34-foot voyageur style canoes with **River Odysseys West** (☎ **800/451-6034;** www.rowinc.com), which offers tours in the style of the fur trappers (except for the high-class tenting accommodations). Price for a 4-day trip on the Missouri is $850 for an adult, $730 for a youth (ages 10 to 16) and $500 for children (ages 5 to 9). Day trips by jet boat are available from **Missouri River Breaks Co.** (☎ **406/453-3035**).

GOLF

The city offers two public golf courses: **Anaconda Hills** on Smelter Hill northeast of town (☎ **406/761-8459**), and the **Robert O. Speck Golf Course** at 29th Street and River Drive North (☎ **406/761-1078**).

HIKING & BIKING

Great Falls has 8 miles of paved River's Edge Trail along the Missouri River from downtown at the Oddfellows Park all the way out past Rainbow Dam to Crooked Falls. There is also an unpaved trail going another 8 miles or so out to the Cochrane Dam. The trail is ideal for hiking, biking, running, walking, and skating. Plans eventually call for more than 30 miles, including improvements to the trail segments on the north shore of the river. The Great Falls Chamber of Commerce can provide you with information and trail maps.

WINTER SPORTS

For skiing and snowmobiling try **Showdown Ski Area,** 65 miles southeast of Great Falls on U.S. Highway 89, near Neihart (☎ **800/433-0022**).

Showdown Ski Area. 65 miles southeast of Great Falls on U.S. Hwy. 89, near Neihart. ☎ **800/433-0022**. Lift tickets $25 adults, $13 juniors and seniors, free for children under 5. Winter, Wed–Sun and all holidays except Christmas and Thanksgiving; daily Dec 19–Dec 24 and Dec 26–Jan 3. Lifts open 9:30am.

This is a full service ski area with three restaurants, a pro shop, and a rental shop. There are 34 trails, two chairlifts, two land lifts, and 1,400 vertical feet of drop. The area is perfect for beginning and intermediate skiers, with long uninterrupted runs for them. Lots of powder. It's not crowded, and the snow base can reach 20 feet. Cross-country ski trails and snowmobile trails are also available. There are a children's program and day care. Just north of Showdown is the Silver Crest Trail System for cross-country skiing, and there is snowmobiling at Kings Hill. Snowmobile and ski rentals are made by calling the ski area.

SEEING THE SIGHTS

Gibson Park, located 1 block north of the Civic Center along Park Drive, is a serene, local favorite, with a large pond (where mallards and Canada geese congregate), playgrounds, flower gardens, and picnic areas. This is a good place to pick up the trail system along the Missouri River, for skating, biking, or hiking. Meriwether Lewis was chased into the Missouri River near here by a grizzly in 1805, at Sacajawea Island. Every Wednesday evening there is a free concert at the band shell. No word on whether the grizzly will be in attendance.

Benton Lake National Wildlife Refuge. 922 Bootlegger Trail, Great Falls, MT 59404. ☎ **406/727-7400**. Fax 406/727-7432. Free admission. Open during daylight hours. Go 1 mile north of Great Falls on MT 87, take a left on Bootlegger Trail, then proceed about 5 miles north to well-marked entrance.

Established in 1929 by President Herbert Hoover, the refuge is physically unimpressive, a small lake in a broad, open, treeless plain. But the 12,283 acres are important nesting grounds for water fowl, especially mallards, pintail, teal, and canvasback. Bird-watching for waterfowl and prairie species is best early in the morning or in the evening. There's a 9-mile auto tour route that takes about an hour, marked with signs to provide information about what you're seeing. Mother Nature is constantly changing the refuge attractions.

Paris Gibson Square Museum of Art. 1400 1st Ave. N. ☎ **406/727-8255.** Fax 406/
727-8256. E-mail: pgsmoa@mcn.net. Free admission. Tues 10am–5pm and 7–9pm, Wed–Fri
10am–5pm, Sat–Sun noon–5pm. Open Mon in summer.

Located in a national landmark building that served as Great Falls' first high school,
Paris Gibson Square is now the cultural and art center of the city. The changing art
shows display the works of artists from around the Northwest, as well as pieces from
the facility's permanent collection. The selection is eclectic, focusing on both contemporary and historical exhibits in a comfortable, beautifully restored space. A recent
$1.5 million fund-raising effort has enabled the gallery to do some major renovations,
including reopening the original front doors. The historical society also has its headquarters here, and displays portions of its collection. The museum cafe serves gourmet
lunches by reservation only, but if you walk in, you may get served. Call ☎ **406/
727-8255** for today's menu and reservations.

✪ **C.M. Russell Museum Complex.** 400 13th St. N. ☎ **406/727-8787.** www.cmrussell.
org. $4 adults, $3 seniors, $2 students. May 1–Sept 30, Mon–Sat 9am–6pm, Sun 1–5pm;
winter, Tues–Sat 10am–5pm, Sun 1–5pm.

You can always divide the world into two kinds of people—those who like cowboy art,
and those who don't. It is a measure of Charlie Russell's greatness that, although he
was a cowboy artist, everybody likes his work. This facility, which includes tours of
Russell's studio and home, is one of the high points of any trip to Montana, and it's
worth going out of your way to see.

Russell and the dime novelists practically invented the West. But the power of his
work is that the personality of everyone portrayed—Indians, cowboys, landscape—
shines through. His long line of imitators have rarely achieved the passion for his subjects that Russell has. Much modern "Western art" concentrates on romantic scenes
and fierce animals. Russell, on the other hand, had something to say about a celebrated but passing way of life. He said it powerfully.

The museum houses a large collection of Russell's work, and it is ably explained by
tour guides. You can spend a few minutes or all day here. There are also a number of
his bronzes, which are much admired, but less interesting, I think, than his paintings.
The artist's studio, also on the tour, contains a lot of things Russell used in his work,
along with many of the Indian artifacts he collected to help maintain his art's authen-
ticity. Russell greatly admired the Indians, and it shows in everything he did.

A number of other excellent artists working on Western themes are shown to good
advantage here as well. Exhibits change several times a year. The museum is currently
undergoing a massive expansion, adding 30,000 square feet of space scheduled to
open in March 2001.

Lewis and Clark National Historic Trail Interpretive Center. 4201 Giant Springs Rd.
☎ **406/727-8733.** Fax 406/453-6157. $5 adults, $4 seniors and students, $2 children 6–17,
free for children under 6. Memorial Day–Labor Day, daily 9am–8pm; Labor Day–Sept 30, daily
9am–5pm; Oct 1–Memorial Day, Tues–Sat 9am–5pm, Sun noon–5pm.

Located on a hill overlooking the Missouri River, this facility is hands down the best
Lewis and Clark exhibit between St. Louis and the Pacific Ocean. I've traveled the
Lewis and Clark Trail in both directions several times, and this offers the strongest feel
for the great explorers' journey that you'll find anywhere. The facility is cleverly
arranged to follow the adventurers' path to each major point along the way. You start
in Washington with Thomas Jefferson's instructions to the Corps of Discovery. Then
you go step-by-step, high-point-by-high-point along the journey. You visit a Mandan
earth house, see the grizzlies, and feel the voyagers sweat as they pull their 1,500-

pound boat along the portage of the Great Falls. Of this portage Clark wrote, "To state the fatigues of this party would take up more of this journal than other notes which I find scarcely time to set down." An excellent facility, it will take a few hours to see properly. The tour guide volunteers are wonderfully informed and entertaining.

Giant Springs State Park. 4600 Giant Springs Rd. ☎ **406/454-3441.** $1 per person, $4 per carload. Take River Dr. east along the Missouri River to Giant Springs Rd. Turn left and go about a quarter of a mile, just past the Lewis and Clark Interpretive Center.

Lewis and Clark also discovered and described the Giant Springs, purportedly the largest freshwater spring in the world, attached in turn to the world's shortest river. The spring is a bright, clear pool that now also feeds a fish breeding facility nearby. It burbles out of the 250-million-year-old Madison Formation, a large water-bearing formation that provides a lot of groundwater throughout the northern West. The springs send out 134,000 gallons a minute into the 201-foot-long Roe River, credited in the Guinness Book of World Records as the shortest in the world. The entire park covers 218 acres. The Montana Department of Fish, Wildlife and Parks also operates a visitors center nearby, where visitors can purchase hunting and fishing licenses. There are several places to admire the dams on the Missouri. The Great Falls that gave Lewis and Clark so much trouble are gone, but you can see a few remnants from overlooks. In the spring, especially, you can see the power of the river flowing through the spillways at Rainbow Dam, spewing mist hundreds of feet into the air, creating the rainbows in the sunshine that so entranced the explorers. Lewis called Rainbow Falls "one of the most beautiful objects of nature."

Malmstrom Air Force Base Heritage Center and Air Park. Malmstrom Air Force Base, east end of Second St. N. past 57th St. ☎ **406/731-2705.** Free admission. Air park: open during daylight hours. Museum: summer, Mon–Sat noon–3pm; spring and fall, Mon–Fri noon–3pm; winter, Mon, Wed, Fri noon–3pm.

The air park has a number of aircraft from various eras of the service, but primarily from the 1950s and 1960s. Included here is the same F-89J Scorpion that is the only plane to test a live air-to-air nuclear missile. Inside is a comprehensive display of military equipment and uniforms from Malmstrom, including the control panel used to fire the base's nuclear missiles. Interpretation of the exhibits is minimal. This is mostly a volunteer effort, and funds are short.

SHOPPING

There are at least 19 antique stores in Great Falls, and the chamber can give you a map of their locations. The **Stagecoach Gallery** (☎ **406/761-8845**), 508 1st Ave. N, combines the antique store with fine art and things Western. **Hoglund's,** 306 1st Ave. S. (☎ **406/452-6911**), has an awe-inspiring selection of cowboy boots and hats. Coffee and books can be found at **Bookmark-it,** 120 Central Ave. (☎ **406/ 453-3500**). **Fantastik Baskits,** at 2114 10th Ave. S. (☎ **800/452-6540**), can provide a gift package of buffalo salami or elk sausage.

WHERE TO STAY

Best Western Heritage Inn. 1700 Fox Farm Rd., Great Falls, MT 59404. ☎ **800/ 548-8256** or 406/761-1900. 240 units. A/C TV TEL. $89 double; $89–$129 suite. AE, DC, DISC, MC, V.

The hotel has a sedate New Orleans motif, and is the preferred business stop-off in Great Falls. It is located a little away from the downtown and closer to the interstate. The rooms are comfortable. It has the largest convention center in Great Falls, and is the only hotel with a gift shop and a fitness center.

Fairfield Inn by Marriott. 1000 9th Ave., S. Great Falls, MT 59405. ☎ **800/228-2800** or 406/454-3000. www.Marriott.com/fairfieldinn. 63 units. A/C TV TEL. $75–$80 double. Children under 18 stay free. AE, DC, DISC, MC, V.

This is a clean, simple, convenient Marriott, up to that chain's exacting standards. There is nothing special about it, but nothing ever goes wrong, either. It's located a little off the south side's main drag, so it is reasonably quiet. It offers a continental breakfast, pool, hot tub, and very good facilities for business travelers.

The Great Falls Inn. 1400 28th St. S., Great Falls, MT 59405. ☎ **800/454-6010** or 406/453-6000. Fax 406/453-6000. E-mail: tgfi@mcn.net. 61 units. $55 double. AE, DC, DISC, MC, V.

This is a hotel away from the bustle, located near the hospital and medical center. The rooms are quiet and clean as well. All have queen-size beds, reclining lounge chairs, refrigerators, and microwaves. The inn has added six new business class rooms with data ports and two telephone lines. There is a continental breakfast but few other amenities—no pool, no restaurant, no lounge. There are a laundry and transportation from the airport, if needed.

WHERE TO DINE

Jakers. 1500 10th Ave. S. ☎ **406/727-1033.** Lunch $4–$9; dinner $10–$20. AE, DISC, MC, V. Mon–Thurs 11:30am–2pm and 5–10pm, Fri 11:30am–2pm and 5–11pm, Sat 5–11pm, Sun 4–9pm. STEAKS/RIBS/FISH.

Jakers offers a very extensive menu in the not-cheap-but-not-expensive-either range. The restaurant is very nicely decorated in dark woods and wide windows. And at least the casino is kept in its own room, instead of ka-chinging in the diners' ears. Carnivores will be well taken care of with the steaks and ribs. The stuffed avocado and crabmeat salad offered with dinner is terrific—it's an unusual offering in lettuce-and-cherry-tomato country.

A SIDE TRIP TO FORT BENTON

Thirty-six miles north of Great Falls on MT 87, you can drop off the high bench along the Missouri River down to the water and the historic town of Fort Benton. The town still faces the river that formed its destiny. There is a pleasant waterfront park, and boat rides on the river are offered on the faux steamboat *Benton Belle,* ☎ **406/466-2628.**

The Lewis and Clark expedition made a critical decision a short distance downstream from Fort Benton, where the Marias River enters the Missouri. The expedition was divided on which was the main branch of the Missouri. The vote was 30-to-2 for the Marias being the main branch. The two who went for the other branch were Lewis and Clark. Had they chosen the other branch, there is a good chance that the expedition would have failed, because they would not have been able to get over the Rockies before winter. A statue of the explorers at this decisive point dominates one end of Front Street in Fort Benton. A small visitor center at the Bureau of Land Management (BLM) office on Front Street offers some information about this event.

BLM manages 149 miles of the Missouri here as a federally designated Wild and Scenic River. The famous **Eye of the Needle,** a high stone arch on the Missouri described by Lewis and Clark, was vandalized in May 1997. The vandals knocked the stone top of the arch into the river, leaving only two stone pillars.

Next to the Lewis and Clark statue is the **Keelboat Mandan,** a full-scale replica 62 feet long and 12.5 feet wide built for the movie *The Big Sky.* In the heyday of keelboating, broad-shouldered men could push a boat upstream at the world record pace of about 2 miles a day. There is also a monument on the riverfront to Shep, a collie sort of dog whose sheepherder master died and was sent East by train for burial. After that, Shep met every train in Fort Benton from 1936 until 1942, waiting for the return of his master.

The first steamboat reached Fort Benton in 1850. This was the farthest upriver the boats could reach and 600 of them stopped here from 1859 to 1870. Furs, goods, and gold were all shipped through the town. **The Museum of the Northern Great Plains,** in the Old Fort Park (20th and Washington; ☎ 406/622-5316), tells the story of settlement. Admission is $2, which includes admission to the Museum of the Upper Missouri at Old Fort Park and Front Street (☎ 406/622-5316). There is a vast collection of farming equipment here, testifying to the fortitude and ingenuity of the settlers on the Great Plains. **The Museum of the Upper Missouri** has an excellent historical collection, including the rifle that the Nez Perce Chief Joseph surrendered at the Bear Paw battle, and the history and personality of Fort Benton as expressed by the artist Charlie Russell, the preacher Brother Van, and the infamous Madame Mustache who was, well, you know.

For lodging, try the newly refurbished **Grand Union Hotel** right on the river. Originally built in 1882 at a cost of $60,000, it has been completely gutted and rebuilt into a modern hotel, restaurant, and lounge. The hotel has 27 rooms, of which three are suites. Rates start at $75 for a double up to $120 for the suites (☎ 406/622-5791).

3 The Rocky Mountain Eastern Front

53 miles W of Great Falls

The eastern front of the Rockies is a more isolated, less populated section of the Montana Rockies, but it is no less beautiful than the peaks and valleys to the West. A great paleontological mystery was solved here. Scientists had discovered many dinosaur fossils in the far eastern part of the state, but no nests or eggs. They wondered why. When fossilized dinosaur eggs turned up along the Rocky Mountain Front—the shoreline of a shallow sea 65 million years ago—paleontologists learned that the dinos had migrated to this area to lay their eggs. You can explore this first discovery site on Egg Mountain near Choteau via a guided tour.

There are two towns with some personality on the front— Choteau and Augusta. Choteau bills itself the gateway to the eastern Rocky Mountain Front. Named for the president of the American Fur Co., who brought the first steamboat up the Missouri, it is one of the oldest towns in Montana.

Tiny Augusta is a cheerful, friendly town that seems pleased with its place in the world. Unlike a lot of small Western towns, it is not hustling to turn itself into something else. It's only about 2 blocks long, with weathered wood exteriors on the buildings, false fronts, and fishing supplies. Folks are out and about, the guy at the gas station gives you full service at the self-service pump, and everybody's on a first-name basis with the county sheriff. A friendly basis, that is to say. The big time in Augusta is the rodeo, which happens the last weekend of June.

ESSENTIALS

GETTING THERE   The closest airport is in Great Falls, about 52 miles from Choteau (see Great Falls above for airport information). From the airport, take I-15 north to the U.S. Highway 89 exit (about 12 miles), then go west on U.S. Highway 89 for 40 miles to Choteau.

To reach the area by car from the northwest, drive on Route 2 along the southern border of the Glacier National Park. At Browning, go south on MT 89. Augusta's position (and that of the front in general) along MT 287 is roughly parallel with that of

Rental-Car Tip

A reliable four-wheel-drive vehicle is strongly recommended for touring the back roads of the Rocky Mountain Eastern Front. Many are unpaved, gravel roads that turn into a slippery mush locally known as "gumbo." Car-rental companies keep such vehicles in stock, but requests for four-wheel-drives should be made weeks in advance. See Great Falls above for information on renting a car.

Great Falls on I-15, which lies to the west about 40 miles. From points south and east of Great Falls, refer to the Great Falls "Essentials" section (above) for appropriate driving directions to this area.

VISITOR INFORMATION For an information packet, write to the regional tourism office for Russell Country, Inc., at P.O. Box 3166, Great Falls, MT 59403; or call ☎ **800/527-5348** or 406/761-5036. In Choteau, write to the Chamber of Commerce at Box 897, Choteau, MT 59422 (☎ **800/823-3866** or 406/466-5316; www.townnews.com/mtchoteauchamber). For hunting and fishing info, contact the Montana Dept. of Fish, Wildlife and Parks at 4600 Giant Springs Rd., Great Falls, MT 59406; or call ☎ **406/454-3441.** Augusta has no visitor information center, but the proprietor of the shop Latigo and Lace says people are welcome to call her at ☎ **406/562-3665** if they want help.

GETTING AROUND The only way to travel this country is to drive. See Great Falls above for information on renting a car.

OUTFITTERS & ORGANIZED TRIPS

Timescale Adventures. P.O. Box 356, Choteau, MT 59422. ☎ **800/238-6873** or 406/466-5410. www.timescale.org. E-mail: dtrexler@3rivers.net. 3-hour day tour, $20 adults, $10 children 12 and under. 1-day program, $75 per person per day. 2-day program, $125 per person. More than 2 days, $60 per person per day. Advance registration is required; space is limited.

Timescale Adventures runs some very popular dinosaur field programs, designed for all levels of interest. The 3-hour seminar is a walk along the Rocky Mountain Front covering identification of dinosaur bones, what a dinosaur egg shell looks like, and what to do when you find a dino bone. The 2-day seminar includes a dig and fossil preservation techniques. In the summer of 1999, Timescale was digging a large meat-eating dinosaur at one of its sites, as well as three duckbill dinosaurs. A new building will be in place by 2000 to increase lab and classroom space. The group also covers lots of geology and can show you how to pan for gold (though they can't tell you where the gold is, necessarily). The program has no age limit, and is perfect for families. The mailing address is Choteau, but the programs originate from the town of Bynum 14 miles north of Choteau on U.S. 89.

✪ **Pine Butte Guest Ranch Summer Trips and Workshops.** HC 58, Box 34C, Choteau, MT 59422. ☎ **406/466-2158.** Reservations required. $1,325 per person per week. Rate includes shuttle from airport, meals, rooms, and the nature program.

The Nature Conservancy's Pine Butte Guest Ranch offers eight learning vacations over the summer covering grizzly bears, mammal tracking, geology, wildflowers, and dinosaurs, to name but a few choices that have been offered in the past. Some have daily hikes, some are overnight or longer. A number of guests have noted that their time at the ranch and the nature workshops made up the best week of their lives.

ESPECIALLY FOR KIDS

The Pine Butte Guest Ranch (see "Where to Stay," below) offers a number of educational programs for youngsters beginning the end of June and ending in mid-August. Past topics have included fly-fishing, dinosaurs, field journals, and storytelling. They are targeted at children ages 7 to 14, and are held at the Old Nelleview School 17 miles west of Choteau. The cost is $15 a day. Call ☎ **406/466-5430** or e-mail belanger@3rivers.net for more information.

A SCENIC DRIVE & A SCENIC MOUNTAIN

The beautiful **Sun Canyon Drive** on Sun Canyon Road starts out west of Augusta along the plains at first, then weaves up the canyon past a 1913 Bureau of Reclamation dam built in the south end of the canyon. The Sun River that carved the canyon was called the Medicine River by the Blackfeet during the time of Lewis and Clark. The canyon is a gray granite jumble with snowcapped peaks in the distance. The area is a weekend getaway spot for residents all along the front. There are fishing, boating, hiking, four-wheeling, and many other outdoor activities in the area. The road up here is a good improved gravel track for the most part, but it can be very rugged in portions, especially if they've been trying to fix it. After you get to the national forest, the road is paved. Go figure.

Egg Mountain (☎ **406/466-5332**) is where Jack Horner of the Museum of the Rockies and Bob Makela discovered dinosaur eggs in the late 1970s. It is now on a portion of land owned by the Nature Conservancy, and the tours are conducted in cooperation with the Museum of the Rockies, the Pine Butte Swamp Preserve, and the Old Trail Museum in Choteau. To get here from Choteau, go 1 mile south on U.S. 287, then 13 miles west on Belview Road. Guided tours only—reservations are required.

SHOPPING

Latigo and Lace on Main Street in Augusta (☎ **406/562-3665**) is an eclectic shop run by Texas native Sara Walsh, who specializes in selling the work of Montana artists but also offers books, games, cappuccino, and knickknacks. There is a spectacular collection of "made in Montana" souvenirs, collectibles, and art. Latigo and Lace can also put your brand on a coffee mug, if you have a hankering.

WHERE TO STAY

AUGUSTA

The Bunkhouse Inn. 122 Main St., Augusta, MT 59410. ☎ **800/553-4016** or 406/562-3387. 9 units. $26–$57 double. No credit cards.

This is the cowboy way. Housed in a building that dates back to 1912 and that is constantly under renovation, the Bunkhouse is sort of a bed-and-breakfast without the breakfast. Proprietor Terry Taillon sends her guests to Mel's Diner across the street. Mel doesn't rent rooms, she says, so she won't serve food. That's the sort of town this is. The rooms are small; there are no televisions or phones, but you shouldn't come to Augusta to watch television anyway. You could sit out on the new second-floor porch above Main Street on Memorial Day weekend and watch Montana's smallest parade as the gray-haired American Legionnaires march to the cemetery to the strains of Sousa marches played on a boom box carried by two of the ladies' auxiliary.

Camping Wagons West. Augusta, MT 59410. ☎ **406/562-3295.** 50 tent sites, 30 RV sites. $10 tent; $20 RV site first night, $15 thereafter. MC, V.

This is just another campground without any particular charm located on the edge of Augusta, but it is a place to put your vehicle or your tent, and it has a view of the mountains from camp. There are also a small associated motel and diner.

JJJ Wilderness Ranch. Box 310, Augusta, MT 59410. ☎ **406/562-3836.** www.triplejranch.com. 6 cabins. $1,022 per week, double occupancy. 1-week minimum stay. Rate includes all meals and ranch activities, and transport from the Great Falls Airport. No credit cards.

The Triple J is a guest ranch located in the extraordinary Sun Canyon near the Gibson Reservoir. It offers everything the outdoorsy type could dream of—horseback riding, fishing, pack trips into the Bob Marshall Wilderness Area (not included in price quoted above), and pure and simple relaxation (sitting and enjoying the views). The cabins accommodate a total of 20 guests, so you're never crowded. Though there are no amenities, it's not due to an oversight. Phones and televisions are forbidden in these parts.

Pine Butte Guest Ranch. HC 58 Box 34C, Choteau, MT 59422. ☎ **406/466-2158.** 10 cabins. Summer, $1,125 per person per week; May 13–June 23 and Sept 17–Oct 6, $825 per person per week. Rates include room, board, naturalist programs, riding ranch facilities, and transportation to and from Great Falls International Airport. AE, MC, V.

Located deep in the Sawtooth Range along the Rocky Mountain Front, Pine Butte Guest Ranch is owned by the Nature Conservancy, a national land preservation and environmental organization. The Conservancy buys and protects property that has special importance ecologically. Seven or eight endangered grizzly bears have made this 15,500-acre Pine Butte Swamp Preserve their home. The preserve is the only place left in the lower 48 states where grizzlies use both the mountain and prairie ranges as they did before settlement of the West drove them to the remnant habitat in the mountains.

Pine Butte Guest Ranch focuses on education, running numerous workshops on appreciating and understanding the natural world, especially the bears in the area. You can also do the usual dude-ranch activities—riding, hiking, swimming, and so on. Pine Butte has been homesteaded since the 1930s but has always been a guest ranch, not a cattle ranch, which accounts in part for the largely undisturbed habitat. Average winter winds of 80 miles per hour have helped keep the riffraff out.

Each of the ranch's log cabins has a river rock fireplace, and is comfortably furnished. The little time you'll be indoors will be spent in the lodge, a handsome pine interior with Western decor and a few photos of Kenneth and Alice Gleason, who owned and ran the place before the Conservancy bought it. There's also a bookstore and nature center.

The Conservancy's preserve is not open to the public, but to get a taste of the country, you can hike some trails in the Bureau of Land Management's Ear Mountain Outstanding Natural Area nearby. This is grizzly country, so be very careful.

Viewforth Bed & Breakfast. 4600 Hwy. 287, Fairfield, MT 59436. ☎ **406/467-3884.** www.3rivers.net/~viewfrth/. 2 units. $80 double first night, $75 thereafter. 7 miles north of Augusta on Route 287.

The best place to stay in Augusta is, strictly speaking, not in Augusta, but a short drive north. Terese and Keith Blanding, long-time Montanans, returned to their home state after a sojourn in Oregon, where they ran a tea room. Only open a short time, the place is very elegant, with soft wash walls the color of clouds.

Both rooms have excellent views of Sawtooth Mountain and Castle Reef in the Rockies. Maybe the nicest thing, though, is the beautiful garden they've put in the front yard. It invites contemplation.

WHERE TO DINE

Buckhorn Bar. Main St., Augusta. ☎ **406/562-3344.** All dishes $3–$8. Daily 8am–2am. BEEF/CHICKEN.

Gordon Dellwo has run this bar in the same location for 40 years, and even hands out key chains to the tourists to commemorate it. His son and daughter-in-law have taken over now, and expanded the kitchen to add steaks and other items to the burgers and chicken that has been the staple fare. The food is decent, the atmosphere classic woody Western, complete with stuffed animal heads, cowboy-hatted patrons, and pool tables.

Mel's Diner. Main St., Augusta. ☎ **406/562-3408.** All dishes $1–$6. No credit cards. Daily 6am–8pm (or later). AMERICAN.

Everyone in town will send you to Mel's for breakfast. It's a tiny place with four booths and one large table. You'll get good food at good prices here. The hours depend on how business is doing.

Outpost Deli. 819 7th Ave. NW, Choteau. ☎ **406/466-5330.** Breakfast $2–$5; lunch and dinner $3–$8. No credit cards. Summer, 6am–9pm; winter, 7am–3pm. SANDWICHES.

This sandwich shop with good sandwiches and excellent milk shakes is a very friendly place. Locals keep their regular coffee cups on a shelf, and they sit together at a large table by the window. But they don't keep to themselves over there. They'll visit with the folks who they don't know and bring them coffee.

Western Bar. Main St., Augusta. ☎ **406/562-3262.** All dishes $4–$15. No credit cards. Personal checks accepted. Daily 10am–2am. AMERICAN.

The main job of both the Western and the Buckhorn is serving beer, not food, but the food isn't bad here, and the Western is very clean for a small-town bar. You can eat at the bar or some inconspicuous tables in the back, near the woodstove. You can also sip a beer or order dinner in the outdoor beer garden. Favorites are Western burgers or cowboy burgers, served by (who else) Lottie and Robert Berger. They also have live music twice a month and sponsor winter and summer fishing derbies. The ice fishing derby in February is Montana's largest.

4 Lewistown

105 miles E of Great Falls; 128 miles N of Billings

Lewistown is not really on the way to any place in particular, so if you find yourself here, you probably meant to come. It is the hub of a large agricultural region in Charlie Russell country, known as the Judith Basin. The town is blessed with mountains, great downtown architecture, stately homes from other eras, and solid and modest citizens who aren't inarticulate agrarian stereotypes. And there are some notable recreational activities here—especially hunting and fishing. Lewistown is also home to two of the best B&Bs in Montana.

   Lewistown is located in a broad valley surrounded by three mountain ranges—the Big and Little Snowies, the Moccasin, and the Judith. This is the center of the Judith Basin. While Charlie Russell lived in Great Falls later, the Judith Basin is where he did his cowboying, and where he fell in love with Montana.

ESSENTIALS

GETTING THERE   Big Sky Airlines (☎ 800/237-7788) provides commuter airline service to and from Billings daily. The **Rimrock Stages depot** (☎ 406/538-3380) is located at 102 W. Main and provides service from and to Billings and Great Falls.

Lewistown is connected to other Montana cities by two-lane U.S. highways that radiate from the town. From Billings, go north 92 miles, then west 31 miles on U.S. 87. From Great Falls, Lewistown is 105 miles east on U.S. 87.

VISITOR INFORMATION   The Lewistown Chamber of Commerce has its offices adjacent to the Museum of the Central Montana Historical Association at Symmes Park at 408 NE Main (☎ **406/538-5436;** www.lewistown.net/~lewchamb). Maps from the Bureau of Land Management, the U.S. Forest Service, and the C.M. Russell Wildlife Refuge, and local maps, are all available. **Travel Montana's Russell Country** includes Lewistown (☎ **800/527-5348** or 406/761-5036). Local road reports are available at ☎ **406/538-7445.**

GETTING AROUND   Rental car agencies in Lewistown include **Budget** (☎ **406/538-7701**) and **Dean Newton Olds, Cadillac, and GMC** (☎ **406/ 538-3455**).

SPECIAL EVENTS   The **Chokecherry Festival,** held on the Saturday following Labor Day, honors that smarter-than-the-average-berry, the chokecherry, one of the few indigenous fruits of the prairie. Generally overlooked by poets and songwriters— no one has ever been the chokecherry of someone's eye, nor has life ever been a bowl of chokecherries—Lewistown attempts to place the chokecherry on its proper pedestal in the berry pantheon with parades, bake sales, and pie cook-offs. It may be that the pit-spitting contest (for distance and accuracy) is not the best PR tool to accomplish this, but the cook-off could launch the chokecherry into the fruit pie hall of fame.

Lewistown lassoed the ✪ **Montana Cowboy Poetry Gathering** when the event got too big for the venue in Big Timber, about a hundred miles south. Each year in mid-August at the Yogo Inn, the cowboys, ranchers, former large animal vets, and other swaybacked and bowlegged Montana literati gather to swap lies and poems. Those of us who always considered "cowboy poetry" an oxymoron have been pleasantly surprised to find a relent-less rhyming vitality to the poetry and an honest and healthy appreciation of fellow poets. There are also a juried arts-and-crafts show, booths full of leatherwork, and other activities. For details on these events, call the Lewistown Chamber of Commerce at ☎ **406/ 538-5436.**

GETTING OUTSIDE
CROSS-COUNTRY SKIING

You have to make your own fun in Lewistown. If you're here in the winter, there is good cross-country skiing in any of the three mountain ranges that ring the valley— the Big and Little Snowies, the Moccasin, and the Judith ranges. There are a number of trails accessible by car in the Judith Mountains north of town, on old logging and mining roads unused except by skiers and snowmobilers when the autumn snows begin to fall. Head north on U.S. Highway 191 to the Maiden Canyon sign, then take a left and follow the road for 5 miles to the trails.

FISHING

High in the Big Snowy Mountains is **Crystal Lake,** about 35 miles southwest of Lewistown. This is a popular and somewhat remote recreational area that offers good fishing, hiking, and camping. You have to travel about 25 miles on gravel road to get there. Take U.S. 87 west of town for 8 miles, then turn south at the sign for Crystal Lake. After about 16 miles it runs into Forest Service Road 275, which you should follow for another 9 miles to the lake. Motorized boats are prohibited, but overnight tent camping is available. For good trout fishing closer to town, try **Big Spring Creek,** which begins south of Lewistown and flows north through town to join the Judith

Must-See in Martinsdale:
The Charles M. Bair Family Museum

The **Charles M. Bair Family Museum** (☎ **406/572-3314;** www.bairmuseum.org) opened in 1995, the legacy of an unusual—and unusually successful—sheepman. Charles Bair came west in 1883 as a conductor on the Northern Pacific Railroad, and then developed the largest sheep ranch in the U.S. His flock at one time numbered 300,000 spread over his 50,000 acres. In one year, he filled 47 railway cars with 1.5 million pounds of lamb.

But sheep was not all Bair accumulated. With his wife Mary and daughters Alberta and Marguerite, the family compiled a treasure trove of European antiques, silver, and American Western paintings by contemporaries C.M. Russell and J.H. Sharp. They also collected Indian artifacts and other Western memorabilia.

The guided tours, which leave every hour on the hour (until 4pm), offer a look into the lifestyle of one of the wealthiest families in Montana. The museum is located 81 miles southwest of Lewistown (or 74 miles north of Livingston) in Martinsdale. From Lewistown, go west on U.S. 87 to the intersection of U.S. 191, then south 39 miles to Harlowton. Go west 23 miles on U.S. 12 to County Road 294, then 2 miles south. From Livingston, go 49 miles north on U.S. 89, then east on County Road 294 to Martinsdale, about 27 miles.

The museum is open from early May to the end of September. In May and September, hours are Wednesday to Sunday, 10am to 5pm, with the last tour offered at 4pm. In June, July, and August, the hours are the same, but the museum is open 7 days a week.

River. You can easily access Brewery Flats on Big Spring Creek about 2 miles outside of town on MT 238. Flatwillow Creek in the Forest Grove area of the Little Snowies provides some rainbow and cutthroat fishing. For **flat-water fishing,** try Upper and Lower Carter's Pond, man-made ponds 6.5 miles north of Lewistown on U.S. Highway 191. There are picnic facilities and overnight camping as well. The **James Kipp Recreation Area** (☎ **406/538-8706**), 78 miles north of town on the western tip of Fort Peck Lake on the Charles M. Russell National Wildlife Refuge, also has fishing, camping, hiking, and a boat ramp. Take MT 191 northeast until it intersects with MT 19, then go north about 35 miles.

GOLF

Lewistown has two golf courses. The **18-hole Judith Shadows Golf Course** (☎ **406/538-6062**) is an alternative-spikes-only facility with a new back nine, located at the end of Marcella Avenue in the northeast corner of town. The **Pine Meadows Golf Course,** a nine-hole layout (☎ **406/538-5885**), is on Country Club Road.

HIKING

At **Crystal Lake** (see, "Fishing," above), there are numerous trails into the Lewis and Clark National Forest, including the Crystal Lake Loop National Recreation Trail. This trail leads to two popular destinations, Ice Caves and Crystal Cascades. There is also good hiking along the Wild and Scenic Missouri River from the James Kipp Recreation Area. The Judith Resource Area of the Bureau of Land Management, Lewistown District Office, Airport Road, Lewistown, MT 59437

(☎ 406/538-7461), can give you information on additional hiking trails in the nearby mountains.

SEEING THE SIGHTS

A little too cutely named, **the Charlie Russell Chew-Choo dinner trains** (☎ **406/538-5436** for information or 406/538-2527 for reservations) runs from Lewistown to Denton and back once each weekend from Memorial Day through the end of September, with special trains on Christmas, New Year's Eve, and Valentine's Day. On the 56-mile round-trip ride, the train crosses three large trestles and navigates a 2,000-foot tunnel during its 3½-hour run through the Charlie Russell country of the Judith Basin. Watch out for train robbers. The food's good, too. The schedule varies, so call ahead. A regular summer run on the train with dinner is $75 per person; the New Year's Eve trip is $119.95 per person

Big Spring, located 7 miles south of Lewistown on County Rd. 466, is the third largest freshwater spring in the world. The spring is the water source for the town, and is considered one of the purest in the nation. It is bottled by the Big Spring Water Company and sold at stores in the western central part of the U.S. The spring also feeds the Montana State Fish Hatchery nearby.

Lewistown became a regional commercial center after a boom in the early part of the 20th century brought on by ranching and mining. The mining, ranching, and banking barons built large homes in a range of styles, primarily Gothic and Victorian. The first to build was a gold miner and organizer of the Empire Bank & Trust, J.T. Wunderlin, and he was soon followed by others, all of whom could afford silk stockings. They lived in **the Silk Stocking District,** which is just northeast of downtown on Boulevard. (Not the section of Boulevard near Symmes Park; if you're here, you're lost.) The Lewistown Chamber of Commerce (☎ **406/538-5436**) can provide information on self-guided tours. The homes, however, are private residences and not open to the public. Start at 220 West Blvd., where there is a plaque outside the Symmes-Wickes house explaining the development of the area. At the top of the hill overlooking the Silk Stocking District, check out the **Fergus County Courthouse** (7th Avenue and Main Street downtown), a gold-domed mission-style courthouse built in 1906.

WHERE TO STAY

Circle Bar Guest Ranch. P.O. Box 61, Utica, MT 59452. ☎ **888/570-0227** or 406/423-5454. Fax 406/423-5686. www.circlebarranch.com. 9 units. $1,330 per adult per week, $1,200 per child 12 and under per week. Rates include meals and ranch activities. No credit cards. 35 miles west of Lewistown; take U.S. 87 west to Windham, then turn south on County Rd. 541 to Utica. Then go 12 miles southwest along the Judith River on a gravel road.

The Circle Bar Guest Ranch is a full-service, year-round guest ranch that offers everything from riding to volleyball. If you want to work a cattle drive, the ranch holds them in June and October. The regular guest season runs from June 1 to September 15, but the ranch also has winter activities available by special arrangement. There's hiking and fishing on the Judith River in summer, bird and big game hunting in the fall, and horse-drawn wagons and sleigh rides in winter. The cabins are roomy log affairs, recently redecorated, with woodstoves, auxiliary heat, and private bathrooms.

Pheasant Tales Bed-and-Bistro. RR1, Box 1615, Lewistown, MT 59457. ☎ **406/538-7880.** www.tein.net/sw. 4 units. $78 double; $156 4-person kitchen suite.

While the Symmes-Wick House offers a turn-of-the-century experience, the Pheasant Tales is a thoroughly modern, beautifully constructed and furnished guest house with some unique touches. Chris and Rick Taylor are both avid pheasant hunters. Chris began preparing gourmet meals with the birds brought down by friends. They became increasingly popular, and hunters told the couple that if they opened a bed-and-breakfast, they would stay there on hunting trips. Chris said that she prefers fixing dinners, so she opened a bed-and-bistro. The results are very impressive. The building is done in reddish pine. The rooms are large and comfortably furnished. With reservations, and for an additional $25, Chris will prepare a gourmet dinner in the evening. The Taylors also raise English setters, and the whelping room is in a portion of the building, so there is almost always a brace of setter puppies providing entertainment in an enclosed area of the lawn. There's an extensive deck, and land to walk on. Good fishing is available nearby as well. Upland game bird hunters can hunt on some leased land for $75 per gun—but no guides are provided. A full breakfast is available on request for $8 per person. Chris will also consider requests for dinner from visitors not staying at the Pheasant Tales if they call ahead and make reservations.

The Symmes-Wicks House Bed & Breakfast. 220 West Blvd., Lewistown, MT 59457. ☎ **406/538-9068.** Fax 406/538-5331. 3 units (2 with private bathroom). $45–$75 double. Rates include breakfast. MC, V.

Charles and Carole Wicks have beautifully restored this 1909 shingle-style, arts-and-crafts home, which sits right in the heart of the Silk Stocking District. Though you can see the exteriors of all the homes in the district, a stay here provides a unique opportunity to view the inside of one. Tiffany glass was used in the windows above the landing on the staircase. Upstairs, the guest rooms are tastefully decorated in two opposing themes: The room facing east, in masculine hunter-green tones, has a sleigh bed and a reproduction Degas figure. The bathroom is a wooden work of art and the chain handle of the water closet is a delightful throwback. The room facing south has a more feminine touch. The bathroom isn't so much a room as it is a tasteful area partitioned off from the main room. In the early 20th century, there was an influx of Croatian stone cutters to Lewistown. Some of their work can be seen on this house, as well as on other buildings in the area.

Yogo Inn. 211 E. Main St., Lewistown, MT 59457. ☎ **800/860-9646** or 406/538-8271. 112 units. $69 double. A/C TEL TV. AE, DISC, MC, V. Pets accepted.

The Yogo Inn looks better on the inside. The rooms are clean, functional, and quiet, but unspectacular. There is a well-kept, interior courtyard that catches the sun and contains one of the motel's two swimming pools. It's popular with business travelers, and everything is functional but not fancy. There's an informal cafe and a more formal dining room, as well as a bar with a big screen television.

WHERE TO DINE

The Whole Famdamily. 206 W. Main St. **406/538-5161.** Lunch and dinner $4–$7. AE, DISC, MC, V. Mon–Fri 11am–8pm, Sat 11am–5pm. SANDWICHES.

This is an inviting, cafe-style restaurant with some character. The sandwiches are your best bet; they are big and reasonably priced. Each night, the dinner menu offers up two new specials. The sandwiches are named for folks—relatives and locals, I guess.

5 The Hi-Line: U.S. Highway 2

Havre: 115 miles NE of Great Falls; Fort Belknap: 46 miles E of Havre; Glasgow: 279 miles N of Billings

If you're not from Montana and find yourself on the Hi-Line, you're probably on the way somewhere else. There aren't a great deal of things up here, except for wheat, birds, and lots of ground squirrels. And an occasional antelope.

There are a number of National Wildlife Refuges along this drive: the gigantic **Charles M. Russell NWR,** and the smaller **Black Coulee, Bowdoin,** and **Medicine Lake**—the latter on the far eastern border of the state. Like most of the refuges nationwide, they are managed primarily for the benefit of birds, especially migratory waterfowl. So this is a good place to bring a bird book, because even if you'll only be driving through, you'll be able to identify a lot of species from the car, like Franklin's gull (a plains gull with black wingtips), the western meadowlark (leave the window open to hear its melodious flute-like song), or the marsh hawk (or harrier, not a true hawk). It flies low to the ground, flapping its wings more often than the gliding hawks, and is gray when mature, brown when young, with a white bar across its rump.

The roadsides up here are dotted with white crosses—memorials to people who have died in auto accidents. Some of them are maintained by friends and family, decorated with flowers, flags, and ribbons. There are a lot of them. Don't be fooled by the long straight stretches of road. Drive carefully.

FROM HAVRE TO FORT BELKNAP

Havre isn't anyone's idea of a vacation spot, but it has its moments. There are some interesting Indian and aboriginal sites, including the nearby **Bear Paw Battleground,** the site of the last major battle between the army and the Indians in the Indian War period. Nearly every tour in Havre itself is a guided tour and requires advance reservations, so please book ahead. The best place to start is the **H. Earl Clack Museum,** located in the Heritage Center downtown, 306 3rd Ave., ☎ **406/265-4000.** The museum is open year-round from 10am to 5pm Tuesday to Friday, and 1 to 5pm on Saturday. You can reserve most of the tours at the museum.

Start your tour of this region just south of Havre on MT 87, coming up from Great Falls. Drive north to Havre until you reach the junction with U.S. Highway 2. Take U.S. Highway 2 east until it converges with Montana's version of Route 66, a state highway running south through the Fort Belknap Indian Reservation. Take 66 through the reservation to the intersection of U.S. Highway 191. Turn left there (or northeast) and drive until the road meets up with U.S. Highway 2 again, about 57 miles.

SEEING THE SIGHTS

Rocky Boys Indian Reservation and the Rocky Boy Powwow. From MT 87 turn east at Boxelder onto Duck Creek Rd. Drive 14 miles to the Tribal Headquarters. Call the Havre Area Chamber of Commerce (☎ **406/265-4383**) for precise dates and further information about the powwow.

Southwest of Havre lies the home of 2,000 Chippewa and Cree Indians on this rather small plot of land at the Western Front of the Bear Paw Mountains. For years the U.S. government tried to keep the Cree from settling in the States, and the tribe was homeless. In 1911, when Fort Assiniboine was abandoned, the Chippewa and Cree had part of the land set aside as a reservation. Then, as now, employment was difficult to come by. Each July the Rocky Boy Powwow is held near Box Elder.

Fort Assiniboine. 3 miles south of Havre on MT 87. Guided tours only, arranged through the H. Earl Clack Museum in Havre. ☎ **406/265-8336** or 406/265-6233. $3 adults, free for children under 6. Open June 1–Sept 1.

This fort was opened in 1879, but by then it was already obsolete. It was intended to protect settlers from Indian attacks, but all the tribes had already been defeated. After the defeat of Chief Joseph in the nearby Bear Paw Battle, the Fort Assiniboine troops didn't have much to worry about. The red brick buildings of the barracks and other quarters are well preserved. After the fort closed, the land around it was turned into the Rocky Boy Reservation. Only guided tours are permitted because the fort is now run by Montana State University as an agricultural research station.

Havre Underground Tours. 120 3rd Ave., Havre. ☎ **406/265-8888.** $6 adults, $5 seniors, $4 children 6–12. Reservations recommended. Summer, daily 9am–5pm, tours 9:30am–3:30pm; winter, Mon–Sat 10am–5pm, tours 10:30am–3:30pm.

This interesting tour of Havre's boisterous history as a railroad and cowboy town provides an interesting look at the past, when racism was rampant. When a devastating fire in 1904 destroyed Havre's business district, the labyrinth of tunnels and basements under the town served as the West's first subterranean shopping mall. A lot of the local businesses in the last century were located here. Their products included honkytonk, gambling, opium dens, and sex for profit. There is also a new railroad museum attached to the underground which focuses on the railroad history in the area.

Wahkpa Chu'gn Bison Kill. Behind the Holiday Village Shopping Mall on U.S. Hwy. 2, west. ☎ **406/265-6417** or 406/265-7550. Tour info available at H.E. Clack Museum. $3.50 adults, $3 seniors, $2 students, free for children under 6. Tours, mid-May to Labor Day, Tues–Sat 1–5pm, 1 evening tour at 7pm, Sun 10am–5pm.

From a steep cliff above the Milk River—Wahkpa Chu'gn—the Assiniboine drove bison off to provide food for the tribe. The jump was used by the Indians from between 2,000 and 600 years ago. The guided tours, which last about an hour, are very informative. And you can't help feeling that after spending some time in the deteriorating shopping mall next door, the bison didn't mind the fall so much.

WHERE TO STAY

On Route 2 in the eastern part of town there is a nice RV campground (right next to the Best Western) called the **Havre RV Park.** There are showers, a saloon, a casino, laundry, and a store. Cost is $22 for an RV, $13 for a tent.

Best Western Great Northern Inn. 1345 1st St., Havre, MT 59501. ☎ **888/530-4100** or 406/265-4200. Fax 406/265-3656. 64 units. A/C TV TEL. $75 double. Rates include continental breakfast. AE, DC, DISC, MC, V.

This is a brand-new entry in the Havre lodging sweepstakes (if that's the word we want) and it is a relatively upscale one. The rooms are fairly large, and there are an indoor heated pool, spa, and steam and fitness rooms. There is no restaurant, but across the street at the Vineyard (see below) or the Mediterranean Room, you can charge your meal to your room. There's a bridal suite for $129 for lovers and a corporate suite for $95 for brokers. The corporate business center with fax, copying, and computer capabilities is open 24 hours a day.

El Toro Inn. 521 1st St., Havre, MT 59501. ☎ **800/422-5414** or 406/265-5414. 41 units. A/C TV TEL. $48–$57 double. AE, CB, DC, DISC.

Although El Toro is just a motel, the Spanish tile and stucco walls give it some character. Rooms are standard, and include a mini-refrigerator and microwave. Coffee is free in the morning and laundry facilities are available.

WHERE TO DINE

PJ's. 15 3rd Ave. ☎ **406/2656-3211.** Breakfast $2–$6; lunch $4–$8; dinner $9–$16. DISC, MC, V. Sun–Thurs 6am–10pm, Fri–Sat 6am–11pm.

You're out on the Hi-Line, driving through Havre, so you might as well eat in a typical Western place. PJ's is across the street from the railway station; there's a poker game in the corner with the clickety-clack of chips, and the boop-boop-boop of the electronic slots. The food is very good, especially the trademark burgers and beef, and the folks are friendly.

Bear Paw Battlefield: The Nez Perce Surrender

One of the most remarkable stories of the Indian Wars culminated here at the Bear Paw Battlefield in Nez Perce National Historic Park, located 26 miles south of Chinook on County Road 240.

In 1877, in what is now northeast Oregon, the Army tried to force a band of Nez Perce Indians under the leadership of Chief Joseph onto a reservation far from their native lands. The Nez Perce decided to escape, trying to reach Canada where they hoped to join Sitting Bull's Lakota, who had already found homes there.

Joseph led 800 of his tribespeople on a 1,700-mile flight through Yellowstone National Park and eventually north to this site, a mere 45 miles south of the Canadian border and freedom.

The tribe was pursued by the army under Gen. Oliver O. Howard all the way. A Civil War hero known as "the praying general," Howard was a deeply Christian man who had developed considerable hostility toward some of the Nez Perce leaders because he considered them heathens. Through a series of brilliant maneuvers, Joseph and his band of warriors, women, children, horses, and cattle escaped or defeated the army at every turn. Even Howard was forced to admit in his memoirs about the chase, "The leadership of Chief Joseph was indeed remarkable. No general could have chosen a safer position or one that would be more likely to puzzle and obstruct a pursuing foe . . . We shall see next how we ought to solve the problem presented us by this shrewd savage."

They fought several battles along the way, but the ubiquitous Col. Nelson A. Miles finally caught Joseph and his band in a snowstorm here at Bear Paw, a rolling, grassy landscape achingly close to the freedom promised by the Canadian border. After a 6-day fight, Joseph surrendered on October 5, 1877.

The Vineyard. 1300 1st Ave., Havre. ☎ **406/265-5355.** Lunch $4–7; dinner $8–$20. AE, DISC, MC, V. Mon–Thurs 11am–2pm and 5–10pm, Fri 11am–2pm and 5–10:30pm, Sat 5–10:30pm, Sun 4–9:30pm. AMERICAN.

Everything about this place, and the Mediterranean Room next door, is overdone. But it is light and airy. The atmosphere may be a little too ferny for some tastes. The food is ordinary American, with enough Mexican and spaghetti to keep the kids happy. The quality is marginal, but since most of the other choices in Havre are fast food, this is a good alternative. Plus, you can dine under an atrium window or in the patio. The place is owned by the same fellow who owns the Best Western across the street.

FORT BELKNAP RESERVATION

The Fort Belknap Reservation was established in 1888, and is now home to the Gros Ventre and Assiniboine tribes. It was named for William W. Belknap, who was secretary of war under President Ulysses S. Grant. The Gros Ventre call themselves the A'a'nin, or White Clay People. They had lived in North Dakota's Red River Valley from 1100 to 1400, gradually being pushed west by competition from other tribes. After coming to the Missouri River country in about 1730, they split into two tribes, the southern branch becoming known as the Arapaho.

The Assiniboine split from the Yanktonai Sioux in the early 1600s, supposedly over a squabble. Two of the first ladies of the tribe fought about a local delicacy, a buffalo

Joseph surrendered his rifle (now in the Museum of the Upper Missouri in Fort Benton). He is believed to have delivered this famous speech, translated by an interpreter:

Tell General Howard I know his heart. What he told me before I have in my heart. I am tired of fighting. Our chiefs are killed. Looking Glass is dead. Toohoolhootze is dead. The old men are all killed. It is the young men who say yes or no. He who led the young men is dead. It is cold and we have no blankets. The little children are freezing to death. My people, some of them, have run away to the hills, and have no blankets, no food; no one knows where they are—perhaps freezing to death. I want time to look for my children and see how many of them I can find. Maybe I shall find them among the dead. Hear me, my chiefs. I am tired; my heart is sick and sad. From where the sun stands now, I will fight no more forever.

That night, White Bird and 200 of his followers slipped away to Canada. Of the 431 remaining, 21 died in the spring. The rest moved to a reservation in Oklahoma, where another 47 of Joseph's people died and many more became ill. Finally, in 1885, 118 Nez Perce who agreed to become Christians were allowed to go to the Lapwai Agency near Lewistown, Idaho. The rest, including Joseph, were settled on the Colville Reservation in Nespelem in northeast Washington state.

Joseph never gave up hope of a return to his homeland in the Wallowa Valley. He met with President William McKinley in 1897, and tried unsuccessfully to purchase the land in 1900. He died at Colville in 1904, age 64. Even in death, he wasn't returned to the Wallowa Valley, but was buried at Nespelem.

heart. They call themselves the Nakota, The Generous Ones. There is also a branch of the tribe at the Fort Peck Reservation to the east.

There is a small **museum** and visitor center at the intersection of MT 66 and U.S. Highway 2 (☎ 406/353-2205). From here you can arrange a tour of the tribes' herd of 300 buffalo and learn a little bit about their culture.

Snake Butte nearby was often used as a site of vision quests, where individuals sought personal supernatural powers or medicine. These powers, if accepted, came with a price. Few who had them lived long lives, so it was said. Snake Butte was quarried for stone by the Army Corps of Engineers for construction of the dam at Fort Peck in the 1930s.

If you head south from here to Hays, then turn to the east, you'll come to **St. Paul's Mission,** established by Jesuit missionaries in 1886. It is a solid stone structure. Next to it is a tiny chapel dedicated to Our Lady of the Little Rockies. A local devotee has carved a statue identical to the miraculous one at Einsiedeld in Switzerland. The chapel was built in 1931. To get here, take MT 66 south from U.S. 2 at Fort Belknap for about 40 miles to the sign for Hays. Turn left (east). In Hays, follow the road south after it turns to gravel. The mission is on the left (east) side of the street about a quarter mile after the road turns south.

Up the road is Mission Canyon a steep, narrow, cool gash in the otherwise open landscape. Just after entering the canyon, you'll see a natural stone arch.

The very brave can climb nearly to the top, and there are several ledges where you can pose for the photographer.

Gros Ventre and Assiniboine Tribes Buffalo Tours. RR1, Box 66, Fort Belknap Agency, Harlem, MT 59526. ☎ **406/353-2205.** Reservations required. Tours are run from the visitor center, located at the intersection of U.S. Hwy. 2 and MT 66 at Fort Belknap. $15–$20 per person (charge based on group size). Open May 1–Sept 30.

The tribes have been rebuilding their bison herd since 1974, starting with 27 animals. There are now about 300 grazing on 10,000 acres of the tribal buffalo reserve. You're likely to see other wildlife on the tour, including golden eagles and America's fastest land animal, the pronghorn. There is also a large prairie dog town that is being considered as a relocation site for the country's rarest mammal, the black-footed ferret. The tour includes insights into the tribes' history, culture, and relationship to the plains and its animals.

FROM GLASGOW TO THE FORT PECK INDIAN RESERVATION & THE C.M. RUSSELL WILDLIFE REFUGE

People moving through here in the northeast extremes of Montana can find themselves a little disoriented by the sheer vastness of the horizons that stretch unbroken all the way to the Dakotas. Although this is mostly wheat country, it's not flat—in fact it is sharply rolling and canyoned country—but open to the eye in all directions.

In 1879, Robert Louis Stevenson rode an immigrant train through here and wrote later: "What livelihood can repay a human creature for a life spent in this huge sameness? He is cut off from books, from news, from company, from all that can relieve existence but the prosecution of his affairs. A sky full of stars is the most varied spectacle he can hope. He may walk five miles and see nothing; ten, and it is as though he had not moved; twenty, and he is still in the midst of the same great level, and has approached no nearer to the object within view, the flat horizon which keeps pace with his advance."

There is a story, usually attributed to an area just over the border in western North Dakota, but in the same sort of landscape, of a lone Indian who watched patiently as a recently arrived farmer plowed into the virgin earth, turning the soil with its deep and tangled roots to begin the civilization and profitability of the already vanishing native prairie. After some time, the Indian came over the farmer, pointed to the plowed earth and said, "Wrong side up."

The story is probably apocryphal, another of the long chain of myths on which the West is built in the American imagination. But there are two contrasting sentiments made flesh here in the northeast corner that illustrate the conflicting impulses of America, progress and preservation.

The first and easiest to spot is the Fort Peck Dam and Lake. Construction of the dam began in 1933, at the height of the Depression, as a way to put men to work and to provide inexpensive water to the growing agricultural area.

The dam is the largest hydraulically earth-filled dam in the world, nearly 5 miles across backing up a lake that is 134 miles long with 1,600 miles of shoreline—more shoreline, it is said, than the entire coast of California. The dam is one of the many Corps of Engineers projects that have turned the cantankerous Missouri River that Lewis and Clark navigated into a tame and regulated lake from the Mississippi River to the Rockies.

Seven thousand men and women went to work on the dam in 1933, and at the peak of employment nearly 11,000 were here. Locally, the attitude toward the dam was ambivalent. The residents were losing their homes to the slowly rising water. On the other hand, they could appreciate the need for jobs, for irrigation water, for electric power, even for a large recreational lake. The story of the dam is told at the **Fort Peck Powerhouse and Museum** (☎ **406/526-3421**). The powerhouse looms over the landscape like a chunky art deco skyscraper that somehow got lost on its way to Des Moines. The museum (it's free and open from 9am to 5:30pm daily) offers tours of the power plant on the hour (the last one leaves at 4:45pm). The museum also houses a fine collection of dinosaur fossils. It's located on MT 24 at Fort Peck Dam.

SPECIAL EVENTS   Fort Peck Lake, backed up by the dam, is the best spot in Montana for walleye fishing. An annual competition, **the Governor Cup,** takes place there each spring. Contact the Corps at P.O. Box 208, Fort Peck, MT 59233 (☎ **406/526-3411**), for the schedule and details.

OUTFITTERS & SEEING THE SIGHTS

The tiny town of Fort Peck is Montana's only planned community, the result of its heyday as the housing base for the workers at the dam in the '30s. It started out as a trading post in 1867, then grew with the dam, then faded when construction was ended. It is testimony to the remoteness of this region that in 1934, months after the U.S. Army Corps of Engineers had begun construction of this $100 million project (big money during the Depression), a New York supplier asked the New York army headquarters how to address some equipment it was sending out to Montana. The army solemnly replied that that there was no such place as Fort Peck—it had been abandoned in the 1880s.

The **Fort Peck Theater** is a large, former cinema built in the '30s for the workers. The surprisingly beautiful theater seats 1,000 people for summer stock. Its season runs approximately from the last week of June to the last week of August, and is operated by the Fort Peck Restaurant and Welfare Council (☎ **800/828-2259**).

Surrounding all those miles of shoreline is the **Charles M. Russell Wildlife Refuge,** named for the famous Western wildlife cowboy artist Charlie Russell. Born in 1864 in St. Louis, Russell was a working Montana cowboy at the age of 16 and drew much of his artistic inspiration from those years. He greatly admired the Indians, and deplored the plowing of the grasslands on the poor soil that would eventually force a turnover every 10 years or so in the ownership of the land in this part of the world. Russell knew that destroying the native grass would destroy the habitat for the animals, the bison would be lost, the Indian conquered. Russell didn't like seeing the West civilized, and he had little use for "settlers."

Turnoffs and campsites are located all along the perimeter of the refuge, as are boat ramps for anglers. Flat Creek, Rock Creek, and Nelson Creek boat ramps are easy to reach, located just off MT 24, which skirts the eastern side of the lake. There are 15 campgrounds scattered along the lake margin. The camping varies from rugged to not-so-rugged. Only two sites—the West End Campground and Downstream Campground—have flush toilets and showers. Both are located near the dam. Contact the Corps of Engineers (☎ **406/526-3411**) for information.

The **Fort Peck Indian Reservation** is home to the Assiniboines and the Sioux. The Sioux, who had been on the reservation by themselves, were joined by the Assiniboine nation after smallpox killed more than half of the tribe farther west along the Missouri River and again threatened the tribe after it resettled near Fort Belknap. The exodus from the deadly disease brought them to Fort Peck. Now the reservation is home to many non-Indians, with less than half of the actual reservation owned by Native Americans.

This area has been extremely important in the fossil world. The world's first Tyrannosaurus rex was discovered in 1902 just south of where the lake is in Garfield County.

The **Garfield County Museum** (☎ 406/557-2517) in Jordan has replicas of the T. rex skull there, along with a duckbill dinosaur and triceratops. It is open June through August. Jordan is located at the intersection of MT 59 and MT 200 in the plains south of Fort Peck Lake. From Miles City, drive north on MT for 83 miles. From Glendive take MT 200 west 111 miles. From Fort Peck Dam, take MT 24 south 59 miles to MT 200, then take MT 200 west 36 miles.

WHERE TO STAY

Big Dome Hotel Bed & Breakfast. U.S. Hwy. 2, Saco, MT 59261. ☎ **406/527-3498.** 6 units with 2 shared bathrooms. $40 double. Rate includes breakfast. MC, V.

Saco is truly a town that you can miss in the blink of an eye, but if you do, you'll miss out on some great stuff, especially this oasis of a lodging. An area renowned for fossils, Saco has a more infamous claim to fame than simple dinosaur relics. It is the mosquito capital of the world (or so we're told): Apparently, there are more mosquitoes per square inch in Saco than anywhere else in the world.

The Big Dome Hotel, built in 1909 as the grand First National Bank of Saco, has been completely remodeled by owners Mark Zuidema and Jody Menge, with many original items from the bank restored, including the vault. All rooms are located on the second floor and are tastefully decorated (the tin ceiling panels were meticulously hand-painted by Jody) and extremely comfortable. The only knock against the place is the railroad tracks across the street. A train rumbling by can be a less than charming noise at 4 in the morning.

The Cottonwood Inn. U.S. Hwy. 2 East, Glasgow, MT 59230. ☎ **800/321-8213** or 406/228-8213. Fax 406/228-8248. E-mail: cwinn@nemontel.net. 92 units. A/C TV TEL. $56–$65 double. AE, DC, DISC, MC, V. Pets accepted.

This motel and convention center is far and away the nicest place in Glasgow: modern and clean, if a little small in the lobby. The rooms are conventional motel rooms. The restaurant, the Prairie Rose Dining Room, is the most popular one in town. It specializes in homemade soups, bread, and pies, all made from scratch. The motel has valet and room service, unusual services out here in the backwoods.

Fort Peck Hotel. Fort Peck, MT 59223 (just off U.S. Hwy. 2). ☎ **800/560-4931** or 406/526-3472. 35 units. $40 double with shared bathroom, $43 double with private bathroom; $66 suite. Rates include continental breakfast. AE, DISC, MC, V.

This registered historic site is an intimate, old-fashioned hotel. Built during the WPA era, it hearkens back to the slower way of life in Montana. There are no televisions or telephones in the rooms, a situation that tends to usher people out into the lobby for (gasp!) conversation. There is a good restaurant that serves dinner in the evenings. The rooms are small but serviceable, with high ceilings and spare furnishings reminiscent of the 1930s and 1940s.

Bozeman, Southcentral Montana & the Missouri Headwaters

by Dan Whipple

8

Relatively unspoiled, yet one of the most heavily visited areas in the state, southcentral Montana is a world-class playground for the outdoor recreational enthusiast. Its biggest draws are the multiple-use mountains that are a haven for hikers and campers, and, without a doubt, the fly-fishing waters of the four major rivers that flow through its valleys—the Madison, Jefferson, Gallatin, and Yellowstone—which double as recreation areas for rafting, kayaking, and canoeing.

During winter months, downhill skiing takes over at Big Sky, which lays claim to having the largest vertical drop of any hill in the United States (4,180 feet). The region is also excellent for cross-country skiing—Lone Mountain Ranch and Bohart Ranch are two of the best Nordic skiing facilities in the state. For a change of pace, make your way south to Yellowstone (see chapter 10).

Bozeman, home of Montana State University, provides the hip, intellectual charm and culture of a college town—good bookstores and restaurants, charming shops, even a brewpub—as well as cultural events that appeal to both the cosmopolitan and cowboy cultures. The Sweet Pea Festival, a celebration of music and the performing arts, is complemented by the Livingston rodeo, one of the best in either Montana or Wyoming.

A few years ago the area around Bozeman bounded by the Bridger, Gallatin, Madison, and Tobacco ranges seemed like an undiscovered bargain for real estate opportunists and others searching for the perfect place to relocate or set up a vacation house. Those times have changed; the communities of Bozeman, Livingston, and Belgrade experienced a boom as newcomers moved in, attracted to the easygoing Montana lifestyle and the wide range of outdoor activities. It's also been discovered by some rebellious Hollywood types who have purchased ranches in the area—writer Tom McGuane, actor Peter Fonda. Hip poet Richard Brautigan lived in Livingston, and a number of writers have made it their home since. Peter Bowen, author of a series of Western detective novels, also lives here.

1 Scenic Drives

The Bozeman-Livingston-Three Forks area is one large intersection. **Interstate 90** runs east to west through this region; and from it, three valley highways extend south. Between Three Forks and Livingston,

I-90 is known for its windiness, especially along the stretch of road from Bozeman to Livingston. The westernmost of the region's three valley highways, **U.S. Highway 287,** runs south from Three Forks, and extends 120 miles south through the Madison Valley to the town of Ennis (a fishing mecca) and West Yellowstone, the western gateway to Yellowstone National Park. From Bozeman, **U.S. Highway 191** runs parallel to U.S. Highway 287 down the Gallatin Valley, past the resort community of Big Sky, to West Yellowstone.

The third highway, **U.S. Highway 89,** runs 57 miles south from Livingston through the Paradise Valley to Gardiner and the north entrance of Yellowstone. Though the area is populated primarily by ranchers and there are few attractions along the way, it's a beautiful drive, especially through Yankee Jim Canyon.

Red Lodge can be reached a few different ways, but the most scenic is reached by taking I-90 to exit 408 at Columbus and heading south on MT 78 through Absarokee and Roscoe for 48 miles. It's a much prettier and less traveled road than the freeway.

DRIVING TOUR #1: THE BEARTOOTH SCENIC BYWAY

Some say that an ideal loop tour is relatively short, runs through lovely scenery, and has excellent roads, facilities, and telephones. If that's your criteria, you won't enjoy the Beartooth Byway. If, however, you'll allow yourself the luxury of a leisurely drive at altitudes of almost 11,000 feet, you will be treated to sights on a route that Charles Kurault called the most scenic road in America.

Begin in Livingston. Drive south, following the Yellowstone River through Paradise Valley, 53 miles to Gardiner. Once inside the park, you can stop off at Mammoth Hot Springs, a geothermal wonderland just inside the park's northern boundary. Then, take the road from Mammoth Hot Springs east to Tower Junction, continuing east to the park's northeast entrance at Silver Gate to pick up U.S. Highway 212 (this is the Beartooth Byway). From here, the road begins to wind upward along the Montana and Wyoming border for nearly 40 ear-popping miles until it reaches the Beartooth Pass (elevation 10,947 feet). From that spectacular altitude, you may well see snow—even in July—as well as miles and miles of mountains across both Wyoming and Montana. The road then drops for 24 miles as the byway continues on to Red Lodge. From Red Lodge, drive north on MT 78 down into the high plains before heading back to the mountains of Bozeman, west on I-90. The entire trip takes between 6 and 8 hours, depending on the time of day you choose to drive it, and the condition of the roads.

DRIVING TOUR #2: U.S. HIGHWAY 287 FROM THREE FORKS TO WEST YELLOWSTONE

Less strenuous on the body and car is the drive along U.S. Highway 287 from Three Forks to West Yellowstone. It passes through the beautiful Madison Valley, which allows for some darn good fly-fishing from the many roadside accesses along the way. You'll also pass Quake Lake, formed when a massive landslide was triggered by the tragic August 17, 1959, earthquake (in which 20 campers lost their lives). The trip from Three Forks to Yellowstone Park's west entrance at West Yellowstone is 124 miles, a 2-hour drive.

To complete the loop on your return, drive north through the Gallatin Valley, where you'll find spectacular views of the Madison Range to the east as you drive through the Gallatin National Forest. Also in sight, on the west side of the highway, is the Gallatin Range, which includes three giants: Hyalite Peak, at 10,298 feet; Mount Blackmore, at 10,154 feet; and Lone Mountain, at the Big Sky resort.

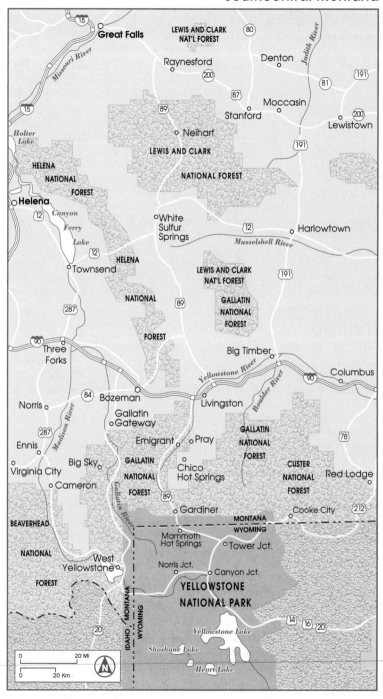

2 Bozeman

82 miles E of Butte; 142 miles W of Billings; 91 miles N of West Yellowstone

Bozeman is a college and tourist town whose cowboy edge has been mostly chipped away to reveal a sophisticated cowboy chic. The vibrant downtown area is filled with independent shops and restaurants. The area bustles all year long—whatever the season, the locals are always out and about.

The great outdoors unites the locals. Bozeman has become the unofficial capital of Montana environmental politics, with several nationally important groups based here. The combination of university and outdoor interests provides a good habitat for them.

Bozeman has experienced its greatest growth during the last 10 years, and it shows little sign of slacking off. Longtime residents worry that the town may be getting a little too chic. The city probably has more nice restaurants per capita than any other town in Montana. The university, Montana State, is a good one, and the students gravitate here for the excellent downhill skiing at nearby Bridger Bowl. The fact that Bozeman is only 2 hours from Yellowstone National Park certainly hasn't hurt its popularity either.

But Bozeman hasn't always been a hotbed of activity. In the 1930s, for instance, local ordinances prohibited dancing anywhere in town after midnight, and in beer halls at any time. It was illegal to drink beer standing up, so all the bars had plenty of stools.

ESSENTIALS

GETTING THERE   Bozeman's **Gallatin Field** (☎ 406/388-8321) serves a wide region in this part of the state. Daily service is available from **Continental** (☎ 800/525-0280), **Delta** (☎800/221-1212), and **Northwest** (☎ 800/225-2525). Commuter flights between Montana cities are available on **Horizon** (☎ 800/547-9308) and **Skywest** (☎ 800/453-9417).

Bus service is available through **Greyhound,** with a terminal at 625 N. 7th Ave. (☎ 406/587-3110). **Rimrock Stages** (☎ 800/255-7655) operates intrastate service to Helena and thence to Missoula or Great Falls, a well as from Bozeman to Billings.

By car, Interstate 90 handles most of the traffic. It is 140 miles along I-90 from Billings to the east and 120 miles from Missoula to the west. For **local road reports,** call ☎ 406/586-1313; for **road conditions statewide,** call ☎ 800/332-6171.

VISITOR INFORMATION   The **Bozeman Area Chamber of Commerce** is located at 690 S. 19th (☎ 800/228-4224 or 406/586-5421; www.bozeman-chamber.com; e-mail: bchamber@avicom.net) but maintains a small information booth off the interstate at 1205 E. Main. There's also an information kiosk at 1001 N. 7th Ave., which is open from Memorial Day to Labor Day. And there is a **Downtown Bozeman Visitor Center** (☎ 406/586-4008) at 224 E. Main. The chamber publishes an extensive **Visitors Guide.** Travel Montana calls this region **Yellowstone Country.** For info from them, call ☎ 800/736-5276 or 406/446-1005.

GETTING AROUND   There are a number of car-rental agencies in Bozeman, including **Avis** (☎ 406/388-6414), **Enterprise** (☎ 800/736-2227), **Hertz** (☎ 406/388-6939), **National** (☎ 406/388-6694), and **Practical** (☎ 800/722-4618)). For taxi service call **All Valley Cab** (☎ 406/388-9999).

A SPECIAL EVENT   Stalking the wild sweet pea may not have been something you'd had in mind while traveling. Reconsider. The **Sweet Pea Festival,** at Lindley Park and throughout Bozeman, (☎ 406/586-4003) is a wonderful diversion in

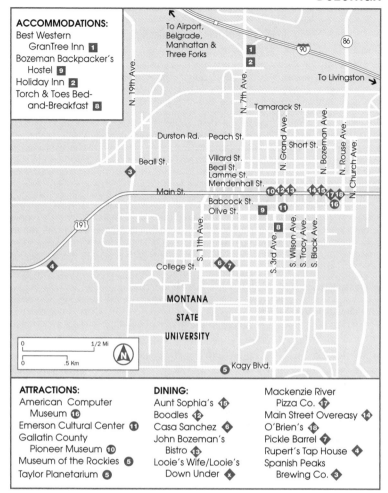

ACCOMMODATIONS:
Best Western GranTree Inn **1**
Bozeman Backpacker's Hostel **9**
Holiday Inn **2**
Torch & Toes Bed-and-Breakfast **8**

ATTRACTIONS:
American Computer Museum **16**
Emerson Cultural Center **11**
Gallatin County Pioneer Museum **10**
Museum of the Rockies **5**
Taylor Planetarium **5**

DINING:
Aunt Sophia's **15**
Boodles **12**
Casa Sanchez **6**
John Bozeman's Bistro **13**
Looie's Wife/Looie's Down Under ✦
Mackenzie River Pizza Co. **17**
Main Street Overeasy **14**
O'Brien's **18**
Pickle Barrel **7**
Rupert's Tap House **4**
Spanish Peaks Brewing Co. **3**

Bozeman. Held the first full weekend each August, it was founded in the early 1900s as a community festival, named for the wild pea that grows in the area. It is a music, arts, and sports festival, with bands from rock to reggae, dance, art, and even a little Shakespeare from the MSU Shakespeare troupe. In keeping with Bozeman's outdoor tradition, the weekend is followed by a week of competitive sports. A Saturday morning run, including one for children, is followed by the Sweet Pea Parade.

GETTING OUTSIDE
ORGANIZED ADVENTURES

✪ **Northern Rockies Natural History Safari** (☎ 406/586-1155; www.beyondyellowstone.com; e-mail nrnh@beyondyellowstone.com) specializes in wild-life and environmental education in Yellowstone and in the Gallatin National Forest. Founded by biologist Ken Sinay—once called "Vesuvian in his enthusiasm"—the group offers guided hikes, snowshoeing, and river drifting to see the wildlife and natural wonders of the area. Full-day trips include guides, transportation, binoculars, spotting scopes, food, and beverages. They can't guarantee what wildlife you'll see but they do guarantee "diverse wildlife and learning opportunities." Rates depend on group size, varying from $410 per person for one person to $120 per person for six, for a full day. Half day is $75 per person.

AdventureWomen, 15033 Kelly Canyon Rd., Bozeman (☎ **800/804-8686** or 406/587-3883; www.adventurewomen.com; e-mail advwomen@aol.com), offers customized trips for "women born to be wild," age 30 and older. Around Bozeman, the company organizes hiking in the Big Sky Country and Yellowstone National Park ($1,595, moderate to difficult), in the Absaroka-Beartooth Wilderness ($1,595, difficult), at a working cattle ranch ($1,595, moderate), and in Glacier National Park ($1,650, moderate to difficult).

BIKING

Panda Rentals (☎ **406/587-6280**) at 621 Bridger Dr. rents bicycles for $15 a day. Rafts and canoes are also available. If you want to try a solo adventure, the staff will tell you how to find a gentle 2-hour float on the lower Madison about 45 minutes from Bozeman, or a 2-hour float on the Jefferson.

They also rent skis and snowboards in winter. **Chalet Sports** (see below) also rents bikes, in-line skates, skis, and snowboards. **Round House Sports Center** (see below) also rents bikes, $18 for a half day and $25 for a full day.

CROSS-COUNTRY SKIING

If you want to explore on your own, many drainages provide excellent skiing around Bozeman. Some local favorites are the 10-mile, moderately difficult **Bozeman Creek to Mystic Lake Trail** that gains 1,300 feet of elevation over its course (go south of South 3rd for 4 miles to Nash Road, then east on Nash Road for a mile to Bozeman Creek Road, then 1 mile south to the parking area), and the **Hyalite Reservoir Ski Loop,** a 4-mile, relatively flat track around the Hyalite Reservoir, also rated moderately difficult (see "Hiking" section for directions). The road may not be plowed or maintained in winter. Two ski mountaineering routes for the adventurous are the 14-mile **Hyalite Ski Loop** and the 5.5-mile **New World Gulch to Mystic Lake** trail.

Bohart Ranch. 16621 Bridger Canyon Rd., Bozeman, MT 58715 (in Bridger Canyon 16.5 miles northeast of Bozeman on U.S. Hwy. 86). ☎ **406/586-9070.** $9 adults, $6 children 7–12. Summer, daily dawn–dusk; winter, daily 9am–4pm.

Next door to the Bridger Bowl downhill area, Bohart Ranch offers 20 miles of groomed and tracked trails for all levels of skiers. There are a biathlon range, a ski school, and ski rentals. In summer, the ranch offers a Frisbee golf course (also known as folf), hiking trails, mountain biking, and horseback riding. Lessons and rentals are also available.

DOWNHILL SKIING

Bridger Bowl. 15795 Bridger Canyon Rd., Bozeman, MT 59715. ☎ **800/223-9609** or 406/587-2111. www.bridgerbowl.com. Lift tickets $31 adults ($26 half-day), $26 seniors, $13 children 6–12, free for children 5 and under. Second Fri in Dec to mid-Apr, daily 9am–4pm.

Not as steep as Teton Village in Jackson Hole, maybe, but pretty steep nonetheless, Bridger Bowl is a great hill for good skiers, with a lot of expert terrain. One of the favorites for the experts here is "skiing the ridge." You take the lift to the top, then climb another couple hundred feet on foot to the very top of the hill, where it is perilously steep and a number of chutes scar the face. There is quite a bit of beginner terrain as well, but the intermediate skier gets squeezed between the two. The lift ticket prices are a bargain as these things go, and there are seldom any lines. You can buy a morning-only, half-day pass at Bridger, which a lot of areas won't let you do. The five double chairs, single quad, and rope tow can haul people up the hill at the rate of 7,300 an hour. With 20 feet of snowfall annually, Bridger sees a lot of powder days. It is also very convenient to town, only 16 miles north on MT 86.

FISHING

At **The River's Edge,** 2012 N. 7th Ave. (☎ **406/586-5373;** www.theriversedge.com; e-mail: rvrsege@mcn.net), Dave and Lynn Corcoran operate a highly professional guiding service that will get you to the stream and get you your fish. They offer fishing trips year-round, rent equipment, and can pick you up at no charge to get to your adventure. They offer float fishing and walking or wading trips. The latter are excellent learning trips, because guides can focus on your fly-fishing skills. They also offer a special program for women only. A guided trip for two costs $300 per day (includes lunch).

Montana Troutfitters, at 1716 W. Main (☎ **800/646-7847** or 406/587-4707; www.troutfitters.com) is a full-line Orvis shop. Opened in 1974, it is Bozeman's oldest operating guide service. Owner Dave Kumlien offers 2-day and 4-day fly-fishing schools to help anglers master the basics of fly casting. It takes a lifetime, of course, to master the fishing itself. Troutfitters offers comprehensive Orvis classes and a 4-day school held at the Gallatin Gateway Inn. Kumlien is especially good at teaching youngsters the basics of the sport. Guided trips cost $300 per day (for two people, including lunch).

The Bozeman Angler, 23 E. Main St. (☎ **800/886-9111** or 406/587-9111; www.BozemanAngler.com) provides guided trips in the Madison, Gallatin, Yellowstone, Big Hole, Jefferson, Bighorn, and Missouri River drainages. Anglers go in hard-sided drift boats, or you can walk along the bank under the tutelage of your guide. The cost is $280 per day for two (includes lunch).

GOLF

Bridger Creek Golf Course at 2710 McIlhattan Rd. (☎ **406/586-2333**) is a scenic and challenging 18-hole layout, 6,400 yards from the back tees; this has been rated one of the 10 best courses in Montana by *Golf Digest.* It costs $24 for 18 holes on the weekend, $22 during the week.

HIKING

There's a beautiful and popular hiking area near Bozeman, known as the **Hyalite drainage** on the Gallatin National Forest. The area includes Hyalite Canyon and reservoir, Palisades Falls Trail, and many trailheads for access to the national forest. A lot of the trails here are steep and difficult walking, though. An excellent introductory hike to get the lay of the land is the half-mile **Palisades Falls National Recreational Trail.** From Bozeman, take 19th Avenue south for 7.5 miles to the Hyalite Canyon Road, and follow the road to the reservoir. Continue east around the reservoir for 2 miles to the East Fork Road, and proceed to the Palisades Falls parking area.

The trail gains 540 feet in a little more than half a mile, which makes it very steep and gives it a rating of "most difficult" for a recreational trail. **Hyalite Reservoir** itself contains cutthroat and grayling, and there are two campsites here. **The Grotto Falls Trail** is a "difficult" 1.25-mile graveled trail to Grotto Falls located 13 miles up the West Fork Road in Hyalite Canyon. For a longer hike, go the 7.2 miles up the **Hyalite Peak Trail** to the peak. There is a 3,300-foot elevation gain on this hike.

If you're interested in combining a little bird-watching with your hiking, you can get a brochure on the *Birding Hotspots of the Gallatin Valley* (Sacajawea Audubon Society, Box 1711, Bozeman, MT 59771). Try Kirk Hill in the foothills transition zone, where you might spot a colorful western tanager or a great gray owl. Take South 19th Street south for 5 miles until the road curves west. The entrance to the preserve is on the left.

LLAMA TREKKING

✪ **Yellowstone Llamas** (☎ **406/586-6872;** fax 406/586-9612; www. yellowstone-llamas.com; e-mail: llamas@mcn.net) offers unique backcountry adventure that combines the simplicity of a rugged trek into Yellowstone and the surrounding area with the civilization of fine dining and no-impact camping. Days begin with a hearty breakfast followed by 5- to 6-mile hikes (per day) in the company of llamas transporting provisions for the gourmet meals—accompanied by wines—that are served at campsites. Afternoons are unstructured, allowing time for the leisurely exploration of alpine surroundings and fishing. A popular 8-mile trip heads for the Black Canyon of the Yellowstone and some of the best trout fishing in the area; longer trips are to the Crazy Mountains and the Thorofare Region of Yellowstone, scenically highlighted by dense lodgepole pines, meadows of wildflowers, and sparkling lakes. No experience with llamas is necessary. The cost is $175 per day, per person. Average length of a trip is 3 to 5 days. No credit cards are accepted. The 10 trips between July 1 and Labor Day are usually fully booked by April.

WHITE-WATER RAFTING

Montana Whitewater (☎ **800/799-4465** or 406/763-4465; www. montanawhitewater.com; e-mail: info@montanawhitewater.com) can get you sprayed in the face by the waters of both the Yellowstone and Gallatin Rivers. You paddle the raft as you fly through the nearly continuous rapids of the Gardiner section of the upper Yellowstone or through the dauntingly named rapids of Snake Bite and Mother Eater on the Gallatin. In addition to the white-water trips, the company offers more sedate scenic trips and "saddle and paddle" outings in which the morning is spent riding and the afternoon rafting. Half-day trips cost $28 to $38 adults, $18 to $28 ages 12 and under. Full-day trips cost $55 to $64 adults, $45 to $50 ages 12 and under.

WHERE TO FIND EQUIPMENT & SUPPLIES

Chalet Sports, on Main and Willson (☎ **406/587-4595**) is a full-line sporting goods store that sells skis as well as rents bikes, in-line skates, skis, and snowboards. They specialize in custom-fitting ski boots, which, as skiers know, is critical to good performance on the slopes. Protective gear is included in the rentals. **The Round House Ski and Sports Center,** 1422 W. Main St. (☎ **406/587-1258**) specializes in bikes and skis, renting and selling both. Bike rentals are available for $18 for a half day and $25 for a whole day. There are in-depth bike clinics on Saturday mornings, including riding and major bike maintenance and overhauls. You can also rent a raft here for $40 a day.

Northern Lights Trading Co., 1716 W. Babcock (☎ **406/586-2225**) is a full-service, high-end store selling gear for everything from kayaking to telemark skiing. While some of the gear might be high-priced, in my experience, in outdoor gear, you get what you pay for. You don't want to go climbing with cheap rope. Canoes, rafts, and kayaks are also available for rent. Northern Lights rents very good rafts for between $275 and $425 a week. Canoes are available for $35 a day and $90 a week.

SEEING THE SIGHTS

American Computer Museum. 234 E. Babcock. ☎ **406/587-7545.** www.compustory. org. $3 adults, $2 children 6–12, free for children under 6. June–Aug, daily 10am–4pm; Sept–May, Tues, Wed, Fri, Sat noon–4pm. Closed major holidays.

This unique museum traces the history of computing technologies from the abacus to the Apple. If you've ever taken electrical tape to the VCR and covered up the flashing clock, this is the place for you. More than 4,000 years of computing circuits are fully explained, from those found in watches and microwaves to automated bank tellers. Though you won't find any T-Rexes here, you can view computing's dinosaurs: slide rules and room-size computers with a mere fraction of the power of today's super-powered miniatures.

Emerson Cultural Center. 111 S. Grand Ave. ☎ **406/587-9797** or 406/586-3970. Free admission. Gallery and shop, Tues–Sat 10am–5pm.

Once a home for school children, this historic building (ca. 1918) was converted in 1993 into a home base for Bozeman's art scene. The center now provides gallery space and studios for more than 40 artists. Visitors will be treated to displays of Tibetan clothing, a collection of handmade papers, and a fiber arts gallery operated by the local weaver's guild. The Cafe Internationale offers fine dining for lunch and dinner.

Gallatin County Pioneer Museum. 317 W. Main. ☎ **406/522-8122.** www. pioneermuseum.org. Free admission. Oct–May, Tues–Fri 11am–4pm, Sat 1–4pm; June–Sept, Mon–Fri 10am–4:30pm, Sat 1–4pm.

Located in the old jail, which was in use until 1982, the museum features county history, focusing in part on law enforcement (as you might expect), the military history of the area, and local daily life of the past. There's a display and memorabilia from local boy, actor Gary Cooper, known as Frank in the days he grew up in Bozeman and Helena. The museum also contains a cell from its days as the jail—kids love this stuff. There's also a research library, a collection of 10,000 historic photos, and a recently donated research library devoted to Lewis and Clark.

✪ **Museum of the Rockies.** 600 W. Kagy Blvd. (on the Montana State University campus). ☎ **406/994-2251.** www.montana.edu/wwwmor/. $6 adults, $4 children 5–18, free for children under 5. Planetarium: $2.50; Memorial Day–Labor Day, daily shows at 1 and 3pm; call for additional showings.

The Museum of the Rockies is a first-class effort that explains the history, wildlife, and people of the Rocky Mountains back through time to the Big Bang. You can walk through time as the exhibits explain the geology and development of the earth in general and the Rocky Mountains in particular. The centerpiece of the museum is the fabulous dinosaur exhibit, which includes a life cast of a Tyrannosaurus rex skull, and the even larger Gigantosaurus carolinii, a recently discovered theropod dinosaur from Argentina. There is also an animated exhibit of a Triceratops and her young, who looks like she is about to attack. You can watch the fossil preparers as they clean recently discovered bones. Also at the museum and almost as popular as the dinosaurs is **Taylor Planetarium,** a state-of-the-art, 40-foot domed multimedia theater whose computer graphics simulator provides the illusion of flying through space in three dimensions. Programs take you from the evening sky to the farthest galaxies and are enhanced by superb visual effects and sound.

SHOPPING

Main Street offers an Old West feel and New West selection, starting at about 7th Avenue and running out to I-90. The chief part of the shopping district is easily accessible on foot. The best of the townie mode is **Vargo's Jazz City and Books,** 1 E. Main (☎ **406/587-5383**), which sells an eclectic mass of new, used, and out-of-print books, CDs, and LPs (or the elusive, vanishing vinyl). The **Country Bookshelf,** 28 W. Main (☎ **406/587-0166**), has an expansive collection of Montana and Western literature. **Poor Richard's News,** 33 W. Main (☎ **406/586-9041**), is the best newsstand and tobacco shop in town. For a real toney Montana flavor, check out **Thomas McGuane Co.,** 121 E. Main (☎ **406/522-9739**). The son of Montana's most famous writer makes and sells handmade knives, from carry-around fishing knives to several-thousand-dollar Damascus steel. Montana and international knife makers have products on sale. The **Thomas Nygard Gallery,** 127 E. Main (☎ **406/586-3636**), sells high-end art from noteworthy artists on American themes, not just Montana. **Chaparral Fine Art,** 24 W. Main (☎ **406/585-0029**), also offers the best in Montana artists. **The Montana Gift Corral,** 237 E. Main (☎ **800/242-5005**), has a wide selection of made-in-Montana gifts, in case you need a moose clock to take home. **Montana Woolen Shop,** 8703 Huffine Lane (☎ **406/587-8903**), has Navajo rugs, sheepskins, and other wool clothing. **Powder Horn Sports,** 35 E. Main, has hunting and fishing gear, guns, expensive outdoor clothing, and the heads of animals from Africa to the Arctic ranged about its walls. Further down Main at 2825 W. Main, the **Gallatin Valley Mall** (☎ **406/586-4565**) has specialty stores, a food court, and the other accoutrements of a mid-sized city mall.

   Big Sky Carvers Outlet Gallery, 324 E. Railroad Ave. S., Manhattan, MT (☎ **406/284-6067**) is a local manufacturer in tiny Manhattan, about 15 miles west of Bozeman on I-90. They make decoys—ducks, geese, and so on—and have garnered a national reputation for their products. This outlet gallery displays some of their fine work on decoys, some bronzes, and a few too-cute bear carvings.

WHERE TO STAY

Bozeman has a full complement of motel chains at its three exits on I-90. In addition to the places listed below, you can stay at the **Hampton Inn** (☎ **406/522-8000**), **Fairfield Inn** (☎ **406/587-2222**), or **Comfort Inn** (☎ **406/587-2144**).

Best Western GranTree Inn. 1325 N. 7th Ave., Bozeman, MT 59715. ☎ **800/624-5865** or 406/587-5261. Fax 406/587-9437. www.grantree.com. E-mail: grantree@grantree.com. 102 units. A/C TV TEL. Summer, $78–$104 double; winter, $69–$99 double. AE, DC, DISC, MC, V.

Located just off I-90 at North 7th Avenue, the GranTree's facility includes a full-service restaurant and coffee shop, Jacuzzi and pool, lounge, and casino. Recently refurbished, the hotel's rooms are clean and spacious. Airport shuttle service is complimentary. The restaurant and lounge have also been completely remodeled.

Bozeman Backpackers Hostel. 405 W. Olive St., Bozeman, MT 59715. ☎ **406/ 586-4659.** 10 bunks, 1 private room. $12 per person; $30 private room. No credit cards.

These bunkhouse accommodations are located in a quiet residential neighborhood near the MSU campus. The bunk rooms are coed, allowing couples to stay together. There's also a private room available. Full kitchen and bath facilities are available to guests. Laundry facilities are on the premises.

Holiday Inn. 5 Baxter Lane, Bozeman, MT 59715. ☎ **800/366-5101** or 406/587-4561. Fax 406/587-4413. E-mail: bozeh1@aol.com. 178 units. A/C TV TEL. Summer, $75–$99 double; winter, $60–$80 double. AE, CB, DC, DISC, MC, V. Pets accepted.

This large, typical Holiday Inn is outfitted for travelers and business folk. The rooms are average-sized, with queen-size beds. Interior rooms overlook a quiet courtyard.

There are a large indoor pool, Jacuzzi, and Nautilus; in-room massage is also available. The hotel is located just off the interstate at North 7th Avenue. It offers a complimentary airport shuttle.

✪ **Howlers Inn Bed-and-Breakfast.** 3185 Jackson Creek Rd., Bozeman, MT 59715. ☎ **406/586-0304.** 5 units. $85–$105 double; $120 chalet. MC, V. Take I-90 east from Bozeman to Exit 319, then go north for 3 miles to the Howlers Inn.

This is both a beautiful B&B and a genuinely unique experience. Located on 42 acres in Bridger Canyon, the Howlers Inn is also home to eight resident wolves, who live in a large penned area adjacent to the main house. The rooms here are large and well appointed, the views of Absarokas and Bridger mountains are marvelous. There's also a rec room with pool table, hot tub, sauna, and well-equipped weight room. Just opened in the spring of 1999 is a two-story chalet that can be rented as either a four-bedroom or two-bedroom unit. The chalet comes with a deck overlooking the wolf pen, the valley below, and the mountains beyond. It also has satellite television. Owner Dan Anstrom worked with wolves and big cats as a volunteer at a refuge in California. When he came to Bozeman, he continued his interest by keeping wolves. Guests can't interact directly with the animals, but they are visible in their pen throughout the day.

Torch and Toes Bed-and-Breakfast. 309 S. Third Ave., Bozeman, MT 59715. ☎ **800/446-2138** or 406/586-7285. Fax 406/585-2749. www.avicom.net/torchntoes. E-mail: tntbb@avicom.net. 3 units, 1 carriage house. $80–$90 double. Rates include full breakfast. Corporate rates available. AE, MC, V. Personal checks accepted.

The Torch and Toes is a homey, friendly B&B in Bozeman's older neighborhood within walking distance of downtown. An eclectic mix of sixties furnishings in the downstairs TV and sitting rooms, "complemented" by a toy crow that hangs on the door of an upstairs guest room, hint at the kind of environment to expect. This is the kind of house where every nook and cranny holds interesting discoveries. The place was named when owners Ron and Judy Hess saw an old photo of the first pieces of the Statue of Liberty to arrive in New York—the torch and her feet. In addition to the B&B's three upstairs rooms, in the backyard there is a 1906 carriage house with a galley kitchen that is perfect for families or groups of friends.

Wingate Inn. 2305 Catron St., Bozeman, MT 59718. ☎ **800/228-1000** or 406/582-4995. Fax 406/582-7488. www.wingateinns.com. 86 units. $79–$135 double. Rates include breakfast. MC, V.

The Bozeman Wingate Inn opened in April of 1999. This is the farthest west that this East Coast chain has ever reached. There is a large and elegantly appointed lobby and breakfast room, where a continental breakfast is served. The rooms are average sized, very clean, and well kept. They include cordless phones, desk phones, and—an unusual amenity for Montana—Internet TV. The chain offers a satisfaction guarantee like Hampton Inns—if you're not satisfied for any reason, they'll refund your money. There is no restaurant or lounge, but there is a pool. The Wingate is located just off Interstate 90 at Exit 305, an area that is developing rapidly.

CAMPING

The **Bozeman KOA** (☎ 406/587-3030) is the city's largest campground, with sites for 100 RVs and 50 tents. It has a natural hot springs pool, laundry, and store, along with rental cabins and tepees. It is located 8 miles south of Belgrade on MT 85. **Bear Canyon** (☎ 406/587-1575; Exit 313) and **Sunrise Campground** (☎ 406/587-4797; Exit 309), though comparable in amenities to the KOA, are scenic public campgrounds. The **Bozeman Ranger District** (☎ 406/587-6920) includes

Langhor, located in the Hyalite Canyon 11 miles south of Bozeman with handi-capped-accessible fishing and fantastic views; **Spanish Creek,** south of Bozeman, with access into the nearby wilderness area; and **Battle Ridge,** a scenic campground in the Bridger Mountains 22 miles north of Bozeman on Highway 86. Other campgrounds in the Bozeman district offer fishing on the Gallatin and hiking trails; contact the ranger district for more information.

The Gallatin National Forest also offers eight primitive **recreational cabins** for skiing or hiking. They are available for $25 per night at various sites around the forest. Very few are accessible by car, however. For information write or call the Bozeman Ranger District, 3710 Fallon St., Box C, Bozeman, MT 59718 (☎ **406/587-6920**). The dates on which these cabins are available or accessible vary.

WHERE TO DINE

The **Leaf and Bean,** 35 W. Main (☎ **406/587-1580**), is a great little coffee shop.

Aunt Sophia's, Looie's Wife. 101 E. Main. ☎ **406/582-0393.** Fax 406/582-0398. Lunch $5–$7; dinner $7–$15. AE, DISC, MC V. Mon–Sat 11:30am–2:30pm and daily 5:30–10pm. ITALIAN.

Aunt Sophia's serves generous portions of reasonably priced Italian food. It has replaced O'Brien's as the lunch spot of choice for some of the Bozeman business crowd. It is not very adventurous, even as Italian food goes, but every dish is carefully prepared. The portions are huge.

Boodle's. 215 W. Main. ☎ **406/587-2901.** Main courses $16–$31. AE, DISC, MC, V. Mon–Thurs 11:30am–2:30pm and 5:30–9pm, Fri 11:30am–2:30pm and 5:30–9:30pm, Sat 5:30–9:30pm, Sun 5:30–9pm. AMERICAN.

Boodle's offers good, if a little expensive, food in a designer Montana atmosphere of dark oaks and nice art. The bar and back bar are the long, saloon-like affairs that you would expect in a Western pub. One of the curious things about Bozeman, in the middle of beef-raising country, is that it is hard to find an unadorned steak without a lot of frippery. Though not really a steak house—they do a little of everything here, from Mexican to Montana—Boodle's offers your best bet. The menu changes every 3 months. The Hawaiian grilled pork tenderloin was good when I was there, and a bison prime rib was on the menu for about $30. There's live jazz on Friday and Saturday after the dinner hour.

Casa Sanchez. 719 S. 9th (at College). ☎ **406/586-4516.** Most dishes $6–$9. DISC, MC, V. Mon–Fri 11am–10pm, Sat noon–10pm, Sun 5–9:30pm. MEXICAN.

This crowded house is home to the best Mexican food in Bozeman. If you consider yourself a nacho connoisseur, Ron's Nachos has what you're looking for: a plate full of chips, shredded chicken, salsa, and jalapeños, topped with mounds of guacamole and sour cream. Burritos, enchiladas, chimichangas, and tacos are the basic food groups on the Casa Sanchez menu; the occasional tostada is thrown in for good measure.

John Bozeman's Bistro. 125 W. Main. ☎ **406/587-4100.** Most dishes $10–$18. AE, CB, DC, DISC, MC, V. Tues–Sat 11:30am–2:30pm and 5–10pm, Sun 9am–2pm. CONTEMPORARY AMERICAN.

This is perhaps one of three—along with O'Brien's and the Gallatin Gateway—most popular and upscale restaurants in town. Recently moved into a renovated 1905 building, the chefs prepare with unabashed zeal an eclectic menu that may include Jamaican jerk chicken breast, classic London broil, or an interesting vegetarian entree. The Santa Fe Setup (a polenta cake with red beans and rice) and the Healthy Happy

Bowl (stir-fried vegetables and soba noodles topped with marinated tofu) are crowd favorites. The atmosphere is a cut above casual.

Looie's Down Under. 101 E. Main. ☎ **406/522-8814.** Reservations recommended. Brunch $8.50; lunch $7–$12; dinner $13–$24. AE, MC, V. Mon 5:30–10pm, Tues–Fri 11:30am–2:30pm and 5:30–10pm, Sat 5:30–10pm, Sun 9am–2pm (brunch) and 5:30–10pm. CONTINENTAL/PACIFIC RIM.

Looie's is run by the same guy who took the Chico Hot Springs restaurant to class A status, and he's working his magic here. The food is excellent and of staggering variety. You can get sushi, lamb, pasta, veal, tempura, or tuna roll. There is a lot of fish on the menu. The scallops were wonderful in a citrus sauce, and the seafood pasta included tuna, sea bass, and artichoke hearts. This is all served up in an informal San Francisco-cafe atmosphere.

✪ **Mackenzie River Pizza Co.** 232 E. Main. ☎ **406/587-0055.** Reservations not accepted. Sandwiches $5–$6; entrees $13–$16. AE, MC, V. Mon–Sat 11:30am–9pm, Sun noon–9pm. PIZZA.

These folks do pizza a decidedly new way, one which matches the decor—funky, in a slightly overdone Western style with a log structure in the middle of the dining room. The tomato-based pizzas are delicious, and there are plenty of old standbys with traditional toppings. Innovations include the pesto-based pizzas from the "Back Forty" side of the menu. Names match the ingredients: the Athenian (feta), Mexican (salsa), and Angler (what else?—smoked trout).

Main Street Overeasy. 9 E. Main St. ☎ **406/587-3205.** Breakfast $3–$7; lunch $5–$7. AE, MC, V. Tues–Sun 7am–2:30pm. BREAKFAST/SANDWICHES.

Chef Erik Carr, who formerly cooked at the Gallatin Gateway Inn, opened this restaurant in 1996, and it rapidly has become a local favorite, especially for breakfast. At this small restaurant located in an office building, you can get old-fashioned oatmeal, a Belgian waffle, eggs Benedict, or cinnamon bread pudding with cream vanilla bean sauce. Lunches consist of large gourmet sandwiches and salads.

O'Brien's. 312 E. Main. ☎ **406/587-3973.** Most dishes $12–$17. DISC, MC, V. Mon–Tues 7am–2pm, Wed–Fri 7am–2pm and 5:30–9pm; Sat 5:30–9pm. CONTEMPORARY AMERICAN.

O'Brien's has a chic, contemporary look to it. No saddles or polished pine, just a quiet dining room with classical music. You'll find such deliciously prepared traditional favorites as pasta with red sauce or filet mignon. There are also some entrees influenced by the Montana surroundings, such as charbroiled breast of pheasant topped with a huckleberry cream sauce, shallots, and mushrooms. Breakfast service has recently been added. However, a friend of mine, who used to eat here every day, says that the place isn't what it used to be. He has moved his luncheon loyalties elsewhere. The whole restaurant is nonsmoking.

Pickle Barrel. 809 W. College. ☎ **406/587-2411.** Most dishes $4–$11. No credit cards. Summer, 10:30am–10pm; winter, 10:30am–10:30pm. SANDWICHES.

For a sandwich and chips, the Pickle Barrel is as good as it gets. It's no coincidence that the Pickle Barrel is located across the street from the college—the customers are mainly college students on tight budgets, but you can count on seeing a smattering of business-types from downtown. The place is tiny, so most people just grab a sandwich and split, but in the late spring, the benches, chairs, and tables outside are crowded with diners. There's another branch downtown at 209 E. Main.

✪ **Rupert's Tap House.** 2711 W. College. ☎ **406/522-8960.** Lunch $6–$8; dinner $10–$20. AE, DISC, MC, V. Mon–Sat 11am–2pm and 4:30–10pm. CONTEMPORARY AMERICAN.

This new addition to the Bozeman restaurant scene has quickly become very popular, especially with the MSU crowd. The food is very good, just adventurous enough and reasonably priced. There are 15 beers on tap. The menu includes a list of unusual entrees, including the honey-glazed pork tostada, a portobello mushroom napoleon, and a Montana trout cakes appetizer. Lots of dinner entrees are available for less than $13.

Spanish Peaks Brewing Co. 120 N. 19th. ☎ **406/585-2296.** www.spanishpeaks.com. Main courses $6–$23. DISC, MC, V. Mon–Sat 11:30am–10:30pm, Sun noon–10:30pm. AMERICAN.

Spanish Peaks Brewing Co. is one of the west's most successful microbreweries. And it didn't get this way because of the food. Nonetheless, the food is a cut above the usual brewpub fare. It consists mainly of chicken and beef prepared in a wood-fired rotisserie. The chef makes daily special appetizers, pasta, main dishes, and desserts. Spanish Peaks is popular with the MSU crowd and is noisy during happy hour.

BOZEMAN AFTER DARK

Bozeman is a college town, so there are lots of places to get a casual drink accompanied by loud music. In addition to **Boodle's,** 215 W. Main, which has live jazz on the weekends, the **Crystal Bar,** 125 E. Main, is a busy place on the weekends. There you can find lots of college students dressed like cowboys—there are scarcely any real cowboys left in Bozeman. **The Molly Brown,** 703 W. Babcock, is also a popular student hangout.

   Shakespeare in the Parks, Montana State University, Bozeman, MT 59717-0400 (☎ **406/994-5885**), is a great touring company that all of Montana has come to appreciate. On top of that, performances are free. Based in Bozeman, the thespian troupe performs throughout the summer at some 50 communities throughout Montana, Wyoming, and Idaho. Some summer weekends find them at their Bozeman stage—located on the MSU campus on 11th Avenue near the corner of Grant Street—for "Shakespeare Under the Stars." Parking is available just north of the MSU fieldhouse.

3 The Madison River Valley: Three Forks & Ennis

Ennis: 54 miles SW of Bozeman; 71 miles N of West Yellowstone

The Madison Valley is an almost mythical place surrounded by spectacular mountain scenery where anglers from the four points of the compass gather to fish. The main attraction is the Madison River, which flows through the valley at the base of the Madison Range, a stretch of peaks that runs toward Yellowstone Park.

   Besides the phenomenal fishing, the historical significance of the Madison Valley makes it a worthy tourist destination. **The Missouri Headwaters State Park** is at the confluence of the Jefferson, Madison, and Gallatin Rivers, where Lewis and Clark paused to take shelter; **Lewis and Clark Caverns,** with its spectacular underground peaks, is just up the road; and **Buffalo Jump State Park,** which has significance among Native Americans, is nearby.

ESSENTIALS

GETTING THERE   The Bozeman airport, **Gallatin Field,** is the closest airport to the valley.

   Greyhound stops at the Sinclair station in Three Forks at 2 Main.

Three Forks is located on I-90, 30 miles from Bozeman, 170 miles from Billings, and 173 miles from Missoula. Three Forks is 66 miles from the capital in Helena. Ennis is 45 miles south of Three Forks on U.S. 287.

VISITOR INFORMATION   The address for the **Three Forks Chamber of Commerce** is P.O. Box 1103, Three Forks, MT 59752 (☎ **406/285-3198**). For the **Ennis Chamber of Commerce,** write to P.O. Box 291, Ennis, MT 59729 (☎ **406/ 682-4388**). For information on **Yellowstone Country,** Travel Montana's region that includes the Madison Valley, call ☎ **800/736-5276** or 406/446-1005.

GETTING AROUND   If you're flying into Bozeman, pick up a car at the airport (see the section on Bozeman for more information). For **road reports** concerning the Madison Valley, call ☎ **406/586-1313;** for **statewide road conditions,** call ☎ **800/332-6171.**

GETTING OUTSIDE

There is plenty of fishing water along the road from Three Forks to Quake and Hebgen lakes along U.S. Highway 287. The first fishing access is **Cobblestone,** just a few miles south of Three Forks on the right side of U.S. Highway 287. If you plan to base yourself in Ennis, the **Valley Garden, Ennis Bridge, Burnt Tree,** and **Varney Bridge** fishing accesses are within minutes of town along 287. Between Ennis and Quake Lake, the accesses begin popping up frequently. **McAtee Bridge, Wolf Creek, West Fork,** and **Reynolds Pass** are all accessible from the roadside. Hebgen Lake, just south of the dam and Quake Lake, are great fishing spots.

On Ennis's Main Street, it seems that every second door houses a fly-fishing outfitter. The Madison River offers perhaps the best trout fishing in the lower 48. The **Madison River Fishing Company,** 109 Main St. (☎ **406/682-4293**), has fishing supplies and a guiding service. If you'd rather go out by yourself, grab a brochure from this shop, which contains a map of the Madison from Ennis to Quake Lake, listing fishing spots and camping and toilet facilities along the way. Greg Doud at **Sphinx Mountain Outfitting,** P.O. Box 111 (☎ **406/682-7336**) can take you hunting, fishing, or riding. **Eaton Outfitters,** Box 351, Ennis, MT 59729 (☎ **800/ 755-FISH**), offers complete fishing services: The guides here will train you in the basics of fly-fishing, take the seasoned angler to spots where the fish are biting, and organize women-only fishing trips. Other outfitters include **Buffalo Jump Outfitting** at Box 649, Ennis, MT 59729 (☎ **888/388-8840**), and the **Tackle Shop,** 127 Main St. (☎ **406/682-4263**). Rates for a guided trip are very similar, usually between $250 and $275 a day.

Wolfpack Outfitters, Box 472, Ennis, MT 59729 (☎ **406/682-4827**), offers horseback riding. Rates begin at $100 per day per person, and overnight pack trips cost $125 per day per person, which includes camping equipment and meals.

SEEING THE SIGHTS

National Fish Hatchery. 180 Fish Hatchery Rd., Ennis. ☎ **406/682-4847.** www.r6.fws.gov/hatchery/ennis/Ennis.htm. Free admission. Daily 8am–4:30pm.

The Ennis National Fish Hatchery is probably the only place in America where you can see white rainbow trout and blue rainbow trout swimming around. The whites are albinos, and the blue a genetic mutant of ordinary rainbows. These fish are for viewing only, and are not released into the wild trout population. Some of the trout in the hatchery ponds weigh more than 20 pounds and are more than 5 years old. The hatchery cultivates seven different strains of rainbow trout brood stock—adult fish that produce eggs and sperm for transportation to other hatcheries, where the fish are raised for release. You can learn about the operation in the small exhibit area, and tour the facility. The 10-mile access road is pretty rough. When some of those huge adults are past their use as brood stock, they too are released into lakes and streams to test fishermen. The hatchery, constructed in 1931, produces more than 25 million rainbow eggs per year.

Lewis & Clark Caverns. Located midway between Butte and Bozeman on U.S. Hwy. 2. ☎ **406/287-3541.** Call for additional park information or to make a group reservation. $5.50 adults, $3 children 6–11. May 1–June 14 and the day after Labor Day to Sept 30, 9am–4:30pm; June 15–Labor Day, 9am–6:30pm. Tours leave as required by demand. Guided tours: May–Sept, daily; Apr–Oct, Sat–Sun.

Lewis & Clark Caverns are named for the famous explorers, but there is no evidence that their party ever saw or visited them. The caverns, which were discovered by surveyor Daniel Morrison in 1902, and were originally known as Morrison Cave, are a succession of vaulted chamber and passageways, thickly hung with stalactites (from the ceiling) and stalagmites (from the ground). There are a series of intricate and mysterious underground formations: massive, gleaming organ pipes; silky, delicate soda straws; intricate filigrees and weirdly hung draperies. One of the areas, the Paradise Room, is growing at the rate of 1 inch per year, which is fast for a cave, but slow for a glacier. A Christmas candlelight tour is held on two weekends in December, and reservations should be made in November for the 200 or so spots available. There are three cabins on the premises with electric heat, $29 in winter and $39 during the touring season.

Madison Buffalo Jump State Monument. 23 miles west of Bozeman. ☎ **406/994-4042.** $4 per car or $1 per person, whichever is cheaper. Open year-round. From the Logan exit off I-90, 7 miles south on Buffalo Jump Rd.

Though the buffalo are mostly gone from the West, there are still a few reminders of their passage. This is one of a few buffalo jumps, or *pishkun,* that have been excavated. Prior to the advent of the horse, the Northern Shoshone and the Bannock drove the bison off this steep cliff to their death (instead of shooting them) on the rocks below. Long rows of rocks funneled the animals to the cliff. There is a well-worn trail up to the base of the cliff, making for a short but steep hike.

✪ **Missouri Headwaters State Park.** 3 miles east of Three Forks on I-90. $4 per car or $1 per person, whichever is cheaper. Go east on County Rd. 205, 3 miles north on County Rd. 286. Follow the signs.

You can easily spend an hour just exploring the interpretive signage at this historic state park. Begin by following the Missouri River out from Three Forks. The headwaters themselves are no great shakes—just another river—but the sunsets from the bank of the river are nothing short of breathtaking. From the headwaters, drive back toward Three Forks where, on the opposite side of the road, you'll see a parking area with interpretive markers. Allow plenty of time to read about Lewis and Clark and Sacajawea, the young Shoshone guide, as well as early Native Americans, trappers, traders, and settlers. Camping and RV units are available as well as access to hiking, boating, and fishing.

Quake Lake. Off U.S. Hwy. 287, 43 miles south of Ennis. ☎ **406/646-7369.** $3 per car. Visitor center Memorial Day–Labor Day, daily 9am–5pm.

Just before midnight on August 17, 1969, a massive earthquake measuring 7.5 on the Richter scale jolted Yellowstone and the Madison River canyon, sending large chunks of mountain into the river. A campsite just below the mountain was covered with rubble and 19 people were buried alive. The rubble that collapsed into the river created a dam and the aptly named Quake Lake. The ghostly fingers of trees that also died when they were inundated still poke skyward from the lake. The visitor center off to the left of the highway offers exhibits, a viewing area, and hourly interpretive talks. The area around Yellowstone and Quake Lake is still very seismically active. For instance, between June 13 and June 22, 1999 more than 630 earthquakes—all of less than a magnitude of 3.5 on the Richter scale—occurred in the area just east of Hebgen Lake. Earthquakes are notoriously difficult to predict, but the constant small seismic activity in the area is a reminder of the area's volatility. The most recent large quake was a 6.1 magnitude quake near Norris Geyser Basin on June 30, 1975. The visitor center has a great deal of information about the area's seismicity and hypotheses of how it got this way.

WHERE TO STAY
IN THREE FORKS

Bud Lilly's Anglers Retreat. 16 W. Birch, Box 983, Three Forks, MT 59752. ☎ **406/ 285-6690** or 406/586-5140. Fax 406/586-8713. 5 units. A/C TEL. $60 double; $135–$155 suite. MC, V.

Just having Bud Lilly mastermind your fishing itinerary is reason enough to stay here, but it's by no means the only reason. Formerly a railroad hotel belonging to Bud's mother, the Anglers Retreat has been refurbished and is now a cozy lodge. Those who fish will love it. (Those who don't would be happier at the Sacajawea Inn, however; see below.)

The three upstairs bedrooms share a bathroom with a claw-foot bathtub and shower (robes are provided); each of the suites has a full bath with shower as well as a fully equipped kitchen. There's also a shady deck, a backyard vegetable and flower garden (help yourself), a washer and dryer, and a comfortable TV room with an extensive library of fishing and Montana videos. But the big draw here is the fishing. Every reservation at the Anglers Retreat includes a personalized, detailed itinerary of where to fish locally, based on your preferences and length of stay.

Sacajawea Inn. 5 N. Main, Three Forks, MT 59752. ☎ **406/285-6515.** Fax 406/285-4210. www.sacajaweahotel.com. E-mail: sac3forks@aol.com. 33 units. TV TEL. $60–$105 double. Rates include continental breakfast. AE, DISC, MC, V.

The Sacajawea Inn would not be out of place as the manor house of a Southern plantation. It is a three-story building with a wraparound porch lined with oversized rocking chairs peering out like old residents over Three Forks' main street. The hotel was built in 1910. The rooms have been renovated since then, with up-to-date amenities, but an ample amount of Old-World ambience still exists. The hotel's restaurant serves dinner year-round and breakfast and lunch during the summer months.

IN ENNIS

In addition to the listings detailed below, the 18 lodgepole pine cabins and 11 motel rooms at the **Sportsman's Lodge** (☎ **406/682-4242**) are especially popular with anglers, who head for the cozy dining room and decks to relax after a day on the river. The Sportsman's Lodge is the only motel in Ennis with a restaurant. **Lakeshore Lodge,** P.O. Box 160, McAllister, MT 59740 (☎ **406/682-4424**), on the shores of Ennis Lake about 7 miles north of town, is a good spot for families. In addition to fishing, there are a playground, a swimming hole, and a marina, where you can rent small boats.

✪ **El Western Resort/Motel.** 1 mile south of Ennis on U.S. 287. ☎ **800/831-2773** or 406/682-4217. Fax 406/682-5207. www.elwestern.com. 29 units. TV TEL. $55–$75 double; $80–$95 kitchen cabin, $115–$175 deluxe kitchen cabin; $160–$325 lodge unit. AE, DISC, MC, V.

It's a little hard to categorize this place, which has some inexpensive log duplex-style motel rooms as well as large, expensive two- and three-bedroom lodge units. The motel portion was built in 1948, and is done with knotty pine interiors and built-in wooden cabinets. The new lodge portions include the Eagle's Loft, a three-bedroom, three-bath two-story cabin with spectacular views of the Madison Range, including Fan Mountain and the Spanish Peaks. You can't go wrong here, and the low end units are as affordable as anything in the valley. There's no restaurant or lounge associated with the property.

Rainbow Valley Motel. 1 mile south of Ennis on U.S. Hwy. 287. ☎ **800/452-8254.** Fax 406/682-5012. 24 units. TV TEL. $60–$100 double. DISC, MC, V.

This motel, on a spacious grassy park area, offers cabin-style rooms, which are well maintained. The rooms are large, comfortable, and affordable. The property offers horse corrals, a heated pool, and a picnic-barbecue area. The walls are thin, though, and noise travels easily from room to room. And beware: The Rainbow Valley Motel was the first place where I couldn't get the shower to work at all. There was a shower head. Water came out of the tap just fine, and plenty hot. But there was no control to shift the flow of water from filling the tub to spraying from the shower head. So I took a bath. Which is fine for a change . . . I guess.

Wade Lake Resort. P.O. Box 107, Cameron, MT 59720. ☎ **406/682-7560.** 5 cabins. $50–$75 double. No credit cards. Drive 40 miles south of Ennis to the Wade Lake turnoff, marked by a sign. Turn west on the bumpy, gravel Wade Lake Rd. and follow the signs about 6 miles to Wade Lake.

The secluded resort, which consists of five cabins, is situated about 40 minutes south of Ennis in a forested canyon on Wade Lake at an elevation of 6,300 feet. The cabins are fairly primitive, with only refrigerators, running water, and a gas stove. Although there are overhead electric lights, there aren't any stand-alone reading lamps by the bed. There aren't even any electric outlets to plug in your computer, and the bathrooms are out back. Bring in food to cook on that stove, because the nearest restaurant is 11 miles back up the road you just came in on. It is very beautiful, though. Wade is part of the Hidden Lake chain in Beaverhead National Forest and has been designated a Montana Wildlife Viewing Site. The area is rich in wildlife, with eagles and osprey nesting on the lake, and moose, elk, bear, and other locals dropping in occasionally. It also helps you remember what real quiet and real darkness are like. During winter months, the resort is a popular cross-country skiing and snowshoeing destination as well.

A GUEST RANCH

Diamond J Ranch. P.O. Box 557, Ennis, MT. ☎ **406/682-4867.** Fax 406/682-4106. www.diamondj.com. E-mail: totalmgt@3river.net. 11 units. $1,150 per person per week, lower for children under 13. Rate includes all meals and activities. AE, MC, V.

Twelve miles east of town, is a 200-acre dude ranch that was among the first established in Montana in the 1930s. Tucked into a narrow canyon in the Madison Range and surrounded by the Beaverhead National Forest, this family-oriented vacation spot lacks the stylishness of some of its competitors but provides adults and children with a good variety of outdoor activities. Overstuffed leather chairs and sofas fill an appealing lounge area in the lodge, and meals are served at long tables in the same building. Children usually dine in a separate room, while their parents socialize at the Branding Iron. Riding is the primary focus here, and rides are organized to suit the abilities and preferences of guests. Other activities include fly-fishing on Ginny Lake, a stocked pond, tennis on the court inside the barn, swimming in the small pool, trap and skeet shooting, volleyball, table tennis, and horseshoes.

CAMPING

Camper Corner RV Park and Campground. Box 351, Ennis, MT (☎ **800/ 755-3474**), is just 50 miles southwest of Bozeman and 75 miles northwest of Yellowstone National Park. It's a full-service campground with hookups, laundry facilities, showers, large spaces, and lots of shade. It's located on the first block north of the intersection of MT 287 toward Virginia City.

Missouri Headwaters State Park has scenic campgrounds with plenty of fishing access. The year-round campground has 20 sites scattered along the river and numerous hiking trails. There is a minimal fee. It's located 4 miles south of Three Forks, on Interstate 90. **Three Forks KOA** is located on U.S. Highway 287, 1 mile south of Exit 274 at I-90. A swimming pool, rec room, playground, and sauna will keep the entire family happy. There are 20 tent and 50 RV sites available at the seasonal campground, open May through September. **Elkhorn Store and RV Park** (☎ **406/682-4273**) is located in Ennis on U.S. Highway 287 and is open from mid-April through November. You can get gas, purchase a hunting license, or rent a video here, and downtown Ennis is just a short drive down the street.

WHERE TO DINE
NEAR THREE FORKS

Wheat Montana Bakery and Deli. I-90 and U.S. 287, Three Forks. ☎ **800/535-2798** or 406/285-3614. Sandwiches $2.50–$4.50. MC, V. Daily 6am–7pm. FRESH BREAD.

This is a very popular place, where Montana-grown wheat is turned into Montanabaked bread. You can build your own sandwich on Montana Wheat bread, take home a couple of loaves, or just get the flour to bake your own. The smell of bread baking inside makes it worth the stop.

✪ **Willow Creek Cafe and Saloon.** 1st and Main, Willow Creek. ☎ **406/285-3698.** Reservations not accepted. Lunch $3–$6; dinner $8–$16. DISC, MC, V. Year-round, daily; call for hours. AMERICAN.

This place is a find, if you can find it—it's located 7 miles southwest of Three Forks on the Willow Creek Road. It's worth the search, though, as Willow Creek is the best restaurant in the Three Forks vicinity (don't let the bullet holes in the ceiling scare you off). Named for the china that sits over the antique cookstove, it began as the Babcock Saloon, a bar established around 1910. In 1980, the property was restored to what is now a remarkable little shelter for antiques, locals, and you. Montana beef is the big seller at Willow Creek, but seafood and chicken are also on the menu. The names of the entrees come from the old mines in Pony, a small town up the road.

IN ENNIS

Madison River Pizza and Bakery, 110 W. Main St. (☎ **406/682-4979**), serves the best pizza in this neck of the woods. **Yesterdays Restaurant and Soda Fountain,** 124 Main St., in the Ennis Pharmacy building (no phone), is an old-fashioned ice-creamparlor-type spot that serves breakfast, lunch, and amazing fountain drinks, shakes, and sundaes. The best place for your morning shot of caffeine is **Westwords,** 101 Main St. (☎ **406/682-7949**), an espresso bar which doubles as a bookstore—or vice versa. Stop in for a quick, to-go cup of coffee and scrumptious, fresh muffin or pastry at **Economy Food Market,** 232 Main St. (☎ **406/682-4213**).

Continental Divide. Main St. ☎ **406/682-7600.** Reservations recommended. Main courses $16–$24. MC, V. Summer, daily 6–9pm; off-season, call for dates and hours. COUNTRY FRENCH.

This is an upscale bistro that would fit nicely into the restaurant scene in Jackson or Bozeman. The Continental Divide has been favorably commented on in many national food magazines. The food is adventurous and well-prepared—tenderloin of elk; free-range chicken mole with Anasazi beans; Cajun, creole, and French dishes. There is an extensive wine and beer selection.

Grizzly Bar and Grille. 1409 U.S. Hwy. 287 N., Cameron, MT 59720. ☎ **406/682-7118.** Main courses $10–$26. AE, MC, V. Mon–Fri 5–10:30pm, Sat–Sun 11am–4pm and 5–10:30pm; hours may vary with the season. AMERICAN.

The address is Cameron, but the restaurant is actually located about 25 miles south of Cameron on U.S. 287. This is the place to eat for folks who forget to take food to cook when they stay at Wade Lake Resort (we won't say who they were). The food here is unexpectedly good, specializing in pasta, seafood, and beef. I had the jumbo prawns grilled on a rosemary skewer, and it was excellent.

Scotty's Longbranch Supper Club and Saloon. 125 Main St. ☎ **406/682-5300.** Main courses $10–$19. MC, V. Mon–Sat 5:30–10pm; hours vary somewhat in winter. AMERICAN.

Scotty's has a sign that reads, "No burgers. No fries." So don't ask. And there is classical music on the CD player. But the atmosphere otherwise is pure Western steakhouse, as is most of the food. You can get a steak béarnaise, though veal parmesan, crab cakes, and shrimp scampi are also on the menu. Scotty's serves twice-baked and baked potatoes, but no fries. The restaurant is located in the rear of the Longbranch Saloon.

Silver Dollar Grill. Main St. ☎ **406/682-7770.** Main courses $12–$19. MC, V. Mon–Sat 5:30–10pm; hours vary somewhat in winter. AMERICAN.

The Silver Dollar Grill is located in the rear of the Silver Dollar Saloon. I think I see a pattern here. The Silver Dollar has more of a cowboy atmosphere than Scotty's, but the food is similar, basically steaks and seafood. You can get an artichoke for an appetizer, which isn't offered everywhere. The cheeseburger is recommended highly, as are the barbecued ribs.

4 The Gallatin Valley

Big Sky: 53 miles S of Bozeman; 48 miles N of West Yellowstone

According to a native legend, the Sioux and Nez Perce once engaged in a bloody battle in the lower Gallatin Valley. On the third day of the fighting, the sun was blotted out and a booming voice told the warriors to forget old wrongs and stop fighting, because they were in the Valley of Peace and Flowers.

Since those days, the sun still mostly shines around here, but the only booming voices heard are those calling you for your tee time or your dinner reservation. The transition of Big Sky from peace and flowers to year-round resort was not entirely without dissension, however. When legendary NBC newsman Chet Huntley—a Montana native—proposed Big Sky, there was an outcry from the budding environmental movement. But Huntley's dream was realized in 1973, and the resort has blossomed into a world-class facility.

The valley is a narrow shining slice of Montana edged by the Absarokas and Gallatin ranges to the east and the Madison Range on the west. The Big Sky Ski Area covers two of the western peaks—Lone Mountain, elevation 11,186 feet, and Andesite Mountain, 8,800 feet.

As far as visitors are concerned, there are three distinct "villages" in Big Sky. The canyon area along U.S. Highway 191 has a haphazard collection of motels, taverns, restaurants, gas stations, and whatnot. The Meadow Village is 2 miles west of the highway, a community of condos, a few overnight lodging places, and the golf course. The main base area for the ski resort is at the Mountain Village, 8 miles west of the highway, with condos, restaurants, and hotels.

The main season in Big Sky is winter, but the Lone Mountain Guest Ranch was once the only destination spot in this valley, and it offers fine, year-round accommodations and activities—dude-ranch style in summer, and cross-country skiing in winter. The summer months bring excellent fly-fishing, horseback riding, and white-water rafting. The Gallatin River was the setting for the film *A River Runs Through It.*

ESSENTIALS

GETTING THERE   Big Sky is about 40 miles south of Bozeman on U.S. Highway 191. Fly into Bozeman's **Gallatin Field** for easiest access to Big Sky.

From the airport, you can ride to the ski area with the **4X4 Stage** (☎ **800/ 517-8243** or 406/388-6404), a company that has a transportation fleet of sturdy four-wheel-drive vehicles. The ride is $36.50 round-trip per person. Or you can take a taxi provided by **Mountain Taxi** (☎ **406/995-4895**) for $57 for two people.

GETTING AROUND   A car gives you the greatest flexibility in getting around this area. The following car-rental agencies are located at the airport: **Avis** (☎ **406/ 388-6414**), **Budget** (☎ **406/388-4091**), **National** (☎ **406/388-6694**), **Thrifty** (☎ **406/388-3484**), and **Rent-a-Wreck** (☎ **406/587-4551**).

For service between condominiums, hotels, restaurants, and activities within the ski area, take the **Snowexpress,** Big Sky's local shuttle bus system, which operates daily between 7am and 11pm, December through April. Skis are allowed and the service is free. The bus operates along routes that completely cover the mountain.

GETTING OUTSIDE

BIKING

Big Sky Resort rents mountain bikes and offers guides. In the summer, you can get an 8-hour bike rental with a lift ticket for $52 a person. Guides are $25 an hour for up to two riders, for a typical 2-hour ride. Call ☎ **406/995-5840.**

CROSS-COUNTRY SKIING

Big Sky Ski Area offers some groomed trails for cross-country skiing. But for the real deal, go to . . .

✪ **Lone Mountain Ranch.** P.O. Box 160069, Big Sky, MT 59716. ☎ **800/514-4644** or 406/995-4644, or 406/995-4734 for outdoor shop. www.lonemountainranch.com. E-mail: lmr@lonemountainranch.com. Full-day trail pass $12, half-day pass $10. The entrance to Lone Mountain Ranch is immediately along the Lone Mountain Trail, the main road to the Big Sky Resort. It's about 2 miles east of the Mountain Village and 4 miles west of the intersection of U.S. Hwy. 191 and Lone Mountain Trail.

Lone Mountain Ranch has 65 kilometers (about 36 miles) of cross-country trails over terrain that will challenge every level of skier. Near the ranch headquarters, in the meadows below, lies some flat terrain that beginners might appreciate. There's also a steeper portion to practice your telemark technique. Intermediate trails with more hills make up about 60% of the area, and expert trails provide plenty of challenging downhill runs. Ski and snowshoe rentals are also available.

DOWNHILL SKIING

✪ **Big Sky Ski & Summer Resort.** P.O. Box 160001, Big Sky, MT 59716. ☎ **800/ 548-4486** for reservations, or 406/995-5900 for snow conditions, or 406/995-5743 for ski school. Fax 406/995-5001. www.bigskyresort.com. E-mail: info@bigskyresort.com. Lift ticket $48 adults, $24 seniors (70 and over), $40 children 11–17 and college students with ID, free for children 10 and under. Half-day (afternoon only) ticket $40.

Tennis, golf, and rock climbing are all very nice, but the real reason to come to Big Sky is to ski. It's a huge hill, with more than 3,500 acres of terrain and 85 miles of trails. You can ski for nearly a vertical mile from the top of the tram at 11,150 feet elevation to the bottom of the Thunderwolf lift, at 6,970 feet. There is terrain here for everybody, with 43% for advanced skiers, 47% for intermediate, and 10% beginner.

Big Sky gets 400 inches of snowfall, offering plenty of powder days. The season begins on Thanksgiving and goes through April. There's an ambitious children's program, offering lessons for kids as young as three, and day care for kids who don't want to ski. Full ski-rental packages are available.

FISHING

According to another Indian legend, folks who drink the water of the Gallatin River will return to the valley before they die. You should no longer drink untreated water out of even high mountain streams, because of the possibility of giardia, an intestinal microbe that you don't want traveling back home with you. I'm not sure if eating the fish that live in the water counts toward the legend, but it's worth a try. Several guides offer half-day and full-day trips for prices ranging from $165 (half-day for two, walking) to $310 (full day for two, floating). For details contact **Lone Mountain Ranch** (☎ **406/995-4644**), **Gallatin River Guides** (☎ **406/995-2290**), or **East Slope Anglers** (☎ **406/995-4369**).

GOLF

Big Sky Golf Course, Meadow Village, ☎ **406/995-5780,** is a striking Arnold Palmer design that is fairly short, fairly open, and harder than it looks on the card. A few of the holes wander next to the West Fork of the Gallatin River, which meanders through the property. Cost is $40 to $52 for 18 holes, $30 to $40 for nine. Tee times available up to a week in advance.

HIKING

As you might expect in an area surrounded by three mountain ranges, the Lee Metcalf Wilderness, the Spanish Peaks Wilderness, and two national forests, the Beaverhead and Gallatin, there is plenty of hiking opportunity not far from Big Sky. An easy, 4-mile hike to **Porcupine Creek** is accessible nearby. Go south 2.7 miles south on U.S. Highway 191 from the intersection with the mountain village road. Turn left at the sign that announces Porcupine Creek, and go about a half-mile to the trailhead. The first mile of the hike wanders along Porcupine Creek, then offers a choice of either a north or south fork. The left (north) fork goes up into the foothills, offering a view of the creek below.

If you want more of a workout, try the **Lava Lake** trail, which is about 13 miles north of the intersection of the mountain village road and U.S. Highway 191 on the highway. Take the Lava Lake turn. The trail climbs steeply and without much relief for 3 miles to an alpine lake in the shelter of three mountains.

Yellowstone National Park is only about 40 miles south of Big Sky, and you can hike there, too. See chapter 10 for specifics.

RAFTING

Both white-water and scenic floats can be arranged through **Geyser White Water,** ☎ **406/995-4989.** Prices are $39 per adult for a half-day Gallatin River trip and $76 for a full-day trip. Kids 6 to 12 are $30 and $57, respectively.

ROCK CLIMBING

If you want to scare yourself to death, **Adventure Skills Guide Service,** ☎ **800/347-1478,** offers rock-climbing lessons for $55 to $65 per person.

WHERE TO STAY

Big Sky offers a wide variety of accommodations, from relatively inexpensive motel rooms to luxury condos. If you'd prefer to rent a condominium, check with the following management companies: **Big Sky Central Reservations** (☎ **800/548-4486** or 406/995-5000; www.bigskyresort.com), **Golden Eagle Management** (☎ **800/548-4488** or 406/995-4800; www.bigskylodging.com), **Big Sky Chalet Rentals** (☎ **800/845-4428** or 406/995-2665; www.bigskychalets.com), or **Triple Creek Realty and Management** (☎ **800/548-4632** or 406/995-4848; www.triplecreek.com; e-mail: sales@triplecreek.com). In winter, expect to pay from $103 to $1,000 per night, double; in summer, $85 to $500 per night, double.

In all the places listed below, rates vary with the season and within the ski season. The highest rates are over Christmas vacation, the lowest in the spring and fall "shoulder" seasons.

As this guide was going to press, the **Summit Hotel** at the Mountain Village was under construction. It's planned to be a 10-story luxury resort complex with ski-in-ski-out proximity to the chairlifts and 98 one-, two- or three-bedroom suites. Rates had not been established. It is scheduled to open in 2000. If you're interested, contact **Big Sky Central Reservations,** ☎ **800/548-4486.**

Best Western Buck's T-4 Lodge. P.O. Box 160279, U.S. Hwy. 191, Big Sky, MT 59716 (on U.S. Hwy. 191 about a half mile south of the intersection of 191 and Lone Mountain Trail). ☎ **800/822-4484** or 406/995-4111. Fax 406/885-2191. www.buckst4.com. E-mail: buckst4@mcn.net. 74 units. $79–$109 double; $94–$219 suite. AE, CB, DC, DISC, MC, V. Pets accepted with additional fee.

Buck's offers a woody, Western ambience on the highway a little away from the ski resort lodgings. The hotel offers large, comfortable rooms in bewildering variety. The motel was started in 1946 as a hunting camp. Buck's T-4 got to the valley before electricity did. It has grown somewhat randomly since then. The current lodge is thoroughly modern, including two hot tubs large enough for the kids to swim in, a hot buffet breakfast, *USA Today* free in the morning, a game room, and all of the other amenities you want in ski-and-Yellowstone area accommodations. The best thing about the place, though, is the restaurant (see "Where to Dine"). Regular motel rooms, suites, and suites with kitchenettes are available for families. Buck's offers numerous ski packages and vacations; inquire when making reservations.

✪ **Gallatin Gateway Inn.** Box 376, Gallatin Gateway, MT 59730. ☎ **800/676-3522** or 406/763-4672. 35 units. A/C TV TEL. $85–$175 double. Rates include continental breakfast. AE, DISC, MC, V.

Located about 28 miles north of Big Sky on U.S. Highway 191, the Gallatin Gateway Inn is a model of historical elegance from the days of luxury railroad travel. The hotel opened in the summer of 1927, as visitors were beginning to come to Yellowstone in large numbers. The Spanish-style building has vast interior spaces, large enough to make it a railroad station all its own. The building recalls prewar elegance, and you almost expect to see Winston Churchill relaxing on the porch with a cigar. With lavish appointments that include Polynesian mahogany woodwork, decoratively carved beams, and high arched windows, the Gallatin Gateway has maintained its proud history of lavish style and refinement. Guest rooms provide a tastefully understated balance to the regal lobby and dining room, where the seasonally changing menu reflects regional specialties. The restaurant prepares hearty, peasant-style dishes with an eye toward imaginative combinations and generous portions. The wine list is extensive.

○ **Golden Eagle Lodge.** P.O. Box 160008, Big Sky, MT 59716. ☎ **800/548-4488** or 406/995-4800. Fax 406/995-2447. www.bigskylodging.com. 17 units. TV. $100 double; $130–$166 suite. AE, DISC, MC, V. The Lodge is located in the Meadow Village on Little Coyote Rd. Take Lone Mountain Trail about a mile from the intersection of Lone Mountain Trail and U.S. Hwy. 191 to the first paved road. Turn right (north) about a quarter-mile to the lodge.

The Golden Eagle Lodge is a small motel in the Meadow Village, run by one of the real estate management companies. It provides basic ski-area rooms, nothing fancy, with enough beds for a family in the suites—queen beds for the grown-ups and bunks for the kids. The prices are relatively low for a destination ski area, though they vary with the Christmas season and other special holidays. You can also get lift ticket-plus-room deals through the lodge.

Huntley Lodge and Shoshone Condominium Hotel. P.O. Box 160001, Big Sky, MT 59716. ☎ **800/548-4486** or 406/995-5000. Fax 406/995-5002. www.bigskyresort.com. E-mail: bigskymail@mcn.com. 294 units. TV TEL. Prime season (Jan 30 to mid-March), $186–$196 double, $229–$443 suite or loft; Christmas season (Dec 25–Jan 2), $220–$230 double, $262–$554 suite or loft; off-season, $160–$170 double, $200–$377 suite or loft. AE, DISC, MC, V.

These are actually two separate places at the foot of the ski slope, with ski-in, ski-out rooms, but they are managed as one. The Huntley Lodge is the less expensive of the two, and the older is the first place Chet Huntley built at Big Sky. It offers rooms with two queens and a bath or larger loft rooms with three queens, a raised seating area, and one bath. The seven-story Shoshone combines the living quarters of a condo with the amenities and services of a hotel. **Big Sky Central Reservations,** which handles reservations for these two places, also manages the other condo properties in the Mountain Village. Weight training centers, saunas, an outdoor pool, gift shops, and ski storage are included at both places.

○ **Lone Mountain Ranch.** P.O. Box 160069, Big Sky, MT 59716. ☎ **800/514-4644.** Fax 406/995-4670. www.lmranch.com. E-mail: lmr@lmranch.com. 24 cabins, 1 lodge, 1 house. Winter: cabin, $1,665–$2,390 first person, $740 each additional person; Ridgetop Lodge, $3,050 first person, $740 each additional person; Douglas Fir House, $2,360 first person, $740 each additional person. Rates include 7 nights' lodging, 3 meals daily, an 8-day trail pass with unlimited access to the ranch's trail system, evening entertainment, a sleigh-ride dinner, a trail buffet lunch, and airport transfers. Summer rates are slightly higher. DISC, MC, V.

Back before there was even a community of Big Sky—never mind a ski area—there was Lone Mountain Ranch. Started in 1926 as a working cattle ranch, Lone Mountain Ranch rapidly blossomed into a year-round destination as a dude-ranch and cross-country ski area.

In the summer, the ranch blends traditional dude-ranch activities—riding, hiking, fishing and eating—with naturalist programs that will improve your understanding of the Yellowstone ecosystem. They'll not only guide you into the Spanish Peaks, but into an understanding of wildflowers, bird habits and habitat, and geology. They offer guided fly-fishing trips, and the shop on the premises is an Orvis outlet. Lone Mountain prides itself on a family atmosphere and has separate activities for children, including animal tracking and wildflower pressing. In the winter the ranch is a cross-country ski destination, with 36 miles of trails (see "Cross-Country Skiing" under "Getting Outside," above).

The accommodations here are varied, from small cabins to the large new Ridgetop Lodge which can host an entire family reunion. Some of the cabins are quite old, remnants from the original ranch, while the new lodge is only 6 years old. All are spacious with private baths and well-maintained pine interiors. They are spread out at wide intervals on the property, assuring quiet and privacy for the guests.

Dining: Lone Mountain's restaurant is good, and open to folks visiting the area who are not staying at the ranch. In the winter, there are a sleigh ride and dinner at the ranch's North Fork cabin, also available to outside visitors, although one night—usually Wednesday—is reserved for Lone Mountain Ranch guests. There are a buffet breakfast and lunch each day. Call after 3pm for dinner reservations at ☎ **406/995-2782.**

Amenities: You can get a massage after a hard day of riding, and they'll arrange guided rafting, fishing, hiking, or climbing trips.

✪ **River Rock Lodge.** 3080 Pine Dr., Big Sky, MT 59716. ☎ **800/995-9966** or 406/995-2295. Fax 406/995-2727. www.riverrocklodge.com. E-mail: lodging@riverrocklodge.com. 29 units. TV TEL. $100–$275 double. Rates include breakfast. AE, DISC, MC, V.

The River Rock Lodge is a substantial, beautiful rock-and-log structure that delivers Montana style with European service. The rooms are large and beautifully appointed, with all the little extras like evening turndown service, the fax version of the *New York Times,* working desks, and champagne or cider upon check-in. The place is fairly new, presenting a lodge atmosphere with small-hotel service, including a multilingual staff. There is no restaurant or lounge, but the hotel provides in-room bars in some of the rooms, a European-style continental breakfast in the summer, and a hot breakfast during ski season. The hotel has been a favorite stopover for television personalities such as Jay Leno and Conan O'Brien.

WHERE TO DINE

At the **Mountain Mall** at the base of the ski area, there are a lot of ski area-type dining and drinking places, including **Dante's Inferno** (☎ **406/995-3999**), which you should avoid if you're allergic to cigars; the **Twin Panda** (☎ **406/995-2425**) for Chinese; and **Mountain Top Pizza** (☎ **406/995-4646**). The **Huntley Lodge Dining Room** (☎ **406/995-5783**) has fine dining, and **Chet's Bar** next door has a bistro menu.

The farther you get from the base of the hill, the better the food gets. In the **Meadow Village,** there are about a dozen restaurants. The **Huckleberry Cafe** (☎ **406/995-3130**) has the best breakfast in Big Sky. The **Blue Moon Bakery** (☎ **406/995-2305**) makes sandwiches. **Rocco's** (☎ **406/995-4200**) is good for Mexican and Italian, and **Cafe Edelweiss** (☎ **406/995-4244;** reservations recommended) for Austrian and German cuisine. **Lone Mountain Ranch** (see "Where to Stay," above) is also in this area.

Finally, in the **Gallatin Canyon** section of town, the **320 Ranch** (☎ **406/995-4283**) offers steaks and wild game. It's located at mile marker 36 on U.S. Highway 191, about 11 miles south of the intersection of Lone Mountain trail and U.S. 191. And the **Half Moon Saloon** (406/995-4533) is a favorite of locals (meaning seasonal ski-area employees and guides), with ribs, burgers, and pasta.

✪ **Buck's T-4 Restaurant.** U.S. Hwy. 191, Big Sky, MT 59716. ☎ **406/995-4111.** Main courses $17–$29. AE, CB, DC, DISC, MC, V. Daily 6–9:30pm. Reservations recommended. CONTEMPORARY AMERICAN.

Buck's offers a very adventurous menu of "Montana cuisine," with nine wild game offerings, including antelope saltimbocca, wild game meatloaf, New Zealand red deer, and applewood smoked bison. Part of the restaurant itself is located in one of the two original buildings that made up the 1949 Bucks T-4 hunting camp, and the setting is very popular with diners. Buck's is in the running for the best-restaurant-in-Montana sweepstakes, and has already been called one of the top 10 ski-area restaurants (by *Snow Country* magazine) and one of the best restaurants in the Rockies (by the *Chicago Tribune*). In the fall of 1999, chef Chuck Schommer was the first Montana chef invited to cook for the James Beard Foundation in New York, sometimes called the "Academy Awards of cooking."

5 Livingston & the Paradise Valley

Livingston: 26 miles E of Bozeman; 110 miles W of Billings; 58 miles N of Mammoth Hot Springs in Yellowstone National Park

Livingston is caught between very cowboy and very hip. As the largest community in the Paradise Valley, it has been discovered by the Hollywood set who want to get away from it all, but still bring some of it with them. Peter Fonda has a ranch here. You might see Dennis Quaid. Or Tom McGuane. Robert Redford is also a fan of the area.

The Paradise Valley is carved out by the Yellowstone River. Along with the two valleys paralleling it to the west— the Gallatin and Madison—this portion of Montana is a fly-fishing paradise. There are lots of fishing guides and tackle shops, and millions of acres to wander in and wonder at.

ESSENTIALS

GETTING THERE   The nearest airport is in Bozeman, **Gallatin Field,** 26 miles west along I-90. It's also possible to fly into Billings' **Logan Airport,** 116 miles east along I-90.

The Gardiner entrance to Yellowstone National Park is 53 miles south on U.S. Highway 89. For local road reports call ☎ **406/586-1313;** for road conditions statewide call ☎ **800/332-2231.** Bus service is provided by **Greyhound.** The bus depot is at 107 W. Park (☎ **406/222-2231**).

VISITOR INFORMATION   The **Livingston Convention and Visitors' Bureau** is located at the Livingston Depot Center (☎ **406/222-0580**). For information on **Yellowstone Country,** Travel Montana's region including Livingston, call ☎ **800/736-5276** or 406/446-1005.

GETTING AROUND   Car-rental agents in Livingston include **Avis** (☎ 406/388-6414), **Hertz** (☎ 406/388-6939), **National** (☎ 406/388-6694), and **Rent-A-Wreck** (☎ 406/587-4551). All have desks at Gallatin Field. Or call a taxi at **VIP Taxi** (☎ 406/222-0200).

GETTING OUTSIDE
CROSS-COUNTRY SKIING

The most popular cross-country ski area near Livingston is the Miller Creek drainage in the Gallatin Forest south of town on Route 87. The drainage is large, and provides terrain for every level of ability, from beginner through expert. **Timber Trails Outdoors Co.** (☎ **406/222-9550**), 309 W. Park St., rents skis and will provide information about ski trails.

FISHING

The biggest industry in Livingston is fishing, mostly fly- fishing. This town is the gateway to classic Montana fly-fishing in the blue ribbon Madison River, the Paradise Valley, and the Yellowstone River that wraps itself around the town. **Dan Bailey's Fly Shop,** 209 W. Park St., ☎ **800/356-4052,** has been in business since 1938. The store offers all manner of fishing tackle for sale, or visitors can rent equipment for an outing. Bailey's can give you some tips on where to fish on your own, or provide a guide for about $290 a day, depending on where you want to go. **Hatch Finders Fly Shop,** 113 W. Park St., no. 3, ☎ **406/222-0989,** can tie your custom flies and also provide outfitters almost anywhere in the state. A full-day guided trip in the Yellowstone River area is about $300 for two anglers (plus Montana fishing licenses).

About a quarter-mile south of town on U.S. Highway 89, **George Anderson's Yellowstone Angler,** ☎ **406/222-7130,** is another fully equipped equipment store and guide service. Anderson also offers a fly-fishing school. **Paradise Outfitters,** 5237 Highway 89 S., ☎ **406/222-6486,** is an Orvis-affiliated guide and outfitter.

Early season fishing before runoff starts—in late April and early May—offers excellent dry fly-fishing. In late May and June, the water on most of the rivers is running high and muddy, but the Firehole River in Yellowstone National Park has a heavy early hatch, and the fishing is good. All fishing in the park is catch and release, which is what many conscientious fishermen prefer nowadays, anyway. The rivers drop in July and August, and there are hatches daily for good fishing. Montana has the best trout fishing in the country, and the area around here is the best trout fishing in Montana.

HIKING

This area is nearly surrounded by the **Gallatin National Forest,** which has 2,000 miles of hiking and riding trails throughout the forest, with more than 800 miles in two congressionally designated wilderness areas—the Lee Metcalf and Absaroka-Beartooth. Popular trails that are relatively easily accessible include **Pine Creek Falls** south of town off the East River Road. The falls themselves are a short walk from the campground at the end of the access road, and Pine Creek Lake is about 4 miles farther along. **Livingston Peak** (or Mount Baldy Trail) is east of town off Swingley Road, and the **Big Timber Canyon Trail** is north of the town of Big Timber. The **Livingston Ranger District of the U.S. Forest Service** (☎ **406/222-1892**) can provide information about trails and access routes to them. **Timber Trails Outdoors Co.** (☎ **406/222-9550**), 309 W. Park St., provides information about and directions to favorite hikes around the Livingston area, free of charge.

HORSEBACK RIDING

R.K. Miller's Wilderness Pack Trips, 409 Cokedale Rd., ☎ **406/222-1717,** offers 7- to 10-day horse packing trips into Yellowstone National Park. And **Planes and Reins,** 17 miles south of Livingston on U.S. Highway 89, will take you up in the air or on the ground. Duane Hodgkinson, ☎ **406/333-4788,** will fly you in his Cessna 182 for a 1-hour airborne tour of the Absaroka and Gallatin mountain ranges. His fee is $125 for three passengers. Or Melody Hake, ☎ **406/333-4146,** can take you horseback riding a little closer to the terrain. **Chico Hot Springs,** ☎ **406/333-4933,** about 22 miles south of Livingston, also offers horseback riding.

RAFTING

Both scenic and white-water rafting and kayaking are available on the Yellowstone River throughout the Paradise Valley. **Rubber Ducky River Rentals,** 4 Mount Baldy Dr., ☎ **406/222-3746,** offers guided trips June through September, or will rent boats and equipment and provide river shuttles. **Chico Hot Springs** (see "Where to Stay," below), ☎ **406/333-4933,** also has raft trips.

SEEING THE SIGHTS

Livingston Depot Center. 200 W. Park St. ☎ **406/222-2300.** $3 adults, $2 seniors and children, free for children under 6. Mon–Sat 9am–5pm, Sun 1–5pm.

The Depot Center is a beautifully restored 1902 railway depot. The museum inside offers a history of the railroad in the development of the area, as well as some steamboating lore. There are videos and interactive displays in this thoroughly modern look at the olden days. This is one of four museums on the city's museum tour. The others are the Natural History Exhibit Hall (see below); the **Park County Museum** (118 W. Chinook; ☎ **406/222-4184;** Memorial Day to Labor Day, daily 10am–5:30pm), which covers the early history of Livingston—you can visit an 1889 train caboose and a Yellowstone National Park stagecoach; and the **International Fly-Fishing Center** at 215 E. Lewis ($3 adults; ☎ **406/222-9369;** Memorial Day to Labor Day, daily 10am to 6pm), with some 10,000 flies on display, and a room with displays showing the evolution of the fishing rod.

The Natural History Exhibit Hall. 120 E. Park St. ☎ **406/222-5335.** $4 adults. June–Sept, daily 1–6pm; Oct–May, Thurs–Sun noon–5:30pm.

This is a thoroughly remarkable facility for so small a town. The exhibit hall creates and displays traveling exhibits, primarily of dinosaurs, from some of the world's greatest museums. The shows differ depending on when you visit. When I was there, there was a display of Chinese dinosaurs, the largest such display ever permitted to leave China. Some of the rarest fossils in the world were on display in tiny Livingston, including *Confusiornis,* an early fossil that has contributed to the understanding of the evolution of birds.

SHOPPING

Livingston is a center of Western art and artists, and there are a dozen galleries in town displaying the work of celebrated Montana artists. For Western wildlife and fly-fishing art, try the **Visions West Gallery** at 108 S. Main, with wood carvings, bronzes, and original oils. Livingston's most famous artist is represented at the **Chatham Fine Art Gallery** at 120 N. Main. Several of Chatham's gauzy Western landscapes are on display inside, along with the works of a few other artists. The **Danforth Gallery,** 106 N. Main, is a nonprofit gallery that changes its shows every 2 weeks during the summer. It specializes in contemporary Western art. The **Wade Gallery,** 116 N. Main, has some original photographs of Edward Sheriff Curtis, who captured the 19th-century Indians on film.

The independent bookstore, imperiled everywhere else in America, seems to be thriving in Livingston. There's **Books, Etc.** at 106 S. Main; **O'Byrnes Bookstore,** 113 W. Park, for first editions; and Sax and Fryer, 109 W. Callendar, which specializes in Western books.

WHERE TO STAY

✪ **Chico Hot Springs Lodge.** 1 Chico Rd., Pray, MT 59065. ☎ **800/468-9232.** www.chicohotsprings.com. E-mail: chico@chicohotsprings.com. 98 units. $45 main lodge with shared bathroom; $85 main lodge with private bathroom; $75–$85 cabin; $90 lodge on the hill with private bathroom; $105–$189 lower lodge with private bathroom. V, MC, DISC.

Chico Hot Springs offers the kind of shabby elegance that makes the West great. Chico is hip without being cool. You'll get fabulous food and pretty good lodging—in bewildering variety—all set in Montana's nearly famous Paradise Valley, with a beautiful view of Emigrant Peak. The lobby of the old hotel has the ambience of an Old West dude ranch. The real place to stay here is the turn-of-the-century main lodge with the bathrooms down the hall and the water in the in-room sinks pumped straight up from the hot pools. No television in the rooms. This is the cowboy way.

Chico has two world-class hot pools, one a naturally toasty 104%, the other a little cooler. In the film *Rancho Deluxe*—screenplay by Paradise Valley resident Tom McGuane—Sam Waterston and Jeff Bridges soak in a Chico hot pool in their cowboy hats. The Paradise Valley's notable residents—McGuane, the late poet Richard Brautigan, Jimmy Buffett—hung out here and attracted other Hollywood types. Independent film director John Sayles and actor Dennis Quaid were spotted in the restaurant on the same day—but not at the same table. Near the northern entrance to Yellowstone, Chico offers a taste of fin de siècle gentility, cowboy style.

The resort has built a new convention center and is building 15 new rooms on the site of the old convention/roller skating facility. The new lodge has large, clean, and bright rooms.

Dining/Diversions: Chico is most famous for its food, served up in two restaurants and a saloon. Vegetables are grown in the resort's own hot-spring-heated greenhouses, which are also open for scheduled visits by guests. The Chico Inn (dinner reservations recommended) offers large steaks and seafood flown in from the coast. There is a fine wine cellar, and a Sunday brunch. I have eaten a lot of antelope in my time, but never any as tender and tasty as that served in this restaurant. The Poolside Grill serves a pizza and burger-based menu. The Saloon attracts locals and guests, and is famous for its bar on the ceiling.

Amenities: Children's program for kids 5 and older, horseback riding, rafting, hiking, and swimming in the hot pools. Cross-country skiing in winter.

The Murray Hotel. 201 W. Park St., Livingston, MT 59047. ☎ **406/222-1350.** Fax 406/222-2752. www.murrayhotel.com. E-mail: info@murrayhotel.com. 28 units. A/C TV TEL. $62–$165 double. AE, DISC, MC, V. Pets accepted.

The Murray once had 100 small rooms with shared baths, back in the days of the horse and buggy. But in the last 8 years, the 1903 hotel has been completely and beautifully restored. All of those rooms have been converted into only 28 suites, each with a private bath, without losing any of the charm of an Old West hostelry. The furnishings are very comfortable, more like those in your living room than those in a hotel room. The Murray has been host to such disparate guests as Will Rogers—who tried to take a horse up to the third floor in an elevator—the Queen of Denmark, and film director Sam Peckinpah. This is an old hotel, and many of the doorways are too narrow for wheelchairs.

Dining: The **Winchester Cafe and Grille** is open for lunch and dinner. Dinner runs from $9 to $23. Try the almond fried prawns.

Amenities: There's a spa on the roof and a weight room in the basement. The Parks Reece Gallery, which has a humorist's eye and an artist's style for viewing the natural world, is located in the mezzanine.

Paradise Inn. Box 684, Livingston, MT 59047 (at the intersection of I-90 and U.S. Hwy. 89). ☎ **800/437-6291** or 406/222-6320. 43 units. A/C TV TEL. $90 double; $130 Jacuzzi suite.

This inn is located by the interstate, which makes it convenient but a little noisy. Other places in Livingston have more charm, but this is a convenient place to sleep. There is an average, but inexpensive restaurant and a lounge on the premises.

CAMPING

The Forest Service has a couple of campgrounds, including **Pine Creek** and **Miller Creek** south of town on Route 87 toward Yellowstone. These provide access to hiking trailheads and Yellowstone River fishing, but amenities are minimal. Suitable for tents, mostly. Nine miles south of Livingston on Pine Creek Road is the **Paradise Valley KOA** (☎ **800/562-2805** or 406/222-0992). Open May through October, the facility has 52 RV spots, 27 tent sites, and an indoor heated pool. **Yellowstone's Edge** (☎ **800/865-7322**) is located on a bluff overlooking the river. It has spaces for large RVs and tents, and includes laundry facilities.

WHERE TO DINE

Chatham's Livingston Bar and Grille. 130 N. Main, Livingston, MT. ☎ **406/222-7909.** Reservations recommended. Main courses $14–$25. AE, DISC, MC, V. Summer, Mon–Sat 5:30–10pm, Sun 5–9:30pm; winter, Mon–Sat 5–9:30pm, Sun 4:30–9pm. CONTINENTAL.

It's a little hard to tell from the street if this place is called Chatham's or the Livingston Bar and Grille. The sign on the door says the former, but on the corner over the street the more conspicuous green neon says the latter. By either name, if you're only going to eat one meal in Livingston, this is the place to go. All the locals will direct you here. The walls are decorated with the original paintings of the owner, Russell Chatham, who opened the place in 1996—as if he doesn't already have enough to do. Some favorites here include the veal-spinach ravioli and the capellini with shrimp.

Grand Hotel. 139 McLeod, Big Timber, MT. ☎ **406/932-4459.** Lunch $4–$8; dinner $14–$22. DISC, MC, V. Daily 11am–2pm (Sun brunch) and 5–9pm. LAMB/SEAFOOD.

This beautiful restaurant is located in downtown Big Timber, about 30 miles east of Livingston, in an 1890 hotel that has been beautifully restored. The main attraction is Big Timber lamb, which is offered as the feature of an extensive menu. The restaurant has also won the *Wine Spectator* Award of excellence 5 years in a row for its all-American wine list of 90 wines. There's also a large selection of Scotch, with 30 different single malts. Owner Larry Edwards has 10 rooms in the hotel for $59 to $145.

The Pickle Barrel. 113 W. Park no. 5, Livingston, MT 59047. ☎ **406/222-5469.** Sandwiches $4.50–$10. No credit cards. Daily 10am–8pm. SANDWICHES.

The sandwiches here are good, and not very expensive. Sit here or carry out. Try the Dragon Slayer, a good Italian sandwich. The perfect place for a quick, filling lunch.

Rumours. 2nd and Callendar, Livingston, MT. ☎ **406/222-5154.** Lunch $4–$7; dinner $11–$16. MC, V. Mon 7am–2:30pm, Tues–Sun 7am–2:30pm and 5:30–10pm. AMERICAN.

This small, elegant restaurant is especially popular at lunch. It advertises itself as serving "yada yada food" —meaning creatively prepared pasta and seafood. It projects a very calm and sophisticated aura with its white interior and big picture windows. The pastries and desserts are worth stopping in for.

The Sport Restaurant and Bar. 114 S. Main, Livingston, MT 59047. ☎ **406/222-3533.** Lunch $4–$10; dinner $8–$20. MC, V. Daily 11am–2am. BURGERS/MEXICAN.

The decor here is different for Montana. You get your Western ambience, with plank floors and the requisite animal heads, but there are also authentic front pages from various newspapers chronicling some of the century's major events. I wasn't very hungry when I ate at the Sport, so I ordered the grilled cheese, which was very good, and it isn't often you can say that about grilled cheese. The Sport has joined in the Montana celebrity parade with visits from Larry Hagman, Brad Pitt, Tom Brokaw, and many others. Originally called the Beer Hall, it became the Sport in 1909. Women weren't allowed in until the 1940s, but the place is now run by a woman.

Uncle Looie's. 119 W. Park St., Livingston, MT 59047. ☎ **406/222-7177.** Lunch $6–$12; dinner $6–$25. DISC, MC, V. Sun–Thurs 11:30am–2pm and 5:30–9:30pm, Fri–Sat 11:30am–2pm and 5:30–10pm. CONTINENTAL.

Everything is made fresh to order at Uncle Looie's. The place has a very comfortable, almost Southwestern feel to it. The most popular dishes include the Penne Looie and the roasted boursin chicken. Veal is available. The wine list is mostly American, but there is a sprinkling of Italian selections as well. For lunch there's a buffet.

6 Red Lodge & the Absaroka-Beartooth Wilderness

60 miles SW of Billings; 62 miles NW of Cody, Wyoming

Red Lodge is not quite a ski resort, not quite a tourist town, yet not quite still a sleepy Western small town, either. It has elements of all three, giving it a homey and still busy feel. The ski area is not large enough to attract the distant destination skiers. It isn't quite close enough to Yellowstone to draw the long-term visitor to the park. While it is slowly losing its small town identity in favor of a resort persona, this hasn't happened completely. The local library for years didn't even have a card catalog. To find a book, you simply asked librarian Bob Moran, who would get it for you.

The town was founded as a coal mining community in the late 1880s, though the mines closed in the 1930s. It's nestled in a steep valley at the edge of the Absaroka-Beartooth Wilderness, and surrounded by the spectacular Beartooth Mountains. Another reason to visit: Red Lodge sits at the northern end of the Beartooth National Scenic Byway, which the late Charles Kurault called the most beautiful road in America.

ESSENTIALS

GETTING THERE   To reach Red Lodge, you'll have to fly into **Logan International Airport** in **Billings** (see the section on Billings "Essentials" in chapter 9). From Billings, take I-94 to Laurel, about 16 miles, then go south on U.S. 212–310. The route diverges after about 12 miles at the small town of Rockvale. Follow U.S. 212 southwest 44 miles to Red Lodge. Rental cars are rare in town, but **Anderson's** (☎ **406/446-2720**) at 210 N. Broadway offers limited rentals. For road conditions concerning the Red Lodge area and closures of the Beartooth National Scenic Byway, call ☎ **406/252-2806** or 307/237-8411. For **statewide weather conditions,** call ☎ **800/332-6171.**

VISITOR INFORMATION   Contact the **Red Lodge Area Chamber of Commerce,** P.O. Box 998, Red Lodge, MT 59068 (☎ **406/446-1718**), for visitor information.

SPECIAL EVENTS   Classical music lovers may want to take in a concert during June's **Red Lodge Music Festival,** which brings professional musicians to town and gives local high school students the opportunity to study with them.

August brings the **Festival of Nations,** an annual get-together of townsfolk from different cultural backgrounds. It's a week-long extravaganza devoted to exploring each of the nationalities—Scottish, Scandinavian, Finnish, Italian, Slavic, English, Irish, and German—of Red Lodge's original settlers.

During winter's last blast in early March, the **Red Lodge Winter Carnival** opens each year with a theme parade on Friday night. The carnival includes a ridiculous fireman's race, often surprisingly good ice sculptures, and a "ski-joring" competition (horse and rider towing a skier over a series of jumps). Call the Chamber of Commerce (☎ **406/446-1718**) for specific dates and information about these events.

And They're Off . . . to the Pig Races, That Is

Bored with the rodeo? Horse racing make you ho-hum? Just head down to the **Bear Creek Saloon;** behind the bar is (what else?) Bearcreek Downs, site of the famed local pig races.

Pig races? After the famous fires in Yellowstone in 1988 created a slow tourist season, the Bear Creek Saloon owners decided that a pig race might generate some visitor interest. They ran the pig races, but the state board of horse racing couldn't decide whether they were legal. Eventually, the Montana legislature stepped in and said pig races were okay by them, provided the proceeds went to charity. So Bearcreek Downs porkers are sending Carbon County students to college.

All the pigs get is a dish full of pig food at the end of their lap around the outdoor arena. The fans get into it. Pig racing has been so popular that they bring the competition inside during winter months.

Even if you don't come for the porcine track meet, this saloon-cum-Mexican restaurant has a lot to offer. It looks and smells like an authentic Western tavern, and the grub is mostly beef, but pretty good. Food is served Friday through Monday 5 to 10pm. Pig races are held Friday through Sunday at 7pm, from late May through September. The saloon is 7 miles east of Red Lodge on Highway 308 in Bear Creek. The saloon is open daily from 5pm to 2am in summer. Call ☎ **406/446-3481** for more information.

GETTING OUTSIDE

GOLF

The **Red Lodge Mountain Golf Course** (☎ **406/446-3344**) is notorious for swallowing golf balls. Water comes into play on 13 of the 18 holes. The signature hole is the 238-yard, par three Number 6, where you hit to an island green from an elevated tee about 80 feet above the hole. The cost is $25 for 18 holes, $15 for nine.

HIKING

The Absaroka-Beartooth Wilderness area is a 950,000-acre wilderness that extends from the boundary of Yellowstone through two national forests. It's some of the most spectacular country in the lower 48 states. Because of its proximity to the park, it is heavily used. There are lots of great hikes, incredible vistas, and pristine lakes with excellent trout fishing. **Granite Peak,** at 12,799 feet, is the tallest mountain in Montana, but it's only one of the 28 mountains topping 12,000 feet in the Absaroka-Beartooth.

For information about trails, camping, and trail conditions, contact the **Beartooth Ranger District Office** of the Custer National Forest, at the south end of town along U.S. Highway 212 (HC49, Box 3420, Red Lodge, MT 59068; ☎ **406/446-2103**).

There are some popular and challenging day hikes not far from Red Lodge. Drive south on Route 212 about 10 miles to County Road 2346, then 2 miles down that road to the **Lake Fork of Rock Creek.** From here you can do a full loop of 19 miles to the West Fork of Rock Creek trailhead, or just walk up a few miles to some fishing in the streams and lakes along the way and return.

Other popular hikes leave from the trailhead at the **West Fork of Rock Creek.** Drive on Highway 71—also the road to the Red Lodge Mountain Ski area, known locally as Ski Run Road. When the road forks, stay left and follow the road for several miles past a number of campgrounds. The road turns to gravel and ends at the Wet Fork trailhead. The hike from here to Timberline Lakes is a 9-mile round-trip of moderate difficulty. If you're not feeling that energetic, you can hike for about a mile to a waterfall. The fishing in Lake Mary near the trail is very good.

If you want to be more ambitious, try the 28-mile hike from the **East Rosebud** trailhead to Cooke City, past the Fossil Lakes. The trail is called The Beaten Path. It is long and strenuous, but not technically difficult, and it gives you a good sample of the terrain of the wilderness. It makes a nice 2- or 3-day backpacking trip. It's about 11 miles to the Fossil Lakes. The trailhead begins at 6,200 feet elevation and rises to the lakes at 9,900 feet. To get to the trailhead from Red Lodge, take U.S. Highway 78 19 miles west to Roscoe. Turn south on Forest Service Road 2177 and drive to the end of the road.

SKIING

Red Lodge Mountain. Box 750, Red Lodge, MT 59068. ☎ **800/444-8977** or 406/446-2610. Lift ticket $34 adults, $28 juniors, $13 children. Half-day ticket $28. DISC, MC, V. Open Nov–Apr. From Red Lodge go south on Broadway past Chateau Rouge and turn right at the sign for the ski area. The road is known locally as Ski Run Rd., but does not have a "real" name, and there is no street sign other than the ski area sign. The ski area is 6 miles up the road.

Red Lodge Mountain is a relatively small, family-oriented ski area that is growing. The size of the skiable terrain recently grew to 1,600 acres of mountain, and plans are in the works for an additional 400 more. There are 2,400 feet of vertical, with more than half the mountain (55%) rated for intermediate skiers, 15% for beginners, and 30% for advanced. There are seven lifts, including two new high-speed quad lifts, and renovation plans include replacement of all the old lifts with new ones. Two-hundred and fifty inches of snow falls annually here. Plus, Red Lodge Mountain has the largest snowmaking operation in the Rockies, so it usually has the earliest opening dates in Montana, with top-to-bottom skiing often available by Thanksgiving. The hill also offers both morning and afternoon half-day passes, not unheard of in the ski industry, but unusual.

SEEING THE SIGHTS

As you've read in other pages, the **Beartooth National Scenic Byway,** a 64-mile stretch of U.S. Highway 212, from Red Lodge to Cooke City, is an incredible piece of road that puts your car at almost 11,000 feet. Make sure a camera is handy when Pilot Peak, the giant spire just outside Cooke City, comes into view.

Beartooth Nature Center. 2nd Ave. N., Red Lodge, MT 59068. ☎ **406/446-1133.** $5 adults; $2.50 seniors and children. Memorial Day–Labor Day, 10am–5:30pm; rest of year, 10am–2pm. Evening and special tours can be arranged for groups.

The Beartooth Nature Center specializes in housing Montana wildlife. These are animals that have been injured, orphaned, or too accustomed to humans to be returned to the wild. The Montana Fish, Wildlife, and Parks Department brings them here for a home. Residents include mountain lions, wolves, coyotes, black bears, sandhill cranes, and other Montana residents or migrants, along with some non-natives (like the Arctic fox) and some domesticated animals. There is a petting zoo for the kids.

Carbon County Peak to Plains Museum. Broadway and 8th Ave., Red Lodge, MT 59068. ☎ **406/6466-1290.** $3 adults; $2 children; free for children 5 and under. Mon–Fri 10am–5pm, Sat–Sun and holidays 1–5pm.

The museum has recently moved into new quarters. Highlights of the facility are a simulated coal mine downstairs (appropriately enough) that recalls Red Lodge's underground past, and the Greenough Collection of cowboy and rodeo gear. The museum is airy and attractively set up to show off the Crow Indian tepee and camp setup and pioneer displays. This is also the place to find out more about "Liver Eatin'" Johnston, who got his name because . . . no, it's too repulsive. You'll have to find out for yourself.

WHERE TO STAY

Bear Bordeaux Bed & Breakfast. 302 S. Broadway, Red Lodge, MT 59068. ☎ **406/446-4408.** 3 units. TV. $45–$85 double. AE, DISC, MC, V.

This is a nice B&B on Red Lodge's main street, presided over by concierge Winston, a handsome golden retriever who always has a stuffed toy in his mouth. The house has a rock-and-stone motif, as well as hardwood floors. The rooms are decorated in mostly Western themes. Each room has a private bath, some with Jacuzzis. There are also gas fireplaces in two of the rooms. Each unit has a television and VCR, and the library downstairs has a collection of 500 movies available to guests. There are also 3,000 books in the library. Rates include a full breakfast, and the proprietor, Sharon Torcaso, will fix lunch and dinner as well if you make reservations in advance.

Chateau Rouge. 1505 S. Broadway, Red Lodge, MT 59608. ☎ **800/926-1601** or 406/446-1601. Fax 406/446-1602. www.wtp.net/chateaurouge. E-mail: chatroug@wtp.net. 24 units. TV TEL. Winter, $68 studio; $85 2-bedroom condo, $15 for each extra person; $99 deluxe condo, $15 for each extra person; summer, $61 studio; $55 2-bedroom condo, $10 for each extra person; $90 deluxe condo, $10 for each extra person. AE, DISC, DC, MC, V.

Though it is run like a motel, the Chateau Rouge is actually a collection of privately owned condominiums. Most are two-story, two-bedroom affairs with a living room and kitchen on the first floor and the sleeping rooms upstairs. The two-story condos have large, fully appointed kitchens, while the studios have small but complete kitchens. All are beautifully appointed and maintained. The only drawback—a minor one in my opinion—is that they are not air conditioned, which can make for warm sleeping on those rare summer days when the mountain temperatures reach the nineties. The place also has an indoor pool. Don't be put off by the faux-Swiss architecture. The Chateau Rouge offers excellent accommodations at a very reasonable price, especially for families.

Comfort Inn of Red Lodge. 612 N. Broadway, Red Lodge, MT 59068. ☎ **888/733-4661** or 406/446-4469. www.wtp.net/comfortinn. E-mail: 1stpic@wtp.net. 53 units. A/C TV TEL. $50–$120 double; $160 suite. Rates include breakfast. AE, DISC, MC, V.

This motel is only 3 years old and is as sparkling clean as a brand-new building. Five suites are available, including a large family suite/meeting room with a giant-screen television. The standard rooms are just standard rooms, but they look like new and are reasonably priced—as low as $80 a night in the busy summer season. Some of the rooms have Jacuzzis, and there are an indoor swimming pool, fitness room, guest laundry, and deluxe continental breakfast.

✪ **The Pollard.** 2 N. Broadway, Red Lodge, MT 59068. ☎ **800/765-5273** or 406/446-0001. Fax 406/446-0002. www.pollardhotel.com. E-mail: pollard@pollardhotel.com. 38 units. A/C TV TEL. $75–$235 double. AE, DISC, MC, V.

The Pollard was built in 1893 by the Rocky Fork Coal Company for $20,000. It recently has undergone a beautiful restoration, which has integrated modern conveniences with historic character and elegance. It has been a stopover for a number of Old West celebrities, including Buffalo Bill Cody, Calamity Jane, and Jeremiah "Liver Eatin'" Johnson. In 1991, the Hotel Company of Red Lodge purchased the hotel and undertook a complete renovation. When it reopened in June 1994, the Pollard was an immediate success and is now considered one of the nicest properties in the state. The hotel has a three-story gallery with a wood-burning fireplace. Six of the rooms have balconies overlooking the lobby. All the rooms are very large, done with manly oak furniture and ladylike flower print comforters. Many of the rooms have Jacuzzis. The entire operation is first-class. I'd like to live here.

Dining: For fine dining in Red Lodge, **Greenlee's at the Pollard Hotel** is the best choice. It's located in a spacious, sparsely decorated dining area off the hotel lobby. The food is excellent. Steaks are grilled over a wood fire. Reservations are recommended. Greenlee's is open daily from 7:30am to 1:30pm and from 5:30 to 9pm.

Amenities: Complete athletic club with aerobic and strength training equipment, free weights, sauna, hot tub, and two racquetball courts. Fax edition of the daily *New York Times* delivered to your room each morning.

✪ **Rock Creek Resort.** HC 49, Box 3500, Red Lodge, MT 59068. ☎ **800/446-1119** or 406/446-1111. Fax 406/466-3688. www.rcresort.com. E-mail: rcresort@wtp.net. 91 units. TV TEL. $88–$285 double. AE, DC, DISC, MC, V.

This property was built in 1963 as a dormitory for members of an international ski racing camp founded by owner Pepi Granshammer. Granshammer is still a very hands-on owner—though he spends much of his time in Vail, Colorado, where he owned property before it became fashionable. He still keeps close tabs on this place, though. In fact he joined me for dessert after dinner the night I ate here.

Rock Creek retains much of the ski atmosphere that gave birth to it. It looks very much like a ski resort, lacking only a ski hill, which is a good 6 miles away. There are a variety of rooms available for every taste and budget. The complex hosts vacationers and businesspeople. The resort offers the Rock Creek Resort Adventure Challenge for groups, based on outdoor adventure games to promote "team building." The lodge provides all the expected amenities: restaurant, indoor pool, sauna, hot tub, and four tennis courts.

The cedar-sided Beartooth Lodge is the main building on the grounds. Just as it was completed in 1991, an electrical fire burned it to the ground; it was rebuilt and opened the following year. It boasts a giant corner fireplace made of river rock and windows that offer mountain views.

Manager Dan Drobney places a high priority on service, making the guests feel special whether they're staying in the deluxe suite or the least expensive room. He wants guests to feel like they're visiting an old friend. He even baked cookies one evening for a couple celebrating their 50th wedding anniversary

Dining: Old Piney Dell serves excellent food. The service is good and the atmosphere is in keeping with a ski chalet owned by an Austrian. It's in a quaint cabin, low-ceilinged, with jazz on the stereo.

Amenities: Restaurant, indoor pool, sauna, hot tub, health club, barbecue area, volleyball and horseshoe area, soccer field, and four tennis courts. The park area in front of the lodge buildings has a stocked trout pond.

CAMPING

There are 16 Forest Service campgrounds available in the Red Lodge area, with sites for over 700 campers. Closest to town are **Sheridan** and **Ratine. Sheridan** is 5 miles southwest of Red Lodge on U.S. Highway 212, then 2 miles southwest on Forest Service Road 379. **Ratine** is 5 miles southwest of Red Lodge on U.S. Highway 212, then 3 miles southwest on Forest Service Road 379. **Parkside, Limberpine,** and **Greenough** are all within a mile of each other and are reached by paved roads. Sites are more developed, with hand pumps for drinking water, picnic tables, and fire pits. They're 12 miles SW of Red Lodge on U.S. Highway 212, then 1 mile SW on Forest Service Road 421.

Basin campground, 6 miles from Red Lodge, is located 1 mile from Wild Bill Lake, a day-use area popular for its fishing access and hiking trails. All of its facilities are wheelchair-accessible. There are also eight Forest Service campgrounds along the Beartooth National Scenic Byway. For information on any of the above-listed campgrounds, contact the **Beartooth Ranger Station** at ☎ **406/446-2103.** Their office is at the south end of town on U.S. Highway 212, and they can inform you of seasonal closings and locations.

For a much less isolated experience, try **Perry's RV Park & Campground** (☎ **406/446-2722**), just 2 miles south of town off U.S. Highway 212 along Rock Creek. Perry's has 20 tent sites and 30 spots for RVs, along with a store and laundry. **The Red Lodge KOA** (☎ **406/446-2634**) is at the other end of town, 6 miles north of Red Lodge on U.S. Highway 212. There are 70 campsites: 46 for trailers, 20 for tents, and 4 for camper cabins. A creek runs through the property, and it is heavily wooded, so you can park in the shade. There's a swimming pool, rec room, playground, and sauna on-site. Both of these private campgrounds are open seasonally, from mid-May through September.

WHERE TO DINE

Bogart's. 11 S. Broadway. ☎ **406/446-1784.** Reservations not accepted. Most dishes $6–$15. MC, V. Daily 11am–9pm. MEXICAN/PIZZA.

Bogart's menu consists of great sandwiches, Mexican entrees, and pizza. The place, as you might have guessed, is named after Humphrey himself. Other than the humble homage of naming sandwiches after some of his movies, don't expect more of a tribute. The chimichangas are toasted to a golden turn, and the chiles rellenos are excellent.

Bridge Creek Restaurant and Wine Bar. 106 W. 12th St. ☎ **406/446-9900.** Lunch $4–$9; dinner $10–$20. MC, V. Mon–Thurs 11am–9pm, Fri–Sat 11am–9:30pm. ECLECTIC.

Bridge Street is a local favorite, with a widely varied, moderately priced menu. Lunches include wraps, sandwiches, and soups, and at dinner there's fish, chicken, steaks, chops, and pasta. The wine bar is a small bright room with an extensive wine list that received the *Wine Spectator* award of excellence in 1998. The atmosphere is casual, sort of California cafe with a Western flavor.

Red Lodge Ale House. 9 & 11 N. Broadway. ☎ **406/446-1426.** Main courses $10–$22. MC, V. Mon–Thurs 4–10pm, Fri–Sun 11am–10pm; Ale House daily until 2am. STEAKS.

This restaurant, which opened in 1998, is decked out in blonde wood furnishings. And as the name implies, there's locally produced ales on tap. The food is American—burgers, steaks, and trout—reasonably priced and competently prepared. It isn't too adventurous, but then again you can't easily ruin it. You can get a T-bone special for $9.95 and an order of baby back ribs for $14.25—bargains in any millennium.

Billings & Eastern Montana

by Dan Whipple

The plains of eastern Montana offer a more subtle beauty than the rugged mountains to the west. A land of rolling hills, dusty bluffs, and occasional rock-walled canyon, this is classic cattle and wheat country, with grass thick and green in the spring, brown and dry in the fall, and white with snow cover in winter. Temperatures can be extreme, hot in the summer under a shimmering sun, and bitter blue-sky cold in the winter, dipping below zero for long stretches.

Eastern Montana has been critical to the settlement of the state and the West. Lewis and Clark trekked along the Missouri River. One of the most famous battles in American history, the Battle of the Little Bighorn, was fought on Montana's eastern plains.

In the old days, travel in eastern Montana was defined by the railroads. Virtually every town with 300 people and a tavern could be visited by train on either the main line or spur. The railroad days are gone, replaced by the Interstate. I-94 cuts a long swath across the state, and I-90 dips south from near Billings to the Crow Reservation in Sheridan, Wyoming, and points south. Well-maintained back roads can take you through the rolling hills of Crow Country and down the canyon-studded Bighorn Canyon National Recreation area.

Billings, though, has its share of splendor. From the heights of the city, you can see three mountain ranges—the Pryor Mountains, the Bighorns, and the majestic Beartooths to the west.

1 Billings

104 miles W of Cody, Wyoming; 123 miles N of Sheridan, Wyoming; 142 miles E of Bozeman; 339 miles E of Missoula; 222 miles W of Glendive

The most populous city in Montana, Billings rivals Missoula for the honor of being the "most citified" place in the state. You'll find real shopping malls here, along with the tallest freestanding hotel west of the Mississippi, and the occasional five o'clock traffic jam. Since its 1880s development by Frederick Billings as a railroad town, the city has evolved into the economic hub for much of the eastern portion of the state and parts of northern Wyoming.

Once a booming oil town, as well as a crossroads for the railroads and interstate highway system, Billings has now positioned itself as the progressive regional medical center for all of eastern Montana, the Dakotas, and Wyoming. The economy, still based on cattle and grain, has been bolstered by 10 years of relative prosperity for the farmers and ranchers who inhabit the eastern edge of the state.

Within the 30 or so square blocks of downtown Billings are beautiful historic build-ings in various stages of restoration, new banks and contemporary business centers, and a few sites that have fallen into disrepair. Though the area has grown suburban-ized, downtown has revived, thanks in part to service businesses and the performing arts center.

ESSENTIALS

GETTING THERE Billings' Logan International Airport is the state's busiest, located atop the rimrocks about 2 miles north of downtown. Intrastate service is pro-vided by **Big Sky Airlines** (☎ 800/237-7788 or 406/245-2300), and regional daily service by **Delta** (☎ 800/221-1212), **Horizon** (☎ 800/547-9308), **Northwest** (☎ 800/225-2525), and **United** (☎ 800/241-6522).

From the west, Interstate 90 cuts through the southern part of the city. To access the downtown, get off at Exit 450 and go north. From the east, coming from Hardin, I-90 meets the end of I-94, 7 miles east of town. Heading west from North Dakota, Glendive and Miles City, I-94 ends at its intersection with I-90 before coming into town. Coming from the north, from Roundup, U.S. Highway 87 turns into a four-lane road before heading west into the Heights, the northeastern part of the city. Follow this road into downtown, or turn right on Airport Road across from **Metra-Park** to reach Logan International Airport.

The bus terminal for **Greyhound** (☎ 800/231-2222) and **Rimrock Stages** (☎ 800/255-7655 or 406/245-5392) is downtown at 2502 1st Ave. N.

VISITOR INFORMATION The **Billings Area Chamber of Commerce,** 815 S. 27th St., Billings, MT 59107 (☎ 800/735-2635 or 406/245-4111), is open Monday to Friday and has brochures, maps, and area information. The area is also part of Travel Montana's Custer Country. You can get a vacation guide from **Custer Country,** Rte. 1, Box 1206A, Hardin, MT 59034 (☎ 800/346-1876 or 406/665-1671; travel.state.mt.us/custer).

GETTING AROUND Billings has adopted a confusing nomenclature for its streets that makes it a little difficult to get oriented. There is, for instance, a 1st Street, dif-ferent from 1st Avenue, and a 6th Avenue S. and 6th Avenue N. which run parallel to each other 12 blocks apart. The heart of the downtown is relatively compact, from N. 27th to N. 29th streets (the eastern and western boundaries) and from 1st to 6th avenues N. (to the north and south).

Virtually the only way to see Billings is to drive yourself. The traditional car-rental companies are ready to help you out, with **Avis** (☎ 800/831-2847 or 406/252-8007), **Budget** (☎ 800/527-0800 or 406/259-4168), **Hertz** (☎ 800/654-3131 or 406/248-9151), and **National** (☎ 800/227-7368 or 406/252-7626) maintaining counters at Logan International Airport.

The city bus service is **Billings Met Transit** (☎ 406/657-8218). You can call a taxi from **City Cab & Silver Eagle Shuttle,** ☎ 406/252-8700.

BLACK OTTER TRAIL SCENIC DRIVE

While not the premier tourist attraction in Billings, the Black Otter Trail Scenic Drive is a good place to get a perspective on the city. It's only about 3 miles long, but it affords a spectacular view of the city and the three mountain ranges in the distance and, on sunny summer days, of high school and college sunbathers who use the bluffs in lieu of a beach. The Black Otter Trail is a rough blacktop road that creeps along the edge of the sheer rimrock overlooking Billings. To get to it, go up N. 27th Street nearly to the airport, then turn right (east) on 310. Watch carefully for signs. The road is not

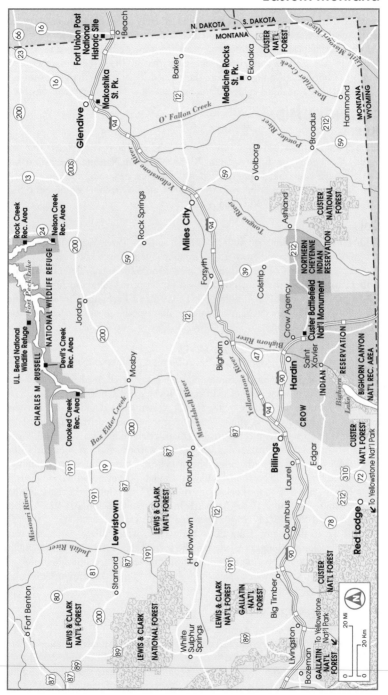

very well marked. The trail has the Boot Hill Cemetery for 40 of the unlucky residents of the town of Coulson, most of whom died with their boots on, as they say. It's also the final resting place of the famous scout, Yellowstone Kelly, who asked to be buried here above the land he scouted. Legend has it that in 1837, the Crow sacrificed a number of horses and young men from these bluffs. They leaped to their deaths as an offering to stop a smallpox epidemic among their tribe. That's the legend, anyway.

GETTING OUTSIDE

FISHING

Though the Yellowstone River runs through the city, it is wide, busy, and often muddy. The best nearby fishing is in the **Bighorn Canyon National Recreation Area.** Fishing guides come and go pretty often in the Billings area, so to find a local one the best bet may be to call or visit the **Base Camp Outdoor Equipment Store** (☎ **406/248-4555**) at 1730 Grand Ave.

GOLF

Lake Hills Golf Club (☎ **406/252-9244**) and the **Peter Yegen Jr. Golf Club** (☎ **406/656-8099**) are the two 18-hole public golf courses in Billings. The private 18-hole **Briarwood Country Club** (☎ **406/256-0626**) and 27-hole **Pryor Creek Golf Course** (**406/256-0626**) offer limited public play. Call ahead for availability. **Circle Inn Golf Links** (☎ **406/259-3351**) and **Par 3 Exchange City Golf Course** (☎ **406/652-2553**) are public par 3 courses. Briarwood is one of the best courses in Montana and Wyoming.

NEARBY PARKS & NATURE PRESERVES

An unusual and worthwhile side trip is to the **Pictograph Caves State Park,** where the remnants of 5,000-year-old communication is preserved on the walls. The caves are more like large stone alcoves than caves in the usual sense. There are 106 cave paintings—pictographs—made by the former residents in red and black paints fashioned from ashes, clay, and animal fat. The true meaning of the paintings is still debated. Perhaps they were ceremonial, perhaps celebrations of a successful hunt or battle. There are many images of shield-bearing warriors. A short (but fairly steep) interpretive trail leads up to the caves. The caves lie in a classic, sheer, broad sandstone canyon. Rabbits and the occasional rattlesnake inhabit the area—so stay on the trails. From Billings take I-90 to the Lockwood exit, no. 452, then follow the signs. The park is open 8am to 8pm April 15 to October 1. In season call ☎ **406/245-0227;** the rest of the year, call ☎ **406/247-2940.** There is a $4 per car fee.

Locals go to the nearby **Lake Elmo State Park,** which offers swimming, windsurfing, picnicking, fishing, and volleyball. It's located about 10 miles north of Billings on U.S. Highway 87. Boat rentals and windsurfing lessons are available in the peak summer months. Gas powered boats are prohibited on the lake. Entrance fees are $1 per person over age 6.

SEEING THE SIGHTS

Some of the artwork on the **Avenue of the Sculptures** along 27th Street (from Exit 450 off I-90 to Logan International Airport) seems almost hidden among the city's buildings. The first work, The *Cattle Drive Monument,* is right outside the Chamber of Commerce's visitor center. *The Trough,* a contemporary piece that looks like a fragment of collapsed concrete, is in front of the Norwest Bank Building at 175 N. 27th. *The Sheriff Webb Memorial Marker* is on the courthouse lawn, and in front of the Yellowstone Art Museum is the *Reineking* statue, at 4th Avenue N. and N. 27th. Finally,

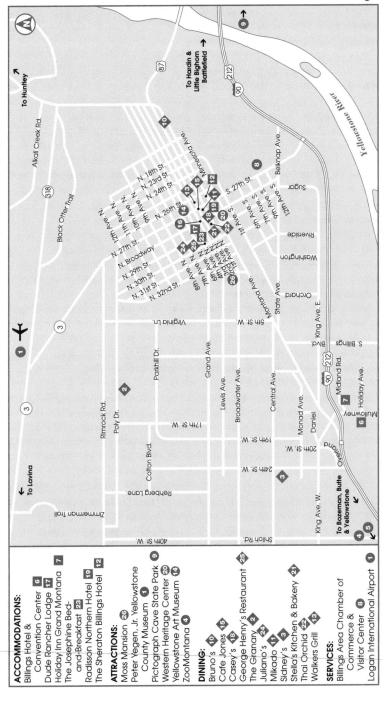

ACCOMMODATIONS:
Billings Hotel &
    Convention Center **6**
Dude Rancher Lodge **17**
Holiday Inn Grand Montana **7**
The Josephine Bed-
    and-Breakfast **28**
Radisson Northern Hotel **19**
The Sheraton Billings Hotel **12**

ATTRACTIONS:
Moss Mansion **26**
Peter Yegen, Jr. Yellowstone
    County Museum **1**
Pictograph Cave State Park **9**
Western Heritage Center **20**
Yellowstone Art Museum **14**
ZooMontana **4**

DINING:
Bruno's **10**
Cafe Jones **15**
Casey's **18**
George Henry's Restaurant **25**
The Granary **2**
Juliano's **24**
Mikado **1**
Sidney's **3**
Stella's Kitchen & Bakery **11**
Thai Orchid **21**
Walkers Grill **13**

SERVICES:
Billings Area Chamber of
    Commerce &
    Visitor Center **8**
Logan International Airport **1**

in front of the airport is the *Range Rider of the Yellowstone*, in memory of cowboy actor William Hart. Hart's boots used to sport fancy spurs donated by local craftspeople, but pranksters stole them so often that Hart now rides spurless.

The Moss Mansion. 914 Division. ☎ **406/256-5100.** www.mcn.net/~mossmansion. $6 adult, $5 senior, $3 children 6–12. MC, V. Summer, guided tour every hour on the hour, daily 10am–4pm; winter, daily 1–3pm. Closed Thanksgiving, Christmas, and New Year's Day.

This massive redbrick three-story mansion was built not for a cattle baron but for Billings banker Preston B. Moss. It was designed in 1901 by American architect Henry Janeway Hardenbaugh and built in 1903. There are many European influences in the house, including a Moorish entry and a Shakespearean library, as well as a French parlor. Oak and mahogany millwork give an elegant feel to the upstairs bedrooms. The mansion hosts various special events during the summer, like a country fair, a garden expo and marketplace, and a doll tea party.

Western Heritage Center. 2822 Montana Ave. ☎ **406/256-6809.** www.ywhc.org. Free admission; donations accepted. Tues–Sat 10am–5pm, Sun 1–5pm.

A lot of Western museums are just vast collections of stuff from bygone eras. But this facility has done an excellent job of interpreting and editing its extensive collection, making the panoramic history of Western settlement accessible to casual visitors. In many other museums, you can get the idea that settlement was a steady procession of triumphant white people. But the Heritage Center includes sensitive displays on the Crow tribe, and on Japanese and other minority settlers. Interactive presentations include videos and recorded memories of three Yellowstone County homesteaders. The museum also has an outreach program, revolving shows, and a gift shop.

Peter Yegen Jr. Yellowstone County Museum. Logan International Airport. ☎ **406/256-6811.** www.pyjrycm.org. Free admission. Mon–Fri 10:30am–5pm, Sat 10:30am–3pm. Closed legal holidays.

The museum, inconveniently located at the airport, has a large collection housed in a 104-year-old cabin owned by the locally prominent McCormick family. Teddy Roosevelt and Buffalo Bill Cody visited the cabin at one time or another. The collection consists mostly of Western history items from Montana and Wyoming, but an occasional odd German 1730 illuminated Bible slips in as well. The interpretation is minimal. The place has the comfortable, musty feel of your grandmother's attic. The volunteers here are encyclopedically knowledgeable about Billings and its history.

✪ **Yellowstone Art Museum.** 401 N. 27th St. ☎ **406/256-6804.** $3 adults. Tues–Wed 10am–5pm, Thurs 10am–8pm, Fri–Sat 10am–5pm, Sun noon–5pm.

Montana art aficionados are justifiably proud of the Yellowstone Art Museum, a leader in the contemporary Western art movement. The museum showcases the best the new West has to offer, from Deborah Butterfield's ranch sculptures to Russell Chatham's gauzy landscapes to Rudy Autio's colorful, erotic ceramics. You won't find many cougars romantically poised to leap in a woodland setting here, but you will find Will James's 19th- and 20th-century drawings, along with an illustrated letter to James from Charles M. Russell, the original Western artist.

ESPECIALLY FOR KIDS: ANIMALS, ANIMALS

ZooMontana. Take Exit 446 north off I-90, head west on King Ave. to Shiloh Rd., then south. ☎ 406/652-8100. $5 adults, $2 children. Summer, daily 10am–8pm; winter, daily 10am–4pm. Closed Thanksgiving, Christmas, and New Year's Day.

This is an ambitious new zoo, only 7 years old and about 15% complete. Current exhibits include bald eagles, river otters, and two of the 300 Siberian tigers remaining in the world. The zoo also has two black-footed ferrets, North America's rarest mammal, and is planning an extensive high plains habitat exhibit. The zoo is also concentrating on northern plains wildlife. This is an excellent place to learn about the wildlife you'll be seeing (and won't be seeing) on your trip through the state. An exit onto Zoo Drive from I-90 should be completed sometime in 2000.

SHOPPING
In the downtown area, the shopping district covers about 4 blocks on N. 29th Street, Broadway, and 1st and 2nd avenues N. The area is heavy in the antique line, but it also has a few boutiques and independent bookshops. The **Yesteryear Antique and Craft Mall,** 114 N. 29th St. (☎ **406/259-3314**), is the first stop for collectors. You can find old bones, fine Western writing desks, and Native American artifacts and jewelry. There are numerous antique stores in Billings, and the Chamber of Commerce has the *Antiquers Trail Guide of Greater Billings,* showing the location of more than two dozen stores.

The **American West Gallery,** 2814 2nd Ave. N. (☎ **406/248-5014**), has a large collection of Indian jewelry, beadwork, dresses, and moccasins for sale. For more contemporary art with a less traditional Western outlook, try the **Toucan Gallery,** 2505 Montana Ave. (☎ **406/252-0122**), which is centered in the city's historic district, offering prints, oils, handmade furniture, and ceramics.

The fashion conscious can find clothing from around the world at the **Cactus Rose,** 202 N. 29th St. (☎ **406/252-9126**). And down the block a little is **Sylvester's Bargain Emporium,** at 2901 1st Ave. N. (☎ **406/245-8083**). **Stillwater Traders** in the Radisson Northern Hotel, Broadway and 1st Ave. N. (☎ **406/252-6211**), offers a densely packed collection of Western clothing, toys, and trinkets. The classic Western department store, where lots of real cowboys get their real clothes, is **Lou Taubert Ranch Outfitters** (☎ **406/245-2248**), now in new quarters at 123 Broadway.

There are some small independent bookstores—a dying breed—in downtown Billings, notably **Thomas Books,** 209 N. 29th St. (☎ **406/245-6754**). **The Book Place,** 2814 1st Ave. N. (☎ **406/256-3500**), specializes in used, rare, and collectible books with a large collection of Western Americana.

For outdoor gear, check out the **Base Camp** (☎ **406/248-4555**), at 1730 Grand Ave., which has a large collection of all the major (and a few minor) outdoor brands.

WHERE TO STAY
Billings Hotel and Conventional Center. 1223 Mullowney Lane, off I-90 at Exit 446, Billings, MT 59101. ☎ **406/248-7151.** 241 units. A/C TEL TV. $59–$79 double; $99–$150 suite; $200 3-room Jacuzzi suite. AE, DISC, MC, V.

This hotel has gone through a number of incarnations, beginning several years ago as a Ramada, then being renovated into a Clarion Hotel, and now being independently operated as the Billings Hotel. Clarion did a 2-year, multimillion-dollar renovation, but the improvements are scarcely visible to the untrained eye. The large lobby is graced by a grand piano and a freestanding fireplace. There is a restaurant and lounge on the premises. Perhaps the best recommendation for this place and the Holiday Inn (below) is that if you are traveling with kids, they are only a few doors down from a large and popular water park, with several large water slides.

Dude Rancher Lodge. 415 N. 29th St., Billings, MT 59101. ☎ **800/221-3302** or 406/259-5561. 57 units. A/C TV TEL. $45–$60 double. AE, DISC, V, MC.

The Dude Rancher offers a Western pine feel in downtown Billings for out-of-town prices. The rooms are comfortable and quiet, but undistinguished, and surround an inner courtyard. The motel offers free parking for guests, king- and queen-size beds, and cable television. There is a coffee shop/restaurant on the premises for a quick bite.

Holiday Inn Grand Montana. 5500 Midland Rd., off I-90 at Exit 446, Billings, MT 59101. ☎ **877/554-7263** or 406/248-7701. Fax 406/248-8954. www.holiday-inn.com/billings-west. 315 units. A/C TV TEL. $59–$69 double; $89 suite; $150 presidential suite. AE, CB, DC, DISC, MC, V. Pets accepted, $10 per night.

The Holiday Inn has recently undergone remodeling. It features an open seven-story atrium with a waterfall that trickles down past three of the lower stories. Rooms in the tower section are newer and a little more expensive than those in the original building, but the furnishings are the same. There's an indoor and outdoor pool, Jacuzzi and sauna, and room service. The Inn especially caters to business meetings and receptions and offers a number of special services.

The Josephine Bed-and-Breakfast. 514 N. 29th St., Billings, MT 59101. ☎ **800/552-5898** or 406/248-5898. www.thejosephine.com. E-mail: josephine@imt.net. 5 units (3 with private bathrooms). $68–$140 double. MC, V.

The Josephine is named for a steamboat that once plied the waters of the Yellowstone between here and St. Louis. It provides turn- of-the-century elegance with a smile. Located within walking distance of downtown, the B&B offers a quiet place amid Billings' urban bustle. Owners Doug and Becky Taylor have put a modern whirlpool tub in one room, but most rooms feature the classic, high-sided, claw-footed tubs familiar from Western movies. The Captain's Room offers a masculine feel, from the pipes on the night table to the four-poster bed. The other rooms have more feminine touches. There are a library, parlor, and dining room for breakfast, and a wraparound porch where you can sit and read. The rooms have cable television, and breakfast is included in the price. Doug's signature dish is a fantastic cheese straw—but don't turn up your nose if you happen be there on the day he makes champagne waffles.

Radisson Northern Hotel. Broadway and 1st Ave. N., Billings, MT 59101. ☎ **800/333-3333** or 406/245-5121. 160 units. A/C TV TEL. $89 double; $99 junior suite; $129 parlor suite. AE, DC, DISC, MC, V.

The Northern Hotel has long been Billings's landmark hotel, going back to the days of the railroaders. It was the finest place to stay from its construction in 1902 until it was destroyed by fire in 1940—although it was rebuilt almost immediately. Early dignitaries that stayed here include painter C.M. Russell, Teddy Roosevelt, and Prince Olaf of Sweden. Recently completely renovated, it has retained its elegance and style. It has a contemporary Western flair, but isn't pushy about it. For business travelers who have to use their computers, it is excellent, with comfortable desks, accessible power outlets, and data ports on the phones in the suites. The parlor suites come with 6-foot conference tables. There is an exercise room.

The Golden Belle restaurant offers a full menu in elegant surroundings. The Saloon hosts lots of long and lean cowboy-hatted types.

The Sheraton Billings Hotel. 27 N. 27th St. (at Montana Ave.), Billings, MT 59101. ☎ **800/588-7666** or 406/252-7400. Fax 406/252-2401. www.sheraton.com/billings. 292 units. A/C TV TEL. $95 double; $150–$199 suite. AE, DC, DISC, MC, V.

With 23 floors, the Billings Sheraton has the distinction of being Montana's tallest building. It is located in the heart of downtown, a short walk from the dining, shopping, and entertainment highlights of the city. There are views from each room, including some views of the distant mountains from the upper floors. The Lucky Diamond Restaurant and Lounge is on the 20th floor, but its main recommendation is the view, not the fare. Parking is available free of charge for guests.

WHERE TO DINE
EXPENSIVE

The Granary. 1500 Poly Dr. ☎ **406/259-3488.** Reservations recommended on weekends. Main courses $15–$35. AE, DISC, MC, V. Mon–Sat 5:30–10pm. STEAKS/SEAFOOD.

This dimly lit establishment is one of the most popular, most recommended, and most expensive restaurants in Billings. Some say the food is well-prepared but poorly presented; however, national and Montana beef councils have bestowed their highest honor to The Granary, so the chef must be doing something right. The outside deck is a favorite haunt for many locals just wanting to quaff late-afternoon beers and cocktails. Owing to next-door neighbors, however, there is no live music, and the deck usually closes down before the summer sun does.

✪ **Juliano's.** 2912 7th Ave. N. ☎ **406/248-6400.** Main courses $14–$22. AE, DC, DISC, MC, V. Mon–Tues 11:30am–2pm, Wed–Fri 11:30am–2pm and 5:30–9pm, Sat 5:30–9pm. PACIFIC RIM/CONTEMPORARY AMERICAN.

Arguably the best restaurant in Montana, Juliano's serves excellent, original food in an elegant atmosphere. It is a little hard to categorize the cuisine. Chef Carl Kurokawa is a native of Hilo, Hawaii, and the menu describes it as "Fun American with European and Asian influences." Privately, Kurokawa says to call it "Carl food." The menu changes monthly. Sometimes you can get seared peppered Montana ostrich or steak topped with crab cakes. The building was originally the stable of the sandstone "castle" next door, built in 1902. A pressed-tin ceiling with Bacchus hoisting a glass covers one of the dining rooms, and there is an outdoor patio for nice days. The service is attentive without being pushy. Juliano's is one of only 585 North American restaurants to receive a DiRoNA Award (distinguished restaurants of North America) in 1998. There is an extensive wine list.

MODERATE

Bruno's. 1002 1st Ave. N. ☎ **406/248-4146.** Most dishes $7–$15. AE, DISC, MC, V. Mon–Thurs 11am–3pm and 5–9pm, Fri 11am–3pm and 5–10pm, Sat 5–10pm. PASTA/PIZZA.

Popular Bruno's original location is the vast old Stockman's bank building on the east side of town by the railroad tracks. The white pizzas are excellent and the pastas are delicious, though you might avoid the ones heavily covered in marinara. A non-smoking area is available.

Cafe Jones. 2712 2nd Ave. N. ☎ **406/259-7676.** Lunch $3–$7. No credit cards. Mon–Sat 7am–7pm. CAFE/SANDWICHES.

Maybe we can call it Western art deco, with a touch of bohemian coffee. The walk-up counter is faced with a melange of broken glass and mirrors. The affordable lunch menu includes an artichoke heart sandwich. You can play one of the cafe's battered board games, say, Yahtzee or Risk, while you eat. The convenient location and great prices attract college students from one of Billings' four colleges, business lunchers, and out-of-towners. There's a new art show each month, featuring a local artist.

George Henry's Restaurant. 404 N. 30th. ☎ **406/245-4570.** Main courses $10–$20. AE, DISC, MC, V. Mon–Fri 11am–2pm and 5:30–9pm, Sat 5:30–9pm. AMERICAN.

Housed in an 1882 home built by Nova Scotia Builder Robert Crowe for his wife and nine children, the pink and floral ambience of George Henry's recalls a 1920s tea room, which, in fact, it once was. The food is mainly American, well prepared and pleasantly served. The restaurant contains stained glass and a lot of original fixtures from the house.

Mikado. 109 N. Broadway. ☎ **406/252-8278.** Lunch $6–$10; dinner $10–$20. AE, DISC, MC, V. Mon–Sat 11am–2pm and 5–10pm. JAPANESE.

This new restaurant is earning good reviews from the locals. It serves well-prepared Japanese food at reasonable prices. There is a small, improvised sushi bar. Entrees are what you'd find in any big city Japanese restaurant—tempura, sushi, bento boxes. The restaurant displays the traditional Japanese concern for service. The atmosphere is open and airy.

Sidney's. Rimrock Mall. ☎ **406/652-6000.** Lunch $5–$9; dinner $6–$10. AE, DC, DISC, MC, V. Mon–Thurs 11am–10pm, Fri–Sat 11am–11pm, Sun 11am–9pm. PASTA/PIZZA.

With the freshest possible ingredients, including their own handmade pasta, Sidney's has created a menu of matchless taste, in every sense of the word. The coconut chicken from their pasta selection is a feast for the palate and eyes, with vegetables and angel hair pasta highlighted by subtle flavors of coconut, lime, and red curry. Popular pizza choices include the Mediterranean and the fajita chicken. The decor is Southwestern fresh, with stucco walls painted in an adobe-colored wash and teal umbrellas covering the patio tables outside. The location at the mall makes this place even more popular, so if you don't want to wait, be sure to come early.

Stella's Kitchen and Bakery. 110 N. 29th. ☎ **406/248-3060.** Breakfast $3–$7; lunch $5–$7. MC, V. Daily 6am–3pm. BAKED GOODS.

Specializing in breakfast and lunch, this combination bakery and kitchen has demonstrated its quality and popularity during more than 20 years in Billings by serving up homemade breads and pastries. Monster Cakes—pancakes—start at $2.30 each but you've got to see 'em to believe 'em.

Thai Orchid. 2926 2nd Ave N. ☎ **406/256-2206.** Lunch and dinner $6–$10; buffet $6. MC, V. Mon–Fri 11am–2pm and 5–10pm, Sat 5–10pm. THAI.

Thai Orchid is a long-established Billings restaurant that has moved from a location in danker quarters to slick, somewhat sterile new digs downtown. Now a spare white room, the restaurant still serves Thai food ranging from hot and spicy to very hot and spicy. There is a daily all-you-can-eat luncheon buffet that is very popular with the downtown office crowd. There may be a line at the height of lunch hour.

Walkers Grill. 301 N. 27th St. ☎ **406/245-9291.** Reservations recommended. Main courses $9–$20. AE, DISC, MC, V. Mon–Sat 5–10pm. AMERICAN BISTRO.

Walkers offers a San Francisco-coastal feel here on the plains. The restaurant is done in an understated light wood, with a hint of a Japanese motif. Diners can look into the kitchen from the dining room. The original chef has moved on, but his two assistants, whom he trained, have taken over and the food remains very good. People come to the restaurant especially for the morel mushrooms served in a port cream reduction, available in the spring and early summer. The restaurant also serves local Montana lamb, getting one or two fresh lambs each week, and using all of it. The lamb stew I had here was excellent, and was huge. President Clinton ate here during his visit to Montana. The wine list is very extensive, including many French wines—often difficult or impossible to find on the plains. Definitely a place that attracts local customers. During dinner hour, all the diners seem to know each other.

BILLINGS AFTER DARK

Casey's, 222 N. Broadway (☎ **406/256-5200**) has been around since 1935. It features a blend of blues, jazz, reggae, and rock leavened with Cajun food, including the "famous gumbo." On Monday nights, there is an open mike, and the locals come in to jam, as do some of the famous touring musicians. The stage has been visited by B.B. King, Chuck Mangione, Vince Gill, and Wynton Marsalis. The ceiling murals are tributes to legendary musicians—Buddy Holly, Billie Holiday, Bob Marley, and many more. One night a mysterious stranger in a dark trench coat sat down at the piano and proceeded to blow the room away with runaway blues. Then he got up and walked out. Never said a word. Never seen again. There are also pool tables and a gift shop. Casey's has recently moved across the street from its long-time location. The old place is now the Mikado restaurant.

A SIDE TRIP TO POMPEY'S PILLAR

A 117-foot-high sandstone butte 29 miles east of Billings holds the only concrete evidence left along the way of the famous journey of Lewis and Clark through the Louisiana Purchase. On July 25, 1806, Capt. William Clark carved his name and the date on the side of the rock. He noted in his famous journals for that day, "The nativs have ingraved on the face of this rock figures of animals &c near which I marked my name and the day of the month and year." Clark then walked to the top and described the panoramic view of the river and plains that can be captured from the top. Clark had to scramble up through the yucca and sagebrush, but visitors now are aided by stairways and enthusiastic and informative volunteer guides who will point out the historic sites and wildlife—from ant lions to eagles' nests.

Clark's name is now locked under a protective glass cabinet, but it has been joined by the carved names of many others, including graffiti from 1882 and onwards. It seems Americans have always been unable to resist inscribing a bare rock surface. The pillar was originally called Pompy's Tower by Clark, who named it after the nickname of the youngest member of their expedition, little Baptiste (Pompy) Charbonneau, the young son of Sakajawea and Touissaint Charbonneau, the expedition guides. Pomp had been ill for the 2 months before the expedition reached this point, and had only recently recovered his strength. Pompey traveled in Clark's dugout, and the captain called him "my boy Pomp."

The park, operated by the Federal Bureau of Land Management, is open from Memorial Day until the first Sunday in October from 8am to 8pm. The fee is $3 per carload during the season. If you happen to be passing during the off-season, however, and the gate is open, no one minds if you visit unescorted. For more information call ☎ **406/875-2233.** To get here, go 29 miles east of Billings on I-94 and take the exit to Pompey's Pillar.

2 The Crow Reservation

54 miles E of Billings

Most Indian reservations in the West are firmly ambivalent about tourism and visitors. The beautiful Crow reservation in southeastern Montana is no exception. While the tribe and its members could use the revenue that visitors generate, they are understandably reluctant to endanger their embattled culture with an influx of outsiders.

Nonetheless, in my experience, the Crow are friendly and open, and are as curious about you as you are about them. Folks in the shops and other facilities will discuss reservation life and culture eagerly and perhaps invite you to ✪ **Crow Fair,** in August, one of the marquee Indian Nation events of the summer-long powwow trail. Powwows are social gatherings, featuring traditional food, dress, and dances that have been passed down through generations. Guests may dance in the "round dance," or when invited to do so by an emcee. Visitors are welcome at powwows. You should take lawn chairs or blankets, since seating is limited. Flash photography is not allowed during contests, and it is polite to ask dancers first before taking their photographs. For more information contact the **Tribal Headquarters** in Crow Agency (☎ **406/638-2601**).

On the other hand, there is very little here to lure visitors that deals directly with the life, culture, and history of the tribe. The most famous and historic site is the Little Bighorn Battlefield, a somewhat ironic inclusion on this reservation. The Crow scouted for Custer, and the Little Bighorn is the site of the cavalry's most infamous defeat at the hands of the Indians.

The origins of the tribe are obscure. They called themselves the Absaroka, the Absarokee or the Apsaalooke, or various other spellings, which early French trappers misinterpreted as "crow." Other sources say that the meaning of the term has been lost. The Crow are a Siouan language group, related to the Hidatsa from whom they separated at the end of the 17th century. In the *Son of the Morning Star,* Evan Connell's wonderful book about the Little Bighorn battle, Connell writes that Col. Gibbon, one of Terry's command, watched a Crow party get ready for a dangerous river swim prior to the battle. They smeared themselves in red paint. "I had the curiosity to inquire the object of this, and was surprised to learn that it was to protect them against the attack of alligators. As the alligator is an animal unknown to the waters of this region, the fact referred to is a curious evidence of the southern origin of the Crows."

The only Crow cultural center is a small one located at **Chief Plenty Coups State Park** (☎ **406/252-1289**). The famous Crow chief Plenty Coups deeded his home and lands as a memorial to the Crow Nation. Today, the park includes the chief's home and a museum, which houses the crow leader's personal items. The park is in the town of Pryor, and the easiest access is from Billings. Drive southeast along I-94 and I-90 to the exit for Highway 416. There are picnic facilities, but no overnight camping. It's open May 1 through September daily from 8am to 5pm. Entrance fee is $4 per car.

On the reservation there are few places to eat. The **Purple Cow Diner** (☎ **406/665-3601**) offers too-fried food just east of the interstate at the Hardin exit on the edge of the reservation. You can get some souvenirs, some beautifully done Indian art work, or books about the tribe at the **Custer Battlefield Trading Post** (☎ **406/638-2270**)—head 15 miles south, where I-90 meets U.S. Highway 212. The new **Little Bighorn Casino** (☎ **406/638-4444**), the Crow entry into the Indian gambling sweepstakes, is nearby.

3 Bighorn Canyon National Recreation Area

Fort Smith: 83 miles SE of Billings

The Bighorn River has carved a steep, sheer canyon out of the rolling plains of the Crow Reservation, which the federal government has seen fit to block with the Yellowtail Dam, creating the 71-mile long Bighorn Lake, extending from near Lovell, Wyoming, deep into the heart of Crow Country.

The lake and recreation area are remote and difficult to get to, requiring long drives on winding roads through typical small Wyoming and Indian reservation towns. The Wyoming and Montana portions of the NRA are not connected by a road. A boater can cruise easily up and down the reservoir, but a driver must make a long, circuitous route to visit both portions.

But a persistent traveler is rewarded by two different experiences. Some of the thousand-foot cliff walls still survive in the Wyoming portion, and the Montana segment offers visitors steep cliff walls; warm, deep water; and excellent boating.

Travel Tip

You can't drive through the **Bighorn Canyon National Recreation Area** from the Montana side to the Wyoming side. To get from one to the other, you must make a very long circuitous drive either east through Sheridan, then north to Lodge Grass, Montana. Or you can go west through Lovell, north to Edgar, Montana, then east through Pryor. It's best to pick a side, and stick to it.

ESSENTIALS

ACCESS POINTS   There are two portions of the NRA and two different access points. The **Wyoming section** is accessible through Lovell, west on Route 14A, then north on Route 37, clearly marked by signs.

On the Montana side, Route 313 south from Hardin goes directly into the National Recreation Area, through the tiny reservation town of Saint Xavier.

FEES   A $5 entrance fee per car is good for 24 hours, or an annual pass is available for $30.

VISITOR CENTERS   Bighorn Canyon is bursting with visitor centers, one for each section of the area. **In Wyoming,** near Lovell, the **Bighorn Canyon Visitors Center** (☎ 307/548-2251) is open daily year-round from 8:15am to 5pm. The facility has a large relief map of the area and a gift shop.

The **Yellowtail Visitor Center** at the Yellowtail Dam (☎ 406/666-3234) offers guided tours of the power plant from Memorial Day through Labor Day. The facility is open from 9am to 5pm. You can also look out at the 1,480-foot-long dam, and down the vertiginous 525 feet to the river below it.

REGULATIONS & WARNINGS   Don't feed the bears. The park has a number of black bears and visitors should stay clear of them. Black bears are not generally dangerous to people, but if a bear becomes habituated to people (or, more importantly, to their food), it is a death sentence for the animal. The bear will almost certainly be destroyed as a nuisance.

Also, most national park area deaths are caused by traffic accidents, drownings, and falls. Bighorn Canyon National Recreation Area, with its winding roads, fabulous waters, and steep cliffs, is a good place to do all three. Use caution in the area.

GETTING OUTSIDE

Bighorn Canyon is primarily a flat water recreation area with excellent swimming, boating, waterskiing, fishing, and scuba diving.

Anglers, take note: **Fishing** regulations are tricky in these parts since the Crow Reservation encompasses nearly all of the Montana portion of the canyon. State fishing licenses are required; though you need a Montana fishing license for fishing on the north end, you have to purchase a Wyoming license to fish on the Wyoming side of the park. One state does not honor the license of the other. Contact the guides and outfitters in the area for more information: **Big Horn Trout Shop** (☎ 406/666-2375), **Quill Gordon Fly Fishers** (☎ 406/666-2253), **Bighorn Angler** (☎ 406/666-2233), and **Angler's Edge** (☎ 406/666-2417).

ON THE WYOMING SIDE

At the very south end of the park, on Route 14A in Wyoming, is the **Mason-Lovell Ranch House,** built as ranch headquarters in 1883 by A.L. Mason and H.C. Lovell.

There are a few surviving log structures. These early ranchers were students of the free-range school of livestock management, so they let their cattle roam throughout the Big Horn Basin. Still on-site are the log structures where the blacksmith worked and the cabins where married employees lived.

Heading north on WY 37, you'll pass **Horseshoe Bend,** where a southern section of the river becomes a lake again. The south side of the park offers some of the more sensational canyon views, and is a prime viewing spot of some of the last wild horses to run free in North America. Boaters can snag provisions at the **Horseshoe Bend Marina** (☎ 307/548-7230), a full-service marina that rents boats, sells fishing supplies, and operates the southernmost boat launch ramp in the park at the head of Bighorn Lake. It's open from Memorial Day to Labor Day—or a little longer, weather permitting.

Leaving Horseshoe Bend, you'll pass the burgundy-colored hills of the Chugwater Formation and enter the **Pryor Mountain National Wild Horse Range,** which has been home to wild mustangs—the virtual emblem of the West, along with the buffalo—for more than a century. Sometimes, you can see these majestic animals from the road. Also just off WY 37 (just across the Montana border) is the **Devil Canyon Overlook,** which offers a taste of the river before the dam was built. Steep, winding canyon walls expose 1,000 sheer vertical feet of gray limestone and orange shale. The river winds through here in an S-shape, over knife-edged cliffs that were carved over millions of years.

Barry's Landing (north on WY 37), with a boat ramp and fishing access, is located at the end of the highway and is the focus for most of the recreational opportunities in the southern part of the park. But before you reach the landing, check out **Hillsboro,** a ghost town that came about after G.W. Barry (of Barry's Landing fame) failed as a miner and rancher and fell into the tourist business.

The self-guided **Canyon Creek Nature Trail** (0.5 miles), which starts at Loop C of the campground at Horseshoe Bend; and the trail from **Barry's Landing** to the campground at Medicine Creek (2 miles), are the only hikes on this side of the park.

ON THE MONTANA SIDE

The **Ok-A-Beh Boat Landing** (☎ 406/665-2216) has a marina and campsites, rents boats, and sells gas and fishing supplies. To reach the boat ramp and fishing access site, turn left after Fort Smith but before the park headquarters and head 11 (somewhat treacherous) miles over the Big Horn Plateau.

A park ranger can help you find the **Om-Ne-A Trail,** which stretches for 3 steep miles along the canyon rim. The **Beaver Pond Trail** is a short trip from the visitor center along Lime Kiln Creek.

WHERE TO STAY

Accommodations on the south side of the park are at Lovell, 3 miles west of the intersection of WY 37 and U.S. Highway 14A.

With one exception, the camping and motels in this area are undistinguished. You can park your RV at **Cottonwood Camp** (☎ 406/666-2391), which is on Route 313 as you enter Fort Smith. Or if you have a boat, there are a number of private and primitive campsites available, where you might run into those bears we warned you about, especially at Black Canyon. Check with the rangers for crowding. When I camped there one night in a friend's boat, I kept kicking something off my sleeping bag, but being a sound sleeper, didn't do much about it. It turned out to be a pack rat who had taken up residence and was raiding the pantry when the hosts were asleep. The entrance to Black Canyon is about 2 miles south on Bighorn Lake from Ok-a-Beh

Marina and then southeast about 1 mile. There is also boat-in camping at Frozen Leg, which is about a mile south on the lake from Ok-a-Beh on the west side of the lake. You can also camp at Afterbay, which is right by Yellowtail Dam.

The **Big Horn Trout Shop** (☎ 406/666-2375) has recently renovated all its rooms, but it's still nothing fancy. The **Quill Gordon Fly Fishers** (☎ 406/666-2253), **Bighorn Angler** (☎ 406/666-2233), **Polly's Place** (☎ 406/666-2255), and **Kingfisher Motel** (☎ 406/666-2326) also offer inexpensive beds for the weary angler.

Forrester's Bighorn River Resort. P.O. Box 7595, Fort Smith, MT 59035. ☎ **800/ 665-3799** or 406/666-9199. Fax 406/666-9179. www.forrester-travel.com. 7 cabins. A/C TEL. $200 per person including all meals; $950 per person (with 3-night minimum stay) including all meals and fishing guides. No credit cards.

This new fishing and hunting log resort with seven cabins overlooking the green Bighorn River flats is hooked up with the fly-fishing giant Orvis. The resort is only about a half-mile north of Fort Smith. The cabins sit on a bluff over the river and the Bozeman Trail, famous in song and movie. Everything is constructed of pine, especially the porches for overlooking the river and watching the sun set in the mysterious West. There are queen-size beds and private baths in each cabin.

4 Little Bighorn Battlefield National Monument

56 miles E of Billings

Perhaps there is no phrase in the English language that serves as a better metaphor for an untimely demise than "Custer's Last Stand." It was on this battlefield, on the dry sloping prairies of southeastern Montana, that George Armstrong Custer met his end. Though the details of the actual battle that took place on June 25, 1876, are sketchy at best, much remains for the visitor to explore and ponder in this mysterious place. The **Little Bighorn Battlefield National Monument** (☎ 406/638-2621) chronicles the history of this world-famous engagement, offering a coherent look at how the battle developed, where the members of Custer's contingent died, and how it might have looked to the swarming warriors.

To understand the history of the battle, you have to go back to 1868, when the U.S. government and the Sioux signed a peace treaty. The terms of that treaty were much disputed on both sides, but it gave the Sioux and Cheyenne title to the Black Hills, and homelands around Fort Laramie in eastern Wyoming and western Dakota territories. Then, in 1873, Custer led an expedition into the Black Hills, where gold had been discovered. Miners flocked to the area. The Indians wouldn't sell the Black Hills—their sacred Paha Sapa—to the whites, and the government knew they couldn't take it without a fight. So, the government issued an order that all wandering bands of Indians were to be sent to reservations by January 1, 1876.

When many tribal bands remained at large past the deadline, Gen. George Crook sent Custer from Fort Abraham Lincoln in South Dakota to force the Indians onto reservations. By some accounts, Custer felt that his great moment was at hand, one that would shower him with glory and catapult him into a run for the White House.

But things didn't turn out quite the way Custer had planned. In June of 1876, about 1,000 lodges of several Indian tribes—the Unkpapa, Blackfeet, Oglala, Brule, Sans Arc, Minneconjou, and Northern Cheyenne—were encamped along the western bank of the Little Bighorn River. These lodges represented about 7,000 people, including at least 1,500 fighting men. They included many of the most famous Indians of the age, Sitting Bull, Crazy Horse, Gall, and Little Wolf.

Before the battle, the Unkpapa, one of the Sioux bands, held a Sun Dance, an agonizing ritual intended to induce visions and honor the sun, the great mystery, Wakan Tanka. Sitting Bull had 50 pieces of skin cut away from each of his arms with an awl and knife. With his face toward the sun, he danced for 2 days and nights, finally falling unconscious. He had a vision of many soldiers falling into camp. This and other omens convinced the assembled Indian army that victory would be theirs.

On the other side, 260 members of the 7th Cavalry under the command of the notorious, glamorous Lt. Col. George Armstrong Custer—or "Yellow Hair," as he was known to the Indians—were marching into the valley of the Little Bighorn to the strains of the Scottish air "Gary Owen."

Custer had a total of 600 men under his command at Little Bighorn. He separated them into three companies, assigning command of the others to Maj. Marcus Reno and Capt. Frederick Benteen. Custer clearly underestimated the force of the Indians. He didn't have much respect for their fighting abilities in the first place, and he appears to have developed no plan to deal with the force amassed against him. Reno said later, "There was no plan communicated to us; if one existed, the subordinate commanders did not know about it . . . I do not think there was any plan." Benteen said the plan was to go "valley hunting ad infinitum."

Custer kept 210 men with him and proceeded toward the Indian encampment at dawn on June 25th. His exact movements are unknown after the forces split. You can ride or walk along the Battle Ridge where Custer and his men fell and look at the stone monuments set up there, most of them reading, "U.S. Soldier, 7th Cavalry, fell here, June 25, 1876." The ridge looks down over the ravine and copse of trees near where the huge Indian village was assembled.

Custer was well known to the Indians from a series of actions, including the destruction of Black Kettle's peaceful village on the Washita River in 1867. He was also known for his scouting of the Black Hills, especially the 1873 expedition in which gold was discovered.

Curiously though, Custer had cut his long, distinctive yellow hair short sometime prior to the battle. So the Indians didn't recognize him. Custer's final fate is still a much debated mystery. One legend says that an Indian woman named Kate Bighead came across the body of the dead Hi-es-tzie—Long Hair. She punctured his eardrum with a sewing awl, so that he could hear better. General Custer had not heard, she said, his own promises of peace in 1868 at the Cheyenne camp on Red River. Or so they say.

ESSENTIALS

GETTING THERE   The monument is located 54 miles southeast of Billings. Take I-94 east to I-90 south, then go just past the Crow Agency to the U.S. 212 exit. The battlefield is located only a few hundred yards to the east.

ADMISSION & HOURS   The entry fee is $6 per car. The tour road is open 8:30am to 5:30pm. The visitor center is open from 8am to 6pm.

VISITOR INFORMATION   The visitor center at the battlefield is small, but it has an electric map explaining the battle; some colorful, low-tech displays of weapons; and photos of the participants. The center hosts some excellent presentations on the battle. The day I was there, a battle-dressed Cheyenne explained many warrior customs and tactics, including some reasons for the mutilations and atrocities that occurred on both sides. You can also purchase an auto-tour tape of the battlefield here, which provides a good overview of the scene.

TOURING THE MONUMENT   Custer National Cemetery, established in 1886, is immediately adjacent to the visitor center, containing the graves of veterans of the Fetterman fight and the Wagon Box Fight in Wyoming and the Battle of the Big Hole in Montana, as well as graves of veterans from more recent wars. A roughly 4-mile drive on a paved road will take you to the **Reno-Benteen Battlefield,** where those two companies waged their own desperate battle against the besieging tribes.

A SPECIAL EVENT   The **Hardin Area Chamber of Commerce,** 21 E. 4th St., Hardin, MT 59034, sponsors **Little Big Horn Days** at the end of June each year, but not here at the monument. The events include a Custer's Last Stand Reenactment. This event is held 6 miles west of Hardin off Highway 87. For information call ☎ **888/450-3577** or 406/665-3577 (www.mcn.net/~custerfight; e-mail: custer-fight@mcn.net). Admission is $15 for adults, $6 for children; it's free for children 5 and under.

5 Miles City

145 miles E of Billings; 70 miles SW of Glendive

Miles City gets its name from Col. Nelson A. Miles—the commander of the Fifth Cavalry who was ordered to return bands of Indians to reservations in the summer of 1876. Even as the world moves on around it, Miles City has been able to retain its Western flair for over a century. In the early days, as portrayed in Larry McMurtry's *Lonesome Dove,* Miles City was a cowboy town on the verge of becoming a leading cattle market; the market came with the arrival of the Northern Pacific Railroad in 1881.

Today, Miles City maintains its cowboy traditions with its annual Bucking Horse Sale—which attracts rodeo stock contractors from all over the country—and the Range Riders Museum, a thorough collection of photographs and firearms from the old days. It's where remote ranchers go when they need barbed wire or tractor axles, and it's the closest business and agricultural center to Billings.

Miles City isn't stuck in the 19th century, though there is still a traditional Main Street with a saloon and lunch counter, and local merchants make conscious efforts to keep up this city's Old West appeal. Its citizens take an active pride in the town's lack of parking meters—a vestige of its civility and small population. It remains, though, a lifeline to the surrounding communities.

ESSENTIALS

GETTING THERE   It's an easy drive up I-94 from Billings. Miles City's Frank Wiley Field is serviced by **Big Sky Airlines** (☎ 800/237-7788 or 406/232-5058), a regional airline. The **Greyhound** station is at 2210 Valley Dr. E. (☎ **406/232-3900**).

VISITOR INFORMATION   The **Miles City Chamber of Commerce,** at 901 Main St., Miles City, MT 59301 (☎ **406/232-2890**), provides maps and guides to the town. You can also get a vacation guide from Custer Country Rte. 1, Box 1206A, Hardin, MT 59034 (☎ **800/346-1876** or 406/665-1671; travel.state.mt.us/custer).

GETTING OUTSIDE

There's an attractive municipal swimming facility at the west end of Main Street, a pond with piers for jumping from, and cottonwood trees surrounding it.

FISHING & BOATING

Miles City isn't classic Montana fishing country, but there is plenty of access to the Yellowstone and Tongue Rivers for walleye, sauger, catfish, crappie, and, occasionally,

---

The Jaycee Bucking Horse Sale

Ever since 1914, rodeo contractors—the men who supply the animals for the West's rodeos—have been meeting in Miles City and lining up their stock. This gathering, which began as an informal event, has now become the Jaycee Bucking Horse Sale, held every May on the third weekend of the month. More than 200 horses are sold at auction from untried stock to spoiled saddle horses. There are parades, rides, and rodeos, as well as wild-horse racing. The downtown area is virtually closed down, and bands play on the streets, and beer is swilled and spilled in public while the city's open container ordinances are suspended. There's also a gun show and a barbecue in the city park. Tickets cost $7 for the Friday night sale session and $8 to $10 for Saturday and Sunday. Children under 12 are $5. Call the Miles City Area Chamber of Commerce (☎ **406/232-2890**) for precise scheduling information.

---

the unusual paddlefish. **Twelve-Mile Dam,** 11 miles south of Miles City on MT 59, then 1 mile south on Tongue River Road, has camping facilities and a boat launch, and a handicapped-accessible fishing platform.

Roche Jaune (which is the original French for "yellow stone") is located in Miles City, and provides a boat launch on the Yellowstone River. **Pirogue Island State Park** is just north of Miles City. Go 1 mile north on MT 22, then 2 miles east on Kinsey Highway, then 2 miles south on a gravel road. Fishing throughout the area is best in late spring and early fall. Stop by **Red Rock Sporting Goods,** 2900 Valley Dr. E. (☎ **406/232-2716**) for gear and information.

GOLF

Miles City has the nine-hole **Town and Country Club golf course** running along the banks of the Tongue River southeast of town. It's relatively short—3,280 yards. For fees and tee times call the pro shop at ☎ **406/232-1500.**

SEEING THE SIGHTS

Range Rider Museum. U.S. Hwy. 12 (on Main St., just outside of town). ☎ **406/ 232-6146** or 406/232-4483. $3.50 adults, $3 seniors, 50¢ children, free for children under 6. April 1–Oct 31, daily 8am–8pm. Closed Nov–March.

The amazing thing about this collection is its size—the Western memorabilia collection includes nine buildings, a frontier town, a Charles Russell gallery, and a gun collection of more than 400 firearms. Included with the weapons are Indian artifacts and French sabers. There are 500 photos of local celebrities in the Wilson Photo Gallery, and a replica of Old Milestown of 1877. Of particular interest are some photos of Cheyenne tribal members taken in the 1890s, although the labeling is reminiscent of old Western racism—one woman is called a "pretty Cheyenne squaw" and a man is called a "fine physical specimen." The photos are very good, though, reminiscent of Edward Sheriff Curtis.

Custer County Art Center. Waterplant Rd. (just over the Tongue River Bridge west of town). ☎ **406/232-0635.** Free admission. Tues–Sun 1–5pm.

The city water plant has been reincarnated as an art museum (specializing in Western pieces) with a notable permanent collection and equally impressive road shows. Listed on the National Register of Historic Places, the museum is actually a piece of work itself. In 1979, the structure was awarded the governor's trophy for best adaptation of a historic structure. Now the building is the home to the Western Art Roundup, an annual show that features the works of Western artists around the time the Bucking Horse Sale is in full swing.

WHERE TO STAY

The **Miles City KOA Campground,** 1 Palmer (☎ 406/232-3991), is shaded by more than 70 cottonwoods and has full hookups, tent sites, a pool, and a store. Take Exit 135 off I-94, go 2.4 miles to Palmer Street, then go left 4 blocks to the KOA.

Best Western War Bonnet Inn. 1015 S. Haynes Ave., Miles City, MT 59301. ☎ **406/232-4560.** Fax 406/232-0363. 54 units. A/C TV TEL. $69–$90 double; $93.60 family suite. Rates include continental breakfast. AE, DC, DISC, MC, V.

This Best Western is the nicest of the collection of motels located just off I-94 at Exit 138. The rooms, which have been flamboyantly painted in green and pink, are clean and comfortable. The lobby has been turned into an airy, sunny breakfast room. There are three "family suites" available with microwave and refrigerators in them. There are also an indoor pool, hot tub, and sauna.

Holiday Inn Express. 1720 S. Haynes, Miles City, MT 59301. ☎ **406/232-1000.** 52 units. A/C TV TEL. $69 double. AE, MC, V.

This relatively new and well-maintained facility is also located just off the Interstate at Exit 138. Visitors always know what they're getting at a Holiday Inn, so it's no surprise that the rooms are dull and comfortable, with all the amenities that business travelers have come to expect, like telephone data ports, and with a pool and whirlpool for the family visitor. The motel is immediately across the street from the New Hunan Restaurant.

Rodeway Inn and Olive Hotel. 501 Main St., Miles City, MT 59301. ☎ **406/232-2450.** 55 units. $42 double. AE, CB, DC, DISC, MC, V.

The Olive looks pretty run-down from the outside, but it is passable inside, and the rooms are larger than you might expect. Joseph Leighton first built the hotel in 1898–99, and it soon became a landmark. At first named the Leighton, it was named by subsequent owners after their own daughter, Olive. It was added to the National Register of Historic Places in 1988, and it has maintained its musty Western charm with beveled glass, multicolored tile floors, and oak reception desk. It also has one of the slowest elevators in the Rocky Mountain West. The hotel promotes the whimsy that it is the place where Gus McRae of *Lonesome Dove* fame slept at the end of the epic cattle drive. This couldn't be the case, because the hotel didn't exist in the 1880s, when the novel was set. However, the West is built on mythology, and it surely couldn't hurt to add one more to the mix. The hotel has an adequate restaurant attached, and a dark, sometimes raucous bar.

WHERE TO DINE

600 Club and the Hole in the Wall Lounge and Supper Club. 600–602 Main. ☎ **406/232-9887.** Breakfast $3–$6; lunch $5–$9; dinner $8–$20. MC, V. Cafe daily 5am–5pm; supper club daily 10am–2pm and 4–10pm. AMERICAN.

These two restaurants with the same kitchen offer steaks and freshly defrosted seafood. You should try a chicken fried steak, or be very brave and get the liver and onions. An Australian lobster tail is available for $20. This is a very popular place in the summer, and there may be a short wait in the supper club on weekends.

Club 519. 519 Main. ☎ **406/232-5133.** Main courses $11–$19. MC, V. Daily 5–10pm. AMERICAN.

Here's another beef place, which is located on the second floor of the Professional Building. It's a dim, quiet, comfortable restaurant, without the cowboy ambience that dominates most of the town. For many years the top floor was the home of the Mile City Club, established in 1884, and visited by Teddy Roosevelt and the Marquis de Mores, both cattle barons from nearby North Dakota.

The New Hunan. 1710 S. Haynes. ☎ **406/232-3338.** Lunch $4–$6; dinner $6–$9. DISC, V, MC. Daily 11am–10pm. CHINESE.

If you tire of the ever-present steaks and burgers on the Miles City tour, head to the New Hunan for respectable Chinese food. The large menu should keep everyone happy, including the kids, who can still get a burger here. There is a very reasonably priced lunch and dinner buffet.

MILES CITY AFTER DARK

The cowboys in their dress hats come out after dark in Miles City, mostly in the bars. The **Montana Bar** (612 Main St.), **Bison Bar** (600 Main St.), and **Range Riders** (605 Main St.) are all within a few steps of each other, and offer a friendly atmosphere for beer, country music, pool, and poker.

6　Glendive

222 miles E of Billings; 196 miles W of Bismarck, North Dakota

In the 1880s, Glendive became a cattle town, and over the last century or so it has gradually become a farming community, producing mostly sugar beets and wheat. The city's most curious attraction is paddlefishing. Every May, thousands of anglers try to snag one of these prehistoric hundred pounders from the bottom of the Yellowstone River. Nearby Makoshika State Park is Montana's largest state park. If you want to stay the night, there's a Best Western (☎ **406/377-5555**) and a Days Inn (off I-94 Exit 215; ☎ **800/325-2525** or 406/365-6011) nearby.

GETTING THERE　　It's a long but easy, 222-mile drive up I-94 from Billings. **Big Sky Airlines** (☎ **800/237-7788** or 406/687-3360) flies to the Dawson County Airport from Billings. The **Greyhound** station is at 1302 Towne St. (☎ **406/365-2600**).

VISITOR INFORMATION　　The **Glendive Chamber of Commerce,** 313 S. Merrill, Glendive, MT 59330 (☎ **406/365-5601**), provides brochures and maps.

PADDLEFISHING

If you're here in the season (May 15 to June 30), you can try to snag a paddlefish. The best spot is at the intake diversion dam on the Yellowstone, 15 miles northeast of town on Highway 16. These large prehistoric monsters are "snagged." That is, they are caught on treble hooks dragged along the bottom of the river. The limit is one fish per fisherman out of the Yellowstone. Fishing tags must be purchased for paddlefish, and several places in town sell them. Ask at the Chamber of Commerce. Other sport fish include sauger, walleye, catfish, ling, and sturgeon.

MAKOSHIKA STATE PARK

Makoshika State Park (☎ **406/365-6256**), is a few blocks from town via the railroad underpass. The name is a variation of a Lakota phrase meaning a "land of bad spirits." The amazing thing about this state park is not necessarily the uncanny resemblance to

Badlands National Park in South Dakota, but the abundance of dinosaur bones that have been removed from under the loess. Erosion has done wonders with the park's upper and most malleable layer, forming magnificent spires in some places and coulees that cut deep into the multicolored valleys in others. Stunted ponderosa pine are scattered over much of the park. The actual skull—*not* a replica or cast—from a young triceratops uncovered in the park is on view inside the visitor center.

A partially paved road—steep and narrow even by Montana mountain standards—winds about 2 miles to an overlook that provides a wonderful view of the badlands. Don't take your RV—the road is narrow and there is nowhere to turn around. Several unimproved roads are available for the adventurous, but they turn to impassable gumbo in the rain, so retreat as soon as any rain begins to fall. The 1.5-mile Diane Gabriel Trail and the 1-mile Kinney Coulee Hiking Trail offer easy to moderately difficult hiking. Once again, rain increases the difficulty of these walks. The clay becomes very slippery. The visitor center (open every day 10am–6pm in summer; Mon–Sat 9–5, Sun 1–5 Labor Day–Memorial Day) has a fine display of the history, prehistory, and geology of the park and includes the skull of the triceratops found here.

A SIDE TRIP TO FORT UNION

Strictly speaking, the Fort Union Trading Post National Historic Site is in North Dakota. The Montana-NoDak border bisects the historic site's parking lot, and the fort itself is a few paces east. But Fort Union is so important to the development of Montana and the West that it should be included in any trip through the eastern part of the state.

For 30 years after 1828, Fort Union was the edge of the frontier—the most important trading post in John Jacob Astor's beaver pelt empire in the Rocky Mountains. This National Park Service site has been spectacularly reconstructed from the original plans. The main gate of the glistening, white-washed wooden stockade overlooks the wide Missouri. Two tall stone bastions stand sentinel over the river at the fort's corners.

Lewis and Clark camped near here on their return trip from the Pacific, on April 25 and 26, 1805. Lewis commented in his journals on the "wide and fertile vallies." The Bourgeois House contains excellent exhibits detailing the life and times of the fur traders. Artist George Catlin visited in 1832, as did Karl Bodmer. The point at which Bodmer painted the fort is a park site, undeveloped, about a mile and a quarter away. By 1867, the beaver were gone from the West. Trade switched to buffalo robes, setting the stage for the slaughter of the buffalo on the Plains. In 1872, the fort was abandoned and the lumber material was used to construct nearby Fort Buford and to fuel steamboats.

Fort Union has been a Park Service site since 1966. Reconstruction started in 1986, and was completed to its current level in 1991. Only about 21,000 people a year visit the site. It is truly an undiscovered jewel of the National Park Service System.

GETTING THERE & VISITOR INFORMATION   From Glendive, take MT 16 northeast to the North Dakota border, then North Dakota 58 north to the fort. Call ☎ **701/572-9083** for more information. There's no admission charge and the park is open from 8am to 8pm during the summer and 9am to 5:30pm in winter.

10 Yellowstone National Park

by Geoff O'Gara

For all the epic wonder of the geysers and the antlered elk and the towering waterfalls, visitors to our nation's first national park often bring home memories more subtle and personal: the fine grades of pastel colors in a small hot spring, or the flight of an osprey above the river, or a spiderweb sagging with steam droplets in the early morning light. And Yellowstone isn't just about beauty: At every turn it raises questions about the mysteries of nature, awakening a curiosity you might have thought died during that long-ago chemistry final.

If we were to set the nation's children loose in this park, free from the distractions of televisions or clocks, I bet we'd produce a huge kiddie corps of aspiring scientists. Because after the initial reaction of wordless awe to a bubbling mud pot or a lumbering bison or a meadow of brightly colored wildflowers, it's human nature to want to know how it all *works*. And only in Yellowstone can you observe firsthand how wolves wander amidst an elk herd seeking prey; or smell the sulfurous vapors venting from the volcanic caldera beneath the plateau; or touch the fireweed and pine seedlings sprouting within the forests burned by the terrifying—but not really harmful—1988 fires.

It was a prescient move in 1872 when the U.S. Congress set aside 2.2 million acres of the West as a geothermal and wildlife preserve and "pleasureing ground." Since then, Yellowstone has been the imperfect, but prominent model for the creation of parks around the world. For Americans, it's become a kind of national touchstone to our wilderness past, visited by more than three million pilgrims a year.

Many choose to take in the major Yellowstone sights—Old Faithful geyser, certainly, and Yellowstone Falls—on a quick trip of only a day or two. Others come on narrowly focused quests: Anglers want to fish the Madison or the Firehole rivers, wildlife watchers seek a glimpse of a grizzly bear or a rufous hummingbird, and snowmobilers compete with the bison to journey snow-packed roadways during the winter. If you smartly plan on a longer stay, you will take away an enormous store of life-long memories.

Despite all we get out of Yellowstone, not much has been put back in recent years. There is a huge backlog of work to be done, from road repair to sewer improvements, far more than can be accomplished with the funding appropriated annually by Congress. There are also issues of ecological health. Imported Mackinaw trout are crowding out the native cutthroat in Yellowstone Lake; bison wandering north out of the park are being shot by hunters; increasing traffic congestion interferes with the movement of wildlife.

But there are success stories, too, such as the reintroduction of wolves to the Yellowstone ecosystem, and the devoted work of park scientists and managers. People who know the park well remain optimistic that our mistakes will not dislodge nature's plan. For 600,000 years, since the last time the Yellowstone caldera blew its top, the forces of nature have been reshaping Yellowstone and populating it with flora and fauna. These things take time, and as much time as you and your family can invest here will be richly rewarded.

1 The Gateway Towns: West Yellowstone, Gardiner & Cooke City

West Yellowstone: 91 miles SW of Bozeman; 30 miles W of Old Faithful; 320 miles NE of Salt Lake City. Gardiner: 79 miles SE of Bozeman; 163 miles SW of Billings. Cooke City: 127 miles SW of Billings

WEST YELLOWSTONE, MT

If all it took to make a thriving community in the West was the addition of more lodging, more restaurants, and more tourist attractions, **West Yellowstone**—just outside the park's west gate—would be a huge success story. By making itself the headquarters for snowmobilers who want to travel the park's roads in winter, the town has created a year-round tourist economy, and attracted an ever-growing number of big hotel chains. The quiet fly-fishing town that I remember is no more; the shops are chock-full of curios and the streets are clogged with tour buses, and, in the winter, noisy snowmachines.

One could argue that West Yellowstone made its Faustian bargain with tourism long ago, when the Oregon Short Line's *Yellowstone Special* train first arrived in 1909. Originally called Riverside, then Yellowstone, the name was grudgingly changed to West Yellowstone in 1920 when Gardiner residents complained that tourists would mistakenly believe the town *was* the park. Not much chance of that. This place is about shopping, not nature, and its biggest offering is a zoo-like look at wildlife in the Grizzly Discovery Center.

ESSENTIALS

GETTING THERE   The **West Yellowstone Airport,** Highway 191, 1 mile north of West Yellowstone (☎ **406/646-7631**), provides commercial air service seasonally, from June through September only, on Delta's commuter service, **Skywest** (☎ **800/453-9417.** If you're driving to West Yellowstone from Bozeman (91 miles), take U.S. Highway 191 south (a pretty drive along the Gallatin River) to its junction with U.S. Highway 287 and head straight into town. From Idaho Falls, take Interstate 15 north to U.S. Highway 20, which takes you directly into West Yellowstone, a 53-mile drive.

VISITOR INFORMATION   Visitor information is available by contacting the **West Yellowstone Chamber of Commerce,** 100 Yellowstone Ave. (P.O. Box 458), West Yellowstone, MT 59758 (☎ **406/646-7701**).

GETTING AROUND   In West Yellowstone, **Avis** (☎ **800/831-2847** or 406/646-7635) is open from May through September. **Budget Rent-A-Car** (☎ **800/527-0700** or 406/646-7882) is open year-round.

Yellowstone National Park

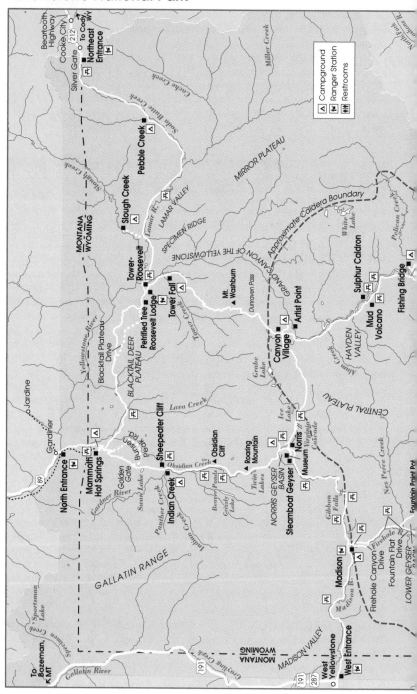

Legend:
△ Campground
🛈 Ranger Station
🚻 Restrooms

To Bozeman, MT

Beartooth Highway
To Cody, WY
212
Cooke City
Silver Gate
Northeast Entrance

Miller Creek

North Fork

Cache Creek

Soda Butte Creek
Slough Creek
Pebble Creek

Slough Creek

MIRROR PLATEAU

Lamar R.
LAMAR VALLEY
SPECIMEN RIDGE

Approximate Caldera Boundary

MONTANA
WYOMING

Tower-Roosevelt
Tower Fall
Petrified Tree
Roosevelt Lodge

Tower Creek
GRAND CANYON OF THE YELLOWSTONE

Mt. Washburn
Dunraven Pass

White Lake
Pelican Creek

Sulphur Caldron
Fishing Bridge

Yellowstone River

Blacktail Plateau Drive
BLACKTAIL DEER PLATEAU

Grebe Lake

Artist Point
Canyon Village

Mud Volcano

HAYDEN VALLEY
Alum Creek

Jardine
Gardiner

Lava Creek
Sheepeater Cliff

Ice Lake

CENTRAL PLATEAU

Bunsen Peak Rd.

89
North Entrance
Mammoth Hot Springs
Golden Gate
Gardner River

Obsidian Creek
Obsidian Cliff
Roaring Mountain

Norris
Museum Virginia Cascade

Swan Lake
Panther Creek
Indian Creek

Beaver Ponds
Grizzly Lake
Twin Lakes

NORRIS GEYSER BASIN
Steamboat Geyser

Gibbon Falls

Nez Perce Creek
Fountain Point Pot

GALLATIN RANGE

Indian Creek

Firehole Canyon Drive
Firehole R. Drive
Fountain Flat Drive
LOWER GEYSER BASIN

Madison

Madison R.

Sportsman Lake
Sphincter Creek

Gallatin River

To Bozeman, MT

Grayling Creek

MADISON VALLEY

MONTANA
WYOMING

West Yellowstone
West Entrance

191
287
191

258

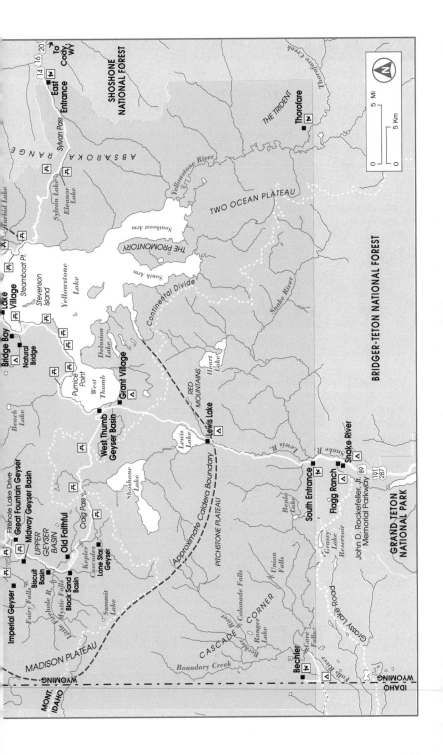

✪ Frommer's Favorite Yellowstone Experiences

Witness the World's Most Famous Geologic Alarm Clock. Old Faithful is known for its reliability, but park timekeepers have to admit that it's slowing down a little with age. Still, about once every 75 minutes you can watch her blow, as she has for at least 120 years. This is the busiest place in the park. While you're there, get a good look at the beautiful and historic Old Faithful Inn. See section 4, "Seeing the Highlights."

Escape to the Backcountry. If the packed benches at Old Faithful gives you the impression that Yellowstone is overrun, venture into the backcountry for a dose of true wilderness. It will restore your spirits and perhaps your belief in national parks. You can go a short ways—up Mount Washburn, or to the Lonestar Geyser—or you can go deep: Try the magnificent Thorofare country south of Yellowstone Lake. Get advice on how to travel safely in bear country, and then have it mostly to yourself—most of the three million annual park visitors rarely leave the roadways. See section 8, "Hiking."

Get Hooked on Yellowstone Trout. There is some fine fly-fishing water inside and just outside the park. Try the Madison, the Gibbon, and the Firehole Rivers, or troll the lakes for native cutthroat, brown, rainbow, and brook trout. When a big trout slaps the twilight surface of the Yellowstone River, Isaac Walton smiles in Heaven. See section 6, "Summer Sports & Activities."

Have a Howling Good Time at Lamar. Since wolves were reintroduced in Yellowstone in 1994, they have surprised biologists by making irregular morning and late afternoon appearances along Slough Creek and in other parts of Lamar Valley in the northeast corner of the park. This less-traveled area of Yellowstone is loaded with wildlife: bison, elk, coyotes, and grizzly bears. You can hike the trails or just set up your spotting scope by the road. See section 8, "Hiking."

Make Like Teddy and Be a Rough Rider. At Roosevelt Lodge, visitors relive the Old West by taking organized rides on horseback, stagecoach, or wagon. A more adventurous alternative is the Old West cookout; you will arrive by either horseback or wagon for hearty, meat-and-potatoes grub. See section 11, "Where to Dine in the Park."

Learn Something at the Yellowstone Institute. You can take classes on everything from wildlife tracking to butterflies to autumn photography from the **Yellowstone Association's Institute,** which inhabits the old buffalo ranch in the park's northeast corner. It's a friendly, communal way to get a more intimate knowledge of the ecosystem. See section 3, "A Park Primer."

Sleep on a Historic Pillow in the Park. Old Faithful Inn, dating back to 1904, is a log cathedral within view of the geyser. Relax with a drink on the second-floor terrace, or climb the timber lattice that holds up the great roof. Original rooms may not all have private baths, but it's still the nicest place to stay in the park. P.S.: Ask for Suite 3014 or Room 229 to watch the geyser erupt from your room. See section 10, "Where to Stay in the Park."

GETTING OUTSIDE

Most people arrive here on their way to the park, but there is no fence along the park's boundary, and some of the best wild country is here to the west. Particularly if you like fishing, the rivers—the Gallatin and the Madison, particularly—are among the best in the West. The following tackle shops offer the full gamut of guided fishing trips and instruction: **Arrick's Fishing Flies,** 125 Madison Ave. (☎ **406/646-7290**); **Bud Lilly's Trout Shop,** 39 Madison Ave. (☎ **800/854-9559** or 406/646-7801); **Eagle's Tackle Shop,** 9 Canyon St. (☎ **406/646-7529**); **Jacklin's,** 105 Yellowstone Ave. (☎ **406/646-7336**); and **Madison River Outfitters,** 117 Canyon St. (☎ **406/ 646-9644**).

Come winter, **cross-country skiers** hit the trails; see "Winter Sports & Activities," in section 7, for information on the most popular routes in the park. Ski rentals are available in West Yellowstone at **Freeheel and Wheel,** 40 Yellowstone Ave. (☎ **406/646-7744**), or **Bud Lilly's,** 39 Madison Ave. (☎ **406/646-7801**).

Snowmobiling is a huge draw for West Yellowstone, where sleds are more common than cars on snow-packed winter streets. In addition to driving machines on the snow-packed roads of Yellowstone—where speed limits are strictly enforced—there are trails in surrounding national forests with fewer restrictions. There are tricks to riding on backcountry snow, and you don't want to get stranded, so if you're inexperienced, rent a guide as well as a machine. All the major hotels and motels in West Yellowstone arrange snowmobile rentals that include gear, and there are numerous independent operations offering rentals and guides, including **Yellowstone Arctic/Yamaha,** 208 Electric St. (☎ **406/646-9636**), and **Backcountry Adventures,** 224 Electric St. (☎ **800/924-7669**).

Expect to pay $125 to $150 per day per snowmobile, and unless you have a helmet and winter gear to protect you from sub-zero windchill, plan on spending another $25 for clothing. Also popular are **snowcoach tours,** offered in vans equipped with tank-like treads to travel on snow. Check with **Yellowstone Alpen Guides Co.,** 555 Yellowstone Ave. (☎ **800/858-3502**), or with snowmobile outfitters, who often offer snowcoach rides as well.

SEEING THE SIGHTS

Grizzly Discovery Center. Grizzly Park (east end of Canyon St., just south of the west entrance to Yellowstone National Park). ☎ **800/257-2570** or 406/646-7001. www. grizzlydiscoveryctr.com. $8 adults, $3.50 children 5–15, free for children under 5. Year-round, daily 8:30am–8:30pm (wildlife viewing until dusk).

For those who haven't the patience to search for and observe from a distance the free-ranging wildlife of Yellowstone, there is this. Although, it seems a pity to come all this way to see caged animals—even *tastefully* caged animals. Now that wolves are back in the park, they have joined the grizzlies here, too. The interpretive center gives a well-mounted and detailed explanation of the grizzlies' and wolves' history in this country, and the difficult and controversial efforts to revive them in the wild. Even in a roomy, landscaped enclosure, you will often see bears and wolves pacing the edge of the fence line—instinctively, these animals want to roam. The animals are well cared for here, and there are wildlife videos and a gift shop in the center, and this is a closer look than you'll likely get with animals in the wild—but did you really come to Yellowstone to look at grizzlies imported from Alaska in an enclosure?

Museum of the Yellowstone. Canyon St. and Yellowstone Ave. ☎ **406/646-7814**. $18 family, $6 adults, $5 seniors and children, free for children under 5. May–Sept, daily 8am–10pm.

Recorded history is brief in these parts, but this museum covers what there is, with a natural emphasis on the days of the luxury trains (the museum is located in the historic 1909 Union Pacific depot). There are also displays on the Yellowstone ecosystem, covering epochal events such as the 1959 earthquake that created Quake Lake, and the

1988 fires. Highlights include Exhibits of Native American art and artifacts and displays on the explorations of the fur-trapping era, along with a mounted grizzly bear known in his animate days as "Old Snaggletooth." There are videos and films on the region's history, as well as occasional "mountain man" demonstrations and lectures.

Yellowstone Imax Theater. 101 Canyon St., West Yellowstone, MT 59758. ☎ **888/ 854-5862** or 406/646-4100. www.yellowstoneimax.com. $7.50 adults, $5.50 children 3–12, free for children under 3. Call for show times.

This theater is next door to the Grizzly Discovery Center. Together they form the centerpieces of a real estate development on the edge of the park, which includes several new hotels. Despite keeping such company, the IMAX concept works pretty well here—there are things an air-borne camera can show you on a six-story-tall screen that you'll never see on your own two feet. Six channels of stereo surround-sound add to the sense of "being there". A show called *Yellowstone* plays fairly often, with swooping views of the canyon and falls and other sights, but there are other big-screen extravaganzas as well.

WHERE TO STAY

Make your reservations early if you want to visit in July or August, or if you're going to spend Christmas to New Year's here. If you're smart, you'll come in the fall, when there are plenty of empty rooms and better rates, and spend your days fishing the Henry's Fork or one of the other great streams in the vicinity. Rates for rooms often reflect the seasonal traffic, and prices fluctuate. Unless noted, all these establishments are open year-round.

West Yellowstone Central Reservations handles booking for many of the hotels (☎ **888/646-7077**). Among the new ones, you'll find chains like the **Marriott Fairfield Inn** (☎ **800/565-6803**) at 105 S. Electric, and the **Days Inn** (☎ **800/ 548-9551**) at 301 Madison Ave., with rooms in the summer costing around $110 a night for a double. There's a bunch of Best Western affiliates, including the **Best Western Desert Inn,** 133 Canyon (☎ **800/528-1234** or 406/646-7376); the **Executive Inn,** 236 Dunraven (☎ **800/528-1234** or 406/646-7681), the largest with 82 rooms; and the **Best Western Weston Inn,** 103 Gibbon (☎ **800/528-1234** or 406/646-7373).

Less expensive options include the **Brandin' Iron Motel,** 201 Canyon (☎ **800/217-4613** or 406/646-9411), with 84 rooms; and the **City Center Motel,** 214 Madison Ave. (☎ **800/742-0665** or 406/646-7337).

The Hibernation Station. 212 Gray Wolf Ave., West Yellowstone, MT 59758. ☎ **800/ 580-3557** or 406/646-4200. www.hibernationstation.com. 35 cabins. TV TEL. $99–$219 per cabin. AE, DISC, MC, V.

The Grizzly Discovery Center re-creates a natural environment, but it's part of something entirely unnatural—a real-estate development. These luxury cabins are furnished Western-style with hand-hewn log beds draped in down comforters, wall tapestries, fireplaces, and enormous bathrooms. They can fit from two to eight people. Like a new saddle, the place may need a few years to get broken in, but it's starting out shiny and tasselled. Every year a few more cabins go up, and the owners say a big lodge will eventually be added. The outdoor sculptures on some of the roofs are eye-catching if not gallery quality, and this place is not exempt from the winter obsession of West Yellowstone—you can rent a snowmobile with your room.

Stage Coach Inn. 209 Madison (corner of Dunraven), West Yellowstone, MT 59758. ☎ **800/842-2882** or 406/646-9575. 80 units. TV TEL. $55–$121 double. AE, DISC, MC, V.

One of the nicer properties in town, Stagecoach Inn is active 12 months of the year, catering to both summertime park-goers and snowmobilers. The lobby is decorated with a Western flair that includes mounts of trophy animals from the American West. Guest rooms are well-appointed with king- and queen-size beds, modern baths, and reading tables. The Coachman restaurant room serves three meals—typically traditional, well-prepared Western fare. The lounge is a popular spot, thanks to several video poker gambling machines, a large-screen TV for sporting events, and a fireplace that warms the room during winter.

Three Bear Lodge. 217 Yellowstone Ave., West Yellowstone, MT 59758. ☎ **800/ 646-7353** or 406/646-7353. 74 units. A/C TV TEL. $73–$108 double. DISC, MC, V.

The cozy, pine-furnished rooms of this family-style inn are located less than 3 blocks from the park entrance. With an outdoor heated pool, indoor whirlpools, and a youth activity center, it is especially suitable for families. Like every other lodging in West Yellowstone, the Three Bear offers snowmobile and cross-country ski packages with or without licensed guides—but unlike elsewhere, their snowcoaches are brand-new. Three Bear Lodge's restaurant and lounge are great spots for refueling and relaxing after a long day of playing in the snow.

✪ **West Yellowstone Conference Hotel Holiday Inn SunSpree Resort.** 315 Yellowstone Ave., West Yellowstone, MT 59758. ☎ **800/HOLIDAY** or 406/646-7365. www. yellowstone-conf-hotel.com. 123 units. A/C TV TEL. $79–$144 double; $90–$200 suite. AE, DISC, MC, V.

This hotel is West Yellowstone's standout offering. From its individual rooms to its restaurant to its conference facilities, this big new resort is first-rate. Small conveniences add up—among them coffeemakers, plush carpeting, hair dryers, microwaves, a big indoor pool, and laundry services. At the activities desk you can arrange fishing and rafting trips, bike and ATV rentals, and chuck wagon cookouts. Snowmobilers who have been rattling around all day relax in the Jacuzzis in the King Spa suites. The Iron Horse Saloon serves regional microbrews, and the Oregon Short Line Restaurant serves Western cuisine including buffalo, elk and, uh, seafood dishes. At the center of the restaurant sits the restored railroad club car that brought Victorian gents to Yellowstone a century ago.

WHERE TO DINE

Just as the chain motels have arrived, so have garden-variety fast-food joints like **Kentucky Fried Chicken,** 120 Firehole Ave. (☎ 406/646-9011). Apart from the choices listed below, **Jocee's Baking Company,** 29 Canyon St. (☎ 406/646-9737), is a small but excellent alternative to steak 'n' eggs breakfast joints. The bakery combines fresh morning pastries with coffee and espresso, and offers deli sandwiches and pizza in the afternoon. Next door at the same address is the **Arrow Leaf Ice Cream Parlor** (☎ 406/646-9776), which brags about its 2,001 different ice cream flavors. For the best variety of coffee drinks and baked goods, visit **Cappy's** (☎ 406/646-9537), part of the Bookpeddler, an excellent little book store in Canyon Square. Also connected to Cappy's is a country store where you can buy coffee by the pound, birch bark bird feeders, and novelty teapots. At **Pete's Rocky Mountain Pizza Company,** 104 Canyon St. (☎ 406/646-7820), you can design your own pizza. Dinner choices include traditional Italian entrees, while hamburgers and the like are served during lunch hour.

Bullwinkle's Saloon, Gambling and Eatery. 19 Madison. ☎ **406/646-7974.** Lunch $5–$8; dinner $9–$24. Summer, daily 11am–2am. MC, V. TRADITIONAL AMERICAN.

Boisterous and noisy crowds, families and fishermen, gamblers and goof-offs fill this restaurant frequently, and they leave well-fed. Both luncheon and dinner menus are packed with traditional entrees: burgers and salads for lunch; chicken, ribs, and steaks at dinner. Try the inexpensive and plentiful Bullwinkle's salad (shrimp included), and check the updated fishing conditions charted on the wall. You can try small stakes gambling on video poker machines, featured in many Montana bars.

The Canyon Street Grill. 22 Canyon St. ☎ **406/646-7548.** Most dishes $5–$11. No credit cards. TRADITIONAL AMERICAN.

You gotta like a restaurant whose slogan is, "We are not a fast food restaurant. We are a cafe reminiscent of a by-gone era when the quality of the food meant more than how fast it could be served." This delightful, 1950s-style spot serves hearty food for breakfast, lunch, and dinner. Hamburgers and chicken sandwiches are popular, accompanied by milk shakes made with hard ice cream. A combo of steak, mashed potatoes, and veggies goes for $10.95.

✪ **Elno's Tavern.** 8955 Gallatin Rd. ☎ **406/646-9344.** Most dishes $4 and up. No credit cards. Daily noon–8pm. Closed first 2 weeks of Dec. AMERICAN.

Locals snowmobile out from West Yellowstone to Elno's (there's a trail that follows U.S. Highway 191) to become their own chefs at the grill here. It's a novel concept, and one that keeps people coming back for more to a restaurant with a fine view of Hegben Lake. If you want to blend in with the locals, go up to the counter and place your order for a steak, teriyaki chicken, hamburger, or hot dog, and keep a straight face when you're handed an uncooked piece of meat. Go to the grill, slap it on, and stand around drink in hand shooting the breeze with other patrons until your food is exactly the way you like it. Steaks and chicken come with your choice of a baked potato or a garden salad, and hamburgers come with chips. Snowmobilers can purchase gas and oil here, too.

The Outpost Restaurant. 115 Yellowstone Ave. (in the Montana Outpost Mall). ☎ **406/646-7303.** Main courses $6–$15. AE, DISC, MC, V. Daily 6am–11pm. Closed Oct 15–Apr 15. AMERICAN.

This fine restaurant is tucked away in a downtown mall. The food is presented in a family-oriented, home-cooking style—exemplified in the beef stew. There's also salmon, steaks, trout, and an excellent salad bar. The opening of so many new establishments in West Yellowstone, many of them linked to snowmobile package deals, has put a dent in the business of this restaurant, which may also suffer from its absence of a bar on the premises. But, overall, it offers solid fare in a quiet, family-friendly atmosphere.

GARDINER

Of all the towns that stand sentry on the roads into Yellowstone, none seems more like a gateway town than Gardiner, in part because of the historic stone arch that marks the entrance through which the earliest visitors passed into the park. It's also practically around the corner from park headquarters in Mammoth. Only here, at the north entrance, are wheeled vehicles allowed into the park year-round, in order to keep a connection open to Montana towns like Cooke City, which in winter can only be reached through the north entrance.

Gardiner sits at the junction of the Gardiner and Yellowstone Rivers, looking like the gritty little mining town it once was. Nobody puts on airs in the coffee shops and bars, and nobody raises an eyebrow when a bison or deer wanders through town. If you need additional information, contact the **Gardiner Chamber of Commerce,**

222 Park St., P.O. Box 81, Gardiner, MT 59030 (☎ **406/848-7971;** www. gardinerchamber.com; e-mail: gardinerchamber@gomontana.com).

GETTING THERE   From Bozeman (the nearest jet service airport), take I-90 26 miles east to Livingston, then take U.S. Highway 89 south 53 miles to Gardiner.

WHERE TO STAY

As with all the gateway towns, make your reservations early if you're coming during the peak season. The steep fall-off in the off-season leads to great discounts—inquire when making reservations.

   Motels with numbers in their names are moving in and filling up during the summer months: the new **Motel 6** (109 Hellroaring Dr.; ☎ **877/266-8356** or 406/848-7520) and the virtually new **Super 8** (on U.S. 89 South; ☎ **800/800-8000** or 406/848-7401) are open year-round with rates during the high season between $80 and $100 for a double.

✪ **Absaroka Lodge.** U.S. 89 at the Yellowstone River Bridge. ☎ **800/755-7414** or 406/848-7414. www.yellowstonemotel.com. E-mail: ablodge@aol.com. 41 units. A/C TV TEL. $50 single; $100 double with kitchenette. AE, DC, DISC, MC, V.

Every room in this lodge has a balcony, many of them with nice views of the Yellowstone River. The lodge's riverbank location—with a nice slope of lawn overlooking the river gorge—is just a few blocks from the village center, and the rooms are well-appointed with queen-size beds. Suites with kitchenettes cost a little more. The owners have been in business here for decades, but they've just put up a modern new building. Like most other properties in town, the lodge has staff ready and able to assist in arrangements with outfitters for fly-fishing, rafting, and, in the fall, hunting.

Best Western by Mammoth Hot Springs. U.S. 89, P.O. Box 646, Gardiner, MT 59030. ☎ **800/828-9080** or 406/848-7311. www.bestwestern.com/mammothhotsprings. 85 units. A/C TV TEL. Summer, $94–$104 double; winter, $57–$67 double. AE, MC, V.

Though a half-mile north of the center of the town, the Best Western also has nicely furnished rooms with spectacular views, and is adjacent to the Mine, one of the better restaurants. There is also a heated pool, and an adjacent casino (Montana allows low stakes gambling.) During winter months you can rent cross-country skiing and snowmobile equipment; winter packages are available.

Rodeway Inn. 107 Hellroaring, Gardiner, MT 59030. ☎ **800/228-5150** or 406/848-7536. 80 units. Summer, $90 double, $129 suite; winter, $45–$75. AE, DC, DISC, MC, V.

This log cabin–style hotel looks like it belongs here, unlike a lot of chain operations. The centerpiece is a 3,000-square-foot rustic lobby, decorated with wild game trophies, and a large second-floor balcony that offers views of Yellowstone scenery and passing wildlife. Family suites that sleep six and luxurious Jacuzzi suites are also available, along with a self-service Laundromat.

WHERE TO DINE

Bear Country Restaurant. 232 Park St. ☎ **406/848-7188.** Breakfast $2–$5; lunch $5–$8; dinner $9–$12. AE, DISC, MC, V. 7am–10pm. TRADITIONAL AMERICAN.

There's nothing fancy about this pleasantly rundown, family-oriented restaurant. Its location across from the park entrance, its early morning hours, and its no-nonsense service are among its attractions. Early in the morning, you'll be among working stiffs fueling up to make a tough living in the mountains. The American fare menu is undistinguished, but the portions are generous: eggs, sausage, pancakes for breakfast; lunch consists of soup-and-sandwich combos; and dinner is strictly meat and potatoes.

The Chico Inn. Old Chico Rd., Pray, MT. ☎ **800/HOT-WADA.** Reservations recommended. Main courses $16–$27. AE, DISC. Summer, daily 5:30–10pm; winter, Sun–Thurs 6–9pm, Fri–Sat 5:30–10pm. CONTINENTAL.

It's 30 miles north of Gardiner, but if you're in the area, stop here for some of the best food in the Rockies, and visit the bar where Peter Fonda's *Easy Rider* motorcycle is enshrined. You'll want to linger over the food, so consider a night's stay in either the old lodge or the newer additions; you can relax and digest in the hot springs. For more details, see chapter 8.

Outlaw's Pizza. Hwy. 89 (in the Yellowstone Outpost Mall). ☎ **406/848-7733.** Reservations not accepted. Most dishes $6–$15. MC, V. Daily 11am–11pm. ITALIAN/SALAD BAR.

This restaurant serves pretty good pizza, which makes it the best in town, as well as fresh soups and decent pasta dishes, plus there's a salad bar and terrific views of the mountains. Try the Gourmet Pizza, with everything on it. Western theme art decorates the walls. You can order take-out.

The Yellowstone Mine. In the Best Western by Mammoth Hot Springs, Hwy. 89. ☎ **406/848-7336.** Reservations not accepted. Breakfast $4–$6; dinner $11–$22. AE, DISC, MC, V. Daily 6–11am and 5–9pm. AMERICAN.

The low-light old-time mining atmosphere may not spark your appetite, but the meals come in healthy portions and the prices are, like those of the hotel itself, reasonable. Steaks and seafood are the restaurant's specialty. There's also a lounge and casino known as the Rusty Rail. Inside you'll find live poker, machine poker, keno—whatever you need for a fix before you head into gambling-free Wyoming. *Note:* If you need food late at night, the Rusty Rail is your only bet—the deep fryer stays open as long as the bar does.

COOKE CITY

If little ol' Gardiner seems just a little too connected to the civilized world, you ought to spend a winter in littler Cooke City or even tinier Silver Gate, just outside Yellowstone National Park's northeast entrance. In the winter, when the cloud-scraping Beartooth Pass closes to the north, supplies for these towns have to come through the park. Better to visit in the summer and take the breathtaking drive north over the pass (U.S. 212 toward Red Lodge), or south along the scenic Chief Joseph Highway (WY 296). For a hundred years, the lifeblood of this town was mining gold, platinum, and other precious metals, but now there is only park tourism, which seems a little anemic by comparison. Less than 100 residents live year-round in the town today, and Silver Gate, right next to the park entrance, is barely in double figures. Contact the **Colter Pass/Cooke City/Silver Gate Chamber of Commerce** at Box 1071, Cooke City, MT 59020-1071 (☎ **406/838-2395**) for information and a map of hiking and snowmobiling trails in the area.

GETTING THERE   From Billings, MT, the nearest city with jet service, drive west on I-90 to Laurel, then south on U.S. Highway 212 to Red Lodge, a total distance of 60 miles; then continue another 67 miles south over spectacular Beartooth Pass, dipping into Wyoming and back up into Montana at Cooke City.

WHERE TO STAY & EAT   A room for the night will be less expensive than in other gateway towns, anywhere from $35 to $80 a night. The 32-room **Soda Butte Lodge** (☎ **406/838-2251**) is the biggest, newest, and poshest motel. It includes the good **Prospector Restaurant** and a small casino; or you can go to the cheaper, bare-bones **Alpine Motel,** also on Main Street (☎ **406/838-2262**). For a bite to eat and a great selection of beers, try the funky **Beartooth Cafe** (☎ **406/**

838-2475). If you find yourself in Silver Gate one evening, stop by the historic **Range Rider Lodge** (☎ **406/838-2359**), a cavernous log building with a huge dance floor.

2 Just the Facts

BEFORE YOU GO

You're only one of three million people heading to the park this year, so plan ahead: to obtain maps and information about the park prior to arrival, contact **Yellowstone National Park,** WY 82190 (☎ **307/344-7381;** www.nps.gov/yell). Information regarding lodging, some campgrounds, tours, boating, and horseback riding in Yellowstone is available from **Yellowstone Park Lodges,** Yellowstone National Park, WY 82190 (☎ **307/344-7311;** www.travelyellowstone.com). For information regarding educational programs in Yellowstone, contact **Yellowstone Association,** P.O. Box 117, Yellowstone National Park, WY 82190 (☎ **307/344-2293;** www.Yellowstone-Association.org), which operates bookstores in park visitor centers, museums, and information stations, and oversees the **Yellowstone Association Institute** and the courses taught at the old buffalo ranch in the park's northeast corner. They also have a catalogue of publications you can order by mail.

GETTING THERE

If interstate highways and international airports are the measure of accessibility, then Yellowstone is as remote as Alaska's Denali National Park or the Serengeti Plains of Africa. But three million people make it here every year, on tour buses, in family vans, on bicycles, and astride snowmobiles.

The closest airport to Yellowstone is in **West Yellowstone,** Montana, which sits just outside the park's west entrance. For information on flying into West Yellowstone, see "Essentials" in section 1 of this chapter.

Visitors can reach the park from the south by flying into **Jackson,** Wyoming (only 14 miles from the southern entrance to Grand Teton), then driving 56 miles through Grand Teton to the southern entrance of Yellowstone. **American Airlines** (☎ 800/433-7300); **Delta** (☎ 800/221-1212); **Skywest,** the Delta Connection (☎ 800/453-9417 or 307/733-7920); and **United Express** (☎ 800/241-6522) all have flights to and from **Jackson Airport.**

To the north, **Bozeman, Montana,** is 87 miles from the West Yellowstone entrance on U.S. 191. Or you can drive east from Bozeman to Livingston, a 20-mile journey on Interstate 90, and then south 53 miles on U.S. 89 to the northern entrance at Gardiner. Bozeman's airport, **Gallatin Field,** provides daily service via **Delta** (☎ 800/221-1212), **Northwest** (☎ 800/225-2525), and **United** (☎ 800/241-6522), as well as **Horizon** (☎ 800/547-9308) and **Skywest** (☎ 800/453-9417) commuter flights. If you're driving to West Yellowstone from Bozeman (91 miles), take U.S. Highway 191 south to its junction with U.S. Highway 287 and head straight into town.

Also to the north, **Billings, Montana,** is 129 miles from the Cooke City entrance. Billings is home to Montana's busiest airport, **Logan International,** 2 miles north of downtown. Daily intrastate service is provided by **Big Sky Airlines** (☎ 800/237-7788 or 406/245-2300); and regional daily service is provided by **Delta** (☎ 800/221-1212), **Horizon** (☎ 800/547-9308), **Northwest** (☎ 800/225-2525), and **United** (☎ 800/241-6522). From Billings, it's a 65-mile drive south on U.S. Highway 212 to Red Lodge, then 30 miles on the Beartooth Highway to the northeast entrance to the park. Keep in mind that the Beartooth Highway (U.S.212), which

---
Travel Tips

Flying into the closest airports to Yellowstone can be an expensive proposition. Often, this involves cramped quarters in a commuter airline, with schedules that change often and even airlines that come and go. You can save significant airfare dollars by flying to **Salt Lake City,** or the more distant **Denver.** Salt Lake City is 390 driving miles from Jackson, a route which takes you through rolling Idaho countryside and alongside the dramatic western slope of the Rockies, then high above it all over Teton Pass. Most Yellowstone visitors plan to drive themselves through the park anyway, so if you don't mind adding a few more scenic hours behind the wheel, this is a smart option.

---

takes you on a high, twisting journey over a spectacular pass, is open only from Memorial Day weekend until late October.

From **Cody, Wyoming,** it's a gorgeous 53-mile drive west along U.S. Highway 16/14/20 to the east entrance of the park. **Cody's Yellowstone Regional Airport** (☎ 307/587-5096) serves the Bighorn Basin as well as the east and northeast entrances of Yellowstone National Park with year-round commercial flights via **Skywest** (☎ 800/453-9417) and **United Express** (☎ 800/241-6522).

Most of the major auto rental agencies have operations in the gateway cities. **Avis** (☎ 800/831-2847), **Budget Auto Rental** (☎ 800/527-0700), **Thrifty Auto** (☎ 800/367-2277), **National Car Rental** (☎ 800/227-7368), and **Hertz** (☎ 800/654-3131) all have operations in Bozeman, Billings, and Jackson. Cody is served by Thrifty, Avis, Hertz, and Budget. **Alamo Auto Rental** (☎ 800/327-9633) serves Billings and Jackson.

ACCESS/ENTRY POINTS

Yellowstone has five entrances. The **north entrance,** near Mammoth Hot Springs, is located just south of Gardiner, Montana, and U.S. Highway 89. In the winter, this is the only access to Yellowstone by car.

The **west entrance,** just outside the town of West Yellowstone on U.S. Highway 20, is the closest entry to Old Faithful. Inside the park, you can turn south to see Old Faithful or north to the Norris Geyser Basin. This entrance is open to wheeled vehicles from April to November and during the winter to snowmobiles and snowcoaches.

The **south entrance,** on U.S. Highway 89/191/287, brings visitors into the park from neighboring Grand Teton National Park and the Jackson area. As you drive north from Jackson, you'll get a panoramic view of the Grand Tetons. Once in the park, the road winds along the Lewis River to the south end of Yellowstone Lake, at West Thumb and Grant Village. It is open to cars from May to November and to snowmobiles and snowcoaches from December to March.

The **east entrance,** on U.S. Highway 14/16/20, is 52 miles west of Cody, Wyoming, and is open to cars from May to September and to snowmobiles and snowcoaches from December to March. The drive up the Wapiti Valley and over Sylvan Pass is especially beautiful, if not marred by road repair delays.

The **northeast entrance,** at Cooke City, Montana, is closest to the Tower-Roosevelt area, 29 miles to the west. This entrance is open to cars year-round, but beginning on October 15, when the Beartooth Highway closes, until around Memorial Day, the only route to Cooke City is through Mammoth Hot Springs. When it's open, the drive from Red Lodge to the park is a grand climb among the clouds.

Regardless of which entrance you choose, when you enter the park you'll be given a good map and up-to-date information on facilities, services, programs, fishing, camping, and more.

Check **road conditions** before entering the park by calling the visitor center at ☎ **307/344-7381.** There always seems to be major road construction in one part of the park or another, so be forewarned.

VISITOR CENTERS & INFORMATION

There are five major visitor and information centers in the park, and each has something different to offer. Unless otherwise indicated, summer hours are 8am to 7pm.

The **Albright Visitor Center** (☎ **307/344-2263**), at Mammoth Hot Springs, is the largest. It provides visitor information and publications about the park, has exhibits depicting park history from prehistory through the creation of the National Park Service, and houses a wildlife display on the second floor.

The **Old Faithful Visitor Center** (☎ **307/545-2750**) is another large facility. An excellent short film describing the geysers, *Yellowstone, A Living Sculpture,* is shown throughout the day in an air-conditioned auditorium. Rangers dispense various park publications and post projected geyser eruption times here. An informative seismographic exhibit is an added attraction.

The **Canyon Visitor Center** (☎ **307/242-2550**), in Canyon Village, between Tower Junction and Lake Yellowstone, is the place to go for books and an informative display about bison in the park. It's staffed with friendly rangers used to dealing with crowds.

The **Fishing Bridge Visitor Center** (☎ **307/242-2450**), located near Fishing Bridge on the north shore of Yellowstone Lake, has an excellent wildlife display. You can get information and publications here as well.

The **Grant Village Visitor Center** (☎ **307/242-2650**), in Grant Village just south of West Thumb on the west side of Yellowstone Lake, has information, publications, a slide program, and a fascinating exhibit that examines the effects of fire in Yellowstone.

Other sources of park information can be found at the Madison Information Station; the Museum of the National Park Ranger and the Norris Geyser Basin Museum, both at Norris; and the West Thumb Information Station.

FEES & PERMITS

Park users are now asked to share more of the burden of park costs with taxpayers, but fees are still moderate: a 7-day pass costs $20 per automobile, and covers both Yellowstone and Grand Teton national parks. A snowmobile or motorcycle pays $15 for 7 days, and someone who comes in on bicycle, skis or foot pays $10. If you expect to visit the parks more than once in a year, buy an **annual permit** for $40. And if you visit parks and national monuments around the country, purchase a **Golden Eagle Passport** for $50: it's good for 365 days from the date of purchase at nearly all federal preserves. Senior citizens can get a **Golden Age Passport** for $10 annually, and blind or permanently disabled visitors can obtain a **Golden Access Passport,** which costs nothing, and entitles them and a guest to free admission into national parks, forests, and wildlife refuges.

BACKCOUNTRY PERMITS   Backcountry permits are free, but you have to have one for any overnight trip, on foot, on horseback, or by boat. Camping is allowed only in designated campsites, many of which are equipped with food storage poles to keep wildlife away. These sites are primitive and well-situated, and you won't feel at all like you're in a campground. If designated campsites in a particular area have already been reserved, you're out of luck. So while you can pick up a permit for hiking or boating the day before beginning a trip, you would be wise during peak season to make a reservation in advance (you can contact the park for reservations for the upcoming year beginning April 1), though it costs $20. The Yellowstone Back-country Office (P.O. Box 168, Yellowstone National Park, WY 82190) will send you a useful "Backcountry Trip Planner" with a detailed map showing where the camp-sites are.

Pick up your permit in the park within 48 hours of your departure, at one of the following visitor ranger stations any day of the week during the summer: Bechler, Canyon, Mammoth, Old Faithful, Tower, West Entrance, Grant Village, Lake, South Entrance, and Bridge Bay. Boating permits can only be obtained at the last four ranger stations.

BOATING PERMITS   Any vessels used on park waters must have a permit. For motorized craft the cost is $20 for annual permits and $10 for a 7-day pass. Fees for nonmotorized boats are $10 for annual permits and $5 for 7-day permits. See "Regu-lations," below, for more information. Rivers and streams are closed to boats of any kind, except for the stretch of the Lewis River between Lewis and Shoshone lakes, which is restricted to hand-propelled craft. Coast Guard–approved personal flotation devices are required for each person boating.

FISHING PERMITS   Permits are required for anglers; the permit costs $10 for 10 days and $20 for the season. Children 12 to 15 years of age must have a permit, but there is no charge, and children under 12 may fish without a permit. Permits are avail-able at any ranger station, visitor centers, and Hamilton stores. The season usually begins on the Saturday of Memorial Day weekend and continues through the first Sunday in November, with some exceptions: Yellowstone Lake opens June 1, and its tributary streams open July 15 (after the bears are done angling). Sections of the Yel-lowstone River also have briefer seasons. Check the park's Web site for current infor-mation: www.nps.gov/yell/fishing.htm.

REGULATIONS

You can get more detailed information about these rules from the park rangers or at visitor centers throughout the parks or at the park's Web site (www.nps.gov/yell/planvisit/rules).

DEFACING PARK FEATURES   Picking wildflowers, or collecting natural or archaeological objects, is illegal. Only dead-and-down wood can be collected for back-country campfires.

BICYCLES   Bicycles are not allowed on the park's trails or boardwalks, but the park is a popular destination for pavement cyclists. Because of the narrow, winding nature of park roads, and the large recreational vehicles with poor visibility, it's recommended that you wear helmets and bright clothing. There are some designated off-pavement bicycling areas—contact the park for more information.

CAMPING   In any given year, a person may camp for no more than 30 days in the park, and only 14 days during the summer season. Food, garbage, and utensils must be stored in a vehicle or container made of solid material and suspended at least 10 feet above the ground when not in use.

CLIMBING   Because of the loose, crumbly rock in Yellowstone, climbing is discouraged throughout the park, and prohibited in the Grand Canyon of the Yellowstone.

FIREARMS   Firearms are not allowed in either park. However, unloaded firearms may be transported in a vehicle when cased, broken down, or rendered inoperable, and on certain trails for access to areas outside the park, with a special permit. Ammunition must be carried in a separate compartment of the vehicle.

LITTERING   Littering in the national parks is strictly prohibited—remember, if you pack it in, you have to pack it out. Throwing coins or other objects into thermal features is illegal.

MOTORCYCLES   Motorcycles, motor scooters, and motor bikes are allowed only on park roads. No off-road or trail riding are allowed. Operator licenses and license plates are required.

PETS   Pets must be leashed and are prohibited in the backcountry, on trails, on boardwalks, and in thermal areas for obvious reasons. If you tie up a pet and leave it, you're breaking the law.

SMOKING   No smoking in thermal areas, visitor centers, ranger stations, or any other posted public areas.

SNOWMOBILING   Snowmobilers must have valid driver's licenses and must stay on the designated unplowed roadways. Snowmobiles must obey posted speed limits.

SWIMMING   Swimming or wading is prohibited in thermal features or in streams whose waters flow from thermal features in Yellowstone. (An exception is the "Boiling River" near Mammoth, where visitors can take a warm soak between 5am and 6pm except during spring runoff.) Swimming in Yellowstone Lake is discouraged because of the low water temperature and unpredictable weather. You can't swim nude in public areas, either.

WILDLIFE   It is unlawful to approach within 100 yards of a bear or within 25 yards of other wildlife. Feeding any wildlife is illegal. Wildlife calls such as elk bugles or other artificial attractants are forbidden.

WHEN TO GO

During the quiet "shoulder" seasons of spring and fall, there are more bison and elk around than autos and RVs. Before the second week in June, you'll be rewarded by the explosion of wildflowers as they begin to bloom, filling the meadows and hillsides with vast arrays of colors and shapes. After that, roads become progressively busier. Traveling before peak season has economic advantages, as well, since gateway city motel rates are lower, as are the costs of meals. Similarly, at the end of the season, after Labor Day weekend, crowds begin to thin and the roads become less traveled. In addition to wildlife and improved fishing conditions in some areas, the fall foliage transforms the area to a calendar-quality image.

In the winter, Yellowstone has a storybook beauty, as snow and ice soften the edges of the landscape and shroud the lumbering bison. Geyser basins appear even more dramatic, the frigid air temperature in stark contrast to the steaming, gurgling waters. Nearby trees are transformed into eerie "snow ghosts" by frozen thermal vapors. Wildlife cluster at the thermal areas to take advantage of the softer ground and more accessible vegetation. Lake Yellowstone's surface freezes to an average thickness of 3 feet, creating a vast ice sheet that sings and moans as the huge plates of ice shift.

The only dissonance to this winter wilderness tableau is the roar of snowmobiles, which inhabit the park's snow-packed roads in ever-growing numbers. Though this is a popular form of recreation, particularly now that the park is linked to snowmobile trails in surrounding national forests, it disturbs some park visitors to approach the gate in winter and find a traffic jam of machines wreathed in exhaust fumes.

You can also enter the park in tracked vehicles that deliver visitors to the Old Faithful Snow Lodge (recently rebuilt and expanded) and tour the park. From the lodge here or at Mammoth—which also stays open to cars during the winter—you can ski, snowmobile, or simply wander around the thermal areas. The only road within the park open for automobile traffic is the Mammoth Hot Springs–Cooke City Road.

SEASONS

Natives of the region describe weather in the Yellowstone ecosystem as predictably unpredictable. Because of the high elevations of the parks, and changing weather systems, the region is characterized by long, cold winters and short, though usually warm, summers.

The first sticking snows typically fall by November 1, and cold and snow may linger into April and May, though temperatures generally warm up by then. The average daytime readings during that time are 40° to 50°F, gradually increasing to 60° to 70°F by early June. So during these months it's a good idea to bring a warm jacket, rain gear, and water resistant walking shoes. The area is never balmy, but temperatures during the middle of the summer are typically 70° to 80°F in the lower elevations, and are especially comfortable because of the lack of humidity. Because this is high altitude, bring plenty of sunscreen to protect yourself in the thin atmosphere, and a wide-brimmed hat. Even during the warm months, nights will be cool, with temperatures dropping into the low 40s, so include at least a light jacket in your wardrobe. Summer thunderstorms are common, so you'll be glad you've included a waterproof shell or umbrella for needed protection.

During winter months temperatures hover in single digits, and sub-zero overnight temperatures are common. You should bring fleece underwear, heavy shirts (not cotton!), vests and coats, warm gloves, and warm, wicking socks. The lowest temperature recorded at Yellowstone was -66°F, in 1933.

AVOIDING THE CROWDS

One of the things you'll discover when you venture down a trail is that the majority of Yellowstone's three million annual visitors aren't going to follow you. Some are afraid of grizzly bears; some are in a hurry; some just don't want the exertion. But Yellowstone rewards those who expend a bit of shoe leather. Half a mile from the Buick, you'll find few people and much better opportunities to smell the wildflowers.

But if you really want a Yellowstone experience that's all your own, head for the backcountry. This is some of the deepest, most exquisite wilderness in the country, and you won't be fighting the mob. While visitation at Yellowstone increases yearly, backcountry permits do not—there were no more visitors in 1997 than there were in 1980, when I took my first trip there. My favorite area is the Thorofare Country, in the park's southeast corner, at the headwaters of the Yellowstone River. Or the high country around the Lamar Valley, including Washburn Peak. But there's so much wilderness here that you will find views of your own.

EDUCATIONAL PROGRAMS

Yellowstone and Grand Teton national parks continue to offer free **ranger-led educational programs** that will significantly enhance a visitor's understanding of the area's history, culture, and wildlife. Most programs run through late September. Detailed information on location and times is listed in the park newsletter, which is distributed at the entrance gates.

On a more informal basis, you'll run into ranger-naturalists roaming the geyser basins and along the rim of the Grand Canyon in Yellowstone, and in areas where wildlife gather in both parks. They are available to answer questions as well.

Evening campfire programs are presented nightly in the summer at campgrounds at Mammoth Hot Springs, Norris, Madison, Old Faithful, Grant, Bridge Bay, and Canyon; and three times weekly at Lewis Lake campground and the Tower Falls Amphitheater. Many of these activities are accessible to the disabled. It's a good idea to bring a flashlight, warm clothing, and rain gear. Rangers also conduct walking, talking, and hiking programs throughout the park.

As one would expect, there are more tours and evening programs in the **Old Faithful** area than anywhere else in the park. The topics of the guided walks, which can run as long as 1½ hours, usually focus on the geysers, their fragile plumbing, and their role in the Yellowstone ecosystem.

Beginning in June, daily hikes in the **Canyon** area head out to the Hayden Valley and the rim of the Grand Canyon; a ranger talk on the art inspired by the falls is held several times a day at the lower platform of Artist's Point. An explanation of the origins of the hot pools and mud pots is conducted daily beginning in June at the **Grant** area as part of a walk of the Lakeshore area of the West Thumb Geyser Basin. The **Lake/Fishing Bridge** agenda includes walking tours of the Mud Volcano area, and along the shores of Yellowstone Lake and Indian Pond. There is an afternoon talk at the Fishing Bridge Visitor Center about managing wildlife like grizzlies and wolves, and a discussion of fisheries management that is held on the west end of the Fishing Bridge. Once a week, a park ranger dressed in mountain man regalia demonstrates the skills of the early mountain men at the Elephant Back Trailhead. Fire ecology, wildlife biology, and aquatic resources are discussed during daily strolls that originate at the Two Ribbons Trailhead of the **Madison** area. Bring mosquito repellent. Some changes are made each year in these presentations; consult the park newsletter that is distributed at the entrance gates.

Two of the more interesting ranger talks are held at **Mammoth Hot Springs;** one is a talk about Yellowstone's diverse wildlife, the second is a historical tour of the original site of Fort Yellowstone, established more than 125 years ago. There is a also a guided tour of the hot springs terraces. The hottest, most dynamic, and oldest geyser basin in the park is at **Norris,** where a popular 1½-hour tour begins at the Norris museum four times daily.

There are also special exhibitions at the various visitor centers around the park. A new film on the teeming microbial life in the park's hot pools began a run at the Old Faithful Visitors Center in 1999, and an excellent exhibit on bison, mounted by the park and Cody's Buffalo Bill Historical Center, is currently quartered at the Canyon Visitor Center.

But you don't have to limit yourself to Yellowstone's natural beauty—you can tour the historic **Lake Hotel** from June 5th through August 15th, meeting at 4:30pm under the porte cochere on the lake side of the hotel; the **Old Faithful Inn** tours begin at the fireplace in the lobby several times a day from May 2 to October 15.

The ranger/naturalist programs are one of several activities youngsters are encouraged to participate in as part of the **"Junior Ranger"** program. For $2, kids can pick up an activity paper at one of the visitor centers, then follow its guidelines for hiking and learning about the park. When they complete the program, their enrollment as Junior Rangers is announced to the public with great fanfare.

Photographers can get some lessons and free advice through **Kodak Presents,** which sends representatives to various locations around the park during the summer.

Check bulletin boards for locations and times or call ☎ **307/344-2263.** Astronomers from the **Museum of the Rockies** in Bozeman, Montana, bring their telescopes and stories to a series of star-gazing sessions throughout the park—contact the museum at ☎ **406/994-2251** for a schedule.

The ❂ **Yellowstone Association Institute** (P.O. Box 117, Yellowstone National Park, WY 82190; ☎ 307/344-2294; www.YellowstoneAssociation.org) operates at the old Buffalo Ranch, on the road through the Lamar Valley to the park's northeast entrance, and offers more than 100 courses, winter and summer, covering everything from wildlife tracking in the snow to wilderness medicine to the history of fur trappers on the plateau. The courses, some of which are offered for college credit, run from 2 to 5 days, with forays into the field, and lectures and demonstrations at the Institute's cramped quarters. Participants are generally friendly and supportive, sharing meals and stories in the common kitchen. Prices are reasonable, and some classes are specifically oriented to families and youngsters.

For folks who want to make a genuine contribution to scientific research in the park, contact **Yellowstone Ecosystem Studies** (P.O. Box 6640, Bozeman, MT 59771; ☎ **406/587-7758;** www.yellowstone.org; e-mail: yes@yellowstone.org). One of its programs, Outdoor Field Studies, puts guests to work in the field following coyotes and wolves with telemetry equipment. You'll pay a hefty fee to participate, but you'll be contributing to crucial wildlife studies by biologist Bob Crabtree. YES also rents cabins at its Science Center in Silver Gate (call ☎ **406/838-2222** for more information).

SERVICES & SUPPLIES

Hamilton Stores is the oldest private concessionaire in the park. The stores are located throughout the park, including Old Faithful, Mammoth Hot Springs, Lake, Fishing Bridge, and Grant Village, and feature gift shops, grocery supplies, and soda fountains. Depending upon the location, you may find a limited supply of fresh veggies and canned goods (as at the Canyon store), plus fishing supplies, souvenirs and, of course, ice cream. Service stations are located at major visitor areas: Old Faithful, Canyon, Mammoth Hot Springs, and Grant Village. Exact locations of all Hamilton stores are listed in the park newspaper you receive at the entrance gates.

If you have medical problems while visiting the park, Yellowstone Park Medical Services provides help at the **Lake Hospital** (☎ **307/242-7241**), an acute-care facility; the Old Faithful Clinic (☎ **307/545-7325**); and the Mammoth Clinic (☎ **307/344-7965**).

ORGANIZED TOURS & ACTIVITIES

A number of tour companies offer bus tours of the park originating in gateway communities: **Powder River Coach USA** (☎ **800/527-6316**) out of Cody offers daylong trips; **Gray Line of Yellowstone** (☎ **800/523-3102**) takes travelers around the park from West Yellowstone, as does **Buffalo Bus Lines** (☎ **800/426-7669**). If you are looking for specialized guided trips—such as photo safaris or snowmobile tours— contact the chambers of the gateway community where you want to begin (see section on Gateway Communities, a few pages back).

Within the park, the hotel concessionaire, **Yellowstone Park Lodges** (☎ **307/344-7311;** ynp-lodges.com) has a variety of general and specialized tours.

Three different **motorcoach tours** are available from all of Yellowstone's villages. For $29 you can explore either the **Upper Loop** (Norris Geyser Basin, the Grand Canyon of the Yellowstone, and Mammoth Hot Springs) or the **Lower Basin** (Old Faithful, Yellowstone Lake, the Hayden Valley); or, for $33, you can do the whole thing, the **Grand Loop.** These are full-day tours, with stops at all the sights and informative talks by the guides. Specialty trips include photo safaris, wildlife trips up the Lamar Valley (try it in winter), and special group charters of the historic yellow "gear-jammers" from the 1930s.

At Bridge Bay Marina, 1-hour **scenicruiser tours** depart throughout the day from June to the end of September for a trip around the northern end of giant Yellowstone Lake. You view the Lake Hotel from the water and visit Stevenson Island, while a guide fills you in on the history, geology, and biology. Fares are $9 for adults, $5 for children 2 to 12. Guided fishing trips on 22-foot and 34-foot cabin cruisers are also available from Yellowstone Park Lodges at Bridge Bay, and you can rent smaller outboards and rowboats.

Buses are replaced in the winter by **snowcoach tours.** These are more vans than buses, mounted on tank treads with skis in front for steering. The snowcoach can pick you up at the south or west entrances, or at Mammoth, and take you all over the park. You can spend a night at Old Faithful and then snowcoach up to Mammoth the next night, or do round-trip tours from the gates or wherever you're lodged in the park. One-way trips range from $40 to $44, while round-trips cost $79 to $88.

Guides tell tales of the areas as you cruise the park trails, and pull over and unload to photograph scenery and wildlife. Snowcoaches aren't the most comfortable mode of transportation, and they're a bit noisy, but they allow larger groups the option of traveling together in the same vehicle. They are also available for rent at most snowmobile locations if you want to do the coaching yourself.

FOR TRAVELERS WITH DISABILITIES

Wheelchair-accessible accommodations are located in the Cascade Lodge at Canyon Village, in Grant Village, in the Old Faithful Inn, and in the Lake Yellowstone Hotel. For a free *Visitors Guide to Accessible Features in Yellowstone National Park,* write to the Park Accessibility Coordinator, P.O. Box 168, Yellowstone National Park, WY 82190, or pick up the guide at the gates or visitor centers. There are **accessible campsites** at Madison, Canyon, and Grant campgrounds, which may be reserved by calling ☎ **307/344-7311.**

Accessible rest rooms with sinks and flush toilets are located at all developed areas except West Thumb and Norris. Accessible vault toilets are found at West Thumb and Norris, as well as in most scenic areas and picnic areas.

Many of Yellowstone's roadside attractions, including the Grand Canyon of the Yellowstone's south rim, West Thumb Geyser Basin, much of the Norris and Upper Geyser Basins, and parts of the Mud Volcano and Fountain Paint Pot areas, are negotiable by wheelchair.

Visitor centers at Old Faithful, Grant Village, and Canyon are wheelchair-accessible, as are the Norris Museum and the Fishing Bridge Visitor Center.

Handicapped parking is available at Old Faithful, Fishing Bridge, Canyon, Norris, and Grant Village, though you'll have to look for it; at some locations it is near a Hamilton store.

3 A Park Primer

A BRIEF HISTORY

A trip to Yellowstone has changed considerably since the days of George Cowan: When he visited the park in 1877, he set a new standard for "roughing it." Cowan was kidnapped from his horse-packing camp and shot by the Nez Perce Indians, then subsisted on roots and coffee grounds as he dragged his paralyzed body for days through the wilderness.

Let's just say the United States government had a bit to learn about how to run the world's first national park. Still does, but it's getting better. For 125 years the National Park Service has been directing traffic at this complex intersection of wilderness and tourism, juggling the protection of powerful natural wonders while allowing for civilized comforts. And if anyone complains that the roads are potholed or the coffee is cold . . . well, George Cowan would *not* be sympathetic.

Yellowstone was never known as a hospitable place. Nomadic Indian bands crossed the plateau, but never settled there, except for a small group of Shoshone known as "Sheepeaters." The first non-Indian to lay eyes on Yellowstone's geothermal wonders was probably John Colter, an explorer who broke away from the Lewis and Clark expedition in 1806 and spent 3 years wandering a surreal landscape of mud pots and mountains and geysers. When he described his discovery on his return to St. Louis, no one believed him, and he settled down to life as a farmer. While he raised wheat, miners and fur trappers followed in his footsteps, reducing the plentiful beaver of the region to almost nothing, and occasionally making curious reports of a sulfurous world still sometimes called "Colter's Hell."

The first significant exploration of what would become the park took place in 1869, when a band of Montanans led by David Folsom completed a 36-day expedition. Folsom and his group traveled up the Missouri River, then into the heart of the park, where they discovered the falls of the Yellowstone, mud pots, Yellowstone Lake, and the Fountain Geyser. But it was an 1871 expedition led by the director of the U.S. Geological Survey, Ferdinand Hayden, that brought back convincing evidence of Yellowstone's wonders, in the form of astonishing photographs by William H. Jackson and drawings by famed western artist Thomas Moran.

Crude hot tubs and "hotels" went up near the hot springs. A debate soon followed over the potential for commercial development and exploitation of the region. Meanwhile, the powers that be also entertained the idea of creating a national park. Many people take credit for this brilliant idea—members of the Folsom party later told a story about thinking it up around a campfire in the Upper Geyser Basin. In any case, the idea caught on as Yellowstone explorers hit the lecture circuit back East. In March 1872, President Ulysses S. Grant signed legislation declaring Yellowstone a national park.

No one had any experience in managing a wilderness park, and many mistakes were made: inept superintendents granted favorable leases to friends with commercial interests in the tourism industry; poachers ran amuck, and the wildlife population was decimated; a laundry business near Mammoth cleaned linens in the hot pool.

By 1886, things were so bad that the Army took control of the park; their firm-fisted management practices resulted in new order and protected the park from those intent upon exploiting it, although the military participated in the eradication of the plateau's wolf population. By 1916, efforts to make the park more visitor-friendly began to bear fruit: Construction of the first roads had been completed, guest housing was available in the area, and order had been restored. Stewardship of the park was then transferred to the newly created National Park Service.

THE PARK TODAY

The job of the National Park Service will never be easy in Yellowstone, where rangers must preserve a natural environment for a wide range of species, including one very demanding creature, the human being. Tourists come from around the world to visit Yellowstone, some with high expectations of creature comforts in the wilderness.

It's challenge enough to provide an unimpaired view of the wildlife, scenery, and thermal features of the park to three million visitors a year. It's even harder to ameliorate the environmental impact of all those feet trodding through the forests, meadows, thermal areas, and wildlife habitat. A number of issues are being debated today that should be the concern of everyone who appreciates Yellowstone: The reintroduction of wolves, their protection, and their impact on livestock around the park; the invasion of Yellowstone Lake by man-introduced species such as Mackinaw trout; the crush of automobile—and now snowmobile—traffic on the roads of this "wilderness"; the "privatization" of park operations like campgrounds, with resulting fees for services; and the diminishing store of undeveloped land around the park, which provides a cushion for Yellowstone's wildlife populations.

The Park Service is determined that the laws of nature should remain unaffected by human intrusion; that's why firefighters let the 1988 fire burn until fears arose about the loss of park buildings and human lives. A similar situation may develop with the wildlife population, which is protected within the park but not without, and therefore has overpopulated certain areas. Herds of elk, deer, and bison have ballooned in size, raising questions about the ecosystem's ability to provide sufficient food; some say the reintroduction of wolves and the rebounding bear population may solve the problem naturally.

Yellowstone's bison herd has grown to more than 3,000 critters in recent years. During winter months, when there's a shortage of food, the shaggy beasts roam beyond park boundaries. Some of the bison carry brucellosis, a virus that, when transmitted to cattle, causes cows to abort fetuses. Though there is no hard evidence of bison-to-cattle transmission, Montana ranchers have successfully demanded that bison that wander north out of the park should be destroyed. Animal rights groups have criticized the shooting of bison—which make no attempt to avoid hunters—as senseless slaughter.

Ranchers have other reasons to fear wolves. For half a century, ranchers around Yellowstone have had nothing to fear from wolves. But when Canadian grey wolves were transplanted to the park's northeast corner in 1995, the move proved astonishingly successful: The wolves reproduced rapidly and immediately began enlarging their range, breaking into new packs and roaming beyond the park boundaries. A few developed a taste for calves and lambs. Lawsuits began to fly, and a federal judge in Wyoming ruled in 1998 that all reintroduced wolves should be removed, on the novel grounds that they were a threat to pre-existing wolf populations (which few people, including the judge, believed existed). The litigation rolls on, and the wolf population continues to grow. At the heart of this fight is a debate over what sort of economy and what sort of culture will shape the Northern Rockies of the future.

Then there are the snowmobilers. They come from the flatlands, singing praises for the fine trail system in and around the park. Long lines at the gates cough exhaust and then roar into the park from December through February. Gateway towns say it boosts their economies in the moribund winter. But the park is developing new plans that may change the way snowmobilers use the park—there's a proposal to keep the road from West Yellowstone to Old Faithful open to cars all winter, for instance. There may be restrictions on engine noise and emissions.

There are summer traffic problems, too, particularly involving house-sized motor homes and trailers navigating the narrow, twisting park roads. They create traffic jams, and force bicyclists off the road. Along with cars, they interrupt the passage of wildlife like bison and elk. Traffic studies suggest the problem will worsen, and the government has shown little inclination to apply its budget surpluses to fixing Yellowstone's beaten up roads.

Wildlife & Where to Spot It

Biologists consider Yellowstone one of the most important wildlife habitats in the world, from the dramatic beauty of the bald eagle or grizzly bear to the less publicized but more unique reptiles and insects of its thermal areas. What particularly distinguishes this collection of wildlife is that the giant herds of elk, the thousands of bison, and all their brethren are free-roaming. Grizzly bears and wolves in the wild are a rarity now in the Lower 48.

Some claim the **bison** (buffalo) that once blanketed the Great Plains were only driven to the Yellowstone Plateau when they were hunted off the plains. Regardless, this herd acts like it's right at home here, wandering along the Yellowstone's main thoroughfares without much regard for the human spectators. They are the largest animals in the park, carrying as much as 2,000 pounds on ballerina-thin ankles. They are easy to view in the summer months, often seen munching grass and rolling in dust pits in **Hayden Valley, Pelican Valley, the Bechler River area,** and in the geyser areas **near the Firehole River.** *A caution:* Keep your distance from these behemoths. Never assume the slow-moving bison are docile; they have poor eyesight and cranky dispositions, and, like moose, they can move with sudden speed to inflict serious injuries on anyone who enters their personal space.

Even biologists have trouble agreeing on how many **bears** there are in Yellowstone, but most will acknowledge that the numbers of the shy bruins are on the rise. I have my own evidence: For the first 10 years I lived in Wyoming, I took several trips into Yellowstone backcountry and never saw a bear, though I saw the marks they left; in the last 5 years, I've seen grizzly bears every year, sometimes along well-traveled roads. In the Yellowstone Ecosystem there are probably 1,000 black bears and at least 500 grizzly bears.

Decades ago, bears used to entertain guests at Yellowstone lodges who sat on bleachers while the bruins foraged in open pit garbage dumps; or the guests hand-fed bears who begged along the park roads. When the dumps were closed in the 1970s and bear-feeding was prohibited, the population of bears plummeted. Diminishing habitat around the park also had an impact. But bears are creative omnivores, and they've found new food sources in the wild; I've also seen them take advantage of wolf kills in the Lamar Valley.

Black bears are most commonly sighted in the spring, sometimes with cubs, in the Canyon–Tower and Madison–Old Faithful areas, where they feed on green grass and herbs, berries, ants, and carrion. The grizzly is their larger, more aggressive cousin, whose unpredictable behavior makes them the likely suspect in the rare instances of bear attacks on humans. Rangers closely monitor their movements during late spring in areas near trout spawning streams and carrion sites to minimize the possibility of an encounter.

Odds of seeing a griz are best during May and June, in the Lamar Valley, Hayden Valley, and the Geyser area, before they retreat into the backwoods for the summer. Backcountry travelers often see bears in the Thorofare Country on the park's southeast border, one of the most remote wilderness areas in the Lower 48, where bears (and avid anglers) journey to the Yellowstone River headwaters for the spring cutthroat trout spawning run.

It is estimated that 63,000 **elk** (wapiti) populate the ecosystem, with about half of them summering in the park—too many for the park's northern meadows, biologists say. You should have no problem telling elk from deer or antelope by their size (typically 900 pounds), the males' large antler racks, and chestnut brown heads and necks, with a distinctive tan patch on their rumps. One herd can usually be located around **Mammoth Hot Springs,** often on the lawn of the main square; others are often seen in the meadows between Old Faithful and Madison Junction.

During winter months the northern Yellowstone herd heads to a winter grazing area near Gardiner. Listen in the fall for the distinctive bugling of the males, a throaty gargle that slips into a piercing high whistle.

Moose are more solitary than elk; they're grumpy loners, and not very patient with the tourists that flock around whenever they appear. Those appearances are usually in alder thickets and marshes around streams, particularly around Canyon and near Jackson Lake Lodge in Grand Teton National Park. They are recognizable by their dark coats, massive antlers, pendulous muzzle, and the fleshy dewlap that hangs beneath its neck like a bell. A moose is capable of traveling at 30 m.p.h.; cows will charge any perceived threat to a calf, and bulls become particularly ornery in the fall. Give them a wide berth.

The **pronghorn,** usually called an antelope, is often sighted grazing near the northern entrance to Yellowstone. These fleet and flighty animals have excellent vision, and they'll take off at 40 mph when photographers try to get near. You might have better luck in the fall, when lonely males wander stoically by themselves. The pronghorn is identified by its short, black horns, tan-and-white body, and black accent stripes.

Not to be outnumbered by their larger cousins, thousands of **mule deer** live within park boundaries. Most often spotted near forest boundaries or in areas covered with grass and sagebrush, the "mulies'" most distinguishing characteristics are their huge ears and a black tip on their tail that contrasts their white rump. Fawns, often in pairs, are typically born in late spring.

For a long time, the **coyote** has been the predator most often spotted by park visitors, but the arrival of wolves has taken its toll on the smaller canine. Coyotes may be seen alone or in small packs—they're particularly visible in winter—with brown to gray coats that grow silvery after the snow falls. Coyotes dig elaborate burrows, where they raise their young and bring their prey—small animals like squirrel and rabbit, larger ungulates like elk and deer that have grown old or ill. They often take on the cringing posture of a beaten dog as they pick over the leftovers of other predators. Biologists estimate there are around 500 coyotes in the park. You'll see them out in the open meadows of the **Hayden Valley,** and you might get lucky and see the interaction between wolves and coyotes in places like **Slough Creek.**

Grey wolves from Canada were reintroduced to the park in 1995, and while many have been killed or relocated, it appears they're here to stay, feasting on the huge elk herd at the northern end of the park. There are more than 100 wolves in the ecosystem today, and they've wandered far to establish new territories, appearing around Jackson to the south and far north into Montana. The **Lamar Valley** is where they were first released, and patient observers at dawn and dusk can sometimes see the Soda Butte Pack along the river or the Rose Creek Pack on the slopes above Slough Creek. Look for ranger Rick McIntyre—he's there most of the summer among the spotting scopes of wolf-watchers in the valley—and ask for his advice, or check at the east gate or Mammoth Visitors Center for the best sighting opportunities.

Alternatives are on the drawing boards—there has even been talk of a park monorail—and it won't be long before Yellowstone follows parks like Yosemite and Grand Canyon with serious proposals to fix the present mess.

"Privatization" has been a watchword since the Reagan era, and increasingly the parks are allowing concessionaires to take over management duties, such as campground management, in order to put private dollars to work where federal funds once did the job. Critics fear that this leads to profit-driven decisions—certainly the expansion of winter activities has made more economic than environmental sense. On the other hand, the beautiful new Old Faithful Snow Lodge is a vast improvement, thanks to Yellowstone Park Lodges. Another effort to raise needed revenues has been the steady increase in entrance and user fees. A good portion of the entrance fee will be funneled back to the park for building maintenance, salaries, roads, and other infrastructure needs.

With the federal budget coming out of the red, and the concessionaires showing some sensitivity to the park's special qualities, things are looking up. But those of us who use the park should take an active interest in the debate over park policies, and make our voices heard.

PLANT LIFE OF THE PARK

The large mammals are the big stars in Yellowstone, but the quieter crowd of flower-lovers will find plenty to enjoy here, too. Flowers and shrubs broadcast bright shades of blues, purples, yellows, and oranges throughout both parks, providing a colorful accent to the forests and meadows.

The volcanic, fire, and glacial events on the plateau have created a tumultuous history of change with an enormous impact on plant life. Plant fossils have been found dating back to the Eocene Epoch, approximately 58 million years ago. At one site in the Lamar Valley, the inspection of petrified tree stumps exhumed by erosion resulted in the identification of 27 distinct layers of forests, one atop the other.

And the plants have evolved with the ever-changing Yellowstone environment. These days the elevation ranges from 5,000 to 13,000 feet, the average low temperature is approximately 30°F, and hundreds of inches of snow fall each year. Plants have adapted to a growing season that in some areas is a mere 60 days in duration. As a consequence, forests once populated with hardwood, like maple, magnolia, and sycamore, are now filled with conifers, the most common of which are pine, spruce, and fir. A smattering of cottonwood and aspen thrive in the cool park temperatures.

Vegetation zones tend to reflect altitude: lower-elevation valleys tend to be dry and grassy, with sagebrush and few trees; forests of fir dominate between about 6,000 and 7,500 feet, followed by lodgepole pine stands and then spruce and more fir up to timberline, with open meadows where wildflowers explode in the spring (remember that spring comes very late here); at high elevations shrubs and carpetlike vegetation take over, and you have to lean over to examine the tiny blossoms.

Attempts by park officials to manage the ecosystem have had an impact, too. Climax forests—a plant succession leading to conifers that create a shady canopy and block the growth of seedlings—had a prolonged reign in Yellowstone because of fire suppression, which contributed to the ferocity of fires in the dry summer of 1988.

4 Seeing the Highlights

Plan carefully, and be patient: this is a wonderland you can return to again and again, sampling a different pleasure each time. All the sites mentioned here are easily accessible along the loop tours detailed in section 5, "Driving the Park." The further you

Hot Spring Hot Spot

Once upon a time, travelers in Yellowstone bathed and did their laundry in the hot springs, but that's not allowed anymore. But there is a spot along the road to the North Entrance, where hot springs run into the Gardiner River and create a series of temperature-graded pools where the public is allowed to take a dip. This stretch of "Boiling River" used to be a late-night skinny-dipping secret, but we can't do that anymore—there's a parking lot, gate, and posted hours. It's still a relaxing way to cap off a day of touring and hiking.

get from the pavement, and the further from July and August you schedule your visit, the more private your experience will be.

You could arrange this list in many different ways. By species, for instance: Where to go for wildflowers, for birds, for bison or wolves. Or by thermal areas, which is certainly the biggest lure for park visits. Or by geology, since the park is a wonderful potpourri of rock and extruding geological eras. But since this list is a variety pack of attractions, I've organized it geographically, following the roadways that form a figure-8 at the heart of the park. We'll begin in the north, then move south, first along the east side, then the west. Get out the oversized map you receive at the gate or by mail, and follow along:

MAMMOTH HOT SPRINGS

At the park's north entrance, 5 miles south of Gardiner, Mammoth Hot Springs is home to spectacular limestone terraces, historic park buildings, and the Mammoth Hot Springs Hotel. It's one of the older park settlements, with stone buildings dating back to the late 19th century, when the army was stationed here at Fort Yellowstone.

There are no geysers at **Mammoth Hot Springs Terraces,** but these stair-stepping hillside hot pools, among the oldest in the park, offer a boardwalk tour of gorgeous pastels in shades of white, yellow, orange, and green created by microscopic bacteria fixed in the sediments. The mineral-rich springs constantly bubble to the surface, depositing travertine as the water cools in contact with the air. It's a vivid illustration of the park's unusual geological situation: a rare geologic hot spot of seismic activity in the middle of the continent, where molten rock still rises close to the earth's surface.

Whether or not you spend the night at the **Mammoth Hot Springs Hotel**—not the most distinguished lodging in the park, but it has historic character—you should drop by the **Albright Visitor Center.** This building once housed Fort Yellowstone's bachelor officers, but you won't find a pool table here today; rather, you'll find displays on park history, wildlife and photography exhibits, smiling rangers dispensing advice, and numerous park publications and maps. A film, *The Challenge of Yellowstone,* is shown throughout the day. A special treat for foreign visitors is the opportunity to get their visas stamped with the official Yellowstone National Park document stamp. For more information call ☎ **307/344-2263.**

TOWER–ROOSEVELT AREA

East of Mammoth Hot Springs you enter a delicious mix of high plains, deep forest, and twisting rivers. Toward the northeast corner lies one of the most beautiful and serene valleys in the Rockies, the **Lamar.** This glacier-carved swath of grassy bottom and forested flanks sits apart from the vehicular chaos at the center of the park; the traffic here is not automobiles but bison, wolves, and elk. If you continue all the way

Petrified Wood

With so many hot pots, mountain peaks, geysers, and bison to gawk at, it's not too surprising that many visitors to Yellowstone fail to realize the park encloses some of the finest examples of petrified forest found anywhere. The trees were preserved, scientists believe, when their organic matter was replaced by volcanic material during one of the many eruptions on the plateau. Some of the tree trunks still stand, particularly in the Specimen Ridge area in the northeast area of the park, and they clearly grew during warmer, swampier days: sycamore, magnolias, and dogwoods are preserved in stone. Check at the Tower Ranger Station for maps showing you where to find petrified wood. This is not a renewable resource: Don't touch or take.

through to the park's northeast entrance, you'll be heading up to the spectacular views of the **Beartooth Highway.**

The area around the Tower–Roosevelt Junction was once a favorite spot of the rough-riding turn-of-the-century U.S. president, Teddy Roosevelt. At **Roosevelt Lodge** visitors can enjoy the kind of simple accommodations the Bull Moose himself liked, with the rustic flavor of the Old West. This is the most relaxed of the park's villages, and a great place to take a break from the more crowded attractions. Get into the cowboy spirit by taking a **guided trail ride,** a **stagecoach ride,** or a **wagon ride.** You can skip the dining room and ride out for an **Old West cookout,** served from a chuck wagon to patrons who arrive by either horseback or wagon. The nearby 132-foot **Tower Falls** is named for the towerlike volcanic pinnacles at its brink and provides an excellent photo opportunity. While in the area, take time to view the petrified forests on **Specimen Ridge,** where a wide variety of fossilized plants and trees date back millions of years. All things considered, Roosevelt is a great place to escape the hordes.

Further south, **Pelican and Hayden Valleys** are the two most prominent remnants of large, ancient lake beds in the park. They are now open meadows in the subalpine zone, so plant life thrives here, providing feed for a population of bison and elk. You might see a bear here, too.

THE GRAND CANYON OF YELLOWSTONE

Hayden Valley flanks the featured attraction of the park's center: the **Grand Canyon of the Yellowstone River,** a colorful, 1,000-foot-deep, 24-mile-long gorge that some can't resist comparing to its larger counterpart in Arizona. Okay, then: this canyon is greener, the water clearer, the air cooler, and it has two dramatic waterfalls, the big one taller than Niagara. As it drops through this gorge, the Yellowstone River in some places moves at 64,000 cubic feet of water per second.

Volcanic explosions and glaciers surging and receding shaped the canyon. The geological story is told in the canyon itself, where hard lava flows formed the lip of the falls and softer rhyolites allowed the river to cut deeply through soft rock of red, orange, tan, and brown hue. Plumes of steam pinpoint vents along the canyon's rock spires, where viewing opportunities are extensive and varied. There are many hikes along and down into the canyon, which is 24 miles long and up to 1,200 feet deep, and you'll be surprised at how few people you encounter away from the parking areas. Many do, though, trek down to the **Brink of the Lower Falls, Uncle Tom's Trail** from the South Rim, and the **Brink of the Upper Falls,** with good reason: breathtaking views. Two other favorite trails are **Inspiration Point** and **Artist Point;** both are handicapped-accessible.

Canyon Village has a sprawling 1950s look, which puts off some visitors. It's also crowded, but you can find many useful services there, and some of the newer lodging is an improvement.

NORRIS GEYSER BASIN

If you travel south from Mammoth on the *west* side of the park, you climb up into Gardiner Hole and pass some interesting rock formations, **Obsidian Cliff** and **Roaring Mountain,** before coming to **Norris Geyser Basin.** Norris is not nearly as famous as the Mammoth terraces or the crowd of geysers around Old Faithful, but there's a lot going on here, from the steaming pools of the **Porcelain Basin** to the eruptions of **Echinus Geyser.** If you're the patient type, you can sit by the blowhole of Steamboat Geyser and hope that this largest of park geysers will erupt . . . be prepared to wait anywhere from 10 minutes to 10 years (last eruption was in 1991!). This is one of the hottest, most active thermal areas on the plateau, at the intersection of three faults in the earth's crust; when they shift, they change the face of the basin, with new geysers popping up and old ones disappearing. The **Norris Geyser Basin Museum** explains geothermal features, and the **Museum of the National Park Ranger** tracks the history of the park's stewards.

OLD FAITHFUL

About a quarter of the world's geysers are crowded into the hills and valleys around Old Faithful, where the hot pools and spouts are divided into three areas, **Lower, Midway,** and **Upper Geyser Basins**. Driving, walking the boardwalks, and even sitting on the crowded benches around Old Faithful, you have to be awestruck. You'll find flatulent mud pots, brilliantly colored pools like **Chromatic Spring,** and geysers with a variety of tricks, from the angled shots of **Daisy Geyser** to the witches' cauldron of **Crested Pool.**

But the grand old dame of geysers, the star of the show, is **Old Faithful.** Over the last 100 years, its eruptions have been remarkably consistent, blowing 21 to 23 times daily with a column averaging about 134 feet and a duration of about 40 seconds. But Old Faithful is part of a dynamic system, subject like the rest of Yellowstone to change. Recent seismic activity has lengthened the intervals between eruptions in recent years. Now estimates posted at the visitor centers are give-or-take 10 minutes; if the last eruption was a long one, you can wait as long as 80 minutes for the next burst. Scientists have measured the geyser's output: from 4,000 to 8,000 gallons of water flies out each time.

Since the geyser is one of the key park attractions, the **Old Faithful Visitor Center** (☎ 307/545-2750) is larger, and has a larger staff, than most of its counterparts. An excellent film describing the geysers, *Yellowstone, A Living Sculpture,* is shown throughout the day in an air-conditioned auditorium—quite a relief on hot July afternoons. Various park publications, up-to-date geyser predictions, and an informative seismographic exhibit are added attractions.

A National Historic Landmark, the shingled, steep-roofed **Old Faithful Inn** was built of local stone and hand-hewn timber, including interior balconies that you can climb several stories above the lobby floor. I happened to be there as a reporter in 1988 when raging forest fires almost reached the building; that was the turning point when park managers abandoned their "let it burn" policy and began fighting the fires. Long-time village employees may be willing to share with you stories of the inn's reported "haunting"!

YELLOWSTONE LAKE

West of Old Faithful, over Craig Pass, or south of Canyon, through the wildlife-rich **Hayden Valley,** is gigantic **Yellowstone Lake,** another natural wonder unique to Yellowstone—it's 20 miles long and 14 miles wide and more than 300 feet deep in places. You would hardly guess, dipping in the frigid water, that the caldera underneath the lake is filling with hot liquid magma, actually tilting the lake northward at a measurable pace. The caldera is the sunken remainder of a huge volcanic blast 600,000 years ago, and another 600,000 years before that, and now that it's filling up . . . well, they say it's due to blow again any century now. Grizzlies work the tributary streams in the spring when fish spawn (some campgrounds are closed), and lots of other wildlife congregate here, including moose and osprey.

The lake has long been a favorite fishing spot, but recent regulations limit your take of large cutthroat trout. This is part of a desperate attempt by park biologists to help the cutthroat come back against a planted exotic fish, mackinaw or lake trout, which dine on small cutthroat. The new rules have discouraged fishermen, and there have been fewer boats on the lake in recent years. You'll see some big sailboats braving the quirky winds of the lake, and experienced paddlers may want to **kayak** or **canoe** into the **south and southeast arms** of the lake, which are closed to motorboats. These deep bays are true wilderness, and great areas to fish and view wildlife. When you pick up a permit, you'll also get a stern warning from rangers to watch out for the changeable weather if you get out on the lake's open water. They're right to urge caution; even the best paddlers risk their lives in a sudden afternoon storm. Also, keep an eye peeled for the rumored **Loch Ness-style monster** that is said to dwell beneath the placid lake surface.

Lake Village, on the north shore of the lake, offers a large range of amenities, including fine restaurants at either the rustic **Lake Lodge** or the majestic 100-year-old **Lake Yellowstone Hotel.** This hotel has Greek columns and a spacious sun room overlooking the lake where classical music is sometimes played; it's very different from the Old Faithful Inn, but a rival for its beauty and history. Just south of Lake Village is **Bridge Bay Marina,** the park's water activity center. Here you can obtain guided fishing trips, small boat rentals, and dock rentals; there's also a store and tackle shop.

WEST THUMB & GRANT VILLAGE

On the south end of the lake, at **West Thumb,** the boiling thermal features extend out into the lake. You can see steaming cones and swirling water created by the action of the underwater hot springs. **Fishing Cone** is rumored to be the place where fishermen used to hook trout and drop them, still on the line, into a hot pot for instant meal preparation. Don't try it—it's illegal to drop anything into a thermal feature. You can walk among the lakeshore pools at the **Central Basin** and look at the colorful thick fudge of the **Thumb Paint Pots.**

Grant Village, named for President Ulysses S. Grant, was completed in 1984 and is the newest of Yellowstone's villages. It has some of the most modern facilities in the park, and it's the least inspired—they should consider tearing it down and starting over, or letting the trees grow back. On the plus side, this area is a great vantage point for watching sunrises and afternoon squalls move across the lake, and you may see **otters** and **cutthroat trout** in the old marina's waters. The **Grant Visitor Center** houses an exhibit that explores the history of fires in Yellowstone.

5 Driving the Park

Yellowstone has approximately 370 miles of paved roads, and in recent years the park has struggled to catch up with a backlog of maintenance—filling potholes, widening

Winter Road Conditions

If you're not an old hand at driving in Wyoming or Montana winters, be cautious about a winter driving trip to Yellowstone. Icy roads and blinding snowstorms take their toll every year. The park itself is largely closed to automobiles in the winter—only the northern entrance is open to wheeled vehicles. The road through Lamar Valley to the northeast gate is kept open to get essential supplies to Cooke City, but from there you can go no farther north into Montana, because the Beartooth Highway is impassable in winter. The rest of the park's primary roads are open during the snowy months to snowcoaches and snowmobiles . . . and bison, which find the packed roads convenient and think nothing of lolling along with a line of frustrated snowmobilers waiting for a chance to pass. Cross-country skiers use trails around Old Faithful and at the northern end of the park. For up-to-the-minute information on weather and road conditions, call the **visitor information center** at ☎ **307/344-7381.**

shoulders, and redoing some roads completely. The wear and tear of heavy RVs and trailers undoes the work as quickly as it's done, and since road construction is limited to the warm months of summer, drivers often encounter delays somewhere along the park's roads. If you travel in July or August, you'll share these frustrations with a lot of other drivers, some of whom never think to look in the rear view mirror when they're trying to wedge their car onto the shoulder so they can gawk at some other gawkers who are presumably gawking at wildlife. But you can see a surprising number of interesting sights along the figure-8 roadways at the heart of the park. You can take in both north and south loops—**the Grand Loop**—in 1 day if a quick blink at each stop is enough for you. Better, though, to take your time, or explore different areas on different trips.

THE UPPER LOOP

The Upper Loop is the shorter of the two loop drives. It's a 70-mile affair that begins at the north entrance. You can drive it either way, but here's the order of sights if you start by going east from **Mammoth Hot Springs** and the park headquarters. You can orient yourself at the **Albright Visitors Center,** then take in the **Blacktail Plateau** or rustic **Roosevelt Lodge** (a good place for lunch); or take a side trip up the ✪ **Lamar Valley** for wildlife viewing at least as far as Slough Creek, **Tower Falls, Mount Washburn** (the highest point in the park), and up over **Dunraven Pass** overlooking the Mirror Plateau. Then head west from Canyon Junction to Norris Junction and north to the ✪ **Norris Geyser Basin,** with pastel pools and a few burbles and spouts, and its fine museum. You'll continue north past **Roaring Mountain** (a travertine cascade by the road, get out only if you have time) and **Obsidian Cliff** (same advice), and then have dinner in the dining room at the historic Mammoth.

You could include the ✪ **Grand Canyon of the Yellowstone** on this Upper Loop tour, though it's a short ways south of Canyon Village, where the loop runs west to Norris. If you're only doing the Upper Loop on this trip, you owe it to yourself to include the canyon.

THE LOWER LOOP

The longer **Lower Loop** covers some of the more famous park landmarks in its 96-mile circuit. Beginning at the south entrance, you would join the loop at the **West Thumb** of Yellowstone Lake, where there are hot springs and mud pots. From here you can begin the loop in either direction, but my description will go east first. The loop skirts the west shore of **Yellowstone Lake** to the handsome **Lake Hotel** at the north end, where the Yellowstone River outlet is spanned by **Fishing Bridge.** The route then encompasses the **Grand Canyon of the Yellowstone, Madison Junction** and the **Firehole Canyon Drive,** the **Lower Geyser Basin** and the **Fountain Paintpots,** the **Midway Geyser Basin,** and the **Upper Geyser Basin** and stalwart **Old Faithful,** where you can top off the day with a meal at historic **Old Faithful Inn.** Then head east over **Craig Pass** to the lake again.

Put the two loops together and you've done the Grand Loop of approximately 166 miles. At its conclusion, you will have seen most of the major attractions in the park.

OUT OF THE LOOPS: ENTRANCES & OTHER DETOURS

Rapturous descriptions of the **Lamar Valley** elsewhere in this guide should encourage you to take a run out of the park's **northeast entrance** (your pass will get you back in the park at no extra cost). The valley is wide and beautiful, with elk and bison grazing by the river, and coyotes, wolves, and grizzly bears making guest appearances. Beyond the park gate you'll find Cooke City, a friendly little town, and then a switchback climb north on the Beartooth Highway, with its spectacular views.

Roads to the other entrances also have allure. If you **head east along the north shore of Yellowstone Lake,** you'll begin climbing into **Sylvan Pass,** the 8,530-foot exit route that will take you through the east gate into the beautiful Wapiti Valley and eventually to the town of **Cody** (see chapter 12 for more on Cody). The north and east shores of the lake have some large-grain beaches where you can sun and swim, or begin a paddling journey to the remote southern corners of the lake. The **south entrance road** skirts **Lewis Lake** and follows the **Gardiner River,** where you'll often see the graceful parabolas of fly-fishing lines at work. You'll also see some of the more severely burned areas from the 1988 fires. Similarly, areas along the **west entrance road** are still marked by the burnt husks of trees, which have a surprising beauty; there are also peaceful views of the **Madison River** along this road.

There are also some trips off the main roads that are worth taking. Try the short **Firehole Canyon Drive** (just south of Madison Junction—there's a one-way loop that goes west)—there's a spring-warmed swimming area on the river here. Drive a short ways into **Slough Creek** in the Lamar Valley in the early morning or late afternoon for a chance at sighting wolves. Drive across the Yellowstone River just south of Canyon Village and drive or hike along the **South Rim.** Drive to the **Mount Washburn** picnic area off Dunraven Pass, and if you're feeling energetic, hike to the top of the 10,243-foot peak.

6 Summer Sports & Activities

BICYCLING

Considering the vast expanse of real estate the parks cover, the challenging terrain, and the miles of paved roads and trails, a cyclist could conclude that the parks are prime areas for biking, on or off the roads.

It looks good on paper, but the reality is more harrowing. The roads are narrow and twisty; there are no bike lanes, so bikers continually fight for elbow room with wide-bodied RVs and trailers, some of which have side-view mirrors that seem designed to decapitate bicyclists. Off-road opportunities are limited because bikes are only allowed on a small number of trails.

Nevertheless, plenty of bicyclists take the challenge. The following trails are available to bikers, but know that you will share the roads with hikers. The **Mount Washburn Trail,** leaving from the Old Chittenden Road, is a strenuous trail that climbs

1,400 feet. The **Lone Star Geyser Trail,** accessed at Kepler Cascade near Old Faithful, is an easy 1-hour ride on a user-friendly road. Near Mammoth Hot Springs, **Bunsen Peak Road** and **Osprey Falls Trails** present a combination ride/hike: The first 6 miles travel around Bunsen Peak; getting to the top requires a hike. A hike down to Osprey Falls adds 3 miles to the journey.

Bike rentals are available in West Yellowstone at **Yellowstone Bicycles** (☎ 406/646-7815) and in Jackson at **Hoback Sports** (☎ 307/733-5335) or **The Edge Sports,** 490 W. Broadway (☎ 307/734-3916).

BOATING

The best place to enjoy boating in Yellowstone is on **Yellowstone Lake,** which has easy access and beautiful, panoramic views. The lake is also one of the few areas where powerboats are allowed; rowboats and outboard motorboats can be rented at **Bridge Bay Marina** (☎ 307/344-7381). Motorboats, canoes, and kayaks can be used on Lewis Lake (about 15 miles north of the south entrance), as well.

FISHING

There are two primary types of anglers in Yellowstone. First are the fly casters, who wade the rivers and trace delicate parabolas in the air, more interested in the artistry and seduction of fly-fishing than in keeping what they catch. There are stretches of the Yellowstone and Madison Rivers where the anglers are packed tippet to tippet and the trout must be punch drunk from catch-and-release.

Then there are the powerboat fishermen who troll the deep waters of Yellowstone Lake. Seven varieties of gamefish live in the parks: native cutthroat, rainbow, brown, brook and lake trout, grayling, and mountain whitefish. Of the trout, only the cutthroat are native, and they are being pressured in the big lake by the larger lake trout, despite efforts to remove the exotic strains by gill-netting. As a result, you can't keep any pink-meat cutthroat caught in Yellowstone Lake; and you *must* keep any lake trout. These limits seem to have diminished the number of fishing boats on Yellowstone Lake in recent years, but they're necessary.

The Yellowstone fishing season typically opens on the Saturday of Memorial Day weekend and ends on the first Sunday in November, except for Yellowstone Lake, which has a slightly shorter season, and the lake's tributaries, which are closed until July 15 to avoid conflicts between humans and grizzly bears, both of which are attracted to spawning trout.

The **required Yellowstone fishing permit** is available at any ranger station, visitor center, or Hamilton Store in the park. Anyone older than 15 needs a fishing permit, which costs $10 for 10 days or $20 for the season. Ages 12 to 15 need a permit, but it's free. Casters under 12 must be supervised by an adult. Season permits can be obtained by mail; write to: Visitors Services, P.O. Box 168, Yellowstone National Park, WY 82190.

In June, one of the best fishing spots is on the **Yellowstone River** downstream of Yellowstone Lake, where the cutthroat trout spawn; anglers head to **Madison River** near the west entrance in July and then again in late fall for rainbow and some brown trout; in late summer, the **Lamar River** in the park's beautiful northeast corner is a popular spot to hook cutthroats in September.

Fishing on **Yellowstone Lake** had been popular until recent years, when regulations designed to bring back the waning population of cutthroat trout have sent some of the trolling powerboats elsewhere. The problem is lake trout, introduced by some "bucket biologist," which compete with and eat the cutthroat. If you catch a lake trout, you *must* kill it, and if you catch a large cutthroat, you *must* throw it back. Certain areas of the lake, like the southeast arm, are closed to motorized boats—this makes it a wonderful area to canoe, camp, and fish at the Yellowstone River inlet.

You can fish the **Yellowstone River** below the Grand Canyon by hiking down into **Seven Mile Hole,** a great place to cast (not much vegetation to snag on) for cutthroat trout from July to September, with the best luck around Sulphur Creek.

Other good fishing stretches include the **Gibbon** and **Firehole** Rivers, which merge to form the Madison River on the park's west side, and the three-mile **Lewis River Channel** between Shoshone and Lewis lakes during the fall spawning run of brown trout.

There is an access for anglers with disabilities at the **Madison River,** 3.5 miles west of Madison Junction at the Haynes Overlook. Here you'll find a fishing platform overhanging the river's edge for 70 feet.

HORSEBACK & LLAMA RIDING

People who want to pack their gear on a horse, llama, or mule must get permits to enter the Yellowstone backcountry, or hire an outfitter with a permit (see below). Other visitors who want to get in the saddle but not disappear in the wilderness can put themselves in the hands of the concessionaire, Yellowstone Park Lodges. Stables are located at Canyon Village, Roosevelt Lodge, and Mammoth Hot Springs. Roosevelt Lodge also offers **evening rides** from June into September. Choices are 1- and 2-hour guided trail rides daily aboard well-broken, tame animals.

If you're looking for a longer, overnight horsepacking experience, contact the park and request a list of approved concessionaires that lead backcountry expeditions. Most offer customized, guided trips, with meals, horses, and camping and riding gear provided. Costs will run from $200 to $400 per day per person, depending on the length of the trip and number of people. In Gardiner, at the north entrance to the park, **Wilderness Connection Inc.** (☎ 406/848-7287) offers horseback trips in the park for groups of two to 10; coming from the south side of the park, try **Press Stephens, Outfitter** (☎ 307/455-2250). Rates begin at $200 per person, per day, and include customized, guided hikes and horseback trips, with meals and lodging in tents or nearby hostelries.

While not a horseback excursion per se, you might also try **Yellowstone Llamas** (☎ 406/586-6872). Beasts of burden carry the heavy gear, leaving you free to wander the trails. They typically cover 5 to 8 miles per day in the park, and serve gourmet meals at the end of the day. Cost is $160 per day, per person.

7 Winter Sports & Activities

Yellowstone's average snowfall of 4 feet every year provides the perfect backdrop for a multitude of winter activities. The north entrance remains open, so you can drive in from Gardiner for a day, and drive back out. You can travel throughout the park by snowmobile (you drive) or snowcoach (someone else does), and spend the night either at Mammoth or at the handsomely rebuilt Old Faithful Snow Lodge. For additional information on all of the following winter activities and accommodations, as well as snowcoach transportation and equipment rentals, contact **Yellowstone Park Lodges** (☎ 307/344-7311). There are also many activities, outfitters, and rental shops in the park's gateway towns.

CROSS-COUNTRY SKIING

The best **cross-country trails** in Yellowstone are: the **Lone Star Geyser Trail,** an 8-mile trail in a remote setting that starts at the Old Faithful Snow Lodge; and the

Fern Cascades Trail, which begins in the Old Faithful Housing area on the south side of the road and winds for 3 miles through a rolling woodland landscape. Energetic skiers can tackle the **Mallard Lake Trail,** though it may take them all day—it departs north of the Old Faithful Lodge area along the north side of the Upper Geyser Basin, then loops north and east to Mallard Lake and back to Old Faithful, 12 miles later.

Equipment rentals (about $12 per day), ski instruction, ski shuttles to various locations, and guided ski tours are all available at the **Old Faithful Snow Lodge** and the **Mammoth Hot Springs Hotel,** the park's two winter lodging options. Discounts are available for multiday rentals of skis or snowshoes. Ski instruction costs $17 per person for a 2-hour group lesson. A half-day guided excursion (two-person minimum) is around $32 per person; a full day is $69 per person. For groups of three or more, the cost is considerably lower: $21 per person for a half day, $48 per person for a full day.

The **Yellowstone Institute** (☎ 307/344-2294) offers winter courses based out of its headquarters at the old Buffalo Ranch in Lamar Valley. Past offerings have included 3-day classes devoted to "Backcountry by Ski," "Yellowstone's Winter World," and "Tracking Yellowstone's Wolves" (it's a howl watching instructor Jim Halfpenny get down on all-fours to demonstrate wolf gaits and "marking").

ICE SKATING

The **Mammoth Skating Rink** is located behind the old Mammoth Hot Springs Recreation Center. On a winter's night you can rent a pair of skates ($1 for an hour; $4 per day) and glide across the ice of this outdoor rink, while seasonal melodies are broadcast over the PA system. It's cold out there, but there's a warming fire at the rink's edge.

SNOWMOBILING

Roads that are jammed with cars during the summer fill up with bison and snowmobiles during the winter. In deference to the shaggier road warriors, moderate speed limits are strictly enforced, but this is still an excellent way to sightsee at your own pace (a driver's license is required for rental). The cost is $120 for a single rider, $135 per day for two at **Mammoth Hot Springs Hotel** or **Old Faithful Snow Lodge.** A quick lesson will put even a first-timer at ease. A helmet is included with the snowmobile, and you can rent a clothing package for protection against the bitter cold. **Warming huts** are located at Mammoth, Indian Creek, Canyon, Madison, West Thumb, and Fishing Bridge. They offer snacks, a hot cup of coffee or chocolate, and an excellent opportunity to recover from a chill. *A caution:* Keep an eye on snow conditions. While it's true that snowmobile trails are groomed for travel, when snow cover is scanty, a normally smooth trip can become something akin to riding on a jackhammer. Also, if engine noise is what you came to Yellowstone to escape, this is probably not for you.

Snowmobile rentals are also available in the **gateway communities** of Gardiner and West Yellowstone, Montana, and at Flagg Ranch (see section 1 of this chapter for recommended outfitters). Most rental shops accept reservations weeks in advance, so reserving at least 2 weeks ahead of time is a good idea. Plan on making reservations for the week between Christmas and New Year's at least 6 months in advance.

8 Hiking

Getting out of your car to view a "wildlife jam" is one way to enjoy the outdoors, but by taking even a short hike, you'll see a whole new side of the park. There are short hikes where you never lose sight of the road or a visitor center; there are moderate hikes where you might spend an afternoon penetrating the forest to visit a spot of secluded beauty; and there are overnight trips where you can hike and camp for days without seeing anyone but the people you brought with you.

My first backcountry trip in Yellowstone was in 1980, when we explored the park's southwest corner around Bechtel Falls and had the area to ourselves. A check 15 years later indicated visitation to that corner hadn't increased at all. So if you want a wilderness experience with privacy, abundant wildlife, hot springs, trout streams, and thrilling scenery, Yellowstone is in fact a wonderful choice.

Part of the reason so few people camp in the Yellowstone wilderness is fear of bears. Bear attacks are extremely rare, and usually involve a sow protecting her cubs, but you should carry pepper spray, just in case; when you camp, secure your food and cooking gear in a tree well away from tents. Park rangers can advise you on current bear activity and safe practices. This is true wilderness, but if you equip yourself properly and learn proper techniques, you'll be safer than you are on a city street. If you go into the backcountry, you need a permit (see "Where to Go & How to Reserve a Spot," below), which also ensures that someone knows where you are.

For those who would rather sleep in a bed, there are still excellent day hikes that allow you to escape the crowd, view wildlife in their own habitat, take in some scenery or climb a peak. Rangers at visitor centers can advise you on a hike to match your interests and abilities, and provide maps of the extensive trail system in the park.

Here is a small selection of good hikes, long and short. In addition to these individual hikes, the **Continental Divide Trail** links many of them together as part of a continuous trail from Mexico to Canada, roughly following the spine of the continent. The Yellowstone Backcountry Office maintains a guide to CDT trails. The Howard Eaton Trail system once went all through the park, but was supplanted by the Grand Loop Road. Sections of the old trail are still maintained and will be found in trail guides, though some of them closely parallel park roads. For a more extensive list of trails and details than what follows here, pick up Mark C. Marschall's excellent *Yellowstone Trails* (Yellowstone Association, $9.95), or the maps provided by the park.

HIKES AROUND MAMMOTH

The **Beaver Ponds Loop Trail** starts in Mammoth at Clematis Gulch (between Liberty Cap and an old stone Park Service residence) and makes a 5-mile loop to a series of beaver ponds, where your best chances of seeing the big-tailed beasts is early morning or afternoon. There are some good views coming and going, including Mount Everts. More ambitious hikers can link up with the **Sepulcher Mountain Trail,** which features a pleasing variety of scenery: hot springs, gardens of oddly shaped limestone boulders, and scenic views from the ridgetops of the Mammoth area. Be in shape for this one, because you'll cover about 12 miles.

Just across the road is the **Mount Bunsen Trail,** a short but steep trip to the summit of this volcanic remnant, with a 1,300-foot gain in elevation. Make the hike early and you can watch the morning sun strike Electric Mountain, which glows with a golden hue. The 2.1-mile trail passes through mosaic burns from the 1988 fires, and when you get to the top you'll have a view from 3,000 feet above the Yellowstone Valley. After topping the peak, you can take an alternative route down the back side to the Osprey Falls Trail (the falls would be another 3 miles of hiking), and come back along the Old Bunsen Peak Road Trail.

HIKES IN THE TOWER–CANYON AREA

It's almost too easy to get a view of **Tower Falls,** by hiking to an overlook only 100 yards from the Tower Falls parking area. Walk a half-mile more—including along some steep switchbacks—and you'll be at the base of the falls for a stunning, and less crowded, view. You can also hike 3.5 miles to the falls from Roosevelt Lodge, a good car-free choice if you happen to be staying there. Begin on the Lost Lake Trail and take a left when the trail forks a half mile from the lodge.

Just south of Canyon Village, the **Chittenden Bridge** crosses from the Loop Road to the South Rim Road near the top of the Grand Canyon of the Yellowstone. You can park and hike either the **South Rim** or **North Rim Trails,** with spurs that drop steeply (but briefly) down to viewing platforms at the Upper and Lower Falls. If you want a more complete and less crowded view of this deep gorge, take the **7-Mile Hole Trail** (which is actually 5.5 miles long) along the north canyon rim. You'll see the Silver Cord Cascade from the rim, and then drop down to the river after a couple of miles in an area where the canyon widens enough for trees. There are some active hot springs along this hike. This is quite a drop (1,400 feet), and hikers should remember that whatever goes down must come up.

Across the road from Uncle Tom's Parking Area (the first parking area to the left after crossing the bridge to the South Rim) is the trailhead for the **Clear Lake/Ribbon Lake Loop Trail.** The hike to Clear Lake is 1.5 miles, a gradual climb across a high plateau, and Ribbon Lake lies less than 2 miles beyond. There is bear activity in this area early in the year, so check with rangers for current conditions before heading out. Views of the plateau improve with each footstep until you find yourself surrounded by a panoramic view of the mountains surrounding the canyon area. During early and late spring it's a bit more difficult because snow runoff and rain can make trails wet and muddy, but that shouldn't be an impediment to anyone interested in the spectacular views. Clear Lake itself is intimately small, and gives you the opportunity to see subsurface activity of the thermal areas below the lake. On a circumnavigation of the lake along a trail, you will see—and smell—venting activity making its way to the surface; in some spots the lake looks like a small, boiling pot. This trail also connects to the **Howard Eaton Trail,** an arduous, 14-mile trail to Fishing Bridge and Yellowstone Lake.

The **Mount Washburn Trail** falls into the "if you can only do one hike, do this one" category. It's a short hike to panoramic views, with wildflowers decorating the way and nonchalant bighorn sheep often browsing nearby. Trailheads are located at the summit at Dunraven Pass (elevation 8,895 feet), and on Old Chittenden Road, where there's more parking available. Either hike is 6 miles round-trip with an increase in elevation of 1,400 feet; however, the climbs are fairly gradual and interspersed with long, level stretches. From the summit, the park will lie before you like a map on a table: You'll see the Absaroka Mountains to the east, Yellowstone Lake to the south, and the Gallatin Mountains to the west and north. In addition to the sheep, you may see marmots and red fox; for a few years, two grizzly bears were regulars rooting in a meadow across from the Dunraven Pass trailhead. You'll be climbing a summit more than 10,000 feet, so pace yourself, and bring a wind shell and warm clothing to fend off the wind that often buffets the top. The hike to the summit is an easy 90-minute walk at a steady pace, which can stretch to 2 hours if you take time for breaks. There's a warming hut in the base of the ranger lookout, with viewing telescopes and rest rooms.

HIKES NEAR OLD FAITHFUL

The popular trail to **Lonestar Geyser** covers a little more than 2 miles of mostly level terrain to the geyser, which rewards visitors with eruptions up to 50 feet tall every 3 hours. The trail follows the Firehole River, with a forest canopy to keep it cool in the summer, widening now and then into broad riverbank meadows. The geyser

---

An Old Faithful Secret

For a spectacular view of Old Faithful from above, take the Observation Point Look Trail, a 2-mile jaunt (beginning at the Old Faithful Visitor Center) that will take you by numerous thermal features on the other side of the Firehole River. Follow the Geyser Hill Trail across the river and then climb the switchbacks to the observation point, then down to Solitary Geyser and back to the Geyser Hill Trail.

---

erupts from a brown cone about 12 feet high, and is surrounded by a meadow pocked by steam vents and thermal features. The path begins from a parking lot on the Old Faithful–West Thumb road just south of the Kepler Cascades. It's partially paved to the geyser and open to bicyclists—this will not be a solitary journey. If you want to try a less busy (and less scenic) route, take the **Howard Eaton Trail** just east of the Old Faithful overpass, 3 miles to the geyser. From the geyser, you can continue on— bicycles can't—over Grants Pass to join the Bechler River Trail to Shoshone Lake. In the winter, skiers and snowmobilers visit the geyser.

From Biscuit Basin you can take a fine 3-mile round-trip hike to **Mystic Falls,** which falls 100 feet to the Firehole River. Continue up switchbacks to the top of the falls and beyond, and you'll link up with the **Little Firehole Meadows Trail** to return to Biscuit Basin, with more views on the way. You can make this trip in less than 2 hours, with only a 460-foot elevation gain.

Fairy Falls plummets a more impressive 200 feet, and can be reached by hiking 2.5 miles on the Fairy Falls Trail, which begins from the Old Faithful-Madison road just south of the Midway Geyser Basin parking area. Hikers who don't mind a slightly longer haul (about 7 miles round-trip) will be rewarded with better wildlife-viewing opportunities by starting from the **Imperial Meadows** trailhead 1 mile south of the Firehole River bridge on Fountain Flat Drive. The hike winds through an area populated by elk along Fairy Creek, then past the Imperial Geyser, where it joins the Fairy Creek Trail and travels east to the base of the falls. The total gain in elevation is only 100 feet. If you turn west instead, you'll find an unmarked trail north to the Imperial Geyser.

HIKES NEAR YELLOWSTONE LAKE

At the north end of the lake, the **Pelican Valley Trail** takes a loop north of the lake around an area loaded with elk, bison, sandhill cranes, trout, eagles, grizzlies, and the new kids on the block, wolves. You can take hikes of different length, up to a 16-mile loop, but a lot of folks, having had their fill of wildflowers and beasts, go no farther than Pelican Creek Bridge, about 3.5 miles in. If you continue on, you'll pass through forest and "bear meadows," where you should be watchful and respectful of wildlife— I once had to make a huge detour around a bison who kept moving up the trail where I wanted to go. This is a daytime-only hiking area, and it's closed in the early summer until July 4 because of bear activity.

The **Elephant Back Loop Trail** is an opportunity to get a bird's-eye view of the island-dotted expanse of Yellowstone Lake, the Absaroka Mountains, and the Pelican Valley. It's a photo opportunity and a fairly easy 2-mile loop, beginning just south of Fishing Bride Junction off the road to Lake Village.

You can walk the north shore of Yellowstone Lake on the **Storm Point Trail,** unless it's been closed, as it occasionally is, due to grizzly bear activity. This easy 2-miler on a level path terminates at a point jutting into the lake where you'll find lovely panoramic views. It begins in the Indian Pond area, 3.5 miles east of Fishing Bridge directly across from the Pelican Valley Trailhead.

HIKES TO REMOTE AREAS

The **Bechler Meadows Trail** enters the southwest corner of the park, an area rich in waterfalls, cascades, and thermal areas that rarely have human visitors. The access is by Idaho Highway 47 from Ashton, Idaho, which will take you to the Bechler Ranger Station in the southwest corner of the park. About 6 miles into the hike, the trail makes several fords of the river as it enters Bechler Canyon, where it passes Collonade and Iris Falls. There are places on this trail where you can view the Grand Tetons in the distance, and hot springs that provide warm bathing in creeks. This is a camping trip—you can cover a good 30 miles, depending on what turns you take—best made late in the summer to avoid high water during creek crossings. You'll need a back-country permit for overnight stays.

The **Slough Creek Trail,** in the Lamar Valley of the park's northeast corner, takes hikers through some of the best wildlife habitat in the park. You can see elk, bison, trumpeter swans, sometimes grizzly bears, and now wolves, who have quite happily taken up residence among abundant prey. The presence of wolves has made this area more popular, and the trail is also used by horse-packers. The trail starts from the road to Slough Creek campground, following the creek's valley north, then crossing a ridge to a second valley. You can hike a few miles, or take your camping gear and head for the park boundary, 11 miles to the north.

The **Thorofare Trail** follows the eastern shore of Yellowstone Lake and then trails the Yellowstone River up into some of the most remote and beautiful backcountry in the Rockies. It's a lot of miles and climbing, but you'll be rewarded with views of the Upper Yellowstone Valley, Two Oceans Plateau, and abundant wildlife. Eventually you'll reach a gorgeous alpine valley just outside the park's boundary, with a ranger station known as Hawk's Rest. Fishermen love this area—so do grizzly bears, especially during the cutthroat trout spawning season. This is the most remote roadless area in the Lower 48, a good 30 miles from the trailhead at the lake, and even the most capable hikers should consider riding with an outfitter. You can cut the journey shorter by getting a boat "shuttle" to the mouth of the lake's southwest arm (call Yellowstone Park Lodges Services, ☎ 307/344-7901). Only nonmotorized boats are allowed into the arm to the Yellowstone River outlet (one year we canoed in, a wonderful trip). Or you can come into Thorofare through Bridger–Teton National Forest to the south (check with the forest's Blackrock Ranger Station).

9 Camping

WHERE TO GO & HOW TO RESERVE A SPOT

The National Park Service has shifted management of five major campgrounds to Yellowstone Park Lodges, the park concessionaire, which means, predictably, higher fees, but also allows you to make reservations ahead of arrival. The other seven campgrounds still managed by the park are available only on a first-come, first-served basis. These lower-cost campgrounds—fees range from $10 to $12 per night—are located at Indian Creek, Lewis Lake, Mammoth, Norris, Pebble Creek, Slough Creek, and Tower Fall. I happen to like the Norris campground, and Slough Creek, which tends to be available when others are full. Check with rangers about campsite availability when you enter the park; generally, you need to arrive early to get a site—some campgrounds fill up as early as 8am.

Yellowstone Park Lodges operates larger, busier campgrounds at Bridge Bay, Canyon, Grant Village, Madison, and Fishing Bridge, where the fees are $15 per night. The **Fishing Bridge RV Park** is the only campground equipped with water, sewer, and electrical hookups for RVs and trailers, though it accepts hard-sided vehicles only (no tents or tent trailers), and the fees are $25 per night. The **Madison campground** is the first to open on May 1, while **Grant Village** is closed until June 21 to avoid bear conflicts during trout spawning season. These campgrounds are larger and busier, and some, like Bridge Bay, are rather barren of trees unless you get a site on the fringes. Some campgrounds close in September, while Madison is open until November 7. Dates vary with weather and road conditions, however, so it's wise to double-check availability of specific camping areas. If you plan on traveling in the busy months of July and August, make your reservations six months ahead of time by calling ☎ 307/344-7311, or by writing Yellowstone Park Lodges, P.O. Box 165, Yellowstone National Park, WY 82190.

Camping is allowed only in designated areas and is limited to 14 days between June 15 and Labor Day, and to 30 days the rest of the year, except at Fishing Bridge, where there is no limit. Check-out times for all campgrounds is 10am. Quiet hours are strictly enforced between the hours of 8pm and 8am.

For those who carry their tents on their backs and want no "neighbors" other than their hiking buddies, there's plenty of room out there. Some areas in the Yellowstone backcountry include delicate habitat—the southeast arm of Yellowstone Lake is an example—and visitors must camp in designated areas for a limited time only. This in no way diminishes the sense of being in a true wilderness, and it helps preserve the wilderness. Check with the **Yellowstone Backcountry office** (☎ 307/344-2160) for rules, reservations, and advice.

WHAT TO EXPECT

Remember, these are campgrounds, not motels, so the amenities are spare. But some have showers and bathrooms and potable water. Check the chart below to determine the level of comfort at each campground. Showers and laundry facilities are available at Canyon, Fishing Bridge and Grant Village, and Madison campgrounds. In addition, campers may use the shower and laundry facilities at Lake Lodge and Old Faithful Lodge.

In the northeast area of the park, the **Tower Fall campground** is near a convenience store, restaurant, and gas station at Tower Lodge, 19 miles north of Canyon Village and 18 miles east of Mammoth. **Slough Creek campground** is located in a remote section of the Lamar Valley near the northeast entrance; the good news is there are fewer people, good fishing, and the possibility of wolf sightings; the bad news is that rest room facilities are pit toilets. **Canyon campground** is the busiest in the park, so it generally requires an early check-in. Sites are assigned by rangers, and are in a heavily wooded area; the store, restaurants, visitor center, and laundry at Canyon Center are nearby. Because it's in an area of spring bear activity, attempts have been made over the years to close the RV park at **Fishing Bridge.** It's still open, but sometimes its opening is delayed, and only hard-sided camping vehicles are allowed here. **Bridge Bay** is located near the shores of Yellowstone Lake, so you get tremendous views, especially at sunrise and sunset. Unfortunately, though surrounded by the forest, the area has been clear-cut, so there's no privacy. It's close to boat launching facilities and the boat rental operation. **Madison** and **Norris campgrounds** are attractive, wooded locations in the heart of the park, close to wildlife activity and near rivers, and so offer excellent opportunities for fishing and hiking. These camp areas seem less like outdoor motels than the big campgrounds on the park's east side.

10 Where to Stay in the Park

For accommodation listings in the gateway towns, see the section on gateway towns in the beginning of the chapter.

Amenities for Each Campground, Yellowstone National Park

(where flush toilets are not available, vault toilets are provided)

Campground	# Sites	Fee	Showers/ Laundry	Flush Toilets	Disposal Stations	Generators Permitted
Bridge Bay*	430	$15	No	Yes	Yes	Yes
Canyon*	272	$15	Yes	Yes	Yes	Yes
Fishing Bridge	340	$25	Yes	Yes	Sewer	Yes
Grant Village*	425	$15	Yes	Yes	Yes	Yes
Indian Creek	75	$10	No	No	No	No
Lewis Lake	85	$10	No	No	No	No
Madison*	280	$15	No	No	Yes	Yes
Mammoth	85	$12	No	No	Yes	No
Norris	116	$12	No	No	Yes	No
Pebble Creek	32	$10	No	No	No	No
Slough Creek	29	$10	No	No	No	No
Tower Fall	32	$10	No	No	No	No

*Reserve through Yellowstone Park Lodges, ☎ **307/344-7311;** TDD 307/344-5395.

The first thing you should know: no televisions. Private bathrooms have arrived. Phones are in place. But no televisions in the rooms.

Railroad companies built most of the Western park hotels and lodges around the turn of the century, and they would offer their Victorian guests a package tour that delivered them by train and stagecoach to what were then considered luxurious resorts with rocking chairs on the verandas and gourmet food. Some of that old-style ambience has been retained at Yellowstone. Even the newer facilities erected by the park concessionaire—the Old Faithful Snow Lodge and the new lodges at Canyon—are suitably matched to older buildings, at least on the exterior. The push for more features may come in the near future, and in fact during recent upgrades at the Lake Hotel the wiring was installed for televisions . . . just in case. While many of the hotels provide beautiful examples of Western architecture and craftsmanship, you'll discover that the lath and plaster walls transmit sound, baths tend to be smallish, and you may just end up walking down the hall to have a shower. The good news in all this is that except for the most expensive suites in the large hotel-lodges, even the most budget-conscious traveler will find a room in the park that fits the pocketbook. Look over the descriptions below carefully, though, because some of the cheaper lodgings are primitive indeed.

Canyon Lodge and Cabins. In Canyon Village (P.O. Box 165), Yellowstone National Park, WY 82190. ☎ **307/344-7311.** www.travelyellowstone.com. 609 units. $105 double; $51–$101 cabin. AE, CB, DC, DISC, MC, V. Closed Sept 13–June 3.

This lodge and cabin complex is one of the newer facilities in the park (it was completed in 1993), but it can't escape the retro-1950s California-style atmosphere of Canyon Village—sprawling and crowded. The lodge is located a half mile from the Grand Canyon of the Yellowstone and Inspiration Point, one of the most popular spots in the park. It offers tastefully appointed but ordinary motel-style accommodations in the three-story building, and in cabins that are scattered throughout the village. You won't find any surprises in the motel units, which have various sleeping configurations designed to accommodate the needs of couples as well as families. The cabins are single-story duplex and four-plex structures with private baths that are

Making Reservations

Yellowstone accommodations are normally open from summer to late October. The winter season begins in mid-December and runs through March, offering snow-mobilers and cross-country skiers accommodations and meals at either Mammoth Hot Springs or Old Faithful Snow Lodge and Cabins. Vacancy increases before June 15 and after September 15. Rooms are typically fully booked during the peak season in July and August, so reservations should be made up to 6 months in advance. For information or reservations at any of the following locations, contact **Yellowstone Park Lodges** at P.O. Box 165, Yellowstone National Park, WY 82190 (☎ **307/344-7311**).

among the largest in the park. They're much nicer than their "rustic" counterparts in other centers, but given the sheer number of units involved, this wouldn't be the place to "get away from it all." The newly opened Dunraven Lodge is tasteful and simple and nicely backed up against forest, away from the traffic of the village.

Grant Village. On the West Thumb of Yellowstone Lake (P.O. Box 165), Yellowstone National Park, WY 82190. ☎ **307/344-7311.** www.travelyellowstone.com. 300 units. $83–$96 double. AE, CB, DC, DISC, MC, V. Closed Oct 4–May 27.

Grant Village is the southernmost of the major overnight accommodations in the park. It was completed in 1984 and is one of the more contemporary choices in Yellowstone. It hasn't got a lot of life, architecturally: The lodge consists of six ordinary-looking, motel-type two-story chalets set back from the water's edge, as well as a reception area and gift shop that are in a separate building near the village entrance. Rooms are tastefully furnished, most outfitted with light wood furniture, track lighting, electric heat, and laminate counters. Nicer and more expensive rooms affording lake views have mullioned windows, one queen or one or two double beds, and full baths. Mid-range rooms are set farther back from the lake and overlook drab grounds that look as if construction was completed only recently. Grant Village is isolated from other park centers, so you're likely to drink in its tiny lounge and eat in one of its two restaurants overlooking the lake. Other guest services located here include a laundry facility, service station, and convenience store.

Lake Lodge Cabins. On Lake Yellowstone (P.O. Box 165), Yellowstone National Park, WY 82190. ☎ **307/344-7311.** www.travelyellowstone.com. 186 cabins. $48–$101 double. AE, CB, DC, DISC, MC, V. Closed Sept 13–June 9.

These cabins, which surround Lake Lodge, face the lake just around the corner north of the Lake Yellowstone Hotel and Cabins. The lodge is an old Western longhouse fronted by a porch and rockers that invite visitors to sit and gaze out across the waters. The floors inside the lodge gleam like a gymnasium, which is what this building brings to mind. Two small rock fireplaces contribute the only ambience to the room, which has virtually no seating. The centerpiece of the room is the reception desk, which is located next to an undernourished gift shop. Eating and drinking take place at a small, uninviting bar area and a cafeteria that serves inexpensive meals. You might wisely choose instead to make the short trek to the Lake Yellowstone Hotel for a more sumptuous meal in a more appetizing setting. Accommodations are in well-preserved, clean, freestanding cabins near a trout stream that threads through a wooded area. There are nature walks around the lodge, but this is a trout spawning area, so access is usually restricted early in the summer when the griz emerge from hibernation. These cabins come in two grades: **Western** cabins provide electric heat, paneled walls, two double beds, and combination baths, while **Frontier** cabins are smaller and sparsely furnished, with only one double bed each and small shower-only baths. You'll need to head outdoors to enjoy the lake views; the only things you can see from your cabin are other cabins.

✪ **Lake Yellowstone Hotel and Cabins.** On the north side of the lake (P.O. Box 165), Yellowstone National Park, WY 82190. ☎ **307/344-7311.** www.travelyellowstone.com. 296 units. $96–$143 double; $77 cabin; $373 parlor suite. AE, CB, DC, DISC, MC, V. Closed Oct 4–May 13.

The Ionic columns, dormer windows, and deep porticos on this yellow frame building faithfully recall the 1891 era when it was built. It's an entirely different world from the rustic Western style of other park places, but when you find yourself sipping a gin & tonic in a wicker chair in the huge sunroom overlooking the lake while someone plays an etude on the piano, you'll appreciate that those Victorians were on to something. The facility was completely restored in the early 1990s, and its better rooms are the most comfortable and roomy in the park. Only the bar leaves something to be desired: Guests are served from what looks like a temporary set-up by the dining room entrance, and then wander with their drinks toward the sunroom with its views of the lake.

Accommodations are in three- and four-story wings in the hotel, in a motel-style annex, and in cabins. The upper-end rooms here are among the nicest in the park, with stenciled walls and traditional spreads on one queen or two double beds. Smaller rooms in the annex are fitted with two double beds and bring to mind a typical motel chain; as an alternative, we'd opt for one of the freestanding cabins. These are decorated with knotty-pine paneling, and furnished with double beds and a writing table—a desirable low-priced alternative. *Note:* if you take a cabin, request a single rather than a duplex, since walls are paper thin; if not, bring earplugs. There's a large dining room, a take-out delicatessen, and a Hamilton store nearby.

Mammoth Hot Springs Hotel and Cabins. P.O. Box 165, Yellowstone National Park, WY 82190. ☎ **307/344-7311.** Fax 307/344-7456. www.travelyellowstone.com. 224 units. $48–$83 double; $245 suite; $48–$77 cabin. AE, CB, DC, DISC, MC, V.

On the site of old Fort Yellowstone, near the steaming terraces of Mammoth Hot Springs and 5 miles from the north entrance, is the only hotel open during both summer and winter seasons on the northern side of the park. It began life as a hostelry in 1911, and was replaced by a lodge, built in 1937, that has been incorporated as a wing in the current Mammoth Hot Springs Hotel. The peaceful scene here, where elk often graze the strips of lawn around the hotel, is somewhat quickened by the flow of tourists stopping by the park headquarters and stores. The hotel itself is less distinguished than the Lake Hotel or the Old Faithful Inn, but its dormer windows and wood floors are attractive, and the high-ceilinged lobby is comfortable and relatively quiet, particularly if you drift into the adjacent Map Room (named for the massive inlaid map of the U.S. on one of the broad paneled walls), with overstuffed sofas and undersized desks for reading, writing, and admiring the scenery through huge windows.

The only high-end accommodations are the suites. Standard rooms and cabins are arranged around three grassy areas, where the resident elk often graze. Rooms offer minimal but apt appointments and various bed arrangements. If you require a tub, be sure and request one when you make your reservation; otherwise, you could get a cramped, old-fashioned shower stall. The cabins here are cottage-style buildings, some with private hot tubs and sundecks. A formal dining room and a fast-food restaurant are both located in a separate building; nearby amenities include a medical clinic,

---

Inside Info

When staying at the **Old Faithful Inn,** if you want to watch the geyser erupt from your room, ask for Suite 3014 or Room 229. The suite is the "best in the house," with a spacious bathroom, bedroom, and sitting room, and goes for $328 a night. Room 229 is a high corner room with views of Old Faithful and the geyser basin, and because it's one of the older rooms, it costs only $54 a night. The problem with 229 is that you have to plan far ahead: people vie for this room, and you probably won't get it if you don't reserve it 18 months before your visit.

---

grocery store, stables, and filling station. In the winter, Mammoth is a take-off point for cross-country skiing and visits by tour bus to the wildlife-rich Lamar Valley.

✪ **Old Faithful Inn.** P.O. Box 165, Yellowstone National Park, WY 82190. ☎ **307/344-7311.** Fax 307/344-7456. www.travelyellowstone.com. 359 units. $52–$242 double; $325 suite. AE, CB, DC, DISC, MC, V. Closed Oct 18–April 30.

There are three hotels within viewing distance of the geyser, including a very nice new one, but this is the crown jewel of Yellowstone's man-made wonders. Seven stories tall with dormers peaking from a shingled, steep-sloping roof, it looks inside like a lodgepole jungle gym—and indeed, you can climb the stairs to its internal balconies, and, with permission, ascend to a widow's walk and crow's nest. Only 30 miles from the west entrance and 40 miles from the south entrance, this is the first place visitors think of when they want a bed for the night, so make reservations far ahead during the busy summer months. The dining room is warmed on cool evenings by a fieldstone fireplace. Like other park properties, this lobby also houses a busy fast-food outlet that serves light meals; there are also a bar and gift shop. Guest rooms are in the main building, and in wings that flank the main lodge. Original rooms are well appointed with conservative fabrics and park-theme art, but may not have private baths; the wing rooms offer better facilities and more privacy.

Old Faithful Lodge Cabins. P.O. Box 165, Yellowstone National Park, WY 82190. ☎ **307/344-7311.** www.travelyellowstone.com. 122 cabins (some without private bathroom). $32–$58 double. AE, CB, DC, DISC, MC, V. Closed Sept 20–May 20.

These are the leftovers from the days when crude cabins littered the landscape around the world's most famous geyser. The ones closest to the geyser were hauled away years ago, but you still get a sense of what tourism was like in the park's early days, especially if you rent one of the **budget cabins,** which are just slightly less flimsy than tents, and have basic beds and sinks, no more. Showers and rest rooms are a short walk away. Next up the scale are the **economy cabins,** which have beds, sinks and toilets . . . but no baths. **Frontier cabins** are the best units, adding a private bath to other amenities. These rustic, thin-walled cabins are an economical way to put a roof over your head in the park, and they're close to a cafeteria and a snack bar. The lodge is perhaps the busiest spot in the geyser area, featuring several snack shops and a huge cafeteria dishing up varied fast food. Just off the lobby is one of the largest gift shops in the park and an old gymnasium that occasionally hosts square dancing and movies.

✪ **Old Faithful Snow Lodge and Cabins.** Old Faithful, P.O. Box 165, Yellowstone National Park, WY 82190. ☎ **307/344-7311.** Fax 307/344-7456. www.travelyellowstone.com. 134 units. $121 double; $101 cabin. AE, CB, DC, DISC, MC, V.

If your last winter (or summer) visit to Yellowstone included a stay at the Old Faithful Snow Lodge, put the memory out of mind. The old dormitory-style lodge was torn down in 1998, and this new, award-winning place could aptly be called the *New Faithful Snow Lodge*. The big beam construction and high ceiling in the lobby echo the Old Faithful Inn, and a copper-lined balcony curves above the common area, where guests can relax in wicker furniture. The rooms are spacious and comfortable (still no TVs!), and a spacious dining room shares a two-sided fireplace with a lounge.

✪ **Roosevelt Lodge Cabins.** P.O. Box 165, Yellowstone National Park, WY 82190. ☎ **307/344-7311** for reservations. 80 cabins (none with private bathroom). $40–$77 cabin. AE, CB, DC, DISC, MC, V.

This is considered the park's hideaway treat, a family-oriented, low-key operation with primitive cabins, horseback rides, and a lodge restaurant that's more like a big ranch house. It's named after Teddy Roosevelt, who loved the northeast area of the park (the lodge is 35 miles from the northeast entrance), and slept in a tent near here. I'd do the same. The bare-bones cabins are called **Roughriders,** and they're furnished with two simple beds, clean linens, a writing table, and a woodstove that may or may not ignite, but in any case probably won't sustain heat on sawdust logs through the night. **Frontier** cabins have their own baths and showers. Better to be outdoors than sharing a cabin wall with strangers and walking through the resort to a crowded shower/restroom to brush your teeth.

The lodge is a rugged but charming stone edifice with a long, deep porch outfitted with rockers so guests can converse with each other, nature, or the squirrels that scurry about. Stagecoach rides, horseback trips, and Western trail cookouts give this place a cowboy flavor that many enjoy, and it's a less pushy, crowded scene than other park villages. Since the cabins are just north of the Grand Canyon of the Yellowstone and Tower Falls, and isolated from crowds at larger hotels and campgrounds, the appeal here is clearly to budget-conscious, outdoor types interested in exploring the northeast part of Yellowstone without having to pay through the nose for accommodations.

11 Where to Dine in the Park

Am I just paranoid about corporate concessionaires, or is there a certain sameness creeping into the menus at the restaurants in Yellowstone's major hotels? The dining rooms at Mammoth Hot Springs Hotel, Old Faithful Inn, and Lake Yellowstone Hotel each has a distinctive ambience, but the cuisine seems less distinguishable and less distinguished than it did a few years ago. Nevertheless, if you plan a visit to one of these big halls, you'll be served by perky youngsters—though some are not so young anymore—with name tags identifying their homes around the world.

If you're not up for restaurant dining, but you don't want to cook over your camp stove the whole time, there is counter-style fast food service at the **Hamilton General Stores** and snacks shops and cafeterias in the villages at Canyon, Mammoth, Grant Village, and the Yellowstone Lake Lodge, and at Old Faithful. Try the new **Geyser Grill** at the Old Faithful Snow Lodge, or the old lunch counter scene at the **Fishing Bridge Hamilton Store.** The **Canyon Lodge Cafeteria** is a fast-food alternative located across the parking lot in the Canyon Lodge area, open from June 1 to September 8.

Canyon Lodge Dining Room. ☎ **307/344-7901.** Reservations required. Breakfast $2–$6; lunch $5–$7; dinner $12–$17. June to mid-Sept, daily 6:30–10:30am, 11:30am–2pm, and 5:30–10pm. AMERICAN.

This is a spacious dining area, with the 1950s feel that infects most of Canyon Village, and when it fills up, it's noisy. The salad bar is long and loaded, but otherwise the fare—steak, chicken, fish, and pasta—is hard to tell apart from what you get at other park restaurants . . . not surprising, since they are all managed by Yellowstone Park Lodges, the park's chief concessionaire. The crowds can be large at Canyon Village, but there is a relaxed and unhurried feel to the place that you don't find at some of the park's other busy points. The dining room is kid friendly.

Grant Village. At Grant Village. ☎ **307/344-7901.** Dinner reservations required. Breakfast $4–$6; lunch $6–$9; dinner $11–$21. AE, CB, DISC, MC, V. June–Sept, daily 6:30–10am, 11:30am–2:30pm, and 5:30–10pm. STEAKS/SEAFOOD.

Breakfast and lunch at the Grant Village restaurant are much like those at the other restaurants in the park, though the chef occasionally surprises diners with interesting items that stray from the norm. Lunch may include pan-fried trout covered with toasted pecans and lemon butter, Wyoming Cheese steak, and a one-third-pound gourmet burger. The dinner menu ranges from honey-lemon chicken to swordfish with lemon dill beurre to blackened prime rib. Quality and ambience here are comparable to those of the better dining rooms at the major park hotels. **The Lake House,** a second restaurant footsteps away, specializes in less expensive fish entrees, including fried clam strips, blackened halibut, burgers, and beer. Meals are served here from 5:30 to 9pm.

✪ Lake Yellowstone Hotel. On the north side of the lake. ☎ **307/344-7901.** Dinner reservations required. Breakfast $4–$6; lunch $5–$7; dinner $8–$21. AE, DC, DISC, MC, V. Mid-May to early Oct, daily 6:30–10am, 11:30am–2:30pm, and 5:30–10pm. PASTA/STEAKS/SEAFOOD.

This is one of most pleasant places to eat in Yellowstone, with a view of the lake stretching south from a big, high-ceilinged dining room that doesn't feel crowded even when it's full. Once again, Yellowstone Park Lodges serve you. Among the variations here are a generous breakfast buffet; alternatives include a tasty traditional country pan breakfast of bacon, eggs, and home fries; a Southwestern pan breakfast seasoned with chilies and salsa; and huevos rancheros. There's also a wide selection of fresh fruit, juices, pastries, and cereals. The dinner menu is equally inviting. Appetizers include duck quesadillas and *spanakopitas* (a tasty Greek pastry stuffed with spinach and cheese), while entrees include breast of duck, fettucine with smoked salmon, and, of course, several beef dishes. The food here is of the quality one expects at a grand hotel.

The deli just off the hotel lobby by the dining room entrance serves lighter fare, including sandwiches, from an area slightly larger than a broom closet. Just down the road, the Hamilton store offers three meals in a section of the store that is shared with tourist items; the best bets here are breakfast or a burger. Inexpensive meals served cafeteria-style are available at the Yellowstone Lake Lodge and Cabins.

Mammoth Hot Springs Hotel. At Mammoth Hot Springs. ☎ **307/344-7901.** Dinner reservations required. Breakfast $2–$6; lunch $6–$9; dinner $8–$21. AE, DC, DISC, MC, V. Summer, daily 6:30–10am, 11:30am–2pm, and 5:30–10pm. STEAKS/SEAFOOD.

At Mammoth, the breakfast buffet features scrambled eggs, French toast, and muffins. Delicious omelets are served with home fries and toast. The midday repast is an array of sandwiches, including teriyaki chicken breast, a grilled vegetarian sandwich, and grilled German bratwurst. Dinner is a bit more substantial, and bears a predictable similarity to its counterparts at other park hotels, all under the same management. The specialty here is shrimp and scallops served over linguine and topped with a curry sauce. At the opposite end of the building, typical restaurant fare is served in a less formal and less pricey dining room.

✪ Old Faithful Inn. Near Old Faithful. ☎ **307/545-4999.** Dinner reservations required. Breakfast $7; lunch $5–$9; dinner $9–$22. AE, DC, DISC, MC, V. May to mid-Oct, daily 6:30–10am, 11:30am–2:30pm, and 5–10pm. STEAKS/SEAFOOD.

There's nothing wrong with the food here, but it pales beside, or beneath, the gnarled log architecture of this distinguished historic inn. Once again, this is Yellowstone Park Lodges fare, similar to that at other park restaurants. Breakfast is strictly buffet, but there's a lot to choose from. The dinner menu is fairly long, with four cuts of prime rib, fish dishes, roasted Cornish game hen, and pastas including a fettucine with artichoke hearts, mushrooms, and olives. There's also a tasty broiled Mexican Caesar salad. As you munch your way through the meal, ponder the task that faced a crew who constructed this building during a miserable Montana winter—hewing the logs, hauling the stone, and forging the metal straps that hold the beams together. I recommend that you have at least one dinner here while you're visiting the park to take in the ambience of the inn.

Old Faithful Snow Lodge. Near Old Faithful (east of Inn). ☎ **307/344-7901.** Reservations not accepted. Breakfast $4–$7; lunch $5–$9; dinner $9–$16. AE, DC, DISC, MC, V. May to mid-Oct and mid-Dec to mid-May, daily 6:30–10am, 11:30am–2:30pm, and 5–10pm. STEAKS/SEAFOOD.

In the well-designed new snow lodge, a spacious restaurant provides an alternative to the Old Faithful Inn dining room. It's a little quieter, a little less expensive, and a little less formal, which is reflected in a menu heavy on burgers and salads. It still has some Yellowstone Park Lodges stalwarts on the menu—teriyaki chicken and London broil—and, again in contrast to the Inn, there is a breakfast menu that goes beyond buffet. If you come in the winter, it's a huge improvement over the cramped restaurant of the old Snow Lodge.

Roosevelt Lodge. At Tower Junction. ☎ **307/344-7901.** Breakfast $4–$7; lunch $6–$12; dinner $8–$21. AE, CB, DC, DISC, MC, V. Summer, daily 7–10am, 11:30am–3pm, and 5–9pm. STEAKS/SEAFOOD.

This is supposed to be the cowboy alternative to the fancier cuisine served at the bigger Yellowstone hotels, but it's really not that special. Like the aging cabins that take you back to the early days of auto camping, Roosevelt's dining area is simple and spare, a collection of tables that take up one side of the lodge's big lobby. Roosevelt beans may be prepared locally, but the food is mostly bland and tastes like the variety that grows in large tin cans. You choose from a short list of entrees and select three side dishes. Better idea: join Roosevelt's Old West Dinner Cookout, and ride by horse or wagon thorough the Pleasant Valley to a chuck wagon dinner that includes cornbread, steak, watermelon, those famous beans, and apple crisp. It's a daily summer event (reservations required) that costs $39 to $50 for an adult, depending on the route of your horseback ride, or $32 if you go by wagon. Children pay less.

11

Jackson Hole & Grand Teton National Park

Grand Teton compares to Yellowstone somewhat the way a Generation X snowboarder compares to an old ski patrol graybeard: younger, flashier, and closer to the bars. The centerpiece is the Tetons, rising spectacularly from the valley like swords of granite and ice. Though Yellowstone has infinitely more geological variety, none of its peaks is so tall and abrupt. The Tetons are a young mountain range in geologic time, and a young national park, on the rolls in its present form since 1950; Yellowstone, by comparison, dates back to 1872. And whereas the geysers of Yellowstone are a pretty long drive from anywhere, you can come off a climb of the Grand and be in a posh Jackson eatery 20 minutes after you hit the valley floor.

That's not a knock on Grand Teton National Park. Jackson, after all, is a spiffy resort town with a little cowboy still in it, nothing to be ashamed of. And within the park's borders are beautiful lakes and rivers, wildlife galore, and lots of recreational opportunities. In the summer, you can climb, hike, boat, balloon, backpack, raft, birdwatch, and fish. In winter, the park and nearby resorts become a magnet for skiers of every style and skill level. Jackson Hole Ski Resort is upgrading furiously to keep its status as a premier national ski resort, and its neighbor on the west side of the mountain, Grand Targhee, has some of the best powder in the Rockies.

1 Jackson Hole

57 miles S of Yellowstone National Park; 432 miles NW of Cheyenne; 275 miles NE of Salt Lake City; 177 miles SW of Cody

Few communities in the Rockies have successfully toed the line between promoting themselves as resort towns and retaining some semblance of indigenous character, but Jackson is giving its best shot. The million dollar homes are sprouting all over the valley, but there is still open space, some memory of the cowboy past, and a somewhat wilted resistance to letting in too much commercial glitz.

The remaining open spaces allow visitors to imagine what it was like early in the 19th century, when fur trappers first camped here (including David E. Jackson, the valley's namesake). They were followed by ranchers, who soon became *dude* ranchers, many of whose guests eventually "went native" and planted roots here. Today, the community holds an interesting mixture of ski bums, blue bloods, nouveau riche in "rustic" mansions, avid outdoor recreationists, and

Jackson

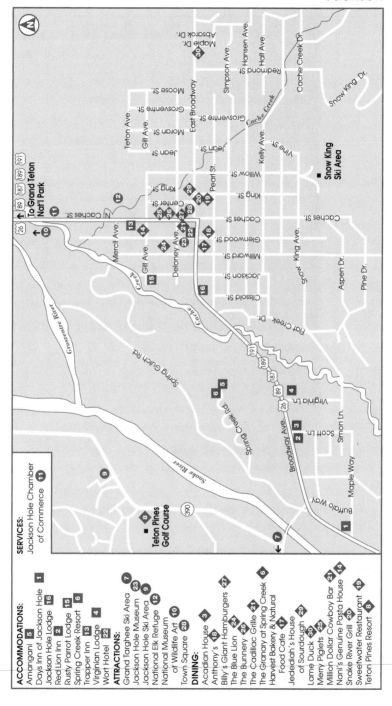

SERVICES:
Jackson Hole Chamber of Commerce ⓫

ACCOMMODATIONS:
Amangani 🔷5
Days Inn of Jackson Hole ◼1
Jackson Hole Lodge ◼16
Red Lion Inn ◼2
Rusty Parrot Lodge ◼15
Spring Creek Resort 🔷6
Trapper Inn ◼13
Virginian Lodge ◼4
Wort Hotel ◼22

ATTRACTIONS:
Grand Targhee Ski Area 🔷7
Jackson Hole Museum 🔷23
Jackson Hole Ski Area 🔷9
National Elk Refuge 🔷12
National Museum of Wildlife Art 🔷10
Town Square 🔷28

DINING:
Acadian House 🔶3
Anthony's 🔶8
Billy's Giant Hamburgers 🔶27
The Blue Lion 🔶24
The Bunnery 🔶26
The Cadillac Grille 🔶21
The Granary at Spring Creek 🔶6
Harvest Bakery & Natural Food Cafe 🔶17
Jedediah's House of Sourdough 🔶29
Lame Duck 🔶30
Merry Piglets 🔶25
Million Dollar Cowboy Bar 🔶21
Nani's Genuine Pasta House 🔶14
Snake River Grill 🔶20
Sweetwater Restaurant 🔶19
Teton Pines Resort 🔶8

Jackson or Jackson Hole—What's the Difference?

You'll likely see every kind of merchandise imaginable fashioned with an image of the Tetons and the words "Jackson Hole, Wyoming" scrawled over it. You may notice that on the map, the town just south of Grand Teton National Park is called Jackson. But your plane ticket says Jackson Hole, Wyoming. But wait a minute—the postmark just says Jackson. The names seem to be used interchangeably, and often this is true. What gives?

The mystery of the town's name is actually pretty simple. Three mountain men ran a fur trapping company in these parts in the 1800s: one named David Jackson, another named Jedidiah Smith, and a third named William Sublette. Mountain men in those days referred to a valley as a hole. As the story goes, Sublette (for whom the county southeast of Teton County is named) called the valley Jackson's Hole, since his friend and partner David Jackson spent a great deal of time in it. That name was shortened, and when the town materialized, it was also named for David Jackson. So the city itself is Jackson, Wyoming, and it lies in the great valley that runs the length of the Tetons on the east side, Jackson Hole.

---

even a few old-time cowboys. The cosmopolitans of this motley crew came not just with a hunger for scenery, but also with a taste for music, art, and good restaurants, too, and the selection here is unrivaled in Wyoming. The big ski hill lures a younger crowd, and the final ingredient for resort status—celebrities—is supplied by low-profile transplants like Harrison Ford.

ESSENTIALS

GETTING THERE   The **Jackson Airport** is located north of town at the southern end of Grand Teton National Park. **American Airlines** (☎ **800/433-7300**) flies in seasonally from Chicago, and regular service is provided from Denver and Salt Lake City by **Delta** and **Delta Connection** (☎ **800/221-1212**), and by **United** and **United Express** (☎ **800/241-6522**).

If you're getting here on your own wheels, come north from I-80 at Rock Springs on U.S. Highway 191/189, or come east from I-15 at Idaho Falls on U.S. Highway 26 and either come through Snake River Canyon on that highway or veer north over Teton Pass on WY 32. If you are coming south **from Yellowstone National Park,** you can stay on U.S. Highway 89, which runs north-south through both parks and into town. For up-to-date weather information and road conditions, contact the Chamber of Commerce (see below), or ☎ **888/WYO-ROAD** (in-state).

VISITOR INFORMATION   The **Jackson Hole Chamber of Commerce** is a source of information concerning just about everything in and around Jackson. Along with the U.S. Forest Service and National Park Service, representatives of the chamber can be found at the informative **Visitors Center,** 532 N. Cache, about 3 blocks north of the town square with a view of the National Elk Refuge. For information on lodging, events, and activities, contact the chamber at P.O. Box E, Jackson, WY 83001 (☎ **307/733-3316;** www.jacksonholechamber.com; e-mail: info@ jacksonholechamber.com).

GETTING AROUND   Once you're on the ground, major car-rental operations serving the airport include **Alamo** (☎ **800/327-9633** or 307/733-0671), **Avis** (☎ **800/331-1212** or 307/733-3422), **Budget** (☎ **800/527-0700** or 307/

733-2206), **Hertz** (☎ **800/654-3131** or 307/733-2272), and **Thrifty** (☎ **800/ 699-1025** or 307/739-9300). Also providing rentals in the area are **Aspen** (☎ **877/22ASPEN** or 307/733-9224) and **Rent-a-Wreck** (☎ **800/637-7147** or 307/733-5014). Downtown at 375 N. Cache is **Eagle Rent-a-Car** (☎ **800/ 582-2128** or 307/739-9999), where you can rent everything from minivans to RVs to snowmobiles. Eagle also provides free pickup and delivery.

Taxi service is available from **All Star Taxi** (☎ **800/378-2944** or 307/733-2888) and **Buckboard Cab** (☎ **307/733-7372**). **Alltrans, Inc.** (☎ **800/443-6133** or 307/733-3135) offers shuttle service from the airport and national park tours. Before you call a cab, remember that many of the hotels and car-rental agencies in the Jackson area offer free shuttle service to and from the airport.

The **Southern Teton Area Rapid Transit (START)** offers bus transport from Teton Village to Jackson daily for $2 (students up to high school age ride free). Winter and summer service runs about hourly between downtown and Teton Village, shutting down around 6pm in the winter, running into the evening during the summer. For specific schedule information, contact START at ☎ **307/733-4521.**

GETTING OUTSIDE
SPORTING GOODS & EQUIPMENT RENTALS
Jackson adventurers may like to flirt with danger, but generally they like to do so fully equipped and handsomely attired. Serious climbers with serious wallets will appreciate the gear at ✪ **Teton Mountaineering,** at 170 N. Cache (☎ **800/360-3595** or 307/733-3595), a block from the square, where you can get carabiners, killer Nordic skis, and high-grade fleece jackets; fishermen are lured to ✪ **High Country Flies,** at 185 N. Center St. (☎ **877/732-7210** or 307/733-7210), and the **Jack Dennis Outdoor Shop** on the square at 50 E. Broadway (☎ **800/570-3270** or 307/733-3270). **Adventure Sports,** at Dornan's in the town of Moose (☎ **307/733-3307**), has a small selection of mountain-bike, kayak, and canoe rentals, and advice on where to go with the gear. When snowboards are put away for the summer, the **Boardroom** switches to BMX bikes and skateboards, at 225 W. Broadway (☎ **307/733-8327**). The competition, in Teton Village, is **Hole in the Wall Snowboard Shop** (☎ **307/739-2687**). **Hoback Sports,** 40 S. Millward (☎ **307/733-5335**), has a large selection of skis, boards, and summer mountain bikes for rent and sale, and a second location at the Snow King (☎ **307/733-5200**). Equally hip, with a smaller but high-quality selection of bikes and skis, is **Edge Sports,** 490 W. Broadway (☎ **307/734-3916**). **Skinny Skis,** at 65 W. Deloney off Town Square (☎ **307/733-6094**), is a year-round specialty sports shop and has an excellent selection of equipment and clothing. For a supply of inexpensive, serviceable factory seconds at steeply discounted prices, head north to the little town of Moose near the entrance to Grand Teton National Park and shop ✪ **Moosely Seconds** (☎ **307/733-7176**). And the friendly folks at **Leisure Sports,** 1075 S. U.S. Hwy. 89 (☎ **307/733-3040**), are year-round as well; they offer mountain bikes, fishing boats, camping equipment, and rafting items in summer. In winter, look for snowmobiles, cross-country skis, and ice-fishing equipment.

BIKING
You can rent a bike and pick up maps at several of the shops listed above, or take a guided trip in Yellowstone, Grand Teton, or the national forest with **Teton Mountain Bike Tours** (☎ **800/733-9788**) or Hoback Sports' **Fat Tire Tours,** 40 S. Millward (☎ **307/733-5335**), who place bikes in the Snow King chairlift for an easy ride up the mountain—and a wild ride down on wheels.

CLIMBING

The sight of the 13,770-foot Grand Teton towering above the valley has been setting hearts pumping for generations. A century ago no one had reached the top; now, thousands have, often carefully roped and cared for by professional guides, who can train novices and have them on top in just a few days. Experienced guides and established routes assure a modicum of safety, but climbing accidents and deaths still occur on the granite and ice of the Tetons. There are two reliable, long-standing guide services: **Exum Mountain Guides,** P.O. Box 56, Moose, WY 83012 (☎ **307/733-2297**), has been around since 1931 and offers climbs on several mountains guided by well-known names in the climbing world—a trip to the top of Teton costs $330. Group preparation classes cost from $90 to $110 per person. **Jackson Hole Mountain Guides,** 165 N. Glenwood St., Jackson, WY 83001 (☎ **800/239-7642**), offers intermediate climbing courses for $100 and a 2-day Grand Teton summit climb for $400. On rainy days, the **Teton Rock Gym,** 1116 Maple (☎ **307/733-0707**), is an inexpensive alternative, setting you loose in its caves and on its walls and climbing ropes for $11 a day.

CROSS-COUNTRY SKIING

With five Nordic centers and a couple of national parks at your feet, plus the 3.5-million-acre Bridger-Teton National Forest, cross-country skiers have plenty of choices. If you're new to cross-country skiing on any level, you might choose to start on the groomed, level trails at one of the Nordic centers. If, however, you have experience in the steep, deep powder of untracked wilderness, visit or call the National Park Service in **Grand Teton National Park** (☎ **307/739-3300**) or the **Bridger-Teton National Forest** in downtown Jackson at 340 N. Cache (☎ **307/739-5500**) and check in before you go.

The local ski shops are an excellent source of unofficial advice about the area's backcountry. Keep in mind that many of the trails used by cross-country skiers are also used by snowmobiles. The **Jackson Hole Nordic Center,** 7658 Teewinot, Teton Village (☎ **307/733-2629**), located on the flats just east of Teton Village, is a small part of the giant facility that includes some of the best downhill skiing around (see "Downhill Skiing," below). The price of a downhill pass does include the price of skiing on the cross-country trails.

Teton Pines Cross Country Skiing Center (☎ **307/733-1005**) offers 8 miles of groomed trails that wind over the resort's golf course. Rates are $8 (see also "Where to Stay," below). **Spring Creek Ranch Touring Center,** 1800 N. Spirit Dance Rd., Jackson (☎ **800/443-6139**), located below the ridge resort (see "Where to Stay" below) maintains 8½ miles of groomed trails, and you don't have to be a guest to enjoy them. The fee for skiers (guests or non) is $8 per day.

At **Grand Targhee** (☎ **307/353-2304**), you can rent or buy anything you need in the way of cross-country ski equipment and take off on the resort's 7.2 miles (12km) of groomed trails.

For those seeking instruction, lessons are available at the Nordic centers, or you can check the schedule of **Teton Parks and Recreation** (☎ **307/733-5056**), which offers inexpensive courses for those who want to ski all day and have brought their own equipment.

For cross-country information in **Grand Teton National Park,** call ☎ **307/739-3300,** or 307/739-3611 for recorded weather information. Also, see section 2, "Grand Teton National Park," below.

DOGSLEDDING

If your idea of mushing is not oatmeal but a pack of yipping dogs, you might want to try your hand at dogsledding, an enjoyable open-air way to tour the high country during the winter. **Jackson Hole Iditarod,** P.O. Box 1940, Jackson, WY 83001 (☎ **800/554-7388**), associated with Iditarod racer Frank Teasley, offers both half- and full-day trips in five-person sleds (the fifth companion is your guide) and you can take a turn in the driver's stand. The half-day ride costs $130 per person, gives the dogs an 11-mile workout, and includes a lunch of hot soup and cocoa before you head back to the kennels. For $225 a head, you can take the full-day excursion out to Granite Hot Springs, a 22-mile trip total. You get the hot lunch, plus your choice of freshly barbecued trout or steak for dinner. Another Iditarod veteran, Bill Snodgrass, leads trips in the national forests around Togwotee Pass with his **Washakie Outfitting** (☎ **800/249-0662**). These trips book up pretty quickly, so call 3 to 4 days in advance to reserve a spot.

DOWNHILL SKIING

Low temperatures, black diamond runs, remote location, and an intimidating vertical drop haven't scared skiers away from Jackson Hole—this is what *attracts* them. The two largest ski resorts in the area have been expanding in recent years, putting in faster chairs, and eliminating long waits in lift lines. The quality of snow on the mountain can vary from year to year, but skiers who seek challenges will not be disappointed. Jackson has three very different ski resorts, which gives visitors some real options.

✪ **Jackson Hole Ski Resort.** 7658 Teewinot, Teton Village, WY 83025. ☎ **307/733-2292** or 307/733-4005, or 307/733-2291 for snow conditions, or 800/443-6931 for central reservations. www.jacksonhole.com. Lift tickets $54 adults, $27 seniors and children 14 and under. AE, DISC, MC, V. Open Thanksgiving to Apr 1, 9am–4pm. From Jackson: Take WY 22 west to Route 390 north to Teton Village, about 5 miles.

Every year it's something new at this resort—in 1998 it was a new gondola, in 2000 it's a high-speed quad on the Apres Vous run. The season is longer; the snow-making will increase. The improvements are designed to move this resort into the elite international ranks; incidentally, prices are moving up too. But there is special grandeur to this ski resort, from its spectacular mountaintop views to its daring black diamond runs. Take the tram to the top of **Rendezvous Mountain** and plunge down Tensleep Bowl if you want to get a taste of skiing on the edge. You'll find an inexhaustible supply of steep runs that require skiing expertise. There are lesser runs to the north, including gentler journeys down the sides of **Apres Vous Mountain** that will better suit an intermediate skier. At the bottom, two small chairs serve beginning skiers.

Luckily, crowded days have been few in recent years— lucky for skiers, at least, if not the owners. With 2,500 acres of skiable terrain, there's plenty of room. Nine lifts, a gondola, an aerial tram, and 62 named runs are available from Thanksgiving through the end of March. (Each ride on the tram costs an extra $3—but you end up only slightly higher than if you take the Sublette Quad Chair up to the top of Rendezvous Bowl.) For an orientation to the mountain, join the Ski Hosts, who gather groups at the top of the Rendezvous lift every hour on the hour to escort newcomers on a tour.

The competition among ski resorts compels growth—not just on the slopes, but in the resort village and real estate developments below. A variety of restaurants, lodging, medical clinic, shops, and entertainment—from sleigh ride dinners to skating rink— make it unnecessary to leave the complex during a ski vacation.

If you've never skied in powder up to your kneecaps, make an early-morning trip to the **Hobacks zone,** just under Cheyenne Bowl, which is set aside for perfect powder mornings. The ski patrol closes it off as soon as the snow gets tracked out.

✪ **Grand Targhee Resort.** Ski Hill Rd., Box SKI, Alta, WY 83422. ☎ **800/TARGHEE** or 307/353-2300. Lift tickets $41 adults, $24 seniors (62 and older) and children 6–14. From Jackson: Take WY 22 over Teton Pass, then ID 33 north to Driggs, then follow sign west (back into Wyoming) to Targhee resort, about 38 miles.

The Grand Targhee resort has struggled to survive, changing ownership, wheeling and dealing with federal land managers and sparring with local conservationists over expansion plans and real-estate development that is necessary to survive in the competitive resort world. None of that affects the snow, which is terrific. Or the deep, forgiving powder from November through spring (more than 500 inches annually), and a more peaceful, less-crowded village that provides a worthy alternative to Teton Village. Many skiers break up a Jackson ski trip by driving over Teton Pass for a day or two on these slopes.

This may also be a better place for less-aggressive skiers. There is a beginner's powder area and hundreds of acres of wide-open powder slopes for intermediates and other cruisers. You can take a Sno-Cat to the Peaked Mountain next door and ski in thigh-deep, untracked snow. The only problem you're likely to encounter is, oddly enough, fog. Now and then the mountain gets socked in with gray moisture, and it can be hard to find your way through the trees. The **Lost Groomer Chute,** a run that takes full advantage of the weather moving west to east, will provide the most insatiable powder hound with enough dust.

Here are a few of the other treats at Targhee: You can ride a sleigh on a starlit evening to a roundtable dinner in a snow-buried yurt; your kids can enroll in the Powder Scouts program, which gives kids ages 6 to 14 a full day of instruction, food, and skiing for $56; a spa offers everything from massage to a mineral mud wrap, along with hot tubs, sauna, exercise room and popular outdoor pool (heated, of course).

Snow King Resort. 100 E. Snow King, Jackson, WY 83001. ☎ **800/533-5464,** 800/522-7669, or 307/733-5200; or **307/734-2020** for snow conditions. Lift tickets $28 adults, $18 seniors and children under 16. Take Cache St. south to Snow King Ave. Turn left and follow signs to resort.

If you enter Jackson from the north on a winter night, the lit slopes of Snow King are an appealing sight. Snow King offers a variety of recreation, from tubing hill to ice rink to snowboard park. Plus, it's conveniently located near the heart of town. It's the oldest ski hill in Wyoming, operating since 1939, and the hotel has attractive moderately priced rooms. The only problem is the skiing itself: What looks pretty neat from a distance at night is in fact a limited number of fairly steep runs that don't offer much variety. The beginner's slope is small and amounts to only 15 percent of the terrain, and there's not enough intermediate snow to satisfy all levels of ability. The two other area resorts are much bigger, with more and longer runs and a greater variety of challenges. "Town Hill," as it's known, has 500 acres of skiable terrain, a triple chair, two double chairs, and a Poma lift.

FISHING

Yellowstone and Grand Teton National Parks are home to some fabled fishing spots (see the park sections for details), but some of the best angling in the region is found outside the park boundaries.

The **Snake River** emerges from Jackson Lake Dam as a broad, strong river, with decent fishing from its banks in certain spots—like right below the dam—and better fishing if you float the river. Fly-fishermen should ask advice at local stores on recent insect hatches and good stretches of river, or hire a guide to keep them company.

✪ **High Country Flies,** 165 N. Center St. (☎ 307/733-7210), has a vast selection of high-quality fishing gear, flies, and fly-tying supplies, along with lessons and guided trips, as well as free advice if you just want to gab about where to cast. The **Jack Dennis Outdoor Shop** on the Town Square, at 50 E. Broadway (☎ 307/733-3270), is a much bigger store with room to display some big boats, and it also offers lessons and guides. There's a smaller edition of the Dennis store in Teton Village (☎ 307/733-6838). **Westbank Anglers,** 3670 N. Moose-Wilson Rd. (☎ 307/733-6483), is another full-service fly shop that sells gear and organizes trips around Jackson Hole.

GOLF

More than one American president has played a round of golf in Jackson, which despite its short putting season has some world-leader-class links. The **Jackson Hole Golf and Tennis Club** (☎ 800/628-9988 or 307/733-3111), north of Jackson off U.S. Highway 89, has an 18-hole course that's rated one of the nation's top 10 resort courses by *Golf Digest* (just ask George Bush or Bill Clinton), as well as six tennis courts. The **Teton Pines Resort and Country Club,** 3450 N. Clubhouse Dr. (☎ 800/238-2223 or 307/733-1005), designed by Arnold Palmer and Ed Seay, is a challenging course; it's hard to imagine that this is a cross-country ski center with 14 kilometers of groomed trails in winter. Both are open to the public.

HIKING

One benefit of having so many mountain ranges converging around Jackson is that you have *choices*—especially when it comes to hiking. The most popular place to go for a stroll in the vicinity of Jackson is **Grand Teton National Park,** which shows off some glorious aspen colors in the fall. Less traveled, but more varied, are the forests that abut the park, particularly **Bridger–Teton National Forest** just east of Jackson. There are fewer amenities, and fewer restrictions, in national forests, and Bridger–Teton and its east-side counterpart, **Shoshone National Forest** encompass a huge piece of mountain real estate, including glaciers, 13,000-foot peaks, and some of the best alpine fishing lakes in the world. Among the mountain ranges included in these forests are the **Absarokas,** the **Gros Ventre,** the **Wyoming,** and the **Wind River Range,** or "Winds," as they're called by locals, which stretch about 120 miles from just southeast of Jackson near Pinedale to the South Pass area and the Red Desert. A **visitor center** located in the log cabin at 340 N. Cache in downtown Jackson (☎ 307/739-5500) provides all of the hiking and access information you'll need for the national forest as well as for the Gros Ventre and Teton wilderness areas. If you want guided hikes, ask at the visitor center.

HORSEBACK RIDING

Some hotels, including those in Grand Teton National Park, have stables and operate trail rides for their guests. For details, contact **Jackson Hole Trail Rides** (☎ 307/733-6992), **Snow King Stables** (☎ 307/733-5781), **Spring Creek Ranch Riding Stables** (☎ 800/443-6139), or the **Mill Iron Ranch** (☎ 307/733-6390).

KAYAKING, CANOEING & SAILING

With the Snake and Hoback rivers and the lakes of Grand Teton National Park, it's no surprise to see all kinds of watercraft towed or tied to the roofs of SUVs in Jackson. Canoeists and kayakers enjoy the upper Snake River, from Jackson Lake Dam down to Moose, and expert kayakers are attracted to the ride through Snake River Canyon and Hoback whitewater. Beginners should be wary of the upper Snake—snags and spring currents have claimed lives, so a guide is advisable. Canoeists paddle Jenny Lake and, with a small portage or two, String and Leigh lakes. The big lake, **Jackson,**

Boating Regulations

If you're going to set out on your own boat, you should know that before launching in the park you'll need a boat permit. Ask at the visitor center at Moose, or call the **National Park Service** at ☎ 307/739-3300 for information. Once you get outside the park, you're in the jurisdiction of the **Bridger–Teton National Forest,** offices in Jackson at 340 N. Cache (☎ **307/739-5500**).

---

attracts sailboats and sea kayaks, but beware of the sudden afternoon eruptions of gusty wind and thunderstorms.

Several operators in Jackson run schools and guide services for beginners, intermediates, and advanced paddlers. The two major outfits are the **Snake River Kayak and Canoe School,** 365 N. Cache, Jackson 83001 (☎ 800/KAYAK-01); and **Rendezvous Sports,** 1035 W. Broadway (P.O. Box 3482), Jackson, WY 83001 (☎ **307/733-2471**).

RAFTING

There are two parts to the Snake River—the smooth water, north of Jackson, and the white water of the canyon, to the south and west. A rafting trip down the upper Snake, usually from Jackson Lake Dam or Pacific Creek to Moose, is not about wild water but about wildlife: Moose, bald eagles, osprey, and other creatures come to the water just like we do. Several operators provide scenic float trips, charging around $30 for several hours on the river. Ask at **Barker-Ewing** (☎ 800/365-1800 or 307/733-1800); **Flagg Ranch,** in the north part of Grand Teton National Park (☎ 800/443-2311 or 307/543-2861); **Fort Jackson River Trips** (☎ 800/735-8430 or 307/733-2583); **Grand Teton Lodge Company** (☎ 800/628-9988); **Lewis and Clark Expeditions** (☎ 800/824-5375 or 307/733-4022); **Signal Mountain Float Trips** (☎ 307/543-2831); and **Triangle X Float Trips** (☎ 307/733-5500).

SNOWMOBILING

Though West Yellowstone is the most popular base for snowmobiling in the Yellowstone area, Jackson has a growing contingent of snowmobile aficionados and outfitters. You don't really need a guide to tour Yellowstone, where snowmobiles are required to stay on groomed roads, and you can also handle Togwotee Pass and the Granite Hot Springs area if you stick to groomed trails. Snowmobilers also head for the rugged Gros Ventre Mountains and the Greys River area, 45 miles west of Jackson. The operators who rent snowmobiles (including the necessary clothing and helmets) also offer guides to take you on 1-day and multiday tours of Jackson Hole and the surrounding area. **High Country Snowmobile Tours,** at 3510 S. Hwy. 89 in Jackson (☎ 800/524-0130), offers touring service for Jackson Hole, Yellowstone, and the Gros Ventre Mountains. **Jackson Hole Snowmobile Tours,** 1000 S. Hwy. 59 (☎ 800/633-1733), offers 1-day trips in Yellowstone and multiday trips along the Continental Divide. In addition to renting snowmobiles, **Wyoming Adventures,** 1050 S. Hwy. 89 (☎ 800/637-7147), also takes trips along the Continental Divide, as well as Grey's River. Typical 1-day outings range from $140 to $180 with pickup and drop-off service, equipment, fuel, a continental breakfast, and lunch at Old Faithful included. Multiday trip prices are from $275 to $400 per day per person (including all equipment, guide, meals, lodging, and fuel), depending on the destination.

Flagg Ranch Snowmobiles, at the south entrance to Yellowstone (☎ 800/443-2311), provides rentals and guided tours from the resort near the park's south gate. Elsewhere in Jackson, snowmobiles can be rented at **Leisure Sports,** 1075 S. Hwy. 89 (☎ **307/733-3040**), and at **BEST Adventures** (☎ **800/562-3948**).

WHITE-WATER RAFTING

The Snake River Canyon's fame has not diminished its Class IV allure to expert paddlers—but they avoid the mid-day crowds and take their white-water jollies more toward twilight. If you want to join them jolting over Lunch Counter Rapids, but you'd rather be in a raft steered by somebody who knows what they're doing (you'll be asked to paddle, and you may feel like your life depends on it), contact **Barker-Ewing** (☎ 800/448-4202); **Charlie Sands Wildwater** (☎ 800/358-8184 or 307/733-4410); **Dave Hansen Whitewater** (☎ 800/732-6295); **Jackson Hole Whitewater** (☎ 800/648-2602); **Lewis and Clark Expeditions** (☎ 800/824-5375); or **Mad River Boat Trips** (☎ 800/458-7238 or 307/733-6203).

OFFBEAT BUT MEMORABLE WAYS TO SEE THE TETONS
AERIAL TOURING

For a much quicker climb to the tops of the mountains, call **Jackson Hole Aviation** (☎ 307/733-4767), at the Jackson Hole Airport, or **Grand Valley Aviation,** Driggs Airport, Driggs, ID 83422 (☎ 208/354-8131 or 800/472-6382). You'll actually be looking down at the summits which climbers strain to top, and you'll get a new perspective on the immensity of the Grand Teton (though you won't get too close—the park has some air-space restrictions). Take your pick: Jackson Hole Aviation offers airplane trips, and Grand Valley offers the Super Teton Ride, in a glider that takes you to 11,800 feet on the west side of the Grand. Flights in the two-seater glider (you and the pilot) cost $140 for an hour; Jackson Hole Aviation charges $225 per hour for its Cessna, which can carry four passengers comfortably.

BALLOONING

It used to be that only fishermen were up at the crack of dawn in Jackson, but now you can add balloonists. The folks at the **Wyoming Balloon Company,** P.O. Box 2578, Jackson, WY 83001 (☎ 307/739-0900), like to fire up early, in the still air that cloaks the Teton Valley around 6 am. Their "float trips" stay aloft for a little more than an hour, cruising over a 3,000-acre ranch with a full frontal view of the Tetons. The journey concludes with a champagne breakfast at the landing site. Flights in a balloon cost $190 per person.

EXPLORING THE AREA

Jackson Hole Aerial Tram Rides. At Jackson Hole Ski Resort, 7658 Teewinot, Teton Village. ☎ **307/739-2753.** $16 adults, $13 seniors, $6 children, free for children 5 and under. Late May–Sept, daily 9am–5pm; mid-June to Aug, daily 9am–7pm. Tram runs approximately every half hour.

Here you can see the Tetons from an elevation above 10,000 feet—but don't expect a private tour. During busy summer days the tram carries 45 passengers, packed in like the skiers that take the lift in the winter. The top of Rendezvous Mountain offers a great view, but it can get pretty chilly, even in the middle of summer, so bring a light coat.

National Museum of Wildlife Art. 2820 Rungius Rd. (3 miles north of town on U.S. Hwy. 89, across from the National Elk Refuge). ☎ **307/733-5771.** $6 adults, $5 students and seniors, free for children under 6. Daily 9am–5pm.

If you don't spot this museum on your way into Jackson from the north, consider that a triumph of design: Its jagged, red-sandstone facade is meant to blend into the steep hillside facing the elk refuge. Within this 50,000-square-foot castle is some of the best wildlife art in the country, as well as exhibits on the elk refuge wildlife and a 200-seat auditorium where there are regular slide shows and lectures on a wide range of subjects. There are 12 exhibit galleries that display traveling shows and collections dating from the 19th century to the present, including John James Audubon and local great Carl Rungius. The museum houses a repository of internationally acclaimed wildlife films, and in the winter it's the take-off point for sled tours of the elk refuge (you can also view the wildlife through spotting scopes on the balcony). Good cafe, too.

Jackson Hole Museum. 105 N. Glenwood (at the corner of Deloney). ☎ **307/733-2414.** $3 adults, $2 seniors, $1 students and children. Mon–Sat 9:30am–6pm, Sun 10am–5pm. Closed Oct–May.

Dedicated local volunteers maintain this repository of early photographs, artifacts, and other items of historical significance, and they'll carefully guide you through the collections. You can browse the exhibits or go down the street to the Historical Society at Glenwood and Mercil to do some research. At the museum, you'll find collections of trade beads, antique pole furniture, pistols, and Indian artifacts, spread out in 3,000 square feet of floor space.

WILDLIFE WATCHING

National Elk Refuge. U.S. Hwy. 26/89, P.O. Box 510, Jackson, WY 83001. ☎ **307/ 733-9212.** Free admission. Visitor center: summer, daily 8am–7pm; winter, daily 8am–5pm.

It's not exactly nature's way, but the U.S. Fish & Wildlife Service makes sure that the elk in this area eat well during the winter by feeding them alfalfa pellets. It keeps them out of the haystacks of area ranchers, and creates a beautiful tableau on the meadowy flats along the Gros Ventre River: thousands of elk, some with huge antler wracks, dotting the snow for miles. Drivers along Highway 89 may also see trumpeter swans, coyotes, moose, bighorn sheep, and, lately, wolves. As autumn begins to chill the air in September, you'll hear the shrill whistles of the bull elk in the mountains; as snow begins to stick on the ground, they make their way down to the refuge. Though the cultivated meadows and pellets help the elk survive the winter, some biologists say this approach results in overpopulation and the spread of diseases like brucellosis.

Regardless, most of us will have few such opportunities to see these magnificent wapiti up close. Each winter from mid-December until March the Fish and Wildlife Service offers **horse-drawn sleigh rides** that weave among the refuge elk. Rides early in the winter will find young, energetic bulls playing and banging heads, while late-winter visits (when the Fish and Wildlife Service begins feeding the animals) wander through a more placid scene. Rides embark from the museum between 10am and 4pm on a first-come, first-served basis. Tickets for the 45-minute rides cost $10 for adults and $6 for children 6 to 12, and can be purchased at the National Museum of Wildlife Art. Ask about a combination pass for the sleigh ride and the museum.

OLD WEST COOKOUTS

If you don't have time or money for the full dude-ranch experience, one alternative is to make a beeline for the nearest guest ranch around mealtime to enjoy Western cuisine served up to the strains of yodelin' cowpokes.

Before you take your appetite to the ranches, check to see if reservations are necessary. The **A/OK Corral,** 10 minutes south of town at 9600 U.S. Hwy. 191 S. (☎ 307/733-6556), will let you ride a horse or a wagon up on Horse Creek Mesa for a steak dinner with a view starry-skied ($40 by horse; $28 by wagon). The **Bar-J Ranch** (☎ 307/733-3370), Teton Village Road, 1 mile north of Highway 22, is a big operation, with room for more than 700 people beneath its awnings. They serve a big meal of BBQ beef, beans, biscuits, and more, and there is cowboy humor and music ($14 for adults; $6 for children under 9; children in laps free). Reservations are recommended. The **Bar-T-5,** 790 E. Cache Creek, Jackson (☎ **800/772-5386** or 307/733-5386), offers a covered-wagon ride through Cache Creek Canyon to the "dining room" for an evening of Western victuals and after-dinner songs from the Bar-T-5's singing cowboys. The covered-wagon dinner runs around $28 for adults, $21 for youngsters 6 to 12; children 5 and under enjoy the night free.

ESPECIALLY FOR KIDS

Snow King may not have the best skiing in the valley, but it caters to kids and families. In the summer, kids can frolic on the **Snow King's Alpine Miniature Golf Course and Alpine Slide** (☎ **307/733-5200**). A round of 18 holes is $4.50 for kids, $5.50 for adults (junkies may purchase the shameful 10-round punch card for $30).

The **Alpine Slide** is the golf course's untamed neighbor. It's a wild ride down the 2,500-foot ophidian highway running from the top of the blue-and-yellow chairlift to the bottom of Snow King Mountain; it's like a water slide without the water.

In the winter, there are ski schools for kids with day-care options at all the ski resorts. Once again, Snow King has something extra: an ice skating rink, which opens in October and features skating and hockey until spring. For prices and hours, call ☎ **307/734-5200**.

SHOPPING

In recent years stores like the **Gap** (on the Town Square; ☎ **307/733-7927**) and **Polo Ralph Lauren** (75 N. Cache; ☎ **307/733-8333**) have opened factory-outlet stores in Jackson, and among the ever-changing array of shops (rents are high; so is turnover) you can find everything from Indian crafts to cowboy boots to Oriental rugs. But these are what you'll find in most resort towns. The areas where Jackson excels are its art galleries and outdoor-wear shops.

Standouts in the outdoor clothing category include **Teton Mountaineering** (170 N. Cache St.; ☎ **307/733-3595**), also a great spot for climbing, camping, and winter gear; and **Moosely Seconds** (150 E. Broadway; ☎ **307/733-7176**), where you'll find surprisingly deep discounts on quality outdoor wear.

Western art is often dismissed by collectors who tire of bighorn sheep on the crags and weather-beaten cowboys on their horses. With the real thing just outside, it's not that alluring to see the Tetons in oils . . . again. But while Jackson has plenty of that genre in stock, some of its two dozen galleries have become more adventurous and sophisticated. The **Martin Harris Gallery,** at 60 E. Broadway, looks down its nose (well, it's located upstairs) at the less sophisticated Western art in neighboring galleries, but it backs up its snobbery with beautifully displayed art, original and contemporary, while still sticking largely to Western themes. Prices are second-story as well. The beauty of Tom Mangelsen's wildlife photography has been somewhat diluted by its display in airports and malls, but Jackson is where he started, and at the **Images of Nature Gallery,** 170 N. Cache, you'll find some of his work signed and numbered. The **Center Street Gallery,** 172 Center St., has the lock on abstract Western art in Jackson. A mile north of town, at 1975 U.S. Hwy. 89 (toward the park), is the **Wilcox Gallery,** which showcases more than 20 painters and sculptors from across the nation.

WHERE TO STAY
IN JACKSON

Clustered together near the junction west of town where Highway 22 leaves U.S. Highway 26/89 and heads north to Teton Village are **Motel 6** (600 S. WY 22; ☎ **307/733-1620**) and the not-just-numerically superior **Super 8** (750 S. WY 22;

☎ **800/800-8000** or 307/733-6833). In the vicinity are the more upscale and expensive **Days Inn,** at 350 S. WY 22; ☎ **800/329-7466** or 307/733-0033, with private hot tubs and fireplaces, and the 73-room **Red Lion Inn,** at 90 W. Broadway (☎ **307/734-0035**).

Jackson Hole Lodge. 420 W. Broadway, Jackson, WY 83001. ☎ **307/733-2992.** 59 units. A/C TV TEL. $80–$130 double; $150–$280 condo. AE, DC, DISC, MC, V.

Though it sits near one of the busiest intersections in Jackson, and it's packed into a small space, this lodge is quiet and well-designed, so that its location in the heart of town becomes a plus. The pool is not just for splashing—you can lap its 40-foot length, sit in one of the whirlpools, take a sauna, or sit out on your own sundeck. Best of all are the condo lodgings, with two upstairs bedrooms, a full kitchen, and a living room with foldout couch. This gives families a little space, and it's affordable.

✪ **Rusty Parrot Lodge.** 175 N. Jackson, Jackson, WY 83001. ☎ **307/733-2000.** www.rustyparrot.com. 32 units. TV TEL. $108–$275 double; $500 suite. Rates include full breakfast. AE, CB, DC, DISC, MC, V.

The name sounds like an out-of-tune jungle bird, but since 1990 the Rusty Parrot has shown excellent pitch, cultivating a country lodge and spa right in the heart of busy Jackson. Located across from Miller Park, the Parrot is decorated in the new-Western style of peeled log, with an interior appointed with pine furniture and river rock fireplaces. One very attractive lure is The Body Sage, where you can get yourself massaged, painted with Austrian moor mud, and treated to all sorts of scrubs, wraps, and facials, for prices ranging from $45 for a hot herbal wrap to $170 for a "Himalayan Experience" that includes aromatherapy, hot-oil massage, and a hot linen pack. The breakfast that comes with your room includes omelets, fresh pastries, fruits, cereals, and freshly ground coffee; food also appears later in the day, but the lodge likes to make that a surprise (sorry). Rooms are gigantic and several have private balconies.

Trapper Inn. 235 N. Cache, Jackson, WY 83001. ☎ **800/341-8000,** or 307/733-2648 for reservations. 50 units. A/C TV TEL. $98–$178 double; $195 suite. AE, DC, DISC, MC, V.

The employees here are some of the most helpful you'll find in Jackson, and they'll tip you off on the best deals in the valley. Just 2 short blocks from the town square, the Trapper is hard to miss if you're walking north on Cache from the town square. On the left side of Cache you'll notice the crazy Trapper guy on the sign. You can walk anywhere downtown within minutes. Though the decor of the rooms is undistinguished, the space is luxurious. In the newest building, erected in 1991, many rooms come with miniature refrigerators; laundry facilities and an indoor/outdoor hot tub are also on hand.

Virginian Lodge. 750 W. Broadway, Jackson, WY 83001. ☎ **800/262-4999** or 307/733-2792. 181 units. A/C TV TEL. $95–$109 double; $125–$165 suite. AE, DC, DISC, MC, V.

It's not brand-new; it's not a resort; it doesn't have a golf course; and the highway is right outside the door, but since its overhaul in 1995, the Virginian is attempting to earn its spurs as one of the better motels in Jackson. Given its location on the busy Broadway strip, that's not likely to happen, but the prices remain reasonable, and it's a busy, cheerful place to stay. There is a large outdoor pool during warm weather, and you can get a room with a private Jacuzzi. Kids can romp in the arcade, families can eat in the Carriage House, and parents can relax in the Virginian Saloon.

Wort Hotel. 50 N. Glenwood, Jackson, WY 83001. ☎ **307/733-2190.** www.worthotel.com. 60 units. A/C TV TEL. $125–$174 double; $150–$295 suite. AE, DISC, MC, V.

Located on Broadway just off the town square—an area constantly in flux with new buildings and new shops—the Wort stands like an old tree, though its Tudor-style two-story building was largely rebuilt after a 1980 fire. Opened in the early 1940s by the wife and son of Charles Wort, an early-20th-century homesteader, it has an older style to it, both in the noisy and relaxed **Silver Dollar Bar** and the quiet, formal dining room (there's a more bustling coffee shop next to it). Rooms aren't Tudor at all—lodgepole furniture and Western artwork are the norm. In the manner of an old cattle-baron hotel, the lobby is graced by a warm, romantic fireplace; another fireplace and a huge, hand-carved mural accent a mezzanine sitting area, providing a second hideaway. Brass number plates and doorknobs welcome you into comfortable, air-conditioned guest rooms with modern decor, thick carpeting, and armoires. The Governor's Suite boasts a traditional parlor.

Dining/Diversions: The famous Silver Dollar Bar is a casual watering hole; the bar itself is inlaid with 2,032 silver dollars, the most precious piece of furniture rescued during the fire. Country-and-western music emanates from the juke box, and live entertainers appear nightly during the summer.

Amenities: A gym, whirlpool, and fitness center.

NEAR JACKSON

Amangani. 1535 NE Butte Rd., Jackson, WY 83002 (on top of East Gros Ventre Butte). ☎ **877/734-7333** or 307/734-7333. 40 units. A/C TV TEL. Summer, $600–$800 double; winter, $500–$700 double. AE, DC, DISC, MC, V.

Chopped into the side of East Gros Ventre Butte, Amangani's rough rock exterior blends well, so that the lights from its windows and pool appear at night to glow from within the mountain. The style is understated and rustic, but every detail is done with expensive style. Walking through the tall-ceilinged corridors or lounging by the outdoor pool, you know not to strike up a casual conversation with your neighbor—this place is all about class and privacy. Owner Adrianne Zecha has resorts like this around the world, from Bali to Hong Kong, and while the designs are tailored to the landscape, the approach is the same: personal service, luxury, and all the little touches. Like CDs in every bedroom. Like cashmere throws on the day beds. Like slate and redwood walls. You can get massages and facials at the health center, or dine at the Grill at Amangani. Some Jackson competitors are jealous: One suggested that Amanresorts operate on the theory that if you set your prices sky-high, a certain clientele feels it has to stay there.

Spring Creek Resort. P.O. Box 4780 (on top of the East Gros Ventre Butte), Jackson, WY 83001. ☎ **800/443-6139** or 307/733-8833. 106 units. A/C TV TEL. $210 double; $375–$1,200 condo. AE, MC, V.

Perched atop East Gros Ventre Butte, 1,000 feet above the Snake River and minutes from both the airport and downtown Jackson, this resort commands a panoramic view of the Grand Tetons and 1,500 acres of land populated by deer, moose, and the horses at its riding facility in the valley below. It seems a little less exclusive now that Amangani has opened next door. But Spring Creek still has much going for it: The rooms divided among four buildings with cabin-like exteriors have fireplaces, Native American floor and wall coverings, refrigerators, coffeemakers, and balconies with views of the Tetons. Most rooms have king- or queen-size beds, and the studio units boast kitchenettes. In addition to its own rooms, the resort arranges accommodations in the privately owned condominiums that dot the butte—large, lavishly furnished, and featuring completely equipped kitchens and sleeping accommodations. There are a pool, two tennis courts within steps of the lodgings, and a concierge who will arrange horseback rides and fishing excursions. Winter skiing at Teton Village is only 15 miles away.

IN TETON VILLAGE

Teton Village is gradually becoming the self-contained resort town now typical of better ski resorts—in the manner of a little Swiss Alps hamlet, it has everything you need, from food to powder to a massage, a short limp from the chairlifts. The village is located on the west side of the Snake River, surrounded by ranchlands that have been protected from development. But you can't get to this side of the river without passing through the clutter and traffic of Jackson's town square, unless you take a narrow little back road from Moose (and that unpaved road shouldn't be burdened with more traffic). While lodging in the town of Jackson tends to be a little cheaper in the winter than the summer, at Teton Village the ratio is reversed—rooms by the ski hill get more expensive after the snow falls.

Very Expensive

Alpenhof Hotel. 3255 W. McCollister Dr., Teton Village, WY 83025. ☎ **800/732-3244** or 307/733-3242. Fax 307/739-1516. www.alpenhof.com. E-mail: gm@alpenhoflodge.com. 42 units. A/C TV TEL. Dec–Apr, $108–$408 double; May–Sept, $78–$324 double. AE, DC, DISC, MC, V. Closed Nov.

No other spot in the village has quite the Swiss chalet flavor of this longstanding hostelry, which has a prize location only 50 yards from the ski resort tram. Four stories tall, with a pitched roof and flower boxes on the balconies, it offers a little old-world atmosphere, as well as excellent comforts and service. The management continues to upgrade, most recently redoing the dining room and deluxe accommodations with brightly colored alpine fabrics, newly constructed handcrafted European furnishings, and tiled baths with big, soft towels. Among the accommodations, you can choose from two junior suites with kitchenettes, five rooms with fireplaces, and four rooms with a shared deck—which you get to by an outside staircase. Economy rooms offer double or queen-size beds, while deluxe units are larger. Your choices for dinner include award-winning and expensive continental fare that is served in The Alpenhof dining room; or pork, game, and pasta, which are staples in Dietrich's Bar and Bistro, a casual second-level dining area overloaded with Bavarian furniture. After dinner, you may relax over cocktails by a stone fireplace, or on the outside deck. If you want to make a reservation at the Alpenhof Web site, you'll have to do it in German.

Jackson Hole Resort Lodging. 3200 McCollister Dr., P.O. Box 51087, Teton Village, WY 83025. ☎ **800/443-8613** or 307/733-3990. Fax 307/733-0244. E-mail: info@ jhresortlodging.com. 125 units. A/C TV TEL. Spring, $52–$64 double, $126 2-bedroom loft, $190–$606 3–5 bedroom home; winter, $90–$100 double, $340 2-bedroom loft, $635–$1,440 3–5 bedroom home. AE, DISC, MC, V.

The wide variety of prices above indicates the wide variety of properties now under the wing of this management group. Most of them are in the Teton Village area, and they range from the relatively inexpensive and simple Crystal Springs Inn to some deluxe private homes that reveal much about the wealth that has moved into Jackson Hole. Also on the roster here are the condos at the Jackson Hole Racquet Club, 4 miles south of the ski resort at Teton Village on 550 acres along the Moose-Wilson Road. The condos are fully equipped with fireplaces, washer-dryer, fully equipped kitchen, and other amenities used by guests who rent when the owners aren't in residence. You can comfortably fit a family in many of these loft-style condos with balconies, and the resort has extras (some require a fee) including tennis courts, a health club, and an indoor pool. Don't expect coddling from the staff, which checks you in and lets you be.

The Resort Hotel. Box 348, Teton Village, WY 83025. ☎ **800/445-4655** or 307/ 733-3657. Fax 307/733-9543. www.ResortHotelatJH.com. 101 units. A/C TV TEL. $99–$299 double. AE, DC, DISC, MC, V.

Major renovations on what was once the Sojourner Inn were completed in 1998, and it was reborn with a less distinctive name but a better facility, with prices that compare favorably to those of surrounding resort properties. Wooden walls, stone floors, overstuffed furniture, and stone fireplaces accent the main reception area. Standard guest rooms in the main lodge provide a comfortable place to hang your hat, especially in rooms with views of either the mountains or the valley floor. Larger rooms in the mountain lodge have living areas with sofa beds and tiled combination baths. Four have kitchenettes. Two restaurants are located on the mezzanine level: The **J. Hennesey Steak House** serves steak and chicken meals family-style, and the **Irish Pub and Grill** offers a place to unwind with simple fare, any beer you can think of including microbrews, pool tables, and sports on television. Summer visitors take advantage of swimming and sunning at the outdoor pool and whirlpools. Winter visitors can ski directly to a locker room with whirlpool or sauna, and drop their skis off for an overnight tune-up.

Teton Pines Resort. 3450 N. Clubhouse Dr., Jackson, WY 83001. ☎ **800/238-2223** or 307/733-1005. 18 units. A/C TV TEL. Summer, $350–$695 suite; rest of year, $125–$485 suite. AE, MC, V.

Arnold Palmer and Ed Seay designed the challenging 18-hole golf course attached to this luxury resort. Don't expect to improve your handicap on this course, but you can soothe your frustrations on the green in the comfortable rooms, which feature, among other things, his and her bathrooms, one with tub, one with shower. An upscale resort like this offers a range of recreation (though some cost extra): tennis, diving, fly-fishing and more. Five minutes away is the Jackson Hole Ski Resort. The dining room, the **Grille at the Pines,** is in the Teton Pines Clubhouse, and it's one of the better places to eat in Jackson, though, in keeping with the rest of the resort, it's pricey.

Moderate

Hostelx. Box 546, Teton Village, WY 83025. ☎ **307/733-3415.** www.Hostelx.com. Summer $40–$50 2–4 people; winter $47–$60 2–4 people.

If you came to Wyoming to ski, not to lie in the lap of luxury, get yourself a room at Hostelx and hit the slopes. It's a great bargain for skiers who don't need the trimmings, and it's not a dormitory, either—private rooms with king-size beds hold up to four people, and there's a coin-op laundry, a game room, a place to prep your skis, and a common room with a fireplace, where ski movies run during the winter. You can walk to the Mangy Moose and other fun spots, and nobody will be able to tell you apart from the skiers staying at the Ritz.

NEARBY GUEST RANCHES

Though there have been ranches in the valley for more than a century, non-Indian residents from the beginning made part of their living hosting visitors from Europe and the eastern U.S. who came to hunt, see the sights, and enjoy the outdoors. Somewhere around the century's turn the term "dude ranching" came into discourse, and Jackson joined Sheridan and Cody as popular Wyoming destinations for folks who wanted a cowboy experience. These days, some visitors would prefer not to be called "dudes"—they come out to work hard on horseback, move cattle, eat wranglers' grub, and pay dearly for it. But many of the dude ranches offer a more relaxed vacation, with riding, river floating, fine food, and plenty of boots-up porch time.

✪ **Flying A Ranch.** 771 Flying A Ranch Rd., Pinedale, WY 82941 (50 miles southeast of Jackson on U.S. Hwy. 191). ☎ **307/367-2385,** or 800/678-6543 in winter. www.flyinga.com. 7 cabins. $1,000–$1,675 per person per week. Rates include all meals and ranch activities. No credit cards.

Nestled at 8,300 feet between the Gros Ventre and Wind River ranges of Wyoming, the Flying A stuns its visitors with panoramic views. Quaking aspen, stream-fed ponds, and curious antelope are hardly disturbed by this exclusive operation, which hosts only 12 guests at a time. Built in 1929, the ranch cabins have been carefully restored, with evocative touches that include wood-burning stoves, handmade furniture constructed of native pine, and regional artwork. Typical of a dude ranch, everything is included: unlimited horseback riding (you have your own horse for the length of your stay), fishing (with lessons, if you wish), mountain biking, guided hikes, gourmet meals, and unlimited hot-tub time. The cabins are rustic on the outside, but have complete bathrooms and fireplaces, porches, and views. The quiet intimacy of this small operation is underlined by a ban on children. It's a 50 mile drive from the ranch to Jackson, where guests make forays to shop and sightsee.

Gros Ventre River Ranch. 30 miles north of Jackson on U.S. Hwy. 89 (P.O. Box 151), Moose, WY 83012. ☎ **307/733-4138.** www.ranchweb.com. 8 cabins. $945–$1,854 per person per week. Rates include all meals. No credit cards. Closed Nov and Apr.

Located in the foothills near the Moose entrance to Grand Teton National Park, the Gros Ventre is a well-established upscale guest ranch that appeals primarily to guests interested in horsebacking in the Gros Ventre Wilderness Area, fly-fishing on 1 mile of private stream, and exploring the parks. Trail rides take you to mountaintops that display dramatic geologic formations and history. The stream appeals to fishermen seeking cutthroat and rainbow trout, while two stocked ponds afford less-skilled anglers a better opportunity to catch something. A staff naturalist conducts a weekly nature hike, and mountain bikes are available for the adventurous.

The main lodge contains two oversized sitting areas with stone fireplaces, cozy reading and sitting areas, and a bar where mixers are provided during the evening cocktail hour. Dinner focuses on the gourmet presentation of beef, lamb, and salmon entrees served with mouthwatering sauces, while the pastry chef dishes up eggs Benedict, omelets, and fresh-fruit pastries every morning. Duplex lodges are enormous, 2,000-square-foot affairs with adjoining rooms and a private porch. The guest bunks are in log cabins neatly clustered near the lodge, each large enough to accommodate four people.

Heart 6 Ranch. 5 miles outside Grand Teton National Park (35 miles north of Jackson on U.S. Hwy. 26/287, Moran, WY 83013). ☎ **307/543-2477.** 15 cabins. $1,072–$1,265 per person per week. Rates include all meals. MC, V.

Slightly more than an hour's drive north of Jackson, just east of the Moran Junction, is the Heart 6, a fistful of fun for families looking to spend some time together in the West. The Heart 6 isn't the fanciest of the guest ranches in and around Jackson Hole, but it's certainly not short on entertainment for the young at heart. Fishing, horseback riding, hiking, or just sitting and talking lead the long list of outdoor activities for the short of breath and the long-winded. A naturalist from the Park Service is also on hand for many of the activities to educate guests on the local wildflowers. The ranch offers an airport shuttle system, Saturday trips to the rodeo in Jackson, and extensive children's programs (counselors look after the kids while parents ride). Baby-sitting service is also available for infants and for children up to age 4. In fact, Heart 6 is the only ranch in the valley that takes care of infants. On rainy days, kids and adults alike can enjoy the recreation center, with bumper pool, Foosball, and Ping-Pong.

⭐ **Lost Creek Ranch.** P.O. Box 95 (off Hwy. 89, 20 miles north of Jackson), Moose, WY 83012. ☎ **307/733-3435.** www.LostCreek.com. 10 cabins. $5,040–$11,600 per cabin per week. Rates include all meals, float trips, and rodeo. Call for discounted group and off-season rates. Corporate rates available. No credit cards. Closed mid-Sept to May.

The Lost Creek is so popular that one guest has stipulated in his will that his family will inherit annual trips after his demise. Reservations are at a premium with a short season, only 10 cabins and a maximum capacity of about 50 guests. If you can get in, this plush ranch offers a range of outdoor activities, crowned by gourmet meals served in a Western lodge with a full frontal view of the Grand Tetons. All the usual dude-ranch activities are available, and then some: Hiking, riding, touring and hiking in the parks, swimming pool, tennis courts, and gourmet meals are part of the package. There are special activities for young folks and baby-sitting at dinner time for kids under 6.

After all that activity, you can pamper yourself—it will cost extra—in the spa. Get a massage, a sea salt body scrub, a fango salicyl bath, a facial, a yoga class or a workout with weights. If you want to get away from the children, there's a lounge with billiards and cards. There is even a skeet-shooting range. Duplex cabins can be rented or sub-divided, since each section is outfitted with queen-size and twin beds, a private combination bath, and refrigerator. There's also a large two-bedroom cabin that has a living area with fireplace and kitchen, and sleeping quarters for seven. Weeks run from Sunday to Sunday and should be booked well in advance.

Red Rock Ranch. P.O. Box 38, Kelly, WY 83011 (30 miles northeast of Jackson on U.S. Hwy. 26/287). ☎ **307/733-6288.** 9 cabins. $1,338 per cabin per week. Rate includes all meals and horseback riding. Minimum 6-day stay (Sun–Sat). No credit cards. Closed Sept–May.

This working cattle ranch makes room for families who want a fun experience amidst the peaceful wilderness of the Gros Ventre Mountains east of Grand Teton National Park. With excellent catch-and-release fly-fishing on the ranch's private stretch of Crystal Creek, horseback riding in the mountains, and activities that include overnighters for the kids, cookouts with live music, trips to the rodeo in Jackson, and weekly country dances, this wonderful family-oriented guest ranch northeast of Jackson is a great spot to bring the whole bunch.

All nine cabins are comfortable log structures built in the 1950s, each equipped with a small refrigerator and charming woodstove (electric heat is also available). The ranch's list of amenities includes a pool hall and bar, and a recreation room for the kids. You'll also find a heated pool to warm your body on chilly Wyoming nights, and if that doesn't do the trick, try the giant hot tub that seats eight people.

The kids will have a blast here. The **Children's Riding Program** (for those 6 and older) is a great learning experience and takes kids all over the ranch by horseback, but the overnight camp out is the real Western treat. After a horseback ride to the upper end of the ranch, the kids (with the help of a couple of wranglers) set up camp and cook supper over an open fire. The night is spent playing games, telling stories, and looking up at a million stars. In the morning they fix their own breakfasts, break down the camp, then mosey on back for a well-deserved rest at the ranch.

CAMPING

There are several places to park the RV around Jackson Hole and a few of them are reasonably priced and not too far away. Most are going to charge around $20, though prices seem to change at the drop of a hat, rising just like local motel prices.

There aren't a lot of campsites for trailers close-in to this resort town anymore, because property values attract more upscale investments. The biggest is the **Virginian RV Campground,** 750 W. Broadway (☎ 800/321-6982), behind the Virginian Motel; there is also the **Wagon Wheel Campground** at 505 N. Cache St. (☎ **307/733-5488**). You'll pay between $30 and $40 for a site. If you're looking to set up a tent, and the parks are full, **Curtis Canyon Campground** (☎ 307/

739-5500) is a great campground up behind the elk refuge in Bridger-Teton National Forest, and it will cost only $10 a night. The **Snake River Park KOA Campground** is also on U.S. Highway 89, 10 miles south of town (☎ **307/733-7078**). In town, the **Wagon Wheel Campground** (☎ **307/733-4588**) is about 5 blocks north of Town Square at the Wagon Wheel Motel and has sites for less than $20. The **Teton Village KOA** (☎ **307/733-5254**), 12 miles northwest of Jackson, has nice shade trees and some sites for $30.

See also section 2, "Grand Teton National Park," below, for details on camping in Grand Teton National Park.

WHERE TO DINE

In addition to the choices reviewed below, you can get smaller, quicker bites to eat at **The Merry Piglets,** 160 N. Cache St. (☎ **307/733-2966**), a snug Mexican restaurant that also serves Thai chicken wraps. **Harvest Bakery and Natural Food Cafe,** 130 W. Broadway (☎ **307/733-5418**), serves smoothies, vegetarian meals, and other breakfast and lunch entrees made from organic ingredients. At the other end of the spectrum is **Bubba's Bar-B-Que,** 515 W. Broadway (☎ **307/733-2288**), a late-night hangout institution dishing out ribs and other meats. If you need a good shot of espresso with your morning paper, stop at **Pearl Street Bagel,** 145 W. Pearl (☎ **703/ 739-1218**), or the **Betty Rock Coffee House & Cafe,** 325 W. Pearl St. (☎ **307/ 733-0747**), where you can sit outside on the deck over an espresso or nosh on a designer sandwich and salad.

EXPENSIVE

✪ **The Blue Lion.** 160 N. Millward. ☎ **307/733-3912.** Reservations recommended. Main courses $15–$28. AE, DC, MC, V. Wed–Mon 5:30–10pm. CONTINENTAL.

In the fast-moving, high-rent world of Jackson dining, the Blue Lion stays in the forefront by staying the same. On the outside, it's a two-story blue clapboard building across from the town park that looks like a comfy family home. On the inside, in intimate rooms accented with soft lighting, diners enjoy slow-paced and elegant meals. The menu features rack of lamb and the usual (in Jackson) wild game specialties, like grilled elk loin in a peppercorn sauce. Fresh fish is flown in for dishes like the wine-basted trout stuffed with Canadian snow crab. Summer diners can eat outside on the patio deck just north of the entrance.

The Cadillac Grille. 55 N. Cache. ☎ **307/733-3279.** Reservations recommended. Lunch $5–$8; dinner $15–$25. AE, MC, V. Daily 11am–3pm and 5:30–9:30pm. CALIFORNIA ECLECTIC.

The 1950s neon and California eclectic cuisine give this restaurant a trendy air that attracts see-and-be-seen visitors more than locals. The chefs work hard on presentation, but they also know how to cook, despite the wide-ranging variety of dishes, from fire-roasted elk tenderloins to garlic-painted Chilean sea bass. The wine list is equally long and varied. The menu in this art deco restaurant changes regularly, but the place itself has become one of Jackson's longer-lived establishments.

The Granary at Spring Creek. P.O. Box 3154 (on top of the East Gros Ventre Butte), Jackson, WY 83001. ☎ **800/443-6139** or 307/733-8833. Reservations recommended. Lunch $8–$15; dinner $15–$28. AE, DC, MC, V. Daily 11:30am–2pm and 5:50–8pm. AMERICAN.

Perched atop Gros Ventre Butte, which is 15 minutes from downtown Jackson, this restaurant at Spring Creek Ranch has one of the best views ever over a plate of roasted monkfish and Tuscan bean and lobster ragout. Across the valley lie the Tetons and down below sits the Spring Creek equestrian center. Lunch is especially pleasant when weather allows dining outside on a wood deck. The menu changes, but you may find elk-flank fajitas at lunch and potato-encrusted red snapper at dinner.

The Grill at the Pines. 3450 N. Clubhouse Dr. off Teton Village Rd., Jackson, WY 83001. ☎ **800/238-2223** or 307/733-1005. Reservations recommended. Main courses $15–$28. AE, MC, V. Mon–Sat 11:30am–2:30pm and 6–9pm, Sun 9am–1pm. ECLECTIC.

This golf resort just happens to be home to what locals consider one of the finest restaurants in the valley. The Grille at the Pines overlooks a placid trout pond and Teton Pines golf course. An impressive menu includes a succulent array of well-prepared steak and veal dishes, as well as the obligatory pastas. The seafood arrives daily—for an appetizer, try the tempura nori roll, with tuna, Dungeness crab and Arctic char; for dinner, there's lamb chops with pear and mint salsa and pistachio couscous.

✪ **Nani's Genuine Pasta House.** 240 N. Glenwood. ☎ **307/733-3888.** Reservations recommended. Main courses $10–$17. MC, V. Tues–Sat 5–10pm. ITALIAN.

The setting is simple but the food is extraordinary at Nani's, where you are handed two menus: a *carta classico* featuring pasta favorites like puttanesca (tomato, anchovy, garlic, and Kalamata olives) and a bowl of mussels in wine broth, or a list of specialties from a featured region of Italy, which might include roasted pheasant and a Fontina cheese melted with eggs and cream from Valle d'Aosta. Your only problem with this restaurant might be finding it—it's tucked away behind a rather run-down motel, and one winter I found two snowmobiles parked where the outdoor tables stood the summer before. Oh well. Maybe it keeps the crowds down. If they knew how good this food was . . .

Snake River Grill. Town Square, Jackson. ☎ **307/733-0557.** Reservations recommended. Main courses $15–$30. AE, MC, V. Daily 5:30–9pm. Closed Nov and Apr. ECLECTIC.

This is a popular drop-in spot for locals, including some of the glitterati who sojourn in the area—Harrison Ford and Uma Thurman to name but a couple. The front-room dining area overlooks the busy Town Square, but there's a more private, romantic room in the back. It's an award-winning restaurant for both its wine list and its menu, which features regular fresh-fish dishes (ahi tuna is a favorite), bourbon-marinated pork chops, and some game meat entrees like venison chops and Idaho trout. The pizzas—cooked in a wood-burning oven—are topped with exotic ingredients like duck sausage or eggplant with portabello mushrooms.

Stiegler's. Teton Village Rd. at the Aspens. ☎ **307/733-1071.** Reservations recommended. Main courses $14–$24. AE, MC, V. Tues–Sun 5:30–10pm. AUSTRIAN/CONTINENTAL.

People often wonder where the von Trapps eat on vacation. Austrian cuisine isn't exactly lurking beyond every street corner waiting to be summoned with a Julie Andrews yodel. But in Jackson, the discerning Austrian has two options: Stiegler's Restaurant or Stiegler's Bar. Since 1983, Stiegler's has been confusing, astonishing, and delighting customers with such favorites as venison St. Hubertus (game dishes are de rigeur at finer Jackson dining establishments). You'll recognize the desserts, at least: Apfelstrudel and Sacher torte? Peter Stiegler, the Austrian chef, invites you to "find a little Gemütlichkeit." Tyrolean leather breeches are, of course, optional.

✪ **Sweetwater Restaurant.** At the corner of King and Pearl. ☎ **307/733-3553.** Reservations recommended. Lunch $5–$7; dinner $13–$18. DC, MC, V. Daily 11am–3pm and 5:30–10pm, shorter hours in winter. AMERICAN.

Though this little log restaurant serves American fare, it does so in a decidedly offbeat way. The eclectic menu includes, for example, a Greek salad, a Baja chicken salad, and a cowboy grilled roast beef sandwich. During the summer, there's outside dining. The dinner menu is just as quirky, and livened by nightly specials; try the unique smoked buffalo carpaccio before diving into the giant salmon fillet smoked on the Sweetwater's mesquite grill. Vegetarians will want to sample the spinach-and-feta casserole that is topped with a cheese soufflé.

MODERATE

Acadian House. 170 N. Millward. ☎ **307/739-1269.** Reservations recommended. Lunch $3–$7; dinner $9–$17. AE, DC, MC, V. Tues–Fri 11:30am–2pm and 5:30–10pm, Sat–Mon 5:30–10pm. CAJUN.

Taking over a building next to the Blue Lion puts the Acadian House in snazzy culinary company, and it seems to be holding its own with its Cajun dishes. The flavor is not as hot as you'll find in the Louisiana swamps, but there's plenty enough cayenne for Rocky Mountain taste buds. Traditional dishes like boudin—a sausage-and-rice bratwurst lookalike—next to red beans and rice, and crawfish etouffée, make appearances with continental-style creations like Cajun pasta. There is, too, an abundance of seafood and fish. If you've never treated yourself to the South's most delicious bottom-feeder, try the catfish, a delicious, blackened-to-perfection delicacy topped with almonds, pecans, and white wine.

Anthony's. 62 S. Glenwood St. ☎ **307/733-3717.** Reservations not accepted. Main courses $10–$17. MC, V. Daily 5:30–9:30pm. ITALIAN.

There was a time when Anthony's was THE Italian restaurant in Jackson, and you would stand in line for a table in an atmosphere of friendly frenzy. The menu has changed little since those days, but Anthony's is no longer top-of-the-line when it comes to dining Italian in Jackson. It's still a favorite place for families, conveniently located if you're staying in town, though there is sometimes still a wait (where isn't there?). The menu features rather heavy items like fettucine with cream, broccoli, and mushrooms, and numerous other pasta dishes.

Lame Duck. 680 E. Broadway. ☎ **307/733-4311.** Most dishes $8–$17. AE, MC, V. Daily 5:30–10pm. CHINESE/JAPANESE.

While Italian food seems to travel well to the Northern Rockies, to find a good Asian-influenced meal you have to search far and wide—or at least up Broadway toward the elk refuge. You may start worrying when you see the drinks menu—yes, you'll get a parasol in your "Pusser's Painkiller"—or the mix of Japanese and Chinese (and even Indonesian) items among the dinner fare, but don't be concerned: This is decent, middle-of-the-road cooking, and the sushi and sashimi are quite good. It's a menu with a sense of humor, including Samurai Chicken, otherwise known as Oriental fajita, and the Six Delicacies, a dish of duck, lobster, shrimp, snow peas, and mushrooms served with a secret sauce. For something to provoke the fire alarm, try the Fireworks Shrimp: shrimp, snow peas, and bamboo shoots mixed with a hot sauce that warrants a beware sign. If you have a larger, limber party, ask for the private tearoom, where you doff your shoes and eat in privacy at a lower elevation.

Mangy Moose. Teton Village. ☎ **307/733-4913.** Reservations recommended for larger parties. Main courses $11–$20. AE, MC, V. Daily 5:30–10pm. AMERICAN.

Coming off the slopes at the end of a hard day of skiing or snowboarding, you can slide right to the porch of this ski area institution. Good luck getting a seat inside, but if you like a lot of noise and laughter, a beer or glass of wine, and a tasty dish like buffalo meat loaf, you'll be patient—it beats getting into your car and driving somewhere. The decor matches the pandemonium: it looks like an upscale junk shop, with bicycles, old signs and, naturally, a moosehead or two hanging from the walls and rafters.

The food is customary Wyoming fare (steak, seafood, and pasta), with a good salad bar and a smattering of Mexican dishes. Try the hot spinach and artichoke-heart dip as an appetizer. There is often music on weekends in the bar, sometimes a well-known name like James McMurtry.

Nora's Fish Creek Inn. 5600 W. WY 22, Wilson. ☎ **307/733-8288.** Breakfast $4–$6; dinner $12–$15. DISC, MC, V. Daily 6am–9:30pm. AMERICAN.

If you like to eat among locals, and if you like to eat a lot, Nora's is the place to hang out, especially at breakfast, where there's all-you-can-eat pancakes and huevos rancheros that can barely stay aboard the huge plates. It's an institution, and if you come here regularly you'll start to recognize the regulars, who grumble over their coffee and gossip about doings in the valley. Prices are inexpensive compared to those at any of the other restaurants in town. Dinner is fish, fish, and more fish, like fresh Idaho trout.

Snake River Brewing Company. 265 S. Millward St. ☎ **307/739-2337.** Main courses $7–$11. Daily noon–11pm. PIZZA/PASTA.

Microbreweries are sprouting (and spouting) all over the country, but this one is a cut above the others, judging from the prizes it's won for its pale ale and zonker stout. In this roomy, high-ceilinged new building, the brewery also serves excellent pizza cooked in a wood-fired oven— try the P.S.T. (prosciutto, spinach, and tomato). There's also pastas, calzones, a spicy brat, and various sandwiches. The 15 brewing vats are all around and above you, sometimes humming a bit too loudly, and you can play Foosball and pool on the mezzanine. Beer lovers will appreciate the happy hour from 4 to 6pm, and there is sometimes live music—jazz or traditional Celtic.

INEXPENSIVE

Billy's Giant Hamburgers. West side of town square. ☎ **307/733-3279.** Most dishes $4–$6. AE, MC, V. Daily 11:30am–10pm. BURGERS.

If you take a wrong turn while entering the posh Cadillac Grill (right instead of left) you find yourself in this cramped 50s-style lunch booth and counter shop . . . and you might just stay. Big, juicy burgers are what you'll get, cooked right there in front of you. You can actually sit in here and order from the fancy Cadillac, perhaps a Maine lobster and a fine sauvignon blanc, but won't you feel silly when the guy in the next booth has a giant cheeseburger in his hand? Go easy on the pocketbook, relax, order a big one and a brewski, with a pile of fries on the side.

✪ **The Bunnery.** 130 N. Cache St. ☎ **307/733-5474.** Breakfast $4–$7; lunch $5–$7. MC, V. Summer, daily 7am–3pm and 5–9:30pm; winter, 7am–3pm. BREAKFAST/ SANDWICHES/SOUPS.

A Jackson mainstay, this bakery and restaurant is a great place to have one of the famous Bunnery breakfasts—perhaps a big soft spinach omelet with sour cream and Swiss, or a Bunner Benedict, served on the Bunnery's OSM (oats, sunflower, and millet) bun. These are cramped quarters, though, and you'll often find yourself waiting in a line that stretches down the boardwalk of the Hole-In-The-Wall Mall just off the square—that's not bad in the summer, but tough on a cold winter morning. Sandwiches like the grilled tuna and cheddar are reasonably priced and the portions are large. The coffee is good. And you might want to pick up a baguette or some other baked goodie on your way out.

Jedediah's House of Sourdough. 135 E. Broadway. ☎ **307/733-5671.** Reservations not accepted. Breakfast $4–$6; lunch $5–$6. AE, DC, MC, V. Daily 7am–2pm. AMERICAN.

You feel like you've walked into the kitchen of some sodbuster's log cabin home when you enter Jedediah's—exactly how they want you to feel, and the servers look as harried as they would have on the frontier. Bring a big appetite for breakfast, and a little patience—you may have to wait for a table, then you may have to wait for food, while you stare at the interesting old photos on the wall and listen to the families packed closely around you. But it's worth it, especially for the rich flavor of the sourjacks, a stack of sourdough pancakes, served with blueberries if you like. The "Diah's" omelet is a big three-egg concoction stuffed with bacon, onions, and cheddar cheese and served with a side of potatoes. During summer months, meals are also served outside on a patio.

JACKSON AFTER DARK

Talented musicians from well-known orchestras around the country do a little slumming in the mountains every summer, participating in the ✪ **Grand Teton Music Festival** (☎ **307/733-1128**) held at Teton Village in the amphitheater next to the tram lift. Under new Music Director Eiji Oue, the classical and contemporary programs have a new exuberance, highlighted by top-notch guest artists from around the world. Tickets are usually available on short notice, especially for the weeknight chamber music performances, which are often terrific.

The **Jackson Hole Playhouse,** 145 W. Deloney (☎ **307/733-6994**), and the **Grand Teton Mainstage Theatre,** 49 W. Broadway (☎ **307/733-3670**), produce musicals, melodramas, and other light fare during the summer months. Get tickets in advance for these shows.

If your idea of theater is a bunch of folks wearing cowboy hats in a bar, visit the famous **Million Dollar Cowboy Bar,** on the west side of the square, where you can dance the two-step to live bands. You can hear yourself talk more easily at the Wort Hotel's **Silver Dollar Bar** at 50 N. Glenwood, where real or imagined cowpokes belly up to the bar. And, yes, those 1921 silver dollars under your glass are authentic. But if you want some high-octane dancing fun led by some talented local hoofers, head out to Wilson (west of Jackson 5 miles on WY 22) and the **Stagecoach Bar** on a Sunday night. It's the only night they have live music in this scruffy bar and hamburger joint, and the place is jammed wall to wall. You'll see, and hopefully join, some folks who really know how to dance, fueled by a lively band including a historical novelist and the first fellow to ski off the Grand Teton (he plays banjo now—must have hurt his head), along with drop-in guitar aces and occasional celebrities (but don't count on Bob Dylan showing up *again*).

2 Grand Teton National Park

12 miles N of Jackson

Since people often think of Grand Teton in conjunction with either Yellowstone National Park or Jackson Hole, they imagine it's been around since the days of exploration, trappers, and ranch homesteads. But, it's a fairly new park, about 50 years old, just as the dramatic Tetons are a fairly young mountain range—a mere 10 million years old, give or take a millennium.

It's also a small park, at least by Yellowstone standards, comprising the eastern slope of this brief mountain range and a portion of the Snake River plain below. It lacks the unique geothermal features of its northern neighbor, but few mountains stand in such dramatic relief as the towering Cathedral Group, "Les Trois Tetons" (or "the three breasts," as cheeky French trappers named them), **Mount Owen, Middle Teton,** and **Grand Teton.** The Grand, as the locals call it, rises highest, to 13,770 feet, and it has lured climbers since the Depression era, when young Paul Petzoldt and a friend scrambled their way to the top in tennis shoes, to the astonishment of locals. Now commercial guides take hundreds of people to the summit every year, while adventurers find new and more difficult climbs in the range, or new ways of challenging themselves, like snowboarding or paragliding off the summits.

But Grand Teton is not merely an amusement park for risk-takers. There are beautiful lakes where you can sail or fish; there are hikes that take you to waterfalls and panoramic views of the valley and mountains. There are historic sites like Menor's Ferry, built a century ago to get folks across the Snake River, and some beautiful old lodges where you can experience holidays the way our grandparents did. Alpine wildflowers explode during the late spring, and hikers will often see elk, moose, trumpeter swans, bald eagles, and sometimes bears. There are peaceful nights under the stars when you might hear a chorus of yapping from coyotes, or, more recently, the throaty howls of wolves.

More than Yellowstone, Grand Teton is a modern park, beset by complex issues that sometimes pit wilderness values against modern conveniences like the commercial airport that operates here, or other uses, like the irrigation water behind Jackson Lake Dam or the cattle that graze the park's meadows.

A BRIEF HISTORY

Your first look at the Tetons, rising like spears from the Snake River plain, will take your breath away. Geologists say these mountains are still growing along a crack in the earth's crust that thrusts the range upward from the west as the valley sinks to the east. The lakebed sediments of the valley floor are actually "younger" than the pre-Cambrian rock of the peaks. Recent earthquakes in the area indicate the fault is still active. Like much of the Rocky Mountains, this range has been sculpted by glaciers, which gouged out the deep U-shaped valleys between the peaks. When the ice sheet that covered Jackson Hole melted for the last time, 15,000 years ago, it left a depression and a big mound of debris—called a terminal moraine—that formed a natural dam at the end of Jackson Lake.

The receding layers of ice created beautiful glacial lakes like Phelps, Taggart, Bradley, Jenny, String, and Leigh; polished the sides of Cascade canyon; and honed the peaks to their present jagged edges. The most prominent remnants of the glaciers are the five that have survived on Mount Moran.

The first human inhabitants of the region appeared as long as 12,000 years ago. Among the tribes who hunted here in the warmer seasons were the Blackfeet, Crow, Gros Ventre, and Shoshone. Summers were spent here hunting and raising crops, then they headed to warmer climes. The trappers and explorers who followed them into the valley were equally distressed by the harsh winters and short growing season, which made Jackson Hole a marginal place for ranching. These early homesteaders quickly realized that their best hope was to market the beauty of the area, which they began doing in earnest as early as a century ago.

The danger of haphazard development soon became apparent. There was a dance hall at Jenny Lake, hot dog stands along the roads, and buildings going up on some choice habitat. In the 1920s, Yellowstone park officials and conservationists met to discuss how the Grand Teton area might be protected, and eventually they enlisted philanthropist John D. Rockefeller, Jr., to acquire lands for a future park. In 1929 a park was established to protect the mountains, while Rockefeller continued buying up ranches at the base of the Tetons, using a dummy corporation to hide his involvement. Wyoming's congressional delegation fought hard against park designation in the valley, so in the 1940s President Franklin D. Roosevelt created the Jackson Hole National

Jackson Hole & Grand Teton National Park

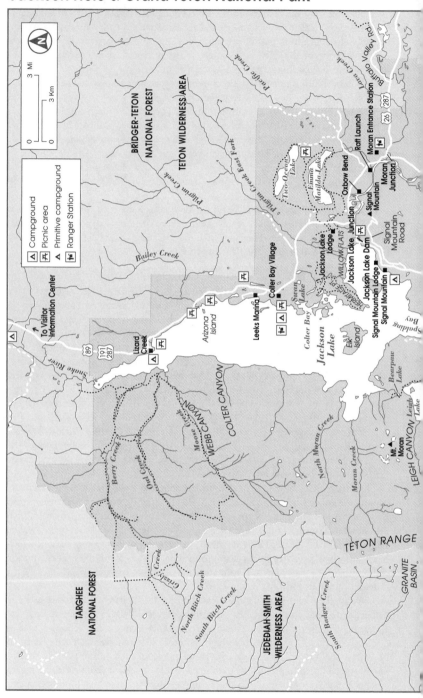

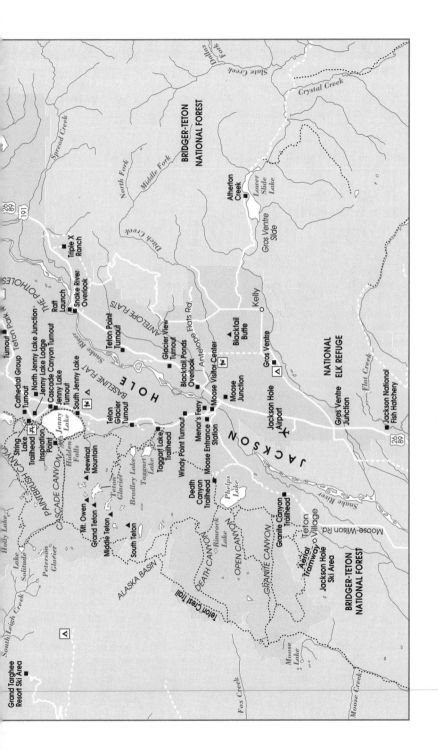

Travel Tip _____

If you're considering a visit to the area's parks prior to the middle of June, you should begin your exploration in Grand Teton before working north to Yellowstone. Elevations are slightly lower and snow melts earlier, so accumulations on trails are reduced and temperatures are moderate.

Monument. It wasn't until 1950 that Grand Teton National Park was expanded to its present form.

JUST THE FACTS
ACCESS/ENTRY POINTS

Like the range of mountains it protects, Grand Teton National Park is a strip of real estate running north-south. Teton Park Road, the primary thoroughfare, skirts along the lakes that pool at the mountains' base. From the **north,** you can enter the park from Yellowstone National Park, which is linked to Grand Teton by the **John D. Rockefeller Jr. Memorial Parkway** (U.S. Highway 89/191/287), an 8-mile stretch of highway, where you may see wildlife through the trees, some of which are bare and blackened from the 1988 fires. When you come this way, you will already have paid your entrance to both parks, so there is no entrance station, but you can stop at **Flagg Ranch,** approximately 5 miles north of the park boundary, and get park information. From December to March, Yellowstone's south entrance is open only to snowmobiles and snowcoaches.

You can also approach the park from the **east,** via U.S. Highway 26/287. This route comes from Dubois, 55 miles east on the other side of the Absaroka and Wind River Mountains, and crosses **Togwotee Pass,** where you'll get your first and one of the best views of the Tetons from above the valley. Travelers who come this way can continue south on U.S. 26/89/191 to Jackson without paying an entrance fee, though they are within the park boundaries.

Finally, you can enter Grand Teton from Jackson in the **south,** driving about 12 miles north on U.S. Highway 26/89/191 to the Moose turnoff and the park's south entrance. Here you'll find the park headquarters and visitor center, and a small community that includes dining and shops.

For details on how to fly into the region, see "Getting There" in section 1, "Jackson Hole," above.

VISITOR INFORMATION

There are three visitor centers in Grand Teton National Park. The **Moose Visitor Center** (☎ 307/739-3399), mentioned above, is a half-mile west of Moose Junction at the southern end of the park; it's open 8am to 7pm daily from June through Labor day, and 8am to 5pm the rest of the year. The **Colter Bay Visitor Center** (☎ 307/739-3594), the northernmost of the park's visitor centers, is open 8am to 8pm from early June through Labor Day, and from 8am to 5pm from Labor Day through early October. There is also **Jenny Lake Visitor Center,** open 8am to 7pm daily from early June through Labor Day and 8am to 5pm from Labor Day through early October. Maps and ranger assistance are available at all three, and there are bookstores and exhibits at Moose and Colter Bay.

To receive park maps prior to your arrival, contact **Grand Teton National Park,** P.O. Drawer 170, Moose, WY 83012 (☎ 307/739-3600). Other key park numbers include emergency park dispatch (☎ 307/739-3300), and recorded information on climbing (☎ **307/739-3604**) and campgrounds (☎ **307/739-3603**). The park's Web site is www.nps.gov/grte.

Other sources of useful information include **Travel Montana,** P.O. Box 200533, Helena, MT 59620 (☎ **800/847-4868;** visitmt.com); **Wyoming Division of Tourism,** I-25 at College Drive, Cheyenne, WY 82002 (☎ **800/225-5996;** www. wyomingtourism.org); **Yellowstone Country,** Box 1107, Red Lodge, MT 59068 (☎ **800/736-5276**); **Jackson Chamber of Commerce,** Box 3, Jackson, WY 83001 (☎ **307/733-3316**); and **Cody Country Chamber of Commerce,** P.O. Box 2777, Cody, WY 82414 (☎ **307/587-2777**).

FEES & BACKCOUNTRY PERMITS

There are no park gates on U.S. Highway 26/89/191, so you get a free ride through the park on that route, but if you want to get off the highway and explore, you'll pay $20 per automobile for a 7-day pass. That's a good deal, and it can be better: If you expect to visit Yellowstone and Grand Teton (admission is good for both) more than once a year, buy a $40 annual permit; or, better, yet, if you visit parks elsewhere in the country, buy a $50 **Golden Eagle Passport,** good for all parks and national monuments for a year from the month of purchase. Senior citizens can get a **Golden Age Passport** for $10 annually, and blind or permanently disabled travelers can obtain a **Golden Access Passport,** which costs nothing. Most of this money goes back into the park where it was collected, so consider it a contribution worth making: In Grand Teton, this revenue has been spent on rehabbing the Jenny Lake Overlook, trail maintenance, and restoring the lakeshore at Jenny Lake, among other things.

For information on camping fees at Grand Teton National Park, see "Camping," below.

Backcountry Permits are required from the Park Service for overnight use of backcountry campsites. The permits are free, but they can only be reserved from January 1 to May 15; thereafter, all backcountry permits are issued on a first-come, first-served basis up to 24 hours before your first night out. Permits are issued at the Moose and Colter Bay visitor centers and the Jenny Lake ranger station. Reservations may be made by writing the **Permits Office,** Grand Teton National Park, P.O. Box 170, Moose, WY 83012, or by sending a fax to **307/739-3438.** Phone reservations are not accepted.

Boating permits are required if you bring your own boat, but they are included in the price of a boat rental. Motorized boats are permitted on Jenny, Jackson, and Phelps lakes, while sailboats, windsurfers, and jet skis are allowed only on Jackson. Boats paddled by humans are permitted on most park lakes and the Snake River, with a permit, which you can get at Moose or Colter Bay. For motorized craft the cost is $20 for annual permits and $10 for 7-day permits. Fees for nonmotorized boats are $10 for annual permits and $5 for 7-day permits. Motorized boating is restricted to designated areas.

State of Wyoming **fishing licenses** are required for anyone over 14 years of age. An adult nonresident license costs $6 per day, $65 for the season. Youth fees (ages 14 to 18) are $10 for 10 days, $15 for the season. (A Wyoming resident pays $15 for a season permit.) You can buy them at sporting goods stores or park visitor centers. The entirety of the Snake River is open for fishing from April 1 to October 31; Jackson Lake is closed October 1 to 31. Because the Snake River flows into, and exits, Jackson Lake, different regulations apply to various sections of the river, and several are closed; the prudent fisherman will become knowledgeable of these laws lest he be fined.

REGULATIONS

BIKES   Though it's not uncommon to see cyclists, bikes are prohibited on back-country trails and boardwalks. Cyclists ride along the roadside in the park where no bike paths currently exist, and this can be harrowing, especially along the many curves in the park where drivers may not be prepared for a sudden encounter with a cyclist. Wear safety gear that includes a helmet and high-visibility clothing, at least.

DEFACING PARK FEATURES   Picking wildflowers or collecting natural or archaeological objects is illegal.

FIREARMS   Firearms are not allowed in the park. However, unloaded firearms may be transported in a vehicle when cased, broken down, or rendered inoperable. Ammunition must be carried in a separate compartment of the vehicle.

LITTERING   Littering in the national parks is strictly prohibited. The park promotes a "Leave No Trace" program for backcountry use, and park rangers will provide you with a list of suggestions to minimize your impact on wilderness. Most important, if most obvious, is that whatever you pack in, you must pack out.

MOTORCYCLES   Motorcycles, motor scooters, and motor bikes are allowed only on park roads. No off-road or trail riding is allowed. Operator licenses and license plates are required.

PETS   Pets must be leashed and are not allowed more than 50 feet from roadways; on trails, boats, or boardwalks; or in the backcountry. They are allowed in campgrounds, but must be restrained at all times.

SEASONS

Spring is an excellent time to visit the park—but remember that spring starts later in Wyoming than in most other parts of the country. In **May and June,** mild days and cool nights intersperse with occasional rain and snow. The snow level usually remains above valley elevation until mid-June. Wildflowers are in bloom, and on a clear day the snow-covered Tetons stand out boldly against a crisp blue sky. Even better, trails are virtually devoid of hikers, though at higher elevations, snow might still block the paths; check in at one of the ranger stations for trail conditions.

   Summer is the most intense season at Grand Teton, with flowers blooming, fish and wildlife feeding, and all sorts of activity crammed into a few months of warm weather, from July to early September.

   In **September,** sunny days and cooler nights alternate with rain and occasional snowstorms, and by the middle of the month, fall colors begin to make their way across the landscape.

   The first big snow usually arrives by the beginning of November (though it's not unheard of in July!). In winter months temperatures stick in the single digits, with sub-zero overnight temperatures common.

AVOIDING THE CROWDS

As with Yellowstone, crowds thin in the park after Labor Day, and you can enjoy sunny days and brilliant aspen yellows well into October. When there are crowds, you can avoid them by staying away from the centers of activity, which are Colter Bay, Jenny Lake, and Moose. Check out the overlooks, photograph the sites, wander through some educational exhibits, then abandon the paved areas for unpaved trails.

TIPS FOR TRAVELERS WITH DISABILITIES

Visitor centers at Moose, Colter Bay, Jenny Lake, and Flagg Ranch provide interpretive programs, displays, and visitor information in several formats, including visual,

Those who are only passing by, and never plan to get far from their cars, can see the full spectacle of these mountains without paying a park entry fee. If you come from the east, you will pass no toll booths on your way south on U.S. Highway 26/89/191, but there are frequent pullouts on the west side of the road that give you a panoramic overview of the Snake River and the Tetons. For that matter, you get a more distant, but equally grand, view of the mountains coming over **Togwotee Pass** on U.S. Highway 26/287.

audible, and tactile. Large-print scripts, braille brochures, and narrative audiotapes are available at Moose and Colter Bay.

Accessible parking spaces are located close to all visitor center entrances; curb cuts are provided, as are accessible rest room facilities.

Campsites at Colter Bay, Jenny Lake, and Gros Ventre campgrounds are on relatively level terrain; Lizard Creek and Signal Mountain are hilly and less accessible. Picnic areas at String Lake and Cottonwood Creek are both accessible, though the toilet at Cottonwood is not.

Accessible dining facilities are located at Flagg Ranch, Leek's Marina, Jackson Lake Lodge, and Jenny Lake Lodge.

More information is available by contacting **Grand Teton National Park,** Drawer 170, Moose, WY 83012 (☎ **307/739-3600;** www.nps.gov/grte).

VIEWING THE PEAKS

The Cathedral Group is composed of **Grand Teton** (elevation 13,770 feet), **Middle Teton** (elevation 12,804 feet), and **Mount Owen** (elevation 12,928 feet). Nearby, almost as impressive, are **South Teton** (elevation 12,514 feet) and **Teewinot** (elevation 12,325 feet).

If you come from the north, and Yellowstone National Park, you will have paid a park entry fee and be entitled to explore along **Teton Park Road,** west of the Snake. You'll be looking at mountains as you drive the east shore of Jackson Lake, and you'll find plenty of opportunities to pull over and snap your shutter. Four miles south of Colter Bay, you can take an unpaved, 1-mile road heading east from the highway to the **Grand View Overlook.** A large, flat area at the end of the road offers a commanding view of the Grand Tetons, and an excellent picnic spot. This road is great for autos, hikers, and bicycles, but not for large RVs.

You'll also get excellent views of the Cathedral Group on the trails and roads that ring **Jenny Lake** (see "Seeing the Highlights," below).

Signal Mountain, southeast of Jackson Lake, may not rank up there with the other Tetons, but you can drive right up it to an excellent lookout spot. Navigating the twisting, narrow road pays off at the summit, where you can gaze out over the valley, Cascade Canyon, Jackson Lake, and the Tetons.

Slightly north of Jenny Lake is the underrated, yet still awesome, **Mount Moran** (elevation 12,605 feet), the fourth-largest peak in the range; its curiously flattened, sheared-off summit is the result of erosion back in geologically volatile times.

SEEING THE HIGHLIGHTS
JACKSON LAKE & THE NORTH END OF THE PARK

A great many people enter Grand Teton National Park from the north end, emerging from Yellowstone's south entrance with a 7-day park pass that gets them into Grand

Teton as well. Yellowstone is connected to Grand Teton by a wilderness corridor through which the **John D. Rockefeller Jr. Memorial Parkway** runs for 56 miles. Along it, you'll see an interesting area of meadows sometimes dotted with elk, the Snake River as it runs into Jackson Lake, and forests that in some places still show the impact of the 1988 fires. Some people complain about the sight of blackened tree trunks, but others are heartened to see the mosaic shapes of natural burn and the soft green of new trees sprouting.

Along the parkway, not far from Yellowstone, you'll pass your first lodging option, the recently modernized **Flagg Ranch** (see "Where to Stay in the Park" below), with gas, restaurants and other services. In the winter this is a busy staging area for the snowcoach and snowmobiling crowd.

JACKSON LAKE　　The north end of the park is dominated by giant **Jackson Lake,** a huge expanse of water that fills a deep gorge left 10,000 years ago by retreating glaciers. Though it empties east into the Snake River, curving around in the languid **Oxbow Bend**—a favorite wildlife-viewing float for canoeists—the water from Jackson Lake eventually turns south and then west through Snake River Canyon and into Idaho. In 1911 potato farmers downstream were instrumental in getting Congress to fund Jackson Lake Dam, which raised the lake about 40 feet and drowned a lot of trees. Now stream flow is regulated at the dam for both farmers and rafters in the canyon, and, for better or ill, we have an irrigation dam in a national park. The dead trees have been cleared out, and the dam was rebuilt in 1989. Elsewhere on the lake, things look quite natural, except when water gets low in the fall.

LEEKS MARINA　　As the road follows the east shore of the lake from the north, the first development travelers encounter is **Leeks Marina,** where boats can launch, gas up, and moor from mid-May to mid-September. There is a casual restaurant serving light fare and pizza during the summer. But drivers also have the option of stopping at numerous picnic pullouts along the lake.

COLTER BAY　　Just south of Leeks is **Colter Bay,** a busy outpost of park services where you can get groceries, postcards and stamps, T-shirts, and advice. If this is your first stop in the park, get maps and information at the **Colter Bay Visitors Center.** Here you can view park and wildlife videotapes and attend a park-orientation slide program throughout the day. Ranger-led activities include museum tours, park-orientation talks, natural history hikes, and evening amphitheater programs. Colter Bay has lots of overnight options, from its cabins to its old-fashioned tent camps to its trailer park and campground. There are also a general store and do-it-yourself laundry, two restaurants, a boat launch and boat rentals, and tours. You can take pleasant short hikes in this area, including a walk around the bay or out to **Hermitage Point** (see "Hiking," below).

The **Indian Arts Museum** (☎ **307/543-2467**) at the Colter Bay Visitors Center is worth a visit, though it is not strictly about the Native American cultures of this area. The artifacts are mostly from Plains Indian tribes, but there are also some Navajo items from the Southwest. The collection was assembled by David T. Vernon, and includes pipes, shields, dolls, and war clubs sometimes called "skull crackers." There are large historic photos in the exhibit area.

JACKSON BAY JUNCTION　　From Colter Bay, the road swerves east and then south again past **Jackson Lake Lodge** (see "Where to Stay in the Park," below), a well-heeled 1950s-style resort with a great view of the Tetons and brushy flats in the foreground where moose often roam. Numerous trails emanate from here, both to the lakeshore and east to **Emma Matilda Lake** (see "Hiking," below). The road then becomes **Jackson Lake Junction,** where you can either continue west along the lakeshore or go east to the park's **Moran Entrance Station.** Here the park's odd entrance configuration comes into play: If you go out through the Moran entrance you are still in the park, and may turn south on U.S. Highway 26/89/191 and drive along the Snake River to Jackson, making most of your journey within the park's borders, though you might not know it.

SIGNAL MOUNTAIN   But if you're here to enjoy the park, you'd probably turn west on **Teton Park Road** at Jackson Lake Junction, and arrive after only 5 miles at **Signal Mountain.** Like its counterpart at Colter Bay, this developed recreation area, on Jackson Lake's southeast shore, offers camping sites, accommodations in cabins and multiplex units, two restaurants, and a lounge with one of the few live televisions in the park. This is also the place to fill up on gasoline and provisions from the small convenience store. Boat rentals and scenic cruises of the lake also originate here.

If you turn east instead of west off Teton Park Road at Signal Mountain, you can drive up a narrow, twisting road to the **top of the mountain,** 1,000 feet above the valley, where you'll have a fine view of the ring of mountains—Absarokas, Gros Ventres, Tetons, and Yellowstone Plateau—that create the Jackson "Hole." Note also the potholes created in the valley's hilly moraines left by retreating glaciers. Below the summit, about 3 miles from the base of the hill, is **Jackson Point Overlook,** a paved path 100 yards long leading to the spot where the Hayden Expedition's photographer, William Henry Jackson, shot his famous wet-plate photographs of Jackson Lake and the Tetons more than a century ago—proof to the world that such spectacular places really existed in the Rockies.

JENNY LAKE & THE SOUTH END OF THE PARK

JENNY LAKE   Continuing south along Teton Park Road, you move into the park's southern half, where the tallest peaks rise abruptly above a string of smaller lakes strung together in the foothills—**Leigh Lake,** the appropriately named **String Lake,** and **Jenny Lake,** which is the favorite of many park visitors. At North Jenny Lake Junction you can take a turnoff west to **Jenny Lake Lodge** (see "Where to Stay in the Park,"below)—the road then continues as a one-way scenic loop along the lakeshore before rejoining Teton Park Road about 4 miles later.

Beautiful **Jenny Lake** gets a lot of traffic throughout the summer, both from hikers who circumnavigate the lake on a 6-mile trail and from more sedentary folks who pay for a boat ride across the lake to Hidden Falls and the short, steep climb to Inspiration Point (see "Hiking," below). The parking lot at **South Jenny Lake** is often jammed, and there can be a long wait for the boat ride, so you might want to get there early in the day. There is also a tents-only campground, a visitor center, and a general store stocked with a modest supply of prepackaged foods, and even less fresh produce and vegetables. You can take a fairly level and easy hike around the south end of the lake to Hidden Falls or grab a ride with the **Teton Boating Company (☎ 307/ 733-2703).**

SOUTH OF JENNY LAKE   South of the lake, Teton Park Road crosses open sagebrush plains with never-ending views of the mountains. You'll pass the **Climbers' Ranch** (see "Climbing," below)—an inexpensive dorm-lodging alternative for climbers—and some trailheads for enjoyable hikes to **Taggart Lake** and elsewhere. Look closely in the sagebrush for the shy pronghorn, more commonly called antelope. This handsome animal, with tan cheeks and black accent stripes, can spring up to 60 miles an hour. If you wander in the sagebrush here, you may encounter a badger, a shy but mean-spirited creature that sometimes comes out of its hole at morning or twilight.

Insider Tips

Some of the best spots aren't highlighted on the map. On the west side of the road from Signal Mountain to the Jenny Lake cutoff, approximately 1.2 miles north of the Spring Lake–Jenny Lake scenic drive cutoff, is an unmarked, unpaved road that leads to **Spalding Bay** (it's an unnamed black line on the Park Service map). You'll travel through bumpy moose habitat before curling down a steep hill to a back bay of the lake, where you'll find a small campsite, boat launch with parking for trucks and boat trailers, and primitive rest room. Use of the campsite requires a park permit, but we think this site provides an excellent opportunity to find seclusion with excellent views of the lake and mountains. The road is easily negotiable by an automobile or sports-utility vehicle; we would not recommend a motor home or towed trailer.

The **Teton Glacier Turnout** presents a view of a glacier that grew for several hundred years until, within the past century, it reversed direction, pressured by hotter summer temperatures, and began retreating.

MOOSE VISITOR CENTER   The road arrives at the park's south entrance again, actually well within the park's boundaries—and the sprawling **Moose Visitor Center,** which is also park headquarters. If you are approaching the park from the south rather than the north, this is where you'll get maps, advice, and some interpretive displays.

Just behind the visitor center is **Menor's Ferry.** Bill Menor had a country store and operated a ferry across the Snake River at Moose back in the late 1800s. The ferry and store have been reconstructed, and you can buy items similar to the ones Menor used to sell here. Nearby is a cabin where a bunch of conservationist conspirators met in 1923 to plot the protection of the natural and scenic quality of the area, an idea that eventually led to the creation of the national park.

Also in this area is the **Chapel of the Transfiguration.** In 1925, this chapel was built in Moose so that settlers wouldn't have to make a long buckboard ride into Jackson. It's still in use for Episcopal services from spring to fall, and it's a popular place to get hitched, with a view of the Tetons through a window behind the altar.

DORNAN'S   This is a small village area just south of the visitor center on an in-holding of private land owned by one of the area's earliest homesteading families. There are a few shops and a semi-gourmet grocery store, a post office, a bar where there is sometimes live music, and a first-rate wine shop, of all things.

OTHER PARK HIGHLIGHTS

The highway route through the park on the east side of the Snake has several turnouts for shutterbugs (better have a wide-angle lens!). Among the stops you can make are the **Glacier View Turnout** (where you can view an area that 150,000 or so years ago was filled with a 4,000-foot-thick glacier) and the **Blacktail Ponds Overlook** (a beaver dam subdivision). Gazing out across **Snake River Overlook** at the plateaus that roll from riverbed to valley floor lends vivid insight into the power of the glaciers and ice floes that sculpted this landscape. If you want to go a ways off-road and down to the river, you can try the **Schwabacher landing** dirt road or the four-wheel-drive trip to Deadman's Bar Overlook.

Only 5 miles north of Jackson on U.S. Highway 26/89/191 you can turn east on the **Gros Ventre River Road** and follow the river east into its steep canyon—a few miles past the little town of Kelly you'll leave the park and be in **Bridger–Teton**

National Forest. In 1925, a huge slab of mountain broke off the north end of the Gros Ventre Range on the east side of Jackson Hole, a reminder that nature still has an unpredictable and violent side. The slide left a gaping open gash in the side of Sheep Mountain, sloughing off nearly 50 million cubic yards of rock and forming a natural dam across the Gros Ventre River half-a-mile wide. Two years later, the dam broke, and a cascade of water rushed down the canyon and through the little town of Kelly, taking several lives. The town of **Kelly** is a quaint and eccentric community with a large number of yurts.

Up in the canyon formed by the Gros Ventre River there are a roadside display with photographs of the slide area and a short nature walk from the road down to the residue of the slide and **Lower Slide Lake,** with signs identifying the trees and plants that survived or grew in the slide's aftermath.

RANGER-LED ACTIVITIES

It's got to be the best bargain in the world: National parks offer all sorts of free presentations and guided hikes throughout the summer days, and the rangers are generally personable and knowledgeable. At Grand Teton, you can sit on the back deck at Colter Bay and chat with a ranger while you look through a spotting scope at twilight, watch an evening slide show at an outdoor amphitheater, or walk among the wildflowers around Taggart Lake with a naturalist who knows their names.

At the north end of the park, based around the Colter Bay Visitors Center, you can take a **lakeshore stroll** with a ranger and learn about the geological and glacial forces that shaped the lake and mountains, or, if that hour-long walk seems too strenuous, sit out on the Jackson Lake Lodge deck and chat with the ranger while you look for moose through the spotting scope. There are summer **campfire programs** nightly from June through September at the Colter Bay amphitheater and the Flagg Ranch campfire (check at the information center). From the Colter Bay Marina (fee charged for boat ride; ☎ **307/543-2811**) you can join a daily cruise around the lake with a ranger telling you what's what.

At the south end of the park there are daily wildflower walks from the **Taggart Lake** trailhead in June and July, **campfire programs** at Signal Mountain and Gros Ventre campground in the evenings, slide shows, and a twilight hike with a ranger around the south shore of Jenny Lake that takes about 3 hours—well worth it. You can also take a trip by boat across Jenny Lake ($5 for adults, $3.50 for children) and hike with a ranger to **Hidden Falls** and **Inspiration Point.** It's not a difficult hike (you could hot-foot it around the lake and save the boat fare), and you may be inspired to go on up **Cascade Canyon** on your own.

ORGANIZED TOURS & ACTIVITIES

✪ **Great Plains Wildlife Institute** (☎ **307/773-2623;** www.wildlifesafari.com) offers trips on open-roofed vans, rafts, and sleighs, and by foot. These tours bring visitors closer to the wildlife than they're likely to get on their own, and guests sometimes participate in radio tracking and other research projects. The **Teton Science School** (☎ **307/733-4765;** e-mail: tss@wyoming.com) is a 30-year-old institution with a cabin campus in the park that offers summer programs for students and adults that discuss the ecology, geology, and wildlife of the park, with workshops in photography and tracking, too. The **Grand Teton Natural History Association** is a not-for-profit organization that provides myriad information about the park, including information for travelers through its bookstores at visitor centers in and around the park. These materials are available by writing the association at P.O. Drawer 170, Moose, WY 83012 (☎ **307/739-3403;** www.granteton.com/gtnha).

SPORTS & OUTDOOR ACTIVITIES

See pp. 337–340 for the section on hiking in Grand Teton.

For lovers of outdoor recreation, Grand Teton offers one of the most accessible play-lands of rock and water in the Lower 48. Hikers can don their boots and motor down trails long or short; mountaineers and technical climbers can head for the highest hills. Paddlers can try the smooth waters of the lakes or get into the livelier flow of the Snake River; there are also waters open to power- and sailboats.

BIKING   The roads in Grand Teton were not built with bicyclists in mind, though the flats of the valley seem perfect for pedaling. The problem is safety—there are huge RVs careening about, and some roads have only narrow shoulders. Teton Park Road has been widened somewhat, but traffic is heavy here; road bikers should try **Antelope Flats,** beginning at a trailhead 1 mile north of Moose Junction and going east. Some-times called **Mormon Road,** this paved route crosses the flats below the Gros Ventre Mountains, past old ranch homesteads and the small town of Kelly. It connects to the unpaved **Shadow Mountain Road,** which actually goes outside the park into national forest, climbing through the trees to the summit. Total distance is 7 miles and the ele-vation gain is 1,370 feet, and you'll be looking at Mount Moran and the Tetons across the valley.

Mountain bikers have a few more options: Try **Two-Ocean Lake Road** (reached from the Pacific Creek Road just north of Moran Junction) or the **River Road,** a 15-mile dirt path along the Snake River's western bank (bison use it, too, so go easy). Ambitious mountain bikers may want to load their overnight gear and take the **Grassy Lake Road,** once used by Indians, west from Flagg Ranch on a 50-mile journey to Ashton, Idaho. A map that shows bicycle routes is available from the Park Service at visitor centers or at Dornan's store at the Moose Junction.

BOATING   Boaters have more choices in Grand Teton than they do in Yellowstone. Motorboats are permitted on Jenny, Jackson, and Phelps lakes. Rafts, canoes, dories, and kayaks are allowed on the Snake River within the park. No boats are allowed on Pacific Creek or the Gros Ventre River. Bigger boats find room on Jackson Lake, where powerboats pull skiers, sailboats move noiselessly in summer breezes, and fishermen ply the waters in search of wily trout. Those who venture on the big lake need to be aware that the weather can change suddenly, and late-afternoon lightning is not uncommon; sailors should be particularly wary of the swirling winds that accompany thunderstorms. **Scenic cruises** of Jackson Lake, as well as twice-a-week floating steak-fry cruises, are available daily at the **Colter Bay** marina from May through September. See "Fees & Backcountry Permits" above for information on boat permits. Boat and canoe rentals, tackle, and fishing licenses are available at **Colter** and **Signal Moun-tain.** Shuttles to the west side of Jenny Lake, as well as cruises, are conducted by **Teton Boating Company** (☎ 307/733-2703).

CLIMBING   Every year there are rescues of climbers who fall or get trapped on Teton rock faces, and many years there are fatalities. Yet the peaks have a strong allure for climbers, even inexperienced ones, perhaps because you can reach the top of even the biggest ones in a single day . . . but not easily. The terrain is mixed, with snow and ice year-round—knowing how to self-arrest with an ice axe is a must—and the weather can change suddenly. The key is to get good advice, know your limitations, and if you're not already skilled, take some lessons at the local climbing schools (see "Getting Outside," in the Jackson Hole section).

Climbers who go out for a day do not have to register or report to park officials, so they should be sure to tell friends where they're going and when they'll be back. Overnight climbers must pick up a free permit. Climbing rangers who can lead rescue efforts are on duty at the **Jenny Lake Ranger Station** at South Jenny Lake from June until the middle of September. The American Alpine Club provides cheap dormitory beds for climbers at the Grand Teton Climbers' Ranch (Climbers' Ranch, Moose, WY 83012). Guided climbs of Grand Teton are offered by **Jackson Hole Mountain Guides** (☎ **307/733-4979**) and by **Exum Mountain Guides** in Moose (☎ **307/733-2297**).

CROSS-COUNTRY SKIING   You can ski flat or you can ski steep in Grand Teton. The two things to watch out for are hypothermia and avalanche. As with climbing, know your limitations, and make sure you're properly equipped. Check with local rangers and guides for trails that match your ability. Among your options are the relatively easy Jenny Lake Trail, starting at the Taggart Lake Parking Area, about 8 miles of flat and scenic trail that follows Cottonwood Creek. A more difficult ski is the Taggart Lake–Beaver Creek Loop, a 3-mile route that has some steep and icy pitches coming back. About 4 miles of the Moose-Wilson Road—the back way to Teton Village from Moose—is unplowed in the winter, and is an easy trip through the woods. You can climb the winding unplowed road to the top of Signal Mountain—you may encounter snowmobiles—and have some fun skiing down. There is an easy ski trail from the Colter Bay Ranger Station area to Heron Pond—about 2.6 miles, with a great view of the Tetons and Jackson Lake. Get a ski trail map from the visitor centers.

FISHING   The lakes and streams of Grand Teton are popular fishing destinations, loaded with lively cutthroat trout, whitefish, and mackinaw (lake) trout in Jackson, Jenny, and Phelps lakes. Jackson has produced some monsters weighing as much as 50 pounds, but you're more likely to catch fish under 20 inches, fishing deep with trolling gear from a boat during hot summer months. The Snake River runs for about 27 miles in the park, and has cutthroat and whitefish up to about 18 inches. It's a popular drift boat river for fly-fishermen. If you'd like a guide who knows the holes, try **Jack Dennis Fishing Trips** (☎ **307/733-3270**), **Solitude Float Trips** (☎ **307/733-2871**), or **Fort Jackson Float Trips** (☎ **800/735-8430**). As an alternative, stake out a position on the banks below the dam at **Jackson Lake,** where you'll have plenty of company and just may snag something. You'll need a Wyoming state fishing license (nonresident $6 for 1 day, $65 for season; $15 for youngsters 14 to 18, no license for under 14), and you'll have to check creel limits, which vary from year to year and place to place.

RAFTING & FLOAT TRIPS   The upper end of the Snake River in the park can be deceptive—its smooth surface runs fast during the spring, and there are deadly snags of fallen trees and other debris. Check with rangers before putting your boat in— they'll discourage you if they think your skills may not match the river—and proceed with caution. It's a wonderful river for wildlife, too, with moose, eagles, and other animals coming, like you, to the water's edge. There are many commercial float operators in the park who will allow you to relax more and look around. They mostly run from mid-May to mid-September (depending on weather and river flow conditions). These companies offer 5- to 10-mile scenic floats, some with early-morning and evening wildlife trips. Try **Triangle X-Osprey Float Trips** (☎ **307/733-5500**), **Barker-Ewing Float Trips** (☎ **800/365-1800**), **Grand Teton Lodge Company** (☎ **307/543-2811**), and **Flagg Ranch Float Trips** (☎ **307/543-2861**).

HIKING
DAY HIKES
Many people cross Jenny Lake, either by boat or on foot around the south end, to hike up into **Cascade Canyon,** a steep but popular journey that takes you first to **Hidden**

Picture Perfect ────────────────────────────────

A meadow near the summit of Signal Mountain presents an excellent opportunity to look to the west for photos of both Mount Moran and the Grand Tetons. The best time to take those photos is before 11am, when the sun will be mostly at your back, or in the early evening, when the sun will backlight the crests to the west.

Falls (less than 1 mile of hiking if you take the boat; 5 miles if you walk around) or another half mile to **Inspiration Point.** You can blame the boat shuttle for the crowds; the easy hike around the south end of the lake is refreshing, uncrowded, and a good prelude to heading up the canyon. Most people go no farther than Inspiration Point, but unless you have a heart condition, you should go on. It's a steep climb to the entrance of the canyon, followed by a gentle ascent though a glacially sculpted canyon. At a fork in the trail around 4 miles from Inspiration Point you can follow either the north fork of Cascade Creek to Lake Solitude (3 miles) or the south fork to Hurricane Pass (5 miles). Try the north fork for a more relaxed day hike. Wildflowers carpet the area, ducks nest along Cascade Creek, and moose and bear may be spotted. The round-trip up into the canyon is about 4½ miles.

A less-taxing alternative to the Cascade Canyon trip mentioned above is a detour to **Moose Ponds,** which begins on the Inspiration Point trail. The ponds, located 2 miles from the trailhead, are alive with birds. The area near the base of Teewinot Mountain, which towers over the area, is populated with elk, mule deer, black bears, and moose. The trail is flat (at lake level), short, and easy to negotiate in 1 to 1½ hours. The best times to venture forth are in early morning and evening.

Just down the road from South Jenny Lake is the trailhead to **Taggart Lake,** a particularly interesting hike that winds through a burned-out area in the process of recovery to a glacial lake. The hike from the parking lot to the lake (a decent fishing spot) is only 1.6 miles along the eastern route, and rarely crowded. After reaching the lake, you can return by the same trail or continue the loop on the **Taggart Lake Trail,** which leads around one end of the pond and loops back to the trailhead through a more heavily forested area. This route adds 0.8 mile to the trip, and the elevation gain is 467 feet. At its highest point, the trail overlooks all of Taggart Lake and the stream that flows from it.

Upon reaching Taggart Lake, a second alternative is to continue north 1.4 miles to **Bradley Lake,** the smaller of the two, and then return to the Taggart Lake Trailhead. Like others in Grand Teton, this hike is best made during the early morning or early evening hours when it is cooler and there is less traffic.

Yet another hike in this busy area begins at the **Leigh Lake Trailhead,** next to String Lake at the String Lake Picnic Area. This trailhead is between Leigh Lake and Jenny Lake (String Lake is essentially a small wet spot between them). The Leigh Lake trail is well marked and relatively flat, and goes through a forested area that is always within sight of the lake. **Picnickers** willing to expend the energy necessary to hike roughly 0.4 mile from the String Lake Picnic Area to the edge of the lake will find themselves eating in a less-congested area that provides spectacular views of the Tetons. The trail continues along the shore of Leigh Lake, but is rather uninteresting; a better option, if time allows, is to return to the picnic area, cross the String Lake inlet, and explore the western edge of Jenny Lake.

Just footsteps from the entrance to the Signal Mountain Lodge is a sign marking the trailhead for the 3-mile **Signal Summit Mountain Trail,** one not generally described in commercial trail books. Though it's well marked, it's not well traveled, since most visitors drive their automobiles in this area. The trail begins steeply, then opens onto a broad plateau covered with lodgepole pines, grassy areas, and wild-flowers. Cross the paved road and you'll arrive at a large, lily-covered pond at the opening of a meadow, home to frogs and waterfowl. The trail then winds along the south and east perimeter of the pond before turning east and heading toward the summit, which will take up to 2 hours. Shortly after passing the pond, you'll come to a fork in the road that converts the trip into a loop trail. Take the northern route and you'll travel the rim of the mountain, meandering to the summit through a forest of sagebrush and pine trees. On the return, a southern trail skirts large alpine ponds where you'll find waterfowl, moose—and, perhaps, black bears.

The day hikes at the north end of the park are less crowded. For instance, the easy but lengthy trip to **Two Ocean Lake** begins off the Pacific Creek Road north of Moran Junction and eventually circumnavigates the lake, with much of the mostly level walk through cool conifer forest. Or there is the **Hermitage Point Trailhead,** located near the marina, which branches out into trips ranging in distance from 1 to 9 miles, mostly in lodgepole pine, with recurring views of the lake and the peaks on the other side. With careful planning, it's possible to start the day with a hike begin-ning at Colter Bay that leads past **Cygnet Lake** across **Willow Flats** to Jackson Lake Lodge (for lunch). Then, after a break, take the path that returns back to Colter Bay in time for the evening outdoor barbecue—all told, that's 9.3 miles round-trip.

Among the loops you can take from this Colter Bay trailhead are trails to **Swan Lake** and **Heron Pond,** the kind of country where wildflowers, Canada geese, moose, beaver, and bears all thrive. The two most prominent flowers here are heart leaf arnicas and the Indian paintbrush. Don't be put off by the fact that the first 200 yards of the Swan Lake/Heron Lake trails, which share the same point of origin, are steep; after reaching the top of a rise the trail levels out and has only moderate elevation gains from that point on. Within minutes, this trail opens to a broad meadow covered with sagebrush and, later in the summer, blooming wildflowers. Here you'll find one of the most spectacular views of Mount Moran, and the peaks reflect on the surfaces of the water.

Finding swans at Swan Lake requires a trip to the south end, where a small island affords isolation and shelter for nests. There are also osprey, kingfishers, and white pel-icans in this neck of the woods. The distance from Swan Lake through a densely forested area to the Heron Pond intersection is 0.3 mile; Hermitage Point is 3 miles from this junction, along a gentle path that winds through a wooded area popular with bears. Circumnavigation from the Colter area is doable in 2 hours.

A shorter hike in the Colter area, the **Lakeshore Trail** is a wide, shady thorough-fare that skirts the bay, leading to gravelly beaches that present views across Jackson Lake of the entire Teton range. The views leap out at you when you arrive at the end of the trail; water laps on the shore and, thankfully, you're out of earshot of the visitor center. This 2-mile loop can be completed in about 1 hour of brisk walking.

LONGER HIKES

If you decide a day hike isn't enough—and you may be quite unhappy if you get to, say, Lake Solitude, and haven't got enough day left to go farther—you must get an overnight permit and camp in one of the various camping zones reserved through the visitor centers. Much longer trips can be strung together into the mountainous back-country, crossing the mountains' spine to **Teton Canyon** on the Idaho side, or, at the north end of the park, exploring deep into the **Jedediah Smith Wilderness.**

Within the park, you can go far behind the day hikes described above—extending a Cascade Canyon hike, for instance, by going north to Lake Solitude, then coming down into **Paintbrush Canyon** (where you can camp, with a permit) and out at String Lake. You can also take the tram to the top of the ski area in Teton Village and follow the **Teton Crest Trail** north into the park, eventually dropping down through **Death Canyon** (another camping area) to **Phelps Lake.** A trip like this is more than 20 miles and will take several days.

The Park Service has a helpful brochure that delineates the 20 or so backcountry camping zones and lakeshore sites. You'll need to reserve sites, and rangers can brief you on the quality of different routes, the bear areas, and "leave no trace" camping techniques.

CAMPING

Since Grand Teton is so much smaller than its counterpart to the north, distances between campgrounds are reduced substantially. As a consequence, selecting a site in one of the five National Park Service campgrounds within the park becomes a matter of preference (rather than geography) and availability. Fees in all campgrounds are $12 per night, and all have modern comfort stations. Campgrounds operate on a first-come, first-served basis, but reservations are available to groups of 10 or more by writing **Campground Reservations,** Grand Teton National Park, Moose, WY 83012. You can get recorded information on site availability by calling ☎ **307/739-3603**. Reservations for **trailer sites** at Colter Bay campground may be made by contacting the **Grand Teton Lodge Co.,** P.O. Box 240, Moran, WY 83013 (☎ **307/543-2855**). Additionally, **Grand Teton Campground** is a concessionaire-operated campground located in the **Flagg Ranch** complex on the John D. Rockefeller Jr. Memorial Parkway. The area has 93 sites with utility hookups, 74 tent sites, showers, and a Laundromat. For reservations, contact Flagg Ranch, P.O. Box 187, Moran, WY 83013 (☎ **800/443-2311**).

All the campgrounds but Jenny Lake can accommodate tents, RVs, and trailers, but there are no utility hookups at any of them. **Jenny Lake Campground,** a tents-only area with 49 sites, is situated in a quiet, wooded area near the lake. You have to be here first thing in the morning to get a site.

The largest campground, **Gros Ventre,** is the last to fill, if it fills at all—probably because it's located on the east side of the park, a few miles from Kelly on the Gros Ventre River Road. It has 360 sites, a trailer dump station, a tents-only section, and no showers. If you arrive late in the day and you have no place to stay, go here first.

Signal Mountain Campground, with views of the lake and access to the beach, is another popular spot that fills first thing in the morning. It has 86 sites overlooking Jackson Lake and Mount Moran, as well as a pleasant picnic area and boat launch. No showers or laundry, but there's a store and service station nearby.

Colter Bay Campground and Trailer Village has 310 sites, some with RV hookups, showers, and a Laundromat. The area has access to the lake but is far enough from the hubbub of the village to offer a modicum of solitude; spaces are usually gone by noon.

Lizard Creek Campground, at the north end of Grand Teton National Park near Jackson Lake, offers an aesthetically pleasing wooded area near the lake with views of the Tetons, bird-watching, and fishing (and mosquitoes; bring your repellent). It's only 8 miles from facilities at Colter Bay and has 60 sites that fill by 2pm.

WHERE TO STAY IN THE PARK

If you plan to visit Grand Teton during a "fringe" season —usually the best, least-crowded time to go, in the fall or spring—you better check first to see not just if there's room at the inn, but if the inn is open at all. The lodgings in the park are run by three

Amenities for Each Campground, Grand Teton National Park

Campground	# Sites	Fee	Showers	Laundry	Flush Toilets	Disposal
Colter Bay	310	$12	yes	yes	yes	yes
Gros Ventre	360	$12	no	no	yes	yes
Jenny Lake*	49	$12	no	no	yes	no
Lizard Creek*	60	$12	no	no	yes	no
Signal Mountain	86	$12	no	no	yes	yes

tents only

different companies, and they all run on different schedules. If you're crazy enough to think the snow will be off the ground by early May, you'll find padlocks on the doors everywhere but at Flagg Ranch, which technically isn't in Grand Teton anyway, but in the limbo of the John D. Rockefeller Jr. Memorial Parkway. Likewise in late fall: By mid-October, there are hardly any beds available in the park, and you'll be bunking in Jackson.

You can get information about or make reservations for Jackson Lake Lodge, Jenny Lake Lodge, and Colter Bay Village through the **Grand Teton Lodge Company,** Box 240, Moran, WY 83013 (☎ **800/628-9988** or 307/543-2811; www.gtlc.com); for Signal Mountain Lodge, contact **Signal Mountain Lodge Co.,** Box 50, Moran, WY 83013 (☎ **307/543-2831;** www.signalmtnlodge.com); and reservations at **Flagg Ranch** are made though Flagg Ranch, Box 187, Moran, WY 83013 (☎ **800/ 443-2311**).

EXPENSIVE

Jackson Lake Lodge. P.O. Box 240, Moran, WY 83013. ☎ **800/628-9988** or 307/ 543-2811. www.gtlc.com. 385 units. TEL. $110–$190 double; $126–$136 cottage; $340–$500 suite. AE, DC, MC, V. Closed mid-Oct to mid-May.

Much the way Old Faithful Inn or the Lake Hotel captures historic eras of Yellowstone tourism, Jackson Lake Lodge epitomizes the architectural milieu of the period when Grand Teton became a park. Unfortunately, that era was the 1950s, an era of right angles, flat roofs, and big windows. Still, the lodge is popular, particularly for its wonderful setting overlooking Willow Flats, the lake in the distance, and towering over it, without a stick in the way, the Grand Tetons and Mount Moran. You don't even have to go outside to see this impressive view—the lobby has 60-foot-tall windows. Guest rooms are in the three-story main lodge and in cottages scattered about the property, some of which have large balconies and mountain views. Lodge rooms are spacious and cheery, and most offer double beds, electric heat, and newly tiled baths. There is also a large outdoor swimming pool. The Blue Heron cocktail lounge is tucked in its own corner of the building, and there are both full-course dining, in the Mural Room, and lighter fare at the Pioneer Grill. Upscale shops selling Western clothing and jewelry are on the main level. At the tour desk you can arrange just about anything legal you can imagine doing in the park, from rafting to riding horses to taking a bus tour up to Yellowstone. Plus, the hotel is an easy 35 miles from Jackson.

✪ **Jenny Lake Lodge.** Box 240, Moran, WY 83013. ☎ **800/628-9988** or 307/733-4647. www.gtlc.com. 37 units. $380 double; $515–$535 suite. Rates include MAP (modified American plan). AE, DC, MC, V. Closed mid-Oct to May.

This lodge justifiably prides itself on seclusion, award-winning food, and the individual attentions that come with a cabin resort kept intentionally small. The Lodge is a hybrid of mountain lake resort and dude ranch, with various activities included in its prices, such as horseback riding, meals, and bicycles. The cabins are rustic on the outside, luxurious within. The name is a misnomer, however, as the lodge is not near the lake but rather sits away from the highway among forested glades, and the lodge functions primarily as a dining establishment. Sofas are clustered around a fireplace to create a beautifully cozy sitting area, and the dining room is tastefully decorated with original works created by local artists; a classical guitarist often accompanies the outstanding gourmet meals (see "Where to Dine," below).

Catering to an older, affluent clientele, the style here is an odd mixture of peaceful rusticity and occasional reminders of class and formality (jackets at dinner are "appreciated"). Generally, though, if you aren't sweating the prices, Jenny Lake Lodge offers a wonderful chance to unwind in an uncrowded, feet-up-on-the-rail atmosphere with, of course, scenery that can't be matched. Accommodations are in pitched-roof log cabins, each fronted by a long, pillared porch. Each cabin has been named for a resident flower (a nice touch) and most have forest views; some can see the lake. Inside are bright braided rugs, dark wood floors, beamed ceilings, log furniture with cowhide upholstery, and tiled combination baths. Rooms have one queen, one king, or two double beds. No televisions, of course.

Located 20 miles from Jackson Airport, it is the southernmost of the park lodges. There are no services at the lodge, but guided pack trips and fishing junkets can be arranged.

MODERATE

✪ **Colter Bay Village.** P.O. Box 240, Moran, WY 83013. ☎ **800/628-9988** or 307/543-2811. www.gtlc.com. 166 units. $31–$116 log cabin; $30 tent cabin. AE, DC, MC, V. Closed late Sept to mid-May.

You might call this the people's resort of Grand Teton, with simpler lodgings, lower prices, and a lively, friendlier atmosphere that seems particularly suited to families. If you're looking to slow the world down on a quiet getaway, pay the price for a Jenny Lake cabin—this place is full of action, but it's outdoor and fun. Situated on the eastern shore of Jackson Lake, 35 miles north of Jackson, Colter Bay Village is a full-fledged recreation center. Guest accommodations are in roughly built but authentic-looking log cabins perched on a wooded hillside; they are clean and simply furnished with area rugs on tile floors, beamed ceilings, and copies of pioneer furnishings—chests, oval mirrors, and extra-long bedsteads with painted headboards. The simple baths have stall showers, and some singles share baths.

If you want to take a trip back to the early days of American auto-travel, when car-camping involved unwieldy canvas tents on slabs by the roadside, you can spend an inexpensive night in "tent cabins." Bring your sleeping bags and sleep on squeaky bunks, and stop that giggling because there's another tent nearby with equally thin walls and small children trying to settle down. The shower and bathroom are down the road a ways, and you'll meet your neighbors there. But it isn't bad—falling asleep with the sound of the woods around you and the glow of the small woodstove, telling stories. There's still another level of common folk accommodation: an RV/trailer park. The village provides an excellent base of operations for visitors, since it encompasses two restaurants, one snack bar, a visitor center, amphitheater, museum, general store, post office, sporting goods shop, and laundry facilities. Scenic cruises and boat rentals can be arranged at the marina. The village operates from mid-May to late September.

Flagg Ranch Resort. P.O. Box 187, Moran, WY 83013. ☎ **800/443-2311** or 307/543-2861. www.flaggranch.com. 92 cabins, 171 RV sites. TEL. Spring and fall, $89 cabin double; winter, $99 cabin double; summer, $131 cabin double. AE, DISC, MC, V.

A few years ago this place by the Snake River just outside Yellowstone National Park was showing its age—the sort of place where a hunter would rent a drafty room to collapse in after a few days in the woods. Not anymore: It's all fixed up, transformed into an all-seasons resort with log-and-luxury ambience.

A century ago there was a military post near here, and travelers in those wagon-road days would stop for a meal when they saw the flag waving—hence, the subsequent name Flagg Ranch, dubbed by original owner Ed Sheffield, who made a swimming hole out of a nearby hot spring and started serving tourists without much initial concern that he was doing so on public land (he eventually got a lease). The only livestock on the ranch these days might be the herds of snowmobiles that gather here in the winter to warm up before entering Yellowstone. In the summer, there are float trips, horseback rides, and excellent fishing in Polecat Creek or the Snake River. The new lodge is a locus of activity, with its double-sided fireplace, fancy dining room, gift shop, espresso bar and pub with large-screen television, convenience store. and gas station. A campground and RV facility are situated on the grounds amidst a stand of pine trees. The newest accommodations are duplex and fourplex log cabins constructed in 1994 that feature king-size beds, spacious sitting areas with writing desks and chests of drawers, wall-to-wall carpeting, and baths with tub-shower combinations and separate vanities.

Signal Mountain Lodge. P.O. Box 50, Moran, WY 83013. ☎ **307/543-2831.** www. signalmtnlodge.com. 80 units. TEL. $85–$180 double. AE, DISC, MC, V. Closed Nov–Apr.

Signal Mountain has a different feel, and different owners, from the other lodgings in Grand Teton, adding to the sense that any place you choose to stay in this park is going to give you a fairly unique atmosphere. What they all have in common is the Teton view, and this lodge, located right on the banks of Jackson Lake, may have the best. For one, it's got lakefront retreats, which you can really inhabit, with stoves and refrigerators and fold-out sofa beds for the kids. Other accommodations, mostly freestanding cabins, come in a variety of flavors, from motel-style rooms in four-unit buildings set amidst the trees to family bungalows with decks, some enjoying beach frontage. There's also a full-size house large enough for a family reunion. The carpeted cabins feature handmade pine furniture, electric heat, covered porches, and tiled baths; some have fireplaces. The recently refurbished registration building has a small TV viewing area, a gift shop, and outdoor seating on a deck overlooking the lake. A restaurant and coffee shop that serve average food share a separate building with a small lounge and gift shop that features Native American crafts. Recreational options include cycling, rafting, waterskiing, and fishing, but note that boat rentals are expensive here. A convenience store and gas station are on the property.

WHERE TO DINE

Flagg Ranch. John D. Rockefeller Jr. Pkwy., Moran. ☎ **800/443-2311.** Breakfast $2–$6; lunch $4–$9; dinner $10–$20. AE, DISC, MC, V. Summer, 7am–1:30pm and 5–9:30pm. TRADITIONAL AMERICAN.

The food at this oasis is better than what's typically found in what most refer to as a "family restaurant," and servings are generous. The dinner menu includes fish, chicken, and beef dishes, as well as home-style entrees like ranch beef stew and chicken pot pie. The ambience is nice as well, during both winter and summer months; wooden chairs and tables with colorful upholstery liven up this newly constructed log building.

✪ Jenny Lake Lodge Dining Room. Jenny Lake Lodge. ☎ **307/543-3300.** Prix-fixe breakfast $14; prix-fixe dinner $41.50, not including alcoholic beverages. AE, MC, V. Summer, daily 7:30–9am, noon–1:30pm, and 6–9pm. CONTINENTAL.

The finest meals in either park are served here, where a cordon bleu chef creates culinary delights for guests and, occasionally, a president of the U.S. All three meals served daily are equally appetizing, but the six-course dinner is the bell-ringer; guests choose from appetizers that may include chilled lobster salad or smoked sturgeon ravioli, buffalo mozzarella and plum tomato salads, and entrees that may include grilled salmon, rack of lamb, or prime rib of buffalo. Desserts are equally decadent. Price is no object, at least for guests, since meals are included in the room charge; nonguests pay a hefty $41.50 per person, and if you don't have quite the right look, your first and only course may be a plateful of chilly snobbery.

John Colter Chuckwagon/Cafe Court Pizza and Deli. Across from the visitor center and marina in Colter Bay Village. ☎ **307/543-2811.** Breakfast $3–$6; lunch $5–$8; dinner $6–$14. DISC, MC, V. Daily 6am–10pm. Closed Oct–Apr. DELI/COMFORT FOOD.

These are the two sit-down restaurants in the village (though there's also a snack shop in the grocery store). Three meals are served daily during the summer months. The **Deli** serves sandwiches, chicken, pizzas, salads, and soup, with prices that range from $4.50 for an individual pizza to $12.99 for a chicken dinner. The **Chuckwagon's** breakfast menu dishes up everything from plain eggs to a Chuckwagon omelet, with a huge and quite wonderful all-you-can-eat buffet available. Lunch is soup, salad, and hot sandwiches; dinner is a buffet with a nightly special each evening. Among the dinner entrees are trout, lasagna, pork chops, beef stew, and New York strip steaks. The ambience is very casual and straightforward, since these restaurants cater mostly to families.

The Mural Room. Jackson Lake Lodge. ☎ **800/628-9988.** Breakfast buffet $8; lunch $6–$9; dinner $16–$22. AE, MC, V. Summer, daily 7am–9:30am, noon–1:30pm, and 6–9:30pm. BEEF/WILD GAME.

Jackson Lake's main dining room is quiet and fairly formal, catering to a more sedate crowd as well as corporate groups; it's also more expensive than other park restaurants. The floor-to-ceiling windows provide stellar views across a meadow that is moose habitat, to the lake and the Cathedral Group. Walls are adorned with hand-painted Western murals (what else?). Three meals are served daily in summer. Breakfast items include a continental breakfast, Belgian waffles, and vegetarian eggs Benedict. Dinner may be a grand, five-course event that includes a shrimp cocktail, French onion soup, and Caesar salad, followed by an entree of Idaho trout, buffalo strip loin, vegetable lasagna, or rack of lamb. On the other side of the wall on which the murals are painted is the **Pioneer Grill,** which serves casual food in a 1950s-atmosphere, soda-fountain-style restaurant. Entrees are lighter and less expensive, and a take-out menu is available. A children's menu is available here. The Blue Heron cocktail lounge is one of the nicest spots in either park to enjoy a cocktail, the other being at Yellowstone Lake Hotel.

Signal Mountain Resort Dining Room. Signal Mountain Resort. ☎ **307/543-2831.** Breakfast $4–$6; lunch $6–$8; dinner $8–$21. AE, DISC, MC, V. Summer, daily 7–10am, 11:30am–2:30pm, and 5:30–10pm. SANDWICHES/MEXICAN/ECLECTIC.

There are actually two restaurants here, serving delicious food in the friendliest style in the park. The fine dining room and lounge are called Aspen's, and the Cottonwood Cafe supplements that top-notch fare with Mexican entrees and sandwich shop fare. You eat up the scenery, too, with a view of Jackson Lake.

Here's an insider's tip: When the bargain-hunting ladies and gentlemen who work for the park's concessionaires head out for dinner, chances are good they land here and

Before arriving in Dubois, practice pronouncing the name without sounding like a city slicker. There are many ways to pronounce it, but only "DO-boys" is correct. Sure, there is the inclination to say "doo-BWAH," but quell that urge—this isn't France.

order Nachos Supreme from the bar menu. A nutritionist's nightmare (and an appetizer, actually), the slew of melted cheese with spicy beef or chicken served on a bed of corn chips topped with sour cream will generally satisfy the appetite of two adults. Since the bar has one of three televisions in the park, and is equipped with cable for sports nuts, the crowd tends to be young and noisy. As an alternative, snacks are served on the deck overlooking the lake, and full meals in a proper dining room. Entrees include chicken pot pie ($9), Mediterranean pasta ($14), and veal saltimbocca, the most expensive entree ($21).

3 A Side Trip to Dubois & the Wind River Range

86 miles NE of Jackson

For years Dubois was a kind of doppelganger to Jackson, a blue-collar logging town with some quietly wealthy folks living on nice ranches up the nearby draws. Now the sawmill is closed, and wealthy folks who want to stay ahead of the latest real estate fashion are wandering over Togwotee Pass and buying up the beautiful Upper Wind River Valley. That means Dubois is poised for resort-dom . . . but it hasn't quite happened yet, which dismays some residents and pleases others. Lying as it does along one of the Yellowstone access roads, Dubois is just far enough from the park entrances to be spared the West Yellowstone gateway syndrome, and if locals keep their heads, they'll protect the great trout streams, uncluttered wilderness, and small-town ambience from uncontrolled growth. So far, so good. It's a fun town, often with several bands playing in the bars on weekends. **To get here** from Jackson, go north on U.S. 26/89/191 to Moran Junction, then east over Togwotee Pass on U.S. Highway 26/287.

Dubois wasn't quite ready for fine Italian dining—its finest restaurant closed its doors and moved to Jackson—but the **Rustic Tavern Steakhouse** (123 E. Ramshorn; ☎ 307/455-2772) does a good job with beef, seafood, and pasta; or you can get a great salad and sandwich on home-baked bread at **Anita's** (106 E. Ramshorn; ☎ 307/455-3828), hidden off the parking lot of Dubois Hardware with a pleasant porch overhanging Horse Creek.

In the lake-dotted Whiskey Basin, just south of town, hundreds of bighorn sheep migrate down in the winter to get away from the deep snows, and so there is a **National Bighorn Sheep Interpretive Center** (907 W. Ramshorn) located just off the highway in the center of town. Just across the street, at the **Dubois Museum** (909 W. Ramshorn), is a look at the past of the town, the Sheepeater Indians, and other interesting artifacts with local flavor. The museum is open 9am to 5pm daily from May through September.

WHERE TO STAY

Absaroka Ranch. P.O. Box 929, Dubois, WY 82513 (10 miles west of Dubois on U.S. Hwy. 26, turn east on Dunoir Rd., and follow signs to the ranch). ☎ **307/455-2275.** 4 two-bedroom units. $1,050 per person per week. Rate includes all meals. No credit cards. Hunting trips in fall. Closed Oct–May.

High in the Absarokas northeast of Dubois is a rustic, comfortable ranch that can host up to 20 people (often families with children in tow). The main lodge, all wood, has the usual and hospitable large stone fireplace for evening gatherings, as a well as a dining area where guests gather around three tables for family-style meals. Menus are eclectic and varied, with a healthful bent. Frittatas, omelets, Greek pizza, and Western fare make appearances, but the chef will cater to the dietary requirements of vegetarians and nondairy eaters. Lunch can be taken outdoors at picnic tables.

The four cabins surround a large, grassy area and a fire pit where evenings are often spent listening to local entertainers. The mainstay of visits here are half- and full-day horseback trips over miles of trails winding through high mountain meadows and cool forests 8,000 feet above sea level. Guides escort guests to nearby streams, and help them learn the tricks for catching wily cutthroat and brook trout. Each cabin has one or two bedrooms, electric heat, and full carpeting. This is a great spot for children, who especially enjoy sleeping in nearby tepees.

Brooks Lake Lodge. 458 Brooks Lake Rd., Dubois, WY 82513. ☎ **307/455-2121.** www.brookslake.com. 12 units. Summer (minimum 3-day stay), $195 lodge room, $215 per person cabin suite; winter, $150 lodge room, $175 cabin suite. Rates include all meals. AE, MC, V. Closed May, Oct–Dec.

For years this remote and historic mountain lodge, once an overnight stop on the slow road to Yellowstone, languished; in 1989 the present owners painstakingly restored and reopened it. It sits above the shores of Brooks Lake, a prize fishing lake surrounded by soaring pinnacles. This is the entry point to some of the most remote and challenging wilderness in the Rockies, packed with elk and trout and grizzly bears. Yet the handsome lodge, with its hand-stripped timbers and deep porch overlooking the lake, is as cozy and comforting as anyone could ask. You can lounge—no one will roust you out of bed until you're ready—or take advantage of the riding stock, guided up steep trails to higher lakes and incredible views. There is a new riding arena where you can get to know your horse. This area is well known to snowmobilers in the winter, and the lodge serves lunch to some who do a loop trip from Togwotee Pass to the lodge—about a 12-mile circuit on unpaved roads. But it's not the sort of noisy, crowded scene you'll find at Yellowstone, and guests get a real treat when they're guided on snowmobiles high up on a ridge overlooking Cub Creek and the Yellowstone backcountry.

Morning coffee and evening desserts are served in the lobby, a misnamed room that is ideally suited to relaxation in front of a fireplace. The price includes all meals, including an afternoon high tea—now there's a special touch. Accommodations are six guest rooms in the lodge and six cabins along the tree line. Cabins are comfortable, spacious affairs that have large decks or porches with views of the lake. Furnishings are Western pine. The most popular cabin for guests seeking seclusion is Trail Boss, a larger one-bedroom cabin with a separate living room.

Cody & Northcentral Wyoming

by Geoff O'Gara

The most livable pockets of the Rocky Mountain West are the deep, broad valleys cupped by its mountain ranges. The mountains provide some protection from the howling storms of the prairies, bank snow to keep the streams running through the summer, and, of course, provide a spectacular backdrop for everyday life in the communities nestled below.

Such a valley runs down the center of Wyoming, cradled by the Bighorn Mountains in the east and the Absarokas and Yellowstone Plateau in the West. Though the area around the town of Cody gets only about 10 inches of moisture annually, founder William Cody recognized a century ago that with a few dams and ditches in the right places, the mountains' snowpack could supply water year-round. Cody's role as a community builder mattered as much to him as his highly promoted "Buffalo Bill" image, and both legacies continue to shape the basin's economy today: A great summer scene of cowboy fun attracts hordes of visitors, and green fields of sugar beets and grains stretch for miles from the mouth of the Wapiti Valley.

While Cody was staking claims to water rights along the Shoshone River around the turn of the century, the U.S. Bureau of Reclamation was backing up that water behind the Buffalo Bill Dam, the world's tallest dam when it was completed in 1910. The reservoir today irrigates some 93,000 acres in central Wyoming, and the swift winds that polished the rock outcrops of the Wapiti Valley now skim the lake's surface and sometimes polish off windsurfers.

The charms of northcentral Wyoming have waylaid visitors on their journey to and from Wyoming's famous national parks since Cody's time. But as the parks become more crowded, an increasing number of travelers find reason to linger longer in these valleys to the east, exploring a wealth of Native American history, geology, mountain scenery, and small-town charm. Highlights include fun-loving Cody (the second most popular destination town in the state, after Jackson), the Bighorn Canyon National Recreation Area (which straddles the Montana-Wyoming border) the gushing hot springs of Thermopolis, and the forests and rivers of Shoshone National Forest and other public lands.

The combination of stunning scenery and historic cattle operations makes the Cody area a natural center for "dude" and guest ranches, where visitors can saddle up and swing a lariat during extended stays. Or, you can mount a more stationary seat in the stands at one of the popular summer rodeos in the area. Cody's rodeo grounds light up every night in the summer, and nearly every town in the basin has its special rodeo weekend. On the Wind River Indian Reservation, the evening outdoor entertainment is often a powwow, featuring drum groups, colorful garb, and various styles of traditional dancing, with visitors welcome and, for the hungry, food stands offering Indian tacos and other treats.

1 Scenic Drives

The two-lane roads of northcentral Wyoming must follow the contours of a craggy landscape, tracking the twists and turns of the river and switchbacking over the mountain passes; the roads are narrow but generally uncrowded, except for the busy summer traffic to Yellowstone's east entrance ("busy," at least, to a Wyoming resident—urban freeway veterans might laugh at my characterization). **U.S. Highway 14/16/20,** the east entrance road (also called the Yellowstone Highway), is the major east-west traverse through this region, following the Bighorn River, then heading west to the park through Greybull and Cody; the breathtaking views as it snakes through the Wapiti Valley and up over Sylvan Pass into Yellowstone make traffic and road repair bearable. West of Cody, almost any road you take will reward you with a canyon or a climb, but many roads narrow and turn to dirt as they delve deeper into the forest. **WY 291** does that, as it follows the **South Fork of the Shoshone River** upstream toward the white-capped peaks of Yellowstone's Thorofare country. Along the way are prominent volcanic rock formations like Castle Rock, a succession of picturesque ranches, and sometimes a lucky glimpse of bighorn sheep before the road ends and you turn back.

Cody is also an alternative starting point for the **Chief Joseph Scenic Highway,** which links up to the **Beartooth Byway** into Montana (see chapter 8).

DRIVING TOUR #1: BIGHORN MOUNTAIN LOOP

Yellowstone is such an iconic American vacation spot that Cody visitors sometimes fail to glance east, at the shining Bighorn Mountains. This moderately easy day trip will open your eyes to an extraordinary mountain range, on a route that encompasses the towns of **Powell** and **Lovell,** as well as the scenic **Shell Canyon area.** Begin in Cody by taking U.S. Highway 14A northeast to Lovell and the **Bighorn Canyon National Recreation Area.** A side trip north along WY 37 provides views of the wild horses of the Pryor Mountain Wild Horse Range and Bighorn Lake from the Devils Canyon Overlook (see chapter 9 for more information on this recreation area).

After crossing the Bighorn River, U.S. Highway 14A rises through the foothills and up the steep flanks of the Bighorns, not far from the footpaths of prehistoric travelers who built the **Medicine Wheel,** a 74-foot stone circle with 28 spokes. Like other mysterious wheel designs in the Rockies, it may have served ancient peoples as an astronomical key (there are 28 days in the lunar cycle) or a long-distance travel marker. To get here, turn off U.S. Highway 14A at the Medicine Wheel sign and hike 1½ miles from the parking area to the site. Though the origin of the wheel is debated—the present wheel was probably constructed about 1200 A.D.—the site is a place of strong medicine, according to Indian spiritual leaders, who conduct fasts and ceremonies here. Visitors are asked not to remove offerings or disturb Native Americans using the site for prayer or fasting. For more information contact the Medicine Wheel Ranger District of the Bighorn National Forest, ☎ **307/548-6541.**

Once you have crested the divide of the Bighorn Mountains, take U.S. Highway 14 southwest at Burgess Junction toward Shell Canyon and the towns of Shell and Greybull. The road drops sharply amidst steeply cut canyons, and you can stop at the **Shell**

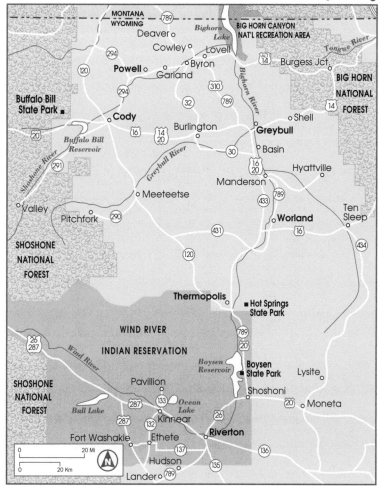

MONTANA
WYOMING
789
Deaver
Cowley
Byron
Lovell
Big Horn
Lake
BIG HORN CANYON
NAT'L RECREATION AREA
Tongue River
294
ALT
14
Burgess Jct.
120
Powell
Garland
310
BIG HORN
NATIONAL
294
32
789
14
FOREST
Buffalo Bill
State Park
Cody
16
14
20
Burlington
Shell
Greybull
20
Buffalo Bill
Reservoir
30
Basin
16
20
Hyattville
291
Greybull River
Manderson
433
789
Valley
Meeteetse
431
Worland
16
Ten
Sleep
Pitchfork
290
434
SHOSHONE
NATIONAL
120
FOREST
Thermopolis
Hot Springs
State Park
WIND RIVER
789
20
26
287
INDIAN RESERVATION
Wind River
Boysen
Reservoir
Boysen
State Park
Lysite
SHOSHONE
NATIONAL
FOREST
Pavillion
133
Bull Lake
287
Ocean
Lake
Shoshoni
26
Moneta
20
132
Kinnear
287
Riverton
Fort Washakie
Ethete
137
136
20 Mi
N
Hudson
135
20 Km
Lander
789

Falls interpretive center and follow a paved path to a close-up view of the creek tumbling and twisting amidst tall granite slabs. As the road flattens out near the town of Shell, you're surrounded by the deep red sandstones of the **Chugwater Formation** set off by the rich greens of cultivated fields. The rock shapes and colors suggest ancient epochs, and indeed this area enfolds some well-packed dinosaur fossil beds. U.S. Highway 14/16/20 takes you back to Cody and the embrace of the Absaroka Mountains and Yellowstone from the west. This driving tour can be enjoyed year-round, though winter drivers should proceed cautiously on the steep grades around Burgess Junction.

DRIVING TOUR #2: BIGHORN BASIN LOOP

This all-day trip keeps to the lowlands of the Bighorn River Basin ("lowlands" in this country is nevertheless more than 3,500 feet above sea level), navigating rolling sagebrush hills, cultivated farmlands, humpy hot spring terraces, and one-pump (formerly one-horse) Western towns.

Depart from Cody and travel south along WY 120 to the tiny burg of **Meeteetse** on the banks of the Greybull River, with its century-old mercantile still open for business. From here, continue on WY 120 to **Thermopolis,** self-proclaimed home of the world's largest free-flowing hot springs (New Zealand does not agree), where the temperature is a constant 135°F. After a relaxing soak and perhaps a brief motor east of the springs for a glimpse of the bison herd that roams the state park, travel northeast on U.S. Highway 16/20 to **Worland,** an important agricultural center. Then, drive east along U.S. Highway 16 to **Ten Sleep,** which lies at the base of another steep-sided canyon cutting down through the Bighorn Mountains. You may want to hike and cast a line in Ten Sleep Creek.

Here, take the Nowood Road north, which joins WY 31 to Manderson and follows the base of the Bighorns. From Manderson, follow U.S. Highway 16/20 north to Basin, take WY 30 west to the junction of WY 120, and continue north to Cody. Along the way, you'll enjoy views of the Bighorn River and the Greybull River Valley, and the uncluttered farms that fan from the rivers. Winter is not too harsh on this loop, which might include a brief detour south of Meeteetse on WY 290 to the **Wood River Ski Touring Park.** A few loops on your skinny skis there and you'll be ready for a soothing soak at Thermopolis. If it's summer, rangers at the state park have a map and key to Legend Rock petroglyph sites north of Thermopolis, where you can hike around the cliffs and then . . . hey, hit the hot pools again for that soothing soak.

2 Cody

52 miles E of the east entrance of Yellowstone; 177 miles NE of Jackson; 214 miles NW of Casper

The legendary scout and showman William F. "Buffalo Bill" Cody really knew how to put on a show, and he also knew where to put a town. Cody, founded by its namesake in 1887, is one of the most beautifully situated communities in Wyoming, near the juncture of rivers that pour from the rugged Absaroka Range. Every summer, Cody puts on a cowtown circus that would do the founder proud, entertaining throngs of visitors on their way to and from Yellowstone 52 miles west. And the way to Yellowstone is nonpareil: Teddy Roosevelt called the Wapiti Valley, "a narrowing swath of grasslands spiked by strange rock formations and fringed by mountains—the most scenic 50 miles in the world."

Stop by Cody before the park's east entrance opens (in mid-May) and it's rather lifeless—an indication of how closely Cody's fate is linked to the park. For 3 months every summer, though, the town parades its Western charm for masses of Yellowstone-bound travelers under cloudless skies. When the sun goes down, the lights come on at the rodeo grounds, and nightly the broncs do a little busting of their own. A world-class museum, a reassembled Old West town, and retail shops all attract visitors. Though lacking the resort density and sophistication of Jackson, Cody's Western charm feels more authentic.

ESSENTIALS

GETTING THERE   Cody's Yellowstone Regional Airport, 3001 Duggleby Dr., Cody, WY 82414 (☎ **307/587-5096**), serves the Bighorn Basin as well as the east and northeast entrances of Yellowstone National Park with year-round commercial flights via **United Express** (☎ **800/241-6522**) and Delta feeder **Skywest** (☎ **800/453-9417**).

If you're driving from **Cheyenne,** travel north on I-25 to Casper, then west on U.S. Highway 20/26 to Shoshoni, where U.S. Highway 20 turns north to Thermopolis.

From there, it's another 84 miles to Cody on WY 120. From **Jackson,** take U.S. Highway 191 to the West Thumb Junction in Yellowstone, drive east along the northern boundary of Yellowstone Lake, and continue on U.S. Highway 14/16/20 to Cody. If you enter Wyoming from the west on Interstate 80, drive north from Rock Springs on U.S. Highway 191 to Farson, WY 28 to Lander, WY 789 to Thermopolis, and WY 120 to Cody. Call ☎ **888/WYO-ROAD** (in-state) or 307/772-0824 for road and travel information.

VISITOR INFORMATION   For printed information on this area of Wyoming, contact the **Park County Travel Council,** 836 Sheridan Ave., P.O. Box 2454, Cody, WY 82414 (☎ **307/587-2777**), or the **Wyoming Business Council Travel and Tourism Division,** I-25 at College Drive, Cheyenne, WY 82002 (☎ **307/ 777-7777**).

GETTING AROUND   If you haven't come by car, you'll probably want to rent one in a state where public transportation is almost nonexistent. **Avis** (☎ **800/331-1212** or 307/587-5792), **Budget** (☎ **800/527-0700** or 307/587-6066), **Thrifty** (☎ **888/794-1025** or 307/587-8855), and **Hertz** (☎ **800/654-3131** or 307/ 587-2914) maintain desks at Yellowstone Regional Airport.

SPECIAL EVENTS   The Buffalo Bill Historical Center is a tremendous resource for unique events in Cody. The April festival of **Cowboy Songs and Range Ballads** features storytelling, poetry, and some fine yodeling and balladry. In mid-June, the **Plains Indian Powwow** brings the Robbie Powwow Garden on the south end of the Buffalo Bill Historical Center parking lot alive with whirling color. Traditional dance competitions are coupled with craft shows and Native American food, and non-Indians are welcomed into round dances. Call the Buffalo Bill Historical Center (☎ **307/587-4771**) for exact dates of these and other events and special exhibits.

Every July 1 to July 4, during the **Cody Stampede,** the streets are filled with parades, rodeos, fireworks, street dances, barbecues, and entertainment, capped by a top-notch rodeo. Call ☎ **800/207-0744** or 307/587-5155 for tickets. For 2 days in July, the cool rhythms of jazz and the brassy sound of big-band and swing music take over the lawn of the Elks Club at 1202 Beck Ave. (next to the Cody Convention Center) during the **Yellowstone Jazz Festival.** Featured musicians come from afar, and all varieties of jazz are heard from 11 am until dark. Call ☎ **307/587-3898** for additional information.

Late in August, the Buffalo Bill Historical Center (☎ **307/587-4771**) stages the **Buffalo Bill Celebrity Shootout,** where celebrities and local shooters test their skills in trap, skeet, sporting clays, and silhouette shooting. It's a more serious test of marksmanship than the melodramatic shoot-out staged every summer evening at 6pm in front of the Irma Hotel, when a group of local actors regress to their flop-dead gunfighter childhoods. In late September, Cody hosts the **Western Design Conference** (☎ **888/685-0574**) at the Cody Auditorium and the Buffalo Bill Historical Center, a gathering of artisans to show off their work in Western-style furniture, decorations, and clothing fashions.

GETTING OUTSIDE

If you'd rather not be a driver in the park's heavy summer traffic, guided Yellowstone National Park day trips are available locally through **Grub Steak Expeditions,** P.O. Box 1013, Cody, WY 82414 (☎ **307/527-6316**); **Buffalo Bill's Yellowstone Country,** 1202 14th St., Cody, WY 82414 (☎ **877/640-8609** or 307/527-5988; www.yellowstonecountryres.com; e-mail: byyccr@trib.com); and **Yellowstone Expedition Services,** P.O. Box 1956, Cody, WY 82414 (☎ **888/808-7990** or 307/ 587-5452; e-mail: yestour@cody.wtop.net).

Cody doesn't have the plethora of organized recreation options that Jackson does, but there is no shortage of places to go outdoors. **Buffalo Bill State Park,** located along the canyon and reservoir 6 miles west of Cody, is a hot spot for recreationists, with opportunities for hiking, fishing, and a variety of water sports. The lake is one of the premier spots for windsurfing in the United States. The park also has facilities for camping and picnicking.

BIKING

Mountain bikes and local trail information are available at **Olde Faithful Bicycles,** 1362 Sheridan Ave. (☎ **307/527-5110;** e-mail: bikecody@wyoming.com). Though there isn't a marked network of bike paths in the Cody area, the Forest Service trails west of town off U.S. Highway 14/16/20 in the Shoshone National Forest are available for biking. For specific trail information, call Olde Faithful Bicycles or the Forest Service at ☎ **307/527-6921.**

CROSS-COUNTRY SKIING

If you favor a groomed course for cross-country skiing, try the **North Fork Nordic Trails** in Shoshone National Forest near the east entrance to the park off U.S. Highway 14/16/20. You can circuit 25 kilometers of trails adjacent to the Sleeping Giant downhill area (see below) and the Pahaska Tepee resort.

DOWNHILL SKIING

Near the east entrance to the park, 50 miles west of Cody, is an inexpensive, family-oriented ski area, cheap but not challenging: **Sleeping Giant Ski Area,** 349 Yellowstone Hwy., Cody, WY 82414 (☎ **307/527-SNOW;** www.westwyoming.com/ Sleeping Giant). *Our suggestion:* Drive north to Red Lodge, Montana, for longer, steeper runs and a bigger resort (see chapter 8); travel time from Cody is about the same.

FISHING

Yellowstone's legendary fly-fishing waters are a short drive away, but you should try the smaller but excellent angling streams west of Cody: **The Clark's Fork of the Yellowstone, the North and South Forks of the Shoshone,** and **Sunlight Creek.** They're located northwest of Cody along Chief Joseph Highway—go north on WY 120, 17 miles to WY 296, (which is Chief Joseph). To the east, the warmer and slower **Big Horn River,** and **Big Horn Lake,** nurture catfish, walleye, and ling for boat fishermen. For advice on the trout streams near Cody, ask at **North Fork Anglers,** 1438 Sheridan Ave. (☎ **307/527-7274;** e-mail: flyfish@wavecom.net), where they stock gear and clothing and also guide short day trips or longer, overnight excursions. If you like to troll or cast from a boat, **Buffalo Bill Reservoir,** 6 miles west of Cody on Yellowstone Highway (U.S. 14/16/20), has produced some big mackinaw, as well as rainbow, brown, and cutthroat trout. You have a shot at landing a rainbow over 15 pounds at **Monster Lake** (☎ **800/840-5137;** www.monsterlake. com), a private 150-acre pond on the Deseret Ranch 10 miles south of Cody. It's strictly catch-and-release for these lunker rainbows and cutthroats, and there's a hefty fee per rod.

GOLF

The **Olive Glenn Golf and Country Club,** 802 Meadow Lane, is an 18-hole PGA championship that is open to the public daily from 6am to 9pm. Greens fees are a modest $20 for nine holes, $35 for 18. Call ☎ **307/587-5551** for tee times.

RAFTING

There aren't a lot of Class IV rapids on the rivers around Cody, but the upper stretches of the North Fork of the Shoshone River rip pretty fast in the spring. The upper river is the province of **Wyoming River Trips,** 1701 Sheridan Ave. (☎ **800/586-6661** or 307/587-6661; www.imt.net/~wyoriver/; e-mail: wrt@wave.park.wy.us), which also runs rafts on the smoother, Class II waters below the dam, along with **River Runners,** 491 Sheridan Ave. (☎ **307/527-RAFT;** www.westwyoming.com/rafting/). Prices run from about $18 to $50, depending on the length and difficulty of the trip.

SNOWMOBILING

The most popular Cody snowmobiling trails originate from nearby Pahaska Tepee Resort, located 51 miles from Cody on U.S. Highway 14/16/20 (see listing in "Where to Stay," below). Don't take the **Pahaska Tepee Trail** over 8,541-foot Sylvan Pass if you're afraid of heights; but if you're not, it connects to the Yellowstone National Park trails and the lengthy Continental Divide Snowmobile Trail, and offers breathtaking views including Avalanche Peak (10,566 feet) and Cody Peak (10,267 feet). The **Sunlight trail system** is located 36 miles north of Cody, and winds through the wilds to a stunning view of the Beartooth Mountains. Sledders start from a parking area at the junction of WY 296 and U.S. Highway 212 and follow the Beartooth Scenic Byway east for 16 miles to a warming hut. To the east, there are 70 miles of snowmobile routes in the Bighorn Mountains. Snowmobiles can be rented at **Pahaska Tepee Resort** and in Cody at **Mountain Valley Engine Service,** 422 W. Yellowstone Ave. (☎ **307/587-6218**).

WINDSURFING

What was once a treeless, windblown reservoir is now, according to *Outside* magazine, one of the Top 10 windsurfing destinations in the continental United States . . . and still a treeless, windblown reservoir. The 8-mile-long, 4-mile-wide **Buffalo Bill Reservoir** sucks wind from three mountain gorges, and the temperature is tolerable from June through September. There is a boat ramp near the campground on the north side of the reservoir just off U.S. Highway 14/16/20.

SEEING THE SIGHTS

✪ **Buffalo Bill Historical Center.** 720 Sheridan Ave. ☎ **307/587-4771.** $10 adults, $6 students (18 and over), $4 youth (6–17), free for children under 6. Admission is good for 2 consecutive days. Group tour rates available by request. Open daily; call for seasonal hours.

This extraordinarily valuable museum casts a scholarly eye on the relics of the West's young history while offering some flash and entertainment for the distracted traveler's eye. From its beginnings in a rustic log building it's grown into a sprawling modern edifice that houses four different museums in 237,000 square feet of space: the Buffalo Bill Museum, the Whitney Gallery of Western Art, the Plains Indian Museum, and the Cody Firearms Museum.

The **Buffalo Bill Museum** is a monument to one of the earliest manifestations of America's celebrity culture, displaying the wares that turned a frontier scout and buffalo hunter into a renowned showman. Posters trumpet his world-famous Wild West shows featuring "Custer's Last Rally" and "Cossack of the Caucasus," and there are some grainy film clips of the show itself. When displays of gaudy gear and gifts from presidents and queens begin to wear on you, shift to more intimate memorabilia from the Cody family.

The **Whitney Gallery** showcases work by the adventurous artists who carried their palettes to the frontier to record firsthand the wilderness beauty, the proud Indian cultures, and the lives of trappers and cowboys in the 19th century. Bygone artists like Frederic Remington, George Catlin, Charlie Russell, Albert Bierstadt, and Alfred Jacob Miller share exhibition space with modern Western artists like Jim Bama and Harry Jackson. Work like Catlin's is invaluable as a historic record of how disappearing Indian tribes looked and dressed, and the same could be said of Russell's cowboys or Bierstadt's landscapes; it's also fine art.

The Plains Indian Museum is devoted to the history of Plains tribes including the Blackfeet, Cheyenne, Crow, Gros Ventre, Shoshone, and Sioux. Exhibits explain the migrations and customs of the tribes, and display art and artifacts including cradle boards, ceremonial dresses and robes, pipes, and beadwork. If you're in Cody in late June, attend the Plains Indian Powwow to see such traditional living gear in use by today's Native Americans (see "Special Events," above).

The Cody Firearms Museum displays weaponry dating back to 16th-century Europe in its collection of more than 4,000 pieces. There are also Boone and Crockett exhibits of world-record game trophies, a stagecoach stop, and an arms manufacturing facility.

Every year the Center features special exhibitions, and a wide variety of educational programs runs throughout the year. Late September's annual Plains Indian Seminar brings in scholars and students for an in-depth examination of Native American issues. The Harold McCracken Research Library is an excellent resource for historic photographs, an archive of cowboy music, and thousands of books and manuscripts.

Tecumseh's Old West Miniature Village and Museum. 142 W. Yellowstone Ave. ☎ **307/587-5362.** $3. June–August, daily 8am–8pm; winter, call for hours.

You have to pass through a trading post of ordinary Western tourist plunder to get to this finely detailed miniature diorama of Western history. It depicts everything from fur trappers floating the rivers to Custer's last moments at Little Big Horn. There is also a small museum of Indian and pioneer artifacts.

✪ **Cody Nite Rodeo.** Stampede Park (on U.S. 14/16/20 as you head west of town toward the Wapiti Valley). ☎ **800/207-0744.** $10 adults, $4 children 7–12, free for children under 7. June–Aug, nightly at 8:30pm.

If you want to see rodeo in Wyoming, Cody offers a sure thing: a nightly dust-up between bulls, broncs, and cowboys, as well as roping, cutting, and kids' events like the "calf scramble." Pay an extra two bucks and you get a seat just above the chutes in the Buzzard's Roost. The 6,000-seat stadium sits out on an open terrace above the river west of town—not a bad place to be on a cool Wyoming evening beneath the stars. Once a year some of the nation's top rodeo competitors show up for the Fourth of July Cody Stampede (see "Special Events," above).

Old Trail Town. 1831 Demaris Dr. ☎ **307/587-5302.** $4. May 15–Sept 15, daily 8am–7pm.

Walking the creaky boardwalks here, you'll pass by gray storefronts and clapboard cabins gathered from ghost towns around the region and assembled on the original town site of Cody City, a short jog from the rodeo grounds. Archaeologist Bob Edgar hasn't wasted any paint on these relics, which include a cabin from Kaycee where Butch Cassidy and the Sundance Kid once conspired, and what must be the largest collection of worn-out buckboard carriages in the U.S. On the west end of the "town" are the relocated graves of a number of Western notables, including John "Liver-eatin'" Johnson, Robert Redford's model for *Jeremiah Johnson.*

The Buffalo Bill Reservoir. 6 miles west of Cody on U.S. Hwy. 14/16/20 at the top of Shoshone Canyon. ☎ **307/527-6076** for visitor center. Free admission. May–Sept, daily 8am–8pm.

The **Buffalo Bill Dam** drops like a slim concrete knife 328 feet into the gorge carved by the Shoshone River west of Cody, and you can walk out atop the dam and look down the steep canyon or back across the deep blue water of the reservoir. Several workers died building it, and when it was completed in 1910, it was the tallest dam in the world. The lake behind it serves anglers, boaters, and windsurfers, while providing irrigation water to farmers downstream. An octagonal visitor center perched next to the dam provides exhibits on the reservoir, wildlife, and area recreation. There is a boat launch along the north lakeshore off U.S. Highway 14/16/20 and a clean, spacious campground that lacks only for adequate shade.

Cody Wildlife Exhibit. 433 Yellowstone Ave. ☎ **307/587-2804.** $4 adults, $2 children over 6. Group rates available. May–Oct, daily 9am–8pm.

Trophy hunters may want to take an envious look at this collection of more than 400 mounted animals from all over the world, displayed in simulated habitats. Others will skip it and head for the park: While there are no elephants, stuffed or otherwise, 53 miles west in Yellowstone, there are plenty of other interesting species, all of them breathing.

WHERE TO STAY

If you want to book lodging before you arrive, contact **Cody Area Central Reservations** (☎ **888/468-6996**).

Buffalo Bill Village Resort: Comfort Inn, Holiday Inn & Buffalo Bill Village Historic Cabins. 17th and Sheridan Ave., Cody, WY 82414. ☎ **800/527-5544.** Fax 307/587-2795. E-mail: jblair@wavecom.net. Comfort Inn: 75 units. A/C TV TEL. $75–$130 double. Holiday Inn: 190 units. A/C TV TEL. $75–$130 double. Buffalo Bill Village Historic Cabins: 83 units. TV TEL. $50–$130 double. AE, CB, DC, DISC, MC, V. Buffalo Bill Village closed Oct–Apr.

This is not exactly a "resort" but an oddly matched cluster of lodgings with a convenient downtown location. The Holiday and Comfort Inns are similar to their chain brethren elsewhere, but the village of aged cabins provides a rustic exterior with a more Western feel, and modern conveniences inside. Family units provide two bedrooms. There is also a brief "Ol' West" boardwalk where you can shop for curios or sign up for tours and river trips, an outdoor heated pool, and several restaurants.

   The Comfort Inn and Holiday Inn are priced identically, and have similar amenities (the rooms at the Comfort Inn, built in 1993, are slightly newer, and breakfast is included in the rate). The rooms at Buffalo Bill Village are simply equipped—bed, phone, and TV—and less expensive.

The Irma Hotel. 1192 Sheridan Ave., Cody, WY 82414. ☎ **800/745-4762** or 307/587-4221. www.irmahotel.com. E-mail: irma@cody.wtp.net. 40 units. A/C TV TEL. $75–$102 double. AE, DC, DISC, MC, V.

Buffalo Bill's entrepreneurial gusto eventually left him virtually penniless, but it also left us this charming old hotel in the heart of town. Cody hoped to corral visitors who got off the train on their way to Yellowstone, and one of his lures was an elaborate cherry-wood bar, a gift from straightlaced Queen Victoria. You can still hoist a jar on Her Royal Majesty's slab in the Silver Saddle Saloon, or spend the night in a renovated room that may have once housed a president or prince. Suites are named after local characters from the town's early days: The Irma Suite, on the corner of the building, has a queen-size bed, a writing table, a vanity in the bedroom area, a small sitting area with TV, and an old-fashioned bathroom with a tub-shower combination. The large restaurant—a bit dark when you come in out of the summer sunlight—serves excellent prime rib and a summer breakfast buffet. Every summer night (except Monday), a gang of mustachioed gunfighters draws crowds as they fire blanks at each other on the porch along 11th Street.

GUEST RANCHES & RESORTS

✪ **Double Diamond X Ranch.** 3453 Southfork Rd., Cody, WY 82414. ☎ **800/ 833-RANCH.** Fax 307/587-2708. www.ddxranch.com. E-mail: ddx@cody.wtp.net. 12 units. $1,460 per adult per week, $1,020 per child per week. Lower rates in shoulder season. Rates include all meals. MC, V. Drive 34 miles SW of Cody on South Fork Rd. (aka WY 291) and look for sign on west side.

Ranches along the South Fork of the Shoshone River don't see the kind of traffic that streams along the North Fork into Yellowstone, but they have scenery to match, including green horse pastures, volcanic rock spires, tumbling river, and snowcapped peaks. Guests visit the Double Diamond X to ride, fish, view wildlife, and just kick back. The horses are saddled and the guests are coddled: bounteous meals, pool, Jacuzzi, children's programs, live evening entertainment, and rockers on the front porch. As with most dude ranches, guests sign up by the week, not the day, and the price includes all ranch activities.

Pahaska Tepee Resort. 183 Yellowstone Hwy., Cody, WY 82414. ☎ **800/628-7791** or 307/527-7701. Fax 307/527-4019. 48 units. Mid-June to August, $96–$105 double; off-season, $60–$85 double. DISC, MC, V. Closed Nov and Apr.

Buffalo Bill's hunting lodge, only a mile from the east entrance to Yellowstone, was dubbed with his Lakota name, "Pahaska" (longhair), when he opened the lodge to park visitors in 1905. Near the top of the beautiful Wapiti Valley along U.S. Highway 14/16/20, Pahaska is a popular winter and summer stop for people visiting Yellowstone and its environs. Far from town and close to the park, it's not unusual to find moose and elk in the neighborhood. It's also useful to have a grocery store, gas station and gift shop, in addition to a dining room with lodgepole beams, a big fireplace, and a good view. The old river-rock fireplace still burns in the main building, overseen by trophy elk on the walls. The Tepee Tavern features Molesworth fixtures.

The cabins scattered on the hill behind the lodge close in the winter, while the A-frames by the lodge are open year-round. Accommodations have no TVs, phones, or air-conditioning, and might best be described as "mini-hotels" with from two to five rooms, each with its own entrance. Some bathrooms have only showers, some tubs—ask.

Pahaska has not kept up with advances in resort amenities, but its location and reasonable prices make up for shortcomings. For a fee, the resort offers trail rides and pack trips, and in the winter you can rent snowmobiles and cross-country ski gear.

Rimrock Ranch. 2728 North Fork Rte., Cody, WY 82414. ☎ **307/587-3970.** 8 cabins. Mid-May to mid-Sept, $1,100 per person per week; children $800 per child per week. 3-day snowmobiling $975. MC, V. Drive 30 miles west of Cody on U.S. Hwy. 16/20/14 (aka Yellowstone Hwy.); ranch is on the south side of highway.

Tucked along Canyon Creek at 6,300 feet above sea level, the Rimrock Ranch has an intimate feel not found on larger dude ranches. The weekly package includes backcountry rides and a roping arena, rodeo trips, fishing, cookouts, and river floats. A small outdoor pool perches next to the lodge with a view down the canyon. In the winter, snowmobile packages are available, including journeys through Yellowstone.

7D Ranch. Sunlight Basin, Box 100, Cody, WY 82414. ☎ **307/587-9885.** www. 7dranch.com. E-mail: ranch7d@wyoming.com. 11 cabins. May–Sept, $1,325–$1,485 per person per week. Discount for children under 13. Rates include all meals. No credit cards. Drive north from Cody on WY 120 to WY 296, then west. Ranch is 35 miles from Cody on north side of the road.

Beautiful Sunlight Creek runs through this venerable ranch, which has a homey, lived-in quality missing in slicker operations. The Dominick family has run the spread for three generations, and they know the nooks and crannies of the Sunlight Basin and the Beartooth Mountains, which guests explore on day-long rides, hikes, and fishing expeditions. Riding and casting lessons, naturalist-led wildflower walks, weekly square dances, and bonfires are all part of the package.

WHERE TO DINE

Arrive in Cody a week before the east entrance to Yellowstone opens, and you might go hungry. That's an exaggeration, but many of the fine restaurants here are shuttered or on reduced schedules until the tourists start to flow, and the park's east entrance is one of the last to open, usually in mid-May.

If you need something less than a formal meal, like a plateful of fuel food or a jolt of caffeine for a busy day, Cody has a good supply of familiar fast-food joints and a few informal, inexpensive places. **Peter's Cafe Bakery,** at 1191 Sheridan Ave. (☎ 307/527-5040), across the street from The Irma, serves a full breakfast starting at 7am, with fresh-baked bagels, pastries, and espresso. **Maxwell's Bakery,** 937 Sheridan Ave. (☎ 307/527-7749) (see Maxwell's Restaurant, below) offers croissants and other fragrant bakery items, along with coffee drinks, in the early hours before the adjacent restaurant opens. There is also the **Cody Coffee Co. & Eatery,** 1702 Sheridan Ave. (☎ 307/527-7879), for coffee drinks, fresh-made pastries, soups, and sandwiches. One of the best places day or night to get a beer-'n-burger (or Rocky Mountain oysters!) is the **Proud Cut Saloon,** 1227 Sheridan Ave. There's a sports bar with a full menu of ribs and pastas and Greek food attached to the **Black Sheep Restaurant,** 1901 Mt. View Dr. (☎ 307/527-5253). And don't forget the big restaurant at the Irma Hotel (mentioned above).

Cassie's Supper Club. 214 Yellowstone Ave. ☎ **307/527-5500.** Main courses $13–$25. AE, DISC, MC, V. Mon–Sat 11am–2pm and 5–10pm, Sun 5–10pm. WESTERN.

Cassie's is the sort of place you might expect and look for in the West: big platters of beef, four bars serving drinks, and a lot of people in a restaurant that can hold more than 400 guests. They've got the routine down, having been in business since 1922. Located along the highway west of town in what was once a "House of Ill Fame," Cassie's is now very respectable and very busy. In the Buffalo Bar, a 20-foot mural depicts horses, cowboys, and shoot-outs, and there is local artwork throughout the club. Hesitant dancers are lured onto the floor by free Western swing lessons several evenings a week. Live music nightly.

✪ **Franca's Italian Dining.** 1421 Rumsey Ave. ☎ **888/806-5354** or 307/587-5354. Reservations recommended. Main courses $14.50–$26. No credit cards. Wed–Sun 6–10pm. Closed Oct 16–May 14. ITALIAN.

Franca Facchetti uses her mother's old-world recipes to cook four-course meals in the sagebrush hills of Wyoming that will transport you to the grape-vined hills of Northern Italy. Italian cuisine is the one exotic that seems to take root in this state, and you have only to taste Franca's loin of veal in tuna sauce to be convinced. Try the ravioli or the popular tortelloni, or get lucky and show up on a night when Franca cooks fresh salmon. The small restaurant—only 24 can be seated at once—is in a turn-of-the-century home a block off Sheridan Avenue. It's been nicely decorated by Franca's artist-husband, and sits atop an impressive wine cellar.

Maxwell's Restaurant. 937 Sheridan Ave. ☎ **307/527-7749.** Lunch $7–$10; dinner $8.75–$16.50. DISC, MC, V. Mon–Sat 11am–9pm. ECLECTIC AMERICAN.

A family restaurant in which "family" does not translate to "bland," Maxwell's has some spicy chicken and pasta dishes to go with its salads, seafood, and beef. The wine list is respectable, and you can order a Philly steak, uncommon in Wyoming. The low-backed booths and varnished wood tables are sometimes packed with boisterous families, raising the noise level and waitress stress, but it's a friendly crowd.

Silver Dollar Bar & Grill. 1313 Sheridan Ave. ☎ **307/587-3554.** Reservations not accepted. Most dishes $5–$8. No credit cards. Mon–Wed 11am–10pm, Thurs 11am–7pm, Fri–Sat 11am–10pm, Sun noon–10pm. BURGERS.

If you're looking for locals, the Silver Dollar is where you'll find them. Located on Cody's main street, the restaurant makes its home in what was once the town's first post office. Though its claim to world-famous burgers may be stretching the truth a bit, the food is hearty and the occasional live entertainment makes for a fun night of music and dancing.

Stefan's Restaurant. 1367 Sheridan Ave. ☎ **307/587-8511.** Lunch $5–$7; dinner $10–$23. AE, DISC, MC, V. Summer, daily 8am–10pm; off-season, Mon–Sat 11am–9pm. ECLECTIC.

Stefan is a restless chef, so the menu of his restaurant today is almost completely different from what he began with a few years ago. Among the entree survivors is a local favorite, a filet mignon stuffed with Gorgonzola cheese, sun-dried tomatoes, and portabello mushrooms. The Southwestern interior decor might lead you to expect an enchilada or two, but there's no predicting—you're just as likely to find a swordfish in an avocado and mango sauce. Experimentation has kept Stefan fresh and his menu deliciously spry. There are separate lunch and Sunday brunch menus, and a "little bites" menu with $3 children's meals.

3 A Side Trip Around the Bighorn Basin

Greybull: 40 miles E of Cody; 60 miles W of Sheridan

The prehistoric past of this region is writ in the rock, and nowhere in Wyoming is that more true than in **Greybull,** named for a legendary albino bison sacred to Native Americans. Though Greybull does little to draw attention to itself, it lies amidst red rock formations rich in fossils and archaeological treasures. **The Greybull Museum** (325 Greybull Ave.; ☎ 307/765-2444) houses one of the largest fossil ammonites in the world, as well as petrified wood, agates, and Indian artifacts. This fine museum is open Monday to Saturday, 10am to 8pm from June to Labor Day, and more restricted hours in the winter. Just north of town you'll find a spectacular 15-mile-long, 2,000-foot-high natural fortress named **Sheep Mountain,** a textbook example of a "doubly plunging anticline," geo-lingo for a natural arch folded into layered rock.

Greybull is a gateway town to the Bighorn Mountains on scenic U.S. Highway 14 up Shell Canyon. Just 7 miles outside of town heading east is the **Stone Schoolhouse,** listed on the National Register of Historic Places. The one-room schoolhouse was built in 1903 of locally quarried sandstone and in recent years was converted to a bookstore/gallery, though its hours are unpredictable. Less than a mile farther along the highway, turn south on Red Gulch Road and drive 5 miles to a signed parking area where you can view dinosaur tracks.

Highway 14 climbs through steep and beautiful **Shell Canyon** (see Driving Tour #1 above) to the Antelope Butte Ski Area, just 38 miles east of Greybull. It's a small ski area with nice views and short lift lines.

Fifty miles south of Greybull and east through little Hyattville brings you to the **Medicine Lodge State Archaeological Site** (☎ 307/469-2234), where prehistoric peoples decorated the sandstone cliffs along Medicine Lodge Creek with carved petroglyphs and painted pictographs of hunting scenes. You can fish the small stream for brown trout. There is a shady, inexpensive, 26-site campground here, open May through October, with no RV hookups. To reach the site and campground, take WY 789/U.S. Highway 16/20 for 20 miles from Greybull to Manderson, then drive 22 miles along WY 31 to Hyattville. In Hyattville, drive north and turn right onto Cold Springs Road. Follow the signs 5 miles to the site.

4 Thermopolis

84 miles S of Cody; 130 miles NW of Casper; 218 miles E of Jackson

Steaming water cascades in glistening streams over pastel-colored terraces and down to the Bighorn River at Hot Springs State Park, one of the undiscovered treasures of Wyoming. Trumpeted as the largest hot springs in the world (it's not quite: New Zealand claims that title), the 134°F water from the Big Spring supplies two indoor/outdoor pool facilities, two hotels, and a state-run soaking spa, with plenty left over to pour over the travertine into the river. The town of Thermopolis—a Greek-Latin neologism for "hot city"—grew up around the hot springs after it was sold to the U.S. government by the tribes of the Wind River Indian Reservation in 1896. Developers dreamt of a health spa to rival Saratoga, but it never happened. What did happen is a small town—peaceful rather than "hot"—with a great place to soak or slide, a nearby canyon of exciting white water, and surrounding hills holding a trove of dinosaur bones and prehistoric petroglyphs.

ESSENTIALS

GETTING THERE   If you're flying into the Thermopolis area, the closest airports are the **Riverton Regional Airport** (55 miles south of Thermopolis, off Highway 26 West at 4700 Airport Rd., Riverton, WY 82501) and Cody's **Yellowstone Regional Airport** (84 miles northeast on WY 120 to U.S. Highway 14/16/20, north on Duggleby Drive to 3001 Duggleby Dr., Cody, WY 82414; ☎ 307/587-5096). There is a small airport in Thermopolis used by private fliers.

United Airlines affiliate **Great Lakes Aviation** (☎ 800/241-6522) is the sole provider of air service into Riverton, with several daily connecting flights to Denver and north to Worland. Cody service is provided by both **United Express** (☎ 800/241-6522) and Delta feeder **Skywest** (☎ 800/453-9417).

To reach Thermopolis from Cody, drive 84 miles southeast on WY 120. From Cheyenne, drive north on I-25 to Casper (178 miles), west on U.S. Highway 20/26 to Shoshoni (98 miles), and north on U.S. Highway 20 to Thermopolis. From Rock Springs, take U.S. Highway 191 to Farson, WY 28 to Lander, WY 789 through Riverton and Shoshoni to Thermopolis. Call ☎ 800/WYO-ROAD in-state or 307/772-0824 for current road conditions.

VISITOR INFORMATION   The **Thermopolis–Hot Springs Chamber of Commerce,** 700 Broadway, Thermopolis, WY 82443 (☎ 800/SUN-N-SPA or 307/864-3192), sends out packets of information about local attractions.

GETTING AROUND   If you've arrived by plane at one of the area airports, you'll need to rent a car to get around. **Avis** (☎ 800/331-1212) and **Hertz** (☎ 800/654-3131) maintain counters at both the Riverton and Cody airports.

GETTING OUTSIDE

Hot Springs State Park (see detailed listing below) offers a variety pack of outdoor activities, from splashing in mineral water to picnicking on the lawn. South and upstream on the Bighorn River is twisting **Wind River Canyon,** a tricky but bountiful fishing and floating section (you'll need permits from the Wind River Indian Reservation), topped by 19,000-acre **Boysen Reservoir,** about 20 minutes from Thermopolis on U.S. Highway 20. The 11 campgrounds on the largely treeless shore of this state park can be a bit buggy and hot in August, but the water attracts boaters to sail, fish, and water-ski. Just south of the dam on the reservoir's northeast shore are two small public beach areas. For more information on the park, contact **Boysen State Park,** Boysen Route, Shoshoni, WY 82649 (☎ **307/876-2796**), or call Wyoming State Parks and Historic Sites headquarters in Cheyenne at ☎ **307/777-6323.**

FISHING

Whether you like fishing lakes or streams, this area has trophy-size opportunities—Boysen grows record-setting walleye, as well as trout and perch, while the Bighorn River, enriched by underground hot springs, grows some fat brown and cutthroat trout. Check locally to be sure you've got the right fishing license: The canyon requires a tribal permit, the reservoir and other stretches of river require a state license—both available at local sporting goods stores. If you have your own boat, or hire an outfitter, you can float and fish from the bottom of the canyon at the Wedding of the Waters, where there is a wheelchair-accessible boat ramp to Thermopolis. During the warmest part of summer, algae can darken the river and hamper fishing, but spring and fall are anglers' dreams. The chamber of commerce can provide the names of fishing guides.

GOLF

The Legion Golf Course is a nine-hole course that overlooks the city from Airport Hill. Call ☎ **307/864-5294** to book a tee time at affordable prices—nine holes for $11 on weekdays and $13 on weekends; 18 holes for $16 and $18. The pro shop offers cart rentals, driving range, and lessons. An adjacent restaurant, the Legion Supper Club (see "Where to Dine," below), is open daily for lunch and dinner.

HIKING

A boardwalk allows you to explore the bulbous travertine terraces without scalding your soles in the hot spring water that flows over them. The paths extend to a suspended footbridge across the Bighorn River, and riverside walkway below. For more earnest hikers, there is a 6.2-mile **Volksmarch Trail,** one of several around the state that are marked with a trademark brown-and-yellow insignia. This one loops through the park and downtown Thermopolis. Just north of town off U.S. Highway 20 you can hike **T Hill,** for a bird's-eye view of Thermopolis, the Wind River Canyon, and the Owl Creek Mountains.

✪ WHITE-WATER RAFTING

The tribes of the **Wind River Indian Reservation** virtually gave away the hot springs, but not the canyon upstream, through which the Wind River tumbles and twists (for reasons no one can explain, the Wind River becomes the Bighorn River as it leaves the canyon). A Shoshone-owned company now takes rafters through rapids named after historic tribal figures like Chief Washakie and Sharp Nose. "Sphincter Rapid" is not an Indian name, but it tells you there are some Class III–IV whitewater thrills ahead. You can run half the canyon or the whole thing, take a more leisurely fishing trip, or camp overnight with **Wind River Canyon Whitewater,** 210 Hwy. 20 S., Thermopolis, WY 82443 (P.O. Box 592, Crowheart, WY 82512, ☎ **307/864-9343** in season or 307/486-2253 during off-season).

HOT SPRINGS STATE PARK

Few state parks in Wyoming are as nice as **Hot Springs** (☎ 307/864-2176), with its shade trees, a band shell, the river running through it, a buffalo herd roaming the eastern portion of the park, and the magnificent hot springs, some of it funneled into swimming pools and slides. It's located at the north side of town off U.S. Highway 20. The park's only shortcoming is that you can't camp overnight, a situation that must please nearby private campgrounds and lodgings. As a Wyoming tourist attraction, the hot springs places a distant third to Yellowstone and Grand Teton national parks, but the lack of crowds allows the town to retain its small-town style.

At the north end of the park, you can climb a few stairs to look down into the bottomless blue-green depths of the Big Spring—the placid surface belies the fact that it pumps around 15 million gallons of aqua vitae a day. The broad shallow pools on the terraces allow some of this water to cool and settle out layers of creamy travertine.

SOAKING IN THE BATHS

You can't just plop yourself down in this 135°F water, but there are three bathing facilities in the park. To get to them, take the loop road—at the north end are the bathing areas. First, and simplest, is the **State Bath House,** a small spa open to the public free of charge thanks to famed Shoshone Chief Washakie. When the tribes sold the federal government the hot springs in 1896—it would later become state property—Washakie noted that the springs had always been a place of peace and neutrality among tribes, and should therefore always be free to all people. The small, clean indoor and outdoor pools aren't for frolicking or swimming laps—just soaking, wading and perhaps conversing with some of the old-timers who come here. You can rent a towel and a locker for under a dollar each, and it's open Monday to Saturday 8am to 5:30pm, Sunday and holidays noon to 5:30pm. On either side of this peaceful place are the more raucous commercial pools.

STAR PLUNGE   The big lure at the Plunge are its three big slides—the kids' favorite "Little Dipper," the outdoor "Super Star," and the enclosed "Blue Thunder," the latter a 300-foot spin around a 60-foot tower that will thrill you to your claustrophobic, free-falling toes. Indoor and outdoor pools, hot tubs, Jacuzzis, a snack bar and an arcade make this the favorite of the young set. On a crowded summer afternoon, there are lines at the slides, splashing all around, and a teenage volume level, but you can still find stillness in the "vapor cave." For more information call ☎ 307/864-3771. Admission is $7 for children over 4 and adults; $2 for children 4 and under; $5 for seniors. It's open daily 9am to 9pm. Closed first 3 weeks of December.

TEPEE SPA   The Spa (☎ 307/864-9250), sometimes called Hot Springs Water Park, is a little more peaceful under its big dome than its neighbor to the east, but it has its share of lively teens and a contingent of young families. The slides are not as big here, but you can hear yelps of delight as bodies zip down the twisting indoor open tube. There is a fast-moving open slide outdoors, too, and often a wet basketball game in the roomy outdoor pool. Soaking pools, a steam room, a sauna, and a game room complete the scene. Admission is $7 for ages 6 to 62; $5 for ages 4 to 5 and 63 and over; under 3, free. Open daily 9am–9pm.

GIFT OF THE WATERS HISTORICAL INDIAN PAGEANT

An annual production, the pageant reenacts the sale of the hot springs and surrounding lands by the Shoshone and Arapaho peoples to the federal government, and thence to white settlers, in 1896. The tribes sold the hot springs and thousands of acres for $60,000, and the pageant makes it out as an act of peace and neighborly brotherhood. In fact, the tribes were starving and desperate, and Chief Washakie was

88 years old and fading. Indians from Wind River are paid to play roles in the pageant, though a troop of local cowbelles are painted up as Indian maidens—normally, you don't often see Native American faces here. Written in 1925 and revived in 1950, the pageant is performed annually during the first weekend in August, along with a powwow. Contact the **Thermopolis Chamber of Commerce** (☎ **800/SUN-N-SPA** or 307/864-3192) for information.

SEEING THE SIGHTS

Hot Springs County Historical Museum and Cultural Center. 7th and Broadway. ☎ **307/864-5183.** $10 families, $2 adults, $1.50 seniors, $1 children under 6. Mon–Sat 8am–5pm.

The original cherry-wood bar from the Hole-in-the-Wall Saloon—Butch Cassidy's hangout—is the biggest draw at this local museum, which has some gems amidst the musty clutter that you learn to expect of rural repositories. Various modes of transportation are represented: a turn-of-the-century stagecoach, a caboose, and a wagon used to tour Yellowstone. Exhibits trace the local economic threads, primarily coal mining, petroleum extraction, and agriculture, as well as the early, crude attempts to erect bathing shacks on the springs. On the lower level are a fully outfitted print shop, general store, and dentist's office. The museum's cultural center features local artwork and crafts on a rotating basis. Call for information on current exhibits.

○ **Legend Rock Petroglyph Site.** Near Hamilton Dome, about 30 miles northwest of Thermopolis. Call the Thermopolis Chamber of Commerce (☎ **800/SUN-N-SPA** or 307/864-3192) to arrange for access to the site.

Petroglyphs—prehistoric drawings inscribed in rock—are scattered throughout the foothills of Wyoming's mountains. Difficult to date and even harder to interpret, these mysterious drawings are nevertheless considered sacred by Indians. Legend Rock is one of the richest petroglyph sites in the Rockies, and it is managed—rather informally—by state agents at Hot Springs State Park. Visitors can pick up a gate key at the park and then drive up WY 120 to the Hamilton Dome turnoff, then continue 8 miles west, partly on a dirt road, to the site. There you can hike up and down Cottonwood Creek to find pecked representations of turtle-like creatures, bird glyphs, hunters, and musicians. To get a good view of some of the panels you need to scramble up on ledges. Weather has taken its toll on this soft sandstone, and so have souvenir hunters—hands off, please! Be sure and ask for a map to the site when you pick up the key between 9am and 5pm at the park office, as the route is not well marked. You can drive down by the creek, but you're better off, particularly when it's wet and muddy, parking up by the gate and taking the short hike down.

Outlaw Trail Ride. Outlaw Trail, Inc., Box 1046, Thermopolis, WY 82443. ☎ **800/ 362-RIDE** or 307/864-2287. W3/trib.com/~outlaw. The ride occurs annually in mid-Aug.

Butch Cassidy was a well-known character around Thermopolis, not by any means the wildest of the outlaws who favored this country. Visitors who want to ride the trails he rode can join the annual Outlaw Trail Ride in August, and journey 100 miles up through the dry, hidden canyons of Hole-in-the-Wall country. Only about 100 people can participate in the weeklong event, and it's BYO horse and sleep on the ground. That hasn't discouraged interest: Every year, the trip is booked up before summer starts.

○ **Wyoming Dinosaur Center.** 110 Carter Ranch Rd., Thermopolis, WY 82443. ☎ **800/455-3466.** $6 adults 19–59, $3.50 children 5–18 and seniors; group rates available. Daily 10am–5pm. Closed Thanksgiving, Christmas, and New Year's Day.

This dinosaur museum is not in some faraway city: It's right here at the site where in recent years paleontologists have been digging up bones from the Jurassic period, 145 million years ago. There are 12 full skeletons on display at the center, as well as eggs, shells, and other remnants from around the world. Except in winter, visitors can take guided tours of dig sites, and then watch workers clean and prepare bones in the laboratory at the center.

WHERE TO STAY

Thermopolis has quite a number of motels and campgrounds with a little age on them, and when you arrive in the busy summer season it's best to have a reservation, or you might land in a room with the amenities of a closet. Recently, chain affiliates have taken a new interest in lodgings here, so the choices are growing.

Holiday Inn of the Waters. Hot Springs State Park, Thermopolis, WY 82443. ☎ **800/HOLIDAY** or 307/864-3131. www.holidayinnthermopolis.com. E-mail: holinn@ trib.com. 80 units. A/C TV TEL. $58–$102 double. AE, DC, DISC, MC, V.

This is no cookie-cutter Holiday Inn—it's a hot springs resort, snug along in the Bighorn River within the state park, with some special amenities . . . and peculiarities. The huge volume of superheated water that surges from the upturned sandstones is piped into the outdoor Jacuzzi next to the big pool. If lolling under the stars doesn't soften you up, take a turn in the health club and submit to the ministrations of a licensed masseuse. Unique to this Holiday Inn are its location in the park, several antique-furnished rooms, and frequent promotions (two weekend nights, dinner, champagne for two for $140 from September to May). Certainly no other Holiday Inn has a restaurant like the Safari Room, arrayed with enough big-game trophies from around the world to make Ernest Hemingway blush and vegetarians gag.

Quality Inn & Suites Plaza Hotel. 116 E. Park St., Thermopolis, WY 82443. ☎ **800/ 228-5161** or 307/864-2939. 36 units. TV TEL. $70–$105 double; reduced rates in winter. AE, DC, DISC, MC, V.

If you'd rather not have a wildebeest staring at you on your way to breakfast, but still want to be in the park, try this alternative, a funky old brick place that once operated as a hostel but now has been nicely fixed up by Quality Inns. Several of the rooms and suites still have working fireplaces, and the new owners have added a swimming pool and Jacuzzi to the inner courtyard. It's an easy walk to pools, but you may enjoy the old-fashioned ambience here enough to linger over your coffee.

Roundtop Mountain Motel. 412 N. 6th, Thermopolis, WY 82443. ☎ **800/584-9126** or 307/864-3126. 12 units. A/C TV TEL. $35–$69 double. DISC, MC, V.

The Roundtop is one of several clean and comfortable budget alternatives in Thermopolis, offering lodging in either a motel or log cabins. A redwood deck and patio complement some of the units, and kitchenettes are available, which puts the Roundtop ahead of its competition. Though not directly adjacent to the hot springs, the motel is located downtown and within a short drive or walk of the mineral baths.

Super 8 Hot Springs. Lane 5 S., Hwy. 20, Thermopolis, WY 82443. ☎ **800/800-8000** or 307/864-5515. Fax 307/864-5447. 52 units. A/C TV TEL. Summer, $75–$85 double, $175 honeymoon suite; winter, $55–$65 double, $145 honeymoon suite. Rates include continental breakfast. AE, CB, DC, DISC, MC, V.

The tile-roofed Southwest style of architecture seems a bit out of place in the Wyoming hills, but it distinguishes this new motel from other Super 8's, and from the many older, somewhat drab lodgings in Thermopolis. Inside, the decor is not particularly distinguished, but there are a big indoor pool, a pleasant lobby and eating area for the free continental breakfast, and a honeymoon suite with a marble Jacuzzi.

CAMPING

The **Fountain of Youth RV Park** (☎ 307/864-3265) has tent and RV sites available almost year-round (they're closed in December and January) and is located 1.5 miles north of town by the river on U.S. Highway 20. The campground features a large mineral pool of its own with RV supplies, barbecue grills, and other sundries available at the camp store. Facilities are wheelchair-accessible and an EMT is on-site. When things are busy in the summer, you may find yourself overhearing the unmuffled conversation of the Harley riders parked in the next slot. The **Latchstring Campground** (☎ 307/864-5262) is a similar facility with almost identical amenities but a little more space and quiet. It's located on U.S. Highway 20 south of Thermopolis.

WHERE TO DINE

Legion Supper Club. At the Legion Golf Club. ☎ **307/864-3918.** Lunch $5–$10; dinner $8–$19. AE, DISC, MC, V. Mon–Sat 11am–2pm and 5–10pm, Sun brunch 10am–2pm. Closed Mon in winter. Turn west off U.S. Hwy. 20 on Broadway, then north on 7th St., which becomes Park St. and climbs Airport Hill to the golf course and supper club. AMERICAN.

Up in the hills above Thermopolis, the Legion's pasta, steak, and prime rib menu is the fanciest fare offered in these parts. Well off the traffic routes, it's got a 360-degree view of the golf course surrounding it. Lunch is a festive affair, with a Mexican menu that includes smothered burritos and a taco salad as well as standard sandwich fare; the crab-and-cheese melt and shrimp salad are local favorites. The cheerful ambience during lunch becomes decidedly more polished and romantic at dinner, when linen tablecloths, flowers, and candles grace the tables and entrees of prime cuts of beef and seafood are served. The restaurant also has a quiet, full-service bar.

✪ **Pumpernick's.** 512 Broadway. ☎ **307/864-5151.** Breakfast $2–$6; lunch $3–$6; dinner $7–$16. AE, DISC, MC, V. Mon–Sat 7am–9pm. AMERICAN.

The three rooms where meals are served at Pumpernick's clearly weren't designed for a restaurant, but the sometimes cramped quarters add a friendly intimacy to good food. In the summer, you can escape the elbows by eating outside in the roomy adjacent arbor. Around town it's sometimes called the Local Yokel Club, and they come for breakfast, lunch, and dinner every day but Sunday. Pumpernick's serves three-egg omelets to breakfast noshers, then crepes and fat specialty sandwiches for lunch. Dinner features generous portions of T-bone steaks and seafood, including sautéed scallops, rainbow trout, and steamed shrimp. They bake their own breads, which they use for hoagies, soup bowls, and dinner loaves. Try the Strawberry Kiss cheesecake for a melt-in-your-mouth treat. The open-air patio is an especially nice place to enjoy your meal during summer.

5 Wind River Valley

Lander: 160 miles SE of Jackson; 117 miles N of Rock Springs; 163 miles S of Cody

The deep curve of the Wind River Valley is shaped by the snowcapped Wind River Mountain range in the West and the Absaroka and Owl Creek ranges in the east, forming a cottonwood-lined bottom that many consider one of the most beautiful areas in Wyoming. A sizable portion of the valley belongs to the Eastern Shoshone and Northern Arapaho tribes of the **Wind River Indian Reservation,** where there is considerable poverty, but also productive ranches and spectacular wilderness reaching up to the Continental Divide. The largest towns are Riverton and Lander, but there are smaller towns like Dubois, Shoshoni, Fort Washakie, and the historical gold-mining town of Atlantic City that reward visits.

RIVERTON

Notched in a big bend of the Wind River is **Riverton,** a settlement that was carved out when the federal government opened the northern portion of the reservation to non-Indian people a century ago. A little too far east to call itself a mountain town, Riverton has established itself as a retail commercial center for west central Wyoming. Contact the **Riverton Area Chamber of Commerce,** First and Main, Riverton, WY 82501 (☎ **307/856-4801**), for information, including useful suggestions for day trips in the area and a list of events. That calendar includes a summer **Riverton Rendezvous and Balloon Rally,** held during the third week in July, when colorful balloons from all over the Rockies rise against the majestic backdrop of the Wind River Range, and the town puts on arts and crafts fairs, rodeo, and even pig-wrestling competitions. Also in the summer, there is a trappers' rendezvous staged at the junction of the Wind River and the Little Wind River, with black powder shooting, Indian dancing, tomahawk throws, and bead-trading. Wyoming's largest **cowboy poetry gathering** is held here in October, and there is a **Winter Carnival** with drag racing on the ice surface of Boysen Reservoir.

GETTING THERE   From Thermopolis, take U.S. Highway 20 south through scenic Wind River Canyon to Shoshoni, then U.S. Highway 26 south to Riverton.

WHERE TO STAY   If you plan to stay overnight in Riverton, your best bet is the **Holiday Inn** (☎ **800/HOLIDAY** or 307/856-8100). Located at North Federal and Sunset, it has 121 rooms that typically rent for an affordable $48 to $79 for a double. Or you could head 24 miles farther west on Wyoming 789 to **Lander** (see below).

SHOSHONI

Shoshoni, which translates as "Little Snow," is located 22 miles east of Riverton on U.S. Highway 26. Peek behind the shabby exterior of the little town and you'll find what are reputedly the world's best milk shakes at the **Shoshoni Drug Store** (they're good, but let's not go too far), some interesting sites for rockhounds amidst abandoned copper mines in the Owl Creeks to the north, and, on Memorial Day weekend, the state's premier **Old Time Fiddlers' Contest.** Contact the **Shoshoni Chamber,** Box 324, Shoshoni, WY 82649 (☎ **307/876-2221**), for more information.

LANDER

If you head 24 miles farther west of Riverton on Wyoming 789, you hit **Lander,** which is tucked snugly into the foothills of the Wind River Mountains where the three fingers of the Popo Agie River draw together. When railroads were the nation's primary mode of travel, Lander was "where the rails end and the trails begin": the take-off point for backcountry trips to hunt, fish, or explore the lake-dotted wilderness that climbs to the Continental Divide. The trains are gone, but this is still where you put on your hiking or riding boots. For more information, contact the **Land of Trails,** 160 N. 1st St., Lander, WY 82520 (☎ **800/433-0662;** www.landerchamber.org).

Just west of town on WY 131 is **Sinks Canyon State Park** (☎ **307/332-6333**), where the Middle Fork of the Popo Agie disappears into a limestone cave and reappears farther down the canyon at a pool with an overlook where you can feed kibble to giant trout (no hooks allowed!). The park has a nature trail, a visitor center with naturalist displays, and tumbling waterfalls for those willing to hike some switchbacks. For a different kind of experience, drive south 37 miles on U.S. Highway 287 to the **South Pass City Historical Site** (☎ **307/332-3684**), which re-creates a gold-mining town from the 1860s—the unlikely high desert setting for a landmark in the history of women's suffrage, when Esther Hobart Morris became the nation's first woman justice of the peace.

Lander has a justly famous Fourth of July parade and Pioneer Days Rodeo (☎ 800/433-0662), and later in July it hosts the **International Climber's Festival** (☎ 307/332-6697; www.climbersfestival.org). Slide shows by climbing greats like Galen Rowell and Royal Roberts, clinics, an equipment show, and afternoons testing skills on the walls of Sinks Canyon and Wild Iris draw to the event hundreds of serious climbers, who unleash their less-serious sides at street dances.

Some of the climbers are resident here, partly thanks to the ✪ **National Outdoor Leadership School (NOLS),** which has been teaching outdoor types responsible ways of enjoying the wilds for more than 30 years, and now has branches all over the world. For course offerings from India to the Winds, write the school's Lander headquarters at 288 Main St., Lander, WY 82520 (☎ 307/332-5300; www.nols.edu).

If you'd rather do less of it yourself, but want an exotic element to your trail adventure, make a date with a llama through the **Lander Llama Company,** 2024 Mortimore Lane, Lander, WY 82520 (☎ 307/332-5624). Their naturalist-led Red Desert trip is as enlightening as it is enjoyable, incorporating ancient Native American history and fossil viewing with stunning Wyoming scenery. If you'd prefer to horse around, check out **Allen's Diamond Four Ranch,** P.O. Box 243, Lander, WY 82520 (☎ 307/332-2995), for guided horseback tours in the Popo Agie Wilderness and Wind River Mountains. The ranch's overnight accommodations are bare-bones—woodstoves, propane lights, bring your own bedding—but the emphasis is on riding, fishing, and seeing the high country. There are special programs for kids.

Winter transforms this country into a snowmobiler's playground, with 250 miles of the **Continental Divide Trail** reaching from Lander all the way to Yellowstone. Call the **Wind River Visitors Council** at ☎ 800/645-6233 for information on this and other snowmobile trails in the area. The **Lander Area Chamber of Commerce,** 160 N. 1st St., Lander, WY 82520 (☎ 307/332-3892), can also provide you with information on the area.

WIND RIVER INDIAN RESERVATION

Note: The starting point for a tour of the Wind River Indian Reservation is Fort Washakie, located 14 miles north of Lander on U.S. 287, or 146 miles from Jackson (U.S. 26/89/191 to Moran Junction, then U.S. 287 over Togwotee Pass to Dubois and then on to the reservation).

More than two million acres of the **Wind River Indian Reservation** surround the town of Riverton, encompassing an area that stretches 70 miles east to west and 55 miles north to south. Wyoming's sole reservation is home to more than 2,800 Eastern Shoshone and 3,700 Northern Arapaho tribal members. It's governed by a joint council made up of representatives from both tribes.

The Shoshone were considered friendly to whites when they first signed a treaty in 1863, and they were given a huge reservation not so much as a reward, but to buffer westward travelers from more hostile tribes to the north like the Sioux and Blackfeet. A reservation that once included parts of Wyoming, Utah, and Colorado was reduced greatly when non-Indians discovered gold, grazing land, and water on tribal lands. Today, the Wind River Indian Reservation is a still-sizable 2.3 million acres, including oil and gas fields, several small communities, and some of the most pristine wilderness—and best fishing—in the United States.

The Northern Arapaho came to Wind River in the late 1870s for what they thought was a temporary placement before moving to their own reservation farther east. However, government promises were forgotten or ignored, and the Arapaho settled in to stay. The two tribes have unrelated languages and a history of warfare, but their relationship has gradually improved.

There are poverty and high unemployment on the reservation, but there is pride, too, quite evident in the finery at the powwows. Outsiders are welcome at these dances, which are held from May to September at various sites (the Wind River Visitors Council can provide a schedule; ☎ 800/645-6233) where you'll see a more open, friendly side of Arapahos and Shoshones, as long as you are respectful. Sun dances are more spiritual affairs, and while visitors are not banned, these moving ceremonies—in which painted dancers go without water and food for 4 days—are not for tourists, and no photographs or videos are allowed.

Services for visitors are not well-developed on the reservation, but you can learn more about the Shoshone tribe at the **Shoshone Tribal Cultural Center** (☎ 307/332-9106) in Fort Washakie, and about the Arapaho tribe at the **St. Stephen's Heritage Center** (☎ 307/856-5110). At **St. Michael's Mission,** in Ethete (5 miles east of Fort Washakie), there is a museum of Arapaho cultural artifacts. There is also a newly refurbished hot spring spa on the reservation, **Chief Washakie Plunge** (☎ 307/332-9106; between Fort Washakie and Ethete) with a pool, Jacuzzi, and private baths. Call for hours.

Sacajawea, the famed Shoshone scout for the Lewis and Clark expedition, is supposedly buried on a reservation that bears her name, west of Fort Washakie. There is some debate about whether she is buried there, but it's a beautiful cemetery on a hill, and worth a visit (ask for directions in Fort Washakie). You might also stop by nearby **Roberts Mission**—John Roberts was an Episcopal minister who lived most of his life on the reservation and had a tremendous influence on the tribes, founding a school and recording useful historical and anthropological information about the tribes. Chief Washakie, the venerated Shoshone chief, is buried in a cemetery along the Little Wind River on the north side of Fort Washakie. He lived to be over 100 and was buried with full honors by the U.S. Army—-the only Indian chief to be so honored.

In late June, Native Americans from around the country converge at Fort Washakie for **Shoshone Treaty Days,** a celebration of Native American tradition and culture. The **Eastern Shoshone Powwow and Indian Days** follow a week later, with one of the West's largest powwows and all-Native American rodeos, including thrilling bareback relay horse races.

There are hundreds of lakes in the reservation high country, and in the summer they come alive with hungry trout—browns, cutthroats, brook, and golden. You can purchase a reservation fishing permit at local sporting goods stores and find your way with maps to Bull Lake and Moccasin Lake by car, or pick up U.S.G.S. topographical maps and head for the high country on foot. Check at **Rocky Mountain Dubbing Company,** 115 Poppy St., on U.S. Highway 287 just south of Lander (less than 1 mile) for permits, maps, equipment, and advice. If you want a guided horseback trip, contact Darwin Griebel at **Paradise Outfitters,** Star Route, Box 2815, Kinnear, WY 82516, ☎ 307/856-2950.

If you want a roof over your head in Wind River country, try the **Holiday Inn** at Riverton (900 E. Sunset, Riverton, WY 82501; ☎ 307/856-8100); or the **Best Western Inn at Lander** (260 Grand View Dr., Lander, WY 82520; ☎ 307/332- 2847).

13 Sheridan & Eastern Wyoming

The Delaware Indians have a term, "*maughwau wama*," which means, roughly, "rising from the plains." As you enter Wyoming from the east, the plains begin to roll like ocean swells, rising, falling, until they break against the Rockies. As the elevation rises the grass grows shorter. Rains taper from dependable downpours to sporadic cloudbursts. The wind races across the surface, combing down the grass, sculpting the snow.

Bison once cloaked these prairies in enormous herds, and people were few. But the modern era brought rapid change. In the 18th century, Indian bands mounted horses that had escaped from Spanish conquistadors, and enjoyed a brief era of prosperity on the plains, hunting the buffalo with great skill. Newcomers poured in: trappers searching for beaver pelts; Mormons pushing west toward Zion; pioneer families and wagons bound for Oregon. But it was the Texas trail drives, moving north, not West, that most shaped the history and culture of eastern Wyoming.

The landscape hasn't change much since then. There's still widely scattered settlements; a few small, irrigated fields; and lots of grass and cattle. The billboards announce: "Welcome to the Cowboy State," but these days it's the coal and oil and gas beneath the prairies that subsidize life in the wide-open spaces. But the cowboy life is still vibrant, if rarely lucrative, and friendly to visitors: You can visit the nightly rodeos in Buffalo, or the country's oldest operating dude ranch, or the best tack shop in the West, Kings Saddlery of Sheridan. You can explore the mostly unchanged landscapes where cattle barons and their hired guns battled homesteaders in the Johnson County War, where Butch Cassidy and the Hole-in-the Wall gang marauded, where Crazy Horse and Red Cloud clashed with the cavalry.

Latter-day adventurers have their own reasons for coming here. What lures many is **Devils Tower,** the corrugated lump of volcanic rock that suddenly rises 1,280 feet from the flatlands of Eastern Wyoming. Climbers come to search for a way up its many challenging routes, and movie buffs who watched *Close Encounters of the Third Kind* come searching for something out of this world. Visitors come also to hike and fish in the Bighorn Mountains, a handsome range somewhat overshadowed by the peaks of the Continental Divide farther west. Almost unnoticed is a precious preserve of prairie habitat, the 1.8-million-acre **Thunder Basin National Grassland.**

The big coal and oil and gas booms that have come and gone and come again during the last 50 years have built up the cities of **Casper**

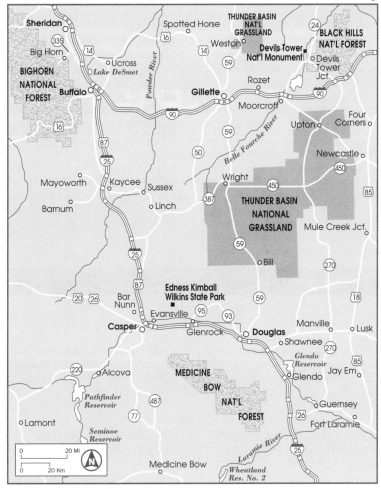

and **Gillette,** rough-hewn towns in a rough landscape, which nevertheless show evidence of the fortunes made off minerals: Gillette has fine new schools and recreation facilities, and both cities have large, modern events centers.

You can explore this region by interstates—I-25 runs north-south, while I-90 dips down from Montana and then east to Devils Tower—or take small highways like U.S. 18 and WY 59 to reach smaller towns and more remote country. But since Sheridan is often the target of travelers to the area, this chapter begins there, exploring south to Buffalo and then east to Gillette and Devils Tower. Then we backtrack to Casper for a look at Wyoming's second-largest city.

1 Scenic Drive: Black Hills Loop

This half-day loop tour begins and ends in Sundance, a town sometimes associated with Butch Cassidy's sidekick, the Sundance Kid. Although the town really wasn't named for him (its namesake is a nearby mountain on which Sioux ceremonies were held) you might guess that the county in which it's located—Crook County—was dubbed for its outlaw past. But Crook County actually takes its name from a U.S. Army general in the Indian Wars, George Crook.

The first stop on the tour is the **courtroom where the Sundance Kid was convicted of horse stealing,** now part of the local museum in Sundance, located in the center of town on Cleveland Street. From here, it's a short and scenic 28-mile drive to **Devils Tower** (21 miles north on U.S. Highway 14, then 7 miles on WY 24 to the monument). From Devils Tower, drive another 9 miles north toward **Hulett,** past red sandstone hills and panoramic views of the Bearlodge Mountains. At Hulett, drive east on WY 24 to **Alva** and **Aladdin,** which hug the border and provide easy access to the neighboring Black Hills of South Dakota. In Aladdin, drive south along WY 111 to Beulah and U.S. Highway 14, then back to Sundance.

You can extend this driving tour by adding on an additional loop: from Sundance to Upton on WY 116 for 30 miles, then on to Moorcroft on U.S. Highway 16 for 20 miles, to Devils Tower Junction on U.S. Highway 14 for 26 miles, then back to Sundance (21 miles). On this route you can soak your feet in the Keyhole Reservoir (between Sundance and Moorcroft), stroll the streets of Moorcroft—a ranching community on the banks of the Belle Fourche River—and you'll probably pass abundant herds of antelope gazing in roadside fields.

2 Sheridan

144 miles N of Casper; 124 miles S of Billings; 156 miles E of Cody

While some towns in eastern Wyoming appear to barely have a grip on the windblown plains, Sheridan looks right at home, its deep roots evident in its well-preserved historic downtown. The Bighorn Mountains cast afternoon shadows in this direction, across the ranches in the foothills where "dude" ranching was defined and perfected. One of the largest Wyoming towns, with 13,900 residents, Sheridan, named after Civil War general Phil Sheridan, retains its small-town charm. Turn-of-the century buildings front Main Street. Mansions of cattle barons still stand, and regular polo matches preserve traces of European influence.

You won't see at first glance many clues to the source of prosperity in more recent times: massive coal deposits to the north and east. After decades of production, the big strip mines are in a slow decline, and tourism is on the rise, with an influx of adventurous mountain bikers, rock climbers, para-gliders, snowmobilers, and cross-country skiers, lured by the Bighorns. Ranching these days is less about beef, and more about providing saddle time for vacation dudes and retreats for wealthy corporate kings. Or queens—Queen Elizabeth of England, who has distant relations here, stopped by in the 1980s—and like any sensible horsewoman would, she dropped by **Kings Saddlery,** known worldwide for hand-tooled tack and ropes.

Sheridan seems sturdier than economic whimsy. Locals have worked hard and raised big bucks to save landmarks like the Wyo Theater and the Sheridan Inn, where you can sit on the veranda as Buffalo Bill once did, auditioning acts for his Wild West Show. The town's future seems assured by its excellent restaurants, some fine ranch-style bed-and-breakfast operations, well-preserved historic sites, polo matches in a beautiful mountain setting, and, of course, those beautiful mountains themselves.

ESSENTIALS

GETTING THERE   The **Sheridan County Airport,** just southwest of town on **Airport Road** (take Exit 25 off I-90), has daily service from Denver on **United Express** (☎ **800/241-6522** or 307/674-8455).

Powder River Transportation (☎ 307/674-6188) provides regional bus service from their terminal at 580 E. 5th. There are two daily buses from Billings, Montana, just over a 2-hour ride away.

If you drive from Billings, take I-90 south 125 miles to Sheridan. From Sheridan you can continue south on I-25, sliding along the eastern side of the Bighorn Mountains, 147 miles to Casper, or drive the full 325 to Cheyenne. From Yellowstone and Cody, follow U.S. Highway 14 across the basin and over the Big-horns, and drop into Ranchester, where you'll take I-25 15 miles south to Sheridan.

VISITOR INFORMATION   The **Sheridan County Chamber of Commerce** and the **Sheridan Convention and Visitors Bureau** (☎ 800/453-3650, ext. 22 or 307/672-2485) are located at the State Information Center, off I-90 at Exit 23—look west from the information center, and the Bighorns are in full view. When perusing brochures, be sure and pick up a copy of the *Main Street Historic District Walking Tour.* Across the street is the **Wyoming Game and Fish Visitors Center** (☎ 307/ 672-7418), with interactive displays and information on wildlife habitats, fishing, hunting regulations, and the best places to spot wild critters. The center is open Monday to Friday 8am to 5pm.

GETTING AROUND   You can rent a car from either **Avis** (☎ 800/331-1212) or **Enterprise** (☎ 800/325-8007) at Sheridan's airport. Or call **Sheridan Taxi** (☎ 307/674-6814).

GETTING OUTSIDE

The **Bighorn National Forest** offers some of the best outdoor recreation in the country, in a wilderness well-stocked with wildlife and not too many humans. For maps and advice, contact the forest headquarters and district office, 1969 Sheridan Ave. (☎ 307/672-0751). You can stock up on camping supplies, get the appropriate licenses, and collect where-to-go advice in Sheridan, and you can also enjoy the town's outdoor amenities, like a picnic lunch in **Kendrick Park** (3 blocks south of Main on Smith). Your options there include seeing a resident herd of elk and bison, jumping in the community swimming pool, and playing a match of tennis on the 24-hour courts. Stroll along the creek, or enjoy the big band that plays free concerts every summer on Tuesday night at 7pm.

For topographical maps and advice on local hot spots for hiking and fishing, check with **Big Horn Mountain Sports,** 334 N. Main (☎ 307/672-6866). In addition to extensive lines of fly-fishing, backpacking, camping, and skiing equipment, they coordinate classes and guided trips through the **Sheridan Recreation Department** (☎ 307/674-6421) and **Sheridan College** (☎ 307/674-6446). Although visitors are encouraged to participate in these classes, reservations—usually 3 months in advance—are necessary. Call for specific course offerings and dates. Past classes have included instruction in fly-tying, kayaking, cross-country skiing, and rock climbing at nearby Tongue River Canyon.

BIKING

In summer, a series of marked trails in Bighorn National Forest allows fat-tire fans to experience more than 1,000 miles of moderate to extreme mountain biking, with some downhill canyon rides exceeding 4,000 vertical feet. Stop by **Backcountry Bicycle** (☎ 307/672-2453) on Main Street for bike rentals and area trail maps. Mountain bikes rent for $25 per day, $110 per week.

EQUESTRIAN EVENTS

Polo? In Wyoming? Well, they ride horses, don't they? Introduced by early English cattle barons, the tradition continues morning and afternoon every summer weekend at **Big Horn's Equestrian Center** (south of Sheridan toward the town of Big Horn at 351 Bird Farm Rd.). Admission (unless a benefit match is scheduled) is free. For further information, contact the center at ☎ **307/674-4812.** For a little cowboy dressage, don't miss **Rodeo Week,** held in mid-July. Call ☎ **307/674-4812** for more information.

FLY-FISHING

The Tongue River is the Bighorns' blue-ribbon stream. There are browns, rainbows, and brook trout up to 20 inches. Inquire at the **Game and Fish Division,** 700 Valley View Dr. (☎ **307/672-7418**), for local catch limits and licenses. For guided fishing trips on private and public land, contact the well-stocked **Fly Shop of the Big Horns,** 227 N. Main (☎ **800/253-5866;** www.troutangling.com).

GOLF

For the golf enthusiast, Sheridan offers several choices, from the **Sheridan Country Club** (west of Sheridan on W. 5th Street; ☎ **307/674-8135**) to the **Kendrick Municipal Golf Course** (on Big Goose Road; ☎ **307/674-8148**), each with 18-hole courses and views of the Bighorns. The latest addition to the area links is the **Powder Horn** (4 miles south of Sheridan on U.S. Hwy. 87; ☎ **307/672-5323**), in the rolling hills at the foot of the Bighorns, with a Western-flavored Back 9 set around a big red barn, with hazards including beaver ponds and streams.

HANG GLIDING

If you're driving down from the Bighorns toward Sheridan on U.S. 14, and you stop at Sand Turn to enjoy the view, you may notice a little strip of pavement pointing over the edge of the steep mountainside. That's the runway where hang gliders and para-gliders take off to soar on the thermal air currents that make this a favorite spot for fliers without propellers. **Eagle Air,** P.O. Box 312, Dayton, WY 82836 (☎ **307/655-2562** or 307/655-9848) is an informally run business, but it offers afternoon and morning lessons when the certified instructors—including a member of the U.S. Women's Hang Gliding Team—are available. The season usually runs April 15 to October 15.

HIKING

Experienced hikers should lace up the hiking boots, strap on your pack, and head for **The Cloud Peak Wilderness Area,** a 189,000-acre, high-altitude preserve southwest of Sheridan. The best hikes are overnighters, including the rugged 6-mile trip to Mistymoon Lake, and then the 11-mile round-trip ascent of 13,175-foot Cloud Peak. Call the Bighorn district of the National Forest Service, 1969 S. Sheridan Ave. (☎ **307/672-0751**), for the locations of trailheads and related information. For an easily accessible short hike take the trail up steep, beautiful Tongue River Canyon (the trail is just outside the town of Dayton, north of Sheridan—get directions from the Forest Service).

SNOWMOBILING & CROSS-COUNTRY SKIING

Snowmobiling has caught on big in the Bighorns, where there are more than 380 miles of groomed and ungroomed trails. There are still some corners reserved for cross-country skiers, including trails around **Sibley Lake.** Take Exit 9 off I-90 north of

Sheridan and drive 25 miles on U.S. Highway 14 to the Sibley Lake turnoff. Contact the Tongue River district of the U.S. Forest Service, 1969 S. Sheridan Ave., Sheridan, WY (☎ **307/672-0751**), for information on local trails and conditions.

SEEING THE SIGHTS

✪ **King's Saddlery and Museum.** 184 N. Main, Sheridan, WY 82801. ☎ **307/672-2702** or 307/672-2755. Free admission. Mon–Sat 8am–5pm.

Don King's Main Street emporium is a cowboy's candy store, with an extensive collection of Western tack, and any size, length, and lay of ropes. Wander the shop to see the tools of the modern cowboy; stop and watch the King brothers hand-tool leather. Then step back in time to their museum, housing one of the largest collections of Indian artifacts and cowboy trappings—including high-back saddles, woolie chaps, Spanish bits, silver spurs, and quirts. Don is often around to chat. Next door is the Kings' new **Bozeman Trail Gallery,** 190 N. Main, which displays Western subject paintings and sculpture, including some artwork featuring polo players.

✪ **Bradford Brinton Memorial Ranch.** 239 Brinton Rd., Big Horn, WY (9 miles south of Sheridan on U.S. Hwy. 87). ☎ **307/672-3173.** $3 adults, $2 seniors and children. May 15–Sept 6, daily 9:30am–5pm.

From a distance, surrounded by cottonwoods, dwarfed by the hills and horizon, the Brinton ranch house doesn't look much different from most other two-story, white wood-frame homes; with a few whitewashed outbuildings, it could be a farm in Iowa. But the house belonged to one of the most successful ranch families in the area, and though the tables are set with china and the shelves filled with gold- and leather-bound volumes, it still could be any mothballed 20-room residence of a forgotten once-important person. But on the walls hangs a collection of art you wouldn't normally find anywhere but in a museum: *Fight on The Little Bighorn* by Frederic Remington, and *When Ropes Go Wrong* by Charles M. Russell. Will James, John Audubon, and a host of other notable Western artists show up in one of the best but least known collections in the Rockies.

Trail End State Historic Site. 400 Clarendon Ave., Sheridan, WY 82801. ☎ **307/674-4589** or 307/672-1729. $2 adults over 18. June–Aug, daily 9am–6pm; off-season, call for hours.

The Kendrick Mansion, the only example of Flemish Revival architecture in Wyoming, sits on 3.8 acres of manicured grounds. John Kendrick, orphaned in Texas, arrived in Wyoming at age 22 on a cattle drive, a Western Horatio Alger. By 1912, he'd built a 200,000-acre cattle ranch and amassed a net worth of one million dollars. The next year, he completed construction on a home so large it took a ton of coal a day to warm its 20 rooms. He later became Wyoming's governor, then U.S. senator. Visitors today can marvel at materials not common in Wyoming: silk, mahogany, Italian marble, Georgia pine beams, and a maple floor in the ballroom. Also on the grounds are a carriage house and the Mandel Cabin, built in 1879, which served as the area's first post office.

The Sheridan Inn. Broadway and 5th, Sheridan, WY 82801. ☎ **307/674-5440.** $3 adults, $2 seniors, free for children 12 and under. Memorial Day–Labor Day, daily 9am–8pm; off-season, call for days and hours.

In 1893, 17 years after the Battle of Little Big Horn, the Sheridan Inn opened and was hailed as the finest hotel between Chicago and San Francisco. The majestic hotel was modeled after Scottish hunting lodges, with dormer windows for each of the 62 rooms, and three impressive river-rock fireplaces. The back bar was imported from

England and the building boasted the town's first electric lights. Buffalo Bill Cody led the grand march for the first dance that opening night. Cody would return annually to stand on the long veranda auditioning riders for his Wild West Show. The Sheridan Inn has hosted a variety of visiting celebrities and dignitaries, including Calamity Jane, Teddy Roosevelt, and Ernest Hemingway. Although it hasn't operated as a hotel since 1965, it houses a restaurant, and fund-raising is underway for ongoing restoration that will eventually allow overnight stays.

The Ucross Foundation. 2836 U.S. Hwy. 14/16 E., Clearmont, WY 82835. ☎ **307/ 737-2291.**

Retreats for writers, artists, and musicians are uncommon in the West, but Ucross has gained a national reputation by providing a quiet, beautiful setting for seclusion and creativity. This ranchland, 25 miles east of Sheridan, was once the headquarters of the Pratt and Ferris Cattle Company, established in 1879 on a 20-mile stretch of the North Platte River. You don't need an artist's residency to stop in and visit **Big Red,** a magnificently restored structure that once served as the main ranch house but today is a showcase of antique furniture; and the **Big Red Gallery,** which every year mounts six exhibits of work produced by artists enrolled in the foundation's residence program. If you're in the area on the Fourth of July, this is the place to be; more than 4,000 people—that's a large town in Wyoming—show up for the fireworks.

WHERE TO STAY

Piney Creek Inn. 11 Skylark Lane, P.O. Box 456, Story, WY 82842. ☎ **307/683-2911.** www.pineycreekinn.com. 5 units. $65–$150 double. Rates include breakfast. No credit cards. Take U.S. Hwy. 87 south from Sheridan 7 miles to Story.

Why pay $90 a night for a generic motel room when for $110 you can stay in the "Hideaway" cabin nestled in the trees and warmed by a fireplace and Jacuzzi? Why pay for two motel rooms, when a family can easily fit in the "Pine Lodge" cabin with its gnarled pine spiral staircase leading to the loft bedroom? Owners Vicky and Mel Hoff try to keep their rates low and their service high. They'll connect you with local horse or wagon rides, or point you at trails to hike. Piney Creek was once one of Wyoming's best kept secrets, but good news travels fast; be sure to book at least 3 months in advance.

✪ **Spahn's Bighorn Mountain B&B.** 70 Upper Hideaway Lane, Big Horn, WY 82833. ☎ **307/674-8150.** www.bighorn-wyoming.com. Reservations should be made 3–6 months in advance. 4 units. $85–$120 double. Rates include full breakfast. MC, V. 15 miles southwest of Sheridan at edge of Bighorn National Forest.

Spahn's Bighorn Mountain B&B prides itself on being the oldest B&B in Wyoming, and it's certainly one of the best. Picture this: a 4-story log cabin surrounded by pines; a common room with a crackling fire, shelves of books, and a piano; and outside, a deck with a 100-mile view of prairie stretching to the east. The rooms glow with varnished peeled logs, and have such country comforts as patchwork quilts and clawfoot tubs. Nightly wildlife safaris visit Teepee Creek in search of moose, elk, and deer, and kids explore the not-so-secret trail underneath nearby Little Goose Falls. There's even a secluded guest cabin called the "Eagle's Nest" that's perfect for honeymooners.

Spear Ranch B & B. 170 Brinton Rd., Big Horn, WY 82833. ☎ **307/673-0079.** E-mail: spearrch@cyberhighway.net. 6 units. $70–$90 double; $150–$175 suite or carriage house (3–5 people). No credit cards.

Pam and Lonnie Wright have restored this beautiful former dude ranch along Little Goose Creek and decorated it with art and antique furniture that give it the comfortable feel of a well-heeled country estate. Several of the rooms have their own fireplaces. The dining and living room areas have a formal air (you can also have breakfast on the patio), and there is a very informal recreation room in the basement with a huge collection of movies. A couple of sweet old dogs will greet you outside if you wander along the creek or the country road that leads to the historic Bradford Brinton Ranch.

GUEST RANCHES

✪ **Eaton Ranch.** 270 Eaton Ranch Rd., Wolf, WY 82844. ☎ **800/210-1049** or 307/655-9285. www.eatonsranch.com. 50 cabins. $1,085 per person per week. June–Sept, 1-week minimum stay required. Rates include all meals and ranch activities and round-trip airport transfers. DISC, MC, V. Closed Oct 2–May 31.

This 7,000-acre working cattle ranch, adjacent to the Bighorn National Forest, is one of the oldest dude ranches in the country. Started in 1879 by three brothers in North Dakota who couldn't seem to keep their freeloading friends from back East away, the Eatons moved to their present location in 1904. Eventually, one of their "guests" felt guilty and offered to reimburse them for their hospitality. They resisted at first, but soon inaugurated the business of dude ranching. Today, the ranch accommodates up to 125 dudes, a more profitable herd than the hoofed variety. Wrangling enthusiasts can sign up for Eaton's annual spring horse drive. With some 200 horses and some 100 miles to cover, the Eton horse drive is one of the last authentic cowboy experiences.

✪ **HF Bar Ranch.** Saddlestring, WY 82840. ☎ **307/684-2487.** www. rockcreekanglers. com. Reservations required at least 6–12 months in advance. 26 cabins. $175 per person per day. Mid-June to mid-Sept, 1-week minimum stay required. Rates include all meals and ranch activities. Round-trip transfers from Sheridan airport can be arranged for an additional $10 per person. No credit cards. Take I-90 35 miles south of Sheridan to Exit 47. Turn west on Shell Creek Rd. for 7 miles to ranch.

With reduced rates and plenty of activities for children, even pony rides for the small tots, the HF Bar Ranch really caters to families—nannies are encouraged to come along too and they get 50% off the daily rate. This hospitable ranch is a real hoedown of old-fashioned fun, with weekly hayrides and square dances. Ice is delivered daily to a wooden box on each of the cabin's front porches, and hearty family-style meals are served in the main lodge. Guests can take daily trail rides or arrange a pack trip to the remote and rustic "mountain camp" 15 miles into the Bighorns. Guests who savvy horses are allowed to ride on their own. The sportsman (or woman) of the group can fish the miles of streambanks, or shoot on one of their five sporting-clay courses, or hunt pheasant and chukar on a private bird reserve. In fall, the ranch outfits hunts for elk and deer.

Paradise Guest Ranch. Box 790, Buffalo, WY 82845. ☎ **307/684-7876.** www. paradiseranch.com. 18 cabins. $1,830–$2,750 double per week, depending on season. Rates include all meals and ranch activities and round-trip airport transfers. No credit cards. Closed Nov to mid-May.

Aptly named, this dude ranch 45 miles south of Sheridan adds modern conveniences to the ambience and activities you expect on a ranch. The log cabins not only have decks with views of the surrounding valley, mountains, or streams, but also come equipped with their own washers and dryers. As with most resort ranches in the West, several trail rides depart daily for guests of all levels of ability. And if you're riding all day, you can get a chuck-wagon lunch. There are ample after-dark activities for the entire family, with evening entertainment in the ranch's French Creek Saloon and recreation center.

Ranch at Ucross. 2673 U.S. Hwy. 14 E., Clearmont, WY 82835. ☎ **800/447-0194** or 307/737-2281. 31 units. A/C TV TEL. $115–$175 double. Rates include breakfast. DISC, MC, V. Closed Oct–Apr.

Once owned by the Apache Oil Company, the Ranch at Ucross has been remodeled and converted to a guest resort and conference center. With 30,000 acres, a rider could go a week without seeing the same place twice. Usually, though, folks just ride for an hour or two ($15 per person per hour). Or they escape with fly rod to the stream. Athletic diehards can hit the tennis courts or basketball backboards. You can complete the day with a dip in the pool. Guests can stay in one of the four rooms in the historic 1912 ranch house, or the one-bedroom cabins. The 15-unit Cottonwood Annex and nine-unit Piney Creek building are comfortable, but not quite as quaint. However, they overlook the creek, have patios or balconies, and are furnished with queen-size beds and queen-size trundles. Meals are served buffet style in a dining room, though you'll find seating outside on the deck as well, or elbow up to the bar in the cozy corner room for a nightcap.

CAMPING

The **Bighorn Mountain KOA Campground,** 63 Decker Rd. (☎ **307/674-8766**), one-half mile north of Sheridan at the Port of Entry exit, has tent and RV sites available from May 25 to September 15. The **Sheridan RV Park** on 3 acres along Little Goose Creek (807 Avoca Ave.; ☎ **307/674-0722**) has 32 RV sites available from April to October 15 for $15 for a full hookup. The **Bramble Motel and RV Park** (2366 N. Main; ☎ **307/674-4902**) has only seven full-hookup sites, but is open year-round.

If you're headed to Cody, or just want to get into the Bighorns, the Forest Service maintains several campgrounds along Highway 14. Contact the USFS Bighorn District (☎ **307/672-0751**) for information on the following campgrounds (in order of distance from I-90): the Tongue River, Tongue Canyon, Sibley Lake, Prune Creek, North Tongue, and Owen Creek. All have tent and RV sites and are open from June through October with a $7 fee.

WHERE TO DINE

✪ **Ciao Bistro.** 120 N. Main. ☎ **307/672-2838.** Reservations recommended. Lunch $7–12; dinner $10–$19. No credit cards. Tues 11–2pm, Wed–Sat 11–2pm and 6–11pm. MEDITERRANEAN.

Wyoming was once considered the last place you'd want to go looking for a gourmet meal, but all that has changed. Sheridan is second only to Jackson in the variety and quality of its restaurants. If you can handle the high prices, this cozy, one-room bistro serves excellent food, such as prawns in cognac cream or a layered pasta dish baked with ham, mozzarella, and béchamel. There's a fine wine list, too.

Golden Steer. 2071 N. Main. ☎ **307/674-9334.** Lunch $4–$8; dinner $10–$20. AE, DISC, MC, V. Lunch Mon–Fri 11am–2pm and 4–9pm, Sat–Sun 4–9pm. STEAKS/SEAFOOD.

Ask around, and the locals point to the north end of town, to the Golden Steer steak house. What can we say? If you crave a big sirloin or a plateful of fried shrimp, this place will satiate your needs. On the weekends, there's live music.

✪ **Sanford's Grub, Pub & Brewer.** 1 E. Alger and N. Main. ☎ **307/674-1722.** Reservations not accepted. Lunch $5–$7; dinner $10–$17. MC, V. Daily 11am–10pm. CAJUN.

The maze of rooms at Sanford's is decorated like the dorm room of a junkman's son: televisions, beer signs, license plates crammed to the rafters. Same with the menu, which leans toward Cajun food but lacks the spice of the real thing. There are 125 different bottled beers available and 37 on tap, including the restaurant's very own Cloud's Peak Raspberry Wheat and Cady House Stout, named for the 1907 historic Sheridan building in which the microbrewery is located. There are nightly specials, and a midnight appetizer menu, available for night owls after 10pm, that features Cajun quesadillas and calamari.

SHERIDAN AFTER DARK

The drinks have been flowing for almost a century from the narrow, deep bar at **The Mint,** at 151 N. Main St. (☎ **307/672-2838**), and it's still a favorite of the cowboys in the area. Every brand imaginable is honored on the knotty pine and cedar walls, and there is a rattlesnake skin more than 8 feet long stretched above the bar (it actually came up here from Texas). But what will capture you are the huge Charles Belden photographs on the walls—you may find yourself quite moved, despite the jolly setting, by these images of the ranching past.

WYO Theater. 42 N. Main, Sheridan, WY 82801. ☎ **307/672-9084.** http://wavecom.net/~wyotheater. Tickets $5–$20. MC, V. Summer performances held at 7:30pm.

The WYO is a model for other old theaters in the West. It was a broken-down movie palace facing the wrecking ball when locals stepped in and saved it, restoring the proscenium and reviving live entertainment in Sheridan. Classical music, local choral groups, touring dance companies, and popular performers like Michael Martin Murphey and Baxter Black fill the house.

3 Buffalo

35 miles S of Sheridan; 182 miles E of Cody

Though Sheridan remains the busy hub of this Wyoming region, it is surrounded by interesting little towns—Dayton, Story, Ranchester—and one big enough to deserve its own slot, Buffalo. A short drive south of Sheridan on I-90, this old ranching town is near the site of the infamous Johnson County War (between cattle- and sheepmen), and not far from the Hole-in-the-Wall country favored by Butch, Sundance, and other outlaws.

Though this was a favorite area of Indian bison-hunting Indian bands, it was not named for a shaggy beast: The original settlers drew names from a hat and someone had written their New York hometown.

The historic downtown area is compact enough to explore on foot, if you don't mind the dip down to Clear Creek. Follow the **Clear Creek Centennial Trail** on a wheelchair-accessible path from downtown to a Green Belt; it joins a 3-mile unsurfaced road to the base of the Bighorn Mountains. Maps are available from the **Buffalo Chamber of Commerce,** 55 N. Main St., Buffalo, WY 82834 (☎ **800/227-5122** or 307/684-5544). You'll see the old **Occidental Hotel** at 10 N. Main, possibly a model for a hotel in Owen Wister's *Virginian,* and now the site of concerts and other community activities. At the excellent **Jim Gatchell Museum,** 100 Fort St., you'll find Native American relics like arrowheads and medicine rattles, as well as cavalry items and the bridle Tom Horn braided while awaiting execution. Open 8am to 8pm from mid-May to mid-October; $2 adults, kids free.

Buffalo lies on the route of the Bozeman Trail, an ill-advised 19th-century shortcut to the gold country of Montana that cut right through the hunting grounds of several resentful tribes. The U.S. Army built forts to protect travelers, and engaged in

Range Wars

The Johnson County War involved no Indians—it was a struggle between immigrant homesteaders and the cattle barons over the open range. One of the skirmishes in that struggle took place at the **TA Ranch**—ask to see the bullet holes—which now hosts guests (Box 313, Buffalo, WY 82834; ☎ **307/684-5833;** www.taranch.com; 13 rooms, $150 per person). The ranch is located 13 miles south of Buffalo on U.S. Highway 87.

skirmishes with the resident Sioux, Cheyenne, and Arapaho. The largest of these was **Fort Phil Kearney** (Exit 44 off I-90; ☎ 307/684-7629), where soldiers endured repeated raids by hostile Indians. Though the original fort is gone, the site today is a national historic site with a visitor center and tours of two major battle sites nearby: the 1866 Fetterman Massacre, in which Crazy Horse and his band overwhelmed a small army contingent; and the Wagon Box Fight, which went the other way. The visitor center is open 6am to 8pm Monday to Saturday, from June to Labor Day; shorter hours the rest of the year, with a $1 admission.

Robert Parker (Butch Cassidy) and his partner, Harry Longabaugh (Sundance Kid), assembled their infamous group of bandits known as the Wild Bunch to rob trains and banks and steal herds of horses and cattle. One of their favorite places to hide was the Hole-in-the-Wall, a red-rock canyon area above the Middle Fork of the Powder River. The **Hole-in-the-Wall,** namesake of the gang led by Butch Cassidy (Robert Parker), is located about 45 miles south of Buffalo near the town of Kaycee. Take I-25 south from Kaycee to the Triple T Road exit, continue south 14 miles to County Road 111, then go west 18 miles to County Road 105, then north 8 miles to U.S. Bureau of Land Management directional sign for Hole-in-the-Wall. It's a 3-mile hike into the actual site. The Hole itself is no more than a notch in a butte, disappointing to folks used to Disney-like re-creations of outlaw hideouts. But for the intrepid on horse or in four-wheel-drive, you can explore the spacious **Outlaw Cave.** There are tepee rings in the surrounding area and large pictographs and stenciled handprints under a rock overhang.

Note: most of this area is private land. Be sure to check with the U.S. Bureau of Land Management office in Buffalo (☎ 307/684-1100) before exploring on your own.

Just a few miles northwest of Buffalo along I-90 is **Lake De Smet,** an excellent fishing and boating destination, with opportunities for picnicking and camping.

4 Gillette

104 miles SE of Sheridan; 240 miles SE of Billings

"Energy Capital of the World," boasts the local chamber of commerce, "where just a century ago it was a frontier land with open ranges." Out on what used to be open range, you can now tour several massive coal mines, like the **Wyodak** (6 miles east of Gillette on WY 51), which scrapes more than 2.7 million tons of coal from its open-pit strip mine on the prairie and burns most of it next door at a 330-megawatt power plant. You can also watch the house-size graders and scrapers and dump trucks work Exxon's 11,700-acre **Caballo Mine.**

The huge coal mines have made Gillette a wealthy community, and it buffers the harsh environment of the high plains with modern community facilities, including a first-class swimming pool and water park. There is still plenty of undeveloped plains habitat, too, particularly in the 1.8-million-acre **Thunder Basin National Grassland.** Anyone who enjoys geological wonders, and anyone who enjoyed *Close Encounters of the Third Kind,* will want to visit the nearby 1,280-foot **Devils Tower** (see section 5, "Devils Tower National Monument," below).

ESSENTIALS

GETTING THERE   **United Express** (☎ **800/241-6522** or 307/685-2280) offers daily commuter flights.

By road, Gillette is 90 miles east from Sheridan along I-90 and approximately 46 miles from Devils Tower National Monument. From Cheyenne, take I-25 north to Buffalo (approximately 100 miles); at Buffalo, turn east on I-90 for 54 miles.

VISITOR INFORMATION   Call the **Gillette Convention and Visitors Bureau,** located at 314 S. Gillette Ave., Gillette, WY 82716 (☎ **800/544-6136** or 307/ 686-0040), for a schedule of local events and/or more-detailed listings of local accommodations. Look for the brochure *Campbell County Natural History Loop Tours,* which presents a brief history of the area and outlines two loop tours through areas populated by deer, pronghorn, turkeys, and other upland birds.

GETTING AROUND   You can rent cars from **Avis** (☎ 307/672-2226) or **Hertz** (☎ 307/686-0550). Call **Yellow Checker Cab** (☎ 307/686-4090) for a taxi.

GETTING OUTSIDE

Outdoor activities are the primary draw here. **Golf** addicts can get their fix at either the **Gillette Country Club,** 1800 Country Club Rd. (☎ **307/682-4774**), or the **Bell Nob Golf Course,** 1316 Overdale (☎ **307/686-7069**). The country club has a nine-hole course; Bell Nob has 18.

Bird-watchers will enjoy the waterfowl of **McManamen Park,** near the corner of Gurley Street and Warlow Drive. And hunters flock (excuse the pun) to the fields and draws to bag deer, antelope, and upland birds.

Note: To obtain an out-of-state hunting license, you must file with the **Wyoming Game and Fish Department** in Cheyenne (☎ **307/777-4601**) by March 15; left-over licenses can be obtained after August 1 in a supplemental drawing. The "Stop Poaching" hotline can be reached at ☎ **800/331-9834.**

To arrange a guided hunting trip, contact **Sagebrush Outfitters,** 22-A Lewis Rd., Gillette, WY 82716 (☎ **307/682-4394**), or the **P Cross Bar Ranch,** Hwy. 14/16 (☎ **307/682-3994**). The P Cross Ranch, run by Marion and Mary Scott, provides fair-chase hunts of deer, antelope, and even trophy bison (call for packages and prices). They also run a small bed-and-breakfast service from their ranch headquarters where summer travelers can put up their horses for $10 to $15 per night, feed not included.

SEEING THE SIGHTS

If you are impressed by big holes and big machinery, visit the **Wyodak Overlook,** 5 miles east of Gillette off U.S. Highway 14/16, and look down into one of the huge strip mines that operate on the plains around the city. The Wyodak Mine is one of the area's oldest, producing more than 2 million tons of coal annually, about half of which goes next door to the Wyodak Power Plant, a 330-megawatt coal-burning steam plant. If you're interested in coal-mine tours in the area, call ☎ **307/682-3673.**

The **CAM-PLEX,** a massive event pavilion, has been the host in recent years of the National High School Rodeo Finals, as well as an array of other exciting events. Call ☎ **800/358-1897** or 307/682-8802 to find out what's scheduled.

The **Campbell County Rockpile Museum,** 900 W. 2nd St. (☎ **307/682-5723**), displays artifacts of the area's past, such as saddles, rifles, arrowheads, plus a horse-drawn sheep wagon and hearse. It's small, but free. Open mid-May to mid-October.

WHERE TO STAY

Best Western Tower West Lodge. 109 Hwy. 14/16, Gillette, WY 82716. ☎ **800/762-PERK** or 307/686-2210. 190 units. A/C TV TEL. $50–$70 double. AE, DC, DISC, MC, V.

This Best Western property is considered by some to be the nicest place to stay in town. It's certainly the largest, and features a heated indoor pool, weight room, and sauna—as well as a lounge and restaurant. Located near Exit 124 just off I-90, the Tower West Lodge is a short drive south from the airport and is also convenient to the Bell Nob Golf Course.

Days Inn. 910 E. Boxelder Rd., Gillette, WY 82716. ☎ **800/329-7466** or 307/682-3999. 141 units. A/C TV TEL. $70–$80 double. Rates include continental breakfast. AE, DC, DISC, MC, V.

Located behind the Holiday Inn, just off the interstate, the Days Inn good-naturedly sends people next door to the Holiday Inn's restaurant. If you don't mind the walk and enjoy saving a few dollars, this very basic accommodation is fine. The Gillette Country Club and the Campbell County Recreation Center are within easy walking distance.

Holiday Inn. 2009 S. Douglas Hwy., Gillette, WY 82716. ☎ **800/HOLIDAY** or 307/686-3000. 158 units. A/C TV TEL. $62–$94 double. AE, CB, DC, DISC, MC, V.

Also off the Interstate, at Exit 126, this Holiday Inn features a heated indoor pool, sauna, and Jacuzzi. When making your reservation, ask where your room is in relation to the lounge: The hotel features live music Wednesday through Saturday nights that just might rock your world a little too much.

CAMPING

The **Circle G Shooting Park,** 32 Shooting Park Dr. (☎ **307/682-3003;** on WY 50 south from Gillette, about 15 miles—look for the Circle G sign on the left), has RV sites for $20 and is open from April through September. The **Greentrees Crazy Woman Campground,** off Exit 124, 1 mile from I-90 (☎ **307/682-3665**), rents RV sites for $30 and charges $10 to $20 for tents. It is open from mid-April through October, with a Jacuzzi, pool, and bike rentals. From May to September, **High Plains Campground,** 1 mile south of I-90 at Exit 129 (☎ **307/687-7339**), lets tents set up for $14 and RVs hook up for $20.

WHERE TO DINE

The Prime Rib. 1205 S. Douglas Hwy. ☎ **307/682-2944.** Reservations recommended. Lunch $4–$9; dinner $7–$18 ($21 16-oz. prime rib, $35 lobster tail). AE, MC, V. Mon–Fri 11am–10pm, Sat–Sun 4–10pm. STEAKS/SEAFOOD.

Locals come to the Prime Rib, one of Gillette's finer dining establishments, to celebrate birthdays, anniversaries, and promotions, A slightly more upbeat mood is noticeable midweek, when the restaurant's keyboard lounge features live piano music on Wednesday nights.

5 Devils Tower National Monument

62 miles NE of Gillette; 230 miles SE of Billings; 110 miles W of Rapid City, South Dakota

Once upon a time, so the Kiowa legend goes, seven sisters were playing with their brother when he suddenly turned into a bear. Fleeing, the girls scrambled onto a small rock and prayed. The rock started to grow, pushing them into the sky. While the bear clawed at the rock's sides, trying to get at the girls, the rock thrust them so high that they became the points of the Big Dipper. The 1,200-foot-tall rock became named in various spellings as Mato Tipila, or "Bear Lodge." The site is sacred to the Sioux and other tribes of the northern plains.

In 1875, Richard Dodge, leader of a U.S. Geological Survey party, mistranslated the Indian name as "Bad God's Tower" and so dubbed it ✪ **"Devils Tower."** In 1906, Congress declared it the nation's first national monument. The tower was further popularized in the 1977 movie *Close Encounters of the Third Kind.*

Any visitor will understand immediately the allure of this striated column of volcanic rock. As darkness shrouds the surrounding hills, Devils Tower stands above the horizon, glowing amber. It rises 1,200 feet above the Belle Fourche River, 867 feet from its base, 310 feet taller than the Washington Monument.

Climbers have been wedging their fingers in its cracks for more than a century, at a rate in recent years of about 5,000 climbers annually. This has led to conflicts with the tribes of the area, who come to the tower to conduct Sun Dances, construct sweat lodges, seek visions, and leave prayer offerings. As a consequence, in 1994, the park superintendent enacted a plan asking climbers to refrain from ascending the peak during times when Indian tribes are most likely to conduct religious ceremonies. A large majority of climbers have complied (88% in 1999), but others filed suit in federal courts to challenge the park's decision. For the time being, the voluntary plan continues, so if you plan to climb, check about closure dates at the visitor center (☎ **307/467-5501**).

Nearby cities worth an extra look are **Sundance,** and the Black Hills gateway community of **Newcastle.** Sundance is within the Black Hill National Forest (on U.S. Hwy. 90, east of Devils Tower; contact the Bearlodge Ranger District, P.O. Box 680, Sundance, WY 82729, ☎ **307/283-1361**, for information on local Forest Service trails and campsites).

Keyhole Reservoir State Park provides the area with outstanding water-based recreation. For more on Keyhole, call ☎ **307/756-3596.** It sits north of Moorcroft on WY 113.

ESSENTIALS

GETTING THERE   From Gillette, take I-90 east to Moorcroft (Exit 154), follow signs to Devils Tower; from Jackson, take U.S. Highway 26/287 to Riverton, then U.S. Highway 26 to Casper, then I-90 through Gillette to Moorcroft (see above); from Sheridan, take I-90 to Gillette, then see above.

VISITOR INFORMATION   The National Park Service maintains the monument and charges a nominal $8 fee to enter the facility ($3 if you're hiking or biking). The most impressive views are from the surrounding countryside, outside the park's boundaries. A number of hiking trails lead around the monument, and camping facilities are available.

The visitor center is open from mid-June to Labor Day, daily 8am to 8pm, and from 8am to 5pm the rest of the year. In addition to a small selection of books, the center features interpretive displays on the geology and history of the area. All climbers are required to register here before attempting an ascent. If you're an experienced climber, it's worth purchasing *Devils Tower National Monument—A Climber's Guide,* by Steve Gardiner and Dick Guilmette (The Mountaineers, 1986), before attempting a climb.

GUIDED TOURS   If you prefer to be led, sign on with **Exum Mountain Guides** (☎ 307/733-2297) or **Jackson Hole Mountain Guides** (☎ 307/733-4979), two Jackson-based climbing outfitters that offer guided climbs of Devils Tower for all ability levels. Especially popular is the four-pitch Durrance Route.

6 Casper

153 miles S of Sheridan; 178 miles NW of Cheyenne; 300 miles S of Billings; 240 miles NW of Denver

Casper is one of those cities that can't get much respect—a homely city blown between the open plains and its own small mountain, surviving by the good grace of the oil and gas industry. Yet its residents are staunch defenders, and whatever may have brought them there, many stay by choice. Its mountain has a small but fun ski area, and there is a lot of wildlife in the vicinity, including more than 75% of the world's pronghorn antelope. Look for mule deer, fox, sage grouse, moose, bighorn sheep, wild birds, and elk, too.

You can also stand in the ruts of the Oregon, Mormon, and Pony Express trails, for Casper stands at the crossroads of westward expansion—a fact it hopes to exploit through construction of the National Trails Center. Fur traders working for John Jacob Astor stopped here in 1812 on their way back East, constructing a hovel from rocks and buffalo hides, perhaps the first Anglo building in Wyoming. Later, the pioneers and Mormons crossed the North Platte River here. Then came the oil miners, who built the first refinery in 1895. Casper boomed. In the crash of 1929, it went bust, losing half of its population. Then came World War II—another boom. And the 1960s—another bust. Next the oil embargo of the 1970s—boom. Then the recession of the 1980s—bust. You get the idea.

Today, Casper is the second-largest city in the state (46,742) and home of its major paper, the *Star-Tribune.*

ESSENTIALS

GETTING THERE   Casper's **Natrona County Airport,** 8500 Airport Pkwy. (☎ 307/472-6688), 10 miles northwest of Casper on U.S. Highway 20/26, provides daily service on **Skywest** (☎ 800/453-9417) from Salt Lake City, and **United Express** (☎ 800/241-6522) from Denver.

Powder River Transportation (☎ 800/442-3682 or 307/266-1094) provides limited local intrastate **Greyhound** bus service from Gillette, Douglas, Wheatland, and Cheyenne.

To reach Casper from **Sheridan,** drive 153 miles south on I-25. From **Cheyenne,** take I-25 north for 180 miles. From **Jackson,** take U.S. Highway 191 to the Moran Junction, then drive 255 miles east on Highway 26/287.

VISITOR INFORMATION   The visitor center, 500 N. Center St., is open from Memorial Day to Labor Day, weekdays 8am to 6pm, weekends 9am to 5pm; the rest of the year it's open weekdays 8am to 5pm. For printed information on this area, contact the **Casper Area Convention & Visitors Bureau,** P.O. Box 399, Casper, WY 82602 (☎ 800/852-1889 or 307/234-5362; www.casperets.com). Wyoming's statewide newspaper, the *Casper Star-Tribune,* is at www.trib.com.

GETTING AROUND   Rent a car with **Avis** (☎ 800/831-2847), **Budget** (☎ 800/527-0700), or **Hertz** (☎ 800/654-3131) at the airport. **RC Cab** (☎ 307/235-5203) and **Rapid Cab** (☎ 307/235-1903) both provide taxi service; there is no city bus in Casper.

A SPECIAL EVENT   Casper draws its largest crowds during the 5-day **Central Wyoming Fair and Rodeo,** though the crowd is largely drawn from the surrounding plains. Each year in mid-July, the fair and rodeo prompts a 6-day carnival of midway madness and hundreds of exhibits, from incredible home-baked goodies to 4-H prize-winning heifers. Call ☎ **307/235-5775** for more information. Admission is $7 gate and rodeo, $3 gate only, $9 to $14 box and chute seats, $25 badge (gate and rodeo grandstand for the week).

GETTING OUTSIDE

To escape the heat of the summer or ski a few runs in the winter, locals take the switch-backs up Casper Mountain —newcomers will want to stop at the pullouts and take in the view of the plains stretching north toward the Bighorn Mountains. The mountain rises 8,000 feet above sea level, and there are campgrounds, hiking trails (try Garden Creek Falls), ski tracks, groomed snowmobile tracks, and mountain biking trails.

Edness Kimball Wilkins State Park is a nice day-use park just 6 miles east of Casper off I-25. Its walking path, canoe launch, picnic tables, and river access appeal to a variety of interests.

Or you can just go to Hell. **Hells' Half Acre,** that is. A bizarre badlands, it's located midway (you can't miss it) between Shoshoni and Casper on U.S. Highway 20/26. You should see plenty of wildlife—particularly pronghorns—in this area.

BIKING

If you want to take a fat tire run on Casper Mountain or its neighbor to the south, Muddy Mountain (appropriately named in the spring), check with the folks at **Backcountry Mountain Works,** 4120 S. Poplar at Sunrise Center (☎ **307/234-5330**), or **Mountain Sports,** 543 S. Center (☎ **800/426-1136**), for information on where to pick up the best trails.

FISHING

Start with a license and information at the **Wyoming Game and Fish Department,** 2800 Pheasant Dr. (☎ **307/234-9185**). For the local skinny on where to fish, or for guided trips on local rivers, hook up with **Choice River Runners** at 513 N. Lennox (☎ **307/234-3870**). For equipment, flies, and rod building, locals recommend **Dean's Sporting Goods,** 260 S. Center (☎ **307/234-2788**), and **Platte River Fly-shop,** 7400 Alcova Hwy. 220 (☎ **307/237-5997**). If you're looking to acquire some big-ticket equipment, look over the extensive canoe and watercraft selection at **Wyoming River Raiders,** 501 Long Ln. (☎ **307/235-8624**).

GOLF

The 18-hole **Municipal Golf Course,** south of downtown on Casper Mountain Road (☎ **307/234-1037**), is the city's only public course. The **Casper Country Club,** 4149 E. Country Club Rd. (☎ **307/235-5777**), and **Paradise Valley Golf Club,** 70 Magnolia (☎ **307/234-9146**), are both private 18-hole courses; call them for eligibility requirements. Both have reciprocal privileges with other U.S. country clubs.

HIKING

Day hikers should head over to Casper Mountain for the area's best trails. Drive south on WY 258 from I-25 to Casper Mountain. The mountain's **Braille Trail** is a great way for visually impaired visitors to enjoy the beauty of Beartrap Meadow, with interpretive Braille markers describing the area's ecology. The **Casper Area Convention and Visitors Bureau** (☎ **800/852-1889** or 307/234-5362) can assist you with maps detailing this and other hiking trails on the mountain.

SKIING

A cheerful little ski area is a big plus in an area of sometimes howling winters, and Casper has a fine one in the **Hogadon Ski Area** (☎ 307/235-8499), situated atop Casper Mountain (drive south on WY 258 from I-25 to Casper Mountain Road). Two double chairs and a Poma lift cover its 60 acres of groomed trails with on-site equipment rentals available through **Ski Hut** (☎ 307/237-5463). There is also a ski school. A series of cross-country ski trails (tickets $4 per person) is groomed for skating and track skiing. The ski area generally opens around the first of December and closes sometime in April. Lift tickets are $20 for adults, $17 for students, and $15 for children. Call for information on seasonal discounts.

SNOWMOBILING

The **Medicine Bow National Forest,** headquartered in Laramie (☎ 307/745-8971), can assist you in planning a local outing on its more than 60 miles of maintained Forest Service trails around Casper Mountain.

WATER SPORTS

Sail, fish, jet-ski, or just splash around at **Alcova and Pathfinder Reservoirs.** These major recreational areas of the North Platte, backwater of dams by the same names, are located 30 miles southwest of Casper on WY 220. Rental boats are available at **Alcova Lakeside Marina** (☎ 307/472-6666).

WHITE-WATER RAFTING

If you want to float the North Platte, more of a pleasant slosh than a white-water experience, call **AJ Outfitters** (☎ 307/473-1196), **RNR** (☎ 307/235-8017), or **Wyoming's Choice River Runners** (☎ 307/234-3870).

SEEING THE SIGHTS

Fort Caspar Museum and Historic Site. 4001 Fort Caspar Rd. ☎ **307/235-8462.** Free admission. Summer, Mon–Sat 8am–7pm, Sun noon–7pm; winter, Mon–Fri 8am–5pm, Sun 1–4pm.

Built from the remnants of Louis Guinard's Platte Bridge, constructed in 1859 to aid travelers in crossing the dangerous Platte, this fort was aptly named Platte Bridge Station. It played a prominent role in the turbulent era of migration and settlement. After a skirmish with the united tribes of Sioux and Cheyenne in the 1860s, in which Caspar Collins died defending the fort, the site was renamed in honor of him. A few years later, it was burned by the Sioux.

Today the site is marked with a collection of fort buildings reconstructed in 1936 by the Works Progress Administration to illustrate the cultural and natural history of central Wyoming. Although visitors may tour the site and interpretive center at any time during the year, the actual buildings are only open May through September. During the summer there are living history festivals and lectures. *A footnote:* Casper is actually named after Caspar Collins as well. But it's the city, not the fort, whose name is misspelled. When a telegraph operator sent word back East of Collins's courageous stand, the operator spelling the officer's name typed a dot rather than a dot-dash. Caspar became Casper.

✪ **Nicolaysen Art Museum.** 400 E. Collins Dr. (Collins and Kimball). ☎ **307/235-5247.** $2 adults, $1 children under 12. 10% discount for groups of 10 or more. Free admission Thurs 5–8pm. Tues–Wed 10am–5pm, Thurs 10am–8pm, Fri–Sat 10am–5pm, Sun noon–4pm.

Culture follows wealth, and this museum, which teeters on the brink of becoming a first-class facility, indicates that Casper has come close to but never quite developed

---

Time Travel

Historic Trails West (☎ **307/266-4868;** fax 307/237-6010; www. goldrushwagontrain.com) organizes trips that take you back in time as you rattle in a wagon, or sway in the saddle, along the ruts of the Oregon, California, and Mormon trails. Trips range in length from 3 hours ($35) to a weeklong Wild West Cattle Drive ($995). Take an Outlaw Trail Expedition to the Hole-in-the-Wall, or watch a re-creation of the Battle of Red Butte. Participants sleep in tepees or tents and may be required to assist in preparing meals and tending to the horses. Travel is by authentic prairie schooners—built to the exact plans held in the Smithsonian. Although dates are tentative and subject to change, most trips are scheduled for June through mid-September and reservations are required at least 6 months in advance.

---

the herd of wealthy patrons that raise museums, symphonies, and other pillars of culture. It's got some of what it takes—a Matisse and a Picasso in the permanent collection—but at times it seems like too much nicely designed space and not enough art or patrons. Still, the staff vigorously tries to coax the artist out of each person who visits. The Discovery Center enhances current exhibits by encouraging individuals to tap into their own creativity through workshops and hands-on experimentation with various art materials. Also exhibited is regional talent from pop art to wax collage, as well as Western landscapes.

Tate Mineralogical Museum. Tate Earth Science Center, Casper Mountain Rd. ☎ **307/268-2447.** Free admission. Mon–Fri 9am–5pm, Sat 10am–3pm.

This museum will either rock your world or fossilize it, depending on how much you enjoy geoscience. Aficionados of fossils will be delighted by dinosaur excavations from the Natrona County area, including a T-Rex skull, and the leg and skull of a brontosaurus. Rockhounds will covet the extensive collection of jade. Cosmos-buffs will enjoy samples of meteorites. And kids can learn from free lectures hosted by visiting paleontologists, archaeologists, or geologists.

Casper Planetarium. 904 N. Poplar. ☎ **307/577-0310.** $2 per person per program. Summer, showings daily at 4, 7, and 8pm.

This is one of only two planetariums in the state, which might be explained by the fact that Wyoming's night sky is so clear and bright, and the stars so visible outside. If you didn't get enough meteorites at Tate, you can travel through the stars at the Casper Planetarium.

WHERE TO STAY

Casper Hilton Inn. I-25 and N. Poplar, Casper, WY 82602. ☎ **800/HILTONS** or 307/ 266-6000. 229 units. A/C TV TEL. $60–$75 double; $125–$150 Jacuzzi suite. AE, DC, DISC, MC, V.

This hotel by the Interstate stands out because of its six-story height, but the fairly pleasant interior is getting a bit run-down—during a recent rainstorm there were several leaks in the skylights above the indoor pool. In addition to the pool, there's a Jacuzzi, a gift shop, and a hair salon. The location is not particularly attractive, hard by the interstate, but it's convenient: The downtown is just to the south, and the Casper Events Center is just up the hill. A restaurant, lounge, and recreation center round out the property's amenities.

Casper Parkway Plaza. 123 W. E St., Casper, WY 82602. ☎ **307/235-1777.** Fax 307/235-8068. 279 units. A/C TV TEL. $55 single, $5 for each additional person. AE, CB, DC, DISC, MC, V.

This sprawling motel by the interstate appears to have been designed by a committee of 8-year-old Lego experts, but in a city with surprisingly few nice places to stay, the Plaza's bustling friendliness wins you over. The lobby is framed by curving stairways leading for no particular purpose to a balcony on the second level, and it can be quite a hike to your room, with many twists and turns. If the journey is long, you may be in one of the older, less spacious rooms—ask to see a newer one, closer to the motel's lobby. The indoor swimming pool is sometimes crammed with kids in town for a soccer or hockey tournament . . . and you might run into the governor, stopping by one of the many conventions held here.

Holiday Inn. 300 W. F St., Casper, WY 82602. ☎ **800/HOLIDAY** or 307/235-2531. 214 units. A/C TV TEL. $84–$99 double; $150 suite. AE, DC, DISC, MC, V.

By far the nicest lodging in town, this Holiday Inn sports an indoor pool area, called the "Holidome," surrounded by foliage and skylights that will have you believing you're outside. A sauna, weight room, and Jacuzzi are nearby, as is a recreation center with a pool table, Ping-Pong table, and basketball court. If that's not enough to keep the kids occupied, a game library is available for overnight check-outs. First-floor rooms convenient to the Holidome are a little more expensive and a lot noisier; your money would be better spent on one of the two Jacuzzi suites far from this bustling center of activity. Located just past the interstate, the Holiday Inn is convenient to downtown Casper.

✪ **Hotel Higgins.** 416 W. Birch St., Glenrock, WY 82637. ☎ **800/458-0144** or 307/436-9212. 9 units, 2 suites. $60 double; $70 suite. Rates include full breakfast. CB, DC, DISC, MC, V. From Casper, take I-25 east for 20 miles to the first Glenrock exit.

Built by area oil tycoon John Higgins in 1916, the Hotel Higgins is located in Glenrock, a small town 24 miles east of Casper. Listed on the National Register of Historic Places, the inn's exterior vinyl siding belies the treasures found within: ornate mahogany and oak woodwork with distinctive decorative touches that include alabaster chandeliers, beveled glass doors, and terrazzo tile floors. In each room you'll find chenille bedspreads and antique curios, but no phones or TVs. The excellent Paisley Shawl restaurant occupies the former ballroom and is one of the best places to eat near Casper (see "Where to Dine," below).

Royal Inn. 440 E. A St., Casper, WY 82602. ☎ **800/96-ROYAL** or 307/234-3501. 38 units. A/C TV TEL. $30–$35 double; $35–$45 double with kitchenette. AE, DISC, MC, V.

The 20-year-old Royal is a two-level hotel located downtown off Center Street on East A Street. Upstairs rooms are $3 cheaper than their downstairs counterparts, which come with a cable TV with HBO, a microwave, and a mini-refrigerator. The only drawback to this lodging is the outdoor pool: It isn't heated. A definite plus is the complimentary airport shuttle; cars can be rented at the hotel.

CAMPING

The Natrona County Parks Department maintains five campgrounds in the Casper area: **Beartrap Meadow** and **Casper Mountain** (approximately 7 miles south of town), plus **Alcova Lake, Pathfinder Lake,** and **Gray Reef Reservoir** (about 30 miles from downtown). All are open from April through mid-October and have tent and RV sites for a $5 fee. For additional information and directions, contact the **Parks Department** at ☎ 307/235-9311. Roughly 9 miles south of town, The Bureau of

Land Management has two campgrounds on Muddy Mountain: **Lodgepole** and **Rim.** Both of these are open from mid-June through October with tent sites for $4. Contact the BLM at ☎ **307/261-7600** for specific directions. The **Fort Caspar Campground,** 4205 Fort Caspar Rd. (☎ **307/234-3260**), near the North Platte River and historic Fort Caspar, offers tent and RV sites year-round for $11 and $16, respectively. Also open year-round, the **Casper KOA,** 2800 E. Yellowstone (☎ **800/423-5155**), charges $15 for tent sites and $20 for full RV hookups.

WHERE TO DINE

Casper is just large enough to attract chain restaurants like **Village Inn,** 325 S. Durbin (☎ **307/234-1614**); and **Perkins,** 4710 E. 2nd St. (☎ **307/265-7339**).

Armour's. 3422 Energy Lane. ☎ **307/235-3000.** Reservations recommended. Lunch $5.75–$7.50; dinner $10–$20. AE, DISC, MC, V. Mon 5–9:30pm, Tues–Fri 11am–1:30pm and 5–9:30pm, Sat 5–9:30pm. AMERICAN.

Blackened beef and chicken entrees are the local specialties at this Casper eatery, one of the city's larger restaurants with seating for more than 100 diners. The menu features typical beef and seafood entrees—prime rib, scampi Alfredo—along with a decent wine list.

Bosco's. 847 E. A St. ☎ **307/265-9658.** Main courses $6–$19. AE, CB, DC, DISC, MC, V. Tues–Fri 11am–2pm and 5pm–closing, Sat 5pm–closing. ITALIAN.

Other than "cowboy" cooking, the only cuisine that seems to shine in Wyoming is Italian, and so it is in Casper, too, where this friendly little restaurant serves excellent food, and stays open as long as the customers keep coming. The scampi is excellent, or you can create your own fettucine dish, choosing from ingredients such as fresh vegetables, lamb, smoked salmon, and shrimp.

El Jarros. 500 W. F St. ☎ **307/577-0538.** Lunch $4–$7; dinner $5–$10. MC, V. Mon–Sat 11am–1:30pm and 5–8:30pm. MEXICAN.

The most popular of Casper's Mexican restaurants, El Jarros consistently packs in crowds for daily specials that are the best value in town. Don't load up on chips and salsa: Although the entrees lack the fire of good Mexican cooking, the servings are generous.

✪ **The Paisley Shawl.** Hotel Higgins, Glenrock (from Casper, take I-25 east for 20 miles to the first Glenrock exit). ☎ **800/458-0144.** Reservations recommended on weekends. Lunch $3–$9; dinner $12–$25. CB, DC, DISC, MC, V. June–Aug, daily 11:30am–1:30pm and 6–9:30pm; Sept–May, Tues–Sat 11:30am–1:30pm and 6–9:30pm. CONTINENTAL.

Only 24 miles separate Casper from the smaller town of Glenrock and the Paisley Shawl, the area's best fine dining establishment. Set inside the grand Hotel Higgins, the Paisley Shawl is the dining complement to an unbeatable guest inn/restaurant combination. Specialties include shrimp scampi, veal Florentine, and the ever-popular Paisley Shawl chicken breast, lauded by locals and *Bon Appetit.* The restaurant is expansive, with seating for 60. There aren't many restaurants in Wyoming that make you feel as if you're indulging yourself by dining there. This is one of them.

7 Fort Laramie National Historic Site

125 miles SE of Casper

On a hot day in 1834, mountain man William Sublette stopped his pack train laden with goods for the Green River rendezvous. Looking at the confluence of the Laramie and Platte Rivers, then to the east, across the dusty plains, and then to the west, toward the mountains, he decided that this was a good place for a trading post. Over the next 15 years, under various owners, the fort served as a hub of the buffalo trade, then as a wayside for weary travelers who needed a break one-third of their way to the Pacific.

In 1849—the year of the California gold rush—the U.S. Army bought the fort to "defend" the rising tide of immigrants from the "savages." The Indian Wars hadn't really started yet, not until 1854, when a lame Mormon-owned cow wandered off and was eaten by a starving Miniconjou. A young lieutenant marched into the Sioux camp and demanded that the cow-eater be turned over for swift justice; soon his troops opened fire on the village, and the wars had begun. Many battles later, warring Indian nations gathered here to negotiate the Treaty of 1868, which gave the Sioux and their allies the Powder River country and the Black Hills for "as long as the grass shall grow and the buffalo shall roam." That turned out not to be very long, after gold was discovered in the Black Hills.

Within a few years, the Army had corralled the Indians onto reservations, the railroad had replaced the wagon trails, the beaver and the buffalo had been exterminated, and the fort abandoned. It wasn't until 1938 that Franklin Roosevelt designated Fort Laramie a national historic site. In its time, travelers from Jim Bridger to Mark Twain stopped at the fort; today almost 100,000 tourists ramble through many of the site's 22 original structures.

For an in-depth look at life at the fort, stop by the **visitor center** before touring the grounds. From mid-May through mid-September, it is open daily 8am to 7pm, and daily from 8am to 4:30pm the rest of the year. The visitor center screens videos about the fort and its role in the settlement of the West, and has an extensive collection of historic photographs. A gift shop sells a wide selection of Western-theme books and gift items. Pick up a copy of the self-guiding tour of the fort's historic buildings before you leave.

Some of the more notable (and restored) buildings you'll see are the **cavalry barracks,** where dozens of soldiers slept, crowded into a single room; **Old Bedlam,** the post's headquarters, which later served as housing for officers, bachelors, and married couples alike; the **guardhouse,** a stone structure that housed the fort's prisoners; and the **bakery,** where the freshest component of the soldiers' daily meals was baked.

Living history programs are conducted every summer, from June to mid-August, when employees dress in period costumes, wandering around the fort and answering visitors' questions. On any given day, you may see a laundress, a baker, or a cavalryman.

Before leaving the fort, consider driving to the **Old Bedlam Ruts** (ask for a map from the visitor center), 2 miles northwest of the fort. The bumpy gravel road allows you to view the rutted trail marks left by the wagon trains of early Western settlers. Look for Laramie Peak and the grave of Mary Homsley, one of the many who died along the trail.

GETTING THERE From Casper, take I-25 past Douglas to U.S. Highway 26 (just before Wheatland), then head east to Fort Laramie. For more information, contact **Fort Laramie National Historic Site,** National Park Service, P.O. Box 218, Fort Laramie, WY 82212 (☎ **307/837-2221**).

Southern Wyoming

14

by Geoff O'Gara

Southern Wyoming has long been less a destination than a land passed through. All the famous trails—the Bozeman, the Californian, the Emigrant, the Mormon, the Overland, and the Pony Express— lead somewhere else. Even today, if you stand on a hill just outside the state capitol of Cheyenne, where two major interstates intersect, you'll see a cluster of mega-gas stations crowded with RVs, autos, and semis, fueling up before speeding east or west.

In the middle of the 19th century, nearly a half-million people passed through Wyoming on the Oregon trail. They paused at Independence Rock only long enough to rest and to carve their names in the stone (it's still there—west of Casper on WY 220). This cross-state journey, which can now be done in a day, took a month in the 1840s. The travelers left behind wagon tracks, cast-iron stoves, worn-out boots, crippled livestock, and their dead. It was no easy passage: They also left behind an average of 10 graves for every mile of trail.

By 1868, the railroad had forged across the plains, following the more southerly route of the Overland Stages. The arrival of the railroad brought shanty towns of gambling tents, saloons and brothels, known as "Hell on Wheels." Left behind as the rails moved on, the makeshift towns collapsed, and a cycle of booms and busts began. New discoveries of coal, oil, gold, and uranium each would spur a revival, followed by another bust.

That legacy colors the character of towns along I-80 today. A new generation of miners dig coal and trona and keep the oil and natural gas flowing. Mineral money builds sparkling new schools and government buildings, but there is still a rough-and-ready quality to the downtown districts.

But unlike the old days, the communities now have a better grip on the landscape. **Cheyenne** is the state capital, home to thousands of government workers. The remnants of the ranching families that once dominated the area come out in force every year for **Frontier Days,** a rodeo extravaganza known the world over. West over the pass in **Laramie,** the University of Wyoming is a cultural and intellectual nexus. From Laramie west, I-80 climbs around Elk Mountain and races across the high desert—a bleak view from behind the windshield, and a sometimes harrowing drive in the blizzardy winter.

To find the unexpected beauty in this land, you have to turn off the interstate. You can head north among the stirring buttes of the Red Desert, read the ancient archaeological record at Fossil Butte, hike the mountain cirque of the Snowy Range, or dip in the clear waters of Flaming Gorge. Two-lane roads lead to chalk buttes and rust-colored mesas. On summer afternoons, the dry air turns humid, the sky black, and lightning dances on the red rims. When the sun breaks again, the cliffs burn copper.

1 Scenic Drives

I-80 runs the length of southern Wyoming along the same path followed by the first transcontinental railroad: straight, fast, convenient, but not often scenic. To an educated eye, though, there are interesting sights along the way.

A geologist, for instance, will be interested in the road cuts made by the interstate— eons of geologic history are revealed. Historians will appreciate the remnants left more than a century ago: take Exit 272, 41 miles west of Laramie, and visit **Little Arlington,** where you'll find what's left of an old stage station and a log cabin, back in the trees. Here along the interstate you'll also see Wyoming's latest contribution to the nation's energy pool: A wind farm of spinning propellers lining the ridges like an infantry on stilts.

But to break the monotony of the long drive across southern Wyoming, you need to take a loop off the interstate. There's great scenery out there. Here are a few diversions worth trying.

DRIVING TOUR #1: THE SNOWY RANGE SCENIC BYWAY: LARAMIE TO SARATOGA

The **Snowy Range Road** (WY 130), designated the nation's second scenic byway, twists up and over the Medicine Bow Mountains south of I-80 and west of Laramie, through corridors of pines, between snow banks (even in mid-summer), and tops Snowy Range Pass at 10,847 feet. During the winter, heavy snows block the pass, but you can reach a ski area (both Alpine and Nordic) on the Laramie side, 6 miles past Centennial.

To reach the Snowy Range Scenic Byway from Laramie, take Exit 311 off I-80 and head west along Snowy Range Road. Once past the little town of Centennial, the road switchbacks steeply up. As you top the pass, you'll see sharp granite peaks to the north, often with skirts of snow, cupping a group of lakes fed by the snowmelt. This is the top of the range, with elevations more than 12,000 feet above sea level. On a summer day you'll have plenty of company at the turnouts—people stopping to look, to fish, to hike a nature trail, to picnic. Half a day of vigorous hiking (if you're adjusted to the altitude) will get you atop Medicine Bow Peak, the highest summit in the range. The road then descends the east side of the range, following French Creek to the **Upper North Platte River** (known as the Miracle Mile), which is popular with anglers. When you come to a T in the road, turn right on 130 and drive 8 miles north to **Saratoga,** a friendly little town where many boats are launched to fish the excellent waters of the Platte. Continue north from here to rejoin I-80 at Walcott Junction.

FINISH THE LOOP: A DIFFERENT WAY BACK TO LARAMIE You can return on I-80 to Laramie, or take a more adventurous route by going north from Walcott on U.S. Highway 30/287 toward Medicine Bow. This road follows the rail-line and, as such, skirts the mountains—in the winter, it's often a better route than the interstate. The landscape is sagebrush plains and hills, where antelope roam. Every 20 miles or so, you'll hit a crumbling town. One of those towns with a little life still left in it is **Medicine Bow,** location of the Virginian Hotel (another model for Owen

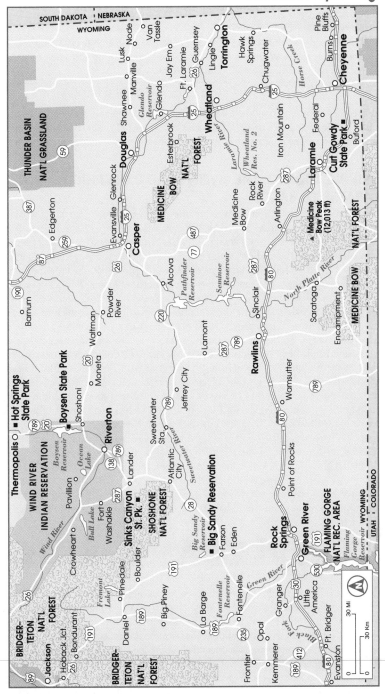

Travel Tip

Because of the altitude of this journey, be alert to weather, especially on the edges of winter. Contact **Wyoming Road and Travel Information** services for regularly updated road conditions at ☎ **888/996-7623.**

Wister's *The Virginian*) and of a watering hole with character, the Diplodocus Bar. (Take a look at the bar itself—a solid slab of jade.) Some of the great historic dinosaur discoveries were made in this area, at nearby Como Bluff. Continue east to finish the loop in Laramie.

DRIVING TOUR #2: THE RIVERS ROAD & NEW HIGHWAY 70: LARAMIE TO BAGGS

This scenic drive goes from Laramie to the town of Baggs along WY 230 and a recently completed stretch of WY 70. **WY 230** (also known as "The Rivers Road") winds its way southwest from Laramie along the Laramie River to the town of **Mountain Home,** where the road dips south into Colorado. Here it makes a loop along CO 127 and 125 for 18 miles, and reenters the state of Wyoming on the other side of the Medicine Bow Range. The route then continues northwest along WY 230 to the old logging town of Encampment. This last portion offers beautiful river scenery with aspen and lodgepole pines, and opportunities for trout fishing. From Encampment, take WY 70 west to Baggs across 58 miles of Carbon County land in the Sierra Madre Mountain Range. Because of the altitude, views can stretch for miles around this virtually uninhabited belt of southern Wyoming. But the altitude also causes road closures in the winter. WY 70 climbs to 9,955 feet to Battle Pass, named for a nearby conflict that took place in 1841. Here it crosses the Continental Divide before descending to the small towns of **Savery, Dixon,** and **Baggs,** three agricultural towns whose total combined population is less than 500. Early settlers came to the area in search of gold and silver. Butch Cassidy celebrated robberies in Baggs, and the quick-triggered livestock detective Tom Horn frequented these parts during the late 1800s.

Turn north off WY 70 onto WY 789 at Baggs, then drive north for 51 miles through high plains ranching country. At Creston Junction, you'll rejoin I-80. From here, you can either drive west to Rock Springs and the Utah border or return to Laramie. You won't have traveled as far as you think, but you'll have seen a lot more along this route than you would have staring at the back of an 18-wheeler along the interstate.

2 Cheyenne

93 miles N of Denver; 180 miles S of Casper

Cheyenne is like a thumbtack pinning down the southeast corner of the state. Legend has it that when Gen. Grenville M. Dodge's surveying crew trudged across the prairie, picking a route for the transcontinental railroad, night came, they were tired, they stopped, said, "Good as any," and thus was born the present site of Cheyenne.

By horse or by highway, you can't miss Cheyenne, not only the largest city in Wyoming (population 55,000) but also its capital. Visitors enjoy the many historic and political sights, from the **Capital Building** to the old **Governors' Mansion.** But the biggest event of Cheyenne, hands down, is the wild and wooly week-long Cowboy Mardi-gras, **Cheyenne Frontier Days.**

Money-Saving Tip

To get the most for your money at Frontier Days, order a 1-day package for $26 that includes a ticket to the afternoon's rodeo and the evening concert; these tickets are good between Monday and Thursday, and must be ordered 6 months in advance. For more information call ☎ **800/227-6336** or 307/778-7222, or check out www.cfdrodeo.com.

ESSENTIALS

GETTING THERE   **United Express** (☎ **800/241-6522** or 307/635-6623) flies daily into the **Cheyenne Municipal Airport** on East 8th Avenue, off Yellowstone Road, but most people choose to fly directly in and out of **Denver International Airport** (☎ **800/247-2336**), 101 miles south of Cheyenne in Colorado on I-25, and rent a car to drive into Wyoming from there.

Go anywhere, **Greyhound** (☎ **307/634-7744**) promises, or hop a **Powder River Transportation** (☎ **307/635-1327**) bus for inner-state destinations from the bus terminal at 120 N. Greeley Hwy.

To get to Cheyenne from **Casper,** take I-25 south for 180 miles. From **Rock Springs** in the southwest part of the state, take I-80 east for 258 miles.

VISITOR INFORMATION   Nearly any question you have about your Wyoming vacation can be answered at the **Wyoming Information Center** at Wyoming Division of Tourism, I-25 at College Drive. The **Cheyenne Area Convention and Visitors Bureau** at 309 W. Lincolnway, P.O. Box 765, Cheyenne, WY 82003 (☎ **800/ 426-5009** outside Wyoming, or 307/778-3133), has a variety of brochures and local maps, like the *Cheyenne Historic Downtown Walking Tour,* and the *Downtown Cheyenne Map.* (A second, centrally located office is at 301 W. 16th St.)

GETTING AROUND   **Dollar** (☎ **800/800-4000** or 307/632-2422) and **Hertz** (☎ **800/654-3131** or 307/634-2131) both have counters at the Cheyenne airport. Should you need a taxi, **Yellow Cab** can be reached at ☎ **307/635-5555.** There is no taxi stand at the airport.

CHEYENNE FRONTIER DAYS

In the world of rodeo, there are three must-see classics: The Pendelton Round-up, the Calgary Stampede, and the "Daddy of 'em all," Cheyenne Frontier Days. Started in 1897, it is both one of the oldest and certainly largest rodeos in the world. The Frontier Days committee, as well as hundreds of volunteers (called the Heels) organize this week-long Western spectacle of parades, rodeo, dances, and concerts each summer, around the last week of July. It's safe to say that this will be the most vivid demonstration of Western hospitality you'll encounter in the modern world.

Though the rodeo lasts for a full 10 days, picking and choosing activities carefully can save you a lot of time and money. Rodeo ticket prices range anywhere from $8 to $18 per person, and nightly shows featuring popular country music acts cost $15 to $20.

VISITOR INFORMATION   Contact the **Cheyenne Frontier Days Committee** for brochures, ticket forms, and information on all shows and activities during upcoming Frontier Days celebrations at Cheyenne Frontier Days, P.O. Box 2477, Cheyenne, WY 82003-2477 (☎ **800/227-6336** or 307/778-7222; www. cfdrodeo.com).

GETTING AROUND DURING THE FESTIVAL Parking is provided at Frontier Park for $5 per vehicle, but shuttle parking is also available and (trust me) makes much more sense. The shuttle picks up visitors at several locations and delivers them to the rodeo grounds; round-trip fare is $4 per carload. The city also runs a special bus service to the park from downtown Cheyenne that stops at nearby campgrounds. Contact the **Cheyenne Area Convention and Visitors Bureau** (☎ 307/778-3133) for bus stop locations and scheduled pickups.

The Parade. Starts at Capitol Ave. and 24th St., runs down Capitol Ave. to 16th Ave., and continues up Carey Ave. to the finish at Carey Ave. and 24th St. Free admission. During Frontier Days, Sat, Tues, and Thurs, commencing at 9:30am.

With the exception of Buffalo Bill's showbiz walk through the streets of Cheyenne in 1898 and a docile march led by Teddy Roosevelt in 1910, Cheyenne's Frontier Days Parade in its early days was similar to a stagecoach holdup. From its start in 1897, guns blazed as cowboys rode through the streets with little regard to form or style. In 1925, things took a turn toward civility when the "Evolution of Transportation" theme was introduced. Today, many horse-drawn vehicles make their way through the streets of Cheyenne as part of the Old-Time Carriage section of the parade. In addition to the carriages and antique cars, marching bands, local clubs, and various Plains Indians groups march. Viewing sites are as near as the closest curb, but you'll want to claim a position 45 minutes before the start.

The Pancake Breakfast. Cheyenne City Center parking lot, corner of Lincolnway and Carey. Free admission. During Frontier Days, Mon, Wed, Fri 7–9am.

Since their inception in 1952, these free breakfasts have become increasingly popular. On Monday, Wednesday, and Friday from 7 to 9am, a cement mixer moves in to mix enough pancake batter to cook more than 100,000 flapjacks for 30,000 people. The breakfasts are held downtown at the Cheyenne City Center parking lot on the corner of Lincolnway and Carey and served by locals, including, sometimes, an unassuming governor.

The Rodeo. Frontier Park, Exit 12 off I-80. ☎ **800/227-6336** or 307/778-7222. Tickets $8–$18. During Frontier Days, daily at 1:15pm.

An anthropologist might see rodeo as a fading ritual to a passing way of life, but don't tell that to the fans who pack the stands at Frontier Days. It's actually one of the most popular spectator sports in the nation, as American as apple pie and baseball, with a Western twist. Cheyenne's annual rodeo draws people from across the nation, and the best of the best cowboys, from Casey Tibbs to Larry Mahan to Ty Murry. Chris LeDoux and George Strait and Garth Brooks have all paid tribute to "Ol' Cheyenne" in song.

Spectators from around the world, young and old, pack into the stands to watch events like steer wrestling, barrel racing, team roping, and the classic event—and Wyoming state symbol—the saddle bronc riding. It's enormous fun, but part of the attraction is that these men and women put themselves in harm's way, working big strong animals with a wild streak. In a world where risk is often an illusion created by entertainers, this is the real thing. Champion bull-rider Lane Frost died in the ring at Frontier Days only a few years ago.

Daily ticket prices start at $8 for bleachers at the far end of the arena; $12 for seats closer to the roping gates; and $18 for the center of the action—the bucking chutes. Each night after the rodeo, top country stars take the stage. Concert tickets range from $14 to $18.

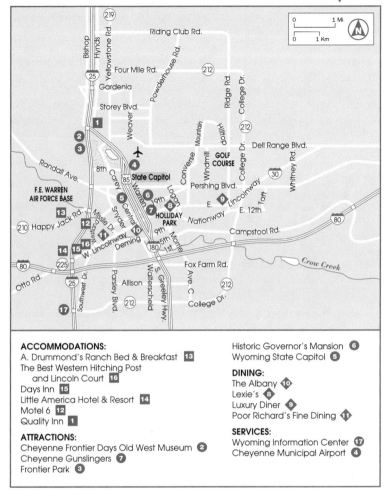

ACCOMMODATIONS:
A. Drummond's Ranch Bed & Breakfast **13**
The Best Western Hitching Post
  and Lincoln Court **16**
Days Inn **15**
Little America Hotel & Resort **14**
Motel 6 **12**
Quality Inn **1**

ATTRACTIONS:
Cheyenne Frontier Days Old West Museum **2**
Cheyenne Gunslingers **7**
Frontier Park **3**

Historic Governor's Mansion **6**
Wyoming State Capitol **5**

DINING:
The Albany **10**
Lexie's **8**
Luxury Diner **9**
Poor Richard's Fine Dining **11**

SERVICES:
Wyoming Information Center **17**
Cheyenne Municipal Airport **4**

SEEING THE SIGHTS

Stop in at the **Nelson Museum of the West** at 1714 Carey Ave. (☎ **307/635-7670**) to see a collection of cowboy trappings, Indian artifacts, taxidermy trophies, and Western memorabilia. Just up the block, bookworms should stop into **City News** (☎ **307/638-8671**), which has an excellent selection of Wyoming writings as well as a dizzying selection of periodicals.

Cheyenne Frontier Days Old West Museum. 4610 N. Carey Ave., Frontier Park, Cheyenne, WY 82001. ☎ **307/778-1415.** www.oldwestmuseum.org. $4 adults, free for children under 12. AE, DISC, MC, V. Mon–Fri 9am–5pm; Sat–Sun 10am–5pm; longer hours during Frontier Days.

Frontier Days has been around long enough that folks have become interested in its history. Sponsors recently decided that a museum could warehouse memorabilia and historic artifacts from the area's ranching culture. The Old West Museum is located next door to the rodeo arena, a convenient place to take a break from the action. It houses a room full of carriages, an interpretive Native American exhibit, photos, a movie, and rodeo stuff.

Cheyenne Gunslingers. Gunslinger Sq., Lincolnway and Carey. ☎ **307/635-1028.** Free admission. Shows held nightly at 6pm, Sat at noon; during Frontier Days, the show runs twice daily at noon and 6pm.

From June through July, this nonprofit Cheyenne group puts on an Old West shoot-out downtown in "Gunslinger Square." You'll recognize it by the stage set of an Old West saloon, jail, and gallows. The volunteer actors love to ham it up. Their show dramatizes a jailbreak, a near-hanging, and a fast-draw—starring a corrupt judge, wily villains, and the white-hat good guys. It's not necessarily the most accurate portrayal of the Old West (and the performers will be the first to admit that), but it is great entertainment for the family.

Street Railway Trolley. Purchase tickets at the Cheyenne Area Convention and Visitors Bureau, 309 W. Lincolnway. ☎ **307/778-3133.** Tour $8 adults, $4 children. MC, V. Summer, 2-hour tours Mon–Sat 10am and 1:30pm, Sun 1:30pm.

No longer used as a mode of mass transit, the local trolley offers visitors a ride around Cheyenne's main tourist sites, including the Governors' Mansion, the Capital, and Cattle Barons' Row. For something different, take a "Ghost" tour departing Fridays at 7:30pm ($6 adults, $3 children). As you visit the Air Force base and the hotel district, you'll hear eerie tails of Cheyenne's haunted past.

Wyoming State Capitol. Capitol Ave. ☎ **307/777-7220.** Free tours by reservation, Mon–Fri 8:30am–4:30pm, except holidays.

In the summer, when the streets of Cheyenne are shaded by large old oaks, it's easy to come upon the capitol building a bit by surprise. It's not a large capitol, as such things go, but traditional, with a gold-leaf dome and carved stone. It was originally built in 1886; the wings were added in 1917, but otherwise, the stately building has undergone little change over the years. Outside, you can stop by two statues: the first woman justice of the peace, Esther Hobart Morris, and the Spirit of Wyoming, the wild bucking horse emblazoned on every license plate in the state. (Interesting side note: The fellow riding Spirit on the license plate was born in my house in Lander, Wyoming.) You can peek inside, but be sure to make reservations at least a week in advance.

The Historic Governors' Mansion. 300 E. 21st St. ☎ **307/777-7878.** Fax 307/777-6472. Free admission. Tues–Sat 9am–5pm.

If you're devoting time to learning about the political history of the state—an excellent way to enrich a Wyoming visit—you should continue 5 blocks from the capitol to the historic governors' mansion. Built in 1904, it housed Wyoming's first families until 1976. Over the years, the decorative styles mixed, and visitors can see everything from Chippendale to Renaissance Revival to art nouveau to the Thermadore oven in the kitchen. There's even a steer-horn chair in the entrance hall. But over the years it's held more interesting personalities than it has accumulated lavish furnishings and worldly antiques. The building itself, with its four Corinthian columns, looks more like an old fraternity house than a governor's mansion. A videotape and tour provide a worthwhile look into the political past of Wyoming's governors.

WHERE TO STAY

A reservation caution: Hotels fill up so fast during Frontier Days that locals sometimes open their homes as bed-and-breakfasts for the week. Unlucky visitors who haven't made reservations up to a year in advance spill into Laramie and Fort Collins motels. Even in those outlying towns, rooms are scarce during the big week.

A caution for those with reservations: During Frontier Days the clock stops and things "get a little Western." Celebrants elbow and slosh plastic beer cups in bars and roam the streets and scream, sing, stomp, and sometimes fall down. Since the historic downtown hostelries, like all old buildings, tend to be thin-walled, guests should not be thin-skinned, and ought to bring ear plugs.

✪ **A. Drummond's Ranch Bed-and-Breakfast.** 399 Happy Jack Rd., Cheyenne/Laramie, WY 82007 (22 miles north of Cheyenne off I-25). ☎ **307/634-6042.** www.cruising-america.com/drummond.html. 4 units. $65–$80 2nd-story room; $100–$125 garden room; $150–$175 carriage house room. Rates include breakfast. MC, V.

A short drive from either Cheyenne or Laramie, the Drummonds' house sits above hills of pine and sage staggering south toward Colorado. Here you can ride mountain bikes in summer, or cross-country ski in winter, or even take a llama to lunch. That's right. For under $10 per person, the Drummonds will pack your lunch by llama. Or guests can bring their own horses; an avid horse-lover herself, owner Taydie Drummond can set your horse up with its own bed-and-breakfast.

Inside, guests can relax in the living room and watch a video, or sit on the porch and gaze. The Drummonds' home isn't historic, or large, or particularly quaint, but it feels exactly like what it is: a home. It's a place to kick back, take walks, pet the animals. Second-story rooms have two beds and share a bath. One of these rooms, aptly named Hummingbird, looks out over Colorado's Rocky Mountain National Park, 75 miles away. The downstairs room has a sliding door that leads to a hot tub. Those in love, or in the lap of luxury, will want to stay in the Carriage House Loft (with private deck, hot tub, gas fireplace, and steam shower).

Best Western Hitching Post Inn and Lincoln Court. 1700 W. Lincolnway, Cheyenne, WY 82001. ☎ **800/221-0125,** 307/638-3301, or 307/638-3302. Fax 307/778-7194. 168 units. A/C TV TEL. Best Western Hitching Post: May–Sept, $79 double; Oct–Apr, $90 double; during Frontier Days, $200 double. Lincoln Court: May–Sept, $60 double; Oct–Apr, $50 double; during Frontier Days, $130 double. AE, DC, DISC, MC, V.

The Hitching Post is where most of the legislators stay during their annual sessions at the capital, so it has an air of importance and deal-making. With that comes good service. It's also got spacious, well-appointed rooms, an indoor pool, and three dining rooms. On busy weekends there is live entertainment in the lounge. Next door is the less expensive Lincoln Court, under the same ownership. It's a 1950s-style motel court, somewhat updated by recent renovations. It also offers a continental breakfast. These motels are located along the motel strip on Lincolnway near the junction of interstates west of downtown Cheyenne.

✪ **Little America Hotel and Resort.** 2800 W. Lincolnway (I-80 at I-25), Cheyenne, WY 82001. ☎ **800/445-6945** or 307/775-8400. Fax 307/775-8425. 188 units. A/C TV TEL. $59–$135 double; during Frontier Days, $119–$149 double. AE, DC, DISC, MC, V.

This is the largest hotel in Wyoming and a noteworthy oasis. The main building and low-rise brick lodges are surrounded by an executive golf course, duck pond, and mature evergreens. The main building harbors a tastefully appointed lounge warmed by a fieldstone fireplace and Navajo rugs; three shops offer boutique clothing, jewelry, and Western souvenirs. Accommodations, in four low-rise brick lodges, all refurbished since 1993, provide 31-inch TVs, balconies, and combination baths with marble counters. Rooms come in three categories: standards, mini-suites with king-size beds, and larger executive suites. Meals and drinks are available in the dining room (just off the lobby), coffee shop, and lounge. The coffee shop serves meals 5am to 1am at amazingly modest prices. The Olympic-size pool is open summer only, but a fitness center and jogging path can be used year-round.

Motel 6. 1735 Westland Rd., Cheyenne, WY 82001. ☎ **800/466-8356** or 307/635-6806. 108 units. A/C TV TEL. $45 double; during Frontier Days, $62 double. AE, DC, DISC, MC, V.

For a family in search of a room at the last minute, this place can be just the ticket. Located just off I-25, this Motel 6 offers basic rooms at a cheap price. There's an outdoor swimming pool, but otherwise amenities are nonexistent. If you've got something a bit fancier in mind, head farther down Lincolnway to the Days Inn and the Best Western Hitching Post.

Quality Inn. 5401 Walker Rd., Cheyenne, WY 82001. ☎ **800/228-5151** or 307/632-8901. 105 units. A/C TV TEL. $32–$58 double; during Frontier Days, $150 double. AE, DC, DISC, MC, V.

If you want to be on the other side of town from the motel strip, nearer to the rodeo grounds, take a right off Exit 12 and you'll find this chain affiliate. Renovation has been slowly progressing, so ask to look at the available rooms before you hand over your credit card. This is a convenient place to be if you're devoting your visit to the rodeo. The Central Cafe and Lounge, and an attached liquor store, are located on the premises.

CAMPING

The Greenway Trailer Park, 3728 Greenway St. (☎ **307/634-6696**), offers paved RV pads and cable TV hookups for $15; $25 during Frontier Days. The biggest campground is the **Restway Travel Park** off Whitney Road, 2 miles east of Cheyenne (☎ **800/443-2751** or 307/634-3811). Catering to RV and tent campers alike, Restway boasts a heated swimming pool, miniature golf, and a store stocked with basic supplies. Fifteen miles east of town at the Hillsdale exit 377, off I-80, the **Wyoming Campground** (☎ **307/547-2244**) has a swimming pool, laundry facilities, and a 24-hour convenience store—as well as a mobile home park in case you want to move. Hookups are around $15, and $23 for Frontier Days.

WHERE TO DINE

The Albany. 1506 Capitol Ave. ☎ **307/638-3507.** Lunch $4–$7; dinner $8–$15. AE, DISC, DC, MC, V. Mon–Sat 11am–9pm. AMERICAN.

The historic Albany, which is located across from the train station, sits in the thick of Frontier Days action. The locals love this place because it's a meat-and-potato restaurant; it has a simple decor of old black and white photos, a bar, and paper napkins, not cloth. Oh, and the prime rib is the best in town.

Lexies. 216 E. 17th St. ☎ **307/638-8712.** Lunch $7–$10; dinner $9–$20. MC, V. Mon 8am–3pm, Tues–Thurs 8am–8pm, Fri 7:30am–9pm, Sat 7am–9pm. AMERICAN.

Locals like to take out-of-town guests to this converted two-story wooden home for lunch. It's conveniently located only a few blocks from the town center. In nice weather, you can sit on the deck and enjoy a glass of ice tea or a microbrew. Sandwiches include the tenderloin steak, the sourdough club, and the pepperjack chicken.

Luxury Diner. 1401-A West Lincolnway. ☎ **307/638-8971.** Breakfast $2–$8; lunch $4–$8. AE, MC, V. Daily 6am–3pm. AMERICAN.

The favorite blue-collar breakfast counter, the Luxury Diner is a real down-home greasy spoon. We say that affectionately, of course, as the food is good, the coffee always hot, and the waitresses sassy. Breakfast all day, of course. The pie: apple. The special: meat loaf. It's the real thing—no Buddy Holly posters, no 45s dangling from the ceiling for that "retro" look. In fact, the small dining area ran as a trolley from 1896 to 1912, before becoming a diner in 1926. Pictures of trains cover the walls, Christmas lights blink around the trim, and the menu says, "Friendliest place in town." They're right.

Poor Richard's. 2233 Lincolnway. ☎ **307/635-5114.** Lunch $5–$8; dinner $7–$19. AE, CB, DC, DISC, MC, V. Sun 5–10pm, Mon–Thurs 11am–2:30pm and 5–10pm, Fri 11am–2:30pm and 5–11pm, Sat 11am–2:30pm (brunch) and 5–11pm. AMERICAN.

With tons of Ben Franklin memorabilia on the walls, Poor Richard's decor conjures up images of statesmanship. Its menu has numerous steak entrees, all served at sturdy oak tables, with cloth napkins and dim lights. It's a hangout for politicians, the place where visitors from around the state come to lobby and talk deals.

3 Laramie

49 miles NW of Cheyenne; 360 miles SE of Yellowstone/Grand Teton; 207 miles E of Rock Spring; 124 miles N of Denver

Though the political capital is 40 miles to the east, Laramie is the cultural capital of Wyoming. It's home to the state's only university, public or private. Unlike Jackson, which has a prefabricated feel designed to appeal to visitors, Laramie has an earnest charm that seems to have developed by accident, and it has been this way for nearly a century. Located just east of the beautiful Medicine Bow Mountains, at an altitude more than 7,000 feet, Laramie is sometimes buffeted by chill winds. But it has university town amenities like bookstores and coffee shops, and a few Western features to boot, including outlying ranchlands and some rowdy downtown bars

ESSENTIALS

GETTING THERE The **Laramie Regional Airport,** 555 General Brees Rd. (☎ 307/742-4164), west of town along WY 130, services daily flights on **United Express** (☎ 800/742-5296) from Denver.

Or go **Greyhound** (☎ 307/742-5188) at **Tumbleweed Express,** 4700 Bluebird Lane (☎ 800/231-2222 or 307/721-7405). The bus stops at several Wyoming cities along I-80, including Rock Springs and Cheyenne.

Laramie is an easy 49-mile drive from Cheyenne on I-80; driving from Salt Lake, it's just more than 300 miles once you hit Evanston. The fastest route from the Yellowstone—Grand Teton area is via U.S. Highway 287 south for 259 miles to Rawlins and I-80 east for 101 miles to Laramie. For information on road conditions call ☎ 888/996-7632.

VISITOR INFORMATION The **Laramie Area Chamber of Commerce,** 800 S. 3rd (☎ 800/445-5803 or 307/745-7339), provides brochures, city maps, and area maps that cover outdoor activities, shopping, dining, and tours for Laramie and the surrounding area.

GETTING AROUND   Avis (☎ 800/831-2222) and **Dollar** (☎ 307/742-8805) maintain counters at Laramie Regional Airport. Taxi service is available through **Laramie Cab and Courier Service** (☎ 307/745-8294).

GETTING OUTSIDE

Curt Gowdy State Park, named for the television sportscaster who hails from Wyoming, is pleasant, if not spectacularly beautiful. Just outside Laramie, and 1,645 acres in size, it's a great spot for a picnic. Or stay the night in one of the five campsites, $5 per night. While there are two lakes here, no swimming is allowed (they provide part of Cheyenne's water supply), but boating is possible (go figure). Call ☎ 307/632-7946 for further information. To get to the park, take I-80 east until you see the exit for WY 210, the scenic back road to Cheyenne.

Southeast of Laramie, on the edge of the Medicine Bow National Forest, are **Pole Mountain** and the **Vedauwoo Recreation Area.** Vedauwoo and the Happy Jack Trailhead near the Summit exit of I-80 have some excellent summer and winter recreational opportunities. The name Veduawoo (pronounced "VEE-duh-voo") is Arapaho for "earth-born." The rock formations—soft-edged blocks shaped like stools, turtles, and mushrooms—were considered the sacred creations of animal and human spirits, and young Indian men sought visions there. Today rock climbers pursue their quests for challenging climbs here, and find tough technical pitches. Other folks see a great place to mountain bike, hike, and scan the vistas. To get there, take I-80 east toward Cheyenne, past the second biggest Abe Lincoln head in these parts (10 miles outside town) to Exit 329, the Vedauwoo turnoff.

SEEING THE SIGHTS

The **Laramie Plains Museum,** 603 Ivinson (☎ 307/742-4448), is a three-story Queen Anne Victorian home built by Laramie settler Edward Ivinson, with furnishings from the 1890s (some furniture was handcarved at the penitentiary). Admission is $4. **The Wyoming Children's Museum and Nature Center,** 412 S. 2nd (☎ 307/745-6332), has enough things to keep kids busy, including a frontier general store where kids can handle things and do face painting. Admission is $2.

The **Laramie River Rodeo** (☎ 307/745-7339) is a summer spectacle. Shows are held Thursday and Friday from June through August at the Fairgrounds (2 miles south of Laramie on U.S. 287 on 3rd Street). **Jubilee Days** (☎ 307/745-7339) is another Western party that runs the second full week in July with rodeos, parades, and fireworks.

The Wyoming Territorial Prison and Old West Park. 975 Snowy Range Rd. (Exit I-80 at Snowy Range Rd. in Laramie; go east). ☎ **800/845-2287** or 307/745-6161. Park admission $8 adults, $6 children 6–12, free for children under 6; dinner theater tickets for both park admission and the Horse Barn Dinner Theater show $26 adults, $17 children. Shows daily 6–9pm.

Formerly a penitentiary where Butch Cassidy (among other famous outlaws) served time, the Territorial Prison transmogrified into an experimental livestock station before becoming the tourist park it is today. Almost everything having to do with frontier life before the turn of the 20th century can be found here, from a funky frontier town, to stage coach rides, to tepees which rent for $16 to $60 per night. Also housed here is the **National U.S. Marshall's Museum,** with exhibits covering 2 centuries of the federal law enforcement agency. The **Horse Barn Theater** features melodrama performances and music revues. Dinner is served in the theater's restored loft.

THE UNIVERSITY OF WYOMING

The university's history began in 1887 with the funding of Old Main, its first building. At that time, there were five professors, two tutors, and 42 students on the 20-acre campus, which included **Prexy's Pasture,** where the school's first president kept his cows. Today, the University of Wyoming has more than 2,000 faculty and staff members and an enrollment of 8,600 drawn from across the United States and 65 countries, though a majority of the undergraduates hail from Wyoming. The university has struggled along with the state's moribund economy, with the legislature holding the purse strings tightly. Some departments have been closed or cut back in

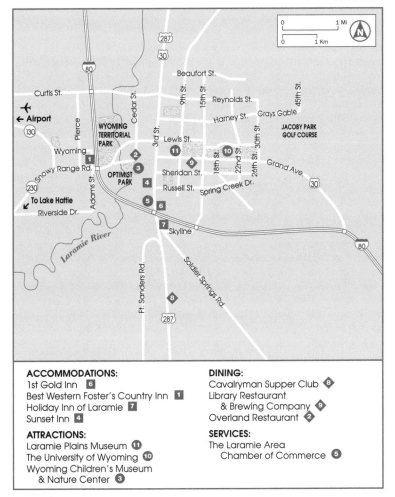

ACCOMMODATIONS:
1st Gold Inn 6
Best Western Foster's Country Inn 1
Holiday Inn of Laramie 7
Sunset Inn 4

ATTRACTIONS:
Laramie Plains Museum 11
The University of Wyoming 10
Wyoming Children's Museum
& Nature Center 3

DINING:
Cavalryman Supper Club 8
Library Restaurant
& Brewing Company 9
Overland Restaurant 2

SERVICES:
The Laramie Area
Chamber of Commerce 5

order to concentrate on other fields—like geology, American studies, and range management—where UW does best.

The campus is puzzling to some visitors, poorly signed and oddly organized, but its elderly sandstone buildings have charm. It has the requisite extensive athletic facilities of a Division I school, a good dinosaur fossil collection, and an interesting piece of new architecture in the Centennial Complex, which houses an excellent research facility, the American Heritage Center.

To catch a glimpse of student life in Laramie, swing by Prexy's Pasture, where students hang, especially in fall. It's located in the heart of the campus, accessed off Ivinson Street or Grand Avenue by turning north on 13th Street (stop at the **Visitors Services Center,** 1408 Ivinson Ave., for a map). Those visiting during the school year may also want to contact **UW Cultural Programs** (☎ **307/766-6666**) to find out what's on the schedule, from classical music to modern dance to international speakers. An auto tour of the campus is worth the effort, if for no other reason than to check out the campus architecture, which ranges from the solid sandstone castles of a century ago to the spaceship designs of today.

With no professional sports teams in Wyoming, the college's football and basketball programs take on special importance. In the fall and winter, fans drive from around the state, despite iffy weather, to root for the **Cowboys** in the university's excellent outdoor stadium and indoor arena. The UW Cowboys have been giant-killers in recent years, knocking off some national top-ranked teams and competing for Western Athletic Conference crowns (the Cowboys became part of the new Mountain West Conference in 1999). For event information and tickets, contact the ticket office at ☎ **307/766-4850;** www.wyomingathletics.com.

In a state where many towns have only small, local collections to display and inform visitors, the university plays an important role with its museum spaces, and most of the exhibits are free. Worth visiting are the **Geological Museum** (☎ **307/766-4218;** located in the Geology Building, northwest corner of Prexy's Pasture), with plenty of dinosaur fossils, open Monday to Friday 8am to 5pm, Saturday and Sunday 10am to 3pm; and the **Rocky Mountain Herbarium** (☎ **307/766-2236**), open Monday to Friday 8am to 5pm. The **Insect Museum** (☎ **307/766-2298;** in room 1408 of the Ag Building, just north of Prexy's Pasture) is primarily a research facility and a bit esoteric to the average visitor; it is open to the public Monday to Friday 8am to 5pm year-round. The **Centennial Complex** (on the east side of campus—look for the volcanic cone, east of 15th Street) houses the **UW Art Museum,** with works by Audubon, Charlie Russell, Thomas Moran, and even Gauguin. It's open Monday to Saturday 10am to 5pm. Also in this modern building—which looks like a volcanic cone tipping sideways—is the **American Heritage Center** (☎ **307/766-4114**), a top-notch research facility with extensive collections of Western history materials but also some unexpected archives, like some of Jack Benny's papers.

SHOPPING

Since Laramie is a university town, it has its fair share of bookstores. There is of course a giant and useful chain store, **Hastings Books Music and Video,** at 654 N. 3rd (☎ **307/745-0312**), but there are also some fine and idiosyncratic locals, including the peaceful **2nd Story Books** and **Personally Recommended Books,** both located at 107 Ivinson (☎ **307/745-4423**), where you can tap into the latest literary currents without the distraction of noise or bustle. **Chickering Books,** at 203 S. 2nd (☎ **307/745-8609**), has a comparable selection of books but is a worthy member of the scene for its selection of classics. To see what's hot on campus, visit the extensive **University Bookstore** 1 block north of Ivinson and 13th (☎ **800/423-5809**). **The Grand Newstand** at 214 E. Grand Ave. (☎ **307/745-5127**) has a more limited and mainstream selection, but an enormous array of periodicals and newspapers.

If you're looking for the gear you need to adventure in the Medicine Bow, try **Cross-Country Connection** at 222 S. 2nd St. (☎ **307/721-2851**) for skiing and climbing equipment (you can rent, too). Searching for something to hang on the wall? **Artisans' Gallery** at 213 S. 2nd St. (☎ **888/616-6409**) specializes in crafts and art work by Wyoming artists. **Earth, Wind, and Fire** (☎ **307/745-0226**), just a few doors down at 220 S. 2nd St., is a pottery lover's dream come true. **Green Gold,** at 215 S. 1st St. (☎ **307/742-0003**), has all the Wyoming jade and most of the silver you'll need.

WHERE TO STAY

The **Sunset Inn,** 1104 S. 3rd St. (☎ **800/308-3744** or 307/742-3741), is a small motel that doesn't have many perks, other than an outdoor pool and indoor hot tub. Doubles cost $40 to $65.

Best Western Foster's Country Inn. 1561 Snowy Range Rd., Laramie, WY 82070. ☎ **307/742-8371.** 112 units. A/C TV TEL. $55–$99 double. Rates include breakfast. AE, DC, DISC, MC, V.

A stone's throw from I-80 (depending on how well you throw), this locally-owned Best Western affiliate is doing its best to come up to speed in the hospitality game. Built around a central parking area, it lacks variety or elbow room, and it's generally crowded with tired drivers off the interstate. The motel offers a free full breakfast, an indoor pool and hot tub, and a restaurant and lounge, as well as an airport shuttle (7am to 11pm).

1st Gold Inn. 421 Boswell, Laramie, WY 82070. ☎ **800/642-4212** or 307/742-3721. 79 units. A/C TV TEL. $49–$85 double. AE, DC, DISC, MC, V.

This rambling two-story motel was once the Laramie Inn, and while it often seems in a state of revision—fixing up older rooms, taking on a new name, hosting a new restaurant—it's still one of the better, more comfortable places to stay in town. Heading west along I-80, take the 3rd Street exit to this hunter-green brick motel. Though the amenities are few (an outdoor pool), the prices tend to be a bit cheaper (but not during football season and Frontier Days, of course).

Holiday Inn of Laramie. Exit 311 of I-80 and U.S. Hwy. 287. ☎ **307/742-6611.** 100 units. A/C TV TEL. $99–$109 double. AE, DC, DISC, MC, V.

In a city that lacks a truly fine hotel, this is one of the best of the bunch. The layout has no particular logic, extending around an inner grass area that goes mostly unused. There's a big indoor pool and hot tub, a restaurant, and a sports bar that fills to the rafters when the UW Cowboys play an away game.

CAMPING

N&H Trailer Ranch, open year-round, is near the University of Wyoming campus at 1360 N. 3rd (☎ **307/742-3158**), and offers laundry facilities and full hookups for $12 a night, as well as weekly and monthly rates. The **Laramie KOA,** off I-80 at 1271 Baker St. (☎ **307/742-6553**), is open from March through November, depending on the snows. Full hookups are $22. For a smaller site near I-80 at the corner of Curtis and McCue, try the **Riverside Campground** (☎ **307/721-7405**). It's open year-round and has tent sites near the Laramie River. RV electric hookups are $12.

WHERE TO DINE

Laramie should do better than it does in the restaurant department, but it has a few good ones. It also has a few chain operations, which serve what their brethren serve all over the country: There's a **JB's** at 3430 Grand Ave. (☎ **307/745-8274**) and an **Applebee's** at 3209 E. Grand Ave. (☎ **307/745-3880**), conveniently close to the campus. You'll find more character in the old downtown area, where thinkers and talkers fuel up on good java at the **Coal Creek Coffee Company,** 110 E. Grand (☎ 307/745-7737); there is sometimes live music in the evenings. You can get a small portion of excellent pasta or pizza at **Grand Avenue Pizza,** 301 Grand Ave. (☎ 307/721-2909), which hides in an old corner space downtown.

The Cavalryman Supper Club. 4425 S. 3rd St. ☎ **307/745-5551.** Main courses $15–$28. AE, DC, DISC, MC, V. Daily 4:30–10pm. STEAKS/SEAFOOD.

This restaurant with an unusual atmosphere and decor, located south of town, is perfect for big appetites; it's also perfect for big spenders with its admittedly high prices. It pays tribute to the 7th Cavalry, a regiment that once used this site as a post on their famous march north to the Battle of the Little Bighorn. Waitresses dress in uniforms resembling those worn by the cavalry. Previously a schoolhouse—and at one time, a brothel—you could say that this is a restaurant with a colorful past. All meals are served with appetizers (sautéed mushrooms), tea, coffee, and dessert. There are always at least eight entrees to choose from, including lobster, prime rib, and lasagna.

✪ **Overland Restaurant.** 100 Ivinson Ave. ☎ **307/721-2800.** Main courses $8–$17. AE, DISC, MC, V. Mon–Thurs 7am–8pm, Fri–Sat 7am–9pm, Sun 8am–8pm. ECLECTIC.

Any time of day, this restaurant proves itself one of the better places to eat, but it shines the most in the evening, when wine lovers can order something from the 2,000-bottle cellar filled with California and Italian wines. Those fine wines will go well with the wild game specials, including venison, ostrich, and Rocky Mountain trout. In the morning, the omelets are delicious. It's a bit of a maze inside, small rooms cobbled together into a restaurant, but that's part of its charm, and in good weather there's pleasant patio dining.

4 A Side Trip for the Outdoor Enthusiast: The Snowy Range & Carbon County

Snowy Range: 32 miles W of Laramie

You can very quickly leave behind the dry plains around Laramie and find yourself up among lakes and forest and substantial peaks in the north end of the Medicine Bow Mountains, known as the **Snowy Range.** Just take WY 130 west, through the foothill town of Centennial and up into the mountains, where peaks rise well over 10,000 feet. Though **Medicine Bow Peak** is 12,013 feet tall, it's a relatively easy day climb, starting at the parking lot by Lake Marie and covering about 5 miles. You can loop around the west side of the cirque in which the peak stands and return on the east side among the lakes. Trails are well marked and you'll meet people as you hike. Just keep an eye on the thunderheads, as you'll be above timberline, exposed if lightning starts to dance. For **detailed trail maps** of the Medicine Bow National Forest, contact the **Medicine Bow National Forest Service** in Laramie at ☎ **307/745-2300.**

If you drive on over the Snowies—it takes only about an hour—you'll drop down into the valley of the **North Platte River,** where you'll find old mining and timber towns like Encampment and Saratoga. **Saratoga** is the roost of several fishing outfits that guide on the North Platte, one of the finest trout fisheries in the state. If you spend the night, you'll probably enjoy the creaky, old-fashioned style of the historic **Hotel Wolf** at 101 E. Bridge St. (☎ **307/326-5525**), or the peaceful (and expensive) spa **Saratoga Inn** (☎ **307/326-5261**), with its own hot spring–fed pool and golf course.

RV & TENT CAMPING

Medicine Bow National Forest (☎ **307/745-2300**) maintains more than 30 public sites from June through September, scattered throughout the range west of Laramie. All are semi-primitive, which means no showers, no electric hookup, no flush toilets. Fees vary from $7 to $10 per night.

GUIDED EXPLORATIONS WITH OUTFITTERS

The Orvis-endorsed **Great Rocky Mountain Outfitters,** at 216 E. Walnut, in Saratoga (☎ **800/326-5390;** www.grmo.com), has been guiding anglers along the Upper North Platte since 1981. They charge $325 for a full-day, two-person drift fishing expedition (including lunch), and $225 for a half-day excursion with no meal. **Platte Valley Anglers,** at the corner of 1st Avenue and Bride Street in Saratoga

(☎ **307/326-5750**), offers drift fishing, white-water fishing, and white-water float trips. Or contact **Medicine Bow Drifters** (☎ **307/326-8002;** www.medbow.com).

5 Rock Springs

258 miles W of Cheyenne; 178 miles S of Jackson

Rock Springs began as a stage station on the Overland trail, named after a natural spring which dried up after extensive mining in the area. In 1894, Jack London wrote of Rock Springs: "It seems to be a mining town . . . It seems to be the Wild and Wooly West with a vengeance." Still true: Rock Springs shows the rougher side of Wyoming, powered by a coal-burning power plant, freight trains roaring through, and all-night truckers stopping for coffee, adding to a pervasive blue-collar sensibility. But it's not without pockets of culture and intellect, particularly at Western Wyoming College.

It's also a pocket of unionism in a conservative state. In 1875, the Union Pacific Railroad demanded more coal to fuel its transcontinental trains, but simultaneously cut wages. When the local miners went on strike, the railroad imported about 500 Chinese laborers. More and more Chinese came to the area, and within a decade, the white miners felt displaced. Animosity festered then burst in 1885, when a mob of laid-off miners murdered 28 Chinese and burned Chinatown to the ground. Now on the site, ironically, stands a church.

Boom followed bust followed boom, and in the late 1970s, oil, gas, and coal caused the area population to double. Wages skyrocketed. So did the crime rate. Motels and bars and quickly assembled prefab homes multiplied. The streets in historic downtown house a high percentage of bars, but it's an attractive area to walk among crumbling brick and wooden false-front buildings. Who knows, you might stumble upon a hidden treasure in one of the many pawnshops.

And you're not far from some fine outdoor attractions: **Fossil Butte National Monument** (see section 7)—an astonishing natural storehouse of ancient plants, insects, and miniature horses—and **Flaming Gorge National Recreation Area** (see section 6 for more information), where a dam has backed up the Green River and made excellent fishing waters above, and fine raft-floating waters below.

ESSENTIALS

GETTING THERE   Continental Express (☎ **800/525-0280**) and **United Express** (☎ **800/241-6522**) fly into the Rock Springs Airport, 15 miles east of town on I-80.

The **Greyhound** bus grumbles in four times a day at 1665 Sunset Dr. (☎ **307/362-2931**).

Northeast of the Flaming Gorge National Recreation Area, Rock Springs squats at the intersection of U.S. Highway 191 and I-80. From Cheyenne, drive I-80 west for 258 miles. From Jackson, take U.S. Highway 191 south for 178 miles. For information on **road conditions** call ☎ **888/996-7623.**

VISITOR INFORMATION   The **Rock Springs Chamber of Commerce,** 1897 Dewar Dr. (☎ **307/362-3771**), puts a positive spin on Rock Springs and its immediate area. The *Sweetwater County Travel Guide,* available from the chamber, is excellent. For maps and information about **Flaming Gorge National Recreation Area,** contact the Green River Forest Service office (☎ **307/875-2871**).

GETTING AROUND   If you need a rental car, **Avis** (☎ **800/331-1212**) and **Hertz** (☎ **800/654-3131**) both maintain counters at the airport in Rock Springs. **Taxi service** is available through **Don's Taxi Service** (☎ **307/382-5207**) or **City Cab** (☎ **307/382-1100**).

SEEING THE SIGHTS

While strolling around town, pop into the **Community Fine Arts Center,** at the Sweetwater County Library, 400 C St., which contains a few original paintings by Grandma Moses and Norman Rockwell. Though not their most famous pieces by any stretch, these are early works that admirers may find notable. The **Rock Springs Historical Museum,** at 201 B St., is a great piece of Romanesque architecture. Formerly City Hall, the building now houses exhibits covering the city's mining history. The **Western Wyoming Community College Dinosaur Skeleton Collection,** 2500 College Dr., has more than 10 dinosaur displays and a few fish and plant fossils. All three museums are free.

For a rundown on upcoming local events, call the county **Events Complex** at ☎ **307/352-6789.**

WHERE TO STAY

The three hotels listed below may not be the fanciest in the state, but they have swimming pools. The **Inn at Rock Springs,** 2518 Foothill Blvd. (☎ **307/362-9600**), offers doubles for $60 a night. The **Comfort Inn,** 1670 Sunset Dr. (☎ **307/382-9490**), offers free continental breakfast every morning and a free cocktail each evening, as well as a heated outdoor pool, hot tub, and exercise room—all for $62 a night. You'll find the same amenities at the **EconoLodge,** at I-80 Exit 104 (☎ **800/548-6621** or 307/382-4217), for $69 a night.

WHERE TO DINE

✪ **Bitter Creek Brewing.** 604 Broadway. ☎ **307/362-4782.** Lunch $5–$8; dinner $10–$17. AE, MC, V. Daily 11:30am–9pm (later Fri and Sat). AMERICAN/ITALIAN.

"Life is too short to drink cheap beer," reads the sign behind the oak bar. If you agree, then Bitter Creek is the place for you. In four fermenting vats, they concoct their own special microbrews, including the popular Mustang Pale Ale, and the cleverly-named Coal Porter, a darker beer with a slight chocolate aftertaste. The menu includes blackened salmon salad, garlic chicken and pesto pizza, and portabello mushroom linguine. Maybe because the prices are a touch high, and the bar doesn't serve hard alcohol, not a lot of locals eat here. But tourists accustomed to the type of brewpubs found in Missoula and Jackson will surely appreciate Bitter Creek's addition to Rock Springs.

Sands Cafe. 1549 9th St. ☎ **307/362-5633.** Breakfast $4–$7; lunch and dinner $6–$15. AE, DISC, MC, V. Daily 7am–10pm. CHINESE.

If you're hankering for Chinese food while in Rock Springs, then head for the Buddha statue across from the Sands Inn. More like a coffee shop than a Chinese restaurant (one side looks like Anywhere, U.S.A., the other like a Beijing storefront), the food is actually quite good. And they deliver.

White Mountain Mining Company. 240 Clearview. ☎ **307/382-5265.** Main courses $11–$22. AE, DISC, MC, V. Mon–Sat 5–10pm. Bar stays open later, depending on crowd. STEAKS/SEAFOOD.

This place was overhauled in 1995 and now is one of the nicer supper clubs in southern Wyoming. The dining room tables are covered with mauve linens, and the barn-style walls give the place the feel of, well, a barn. Like any other supper club, this one serves a mean prime rib, of which they are very proud, but the deep-fried shrimp is a close second.

6 Flaming Gorge National Recreation Area

24 miles W of Rock Springs

By May of 1869, the Union Pacific had laid its tracks across Wyoming and pinned them to the eastbound rails with a golden spike. The town of Green River, 15 miles west of Rock Springs, was only a year old. And that May, 10 frontiersmen and ex-soldiers climbed off the train, lead by a veteran who'd lost his arm in the Civil War. They jumped into stout wooden boats and set down the Green River. As they slid through red canyons with the cliffs peaking high above, almost singed yellow along their rims, they named the place "Flaming Gorge."

The expedition continued down the Green and merged into the Colorado, into the Grand Canyon, weaving through boulders, portaging sandbars, and being sucked through rapids. Three men decided to hike out rather than risk the rapids. They were later found bristling with arrows. The remaining seven survived. And the leader would go on to map and record the *Great American Desert* and later to help organize and then direct the U.S. Geological Survey. The one armed-man, the famous river runner was, of course, John Wesley Powell.

Today a 455-foot damn, 15 miles into Utah, backs the river onto itself for 91 miles, nearly to the town of Green River. Each summer, jet-boaters, water skiers, and anglers skim the surface of the reservoir, while paddlers drop in below the dam for scenic and adventurous floats in the wake of Powell's boats.

ESSENTIALS

GETTING THERE   Take I-80 west from Rock Springs for 15 miles to the town of **Green River** at the junction of WY 530. (See "Driving Tour," below for information on driving through the area.)

VISITOR INFORMATION   Stop at the U.S. Forest Service's **visitor center** in **Green River** at 1450 Uinta Dr., Green River, WY 82935 (☎ 307/875-2871) to pick up maps and brochures, including detailed information about hiking and mountain-biking trails.

ADMISSION & REGULATIONS   Admission to the 200,000-acre Flaming Gorge National Recreation Area is $2 per day, $5 for 16 days. The Forest Service's regulations here are mostly common sense, aimed at preserving water quality and protecting the forest and historic sites. In addition, Wyoming and Utah fishing and boating regulations apply in those states' sections of the recreation area. Dogs are permitted on trails, but not indoors, and should be leashed at all times. For more information, call the Green River Game & Fish Department office, ☎ **800/843-8096,** or the Green River office of the U.S. Forest Service (☎ **307/875-2871**).

A DRIVING TOUR

As you drive south on WY 530, the cactus and sagebrush-filled **Devils Playground** badlands and the humpbacked rock formations of **Haystack Buttes** will be to your right. WY 530 runs the length of the recreation area's west side and provides access to the Flaming Gorge Reservoir at the **Buckboard Crossing Area,** 20 miles south, where a full-service marina is in operation during the summer.

At the **Buckboard Marina** (☎ **307/875-6927**), a 14-foot boat can be yours for $8 an hour or $60 a day. (You can rent a waterskiing boat for $20 an hour and $250 a day.) From Buckboard, it's another 25 miles to Lucerne Valley and the **Lucerne**

Marina across the border in Utah (☎ **435/784-3483**). During the summer season, you can rent a houseboat, minimum of 3 nights, for $598 (36') or $950 (50'). For the whole week, the smaller boats go for $1,060 and the larger ones for $1,650.

From WY 530, pick up UT 44 just across the state line in Manila, Utah. UT 44 runs south then east for 27 miles to pick up U.S. Highway 191. Along this route you'll catch glimpses of Utah's Uinta Mountains to the west and may see bighorn sheep in nearby **Sheep Creek Canyon,** which has been designated a special geological area by the Forest Service because of its dramatically twisted and upturned rocks. A mostly paved 11-mile loop road cuts off from UT 44, offering a half-hour tour of this beautiful, narrow canyon, with its lavish display of rocks that have eroded into intricate patterns, a process that began with the uplifting of the Uinta Mountains millions of years ago. This loop may be closed in winter.

Eventually, you'll come to the **Red Canyon Overlook** on the southern edge of the gorge, where a rainbow of colors adorns 1,000-foot-tall cliffs. In Wyoming, highways are farther from the rim, offering fewer opportunities to see the river and its canyons than in Utah. Here, you'll be able to drink them in. The **Red Canyon Visitor Center** (open 9:30am to 5pm in summer) is nearby, as is **Flaming Gorge Dam.**

To head back to Wyoming, take U.S. Highway 191 north and south away from the eastern edge of the gorge. From the junction of UT 44 and U.S. Highway 191, it's 16 miles to the border. Once you're at the state line, it's 30 miles to the turnoff for **Firehole Canyon,** an access to the gorge that offers views of the magnificent spires known as **Chimney Rocks.** Keep going north on 191 and you'll hit I-80 again.

GETTING OUTSIDE

For more information about the Utah portion of Flaming Gorge National Recreation Area, including additional outdoor recreational activities and outfitters, lodging options, and other nearby sites of interest, see *Frommer's Utah.*

BOATING   During the summer, the **Buckboard Marina** (☎ 307/875-6927) rents 14-foot boats for $8 an hour and $60 a day. Or if big-engine waterskiing boats are more your speed, they rent those for $20 an hour and $250 a day.

From Buckboard, it's another 25 miles to Lucerne Valley and the **Lucerne Marina** across the border in Utah (☎ **435/784-3483**). During the summer season, you can rent a houseboat, minimum of 3 nights, for $598 (36') or $950 (50'). For the whole week, the smaller boats go for $1,060 and the larger ones for $1,650.

CAMPING   The U.S. Forest Service maintains about 20 sites in the area. Visit their office in Green River (listed above) for maps and other information.

FISHING   For fishing information and excursions, call **Creative Fishing Adventures** (☎ 435/784-3301) or **The Good Life Guide Service** (☎ 307/786-2132 in winter or 801/784-3121 in summer). Cliff at Good Life will take two people out for 4 hours in the morning for $200.

WHERE TO DINE

Penny's Diner. 1170 W. Flaming Gorge Way, Green River. ☎ **307/875-3500,** ext. 550. Breakfast $5; dinner $7. Daily 24 hours. DISC, MC, V. AMERICAN.

Step back in time at the retro Penny's Diner. Although more replica than Real McCoy, this is a classic greasy spoon for all the right reasons: lots of chrome, a juke box, open short-order grill, milk shakes, cherry pie a la mode, weak coffee, and—of course—breakfast served all day.

7 Killpecker Sand Dunes & Fossil Butte National Monument

Killpecker Sand Dunes: 36 miles W of Rock Springs; 140 miles SE of Jackson

KILLPECKER SAND DUNES

North of Rock Springs and east of Eden (we're not kidding . . . it's a small town) swell the **Killpecker Sand Dunes** —the largest active dunes in North America. Here hikers can scale and descend the heaving hills of white sand, where the noon heat shimmers and the midnight cold cuts. Rock climbers trek to **Boar's Tusk,** a standing volcanic plug, while ethnography buffs seek the **White Mountain Petroglyphs;** and photographers with high-powered telephoto lenses should be on the lookout for wild horses.

Bird-watchers will especially enjoy the **Seedskadee Wildlife Refuge,** where they may see geese, sandhill cranes, and great blue herons along the miles of marshes along the Green River.

GETTING THERE   To get to the dunes, drive WY 191 north from Rock Springs 36 miles to Eden. Turning east, you'll bump along at least 20 miles of gravel road. Bring a compass, plenty of emergency water, and a map. It's best to contact the Bureau of Land Management (☎ 307/352-0256) before blazing the trail on your own. *Note:* When it rains, the bentonite on these rough roads turns to glue, and smart drivers stop trying.

FOSSIL BUTTE NATIONAL MONUMENT

Standing at the base of Fossil Butte, gazing up 1,000 feet at the rust and ochre stained cliffs, with the crackling desert wind rattling sage and tumbleweeds, you'd never guess that eons ago you'd have been looking up from the bottom of a sub-tropical ocean. Some 50 million years ago, during the Eocene Epoch, millions of fish wriggled across this sky. With the ebb and flow of millennia, they sifted into the mud, and fossilized.

Today, on weekends, visitors can join paleontologists and dig for the ancient remains of fish, insects, turtles, birds, and even bats. You can hike (be watchful for rattlesnakes) or learn more about the geology of the area at **Fossil Butte Visitor Center** (☎ 307/877-4455). It's open daily 8am to 5pm in summer, but only until 4:30pm during the rest of the year, and closed during holidays and bad snow.

GETTING THERE   Head east on I-80 past Green River, then exit onto U.S. Highway 30. Go about 40 miles though Kemmerer, a few more miles further east, then follow the signs 3½ miles to the visitor center.

ALSO WORTH A LOOK   No need to rush through Kemmerer, an old mining town with a pleasant central square and some fine old buildings, set along the Hams Fork River. Why not visit the very first **JCPenney store** and the original home of its founder, James Cash Penney? The store, despite being both small and historic, is a regular JCPenney, open year-round. The house is open 11am to 6pm in summer, with free admission. The "mother" store is located on the town's central square, at 722 JCPenney Drive; the home is 1 block north on the same street.

Appendix: Montana & Wyoming in Depth

by Geoff O'Gara

Years ago, when I tired of the suits and flat horizons of Washington, D.C., I went to the Library of Congress and looked up Wyoming in the subject index. There were only a few listings; one of them was the 1930s Federal Writers Project Guide to Wyoming. In it was this wonderful line, which set my compass west: "In Wyoming, the past presses so closely on the present."

When you travel through this uncluttered country, the old stories come easily to life. The setting is still here as it was: the remote wilderness of Yellowstone's Thorofare country, the Gallatin valleys where Sacajawea led Lewis and Clark, the sandstone arroyos of Butch Cassidy's Hole in the Wall country. The written history of the West begins only a few generations before us, and the premature myth of the "Wild West" spills over into our own century, when a last gunslinger or two grew old in Hollywood.

There's a little more pavement than there was 75 years ago, but the open horizon and hospitality are still here in Montana and Wyoming. There are still so many remote places beyond the view from the interstate, and so many people who invest their sweat and their wit in creating independent lives. When you take your first look around, this is what many travelers enjoy about Montana and Wyoming. When you take your second, third, and fourth look around, you realize how much more there is yet to discover.

1 The Natural Environment

In Montana and Wyoming, the earth seems to have turned itself inside out, its hot insides leaking into hot springs and geysers, its bony spine thrust right through the skin of the continent to form the Continental Divide. It's a geologist's dream, with ancient Pre-Cambrian rock uplifted to the surface and rich pools of oil hidden all over the region. And to a biologist it's heaven, one of the last regions in the world with enough open space for rangy animals like elk and pronghorn and grizzly bears to roam free.

Plains, basin, and range alternate in the Northern Rockies environment, all set at a high-altitude environment that suffers extremes of weather and temperature. These dramatic, changing landscapes make Montana and Wyoming two of the best driving states in the country for travelers who like their scenery dynamic and dramatic.

The western side of both states is mountainous, dragging moisture from the clouds moving west to east, storing it in snowpack and alpine lakes. Because the ridge of the Rockies wrings moisture from the atmosphere, you find deeper, denser forest extending far to the west, while on the east side, the lodgepole, pine, spruce, and fir forest gives way in the foothills to the Great Plains, a vast, flat land characterized by sagebrush, native grasses, and cottonwood-lined river bottoms.

But a lot of the landscape dates back over 100 million years when the collision of tectonic plates buckled the earth's crust and thrust these mountains upward; later, glaciers (of which some vestiges remain) carved the canyons and left moraine hills at the mountains' base. The tallest peaks in Wyoming are located within the Wind River Range, which rises from the high plains of South Pass north of Rock Springs and runs northwest to the Yellowstone Plateau. Nine of the peaks in the Winds have elevations over 13,000 feet; **Gannett Peak,** at 13,785 feet, is the highest in the state. Several other mountain ranges append to Yellowstone from the south—including the Absarokas and the stunning Tetons—and from Yellowstone north into Montana run more dramatic ranges, including the Gallatin, Madison, Missions, Bitterroots, Cabinets and Beartooths, where you'll find Montana's highest point, **Granite Peak,** at 12,799 feet.

The **Continental Divide** enters Montana from Canada and traces a snaking path through these mountains, south toward Butte and then southwest to form the state's southwest border with Idaho. From there, the Divide heads west, crossing into Yellowstone National Park just south of West Yellowstone and then turning south in Wyoming. Both Montana and Wyoming have rivers flowing west to the Pacific and east to the Atlantic—near the divide you'll find several Atlantic and Pacific creeks.

You'll also find here the headwaters of major river systems—the Flathead and Clark Fork heading west into the Columbia from Montana, along with the Snake from Wyoming; the Yellowstone and North Platte and Madison joining the Missouri bound east; and the Green from Wyoming emptying into the Colorado heading south. These rivers are the lifeblood of the region, supplying irrigation and fisheries and power from dams. Montana also boasts the country's largest freshwater lake west of the Mississippi: **Flathead Lake. Yellowstone** and **Jackson lakes** are Wyoming's two largest natural bodies of water, located within national parks in that state's northwest corner.

Montana is greener, with more abundant alpine wilderness and bigger rivers, while Wyoming has been dealt a more interesting hand of natural wonders: Waterfalls, geysers, and other geothermal oddities are synonymous with Yellowstone; **Devils Tower,** near the state's Black Hills region of the northeast, is a natural landmark of clustered rock columns that rise more than 1,280 feet above the surrounding plains. At Wyoming's Red Desert, south of Lander, the Continental Divide splits to form an enclosed basin where no water can escape, and nearby you find **Fossil Butte National Monument,** an archaeological treasure chest of fossilized fish and ancient, miniature horses.

The states are characterized by unusually long, cold winters and short summers of hot days and cool nights. Temperature ranges are dramatic, and are largely dependent on elevation. Except along the far western edge of Montana, precipitation here is less than 30 inches a year. It's considerably less as you journey east and south. But the snowpacks in the high mountains—over 200 inches accumulate in some areas—are like a water bank, melting through the summer and keeping the rivers running.

2 Environmental Issues

The environmental issues that get attention in the Northern Rockies usually have to do with the parks: How do we stop the building of second homes around the edges? How do we reduce the impact of cars and snowmobiles? How do we keep the free-roaming herds of elk and bison from spreading brucellosis—a disease that causes cattle to abort—outside the park?

But the real impacts are occurring outside the parks, in areas less popular and less noticed. Oil and gas development continues in "elephant" fields around the region, particularly south of Jackson, Wyoming. Big mining operations have been proposed in delicate areas like the Stillwater Complex in southern Montana.

Ranchers and farmers have always been powerful in this region—they can take the time to work in the legislature during the winter—and they often want wildlife protection to take a back seat to livestock and irrigation and farming. Grazing leases on state and federal lands are considered a property right, and agencies have not always been vigilant about overgrazing and habitat damage. But the livestock industry's power seems to be waning—certainly the reintroduction of wolves in Yellowstone showed new muscle in the region's conservation forces. Exotic species present a new problem, particularly in the fisheries, where lake trout crowd out native cutthroat, and whirling disease has infected some of the region's trout streams.

Logging in the northern Rockies has cost the region not just scenery but critical wildlife habitat. But the timber industry, too, has seen better days—over the last 20 years, money-losing sales on public lands have been challenged and sometimes stopped. Forest managers are modifying plans to reduce the amount of logging in slow-growth forests.

As these longtime stalwart industries of the region decline, tourism is advancing. It brings its own problems: traffic, building construction, and other impacts, as well. Stay tuned.

3 The Northern Rockies Today

New people are moving to the northern Rockies, but they are quite different from the people who came before them. Those people were homesteaders, putting down roots and raising families, building communities and "going native." The much greater wealth and mobility of today's Americans have brought a different crowd. Many are tourists who decided on an earlier visit that this was where they would retire. Many come only for a particular season, spending the rest of the year at another, often urban, home. A growing number make their livings long-distance, through a modem or mail. Cities with scenery and recreation are thriving—Missoula, Jackson, Bozeman—and the new residents are bringing some cosmopolitan tastes.

Some dabble in ranching, but even the old-timers find that a hard business to make a living at. The CEOs who've built mansions in Jackson may save as much on income taxes annually by living here (where there's no state income tax) as a Meeteetse rancher makes off his cattle in a year. Once they're here, they may resist growth—trying to shut the gate behind them.

Whether Wyoming and Montana can build year-round economies with tourism as the engine remains to be seen. The natives remain practical, sometimes stoical people—they know you have to change and adapt. They've learned the lessons of this region's short history, so they have no illusions about a past golden age. They also know the value of patience, and withholding judgement, and that's what they're doing in regard to the newcomers and the new economy—they know that if you wait 5 minutes, in this country, the weather will likely change again.

4 History 101

MONTANA

IN THE BEGINNING   The first people to wonder at the Big Sky was Folsom Man, who arrived sometime after the end of the last Ice Age about 12,000 years ago, and hung around until superseded by the Yuma culture about 6,800 years ago.

About 3,000 years ago, more modern Indian culture began to emerge, eventually evolving into the Kootenai, Kalispell, Flathead, Shoshone, Crow, Blackfeet Chippewa, Cree, Cheyenne, Gros Ventres, and Assiniboine that lived across the state when Europeans first encountered them.

These tribes got their meat by still hunts—setting fire to the prairie and then surrounding their quarry—or by drives. There have been more than 400 pishkun, or buffalo jump sites, uncovered in Montana, and you can see a few of them preserved on your travels through the state. Buffalo provided food, clothing, shelter, and ornament for the tribes.

EUROPEAN EXPLORERS   The first European to enter Montana was Pierre Gauliter, Sieur de Varennes de la Verendrye.

Verendrye, like many after him, had heard of a river that flowed to the western sea and was looking for the Northwest Passage. He came in 1738, but retreated. His sons, Pierre and Francois, returned in 1743 and described the "shining mountains," generally believed to be the Bighorns of southern Montana and northern Wyoming. But threats of a looming Indian war, and perhaps the reports of the rugged country that was ahead of them, discouraged the brothers and they returned to Montreal. No other white men came to the country for 60 years.

Those white men were with the expedition of Lewis and Clark, the great journey of discovery on the Western landscape. The explorers reached the mouth of the Yellowstone River on April 26, 1805, and pushed upriver to the Shoshone, where they were warmly greeted, the result of having coincidentally brought

Dateline

- **11,000 B.C.** Earliest evidence of man in Montana.
- **1620s** Arrival of the Plains Indians.
- **1803** The eastern part of Montana becomes a territory through the Louisiana Purchase.
- **1805-06** Lewis and Clark journey through the northern Rockies to and from the Pacific coast.
- **1864** Montana becomes an official territory; gold is discovered at Last Chance Gulch in Helena.
- **1876** Defeat of George A. Custer at the Battle of the Little Bighorn.
- **1877** The surrender of Chief Joseph of the Nez Perce in the Bear Paw Mountains.
- **1880** The Utah and Northern Railroad enters Montana.
- **1883** The Northern Pacific Railroad crosses Montana.
- **1889** Montana, on November 8, becomes the 41st state in the Union.
- **1893** The University of Montana in Missoula and Montana State University in Bozeman are founded.
- **1910** Glacier National Park is established.
- **1914** Women's suffrage amendment passes.
- **1917–19** Missoula native Jeannette Rankin becomes the first woman elected to U.S. Congress and votes against U.S. participation in World War I.
- **1940** Fort Peck Dam is completed. Jeannette Rankin is again elected to the U.S. House of Representatives;

continues

she is the only member of Congress to vote against U.S. involvement in World War II.

- **1965** Construction of Yellowtail Dam is completed.
- **1973** Montana's third state constitution goes into effect; it includes the right to a clean and healthful environment and the goal of preserving the cultural integrity of the state's Native Americans.
- **1983** Anaconda Copper Mining Company shuts down.
- **1986** Montana spends $56 million on environmental protection programs.
- **1995** Wolves are reintroduced to Yellowstone. Daytime speed limits are abolished.
- **1998** New, $6-million Lewis & Clark National Historic Trail Interpretive Center opens in Great Falls.

Shoshone chief Cameahwait's long-lost sister Sacajawea with them as one of their guides.

They continued on through the Bitterroot Valley and eventually over Lolo Pass and on into Idaho. They returned the following year and sped through the state—it was downstream now—along two different routes, meeting again at the mouth of the Yellowstone.

SETTLEMENT   The first industry in Montana was trapping, as John Jacob Astor, Alexander Ross, and William Ashley brought in their hearty voyageurs to clear the country of beaver for the European hat market.

The first steamboat landed at Fort Benton—the westernmost navigable section of the Missouri River—in 1859. Until 1862, some four cargo boats a year landed there. But after gold was discovered at Bannack, that number increased to 39 boats a year.

The discovery of gold opened Montana's Wild West period for real, a period you can see preserved in the Bannack/Virginia City/Nevada City sites. The fact that these towns were 400 miles from official justice attracted bad men from all over the West.

In 1864, as a semblance of order was restored in the Wild West, and as "traces of color" were being found in Last Chance Gulch in present-day Helena, the Montana Territory was formed and Sidney Edgerton became the first territorial governor. The capital was moved to Virginia City and a constitutional convention was called as the first step toward statehood. A constitution was drafted and sent to St. Louis for printing. It was, alas, lost somewhere along the way.

In 1884, another constitutional convention drafted another constitution. This one didn't work either, for one reason or another, and in 1889, under Congressional Enabling Law, the now well-practiced delegates came up with a third one. Taking no chances, they prefaced it with the Magna Carta, the Declaration of Independence, the Articles of Confederation, and the U.S. Constitution. Montana finally became a state in November 1889.

TROUBLE BETWEEN THE INDIANS & THE SETTLERS   Montana's Indian tribes were not at first invariably hostile to the whites, and signed a number of treaties signaling their peaceful intentions. But the influx of settlers and the confinement of tribes to the reservation resulted in dissatisfaction among the original inhabitants, and escalating hostilities against the whites. In 1876, the War Department launched a campaign against the Sioux and Cheyenne. At the end of June that year, this culminated in the **Battle of the Little Bighorn** and the death of all of the command under Gen. George Armstrong Custer.

The Indian victory was only a temporary setback for the whites, however, and by 1880 all the Indians had been settled on reservations. The last action of the Indian War period occurred in Montana with the heroic flight of Chief

Joseph's Nez Perce from their northern Idaho reservation toward Canada in 1877.

INDUSTRIALIZATION   When copper was first discovered in the silver mines in Butte, no one could have foretold its effects on Montana's future. This vast territory, full of prospectors and railworkers, soon became the home of two of the richest men in America, who would not only seize political power within the territory, but take complete control of the everyday lives of its citizens. As copper wiring became an integral part of several new electrical technologies, Butte became an important resource for America. One of the first men to profit was Marcus Daly, an Irish immigrant, who came to Butte in his mid-30s and purchased his first silver mine. The mine proved to yield incredibly large amounts of the purest copper in the world instead, and soon a smelter was built near the source at Warm Springs in Anaconda, the town that took its name from the company Daly founded.

William Clark, the other baron of the copper mines, was a Horatio Alger type. An average youth from Pennsylvania, he rooted around in mines until, like many others on the mining circuit, his efforts took him to Montana. His wealth was quickly amassed from a keen business acumen that prompted him to purchase mining operations, electric companies, water companies, and banks. Though his interest in wealth was most assuredly magnificent, it was an inflated ego that drove him to the political arena. His was the major voice in the territorial constitution proceedings in 1884, and when Montana held its last territorial election, Clark was determined to get into public office as Montana's representative.

The war that commenced between these two men was rooted in Clark's determination to hold political office and Daly's unwillingness to see him do it. Montana finally became a state in 1889, after 5 tough years of appeals to the U.S. Congress. The bellicose millionaires were so set on controlling the young state's political interests that they bought newspapers or created them just to have a printed voice. They stuffed money into the pockets of voters and agreed on nothing. In Montana's first congressional election, Clark fell three votes shy of his bid, and the legislature adjourned without ever selecting a second senator. So in Montana's embarrassing first years as a state it had but half of its due representation in Washington, all because of two pigheaded millionaires who couldn't accept the victory of the other.

The fight for capital status came along in 1894. Helena had been the capital, but the constitution held that the site must be determined by the voters. Daly wanted his newly created Anaconda to be the capital. Clark, with interests of his own in Helena, wanted that city to remain the capital. Given Clark's record, it seemed that Helena was doomed. But the fact that Anaconda was ruled by the strong arm of the Anaconda Mining Company caused voters to turn to the diversified ways of Helena. For once in his life, William Clark was not only rich, but appreciated by the masses. Or so it seemed.

With his thirst for public office revitalized, Clark did his damnedest to buy his way into the U.S. Senate, and pulled it off. Daly, infuriated by the way his bitter enemy achieved his seat, demanded an investigation by the Senate. The investigation uncovered a wealth of impropriety on Clark's part, so he resigned and went home to Montana kicking and screaming. Down, but for some crazy reason not out, Clark took a deep breath and plunged immediately back into the thick of things. Once when Robert Burns Smith, governor of Montana and hardly an ardent admirer of Clark's, was out of town, Clark arranged for his friend, A.E. Spriggs, the lieutenant governor, to accept his resignation and in the stead of Governor Smith, appoint Clark to the Senate. This lunatic act embarrassed the state of Montana, causing Smith to nullify the appointment upon his return. Meanwhile, Daly had sold his Anaconda Copper Company to Standard Oil to form the Amalgamated Copper Company, and Clark was now up against a nameless, faceless opponent.

He chose to link his fate with another, younger copper king, Augustus Heinze, who had a reputation as a briber of courts, hoping to form an alliance that Amalgamated couldn't match. Heinze was more influential at this point than the older, less active Clark, and the two soon had complete control of the mining world in Montana. It seemed as if Clark's last wish—to garner the Senate post he had been denied for so long—was to be realized with Heinze's help. And rather anticlimactically, it was. Clark served his state as a senator from 1901 to 1907.

Though the discovery of copper in Montana was important, it is now commonly thought of as just another chapter in the history of the state's misuse of natural resources, as evidenced by the Berkeley Pit in Butte, an ugly, massive hole in the earth that today stands vacant. Montana's copper mining industry also brought its share of unmitigated disaster to future generations. Marcus Daly died in 1900 without control of his beloved Anaconda Copper Company. Augustus Heinze sold his interest in mining in 1906 and lost his fortune on Wall Street. William Clark, who at one time in his life was believed to be earning $17 million a month, died in 1925 at the age of 86 in New York with a net worth estimated at $150 million. Their legacy: a reputation as the ultimate robber barons and polluters.

THE 20TH CENTURY At the beginning of the 20th century, Montana experienced a boom of a different type. The Indian Wars had ended, and white settlers declared the land a safe and fertile haven for the farming lifestyle. The U.S. government helped things along in 1909 when it passed the Enlarged Homestead Act, giving 320 acres to anyone willing to stay on it for at least 5 months out of the year for a minimum of 3 years. Homesteaders came from all over the country to stake a piece of land, and the sweeping northern plains were advertised shamelessly by railroad companies and real estate agencies as ideal for farming.

Sentiment for the homesteaders was never good, and the generalization that homesteaders were stupid, dirty people became increasingly popular. Even the renowned cowboy artist Charlie Russell, who had no stake in the matter, expressed antifarming sentiments. The truth is, Montana's agricultural backbone was created by these extraordinary people who came west to settle farms. Wheat became—and still is—the major crop in such areas as the Judith Basin in the center of the state and Choteau County north of Great Falls.

As more and more homesteaders came to settle in Montana and farming became a mainstay of the state's economy, women began to emerge from their submissive roles in the home and take part in a suffrage movement on a large scale. In the middle of it all, though isolated by geography, was young Jeannette Rankin from Missoula. In 1914, voters narrowly passed the amendment for women's suffrage; 2 years later, Rankin became the first woman elected to the U.S. Congress. Though her stay was brief, she was there long enough to vote against United States involvement in World War I. In 1940, she was elected once more to the U.S. House of Representatives, and, as an avowed pacifist, became the only member of Congress to vote against American involvement in World War II.

When the Great Depression hit Montana, farming was enduring some rather dry difficulties, and jobs were nowhere to be found. Roosevelt's New

Deal was a lifesaver. Without the jobs created by the Civilian Conservation Corps and the Works Progress Administration, the state might have never recovered its economic balance. The most tangible salvation came when work began on the Fort Peck Dam in the mid-1930s, employing more than 50,000 workers over the course of its construction. The earth-filled dam, the largest of its kind in the world, took almost 5 years to complete.

Since the 1950s, the story of Montana has been an evolving one, with tourism and agriculture playing key roles. While farming and cattle-ranching methods have become much more sophisticated, many of the younger generation, expected to carry on the farming tradition, have opted to settle in the larger cities. Though agriculture still drives the economic engine of the state, tourism makes a huge financial contribution, and the face of ranch life has changed. Empty nests in ranches are now filled with guests paying to participate in ranch activities.

WYOMING

IN THE BEGINNING The earliest indications of man in Wyoming date back 20,000 years. No one knows the identity of these early inhabitants, nor can anyone say with certainly who created the Medicine Wheel in the Bighorn Mountains or the petroglyphs carved in rocks in various parts of the state. The earliest known settlers in what is now Wyoming were the Crow, Sioux, Cheyenne, Arapahoe—tribes that came from the east, of the Algonquin language family—and the Shoshone and Bannock, who came from the Great Basin, more closely related to the peoples of Central America. The lifestyles of these tribes were greatly changed by the arrival of two European innovations—the horse and the gun—which brought on the flamboyant Plains Indian culture of the 18th and 19th centuries. The first white men in Wyoming were fur trappers, and the first of them was John Colter, who left the Lewis and Clark expedition in 1806 to wander south through Yellowstone and possibly Jackson Hole.

SETTLEMENT The Oregon Trail and other major pioneer routes west cut right through Wyoming and the territories of the Sioux, Shoshone, Arapaho, and other tribes. Without much regard for the people they were displacing, the non-Indians killed a great deal of the game the Indians depended on; Indian bands, in turn, harassed and sometimes attacked the travelers. Indian tribes were increasingly pushed west into tighter spaces, and there was warfare among tribes; Shoshone Chief Washakie often allied himself with the non-Indian newcomers against enemies like the Sioux and Crow.

Dateline

- **1807** John Colter explores the Yellowstone area, coming as far south as Jackson Hole.
- **1812** Fur trader Robert Stuart discovers South Pass, the gentlest route across the northern Rockies.
- **1843** Pioneers begin traveling west on the Oregon Trail through Wyoming.
- **1848** U.S. Army moves into Fort Laramie to protect Oregon Trail travelers from Indians.
- **1852** The first school in the state is founded at Fort Laramie.
- **1860** The Pony Express begins its run from Missouri to California, through Wyoming.
- **1867** The Union Pacific Railroad enters Wyoming.
- **1868** Treaty of Fort Bridger creates the Shoshone Reservation in northwest Wyoming.
- **1868** The Territory of Wyoming is created by Congress.
- **1869** Wyoming Territorial Legislature grants women the right to vote and hold elective office.
- **1870** Esther H. Morris becomes the nation's first female justice of the peace.

continues

- **1872** Yellowstone National Park is established as the nation's first national park.
- **1884** First oil well drilled in Wyoming.
- **1886-87** Great blizzard decimates ranches of eastern Wyoming, sending many "cattle barons" into bankruptcy.
- **1889** The state constitution is adopted.
- **1890** Wyoming becomes the nation's 44th state.
- **1892** The Johnson County War breaks out over a dispute about cattle rustling.
- **1897** The first Frontier Days rodeo is staged.
- **1906** Devils Tower is established by President Roosevelt as the country's first national monument.
- **1910** Buffalo Bill Dam is completed.
- **1925** Nellie Taylor Ross becomes the nation's first female governor.
- **1927** Man claiming to be Butch Cassidy visits Wyoming from Washington, suggesting outlaw was not killed in Bolivia.
- **1929** Grand Teton National Park is established, consisting of only the peaks.
- **1929** Oil thefts discovered on federal land at Teapot Dome, a scandal that rocks the Harding Administration.
- **1950** National forest and private lands added to form Grand Teton National Park as it is today.
- **1965** Minuteman missile sites are completed near Cheyenne.
- **1973** The Arab oil embargo sends oil prices skyrocketing, instigating a huge oil drilling boom in Wyoming.
- **1988** Five fires break out around Yellowstone National Park, burning through the summer and blackening approximately one-third of the park.

continues

In a series of treaties, beginning with the Fort Laramie Treaty of 1851, the tribes gave up rights to some of their homelands in return for reservations and other considerations. The discovery of gold in areas like the Black Hills and South Pass, and the routes of settlers, led to numerous treaty violations and continued conflict. Tribes in the east were being evicted and shipped west. U.S. Army troops were sent out. Treaties were modified and broken; some tribal leaders, recognizing the inexorable advance of the whites, and the decline of the health and culture of their own people, decided the only alternative was to fight the invaders.

TROUBLE BETWEEN THE INDIANS & THE SETTLERS Sitting Bull and Crazy Horse of the Hunkpapa Sioux joined forces with members of the Cheyenne and Arapaho tribes along the Little Bighorn River. It was here in June, 1876, that the greatest gathering of Indians ever assembled defeated George Custer and his men in certainly the greatest consolidated Indian victory. Inevitably this led to a backlash, a series of attacks on Indian communities, culminating in the death of Sitting Bull and the massacre of Big Foot and his Sioux followers in 1890 at Wounded Knee, South Dakota. Chief Washakie of the Shoshone was one of the few great Indian leaders still alive, though his star was diminished by his decision to ally his tribe with the whites. That alliance got his people one of the finest reservations in the West —and the only one in Wyoming. Then the U.S. Army moved the now threadbare Arapaho, traditional enemies of the Shoshone, to Wind River "temporarily," and the two tribes began an uncomfortable cohabitation that continues to this day.

INDUSTRIALIZATION & THE 20TH CENTURY Big cattle operators moved into Wyoming in the 19th century, running their cattle on the open range and controlling the territory's economy and political scene through organizations like the Cheyenne Social Club. A couple of severe winters in the 1880s, and the influx of new settlers building fences raised tensions. When the cattle "barons" brought in hired guns to clear out the newcomers, the Johnson County War of 1892 erupted. The wealthy cattlemen claimed the newcomers were rustlers. But that show of muscle was futile in halting the longtime decline of the big livestock owners. Though the ranch community would long dominate Wyoming politics, the true economic hammer in the state would soon be the energy industry.

The state's fate has been closely tied to oil and gas and coal, with the economy rising and falling in synch with world prices. The boom and bust of the energy industry has prompted repeated calls for a more diversified economy, but the state has largely missed the joyride of the Clinton years.

- **1995** Wolves are reintroduced to Yellowstone.
- **1996** The National Park Service institutes voluntary ban on climbing Devils Tower during June to respect Native American religious ceremonies; climbers file suit to overturn action.

5 Recommended Books

BOOKS

FICTION   Start with some classics: A. B. Guthrie's *The Big Sky* (Houghton Mifflin, 1947) is now a Montana classic, as is Owen Wister's *The Virginian* (Macmillan, 1929), set in frontier Wyoming. Then move on to contemporary fiction, where the shelves are getting crowded with work by authors who've moved here or visited. Don't fail to read the classic fly-fishing novella, *A River Runs Through It* (University of Chicago Press, 1976) by Norman Maclean. *Fool's Crow* (Viking Penguin, 1986) by James Welch (a native Montanan, in two senses of the word) and *Heart Mountain* (Viking Penguin, 1989) by Gretel Ehrlich are fictional stories which revolve around Native American and Asian characters. Annie Proulx's *Wyoming Stories* (Harcourt Brace Jovanovich, 1999) is a recent addition by a fine writer who's spent considerable time around Sheridan. Poet James Glavin's beautifully written *The Meadow* (Henry Holt, 1992) is set in the Tie Siding area of southeast Wyoming.

Montana is fortunate to have the best of its literature compiled in one volume, *The Last Best Place* (University of Montana Press, 1988), the definitive anthology of Montana writings, from Native American myths to contemporary short stories.

NONFICTION   Novelist Ivan Doig wrote a beautiful memoir about his youth in Montana, *This House of Sky* (Harcourt Brace Jovanovich, 1978). Gretel Ehrlich's *The Solace of Open Spaces* (Viking Penguin, 1986) is a telling account of Wyoming ranch life that is beautifully written and evocative. Both are real-life illustrations of the experiences many are seeking when they visit the West. If you're interested in obscure facts, *Wyoming Place Names* (Mountain Press, 1988), by Mae Urbanek, and *Names on the Face of Montana* (Mountain Press, 1983), by Roberta Carkeek Cheney, will engross you. Also full of random and amusing trivia is *Wyoming Almanac* (Skyline West, 1989) by Phil, David, and Steven Roberts.

If your interests lean more toward geography, check out the *Roadside Geology of Montana* (Mountain Press, 1986), by David Alt and Donald W. Hyndman, and the similar *Roadside Geology of Wyoming* (Mountain Press, 1988), by David R. Largeson and Darwin R. Spearing.

HISTORY   Perhaps the best, and easiest, read about the history and culture of Montana is found between the covers of *Montana, High, Wide and Handsome* (University of Nebraska Press, 1983), written by Joseph Howard and first published in 1944. You'll find copies in used-book stores.

Index

FROMMER'S® COMPLETE TRAVEL GUIDES

Alaska
Amsterdam
Arizona
Atlanta
Australia
Austria
Bahamas
Barcelona, Madrid &
  Seville
Beijing
Belgium, Holland &
  Luxembourg
Bermuda
Boston
British Columbia & the
  Canadian Rockies
Budapest & the Best of
  Hungary
California
Canada
Cancún, Cozumel &
  the Yucatán
Cape Cod, Nantucket &
  Martha's Vineyard
Caribbean
Caribbean Cruises & Ports
  of Call
Caribbean Ports of Call
Carolinas & Georgia
Chicago
China
Colorado
Costa Rica
Denmark
Denver, Boulder & Colorado
  Springs
England
Europe

European Cruises & Ports
  of Call
Florida
France
Germany
Greece
Greek Islands
Hawaii
Hong Kong
Honolulu, Waikiki &
  Oahu
Ireland
Israel
Italy
Jamaica
Japan
Las Vegas
London
Los Angeles
Maryland & Delaware
Maui
Mexico
Miami & the Keys
Montana & Wyoming
Montréal & Québec City
Munich & the Bavarian
  Alps
Nashville & Memphis
Nepal
New England
New Mexico
New Orleans
New York City
New Zealand
Nova Scotia, New Brunswick
  & Prince Edward Island
Oregon
Paris

Philadelphia & the
  Amish Country
Portugal
Prague & the Best of the
  Czech Republic
Provence & the Riviera
Puerto Rico
Rome
San Antonio & Austin
San Diego
San Francisco
Santa Fe, Taos & Albuquerque
Scandinavia
Scotland
Seattle & Portland
Singapore & Malaysia
South Africa
Southeast Asia
South Pacific
Spain
Sweden
Switzerland
Thailand
Tokyo
Toronto
Tuscany & Umbria
USA
Utah
Vancouver & Victoria
Vermont, New Hampshire
  & Maine
Vienna & the Danube Valley
Virgin Islands
Virginia
Walt Disney World &
  Orlando
Washington, D.C.
Washington State

FROMMER'S® DOLLAR-A-DAY GUIDES

Australia from $50 a Day
California from $60 a Day
Caribbean from $70 a Day
England from $70 a Day
Europe from $60 a Day

Florida from $60 a Day
Hawaii from $70 a Day
Ireland from $60 a Day
Italy from $70 a Day
London from $85 a Day

New York from $80 a Day
Paris from $85 a Day
San Francisco from $60 a Day
Washington, D.C.,
  from $60 a Day

FROMMER'S® PORTABLE GUIDES

Acapulco, Ixtapa &
  Zihuatanejo
Alaska Cruises & Ports of Call
Bahamas
Baja & Los Cabos
Berlin
California Wine Country
Charleston & Savannah
Chicago

Dublin
Hawaii: The Big Island
Las Vegas
London
Maine Coast
Maui
New Orleans
New York City
Paris

Puerto Vallarta, Manzanillo
  & Guadalajara
San Diego
San Francisco
Sydney
Tampa & St. Petersburg
Venice
Washington, D.C.

FROMMER'S® NATIONAL PARK GUIDES

Family Vacations in the
  National Parks
Grand Canyon

National Parks of the
  American West
Rocky Mountain

Yellowstone & Grand Teton
Yosemite & Sequoia/
  Kings Canyon
Zion & Bryce Canyon

FROMMER'S® MEMORABLE WALKS

Chicago
London

New York
Paris

San Francisco
Washington D.C.

FROMMER'S® GREAT OUTDOOR GUIDES

New England
Northern California

Southern California & Baja
Southern New England

Washington & Oregon

FROMMER'S® BORN TO SHOP GUIDES

Born to Shop: China
Born to Shop: France

Born to Shop: Italy
Born to Shop: London

Born to Shop: New York
Born to Shop: Paris

FROMMER'S® IRREVERENT GUIDES

Amsterdam
Boston
Chicago
Las Vegas

London
Los Angeles
Manhattan
New Orleans

Paris
San Francisco
Seattle & Portland
Vancouver

Walt Disney World
Washington, D.C.

FROMMER'S® BEST-LOVED DRIVING TOURS

America
Britain
California

Florida
France
Germany

Ireland
Italy
New England

Scotland
Spain
Western Europe

THE UNOFFICIAL GUIDES®

Bed & Breakfasts in
  California
Bed & Breakfasts in
  New England
Bed & Breakfasts in
  the Northwest
Beyond Disney
Branson, Missouri
California with Kids
Chicago

Cruises
Disneyland
Florida with Kids
Golf Vacations in the
  Eastern U.S.
The Great Smoky &
  Blue Ridge
  Mountains
Inside Disney

Hawaii
Las Vegas
London
Miami & the Keys
Mini Las Vegas
Mini-Mickey
New Orleans
New York City
Paris

Safaris
San Francisco
Skiing in the West
Walt Disney World
Walt Disney World
  for Grown-ups
Walt Disney World
  for Kids
Washington, D.C.

SPECIAL-INTEREST TITLES

Frommer's Britain's Best Bed & Breakfasts and
  Country Inns
Frommer's Britain's Best Bike Rides
The Civil War Trust's Official Guide
  to the Civil War Discovery Trail
Frommer's Caribbean Hideaways
Frommer's Food Lover's Companion to France
Frommer's Food Lover's Companion to Italy
Frommer's Gay & Lesbian Europe
Frommer's Exploring America by RV
Hanging Out in Europe
Israel Past & Present

Mad Monks' Guide to California
Mad Monks' Guide to New York City
Frommer's The Moon
Frommer's New York City with Kids
The New York Times' Unforgettable
  Weekends
Places Rated Almanac
Retirement Places Rated
Frommer's Road Atlas Britain
Frommer's Road Atlas Europe
Frommer's Washington, D.C., with Kids
Frommer's What the Airlines Never Tell You

Next time, make your *own* hotel arrangements.

<u>Yahoo! Travel</u>